"John Burkhard has an unparalleled, and en literature on the 'sense of the faith' in the life the topic is the fruit of meticulous research tl .... and encompasses an astounding array of sources. The "Sense of the Faith'" in History distills Burkhard's scholarship into a single volume that maps the theme in detail, providing an accessible overview of past and present theologies. This volume is a great gift for anyone interested in gaining insight into a topic that is foundational to Pope Francis's desire for a more synodal church."

—Richard Lennan, Boston College School of Theology and Ministry

"This major work on 'the sense of the faith' gives further evidence for why John Burkhard is one of the most important Catholic theologians working in the field of fundamental theology today. His extraordinary erudition, clarity of thought, and capacity for synthesis are all on full display in these pages, as is his deep commitment to the welfare of the church. Almost six decades since the close of the council, our church is still struggling to fully embrace the council's teaching that all the baptized faithful receive and penetrate the gift of God's Word and so contribute in crucial ways to the life and mission of the church. Burkhard's book is certain to help this central teaching gain wider acceptance and deeper appreciation in the church today."

—Richard R. Gaillardetz, Boston College, author of *By What Authority? Foundations for Understanding Authority in the Church*

"For decades John Burkhard has been tracking the emergence of the doctrine of the 'sense of the faith' in official church teachings and influential theological contributions and debates. Here he offers his fullest assessment of these materials. This is an immensely important resource for understanding this history and identifying unresolved issues."

—Bradford E. Hinze, Fordham University

"With his encyclopedic knowledge of research into the topic of *sensus fidei*, John Burkhard does the church a great service with this book. He highlights the indispensable role the people's 'sense of the faith' plays in the transmission of Christian faith throughout history. Above all, he shows the need for the church to be attentive continually to this expression of the lived faith of the people of God. For anyone wanting to understand Pope Francis's vision of 'a synodal church . . . a church which listens,' this book is a sure guide."

—Ormond Rush, Australian Catholic University

"After having provided us over many decades with precious lists of annotated bibliography on the theme of *sensus fidei*, John J. Burkhard now comes out with a historical and systematic analysis on this crucial category of theological discourse. He demonstrates how central and vital *sensus fidei* is for the whole of theology. It is not only ecclesiology or fundamental theology that needs to recognize and study in depth this category, but also the theology of sacraments, the liturgy, and moral theology can benefit from the richness of this idea. This book can rightly be considered the *opus magnum*, the *Lebenswerk* (Life's work) of a refined scholar of the history of theology and its traditions, as is John J. Burkhard. His analysis and his perspective are all played out in the theological climate of the Second Vatican Council and the post-conciliar reflections regarding the rediscovery of *sensus fidei*."

> —Antonio Autiero, Professor Emeritus of Moral Theology, University of Münster

The "Sense of the Faith" in History

Its Sources, Reception, and Theology

John J. Burkhard, OFM Conv

LITURGICAL PRESS
ACADEMIC

Collegeville, Minnesota
www.litpress.org

Excerpts from *Vatican Council II: Constitutions, Decrees, Declarations; The Basic Sixteen Documents*, edited by Austin Flannery, OP, © 1996. Used with permission of Liturgical Press, Collegeville, Minnesota.

Excerpts from the English translation of the *Catechism of the Catholic Church* for use in the United States of America copyright © 1994, United States Catholic Conference, Inc.—Libreria Editrice Vaticana. English translation of the *Catechism of the Catholic Church: Modifications from the Editio Typica* copyright © 1997, United States Catholic Conference, Inc.—Libreria Editrice Vaticana. Used with Permission.

| 1 | 2 | 3 | 4 | 5 | 6 | 7 | 8 | 9 |

Library of Congress Cataloging-in-Publication Data

Names: Burkhard, John J., 1940- author.
Title: The "sense of the faith" in history : its sources, reception, and theology / John J. Burkhard, OFM Conv.
Description: Collegeville, Minnesota : Liturgical Press Academic, [2022] | Includes bibliographical references and index. | Summary: "This book locates the historical roots of the Catholic teaching of "sense of the faith" (sensus fidei) and its emergence at Vatican II"— Provided by publisher.
Identifiers: LCCN 2021039603 (print) | LCCN 2021039604 (ebook) | ISBN 9780814666890 (paperback) | ISBN 9780814666906 (epub) | ISBN 9780814666906 (pdf)
Subjects: LCSH: Sensus fidelium—History. | Catholic Church—Doctrines. | Vatican Council (2nd : 1962-1965 : Basilica di San Pietro in Vaticano)—History.
Classification: LCC BX1746 .B87 2022 (print) | LCC BX1746 (ebook) | DDC 262/.02—dc23
LC record available at https://lccn.loc.gov/2021039603
LC ebook record available at https://lccn.loc.gov/2021039604

In memoriam
Reverendi Dionysii Gallagher, OFM Conv,
ac magistrorum meorum,
qui in studentibus pluribus
amorem studii et litterarum
incenderunt.

Contents

Preface

The Second Vatican Council vindicated the role of every believer in the church to witness to the church's faith and to participate in understanding, formulating, and determining that faith. Vatican II spoke of the *sensus fidei* ("the sense of the faith") and the *sensus christianus fidelium* ("the Christian sense of the faithful") to express this teaching. In many ways, the emergence of the teaching on the "sense of the faith" at the council was quite unexpected. However, as the council unfolded, bishops and theologians refined the teaching and in the end it emerged with greater clarity. Subsequent theological development after the council has greatly contributed to clarifying the "sense of the faith" and moved it to the center of the church's life. And yet, most people in the church either do not know what the teaching means or have not even heard about it. As important as the teaching is, and as fruitful as it can be in renewing the vitality of the church, to this day it hardly impacts the church. In many respects, what the terms the "sense of the faith" and the "sense of the faithful" try to express is not a novelty. The terms attempt to reconnect with the earlier teaching that stressed the unity of everyone in the church in the one faith and their responsibility for its purity and transmission.

From the beginning of this project I have wanted the book to take the sources of the "sense of the faith" seriously and make them available to scholars and the general public. Many studies have pointed out these sources, but by and large they have not appeared in English. My intention is to cite them in their original languages and translate them when necessary, while also placing them in their historical context and in the context of their authors' thought. In this way I hope that readers will have the evidence they need to make up their own minds about the meaning and scope of this seminal teaching of Vatican II.

I proceed chronologically by examining in chapter 1 the emergence of the terms the "sense of the faith" and the "sense of the faithful" in the light of the ecclesial crisis of the Great Western Schism in the fourteenth and fifteenth centuries followed by the Reformation and the Tridentine reform. What factors from these events formed the terms and how did they in turn form the church's understanding of teaching authority in the church? Chapters 2, 4, and 5 examine the explicit emergence of the terms in the nineteenth century. The thought of Johann Adam Möhler, Giovanni Perrone, John Henry Newman, and the Roman school are studied. Chapters 6 and 7 examine the contributions to the "sense of the faith" of several influential twentieth-century theologians in the years shortly before Vatican II. The contributions of the ordinary faithful in the nineteenth- and twentieth-century definitions of Mary's immaculate conception and her assumption into heaven played a unique role in the church's process of defining two recent Marian dogmas. What does this process say about the role of the laity in arriving at a deeper understanding of the faith as summarized in the term the "sense of the faithful"? I examine these questions in chapters 3 and 8. In chapter 9 I study how these terms found their way into the documents of Vatican II from the first formulation of the pre-conciliar preparatory texts. What happened to the terms as the conciliar fathers discussed such thorny issues as revelation and tradition and the nature and mission of the church? What were the contexts in which the "sense of the faith" and the "sense of the faithful" emerged at the council? How do they fit into the ecclesiology of Vatican II? Chapter 10 examines how the "sense of the faithful" has been received in the period after the council, in canon law and the *Catechism of the Catholic Church*, in the teachings of the popes, and the actions of the Congregation for the Doctrine of the Faith. What do the various statements of the International Theological Commission reveal about the meaning of these terms and of their growing acceptance in the church? What remains to be done in the process of reception? In chapter 11 I conclude with some observations and suggestions about formulating a theological understanding of the "sense of the faith" and the "sense of the faithful."

In the vast theological literature on the terms the "sense of the faith" and the "sense of the faithful" before, during, and after Vatican II, English-speaking authors have preferred the Latin expressions. In the early stage of writing the book, I repeated these Latin expressions again and again in the text. Eventually, it dawned on me that if the reality represented by the Latin terms *sensus fidei* and *sensus fidelium* is going to be understood and received by the whole church, it is necessary to refer to them in the vernacular.[1] Using the Latin only perpetuates the strangeness and formality of the terms, while the vernacular makes them accessible to everyone. And so, I have decided in general to refer to these terms by their English equivalents. It is my hope that this effort will help in the continuing process of their reception by the whole church—by those trained to understand Latin and those for whom Latin is entirely foreign. I have used the convention of enclosing the English terms in quotation marks to indicate the technical character of these expressions. I look forward to the day when the quotation marks, too, can be removed because the meaning and import of the terms will be more broadly understood in the church.

I wish to thank the many theologians and scholars who have helped me throughout the long process of writing this book. I thank Dr. Ormond Rush who first suggested I write the book. Dr. Bradford E. Hinze also gave the project added impetus by inviting me to give a plenary presentation on the "sense of the faithful" to the members of the Catholic Theological Society of America in June 2015. I thank Msgr. Paul McPartlan who invited me to share the results of my research with the faculty and doctoral students of the School of Theology and Religious Studies of the Catholic University of America. My former academic dean and colleague at the Washington Theological Union, Dr. James A. Coriden, has been generous in sharing his time and insights on the text as it unfolded. My thanks, too, to professors Bradford E. Hinze, Brian P. Flanagan, John P. Galvin, and Paul Lakeland who have shared their observations on various chapters in the course of the composition of the book. I also want to thank my confrere Friar Christopher Garcia, who graciously helped obtain books and photocopies of articles for me from the library of The Catholic University of America. A special word of thanks to the librarians at the Woodstock Theological Library at Georgetown University for providing me with access to the amazing treasures of this collection. I could not

1. This is generally the case among German authors, who regularly refer to the "Glaubenssinn" and the "Glaubenssinn der Gläubigen." French-speaking authors, too, often speak of "le sens de la foi" instead of the Latin *sensus fidei*.

have written this book without these resources. Finally, my thanks to Hans Christoffersen who showed an interest in my book early in the process of its conception and who encouraged me to complete the manuscript. I am indebted to Liturgical Press for agreeing to publish my book.

Chapter One

The "Sense of the Faith" before, during, and after the Council of Trent

The terms the "sense of the faith" and the "sense of the faithful" have been accepted and employed in theology since Vatican II. The council itself employed the term the "sense of the faith" (*sensus fidei*) in articles 12 and 35 of the Dogmatic Constitution on the Church and in article 9 of the Decree on the Ministry and Life of Priests, and the term the "Christian sense of the faithful" (*sensus christianus fidelium*) in article 52 of the Pastoral Constitution on the Church in the Modern World. Subsequent Roman statements and countless articles on the meaning and applicability of the terms have been published in the postconciliar period.[1] Although the terms enjoy increasing acceptance in the Catholic Church, not all understand the "sense of the faith" and the "sense of the faithful" in the same way or ascribe the same degree of importance to

---

1. See the author's surveys of the literature up to 2001: "*Sensus fidei*: Theological Reflection since Vatican II (1965–1989)," *The Heythrop Journal* 34 (1993): 41–59 and 123–36, and "*Sensus fidei*: Recent Theological Reflection (1990–2001)," *The Heythrop Journal* 46 (2005): 450–75 and 47 (2006): 38–54. The author hopes to complete a third survey that will cover the last twenty years. Also helpful for its survey of the literature is Daniel J. Finucane, *Sensus Fidelium: The Use of a Concept in the Post–Vatican II Era* (San Francisco – London – Bethesda, MD: International Scholars Publications, 1996).

them. Unfortunately, little attention has been devoted to the question of the origin of these terms in the English literature.[2] This chapter will consider the antecedents of the use of the terms the "sense of the faith" and the "sense of the faithful" in Roman Catholic theology in the years before and after the Council of Trent (1545–1563).

Before Trent

Thomas Netter, O Carm (ca. 1375–1430)
The Carmelite friar Thomas Netter of Walden was an English theologian and apologist who was active in the early fifteenth century.[3] His principal work, entitled *Doctrinale antiquitatum fidei ecclesiae catholicae contra Wiclevistas et Hussitas* (The Ancient Doctrines of the Faith of the Catholic Church against the Followers of Wycliffe and Hus) aimed at refuting the teachings of his countryman John Wycliffe (c. 1330–1384). Clamors for reform of the church had long been in the air and were exacerbated by the schism in the Western church over the papacy. Wycliffe was active when the popes resided in Avignon (1309–1377), while in Bohemia, Jan Hus (c. 1372–1415) took up the challenge of the need for reform after the popes had returned to Rome in 1377. During this period claimants to

2. In what follows, I have been greatly helped by several recent doctoral dissertations in German that have addressed the history of the use of *sensus fidelium* before Vatican II. See Robert W. Smucker, *Sensus Fidei. Der Glaubenssinn in seiner vorkonziliaren Entwicklungsgeschichte und in den Dokumenten des Zweiten Vatikanischen Konzils*, Theorie und Forschung, vol. 560, Theologie, vol. 36 (Regensburg: Roderer Verlag, 1998); Christoph Ohly, *Sensus fidei fidelium. Zur Einordnung des Glaubenssinnes aller Gläubigen in die Communio-Struktur der Kirche im geschichtlichen Spiegel dogmatisch-kanonistischer Erkenntniss und der Aussagen des II. Vaticanum*, Münchener Theologische Studien, III, Kanonistische Abteilung, vol. 57 (St. Ottilien: EOS Verlag, 1999); and Dominik Burghardt, *Institution Glaubenssinn. Die Bedeutung des sensus fidei im kirchlichen Verfassungsrecht und für die Interpretation kanonischer Gesetze* (Paderborn: Bonifatius Verlag, 2002).

3. On Thomas Netter, or Thomas of Walden (Waldensis), see Kevin J. Alban, "Thomas Netter: Carmelite and Theologian," *The Teaching and Impact of the 'Doctrinale' of Thomas Netter of Walden (c. 1374–1430)*, Medieval Church Studies 7 (Turnhout: Brepols, 2010), 9–28, and Donald Nicholl, "Netter, Thomas," in *New Catholic Encyclopedia*, vol. 10 (New York: McGraw-Hill, 1967), 363.

the papacy lived both in Rome and in Avignon.[4] The question of who was the legitimate pope was not decided until Martin V was elected in 1417.[5]

The ecclesiological issue of the papacy was inextricably intertwined with the secular politics of the day—that is, with the struggle for power and influence among the kings of France, Aragon (Spain), Germany-Hungary, and the kingdom of Naples. In this struggle, the papacy was treated as a pawn in the game of chess being played in the empire and in the church. The ecclesiastical and political confusion of the times needs to be adverted to when reading the *Doctrinale*. This was not a time when theology could be pursued peacefully and without worry. Theology and reform writings involved real personal risk.[6] This was the climate in which Thomas Netter composed his *Doctrinale* (c. 1421) and which demanded a pronounced apologetical cast to the work. Wycliffe is quoted frequently and refuted with the help of the teachings of the fathers of the church, especially St. Augustine.

The *Doctrinale* is divided into six books: Christ (book 1), the Church (book 2), religious life (books 3 and 4), the sacraments (book 5), and various ecclesiastical practices (book 6).[7] The eighty-three chapters of book 2 are of special interest to us. In general, book 2 devotes a great deal

---

4. In fact, from 1409 there were three popes with the election of John XXIII at Pisa. In the words of J. N. D. Kelly, "While there were still three claimants to the papacy, John commanded the widest support, with France, England, and several Italian and German states recognizing him. With the help of Louis of Anjou . . . he was able to establish himself in Rome." *The Oxford Dictionary of Popes* (New York: Oxford University Press, 1986), 238.

5. On this painful situation in the Western church and the widespread confusion surrounding it, see Karl August Fink, "The Western Schism to the Council of Pisa," "The Nationalist Heresies: Wyclif and Hus," and "The Council of Constance: Martin V" in *Handbook of Church History*, vol. 4: *From the High Middle Ages to the Eve of the Reformation*, ed. Hubert Jedin and John Dolan and trans. Anselm Biggs (Montreal: Palm Publishers, 1970), 401–25, 443–48, and 448–68, and Yves Congar, "Du Grand Schisme d'Occident au Concile de Florence: Ébranlements. Crise de la conscience ecclésiologique," *L'Église de saint Augustin à l'époque moderne* (Paris: Cerf, 1970), 297–338. Apropos of Thomas Netter, see Kevin J. Alban, "The Framework of Netter's Theology," *The Teaching and Impact of the 'Doctrinale' of Thomas Netter of Walden*, 29–59.

6. Remember that Jan Hus, even though his safety had been assured, was executed at the Council of Constance (1414–18).

7. See Kevin J. Alban's outline of the contents of the *Doctrinale* in his *The Teaching and Impact of the 'Doctrinale' of Thomas Netter of Walden*, xi–xiii.

of attention to the question of the church's hierarchical structure and its authority: the apostle Peter and the papacy, councils, bishops and other offices in the church, and the clergy. What is of interest to the question of the "sense of the faith" is that we already find the argument that will be made by theologians after the Council of Trent on the importance of the witness of the entire church to the revelation entrusted to it by Christ and the apostles. The explicit term the "sense of the faithful" is not found in Netter's *Doctrinale*, but its roots are definitely there, and this in a work that is consciously centered on the church as hierarchical. What, then, do we find in Thomas Netter's thought?

One of the arguments employed by Netter was his conviction that the whole church was preserved from error when it professed and lived the faith. In book 2 of the *Doctrinale*, he takes up the question of whether the church possesses the truth of Christ and is preserved from error. In article 5 of chapter 18, entitled "That the Church Founded on the Creeds Is Necessarily Apostolic and One," he writes:

> This is the formula that John used at the end of his gospel, "This is the disciple who is the witness to these things," to which the Church adds: "And we know because his witness is true" (John 21:24). For the witness of the universal Church cannot be lacking in anyone who either believes it or teaches it. In this case, it is no small matter that then the apostles and the first believers, just as today those who believe are called "witnesses of Christ," as the Scriptures attest in many places (Acts 1:22; Acts 1:8; Rev. 22:9). This witness is infallible and cannot be nullified.[8]

In article 7 of chapter 19, however, Netter asks whether in matters of serious doubt concerning the faith, the lay faithful should be consulted.

---

8. "Haec forma cum Johannis diceret expleto evangelio, 'Hic est discipulus ille qui testimonium perhibet,' subiungit Ecclesia, 'et scimus quia verum est testimonium eius.' Non enim deesse potest testimonium universalis Ecclesiae alicui secundum eam credenti, vel docenti. Et ad hoc non modicum facit quod Apostoli et primaevi credentes, sicut nunc fideles, ita tunc dixerunt se 'testes Christi,' passim per Scripturas. . . . Hoc autem testimonium et infallibilis est et evacuari non potest." *Doctrinale antiquitatum fidei ecclesiae catholicae contra Wiclevistas et Hussitas*, vol. 1, ed. Bonaventura Blanciotti (Venice: Typis A. Bassanesii, 1757), II: 18, no. 5, cols. 332E–333A. Accessed online. The Bonaventure Blanciotti edition of the *Doctrinale* is now available as a photocopied reprint by Nabu Press, 2012. My translation.

Even though he argues for the priority of the bishops gathered in ecumenical councils for deciding delicate and complex questions of the faith, he makes it clear that the lay faithful continue to play a role as witnesses of the faith and that their witness is to be included. He writes:

> Nevertheless, I am certain that the faith of the Church founded on the creeds does not exclude the witness of lay believers. Indeed, it includes their witness because they have firmly laid hold of the faith in their hearts. They have not known the faith with the help of technical terms free of every heretical association, but they drink from the recollections of those to whom they succeed.[9] That is why Augustine counseled us to have recourse to the source that Christ's bishops and teachers provide. Then it is possible to drink a purer drink and arrive at even deeper understanding. In this way we drink in the waters of faith, the source of truth that first gushed forth in rivers. In the end, indeed, faith guarantees that the streams of [God's] believing people shall not cease to flow.[10]

What strikes us in these two quotations is Netter's awareness of an important role played by the lay faithful in the church. Netter appears to assume that there is an intimate and irrefragable bond between the bishops as teachers of the faith and the faith of the whole people of God. The

9. Netter works with an elaborate and rich theory of succession: the bishops succeed to the apostles; the popes succeed to Peter; the doctors (*magistri*) of the church succeed to the teachers mentioned in the New Testament; priests succeed to the seventy-two disciples sent out by Jesus on mission (see Luke 10:1-20); and the laity succeed to those who precede them in the faith. According to Kevin J. Alban, quoting Netter, the church teaches "the whole succession of the faithful from Christ's first congregation on the banks of the Jordan to our own day, and from there to the end of the world." See *Doctrinale* II, chapter 17, article 5, col. 327 E quoted in *The Teaching and Impact of the 'Doctrinale' of Thomas Netter of Walden*, 106.

10. "Certus sum tamen, quod fides Ecclesiae symbolicae testimonium laicorum fidelium non excludit; immo includit: sed quia fidem illam, quam corde firmissime conceperunt, non sciverunt sub congruis terminis, liberis ab omni intricatione haeretica, successorum suorum propinare memoriis; idcirco ad fontem Sanctorum Christi Antistitum et Doctorum consulit nos Augustinus recurrere, ubi haustus magnae intelligentiae potest haberi profundior, et potus sincerior; et inde potare aquas fidei, unde fons veritatis primo manavit in rivulos; immo fine quibus rivuli populorum fidelium sicci remanerent a fide." *Doctrinale*, col. 340 D-E.

bishops enjoy priority in teaching, but that teaching can never be separated from the all-encompassing faith of the church's believing members. *In nuce*, we have here the outlines of what the generation of theologians after the Council of Trent will teach and what will come to be called the "sense of the faith" in a later period.

Antoninus of Florence, OP (1389–1449)

Antoninus was born in 1389 in Florence, the see of which he would eventually become the archbishop.[11] After completing his novitiate in the Order of Preachers at Cortona, he was assigned to the priory in Fiesole, a newly established reform community that followed a strict observance of the Rule. Obviously destined for leadership, Antoninus became the prior of the Dominican reform communities in Cortona, Fiesole, Naples, Rome, and finally his native Florence, where he established San Marco, a convent and church of the reform. Between 1432 and 1445, Antoninus was vicar general of Dominican priories of the strict observance in Italy. He became archbishop of Florence in 1446. Antoninus clearly proved to be an effective administrator, who could be flexible when necessary, but who did not shy away from being decisive and severe on occasion.[12] His short episcopacy was marked by efforts to reform the church in Florence. After his death in 1449, Antoninus was venerated locally and canonized by Pope Hadrian VI in 1523. He was a student of the theology of Aquinas and carried out an energetic program of writing, especially on pastoral or moral subjects.[13] In fact, he was among the first to write a text on moral theology, his *Summa theologica moralis*, written in the 1440s.

---

11. See James B. Walker, "Antoninus, St.," in *New Catholic Encyclopedia* (New York: McGraw-Hill, 1967), 1:646–47; and Ronald C. Finucane, "The Reforming Friar-Archbishop, Antoninus of Florence (1389–1449, cd. 1523)," *Contested Canonizations: The Last Medieval Saints, 1482–1523* (Washington, DC: Catholic University of America Press, 2011), 167–206.

12. Like many other ecclesiastical leaders in his day, Antoninus even employed torture on occasion.

13. These include his *Confessionale* or manual for priests administering the sacrament of penance and the *Chronicon*, a chronicle intended to provide guidance for men and women living in the world. Like the *Confessionale*, it was a practical treatment that formed a resource for preachers and pastors.

Antoninus divided his *Summa moralis* into four books.[14] Book 1 treats Aquinas on the soul, its faculties and passions, and sin and law. Book 2 continues his treatment of sin. Book 4 treats the theological and cardinal virtues and the gifts of the Holy Spirit. But it is in Book 4 that Antoninus treats the different states of life in society, including political life, as well as religious and clerical life in the church. In book 3, too, he deals with the papacy and councils—the lively ecclesiastical topics of his day.[15]

It is precisely against the backdrop of Antoninus's engagement in the secular society of his day—namely, the political life of Florence and the highly charged ecclesiastical life of the Order of Preachers and in the church at large—that Antoninus's knowledge of the church's tradition plays such an important role. In terms of the focus of this book on the "sense of the faith," Antoninus is another witness, like his Carmelite contemporary Thomas Netter, to the role of the ordinary faithful in supporting the witness of the church to the Christian faith. In book 3, Antoninus wrote the following:

> There is no reason to object if it be said that a council does not err, because Christ prayed for his Church that it not fail . . . for although a general council is concerned with the whole universal Church, it is in this instance only the universal Church in a representative sense, because the universal Church is constituted by the gathering of all believers. All the faithful of the earth, then, constitute the universal Church in its fullness, whose head and spouse is Christ himself. True,

---

14. The *Summa theologica moralis*, sometimes cited simply as the *Summa moralis*, was published posthumously in 1477. See the edition printed in Verona in 1740 and reproduced in Graz: Akademische Druck und Verlagsanstalt, 1963.

15. The Council of Constance was held in 1414–1418 and Ferrara-Florence(-Rome) from 1438 to 1445, both of which dealt with the role of councils in the life of the church. Antoninus could not have escaped the tensions between conciliar theory and the pope's primacy. Directly or indirectly, these discussions must have influenced Antoninus's thinking. The complexity of the issues surrounding the Council of Basel and the council that met successively in Ferrara, Florence, and finally in Rome has never been satisfactorily addressed. The manifold of issues surrounding these councils cries out for interdisciplinary attention, given the weightiness of the issues they sought to address, especially regarding the relations between the churches of the East and the West.

the pope is the vicar of the same Christ, but he is not the real head of the Church.[16]

Antoninus does not speak of the "sense of the faithful" in this context, since such terminology has not yet emerged, but he clearly envisions an indispensable role of the ordinary faithful in constituting the church and so in expressing its belief. As we will see with authors after the Council of Trent, the fifteenth to the seventeenth centuries understood "church" to mean the entirety of believers and not just its hierarchical leadership. For this reason, Antoninus should be numbered among the theologians who understood the church as "the whole body of believers"—the *universitas fidelium*.[17]

---

16. "Nec obstat, si dicatur, quod concilium non potest errare, quia Christus oravit pro ecclesia sua, ne deficeret . . . nam licet concilium generale totam ecclesiam concernat, tamen ibi vere non est universalis ecclesia, sed repraesentative, quia universalis ecclesia constituitur ex collectione omnium fidelium. Unde omnes fideles terrae constituunt totam universalem ecclesiam, saltem cuius caput et sponsus est ipse Christus; papa autem est vicarius ipsius Christi, et non est verum caput ecclesiae." *Summa Moralis* III, 23. Quoted by Ulrich Horst, "Papst, Bischöfe und Konzil nach Antonin von Florenz," *Recherches de théologie ancienne et médiévale* 32 (1965): 76–116, at 102.

17. Because of his defense of the role of councils in the life of the church, Antoninus would play an unanticipated role at Vatican I. John W. O'Malley has vividly narrated and critically assessed the intervention of the Dominican Cardinal Filippo Maria Guidi in which Guidi enlisted Antoninus in support of the minority bishops' defense of the historical role of the bishops in the church. To some bishops of the majority this meant that Guidi had tipped his hand and revealed his Gallican leanings. That very day, Pius IX summoned Guidi and berated him for his intervention. It was at this meeting that Pius is reported to have uttered the rash claim that he, the pope, was tradition, and he, the pope, was the church ("I, I am tradition. I, I am the Church"). See *Vatican I: The Council and the Making of the Ultramontane Church* (Cambridge, MA: The Belknap Press, 2018), 208–14 ["The Guidi Affair"]. Ulrich Horst, too, has related the efforts of bishops of the majority to question the minority's interpretation of Antoninus's true position. See "Papst, Bischöfe und Konzil nach Antonin von Florenz," 112–16. On how Antoninus's position is to be understood in terms of the Dominican interpretation on papal infallibility over the centuries, see Ulrich Horst, *The Dominicans and the Pope: Papal Teaching Authority in the Medieval and Early Modern Thomist Tradition*, trans. James D. Mixson (Notre Dame, IN: University of Notre Dame Press, 2006), 3, 32, and 57–58. On Cardinal Guidi, see Ulrich Horst, "Kardinalbischof Filippo Maria Guidi O.P. und das I. Vatikanische Konzil," *Archivum Fratrum Praedicatorum* 49 (1979): 429–511.

The Council of Trent (1545–63)

Pope Paul III (1534–49) convoked the Council of Trent, at the strong urging of Emperor Charles V, to address the challenges and teachings that emerged out of the Reformation begun by Martin Luther.[18] Before Vatican II, no other ecumenical council had addressed so many matters of the faith and issued so many decrees. The primary intent of Trent was to teach as clearly as possible what the Catholic Church had maintained through the centuries, and only secondarily to refute what the bishops at the council saw as the errors of the Reformers. It did not intend to break new ground on the doctrine of the church but to state it as clearly, persuasively, and authoritatively as possible. Its secondary purpose was to launch a program for the reform of the church.

The student of the Council of Trent needs to tread very carefully on the council's terrain, a warning that has not always been heeded by interpreters who came after the council and saw in it the fixed, permanent, and perfect expression of the Catholic faith. The words "Trent" and "Tridentine" came to represent an entire program of doctrine and Catholic practice. In time, Trent took on the aura of authority enjoyed by such earlier councils as Nicaea (325) and Chalcedon (451), rather than the more limited scope of Lyons II (1274) and Florence (1438–43). Trent has often been taken as the final word of what the Catholic Church represented at the time of the council itself and eventually what it came to represent as well. It is, therefore, sobering to observe the degree of continuity Trent exhibited with the mentality and formulations of the pre-Tridentine church, at the expense of the often-grandiose assumptions of later post-Tridentine authors.

In his treatment of the "sense of the faith" in the documents of the Council of Trent, Yves Congar cites a number of references where the already traditional formulas we have glimpsed in Thomas Netter are used to express the church's teaching. On the matter of the real presence of

---

18. On the Council of Trent, see Hubert Jedin, *History of the Church*, vol. 5: *Reformation and Counter Reformation*, ed. Hubert Jedin and John Dolan, trans. Anselm Biggs and Peter W. Becker (New York: Seabury Press, 1980) 431–98 (chapters 32–37), and John W. O'Malley, *Trent: What Happened at the Council* (Cambridge, MA: Belknap Press, 2013). Hubert Jedin's two-volume *A History of the Council of Trent*, trans. Ernest Grag (London: Thomas Nelson, 1957–1961) remains the classic text on the council.

Christ in the Eucharist, Congar refers to Session XIII's "Decree on the Most Holy Eucharist," where the bishops describe "those who deny the reality of Christ's flesh and blood, contrary to the universal understanding of the Church."[19] The reader should take note that it is the entire church that stands behind the bishops' rejection of errors regarding the Eucharist and not just their apostolic authority, however correct that also is. Describing those who denigrate Christian marriage as those who "have not only thought basely about this revered sacrament . . . but have said and written a great deal that is foreign to the understanding of the Catholic Church and to custom from the time of the apostles," the decree *Tametsi* defended the sacramentality of Christian marriage in conformity with the entire church's understanding of it at Session XXIV.[20] Finally, Congar speaks of the issue of justification discussed at Session VI and cites Trent as describing those who object that "the words [of St. Paul] are to be understood in the sense which the perennial consent of the Catholic Church has maintained and expressed."[21] The reader should take notice from this third quotation that Trent was already aware of the use of the terms "sense" and "consent" in conjunction with official formulation of the church's belief. Such traditional formulations will play a more pronounced role in the theological discussion after Trent often, but not always, in the service of more apologetical goals dictated by the polemics of the period.

19. "Quibus veritas carnis et sanguinis Christi negatur, contra universum ecclesiae sensum detorqueri." See Henricus Denzinger and Adolfus Schönmetzer, eds., *Enchiridion symbolorum, definitionum et declarationum de rebus fidei et morum*, 33rd ed. (Freiburg: Herder, 1965), 1637. Hereafter I refer to this work with the standard abbreviation of DS. I have slightly emended the translation of Norman P. Tanner, *Decrees of the Ecumenical Councils*, vol. 2 (Washington, DC: Georgetown University Press, 1990), 694. On the positions of the Reformers and the teaching of Trent, see David N. Power, *Eucharistic Mystery: Revitalizing the Tradition* (New York: Crossroad, 1992), 250–63 ["Reformation and the Council of Trent"].

20. "Multa ab ecclesiae catholicae sensu et ab apostolorum temporibus probata consuetudine aliena, scripto et verbo asseruerunt." See DS 1800 and Tanner, slightly altered, 754.

21. "Cum vero Apostolus dicit, iustificari hominem 'per fidem' [Rom. 3:22], et 'gratis' [Rom. 3:24], ea verba in eo sensu intelligenda sunt, quem perpetuus Ecclesiae catholicae consensus tenuit et expressit." See DS 1532 and Tanner 674. Congar mentions several other instances, but these usually involve the Latin predicate form "sentire," to mean, to understand.

After Trent

Melchior Cano, OP (1509–60)

Many commentators on the "sense of the faith" and the "sense of the faithful" have pointed to the use of these terms in some form or other by important post-Tridentine authors. Thus, Melchior Cano, OP (1509–60) in his posthumously published classic *De locis theologicis* twice spoke of the importance of the "general consent of the faithful" (*communis consensus fidelium*) or the witness to the Catholic faith by the whole church, as a source for determining the content of the faith.[22] In his list of the "authoritative witnesses," or *loci*, of the Christian faith, Cano distinguished between "proper" authoritative witnesses and "foreign" or external authoritative witnesses. Scripture and tradition constitute the very content of revelation, while five other authoritative witnesses are interpretative sources, among which Cano lists the entire or "catholic" church (*ecclesia catholica*). The other authoritative sources are the ecumenical councils, the Roman Church in the person of the pope, the fathers of the church, and the scholastics.[23] It is evident that for Cano the church taken as a whole is an authoritative witness of the truth of the Catholic faith.[24] Thus, in book 3, chapter 4, Cano speaks of "what is proven by the common consent of the faithful in the Church" regarding matters derived from the church's tradition and not merely from human design or ingenuity, as "the

---

22. Cano's *De locis theologicis* appeared in 1563 (Salamanca: Mathias Gastius, 1563). It was recently reissued to commemorate the fifth centenary of its appearance in an edition edited by Juan Belda Plans (Madrid: Biblioteca de Autores Cristianos, 2006), and can also be found online. On Melchior Cano, see Yves Congar, *A History of Theology*, trans. Hunter Guthrie (Garden City, NY: Doubleday, 1968), 163–65 and Patrick W. Carey, "Cano, Melchior" in *Bibliographical History of Christian Theologians*, ed. Patrick W. Carey and Joseph T. Lienhard (Peabody, MA: Hendrickson Publishers, 2002), 114–16.

23. See the treatment by Walter Kern and Franz-Josef Niemann, *Theologische Erkenntnislehre* (Düsseldorf: Patmos, 1981), 49–53 ["Theologische Erkenntnislehre bei Melchior Cano"].

24. This truth does not contradict the legitimate need for ecclesiastical institutions such as councils with their episcopal representatives, or the papacy, or the foundational insights of the fathers of the church, or the contributions of learned theologians. The spontaneity of the faithful and the institutional-hierarchical element in the church do not cancel each other out.

third way" for determining the faith.[25] Later, in book 4, chapter 4, Cano is at pains not to play off the "gathering of all believers" against church leaders since both ultimately converge in officially witnessing to the faith: "It is not only the universal Church, that is, the gathering together of all who believe, that possesses the eternal spirit of truth, but the leaders and pastors of the Church, too, possess it."[26] To this claim he adds: "Whatever the Church holds as true, that is, the gathering of all believers, the same can be affirmed of the pastors and teachers of the Church who cannot err in matters of faith, for whatever they teach the faithful people pertains to the faith of Christ and is completely true."[27]

Robert Bellarmine, SJ (1542–1621)

After Cano, no less an imposing ecclesiastic than Cardinal Robert Bellarmine, SJ (1542–1621), also defended the infallibility of the whole church.[28] In 1576, Bellarmine was entrusted with the new chair for "Controversial Theology," a course that addressed the errors of Reformation thinkers. The years of teaching at the Jesuit Roman College resulted in the classic *Disputationes de controversiis christianae fidei adversus huius temporis haereticos* (Disputations against the Heretics of Our Time on Matters of Faith).[29] Book 2 addressed the infallibility of Christian truth as taught in

---

25. "Quidquam est nunc in ecclesia communi fidelium consensione probatum." Accessed online as *Documenta catholica omnia. Omnia paparum, Conciliorum, SS. Patrum, Doctorum Scriptorumque Ecclesiae qui ab aevo apostolico ad usque Benedicti XVI tempora floruerunt.* See *De locis theologicis*, p. 117. My translation.

26. "Non solum ecclesia universalis, id est, collectio omnium fidelium hunc veritatis spiritum sempiternum habet, sed eundem habent etiam ecclesiae principes ac pastores." Ibid., 149. My translation.

27. "Quicquid ecclesia, hoc est, omnium fidelium concio teneret, id verum esse. Haec autem illud affirmat pastores ecclesiae doctores in fide errare non posse, sed quicquid fidelem populum docent, quod ad Christi fidem attineat, esse verissimum." Ibid., 149. My translation.

28. Two references from Bellarmine are cited in the International Theological Commission's *Sensus fidei in the Life of the Church*," article 32 (London: Catholic Truth Society, 2014), 20–21. The text is also available online at www.vatican.va. On Robert Bellarmine, see John Patrick Donnelley, "Bellarmine, Robert" in *Bibliographical Dictionary of Christian Theologians*, ed. Patrick W. Carey and Joseph T. Lienhard, 64–66.

29. The *Disputationes* enjoyed enormous success and were often reprinted. The edition I consulted was printed in Rome at the Typographia Giunchi et Menicanti in 1836. The references in the footnotes are to this version.

the Roman Catholic Church. After reviewing the standard questions of the content of revealed truth as represented by the infallible teachings of the church and the various councils of the church that have taught Christian truth authoritatively, Bellarmine addressed the subjects of this infallibility. In chapter 2, he writes: "Secondly, a General Council represents the universal Church and therefore has the consent of the universal Church. For this reason if the Church herself cannot err, neither can an approved legitimate ecumenical council err."[30] The direction of the argument should be noted. An ecumenical council represents the prior truth taught by the universal church; it does not express this truth for the first time. The truth is antecedently there in the believing church.

In chapter 14 of book 3, Bellarmine again takes up the impossibility of the church teaching erroneously. At somewhat greater length he writes:

> Our position is that the Church cannot err, whether in matters of what is absolutely necessary, or in such other matters that it proposes to be believed or put into practice, whether they are found expressly in Scripture or not. Again we assert that the Church cannot err, by which we mean both the entirety of the faithful and the whole of the episcopate. Thus, the meaning of the proposition that "The Church cannot err" is that what all the faithful hold as pertaining to the faith is necessarily true and pertains to the faith, just as what all the bishops teach as pertaining to the faith is necessarily true and pertains to the faith.[31]

According to Bellarmine, revealed truth is taught and lived by both the body of the faithful and by the body of the bishops—both together, that is, the church as universal. For the bishops to claim that they alone teach Christian truth would not make sense to Cardinal Bellarmine. In council the bishops teach, of course, but they teach what the faithful already

---

30. "Secundo, Concilium generale repraesentat Ecclesiam universam, et proinde consensum habet Ecclesiae universalis; quare si Ecclesia non potest errare, neque Concilium oecumenicum legitimum, et approbatum potest errare," vol. 1, 49. My translation.

31. "Nostra igitur sententia est, Ecclesiam absolute non posse errare, nec in rebus absolute necessariis, nec in aliis, quae credenda, vel facienda nobis proponit, sive habeantur expresse in Scripturis, sive non; et cum dicimus, Ecclesiam non posse errare, id intelligimus tam de universitate fidelium, quam de universitate episcoporum, ita ut sensus sit eius propositionis, ecclesia non potest errare, id est, id, quod tenent omnes fideles tamquam de fide, et similiter id, quod docent omnes Episcopi, tamquam ad fidem pertinens, necessario est verum de fide," vol. 1,124. My translation.

believe and practice in their lives. As we have seen above, Bellarmine had sound precedent in what the Council of Trent itself had taught about the Eucharist on the basis of the constant witness of the faithful. For Cano as well as for Bellarmine, the authority of the faithful as true witnesses to the Catholic faith is not a theological novelty. It was simply taken for granted.

Gregory of Valencia, SJ (1549–1603)

Gregory of Valencia, SJ (1549–1603), was among the first post-Tridentine authors to mention the role of the "sense of the faithful" in keeping the church free from errors regarding the faith. Like Bellarmine in Rome, Gregory was charged with teaching the new "controversial theology," but for the Spaniard Gregory it was in Germany at Dillingen and Ingolstadt.[32] In 1591, he published his *De rebus fidei hoc tempore controversis* (On the Controversies of Our Time regarding Matters of Faith), which included the influential *Analysis fidei catholicae* (An Analysis of the Catholic Faith) in which he developed his ideas on ecclesial infallibility.[33] There Gregory wrote:

> Definitions of the faith should, as much as possible, take into account the consent of the faithful. This is because the faithful who form the Church also preserve divine revelation in an integral and pure form, with the help of the Holy Spirit, so that in its entirety the Church cannot err, as is clear from what was said above about the seventh mark of the Church. Nonetheless, on this matter I do not insist that the Pope must inquire about the understanding of all the faithful on a given controverted matter. For such a thing cannot be done, and if it is impossible, he is not bound to do so. In general, when it comes to controverted points

32. On Gregory, see Gerald van Ackeren, "Gregory of Valencia," *New Catholic Encyclopedia* 6 (New York: McGraw-Hill, 1967), 799.

33. See Gregory's *De rebus fidei hoc tempore controversis libri, qui hactenus extant omnes* (Lyons: Apud Haeredes Gulielmi Rovilli, 1591), 92A. The *Analysis fidei catholicae* is book 8 of the above-named work. It consists of twelve chapters and can be found on pages 66–93. The following chapters deal with the sources for determining what can be defined by the church, that is, *De quibusdam quasi definiendi regulis, quae in determinandis fidei controversiis consuli debent*: Chapter 5: *Primum de sacra Scriptura* (71–77); chapter 6: *De traditionibus apostolicis* (77–86); chapter 7: *De conciliis* (86–91); chapter 8: *De consensu doctorum* (91–92); chapter 8: *De consensu fidelium* (92); chapter 9: *Quem modum debeat tenere Pontifex in definiendo secundum praedictas regulas* (93).

of the faith, such matters far exceed the common comprehension of the faithful. And so, all I am asserting is that when a controversy arises in a matter of belief, such as might be the case in a situation of public devotion commonly practiced by the Christian peoples, or if the opinion of some gives rise to a general situation of scandal or some offense, and so forth, then, to the extent that the faithful agree in their understanding, it must be said that the Pope can and must rely on the understanding of the Church. And in my opinion this is what Thomas Waldensis seems to have intended when he says: "It is for the Church, when determining a doctrine of the faith, not to exclude the witness of the ordinary faithful but to include it, even if they [the faithful] are not wont" (he says) "to be questioned—something that is hardly appropriate in validating an explanation of its [the official Church's] understanding."[34]

Finally, in his conclusion to chapter 12, Gregory summarizes his understanding of the mutual relationship of the faithful to the papal office. He writes:

> If such authority as is needed to achieve its perpetual purpose is found in the true Church of the faithful and flourishes there, then it is necessary that the Church of the faithful is of such a nature that it is a Church that "adheres" to the Roman Pontiff "as united to the Pastor of the flock" (as Cyprian says) (since the very thought of excluding the Roman

---

34. "Est etiam in definitionibus fidei, sicut supra diximus, habenda ratio, quoad fieri potest, consensus fidelium, quoniam et ii sane, quatenus ex ipsis constat Ecclesia, sic Spiritu sancto assistente divinas revelationes integre ac pure conservant, ut omnes illi quidem aberrare non possint, sicut patet ex superius dictis circa septimam Ecclesiae proprietatem. Neque tamen idcirco volo, debere Pontificem, de quavis controversia, fidelium omnium sententiam inquirere. Hoc enim neque fieri potest, neque si posset; expedire. Fere enim huiusmodi sunt quae in controversiam fidei adducuntur, ut captum vulgarium fidelium longe superent. Illud solum contendo: Si quando de re aliqua in materia religionis controversa constaret, fidelium omnium concordem esse sententiam (solet autem id constare vel ex ipsa praxi, alicuius cultus communiter apud Christianos populous recepta, vel ex scandalo et offensione communi, quae ex opinione aliqua oritur, etc.) merito posse ac debere Pontificem illa niti, ut quae esset Ecclesiae sententia infallibilis. Atque hoc mihi tantum voluisse Thomas Waldensis videtur, cur ait, *Ecclesiam, cuius est determinare doctrinam fidei, testimonium communium fidelium non excludere, sed includere, tametsi non soleant* (inquit) *interrogari, quod minus commode valeant sententiam explicare suam.*" *Analysis fidei catholicae* book 8, chap. 9, p. 92A. My translation.

Pontiff is impious.) If the true Church of the faithful exists, then the same Roman Pontiff, the successor of St. Peter, is to be found there.[35]

In the mind of Gregory, the whole church is found in the communion of the faithful with the Roman pontiff.[36] There is no church without the body of the faithful and the faithful do not constitute a body without divinely willed leadership. So, too, the whole church believes and teaches infallibly both in the body of believers and in the leaders of the church.

Francisco Suárez, SJ (1548–1617)

Francisco Suárez, SJ (1548–1617), Gregory's Spanish contemporary and confrere, spent his whole adult life teaching theology, briefly in Rome but mostly in Spain at Avila, Segovia, Valladolid, Salamanca, and principally in Coimbra, Portugal. Suárez was a prolific theologian and philosopher, whose collected writings number thirty volumes in the Paris edition of 1872–78.[37] Suárez treated the infallibility of the church in his *Tractatus de fide* (Treatise on the Faith) and in his *Theologiae Summa, seu Compendium* (A Summa of Theology or The Compendium).

In the fifth disputation of the *Compendium*, he discusses the rules of infallibility for the object of faith. In section 6 he asks, "Is the universal Church an infallible rule of faith?" He begins the discussion with a rather startling statement: "Take Note: From the beginning of the world there has always been the Church, that is, the gathering of the faithful, espe-

---

35. "Si ad eundem etiam finem perpetuo ea auctoritas in vera Ecclesia fidelium prae-sens ut vigeat, necesse est (quod cogitare impium est) aut illa est, quae Romano Pontifici *tanquam pastori suo grex, adunata* (ut Cyprianus inquit) *adhaeret*: Si in ea ipsa vera Ecclesia fidelium ille idem Romanus Pontifex (ut successor Divi Petri is est)." Ibid., book 8, chap. 12, p. 93B. My translation.

36. By the late sixteenth century, then, in someone like Gregory we see growing atten-tion to the office of the papacy, in addition to the bishops as leaders and pastors of the church. The influence of the papacy will continue to increase in subsequent centuries, culminating in the definition of the primacy of the pope at Vatican I (1869–1870) in the Dogmatic Constitution *Pastor aeternus*.

37. D. M. Andrei, ed., *Opera Omnia* (Editio nova; Paris: Ludovicus Vivès). On Fran-cisco Suárez, see José María Dalmau, "Suárez, Francisco," in *New Catholic Encyclopedia*, vol. 13 (New York: McGraw-Hill, 1967), 751–54, and Jack Treloar, "Suárez, Francis," in *Biographical Dictionary of Christian Theologians*, ed. Robert W. Carey and Joseph T. Lienhard, 483–84.

cially among the Jewish people. In the present matter, however, we are dealing with the catholic and apostolic Church, which is the gathering of baptized believers, who worship God under one head and with [one] sacrifice and by the sacraments instituted by Christ."[38] Then, he adds: "It is a matter of faith that the universal Church, that is, the Church of Rome, cannot abandon the faith by heresy" (*Dico* 1) nor by "invincible ignorance" (*Dico* 2).[39] It is clear from the outset how Suárez understands the church: it is a gathering of everyone who believes in Jesus Christ. The element of communion in faith and life (*communio*) was still dominant in the early post-Tridentine period, that is, before the theological turn to the church as "a perfect society" (*societas perfecta*) under the growing influence of the Enlightenment,[40] and was still primary for Suárez. Next, he adds the following comment:

> Although what the Church believes as merely pious and probable is not necessarily true, whatever the whole Church agrees to on a matter of this sort is to be held not only as not erring in a matter of practice (as is evident), but also as a speculative matter. Because the whole Church, even when it is regarded as a gathering of human beings, in which many wise persons are found, has the highest authority humanly speaking,

38. "Nota: Semper ab initio mundi fuit Ecclesia, id est fidelium congregatio, et specialis quidem in populo Judaeorum; hic autem agimus de Ecclesia catholica et apostolica, quae est congregatio fidelium baptismorum, quae sub uno capite ac sacrificio et sacramentis a Christo institutis, Deum colit." *Theologiae R. P. Fr. Suarez, S.J., Summa, seu Compendium*, 2 vols. (Paris: Apud Garnier Fratres, 1877), vol. 2, cols. 1070–71. My translation.

39. "De fide est universalem seu Romanam Ecclesiam non posse a fide per haeresim deficere. . . . Haec Ecclesia non potest errare in iis quae credit certa de fide, etiam per invincibilem ignorantiam." Ibid., 1071. My translation.

40. Christoph Ohly makes this point in his dissertation on the "sense of the faith." See *Sensus fidei fidelium: Zur Einordnung des Glaubenssinnes aller Gläubigen in die Communio-Struktur der Kirche im geschichtlichen Spiegel dogmatisch-kanonistischer Erkenntnisse und der Aussagen des II. Vaticanum* (St. Ottilien: EOS Verlag, 1999), 52–54, 57, 76. Ohly points to two indicators of Enlightenment thinking on the "perfect society." First, the church understands that it must justify its existence and its works by the benefits it brings to society. Second, to Enlightenment thinkers, "society" is understood as constituted by "contractual" obligations and commitments mutually entered into by civil society and the church. See also Patrick Granfield, "The Church as *Societas Perfecta* in the Schema of Vatican I," *Church History* 48 (1979): 431–46, and Knut Walf, "Die katholische Kirche— eine 'societas perfecta'?" *Theologische Quartalschrift* 157 (1977): 107–18.

so too is it likely that these learned persons of the Church are aided by the special guidance of the Holy Spirit (*Dico* 3).[41]

Suárez, then, goes out of his way to insist that the "whole Church" is involved in determining matters of the faith "with certitude," but also to truths that are "probable." Moreover, the probability is more than practical, since it includes speculative truth as well. A practice of the faithful then can flow over into the very understanding of the faith and its formulation as speculative.

But that is not all for Suárez, who proceeds in his fourth assertion to maintain the following:

> Although the Church is infallible in believing, nevertheless when understood as a whole, it is not sufficient as a living rule of the faith in the matter of teaching officially. By no means are all the faithful in total agreement on a matter of faith to be defined, and this pertains to most of the faithful who are from the lay state. To teach by defining something *ex cathedra* is a matter of the "keys," and constitutes an act of special power bestowed by Christ for leading the Church in matters of doctrine. Christ, however, does not entrust this power to the whole Church but to its head (*Dico* 4).[42]

I want to focus on the distinction between "infallibility in believing" and "infallibility in teaching."[43] Suárez does not separate both forms of

---

41. "Quamvis ea quae credit Ecclesia tantum ut pia ac probabilia, non clare constet esse vera, tamen si tota Ecclesia in aliqua ejusmodi re conspiret, tenendum est non tantum in ea non errare practice (quod manifestum est), sed nec speculative; quia tota Ecclesia, etiam spectata ut humana congregatio, in qua sunt plures viri sapientes, habet humano modo summam auctoritatem, et verisimiliter isti doctores Ecclesiae, speciali illustratione Spiritus sancti adjuvantur." Ibid., 1071. My translation.

42. "Licet Ecclesia sit infallibilis in credendo, tamen secundum se totam sumpta, non est sufficiens viva fidei regula in docendo: quia non omnes omnino fideles possunt simul convenire ad aliquid de fide definiendum, nec hoc spectat ad plurimorum fidelium statum maxime laicorum. Docere enim ex cathedra definiendo, spectat ad clavem, estque specialis potestatis actus a Christo datae ad regendam in doctrina Ecclesiam; Christus autem non dedit hanc potestatem toti Ecclesiae corpora, sed capiti." Ibid., 1071–72. My translation.

43. See Gustave Thils, "L'infaillibilité de l'Église *in credendo et in docendo*," *Salesianum* 24 (1962), 298–336, and his *L'infaillibilité du peuple chrétien "in credendo." Notes de théologie posttridentine*, Bibliotheca Ephemeridum Theologicarum Lovaniensium 21 (Louvain: E. Warny, 1963).

infallibility, but he does distinguish them. A dimension of "infallibility in believing" is the power or ability to "define infallibly." He says nothing about "infallibility in teaching" as being in any way superior to "infallibility in believing," only that they are not the same.

Finally, Suárez concludes section 8 on the pope's competence to define infallibly without a general council with the following answer to an objection:

> I respond that any given Pontiff is truly a Pontiff in a matter of the faith after the sufficient consent of the whole Church has been received, and has thus been approved, so that all are held to obedience, even in definitions of the faith (*Objectio* 3).[44]

Once again, Suárez does not resolve the question in terms of an "either/or" alternative, but sees the internal connection between an act of defining (the pope) and the corresponding act of receiving (the faithful). Such an attitude of mutual cooperation and "conspiring" in a complex act of believing/teaching is characteristic of a communion ecclesiology that sees the church as a gathering of the faithful and their pastors. A spirit of mutuality will prove difficult to maintain in an ecclesiology of divided competencies, as in an ecclesiology of the church regarded as "a perfect society" (*societas perfecta*). Unfortunately, such an ecclesiology will win the day in the eighteenth and nineteenth centuries.

Denis Pétau, SJ (1583–1652)

Finally, the French patrologist and theologian Denis Pétau, SJ (1583–1652), is another valuable witness of the acceptance of the role of the whole church in the understanding of Christian revelation.[45] Pétau represents positive theology, a movement that emerged in the late sixteenth

---

44. "Respondeo esse de fide hunc pontificem esse verum pontificem postquam sufficienti totius Ecclesiae consensu receptus est, et ita approbatus, ut omnes illi obedire teneantur, etiam in fidei definitionibus." Ibid., 1075. My translation.

45. On Pétau, see Francis X. Murphy, "Petau, Denis (Petavius)," in *New Catholic Encyclopedia*, vol. 11 (New York: McGraw-Hill, 1967), 199–200; Patrick W. Carey, "Petavius, Dionysius," in *Biographical Dictionary of Christian Theologians*, ed. Patrick W. Carey and Joseph T. Lienhard (Peabody, MA: Hendrickson Publishers, 2002), 413–14; and Leo Karrer, *Die historisch-positive Methode des Theologen Dionysius Petavius* (Munich: Max Hueber, 1970).

and seventeenth centuries. Thanks to the painstaking advances in the humanities and in theology that came from collecting and comparing various manuscripts from patristic, medieval, and Renaissance sources, the historical-critical method emerged and would be refined well into the twentieth century. Theologians like Pétau were able to concentrate on the content of their sources. The fathers and the great scholastics were mined less for proofs of predetermined theses than for what they taught on their own terms. The burgeoning study of history held greater attraction for these scholars, and efforts at producing a critical text from a wide and often confused state of the manuscripts promised future benefits.[46]

In the course of his many years of teaching, Pétau produced his *Opus de theologicis dogmatibus* (A Study of the Dogmas of Theology) in eight large volumes.[47] The work includes volumes on God and the divine properties, the Trinity, angels, creation, law and gospel, and the incarnation of the Word. In the course of his treatment regarding Christ, Pétau includes a veritable tract on Mary.[48] In chapter 2, he takes up the question of the Blessed Virgin's immaculate conception. First, Pétau points out that the doctrine is not universally accepted by Christians and has not been officially defined. In order to argue for the truth of Mary's immaculate conception, Pétau reports on a variety of patristic and scholastic witnesses to its truth.[49] This source is understandable from the point of view of a

---

46. On positive theology see Hubert Jedin, "The Rise of Positive Theology," in *History of the Church*, vol. 5: *Reformation and Counter Reformation*, ed. Hubert Jedin and John Dolan, trans. Anselm Biggs and Peter W. Becker (New York: Seabury Press, 1980), 546–55; Yves Congar, *A History of Theology*, trans. Hunter Guthrie (Garden City, NY: Doubleday & Company, 1968), 170–75 ["Scholastic Theology and Positive Theology"]; and Leo Karrer, *Die historisch-positive Methode des Theologen Dionysius Petavius* (Munich: Max Hueber, 1970).

47. See *Dogmata theologica Dionysii Petavii, dissertationibus ac notis F. A. Zachariae, aliorumque, necnon Adriani Leclerc*, 8 vols. (Paris: Apud Ludovicum Vivès, 1865–67).

48. Pétau treats the following Mariological questions in Book 14: Mary's personal holiness and her freedom from personal sin (chapter 1); Mary's freedom from Original Sin (chapter 2); Mary's virginity (chapter 3); Mary's perpetual chastity and her marriage to Joseph (chapter 4); Mary's virginity *in partu* (chapters 5–6); Mary's virginity and erroneous opinions in understanding the doctrine (chapter 7); erroneous opinions on devotion (*cultus*) to Mary (chapter 8); and Mary's mediatorial role (chapter 9).

49. These witnesses include Augustine, Hilary of Arles, Fulgentius of Ruspe, Ferrandus of Carthage, Ildephonse of Toledo, Peter Damian, Rupert of Deutz, Anselm of Bec/

consensus of the fathers, but Pétau goes further in drawing on what he calls the "universal sense of all the faithful." Let us examine Pétau's line of reasoning on the matter. He writes:

> I understand that not only did the Virgin lack every personal and actual (as it is called) sin, but indeed even original sin. Yet even though I hold this conviction, I do not want to insist that it is a matter of faith, nor do I believe that anyone should be damned or censured who thinks otherwise. For this reason then I am ready to accept internally what has been prescribed by Roman pontiffs and the Council of Trent, that is, by the catholic and Roman Church. Moreover, what motivates me to be more inclined to this point of view in particular is precisely the universal sense of all the faithful. Those who hold this [teaching] in the recesses of their minds and are profoundly committed [to it], can by such references and official sources testify that there was no other creature of God who was more chaste, pure, innocent, and that therefore there never was another to whom all stain and blemish of sin was more foreign (paragraph 9).[50]

Canterbury, Hugh of St. Victor, and Bernard. He also adds the Franciscan Pope Sixtus IV, who in 1476 approved the feast of the Immaculate Conception with its own Mass and Office. Furthermore, Pétau refers to the decision of the bishops at the fifth session of the Council of Trent to refrain from teaching the doctrine formally by simply allowing the decision of Sixtus IV to stand. ("The same holy council, however, also declares that it is not its intention to include in this decree, when it is dealing with original sin, the blessed and immaculate virgin Mary, mother of God, but rather that observance must be given to the constitutions of Pope Sixtus IV of happy memory, in accord with the penalties included in those constitutions, which the council renews.") *Decrees of the Ecumenical Councils*, ed. Norman Tanner, vol. 2, 667. See *Dogmata theologica Dionysii Petavii*, vol. 8:49. We will examine the dogma of Mary's immaculate conception in depth below in chapter 3. On Pope Sixtus IV, see J. N. D. Kelly, *The Oxford Dictionary of the Popes* (New York: Oxford University Press, 1986), 250.

50. "Virginem existimo non solum omni proprio et *actuali*, ut vocant, delicto caruisse, verumetiam originali: sed eatenus persuasum illud habeo, ut hoc ad fidem spectare nolim; neque damnandum credam, aut severius appellem qui secus sentiat: nec alia ratione denique tueri sim paratus animo, quam quae ab Romanis pontificibus et Tridentina synodo, id est ab Ecclesia catholica, Romanaque praescribitur. Movet autem me, ut eam in partem sim propensior, communis maxime sensus fidelium omnium; qui hoc intimis mentibus, alteque defixum habent, et quibus possunt indiciis officiisque testantur nihil illa Virgine castius, purius, innocentius, alienius denique ab omni sorde, ac labe peccati procreandum a Deo fuisse." *Dogmata theologica Dionysii Petavii*, vol. 8, 49–50. My translation.

Pétau's use of the phrase "the universal sense of all the faithful" is an important linguistic marker in the history of the emergence of the doctrine of the role played by the entire church in grasping, proclaiming, and understanding the truth of Christian revelation. Far from representing something novel in Catholicism, the "universal sense of all the faithful" aptly expresses a long-held conviction in the church.

Conclusion and Prospect

Our short excursion through the use of the terms the "infallibility of the Catholic Church" and the "sense of the Church" or the "consensus of believers" from the fifteenth to the seventeenth centuries has led to the result that the church was familiar with the idea that all believing Christians played a role in confessing and witnessing to the truth of Christian revelation. The time frame has stretched from a century and a half before the Council of Trent up through the apologetical writings of the sixteenth and seventeenth centuries and the emergence of positive theology with Denis Pétau in the seventeenth century. When, therefore, theologians in the nineteenth century began to speak of a "sense of the faith" and the "sense of the faithful," the idea was not an entirely novel one. As we shall see, the focus will change from the infallibility of the entire church ("infallibility in believing") to a different terminology associated with the "sense" of what the whole church believes and witnesses. By locating infallibility actively in the teaching authority of the pope and the bishops at Vatican I to the exclusion of the lay faithful, something important will be lost in the church's consciousness. The effort to redress the imbalance introduced by severely restricting the faithful in the church's infallibility will now be addressed by another traditional concept, that represented by the Latin nouns *sensus* and *consensus*. How Catholic theology arrived at this insight is the goal of the chapters that follow.

Chapter Two

Conscious Stirrings
of the "Sense of the Faith"
in Nineteenth-Century Germany

Two quite different movements in nineteenth-century German Catholicism contributed to advancing the theological insights that would eventually come to be expressed by the terms the "sense of the faith" and the "sense of the faithful" at Vatican II. The first movement was the pioneering work of the Tübingen School of Theology, a robust Catholic theology that emerged out of the ruins of the French Revolution and the Napoleonic Wars. The critical situation in Europe, and in Germany in particular, called for a bold reaction that assumed form at the University of Tübingen. Among these creative theologians, Johann Adam Möhler helped to recover the role of the Holy Spirit in Catholic theology and so to rediscover and deepen the understanding of tradition as a living and dynamic force in the church. The other contribution came from a small group of German-speaking canonists who discovered the possibilities for ecclesiology of the three offices of Christ as prophet, priest, and king. How might this christological insight into the ministry of Jesus enrich a theology of ministry in the church? Let us now examine these two fruitful avenues to the discovery of the "sense of the faith" in Catholicism.

Johann Adam Möhler (1796–1838)

Commentators commonly point to the influence of the Tübingen School on theology in the nineteenth, twentieth, and twenty-first centuries, with special attention to the thought of Johann Adam Möhler.[1] The Tübingen School, and Möhler in particular, represent something new in the emergence of modern theology. Yves Congar pointed out the disastrous effects of Napoleon's rule and wars on university education in France and Germany. He wrote: "The French Revolution and the Napoleonic Empire, coming after a period of relative stagnation in Catholicism at the end of the eighteenth century, had done away with a large number of universities and research centers, especially in France."[2] Thus, Möhler and the other members of the Tübingen School were in an advantageous position to build something new and vital, and that was precisely what they succeeded in doing.[3] The Tübingen School developed new insights into Catholic life, theology, pastoral ministry, and Catholic identity.[4]

1. On the life, writings, and contributions of Möhler, see Paul-Werner Scheele, "Johann Adam Möhler (1796–1838)," in *Katholische Theologen Deutschlands im 19. Jahrhundert*, 3 vols., ed. Heinrich Fries and Georg Schwaiger (Munich: Kösel Verlag, 1975), 2:70–98 and Bradford E. Hinze, "Möhler, Johann Adam" in *Biographical Dictionary of Christian Theologians*, ed. Patrick W. Carey and Joseph T. Lienhard (Peabody, MA: Hendrickson Publishers, 2002), 365–68.

2. And Congar added, "There existed in Germany, before 1789, eighteen Catholic university centers; in 1815 there were no more than five faculties of theology," including Tübingen. *Tradition and Traditions: An Historical Essay and a Theological Essay*, trans. Michael Naseby and Thomas Rainborough (New York: Macmillan, 1966), 196. On the period from the mid-seventeenth through the eighteenth century, see the description by Congar, *A History of Theology*, trans. and ed. by Hunter Guthrie (Garden City, NY: Doubleday & Company, 1968), 177–89.

3. Donald J. Dietrich has written: "Sailer and the Tübingen school fostered by Drey provide a unique case of theological vitality during the first thirty years of the nineteenth century. With the exception of Sailer and the Tübingen school, there was little enduring religious scholarship during this period. Guided by their insights, the theology of the magisterium could now be analyzed with greater rigor with respect to its connection to the Church as a community." See his "German Historicism and the Changing Image of the Church, 1780–1820," *Theological Studies* 42 (1981): 46–73, at 72. And Congar wrote: "The Catholic school of Tübingen is a more or less unique case of theological vitality during the first thirty years of the nineteenth century." *Tradition and Traditions*, 196. Finally, Leo Scheffczyk called the nineteenth century the "classical period" of reflection on the church "when a deeper understanding of the mystery of the Church arose in theology." See *Sensus fidelium*—Witness on the Part of the Community," *Communio* 15 (1988): 182–98, at 188.

4. See the collection of studies edited by Donald J. Dietrich and Michael J. Himes, *The Legacy of the Tübingen School: The Relevance of Nineteenth-Century Theology for the Twenty-First Century* (New York: Crossroad, 1997).

Möhler's contribution was his deepening of the understanding of tradition and its relationship to the nature of the church. The members of the Roman School—Giovanni Perrone, Carlo Passaglia, and Clemens Schrader—were indebted to Möhler and drew on his writings. It was Perrone who mediated Möhler's ideas on the active nature of tradition to John Henry Newman and thereby confirmed Newman's own emerging ideas on the "consensus of the faithful" and on the development of doctrine. No other nineteenth-century theologian capitalized on the "sense of the faith" to the extent that Newman did, but the general thrust of theology emerging from the Tübingen School definitely changed the way Catholic theology would be practiced after Möhler.

Möhler did not employ the term the "sense of the faithful" but his teaching on tradition already included the reality *avant la lettre*. In his own early attempt to draw on the richness of the resources in Catholic theology, Möhler went beyond the standard post-Tridentine meaning of tradition and retrieved the understanding of the early church fathers. Theologians after Trent generally understood tradition as the body or deposit of fundamental doctrines of the faith.[5] These doctrines had been revealed to the apostles and passed on by them to their successors. It was the duty of the church to guard these doctrines and hand them on to future generations in all their purity. This objective meaning of tradition was concerned with the dogmatic content of the Christian faith as a more or less self-contained and self-explanatory system of truths. Möhler noted how Irenaeus and Tertullian understood tradition in a more dynamic and organic sense that included the subjects who witnessed to revelation and handed it on in a living way. Möhler was able to do so because he reconceived the nature of the church. Tradition is inconceivable apart from the church, and the church participates in the ongoing process of handing on revelation.

In 1825, Möhler published *Unity in the Church or the Principle of Catholicism: Presented in the Spirit of the Church Fathers of the First Three*

---

5. This is sometimes called the "objective sense" of tradition. See Walter Kasper, *Die Lehre von der Tradition in der Römischen Schule*, Walter Kasper Gesammelte Schriften, vol. 1 (original edition, 1962; Freiburg: Herder, 2011), 100 [31], 117 [43], 282–83 [167–68]. Kasper also lists the exceptions to this rule: Thomas Stapleton, Johannes Driedo, and Adrian and Peter von Walenburch. Ibid., 117 [43].

Centuries.[6] Christoph Ohly has shown how in this work Möhler moved away from his earlier understanding of the church as a "religious institution" that in its authoritative teachers was entrusted with the task of proclaiming divine doctrine.[7] Instead, for Möhler the idea of the church as a "community" in the Holy Spirit emerged as dominant. The community of the baptized is filled with and led by the Spirit.[8] Already in *Unity in the Church*, then, Möhler was developing his understanding of the church hand in glove with his understanding of living tradition. In part 1, chapter 2 he writes:

> Tradition is also always the name for the word that was first spoken and is continually expounded in a living way in the Church; it is then

6. Translated by Peter C. Erb (Washington, DC: Catholic University of America Press, 1996).

7. See *Sensus fidei fidelium. Zur Einordnung des Glaubenssinnes aller Gläubigen in die Communio-Struktur der Kirche im geschichtlichen Spiegel dogmatisch-kanonistischer Erkenntniss und der Aussagen des II. Vatikanum* (St. Ottilien: EOS Verlag, 1999), 44. Hermann Josef Pottmeyer has examined Möhler's early ecclesiology in even greater detail and shown how Möhler moved away from his former ecclesiological leanings, characterized by the statist influences of Josephinism, by drawing on the role of the Holy Spirit. He writes: "With this pneumatological view of the Church, according to which the hierarchy is an organ of the Spirit, he has taken a decisive step away from the external, more sociological understanding of the Church to the view of the Church represented in his *Unity of the Church.*" *Unfehlbarkeit und Souveränität. Die päpstliche Unfehlbarkeit im System der ultramontanen Ekklesiologie des 19. Jahrhunderts* (Mainz: Matthias-Grünewald, 1975), 134–42, at 140. Pottmeyer even speaks of Möhler's tendency toward ecclesiological "positivism" regarding his early understanding of tradition. Ibid., 139. Robert Wolfgang Schmucker has also pointed out the limitations of Möhler's first ecclesiological attempts of 1823–25 and drew on Pottmeyer's study to good effect. During these years, Möhler was influenced by stratified ideas of the difference between the bishops as teachers and the faithful as led by the bishops. See *Sensus Fidei. Der Glaubenssinn in seiner vorkonziliaren Entwicklungsgeschichte und in den Dokumenten des Zweiten Vatikanischen Konzils* (Regensburg: S. Roderer Verlag, 1998), 20–32, especially 21–23.

8. The ecclesiology of *Unity of the Church* has been characterized as pneumatological. The inner power of the Spirit unites all in the church and is propelled outward to express the church socially and externally in history. The church is neither a purely external society of those who believe in Christ nor a purely internal gathering of believers in the Spirit but both in reciprocal relationship. The Holy Spirit is the bond uniting the interior life of faith and expressing the exterior as the communion of the saints. At this stage, the character of the church as mystery for Möhler comes to clear expression.

immediately embodied again for the future. . . . The proof from tradition is a call upon the Christian consciousness that always existed and existed among all. . . . If this side of tradition is directed more toward the external, another draws itself more toward the internal, namely, to demonstrate the identity of the Christian consciousness of each individual member or of a specific generation with the consciousness of the whole Church. . . . By an inner necessity the love of Christ, through the Holy Spirit, unites individual believers with the contemporary totality of believers. . . . By tradition, then, as soon as the life of the Church has developed in the believer, that believer will be conscious that his or her Christian consciousness agrees with and is the same as the enduring consciousness of the Church. . . . The believers of all times are thus present to us in tradition. They appear as integrating members of a whole: they teach, admonish, and direct us properly so that we accept nothing as apostolic doctrine unless accepted by all believers from the time of the apostles.[9]

In this passage, the active participation of each believer within the church as the totality of believers comes to clear and powerful expression. This is what those following him will call the "sense of the faithful." Of course, Möhler did not dismiss or denigrate the role of the bishops and the pope, since he envisions them as organically united with the community of the baptized. He was concerned with a fuller vision of the church, not a truncated or narrow one.

At this stage, Möhler came under the influence of German Romanticism's understanding of life as organic and of a "people" as a unique expression of community identity and its history—ein Volk.[10] His interest shifted from an exclusive concentration on the official hierarchical witnesses to the content of revelation to the consciousness of the faith of all believers. As Ohly writes: "The sense of the faith is not individualized by Möhler but is consciously integrated into the structure of the Church as a community. Every single believer is related to the whole and receives

9. *Unity in the Church*, 107–9.

10. Dietrich has explained it this way: "The Aufklärung vision of progress was reformist; their sense of future time was controlled by their immersion into past time and was modified by the realization that *every nation, every historical epoch, had its own merit, its own unique spirit.*" "German Historicism and the Changing Image of the Church," 51. My italics.

the 'internal power of faith' only out of this whole."[11] In such a view, what we today call the "sense of the faithful" is virtually identical with Möhler's understanding of tradition as the living transmission of the faith by all the faithful.[12]

In 1832, Möhler published a second book on the church, *Symbolism: Exposition of the Doctrinal Differences between Catholics and Protestants as Evidenced by the Symbolical Writings.*[13] In this work, Möhler chose to develop an ecclesiology that was centered on the Christological mystery of the incarnation of the word of God. He applied the Council of Chalcedon's Christology to the church itself: the two natures of the hypostatic union can be employed to explain the two dimensions of the church, its socio-historical visibility and the inner life of grace. The church and the incarnation are related to one another insofar as the church is fashioned after the incarnate Word as another expression of the mystery. The church, then, truly is the Body of Christ. Such ideas added greater concreteness to the ecclesiology developed in *Unity in the Church*, and Möhler was better able to express the meaning and role of the church's hierarchical offices, ministry, authority, and sacraments. In the words of Robert Schmucker: "The authority of the Church and its offices is objectively founded in the reality of Christ."[14]

Möhler developed his christologically based theology of the church by drawing on various aspects of classical christological thought. In the following quotation, he highlights the relationship between the church and the historical concreteness of the economy of salvation:

> By the church on earth, Catholics understand the visible community of believers, founded by Christ, in which . . . the works wrought by him during his earthly life, for the redemption and sanctification of mankind are, under the guidance of his Spirit, continued to the end of the world.[15]

11. *Sensus fidei fidelium*, 46.

12. It is important to note that for Möhler there was a shift from the "sense of the faithful" as an explanation of the infallibility of the Church to the "sense of the faith" as the expression of tradition. Tradition, not infallibility, was central for him.

13. Translated by James Burton Robertson (New York: Crossroad, 1997 [originally appeared in 1843]).

14. *Sensus fidei*, 28.

15. *Symbolism*, §36, 258.

Next, Möhler draws out the implications of a christologically oriented ecclesiology. The church is grounded in the mystery of the incarnation of the Logos, the word of God, and conforms to God's pedagogy vis-à-vis our human nature and needs.

> Thus, to a visible society of men and women is this great, important, and mysterious work entrusted. The ultimate reason of the visibility of the church is to be found in the incarnation of the divine Word. Had the Word descended into the hearts of men and women without taking the form of a servant, and accordingly without appearing in corporeal shape, then only an internal, invisible church would have been established. But since the Word became flesh, it expressed itself in an outward, perceptible, and human manner. It spoke as man to man, and suffered, and worked after the fashion of men and women, in order to win them to the kingdom of God, so that the means selected for the attainment of this object fully corresponded to the general method of instruction and education determined by the nature and the wants of humans.[16]

Then, he explains how these human means of saving humankind correspond to humankind's social nature and the role that institutions play in communicating truth and grace.

> This decided the nature of those means, whereby the Son of God, even after he had withdrawn himself from the eyes of the world, wished still to work in the world and for the world. The Deity having manifested its action in Christ according to an ordinary human fashion, the form also in which his work was to be continued, was thereby traced out. The preaching of his doctrine needed now a visible, human medium, and must be entrusted to visible envoys, teaching and instructing after the accustomed method. Men must speak to men and hold intercourse with them, in order to convey to them the word of God. And as in the world nothing can attain to greatness but in society, so Christ established a community, and his divine word, his living will, and the love emanating from him exerted an internal, binding power upon his followers, so that an inclination implanted by him in the hearts of believers corresponded to his outward institution. And thus a living, well-connected, visible association of the faithful sprang up, of which

16. Ibid.

it might be said, There they are, there is his church, his institution in which he continues to live, his Spirit continues to work, and the word uttered by him eternally resounds.[17]

Finally, he stresses the continuity of the visible church with the mystery of the incarnation. The historical reality we call church is composed of divine and human traits.

> Thus, the visible church, from the point of view here taken, is the Son of God himself, everlastingly manifesting himself among men and women in a human form, perpetually renovated, and eternally young—the permanent incarnation of the same, as in holy scripture, even the faithful are called "the body of Christ." Hence it is evident that the church, though composed of men and women, is yet not purely human. Rather, as in Christ the divinity and the humanity are to be clearly distinguished, though both are bound in unity, so is he in undivided entireness perpetuated in the church. The church, his permanent manifestation, is at once divine and human—the union of both. He it is who, concealed under earthly and human forms, works in the church. Therefore it has a divine and a human part in an undivided mode, so that the divine cannot be separated from the human, nor the human from the divine.[18]

Despite the different starting point and the difference of perspective, Möhler remained true to his understanding of tradition as developed earlier in *Unity in the Church*. Thus, he writes:

17. Ibid., 259

18. Ibid., 259. I have emended the translation, paragraphs, and punctuation slightly. The christological analogy was taken up by Vatican II in The Dogmatic Constitution on the Church: "It is therefore by no mean analogy that it is likened to the mystery of the incarnate Word. For just as the assumed nature serves the divine Word as a living instrument of salvation inseparably joined with him, in a similar way the social nature of the church serves the Spirit of Christ who vivifies the church towards the growth of the body" (art. 8). Norman P. Tanner, *The Decrees of the Ecumenical Councils*, vol. 2 (Washington, DC: Georgetown University Press, 1990), 854. However, it should be noted that the document does so in a context that is also clearly pneumatological. In an essay written before Vatican II, Yves Congar warned of the dangers of misunderstanding the christological analogy when it is considered in isolation. See "Dogme christologique et Ecclésiologie: Vérité et limites d'un parallèle," in *Das Konzil von Chalkedon: Geschichte und Gegenwart*, 3 vols., ed. Alois Grillmeier and Heinrich Bacht (Würzburg: Echter, 1954), 3:239–68.

Tradition is the living word, perpetuated in the hearts of believers. To this sense, as the general sense, the interpretation of holy scripture is entrusted. The declaration which it pronounces on any controverted subject, is the judgment of the church, and therefore the church is judge in matters of faith. Tradition, in the objective sense, is the general faith of the church through all ages, manifested by outward historical testimonies.[19]

And again, later in the same work:

Tradition we have hitherto described as the consciousness of the church, as the living word of faith, according to which the scriptures are to be interpreted and to be understood. The doctrine of tradition contains, in this sense, nothing else than the doctrine of scripture. Both, as to their contents, are one and the same.[20]

It should be noted, furthermore, that it is precisely in his *Symbolism* that Möhler comes closest to expressing what the term the "sense of the faith" has come to purport. He writes:

It is taught that *the divine Spirit*, to which are entrusted the guidance and vivification of the church, *becomes in its union with the human spirit in the church a peculiarly Christian tact, a deep sure-guiding feeling, which, as it abides in truth, leads also into all truth.* By a confiding attachment to the perpetuated apostleship, by education in the church, by hearing, learning, and living within her pale, by the reception of the higher principle which renders her eternally fruitful, *a deep interior sense* is formed that alone is fitted for the perception and acceptance of the written Word, because it entirely coincides with the sense, in which the sacred scriptures themselves were composed.[21]

In Möhler's writings, from the early period of his lectures in the early 1820s to his first book on the church, *Unity in the Church* (1825), and finally to his second book, *Symbolism* (1832), we note a development in his thought about the church. From a hierarchical society or institution

---

19. *Symbolism*, §38, 279. I have emended the translation slightly.
20. Ibid., §41, 292. I have emended the translation slightly.
21. *Symbolism*, §38, 277. My italics.

charged with teaching Christian dogma and its educative value in the eyes of the Enlightenment, Möhler moved from a secular social model to envision the church as a mystery. In *Unity in the Church*, it is a mystery of the Spirit, while in *Symbolism* it is a mystery of Christ the incarnate Word. Whatever the relationship between his more pneumatological and his more christological ecclesiologies, Möhler remained firm in his conviction that the church was the entirety of believers and that tradition was entrusted to all as a living and dynamic process of handing on the faith.[22]

Nineteenth-Century Roman Catholic Canon Lawyers

The German Catholic canon lawyer Christoph Ohly has examined an area of the history of the "sense of the faith" that has received little attention by English-speaking scholars. How and to what extent did Roman Catholic canon lawyers in the nineteenth century contribute to the understanding of the "sense of the faith" in this critical century? Ohly has singled out two Germans for consideration, both of whom were married laymen incidentally, the professor at the University of Bonn, Ferdinand Walter (1794–1879) and the professor at the universities of Berlin, Munich, and

---

22. For various assessments on Möhler's ecclesiologies—(1) they are independent treatments, (2) there is continuity from one to the other, and (3) the approaches are complementary—see the judgments of the following scholars. Yves Congar, "Sur l'évolution et l'interprétation de la pensée de Moehler," *Revue des sciences philosophiques et théologiques* 27 (1938): 205–12, and idem, *L'Église de saint Augustin à l'époque moderne* (original edition, 1970; Paris: Cerf, 1997), 417–24 ["Le renouveau dans le climat du romanticisme allemand"]; Josef Rupert Geiselmann, "Der Wandel des Kirchenbewusstseins und der Kirchlichkeit in der Theologie Johann Adam Möhlers," in *Sentire ecclesiam. Das Bewusstsein von der Kirche als gestaltende Kraft der Frömmigkeit*, ed. Jean Daniélou and Herbert Vorgrimler (Freiburg: Herder, 1961), 531–675; Philip J. Rosato, "Between Christocentrism and Pneumatocentrism: An Interpretation of Johann Adam Möhler's Ecclesiology," *The Heythrop Journal* 19 (1978): 45–56; Bradford Hinze, "The Holy Spirit and the Catholic Tradition," in *The Legacy of the Tübingen School*, ed. D. J. Dietrich and M. J. Himes, 75–94; Peter C. Erb, "Introduction," *Unity in the Church*, 1–71; Michael J. Himes, *Ongoing Incarnation: Johann Adam Möhler and the Beginnings of Modern Ecclesiology* (New York: Crossroad, 1997); and James Ambrose Lee II, "Shaping Reception: Yves Congar's Reception of Johann Adam Möhler," *New Blackfriars* 97 (2016), 693–712. On Möhler's changing views about episcopacy and the universal episcopate vis-à-vis the papal office, on the importance of the hierarchy in general for the church's mission, and on changing views regarding infallibility, see H. J. Pottmeyer, *Unfehlbarkeit und Souveränität*, 134–42.

finally Vienna, George Phillips (1804–72). Both enjoyed long teaching careers and experienced firsthand the vagaries of the nineteenth-century discussions on the "sense of the faith" and papal infallibility.

Ferdinand Walter (1794–1879)

Ferdinand Walter developed his understanding of the relationship of the laity to the hierarchy in his textbook *Lehrbuch des Kirchenrechts aller christlichen Confessionen* (A Textbook of Canon Law in All Christian Confessions). A popular resource at the time, the textbook went through fourteen editions between 1822 and 1871.[23] One of the features of the then-standard theological presentation of the church included the distinction of the church into the "teaching Church" (*ecclesia docens*) consisting of the bishops and their assistants, the priests, who actively teach the truths of the faith, and the "learning Church" (*ecclesia discens*), which consists of the rest of the members of the church who passively accept the hierarchy's teaching. Although Walter did not reject the distinction outright, he certainly changed the way it was understood by extending the meaning of the "learning Church" to include more than the laity's merely passive acceptance of the hierarchy's teaching. Walter did this by developing the notion of the "priestly dignity" of all believers[24] and by

23. The original title of the textbook through the first three editions was *Lehrbuch des Kirchenrechts mit Berücksichtigung der neuesten Verhältnisse* (A Textbook of Canon Law with Special Attention to Recent Circumstances). Ohly points out how the first four editions of the *Lehrbuch* hardly differed from the then-standard theological presentation of the church as a freely entered "association" [Verein] and a public, civic "institution" [Anstalt] that met the Enlightenment's expectation that the church would teach the citizens of the state the truths of Christian revelation and thereby serve the needs and expectations of the broader secular society. Even so, Walter departed from the standard presentation by rejecting the other component of the church as a society, namely, that the church fulfilled this expected duty on the basis of a "contract" between the church and the civil authorities. The church fulfilled these tasks because Christ had entrusted this mission to it. See C. Ohly, *Sensus fidei fidelium*, 52–53.

24. In the sixth edition of the *Lehrbuch*, Walter wrote: "Since in the Church all the faithful are sanctified and come to share in Christ's life as members, so too do they possess in this sense a priestly dignity corresponding to these exercises, [a dignity that] is determined by prayer and other internal expressions of religion." Later, in the eighth edition of the *Lehrbuch*, the "priestly dignity" of the faithful is extended beyond "the fellowship of prayer" to include "teaching" [das Lehramt] and "public ecclesiastical discipline" [die

employing the distinction of the three offices of Christ in the church, as priest, prophet, and king.[25] Ohly maintains that Walter was able to do this successfully because he broadened the understanding of the church as the official teacher of Christian revelation to include Möhler's understanding of the church as a "community" and the "Body of Christ." The various editions of Walter's *Lehrbuch* show a growing conviction of the church as a community that derives its very life from Christ and so cannot be summed up neatly in terms of its duty to teach the truths of Christian revelation to the citizens of the state. This insight permitted Walter to hold together the tension between the church of a corps of office holders who possess authority and the ordinary faithful who are called to "collaboration" (Mitwirkung).[26] In effect, Walter rejected the Enlightenment's theology of the church as a mere civil "association" that the individual believer freely enters. How, then, did Walter understand the three offices of sanctifying, teaching, and governing, and what effect did this insight have on the emergence of the "sense of the faith"?

Christoph Ohly has shown how, in the course of the second Christian millennium, the division of the church's ministerial authority gave rise to an ultimately unsustainable division into two quite separate, though mutually related, "powers"—the power of orders and the power of jurisdiction. The full ministry of the church defies such an overly neat and

---

äuseren Kirchenzucht]. Quoted by Ohly, *Sensus fidei fidelium*, 57. Ohly's judgment here is worth noting: [Without sacrificing the hierarchical structure of the church's constitution, Walter] "gained a hearing for the 'sense of the faith' vis-à-vis the magisterium and thereby opened up an ecclesiological meaning for participation in the ministry of teaching (*munus docendi*) of the Church." Ibid.

25. Pottmeyer comments on Walter's use of the three offices as follows: "The extreme accent on the duty to teach leads him to employ the up-to-then scarcely known triple distinction of ecclesiastical power by introducing its own proper power to teach." *Unfehlbarkeit und Souveränität*, 146. Unlike Ohly, however, Pottmeyer did not pursue the use of the distinction in Walter's thought. Instead, Pottmeyer was interested in charting the "development" of the teaching on infallibility in the nineteenth century.

26. In the sixth edition, Walter wrote: "Christ himself has established the Church as visible, one, universal, apostolic, true and holy and as the necessary community of salvation." Later, in the fourteenth edition, Walter wrote of the church that beyond its institutional duties of education and formation, "life streams forth from its head and binds the faithful together, [the Church is then] a body in which the work of redemption is constantly present and effective." Quoted by Ohly, *Sensus fidei fidelium*, 56–57.

simplistic distinction, in which the underlying unity of the ministerial responsibility is difficult to sustain and properly express. In his treatment, Ferdinand Walter attempted to address these unsatisfactory distinctions and tensions by turning to a threefold "power" instead.[27] In terms of the emergence of the "sense of the faith," however, the threefold distinction opens up new possibilities for participation in ministerial responsibility beyond the ordained in the church.[28] This opening up of ministerial

27. While Walter's distinction into three "powers" better addresses the fullness of the church's ministerial responsibility, it still preserves the unhelpful plurality of separable "powers." The issue of *postestas ordinis et iurisdictionis* (power of orders and of jurisdiction) is too complex to enter into in the present context. To treat the problem adequately would take us far afield and ultimately distract from the issue at hand. For a detailed presentation, see Laurent Villemin, *Pouvoir d'ordre et pouvoir de juridiction. Histoire théologique de leur distinction*, Cogitatio Fidei 228 (Paris: Cerf, 2003). The Second Vatican Council decided the matter in favor of a single power, which it called *sacra postestas* (sacred power), but that has three inextricably linked areas of activity. See the Dogmatic Constitution on the Church, chapter 3, "The Hierarchical Constitution of the Church and in Particular the Episcopate," art. 18 and the subsequent application to ecclesiastical offices in arts, 19–29. These areas of activity are modeled on the threefold office of Christ as prophet-teacher, priest-sanctifier, and king-shepherd. See Klaus Mörsdorf, "Ecclesiastical Authority," in *Sacramentum Mundi: An Encyclopedia of Theology*, ed. Karl Rahner, 6 vols. (New York: Herder and Herder, 1968–70), 2:133–39; Karl Rahner, Alois Grillmeier, and Herbert Vorgrimler, *Commentary on the Documents of Vatican II*, ed. Herbert Vorgrimler, 6 vols. (New York: Herder and Herder, 1967), 1:153–230; Winfried Aymans, "Begriff, Aufgabe und Träger des Lehramts," *Handbuch des katholischen Kirchenrechts* (Regensburg: F. Pustet, 1983), 533–40; Eugenio Corecco, "Natur und Struktur der 'sacra postestas' in der kanonistischen Doktrin und im neuen CIC," *Archiv für katholisches Kirchenrecht* 153 (1984): 254–383; Peter Hünermann, "Die hierarchische Verfassung der Kirche," in *Herders theologischer Kommentar zum Zweiten Vatikanischen Konzil*, ed. Peter Hünermann and Bernd Jochen Hilberath, 5 vols. (2nd ed.; Freiburg: Herder, 2004–2006), 2:404–60; and Christoph Ohly, "Officium ecclesiasticum. Ein rechtsprachlicher Vorschlag," *Archiv für katholisches Kirchenrecht* 177 (2008): 56–72.

28. On the three offices, see John Henry Newman, "The Three Offices of Christ," *Sermons Bearing on Subjects of the Day* (London: Longmans, Green & Co., 1918), 52–62; Josef Fuchs, *Magisterium, Ministerium, Regimen. Vom Ursprung einer ekklesiologischen Trilogie* (Cologne, 1941), French translation by Yves Congar, "Origines d'une trilogie ecclésiologiques à l'époque rationaliste de la théologie," *Revue des sciences philosophiques et théologiques* 53 (1969): 186–211; Juan Alfaro, "Die Heilsfunktionen Christi als Offenbarer, Herr und Priester," in *Mysterium Salutis: Grundriss heilsgeschichtlicher Dogmatik*, ed. Johannes Feiner and Magnus Löhrer, 5 vols. (Einsiedeln: Benziger, 1965–1976) 3/1:649–708; Ludwig Hödl, "Die Lehre von den drei Ämter Christi in der dogmatischen Konstitution

responsibility in the church is Walter's contribution to the emergence of the "sense of the faith."

In the various editions of his *Lehrbuch*, Walter saw the tasks of teaching, sanctifying, and leading as interconnected. For each of these responsibilities, he discerned the role and the participation of the faithful in accomplishing them. In this way, according to Ohly, Walter prepared the way for Vatican II's interpreting the "sense of the faith" in terms of the responsibilities of everyone in the church for teaching, sanctifying, and leadership.

Ohly pointed out "a dialogical ordering of the special and the universal priesthood"[29] in Walter's understanding of the ministry of sanctifying (*munus ministeriale*). In Walter's own words, the faithful "officially intervene as the community at prayer in the inner and mysterious life of the church—at the Sacrifice of the Mass, in intercession for sinners, and in the prayer for the ordination of ministers.[30] In these cases, it is true that the priest alone posits the external act, while the community really collaborates in the realm of the Spirit."[31]

The responsibility for leadership (*munus regiminis*) presents an interesting case, since in the nineteenth century non-clerics still played a meaningful role in the appointment to ecclesiastical office and in exercising oversight in regards to church property and church goods. Today, most of these opportunities have been eliminated, but in Walter's day, and in the earlier history that he would have known, such actions were real "exercises of co-responsibility." In the words of Walter, "The laity

---

des Zweiten Vatikanischen Konzils über die Kirche," in *Wahrheit und Verkündigung. Michael Schmaus zum 70. Geburtstag*, 2 vols., ed. Leo Scheffczyk, Werner Dettloff, and Richard Heinzmann (Munich: F. Schöningh, 1967) 2:1785–1806; Yves Congar, "Sur la trilogie: Prophète—Roi—Prêtre," *Revue des sciences philosophiques et théologiques* 67 (1983): 97–115; Joseph H. Crehan, "Priesthood, Kingship, and Prophecy," *Theological Studies* 42 (1981): 216–31; Peter Drilling, "The Priest, Prophet and King Trilogy: Elements of Its Meaning in *Lumen Gentium* and for Today," *Église et théologie* 19 (1988): 179–206; and Peter De Mey, "Sharing in the Threefold Office of Christ, A Different Matter for Laity and Priests? The *Tria Munera* in *Lumen Gentium, Presbyterourm Ordinis, Apostolicam Actuositatem* and *Ad Gentes*," in *The Letter and the Spirit: On the Forgotten Documents of Vatican II*, ed. Annemarie C. Mayer (Leuven: Peeters, 2018), 155–79.

29. Ohly, *Sensus fidei fidelium*, 66.

30. Is it possible to see these three areas as expressions of the sacraments of the Eucharist, reconciliation, and orders?

31. Quoted by Ohly, ibid., 66–67.

participate appropriately in most areas of public ecclesiastical discipline, namely, appointments to ecclesiastical offices, as well as what pertains to the administration of church property."[32] Ohly points out that the role of the laity in these cases involves more than merely external or consequent assent but includes "an active, contributory element."[33]

Finally, as regards the responsibility to teach (*munus magisterii*), Walter makes it clear that the faithful play a role here too. In light of their professions or walks of life, their responsibilities as parents, and their theological expertise, the laity truly contribute to the teaching activity of the church in the fullest sense.[34] This responsibility is based on the place they occupy in the world and the expertise they have gained from their involvement there. In this context it is noteworthy how Ohly mentions Walter's influence in this regard. He saw Walter leading the way to Vatican II. Walter took the "first steps of conciliar co-responsibility of all the faithful regarding the official teaching responsibility in the canonical language of his day. Because of their being bound to one another in the church the laity have the possibility, and even the responsibility, of offering their advice, their viewpoint, and thus their influence on the life of the church in matters of teaching."[35] Ohly concludes his treatment of Walter with high praise: "[In Ferdinand Walter] the 'sense of the faith' finds expression in an important exponent of German canon law."[36]

George Phillips (1804–72)

The understanding of the "sense of the faith" in conjunction with the threefold responsibilities of Christians in preaching, sanctifying, and leading was also advanced by another important canon lawyer of the

---

32. Quoted by Ohly, ibid., 67.

33. ". . . ein agierendes Element." Ibid.

34. Ohly explains Walter's position here in terms of the role the laity played at various councils of the church in the past, whether as secular rulers who convoked the councils or were influential in calling them, or the lay theologians who were active at these councils. In these historical data, however, can be found the seeds of a much broader understanding of "theological competence." In fact, Ohly mentions the role of the consultation of the laity by Pope Pius IX before he issued his *ex cathedra* teaching on Mary's immaculate conception. Ibid., 68–72.

35. Ibid., 70.

36. Ibid., 72.

nineteenth century, George Phillips.[37] The German canonist and legal historian, who was of English and Scottish parentage but born and educated in Germany, was a convert to Catholicism. Like Walter, Phillips took up the threefold division of ministry and so helped to extend and solidify its use in the Catholic Church. What is not clear is the extent to which Phillips's own understanding of the threefold ministry is ultimately fully compatible with the teaching of Vatican II.[38]

In a study of Phillips's influence on the development of the threefold ministry, Ludwig Schick has shown how Phillips was influenced by both Johann Adam Möhler and John Calvin.[39] From Calvin, Phillips borrowed the christological model of Christ as prophet, priest, and king and applied it to Möhler's understanding of the church as the Body of Christ. What resulted was another way of understanding the threefold ministry as applied to the church.[40] Despite his reliance on Möhler, Phillips entertained quite different ideas about the nature of the church. We saw above that Möhler's understanding was pneumatological and incarnational. This is not the case with Phillips's ecclesiology, which is marked by other categories entirely: authority, strict hierarchy, the subordination of the laity to the ordained, and an ultramontanist understanding of the papacy. When we compare Möhler's frame of reference to Phillips's understanding of the church, we see how different their ecclesiologies really are.[41]

---

37. On Phillips's life, writings, and contributions to theology, see Johannes Neumann, "George Phillips (1804–1872), in *Katholische Theologen Deutschlands im 19. Jahrhundert*, 2:293–317.

38. Christoph Ohly takes an affirmative stance on Phillips, pointing out his positive influence, but without being blind to the limitations in his thought. See *Sensus fidei fidelium*, 72–88 ["Der Rechtshistoriker und Kanonist George Phillips"].

39. "Die Tria-Munera in den Schriften George Phillips und in den Dokumenten des II. Vatikanischen Konzils—Ein Vergleich," *Österreichisches Archiv für Kirchenrecht* 32 (1981): 59–78. See also idem, "Die Drei-Ämter-Lehren nach Tradition und Zweitem Vatikanischen Konzil," *Internationale Katholische Zeitschrift* 10 (1981): 57–66 and idem, *Das dreifache Amt Christi und der Kirche: Zur Entstehung und Entwicklung der Trilogien* (Frankfurt & Bern: Peter Lang, 1982).

40. "Insofar as Phillips combined these two theological points of view, he constructed the ecclesiological trilogy." See "Die Drei-Ämter Lehren nach Tradition und Zweitem Vatikanischen Konzil," 65. See also ibid., 67.

41. Möhler's inspiration for the church as the Body of Christ is the fully developed metaphor-concept found in Colossians and Ephesians. Phillips, on the other hand, is motivated by the metaphor of the human body, its organic unity and hierarchical

It is important to note at the outset, however, that Phillips does not lose sight of the corporate character of the church, which he characterizes as "the gathering of those called to be members with Christ."[42] The same is true of the dignity of its members, as the following quotation illustrates:

> Just as all men originate with Adam, the first man, as regards their humanity, so too should all be derived spiritually from Christ, the new Adam. They should be Christians, that is, members of his body, the Church. They are not Christians because they are devotees of his teaching, but they are his brothers. Just as he put on human nature, so should men and women put on his divinity. They should be *christoi*—kings like him who have been anointed and crowned.[43]

Against the background of the underlying unity of all with Christ, we still must point out how for Phillips this takes place in a highly hierarchical view of the church. According to Phillips:

> The earthly kingdom is organically structured like the heavenly kingdom, but also like the human body, whose invisible head is Christ, and who takes his place as visible head, the successor of Peter. The entire order is connected to him, and is expressed in the hierarchy, as it is called, that is, in the holy ordering of its rulers.[44]

Against this foundation of papal authority, then, Phillips envisions the bishops following in their turn, and then the priests and deacons, and finally the lay faithful:

---

ordering. The language sounds reminiscent of Möhler's use, but Phillips's framework is quite different. In the end, Phillips drops mention of the church as the body of Christ, since in the meantime the concept of the church as the kingdom of God on earth has superseded it. Thus, according to Schick, "In his late *Lehrbuch des Kirchenrechts* (A Textbook on Canon Law) [1859–62, revised in 1871] he has returned completely to the idea of the Church as institutional and bound by its constitution in law. In this work he no longer employs the idea of the 'body of Christ.' The reason can be found in the fact that he became increasingly aware that an understanding of the Church as expressed by its constitutional law better grounded the authority of the pope and the monarchical-hierarchical view of the Church than the concept of the body of Christ could do." Ibid., 65n.

42. *Kirchenrecht*, 7 volumes (1845–69) 1:13. Reprinted in Graz in 1959.

43. *Kirchenrecht*, 1:12. Quoted by Ohly, *Sensus fidei fidelium*, 79.

44. *Kirchenrecht*, 1:14. Quoted by Schick, 67–68.

The laity [participate in the threefold ministry] by offering themselves in prayer, and by teaching, to the glory of God, each one in his circle of influence . . . and finally even though never directly in ecclesiastical governance itself, still to the extent that each one can exercise a not insignificant influence, in accordance with the Church's [constitutional] law.[45]

What is one to make of Phillips attributing the roles of prophet, priest, and kingly ruler to the faithful? How far do they extend? Where are they exercised concretely? Are they completely dependent on the hierarchy? Phillips offers the reader tantalizing hints but ultimately his view is unsatisfying. Perhaps the most one can say is that Phillips contributed modestly to the thought and direction of Möhler's ecclesiology by applying the threefold ministry to it.

At a later time, when the church chose to reflect more deeply on its nature at Vatican II, the framework of the threefold ministry was available to the church, thanks to the modest efforts of the laymen Ferdinand Walter and George Phillips.

---

45. *Kirchenrecht*, 1:296–97. Quoted by Schick, 69.

Chapter Three

The Role of the "Sense of the Faith" and the Definition of Mary's Immaculate Conception

The definition of Mary's immaculate conception played a significant role in the emergence of the "sense of the faithful" in the church of the nineteenth century. In addition to the spread of devotion to the Blessed Virgin among the faithful, especially through the popularity of the Miraculous Medal, the theologian Giovanni Perrone, in preparation for a possible definition of the dogma by the pope, examined the nature and role of tradition in the church and its relationship to the immaculate conception.

This chapter will examine the emergence of the "sense of the faith" against the backdrop of Pius IX's definition of the immaculate conception in 1854. The ordinary faithful played an essential role in maintaining the conviction of Mary's immaculate conception, even in the face of widespread questions from theologians. The popes supported the doctrine primarily by enhancing its celebration liturgically. Theologians wrestled with thorny underlying theological conundrums and communicated their insights to the faithful by their teaching but also their preaching. The bishops, too, supported the belief by liturgical means and by promoting Marian devotion. And the process continues even in our day as all in the church struggle to find new meaning under the circumstances of changing Marian devotion and the demands of new theological imperatives. In each of these stages, the "sense of the faith" was and is active as the whole church strives to understand and proclaim its Marian belief.

Before considering the process that led to the definition of Mary's immaculate conception and in particular the role of the "sense of the faith," let us examine the labyrinthine paths which the doctrine took in East and West. I propose to study the liturgical and devotional life of the church and the theological discussions that clarified the meaning of Marian devotion to the immaculate conception.

History of the Liturgy and the Theology of the Immaculate Conception

The modern dogma of Mary's immaculate conception presented formidable theological challenges to its definition. The doctrine could not be found clearly attested to in Scripture, and the historical sources, too, were not without their problems. In the case of Mary's immaculate conception, three issues demanded attention: (1) the ambiguity in both East and West regarding the moment when Mary the Mother of God (*Theotokos*) could be said to be all holy; (2) the doctrine of original sin in St. Augustine and its effects on the subsequent history of the question especially in the West; and (3) the necessity of maintaining the biblical doctrine that all men and women are in need of redemption.

Evidence from the Liturgy

The perfect holiness of Mary was not accepted without question in the earliest centuries of the church. Tertullian († c. 220), Origen († 253/254), John Chrysostom († 407), Cyril of Alexandria († 444), Theodore of Mopsuestia († 428), and many other bishops and theologians pointed to difficulties with a doctrine of the total absence of sin in Mary.[1] Other writers, however, defended her preeminent holiness, so that with time the conviction of Mary's holiness advanced in the East. Preeminent among them was the Syrian Jacob of Serug (c. 450–c. 520), who was followed

---

1. See the treatment by Brian K. Reynolds, "The Immaculate Conception," *Gateway to Heaven: Marian Doctrine and Devotion, Image and Typology in the Patristic and Medieval Periods* (Hyde Park, NY: New City, 2012), 1:331–37. To date, only the first volume of a proposed two-volume work by Reynolds has been published. The problematic biblical passages are usually Jesus's sayings about Mary and his family members in Mark 3:31-35 (parallels Matt 12:46-50 and Luke 8:19-21) and Mary's presumptuousness in urging Jesus to perform his first miracle at Cana in John 2:1-11.

by others in the East.[2] From the sixth century onward, in fact, the tide turned to a growing acceptance of Mary's perfect holiness and the absence of sin in her life. The Marian homilies of Theoteknos of Livias (late sixth to seventh century), Sophronius of Jerusalem (c. 550–638), Germanus of Constantinople (bishop from 715 to 730), Andrew of Crete (660–740), and John of Damascus (c. 675–753) frequently rhapsodize Mary as being without sin. At first she is praised for being purified and strengthened with grace at the annunciation, in preparation for the incarnation of the son, and then eventually within her mother Anne's womb. Still, it must be forthrightly admitted that the Eastern fathers do not always consider the peculiarly Western perspective on the question—namely, Mary's preservation from the stain of original sin.[3] This focus is peculiar to Western thinkers, particularly after St. Augustine (354–430), who concentrated heavily on the fact of original sin. Instead, the Eastern fathers speak with growing conviction that Mary was purified from the first moment of her existence in the womb.[4]

The feasts of Mary's nativity and her purification develop the motif of sinlessness. The nativity of Mary was among the four major Marian feasts

2. See Reynolds, *Gateway to Heaven*, 1:337.

3. According to Reynolds: "Thus when Germanus addresses the Virgin as the 'wholly immaculate One,' and Andrew writes of the extraordinary events surrounding Mary from, and even before, her conception, and speaks of the Virgin's life as being 'without spot of stain, utterly filled with every pure and holy quality, a life such as the world cannot grasp,' this does not mean that they were affirming the Immaculate Conception, although it could be argued that such statements laid the groundwork for the doctrine." *Gateway to Heaven*, 1:342.

4. Some of the fathers understood that Mary had been purified already in Anne's womb in anticipation of her conceiving the Son of God. It was felt that John the Baptist had been purified of sin in Elizabeth's womb when Mary visited Elizabeth and John leapt in his mother's womb at Mary's greeting. The reason for the purification was John's exalted mission to announce Jesus as the Messiah. So, too, the fathers understood that Mary had been purified, but at an earlier point of prenatal development, and that in view of her greater mission to be the Mother of God. In general, however, they are not very specific as to the exact moment of her purification or of her being preserved from sin. But the tendency grew among the Eastern bishops to regard Mary as having been preserved from all sin from the first moment of her existence. In the East, Mary's holiness emerged out of the very fact that she is the Mother of God and as such was preserved from all sin, both in the womb and throughout her life.

in the Eastern church that included Mary the Mother of God, the dormition of Mary, the nativity, and the purification.[5] According to Pierre Jounel, the nativity of Mary owes its origin to the commemoration in the sixth century of the founding of a church in Jerusalem a century before. This church originally commemorated the cure of the sick man by Jesus at the pool of Bethsaida (see John 5:1-19), but within a century its focus had shifted to Mary's birth and so was named after her. As Jounel remarks: "All the Churches, with the exception of the Syro-Nestorian Church, also celebrated the Nativity of Mary and her Entrance into the Temple. The spread of the Marian feasts of Jerusalem was an accomplished fact by the sixth century."[6] In the West, Rome soon followed suit, and proper prayers for the Mass can be found in the Gelasian (mid-eighth century) and the

---

5. We will consider the emergence of these feasts in greater detail in chapter 8, especially from the point of view of how devotional and liturgical practice led the church to deeper theological reflection on the doctrinal meaning of Mary and the mysteries that surrounded her life and her final moments. Clément Dillenschneider examined the meaning of the theological adage *lex supplicandi statuat legem credendi* and the role it plays in forming the "sense of the faithful." See my presentation of Dillenschneider in chapter 7. There, in footnote 33, I offer a short history and explanation of this rich and often neglected source.

6. Pierre Jounel, "The Veneration of Mary," in *The Church at Prayer*, vol. 4: *The Liturgy and Time*, ed. Aimé Georges Martimort (new edition; Collegeville, MN: Liturgical Press, 1986), 130–50, at 131–32 ["The Marian Feasts in Jerusalem"]. Around 715, Andrew of Crete preached four sermons dedicated to Mary's nativity in which he extolled her incomparable holiness. See J.-P. Migne, *Patrologia Graeca* 97, cols. 1046–1110. According to Luigi Gambero: "Andrew's witness to the Church's faith in the exceptional holiness of the Mother of the Lord is absolutely remarkable. He affirms more than once that the Blessed Virgin lived her whole life without being contaminated by any moral stain. The insistence with which the bishop of Crete returns to this point is so strong that some have seen him as an exponent of the Immaculate Conception. Even if we cannot accept this thesis without hesitation, we must at least recognize that Andrew had a highly elevated concept of the Virgin's sinlessness and holiness. . . . We have to keep in mind that the bishop of Crete did not share the notion of original sin that the Latin theologians had already formed. Therefore, it is understandable that he could speak in these terms without considering the problem of the presence or absence of original sin in Mary. Instead, Andrew appears to have believed that God prepared the holy Virgin in advance, on both the moral and the personal level, to make her worthy and capable of being God's Mother." Luigi Gambero, "Andrew of Crete," *Mary and the Fathers of the Church: The Blessed Virgin in Patristic Thought*, trans. Thomas Buffer (San Francisco: Ignatius Press, 1999), 391–99, at 392–93.

Gregorian (early ninth century) sacramentaries. Nevertheless, according to the historian of the liturgy Bernard Capelle, "The fate of the feast in the West was at first hesitantly received."[7] He points out how the feast was accepted in Gaul by the late seventh century and celebrated with greater solemnity in Rome in the thirteenth and fourteenth centuries.

The history of the fate of the celebration of the conception of Mary by St. Anne was even more checkered than that of Mary's nativity. The East had celebrated a feast from the eighth century, but as Sévérien Salaville has noted, the feast "did not develop under the influence of theological preoccupations, amid struggles and controversies, as was the case in the West. It is a phenomenon of Marian piety that simply burst on the scene in time and in a completely natural way occasioned dogmatic expressions, namely, declarations of the holiness of the Mother of God from her beginning, a doctrine that had been admitted long before the feast itself."[8] In the West, after it was introduced into England around 1050, it became the feast of Mary in the twelfth century. Of special importance in this regard was the English Benedictine Eadmer of Canterbury (c. 1064–1124), who established the feast on solid theological footing.[9] The feast became especially popular in Normandy, and according to Jounel, "Norman students brought it to Paris, whence it spread in turn, though not without opposition from some theologians. . . . Beginning in the thirteenth century it had the consistent support of the Franciscans, who adopted the feast as early as 1263, celebrating it in their convent in Rome."[10]

7. Bernard Capelle, "Les fêtes mariales," in *L'Église en prière*, ed. Aimé Georges Martimort (Paris: Desclée, 1961), 766–85, at 779.

8. Sévérien Salaville, "Marie dans la liturgie byzantine ou gréco-slave," in *Maria. Études sur la sainte Vierge*, 8 vols., ed. Hubert du Manoir (Paris: Beauchesne, 1949–1971), 1:247–326, at 254.

9. See Luigi Gambero, "Eadmer of Canterbury," *Mary in the Middle Ages: The Blessed Virgin Mary in the Thought of Medieval Latin Theologians*, trans. Thomas Buffer (San Francisco: Ignatius Press, 2005), 117–23 and Heinrich M. Köster, "Der Beitrag Eadmers zur theologischen Erkenntnis der Unbefleckten Empfängnis," in *Im Gewande des Heils: die Unbefleckte Empfängnis Mariens als Urbild der menschlichen Heiligkeit*, ed. German Rovira (Essen: Ludgerus Verlag, 1980), 61–70. The works of Eadmer can be found in *Eadmeri Monachi Cantuarensis tractatus de conceptione Sanctae Mariae*, ed. Herbert Thurston and Thomas Slater (Freiburg: Herder, 1904).

10. Pierre Jounel, "The Veneration of Mary," 139–40. Bernard Capelle points out that the feast was adopted by the Franciscan Order at its General Chapter held in Pisa in 1263,

The feast, however, suffered from the debilitating lack of thematic focus. What was being celebrated: the miraculous conception of Mary by her sterile parents, now beyond the years of conceiving life? A conception by Anne and Joachim that God miraculously preserved from the sinful passions of normal human sexual intercourse? A conception that preserved Mary from the stain of original sin from the first moment of her sentient life? A conception that preserved Mary from the stain of original sin from the moment of her animation, an event that was regarded to take place some thirty-five to eighty-two days after the creation of the body, according to the medical opinion of the time? Only clarity on the theological points that underpinned these issues could bring about agreement of Mary's immaculate conception. Such clarity, however, was still lacking.

The task would not be accomplished all at once but would require several generations of sifting through general assumptions among the laity and the ordinary members of religious orders, as well as among the more theologically educated bishops and theologians. The mere fact of celebrating the conception of Mary did not assure that the doctrinal center of the celebration was recognized as her complete freedom from original sin from the very first moment of her existence, and that with a view to her role of being the Mother of God. Between the eventual official teaching of the Catholic Church and the many possibilities of understanding Mary's conception there were a great many divergent interpretations.[11]

---

prescribing it for the entire order. "Les fêtes mariales," 783. Recently, Marielle Lamy has defended the position that the feast of Mary's conception had its origins in the West in Normandy. From there it spread to England, where it was warmly welcomed in Canterbury, Winchester, and elsewhere. See *L'Immaculée Conception: Étapes et enjeux d'une controverse au moyen-âge (XIIe–XVe siècles)*, Collection des Études Augustiniennes, Série Moyen Âge et Temps modernes, no. 35 (Paris: Institut d'Études Augustiniennes, 2000): 33–37 ["Les débuts obscurs de la fête en Angleterre"] and 38–42 ["Premières controverses en Angleterre"]. Lamy's examination of the often heated controversy of Mary's immaculate conception from the twelfth to the fifteenth centuries is now the indispensable source for studying the influences on the doctrine, its sources, and its historical unfolding. The importance of Lamy's study will be even clearer in the section below on the theological issues involved with Mary's immaculate conception.

11. Lamy has traced the confusion surrounding the understanding of what the feast meant to the laity, ordinary religious, bishops, popes, and theologians. See "Diffusion de la doctrine immaculiste et développement du culte," *L'Immaculée conception*, 381–86.

Resuming our discussion of the history of the acceptance of the feast of Mary's conception, Jounel and Capelle point to the eventual adoption of the feast in the fourteenth century by the popes in Avignon.[12] Finally, Sixtus IV (1471–84), a Franciscan pope, established the feast for the diocese of Rome in 1477. Only in 1708 did Clement XI extend the feast throughout the entire church in the West.

A more widespread liturgy of Mary's immaculate conception solidified the Marian piety and devotion of the ordinary faithful. In Eastern Christianity, there had long been the conviction of Mary's holiness and Mary was celebrated with a growing number of feasts and with an increasing clarity about her role in salvation history and her prominence among the saints. Mary's holiness made complete sense in light both of her status as the God-bearer, or Mother of God, and her virginity. Insights about Mary grew out of faith convictions regarding her son—especially the Council of Nicaea's defense of the full and equal divinity of Jesus Christ. A difference of theological accent between Christians of the East and West would eventually lead to differing doctrinal formulations within a shared liturgical veneration of Mary. Whereas the East has eschewed the multiplication of dogmas, preferring to remain content with the teachings of the first seven ecumenical councils and drawing on their power to unite and enliven the church, the West has been attracted by the intrinsic logic and cohesiveness of Christian truths to the point of refining them more and more and eventually even proceeding to the culminating act of officially defining them as revealed by God. Both East and West value the importance of the liturgical celebration of the truths of Christian revelation, but with different accents. In both traditions the liturgical dimension has enjoyed a certain primacy over the element of dogmatizing a given belief.

Benefits of Theological Development

If the liturgical celebration of Mary's immaculate conception moved forward by fits and starts, this was even more true of how the doctrine was received by theologians. Most of the second Christian millennium was given over to arguing for and against it. So-called maculists steadfastly

---

12. Bernard Capelle, "La liturgie mariale en Occident," in *Maria*, ed. Hubert du Manoir, 1:215–45, at 226–27.

resisted the doctrine practically up to the time of its definition in 1854. What, then, accounted for the stubborn rejection of the doctrine by theologians for so long? This question brings us to our second major consideration regarding the immaculate conception, particularly in the West—the role of the doctrine of original sin in coming to an agreement about Mary's immaculate conception.

The doctrine of original sin played a major role in the theological reflection of St. Augustine, especially in his dealings with the Pelagians.[13] The Western church, in fact, was so profoundly affected by Augustine's theology of grace that its subsequent history has remained deeply indebted to him. And yet Augustine's thought was not without its ambiguities and misconceptions, so that changes in the understanding of original sin were inevitable.[14] Western theologians would have to move beyond the flaws in Augustine's theology of sin and grace in a historical development that would result in the more balanced formulations of the Council of Trent.[15]

13. See the excellent presentation of Peter Brown, "Julian of Eclanum" in *Augustine of Hippo: A Biography* (new ed.; Berkeley and Los Angeles, CA: University of California Press, 2000), 383–99, where the author not only historically, philosophically, and theologically contextualizes Augustine's controversy with the Pelagians, but where he also frankly and forthrightly points out the assumptions of late Latin antiquity regarding the unavoidability of sexual passion and the intensity of the sexual act itself. These contexts, according to Peter Brown, explain the emphasis Augustine placed on this aspect of his doctrine of original sin, an aspect that is at once intensely physical and psychological.

14. On Augustine's thought, see Athanase Sage, "Péché originel: naissance d'un dogme," *Revue des études augustiniennes* 13 (1967): 211–48, idem, "Le péché originel dans la pensée de saint Augustin, de 412 à 430," *Revue des études augustiniennes* 15 (1969): 75–112, and Jesse Couenhoven, "St. Augustine's Doctrine of Original Sin," *Augustinian Studies* 36 (2005): 359–96. For a study of the roots of Augustine's thought, see Pier Franco Beatrice, *The Transmission of Sin: Augustine and the Pre-Augustinian Sources*, trans. Adam Kamesar (New York: Oxford University Press, 2013). Still very helpful for understanding the development of the doctrine of original sin and its modifications over time is Karl Rahner, "Original Sin" in *Sacramentum Mundi: An Encyclopedia of Theology*, 6 vols., ed. Karl Rahner (New York: Herder and Herder, 1969), 4:328–34 and his classic study "Erbsünde und Monogenismus" in Karl-Heinz Weger, *Theologie der Erbsünde*, Quaestiones Disputatae 44 (Freiburg: Herder, 1970), 176–223.

15. See Alfred Vanneste, "La préhistoire du décret du Concile de Trente sur le péché originel," *Nouvelle revue théologique* 86 (1964): 355–68 and 490–510, and idem, "Le décret du Concile de Trente sur le péché originel," *Nouvelle revue théologique* 87 (1965): 688–726 and 88 (1966): 581–602.

One of these Augustinian flaws was the focus on the role of the sexual act in conception. Since every person begins existence with the sexual union of a father and a mother, Augustine connected the universality of sin with the act of procreation.[16] This misguided emphasis on the connection between the sexual act and the real guilt of original sin placed the West in a quandary for centuries. Given the connection he established between the reality of the guilt of original sin and the origin of each person through the physical act of procreation, Augustine could not see his way to exempt Mary from the fate we all share, because she, too, had been conceived by her parents, Joachim and Anne, in the normal way, and that would have involved the sin-tinged passions of the act of sexual union.[17] Augustine bequeathed this legacy to subsequent generations of theologians in the West, so that the common teaching among Latin

16. Only Jesus was exempted from this anthropological law because he was conceived in a unique way through Mary's virginal conception of him "by the overshadowing of the Holy Spirit." Jesus was truly human while remaining the eternal word of the Father. In the background of Augustine's teaching lay two other indispensable presuppositions for it. Augustine, like all of his contemporaries and successors until recently, took the historicity of the biblical accounts of the creation and fall of Adam and Eve for granted. This meant that everyone born after Adam had inherited his guilt. Although Adam's guilt was primary, it was de facto passed on by the procreative act of sexual intercourse. Moreover, the universality of human guilt in Adam was confirmed for Augustine by his mistaken translation of Romans 5:12. Following the Latin version before him, Augustine understood the phrase *in quo* as "in whom (namely, in Adam) all have sinned." But the Greek phrase *eph' hō* is more correctly translated as "inasmuch as" or "because" all sinned, which need not entail some connection inherited from Adam but an association of all sinners with Adam. The consequence of Augustine's insisting on the literal idea of "in whom" meant that every human being born after Adam had to have inherited guilt from Adam. In Augustine's mind, the human experience of being physically overwhelmed in the act of sexual union pointed powerfully to the universality of sin. On Romans 5:12, see Joseph A. Fitzmyer, *Romans: A New Translation with Introduction and Commentary*, The Anchor Bible 33 (New York: Doubleday, 1993), 411–17, where he indicates eleven possible meanings of the phrase *eph' hō*.

17. Brian Reynolds draws on the writings of Augustine to explain the connection of the physical act of conception with the presence of concupiscent passion in the parents. For instance, he writes: "Mary, instead, could not have been conceived without original sin given that she was the product of the sexual union of her parents, Joachim and Anne. While for Augustine the consequences of original sin were absent in Mary due to the grace of God, this does not mean that he believed in the Immaculate Conception since he does not say that grace actually blocked the transmission of the original fault." *Gateway to Heaven*, 1:346–47.

theologians was that Mary had not been immaculately conceived. The knot Augustine had tied of human generation, the universality of sin with the need to be saved, and the necessity of being baptized as the means to salvation needed to be untied.[18] Was there another way to envision the need of all humanity to escape its estrangement from God and God's bestowal of grace than the one Augustine had formulated?

We saw above how Eadmer of Canterbury had found another way, but it was not entirely of his doing. Eadmer has been taught by St. Anselm (1033–1109) and it was Anselm who subtly shifted the understanding of original sin from each person's inheriting a state of guilt from Adam to each one's being conceived without grace. Original sin was less a matter that one had been conceived in sin than that each person came under the universal condition of being deprived of grace and holiness from conception.[19] All men and women were deprived of grace so that in Christ, God could lavish upon them God's very life. The sexual act of procreation was not constitutive of the state of original sin. The salvific will of God is directed toward all human beings without exception, and that because all were truly in need of God's grace.[20] Anselm provided the knife that

18. Augustine laid great stress on the practice of infant baptism. Since the creed spoke of "baptism for the forgiveness of sins" and infants as well as adults were in need of baptism, he concluded to the presence of true guilt—even in infants incapable of sinning personally.

19. Theologians after Vatican II distinguish more clearly between "personal sins" and the guilt of "original sin." When the latter term is used to express the individual's inherited state of being deprived of grace, it is, in this instance, more properly sin in an "analogical" sense. Karl Rahner writes: "For some centuries at least the teaching on original sin is used only 'analogously,' since it means primarily subjective, personal sin and the state of the actual sinner resulting from this. But in such an analogy it is clear that the two analogates differ in every respect from one another as much as they agree with one another. If this is true, it might be just as well to avoid a common term for the two analogates (in order not to obscure or overlook the difference) as it is to bring out the resemblance by seeing them together under a common but analogous term." See his "Yesterday's History of Dogma and Theology for Tomorrow," *Theological Investigations* 18, trans. Edward Quinn (New York: Crossroad, 1983), 3–34, at 26.

20. Here is how Brian Reynolds expresses Anselm's contribution: "[Anselm's] theory of original sin opened up new possibilities. His argument that it was the absence of the state of original justice, lost as a result of Adam's disobedience, which was transmitted when a new life was generated, resulting in a will that was easily corrupted, and not any inherent sinfulness transmitted in the male seed, meant that it was possible to overcome

would cut the Gordian knot Augustine had tied.[21] Future generations of theologians would benefit from Anselm's insight, and thereby both clarify the concepts employed to express a doctrine of original sin and also resolve the issue of Mary's spotless conception.

As the heyday of high scholasticism dawned, the majority of Western theologians continued to support the common opinion that Mary had been conceived with original sin but that she had also been sanctified at some stage in her mother's womb prior to her birth. If Christ came to save all human beings, then he came as universal savior, and that must have included his mother, Mary. Given the universality of this soteriological principle, she too must have been in need of redemption. In some form or other this was the opinion of Alexander of Hales (c. 1186–1245) and Bonaventure (1221–74) among the Franciscans, and Albert the Great (c. 1200-80) and Thomas Aquinas (1225–74) among the Dominicans.[22] A generation later John Duns Scotus (c. 1265–1308) would cautiously present the opinion that Mary had been preserved from all stain of sin,

---

the obstacle posed by Mary's natural conception because it decoupled the issue of whether the procreative act was inherently lustful from the question of the means of transmission of original sin. . . . Effectively, Anselm had offered the first viable alternative to Augustine's teaching on the transmission of original sin, which was of major importance for the question of the Immaculate Conception, though it took several centuries for the full implications of his theory to be worked out." *Gateway to Heaven*, 1:352.

21. Anselm himself denied Mary's immaculate conception, not perceiving the implications of his own breakthrough, and continued to support the idea that Mary had been purified in St. Anne's womb. In his later work *Cur Deus homo* (1094–97), he writes: "Moreover, the virgin, from whom that man was taken of whom we are speaking, was of the number of those who were cleansed from their sins before his birth, and he was born of her in her purity" (book 2, chapter 16), *St. Anselm, Basic Writings*, trans. S. N. Deane (2nd ed.; Lasalle, IL: Open Court, 1962), 283.

22. See the discussion of the theological opinions during this fertile period by Georg Söll, *Mariologie*, 164–77 ["Der Werdegang des Glaubens an die Erbsündenfreiheit Mariens"] and Marielle Lamy, *L'Immaculée Conception*, "Deuxième Partie: La doctrine immaculiste à l'âge d'or de la théologie scolastique: de la négation à la reconnaissance (c. 1240-1305)," 235–378. Helpful summaries can be found in Brian Reynolds, *Gateways to Heaven*, 1:360–69, Benoît-Dominique de La Soujeole, "L'Immaculée Conception proprement dite" and "La préservation de tout péché," *Initiation à la théologie mariale* (Paris: Parole et Silence, 2007), 157–63 and 165–70 respectively, and Dominique Cerbelaud, *Marie, un parcours dogmatique*, Cogitatio Fidei 232 (Paris: Cerf, 2003), 147–53.

including original sin. The Scotistic breakthrough was the insight that Mary had indeed been saved, but saved not by a *purification* but by *preservation from sin* in view of her son's redemptive act. The divine intention in saving humankind included the intention to preserve Mary from all sin, both original and personal.[23] Building on the devotion of the English church to the feast of Mary's conception and on the theological contributions of Anselm and Eadmer, Scotus turned the page on the long history of Augustine's authoritative teaching that Mary, too, had been conceived with original sin.[24] It would take several more centuries, however, before the Scotistic opinion would prevail outside the Franciscan Order, so weighty were the authorities of Augustine, Peter Lombard's *Sentences*, and Aquinas.[25]

23. For Scotus's *De immaculata conceptione beatae virginis* in his *Ordinatio* Book III, distinction 3, quaestion 1, see *Four Questions on Mary*, trans. Allan Wolter (Santa Barbara, CA: Old Mission Santa Barbara, 1988), 36–62, with Latin text and Wolter's English translation on facing pages. See also George Tavard, "John Duns Scotus and the Immaculate Conception," in *The One Mediator, the Saints, and Mary*, Lutherans and Catholics in Dialogue 8, ed. H. George Anderson, J. Francis Stafford, and Joseph A. Burgess (Minneapolis: Augsburg Press, 1992), 209–17. Marielle Lamy discusses the influence of the English strain of thought on Scotus and his definitive formulation in *L'Immaculée Conception*, 336–78 ["Les fruits de la tradition insulaire"]. Lamy devotes special attention to the controverted question of whether the master, William of Ware, influenced his student, Scotus, or whether William conceded Scotus's surer theological insight on Mary's immaculate conception. Lamy presents Scotus's view in detail on pages 367–78.

24. The question of whether Scotus himself held the immaculate conception to be a certain teaching or a probable opinion is hotly debated by scholars of the period. Lamy has carefully scrutinized the differences in Scotus's own writings—the text from his *Ordinatio* written at Oxford, and the subsequent texts, especially the various incomplete *Reportationes*. Here is how she diplomatically concludes her analysis of the question: "It would appear that Duns Scotus deliberately covered his tracks. The ambiguities and hesitations in the texts are certainly indirect witnesses to this . . . and do not authorize us to make of him the legendary herald of the immaculate conception. If we were to take stock of the various arguments, the debate strikes us as pointless in the end. More than the views of Scotus, who apparently did not judge it wise to put them on display himself, what matters in our mind are the traces his discussion left in the minds of his contemporaries. Ignoring the nuances and the careful expressions he employed, his contemporaries very quickly interpreted them in a univocal sense." *L'Immaculée Conception*, 378. The "sense of the faith," then, was active among the theologians who came after Scotus.

25. For this period extending over the fourteenth and fifteenth centuries, see Georg Söll, *Mariologie*, 174–93.

In connection with the eventual dominance of the Scotistic teaching, mention needs to be made of the premature definition of Mary's immaculate conception by the Council of Basel.[26] This event is often passed over in silence in histories of the doctrine, or is at most relegated to an obscure reference.[27] In a treatment of the "sense of the faithful," it is at least of historical interest to inquire further as to what was going on when the bishops and theologians at Basel decided to define this doctrine.

By the time Basel treated the question of Mary's immaculate conception, Pope Eugene IV had abandoned his support of the council and had instead convened another, first at Ferrara and a year later transferred to Florence.[28] Canonically, Basel no longer met the requirements for a valid council, but that is not how the participants of Basel saw the matter. The maculist position had been defended by the prior general of the Dominicans, John of Montenegro, and his Dominican confrere, John of Torquemada, while John of Segovia defended the immaculist view. In the end, on September 17, 1439, Basel issued a statement favoring Mary's immaculate conception and declared the following:

> Indeed, we define . . . the doctrine that the glorious virgin Mary and Mother of God, . . . was never in fact subject to original sin but was always free from all original and actual guilt—the holy and immaculate one. This pious teaching is in accord with the Church's cult, the Catholic faith, right reason, and Holy Scripture and is to be approved, held, and

26. On the Council of Basel, see Karl August Fink, "Eugene IV and the Council of Basel-Ferrara-Florence," in *Handbook of Church History*, ed. Hubert Jedin and John Dolan, trans. Anselm Biggs (New York: Herder and Herder, 1969), 4:473–87.

27. Dominique Cerbelaud, *Marie un parcours dogmatique*, 155–56, is an exception. The standard reference for Basel now is Marielle Lamy, who has studied in great detail the controversies between the Franciscans and Dominicans leading up to the council. See *L'Immaculée Conception*, 591–620 ["Le 'Lobbying' des immaculistes et son aboutissement au Concile de Bâle"].

28. The Council of Ferrara-Florence (1438–43) is universally recognized by Catholics as an ecumenical council. But Ferrara-Florence was preceded by another council at Basel (1431–47) that, convened by Pope Eugene IV, began as ecumenical and followed in the footsteps of the Council of Constance (1414–18). Constance had ended the Great Western Schism and defended a moderate form of conciliarism in its document *Haec sancta synodus* designed to promote the reform of the papacy. The council's specific decisions for implementation of the reform of the papacy were spelled out in the document *Frequens*.

embraced by all Catholics. Furthermore, we declare that no one is to preach or teach as licit anything contrary to it.[29]

In addition, the council confirmed December 8 as the feast of the Immaculate Conception, commanded religious orders to observe it as a day of obligation, and offered the faithful the benefit of indulgences on the feast. Regarding Basel, Georg Söll observed:

> From a critical-theological point of view, the formulation could hardly have been considered satisfactory at the time, even though the Council willed to issue a dogma of the faith. Nonetheless, the immaculate conception had become an object of a conciliar decision, and in the following years was accepted in Spain, France, Switzerland, Germany, Austria and Belgium, as well as by the universities of Paris, Cologne, Mainz and Louvain. Without a doubt it influenced further theological discussion as well as the liturgy and the devotion of the faithful.[30]

Because of the dominance of Thomas Aquinas's thought, the Dominicans resisted Scotus's solution for centuries. Ever since Sixtus IV's decision in *Grave nimis* (1483) in favor of the doctrine, its acceptability and popularity among theologians and the faithful at large grew steadily.[31] The papacy usually tolerated the Thomistic opinion and even defended the right of the Dominicans to teach their opinion to members of their order.[32]

---

29. "Nos vero . . . doctrinam illam disserentem gloriosam Virginem Dei Genitricem Mariam . . . numquam actualiter subiacuisse originali peccato, sed immunem semper fuisse ab omni originali et actuali culpa sanctam et immaculatam, tamquam piam et consonam cultui ecclesiastico, fidei catholicae, rectae rationi et sacrae scripturae ab omnibus catholicis approbandam fore, tenendam et amplectandam, definimus et declaramus nullique de cetero licitum esse in contrarium praedicare seu docere." Quoted by Söll, *Mariologie*, 182, from J. D. Mansi, *Sacrorum conciliorum et decretum collectio nova et amplissima collectio*, 53 vols. (Florence/Venice/Paris/ Leipzig, 1759–1927) 29:182–83. My translation.

30. Söll, *Mariologie*, 183. From the perspective of the present study on the role of the "sense of the faithful," I direct the reader's attention to the observation in the definition that the teaching is "in accord with the Catholic faith." It is likely that here is yet another witness before the Council of Trent of the role of the faithful in expressing the church's faith.

31. Georg Söll has canvassed this long period of theological gestation of the doctrine of Mary's immaculate conception in *Mariologie*, Handbuch der Dogmengeschichte, vol. 3, fascicle 4 (Freiburg: Herder, 1978), 198–207 ["Das Immaculata-Dogma im letzten Widerstreit"].

32. In the bull *Sollicitudo* (1661), Alexander VII maintained: "The faithful believe that [Mary's] soul, from the first moment of its being formed and being breathed into her

But with the passage of time, a series of popes began to limit this freedom and to favor the teaching of the Scotistic view. By the mid-seventeenth century, the controversy was more or less drained of all vitality, and when Alexander VII (1655–67) issued the Bull *Sollicitudo omnium ecclesiarum* on December 8, 1661, favoring the doctrine but not defining it, the die had been cast in favor of those who supported the immaculate conception.[33]

The controversy continued throughout the seventeenth and eighteenth centuries, but it was only a matter of time before theological conviction caught up with the acceptance of the faith and devotion of the faithful that in some countries had been nourished by the liturgical celebration of the feast already for several centuries. The most prominent way in which the papacy advocated in behalf of Mary's immaculate conception was to approve of the liturgical celebration of the doctrine in the Office of the Hours and at a Mass commemorating Mary's immaculate conception. In this way, more than through direct intervention in the theological tendencies of the schools of theology and the theologies championed by the universities,[34] the papacy nourished the "sense of the faith" regarding Mary's immaculate conception.[35]

---

body, has been preserved from the stain of original sin by a special privilege of divine grace with a view to the merits of her Son Jesus Christ, the Savior of humankind, and that in this sense the feast of her Conception is be honored and celebrated solemnly." Despite the directness of this statement, the pope still refused to condemn the position of the maculists as "heretical" and he rejected the accusation that those who did not accept the doctrine committed a mortal sin. See Söll, *Mariologie*, 204–5.

33. The actions of two preceding popes of the seventeenth century facilitated Alexander VII's decision. In 1617, Paul V (1605–21) forbade anyone in the church to teach publicly that Mary had been conceived with original sin (*Sanctissimus*, dated September 12, 1617). Paul's successor, Gregory XV (1621–23) extended the prohibition to include even private communications (June 4, 1622).

34. The magisterium of the popes and the bishops has long valued and respected the contributions of a broad variety of theological schools. The principle is that revelation is so rich and its understanding so implicated with various epistemologies that no one school can embrace the fullness of Christian truth. In their definitions, ecumenical councils generally have avoided deciding between schools of thought, preferring to reassert the most basic elements necessary to preserve the truth of revelation while granting considerable freedom of thought to the schools. See Karl Rahner and Herbert Vorgrimler, "Schools of Theology," in *Dictionary of Theology*, trans. Richard Strachan, David Smith, Robert Nowell, and Sarah O'Brien Twohig (2nd ed.; New York: Crossroad, 1981), 466–67.

35. In the words of Brian Reynolds: "Throughout the history of the Church it has been accepted that practices and beliefs that are embraced by large numbers of the people may

Definition of Mary's Immaculate Conception and the Role of the "Sense of the Faithful"

The ideas of Johann Adam Möhler about living tradition influenced the Jesuits who taught at the Roman College. In turn, they influenced the development of the notion of the "sense of the faithful" as it was applied to Pope Pius IX's definition of Mary's immaculate conception in 1854. This is true especially of Giovanni Perrone, the teacher of subsequent professors at the Roman College, Carlo Passaglia and Clemens Schrader, and their students, Johannes Baptist Franzelin and Matthias Joseph Scheeben.[36] In the hands of these Roman masters the notion of the "sense of the faithful" was more widely accepted in theology.

The Roman School: Giovanni Perrone, SJ (1794–1876)

The renewal of theology at the center of Catholicism was a reaction both to Napoleon's humiliation of the Roman Pontiff Pius VII (1800–23) and to the limits of Baroque theology as it faced the challenges to Catholic thought posed by the various philosophical, social, and political currents in nineteenth-century Europe.[37] The so-called Roman School of theology

---

be of divine inspiration, although it requires the discernment of the Magisterium to determine whether this is in fact so." *Gateway to Heaven*, 1:353. The words of Marielle Lamy are more cautious. She writes: "This [survey] leads us to another conclusion: the role played by the mendicant orders was doubtlessly determinative. The members of these orders who had received doctorates were not only university careerists but many of them were also pastors and preachers. To a certain extent they were able to popularize the learned theology they had received. It is hard to identify any influence from the opposite direction though. Even if our vision of the nature and origin of our sources is somewhat distorted, one can hardly attribute to the people the primary role in the dynamic expansion of the feast of the Conception and of the immaculist doctrine. Nevertheless, it seems that the people did not require too much persuasion but closely followed the lead of their pastors in solidifying this new devotion." *L'Immaculée Conception*, 465–66.

36. On the Roman College, see Gerald McCool, *Catholic Theology in the Nineteenth Century: The Quest for a Unitary Method* (New York: Seabury, 1977), 81–87 ["Renascent Scholasticism"].

37. On this turbulent period, see Roger Aubert, Johannes Beckmann, Patrick J. Corish, and Rudolf Lill, *History of the Church*, vol. 7: *The Church between Revolution and Restoration*, ed. Hubert Jedin and John Dolan, trans. Peter Becker (New York: Crossroad, 1981). See also John W. O'Malley, "Catholicism and the Century of Lights," *Vatican I: The*

emerged, flourished, and was transformed both by political events on the Italian peninsula and by the life and politics at the papal court.[38] A more pronounced scholastic phase known as "neoscholasticism" characterized the Roman School from 1879 on, the year of the publication of Leo XIII's encyclical *Aeterni Patris*. We are interested primarily in the contribution of Giovanni Perrone at the Roman College to the emergence of the "sense of the faithful" in recent Catholic theology and the process of the definition in 1854 of Mary's immaculate conception.

In the course of an illustrious career as professor (1824–53) and then rector and prefect of studies (1853–76) at the Roman College, Giovanni Perrone distinguished himself by writing an enormously popular textbook of theology in eight volumes,[39] as well as his magisterial study of the immaculate conception, *De immaculato B.V. Mariae conceptu an dogmatico decreto definiri possit. Disquisitio theologica* (The Concept of the Immaculate Conception and the Possibility of Its Dogmatic Definition: A Theological Disquisition) (1847).[40] In addition to this theological output, Perrone is also important because of his personal contact with John Henry Newman and its ultimately beneficial outcome regarding Newman's life in the Catholic Church as a recent convert, as well as his ideas on the "sense of the faithful" and on the development of doctrine.[41] What, then, did Perrone hold regarding the "sense of the faithful"?

Council and the Making of the Ultramontane Church (Cambridge, MA: Belknap Press, 2018), 23–54.

38. See Aubert, Beckmann, Corish, and Lill, *History of the Church*, vol. 8: *The Church in the Age of Liberalism*, ed. Jedin and Dolan, trans. Becker (New York: Crossroad, 1981) and John W. O'Malley, *Vatican I: The Council and the Making of the Ultramontane Church*.

39. See the *Praelectiones theologicae* (Rome: Typis Collegii Urbani, 1835–42, and an expanded edition in 1854–55). The *Praelectiones theologicae* (Lectures on Theology) eventually saw forty-three editions and printings (1835–99).

40. I am closely following the treatment by Walter Kasper in his 1962 doctoral dissertation *Die Lehre von der Tradition in der Römischen Schule*, recently reissued as vol. 1 of Walter Kasper Gesammelte Schriften (Freiburg: Herder, 2011). The pagination of the original 1962 edition is indicated in the margins of the 2011 reprint, and makes for handy consultation of either edition.

41. Roger Aubert has written of Giovanni Perrone that "to his credit . . . the relatively new treatment of the relationship between reason and faith was introduced into classical theology. He also sensed the importance of positive theology, which during the pontificate of Pius IX came to full bloom in the Roman College under his students Carlo Passaglia

Perrone's interest in the "sense of the faithful" was piqued by the question of the definability of the doctrine of Mary's immaculate conception. In 1843, Cardinal Luigi Lambruschini published his *Dissertazione polemica sull'immacolato concepimento di Maria* (A Polemic Dissertation on the Immaculate Conception of Mary), which called for the definition of the doctrine.[42] Pius IX (1846–78) was favorably inclined to accede to the request, but the weakness of the arguments from Scripture and from the fathers, and the absence of unanimity among the theological schools, gave him reason to pause. Independently, Perrone decided to take up the challenge posed by the problems in the sources and witnesses. Was there perhaps another way of looking at the issue in light of the church's tradition?

Perrone's presentation in *De immaculato B.V. Mariae conceptu an dogmatico decreto definiri possit* is divided into two parts.[43] In part 2, Perrone develops a theological argument in support of the Marian defi-

---

and Johannes Franzelin." *History of the Church*, vol. 8, 46–47. T. Howland Sanks, too, views Perrone positively: "His reputation was world-wide . . . and his influence great. . . . He had great respect for and knowledge of the Christian tradition as well as familiarity with the contemporary theologians of his time, both Catholics and Protestants. He was particularly influenced by Möhler." *Authority in the Church: A Study in Changing Paradigms* (Missoula, MT: American Academy of Religion, 1974), 22. On Perrone's ultramontanist leanings, see Richard F. Costigan, "Giovanni Perrone, S.J., 1794–1876," *The Consensus of the Church and Papal Infallibility: A Study in the Background of Vatican I* (Washington, DC: Catholic University of America Press, 2005), 165–85.

42. Rome: Edizione Propaganda Fidei, 1843. On Lambruschini, see L. Pasztor, "Lambruschini, Luigi," in *New Catholic Encyclopedia*, vol. 8 (Detroit, MI: Gale Group, 2003), 307–8. Not to be lightly discounted was the effect of the three appearances of the Virgin Mary to St. Catherine Labouré, a sister of the Daughters of Charity of St. Vincent de Paul. According to Catherine, in 1830 the Virgin Mary appeared to her and requested that she be honored by a medal that bore her likeness and the prayer "O Mary, conceived without sin, pray for us who have recourse to you." The archbishop of Paris, Hyacinthe-Louis de Quélen (1821–39) accepted Catherine's vision as genuine and worked to spread devotion to the medal. The so-called Miraculous Medal enjoyed enormous popularity at the time and for decades thereafter, and contributed to the popular acceptance of Mary's immaculate conception by devout Catholics in France and throughout the world. See René Laurentin, *Catherine Labouré: Visionary of the Miraculous Medal*, trans. Paul Inwood (English translation © Sisters of Charity of St. Vincent de Paul, 1983; Boston, MA: Pauline Books & Media, 2006), especially 34–49 ["The Apparitions (April–December 1830)" and 53–61 ["The Medal at Last"]. See also Söll, *Mariologie*, 206.

43. Part 1 is an examination of the data from Scripture, the fathers, and the magisterium.

nition based on his understanding of living tradition and his argument from the "sense of the faithful." In chapter 2, "The Reasons Why These Conditions Can Be Met," Perrone answers the question as to whether the conditions for a definition are in fact met in the case of the immaculate conception. He answers that they are because of the status of tradition regarding the doctrine. He writes:

> For these reasons we assert that the Churches have preserved the doctrine handed down from Christ and the apostles and this because it has been transmitted to those after them [the apostles] by reason of the succession of bishops, inasmuch as, by instituting others to be their successors, they have certainly handed on that which they received from their predecessors. Moreover, they handed on Christian doctrine by actions of an active magisterium, by usages and practices, and by instituted rites and other such actions. . . . Accordingly, although the Fathers on this or that point were completely silent, it should not be concluded that this tradition or doctrine lacked all force in the Church. In fact, sometimes it [true doctrine] can be found in what is rejected as living doctrine, but then is later shown by the fact that many Fathers and doctors have accepted it in their subsequent writings. . . . Therefore, the perpetual magisterium of the Church, practice or custom as confirmed by the records, *and the general sense of the pastors and the faithful* are adequate for determining doctrine in force in the same Church.[44]

44. "Ex his assequimur, ecclesias conservasse doctrinam a Christo et ab Apostolis traditam eamque per episcoporum successionem posteris transmisisse, quatenus ipsi nimirum ceteros instituendo ad successores transmiserint quod a praecessoribus acceperant. Transmiserant autem tum activi opera magisterii, tum usu et praxi, tum institutis ritibus, aliisque eiusdemmodi. . . . Quamvis proinde Patres de aliquo peculiari doctrinae articulo vel parce admodum disseruerint, vel etiam, quia nulla sese eis obtulit occasio, penitus siluerint; non ideo tamen concludendum, traditionem aut doctrinam illam in Ecclesia minime viguisse. Quinimo contingere quandoque potest, ut nonnulli Patres ac doctores ea interdum in scriptis habeant suis, quae vigenti doctrinae repugnant. . . . Satis igitur est ad cognoscendam traditam doctrinam in Ecclesia vigentem iuge eiusdem Ecclesiae magisterium, praxis seu consuetudo, quae monumentis firmetur, et communis ipse pastorum ac fidelium sensus." *De immaculato B. V. Mariae Conceptu,* 142–43. The translations that follow are mine. My italics. Among patristic witnesses to the "sense of the faithful," Perrone cites Irenaeus, Tertullian, Pope Stephen's letter to Cyprian, Paulinus of Nola, Epiphanius, Jerome, Augustine, and Vincent of Lérins. Among authors from the second Christian millennium, he mentions Melchior Cano and Gregory of Valencia. See ibid., 143–45.

In the four remaining paragraphs of chapter 2, Perrone goes on to mention the *communis fidelium sensus*, the *communis sensus*, and the *fidelium consensus* five more times. It is clear that to him the patristic, Tridentine, and post-Tridentine teaching of theologians regarding the "sense of the faithful" is of central significance.

In chapter 4, "On the Immaculate Conception of the Virgin and Its Dogmatic Definition," Perrone returns to the argument from the "sense of the faithful." He writes:

> In order for a dogmatic definition to be issued, it suffices that the article concerned is at least *implicitly* contained in the sacred scriptures, and that its seeds as it were germinate and are contained in the primitive tradition. Even though Scripture and the earliest Fathers are silent on the matter, the tradition is at least maintained by the magisterium of the Church and by the general conviction of the faithful, until at last the occasion arises that opens up the possibility that the doctrine has indeed been divinely revealed whether in the writings of the Fathers or as attested to in other sources.[45]

He even quotes Denis Pétau in support of his position and claims that "because of the wonderful conviction and consensus of the faithful," Pétau too was able "to freely consent to this pious opinion" of Mary's immaculate conception.[46] Since the argument from tradition was so central to Perrone's understanding he could write:

> I have spoken of *divine and apostolic traditions* because otherwise there would be no probable and solid explanation that could be adduced for the strength of the firm and universal consensus over many centuries

---

45. "Ad dogmaticam edendam definitionem id satis Ecclesiae est, ut *implicite* saltem articulus, quo de agitur, in sacris habeatur litteris, ac eius veluti semina, quae deinceps progerminent, in primitiva contineantur traditione; vel etiam ut silentibus Scripturis ac primis etiam Patribus, saltem traditio in Ecclesiae magisterio, et communi fidelium persuasione servata fuerit, donec data tandem occasione, doctrina quae fuerat revelata divinitus sive per Patrum scripta, sive per alia monumenta in apertum veniat." Ibid., 154. Italics in the original.

46. "Hac pene mirabilis fidelium suasione et consensus permotum sese fatetur Petavius ad piam sectandam sententiam." Ibid., 156. He then quotes Pétau's support for the immaculate conception in his *De Incarnatione*, book 14, chapter 2, §10.

by the faithful and the pastors of the Church, as well as the ancient [Marian] cult in both the Eastern and the Western Churches.[47]

A second important idea regarding the "sense of the faithful" developed by Perrone was his notion of the *conspiratio* of the bishops and the faithful as the expression of their witnessing to and confessing the truth of revelation. Perrone asks what can be said about the true sense of the church regarding Mary's conception.[48] He responds by referring to certain "pointers and exhibits" (*indicia ac manifestationes*) that argue in favor of the doctrine. These include "public acts, liturgies, a feast, prayers." Then he adds another indication: "the bishops and the faithful breathing in unison as it were" (*pastorum ac fidelium in unum veluti conspiratio*).[49] The bishops and the faithful in their mutual action resemble the two lungs of a person that breathe together in unison.[50] Perrone returns to the idea later. He writes:

> Third, on the contrary, the proclivity of the Church, indeed the *conspiratio*, is in the direction of this pious opinion and indeed is its clear meaning. This opinion is the most ancient one. . . . Therefore, it is crystal-clear that the pointers give evidence of the cult surrounding this mystery and its determinate object. And fourth, the unanimous agreement of the pastors and the faithful have existed for many centuries and

47. "Dixi *traditionis divinae atque apostolicae*; neque vero id solum quia secus nulla ratio adduci probabilis posset tam constantis, tamque firmae atque universalis consensionis ad plura secula vigentis tum fidelium tum Ecclesiae pastorum, nec non cultus adeo antiqui in utraque Ecclesia orientali et occidentali." Ibid., 159. Italics in the original.

48. "Quid de germano Ecclesiae sensu circa B. Virginis Conceptionem sentiendum videatur, disquiritur." *De immaculato B. V. Mariae conceptu an dogmatico decreto definiri possit*, part 1, chapter 15 (§III).

49. "In catholicae Ecclesiae sensum quoad aliquam sententiam inquirere perinde quidem est atque investigare, in quam illa partem animum suum proclivem magis patefecerit. Huius vero propensionis indicia, ac manifestationes, sunt publica eius acta, liturgiae, festa, orationes, pastorum ac fidelium in unum veluti conspiratio." *De immaculato B. V. Mariae conceptu an dogmatico decreto definiri possit*, 101.

50. With the notion of *conspiratio*, Perrone closely approximates the teaching of Vatican II that the "sense of the faithful" includes all the members of the church. In a sense, Perrone's use, and as we will see, especially with John Henry Newman's adoption of the notion, *conspiratio* of the bishops and the faithful renders the meaning of the "sense of the faithful" of Vatican II.

is clear from liturgies, feasts, liturgical texts, controversies surrounding the faith, and even preaching. Therefore, it must be held all the more as the general "sense of the Church" theologically speaking.[51]

The image proved seminal and was employed by Pius IX in his definition of the immaculate conception. It deeply affected John Henry Newman, who adopted it and further developed it.

Perrone was able to retrieve both ancient and more recent teachings because his theology of the church was nourished by Möhler's ecclesiology in his *Symbolism*.[52] The "sense of the faithful" and the act of "breathing in unison of the bishops and the faithful" made sense to him because they expressed the nature of the church's living tradition.[53]

---

51. "3. E contrario quae Ecclesiae propensionem, immo et conspirationem erga piam sententiam, adeoque eius sensum patefaciunt, esse antiquissima. . . . deinde luculentissima esse, quippe quae et cultum huius mysterii ac determinatum obiectum exhibent. 4. Unanimem pro eadem pia sententia pastorum ac fidelium consensionem ad plura secula extitisse, quaeque per liturgias, per festa, per euchologia, per fidei controversias, per conciones denique patefacta est. Quanti vero faciendus sit communis eiusmodi Ecclesiae sensus in re theologica." Ibid., 109.

52. In this section he even quotes at length Möhler's *Symbolism*, §58. See ibid., 142n2. Earlier he had referenced Möhler's *Symbolism*, §39. See ibid., 136n1. Walter Kasper frequently points out the influence of Möhler on Perrone's thought. See *Die Lehre von der Tradition in der Römischen Schule*, 164 [79], 170 [83], 172 [85], 195–96 [102–3], 266 [155], 272 [159], 274 [161], 284 [168], 297 [178], and 299 [180].

53. Perrone's book was subjected to harsh criticism by two members of the Roman Commission established by Pius IX in 1848. Filippo Cossa was professor of dogmatic theology and a colleague at the Roman College and Bishop Vincenzo Tizzani was a consultor on the Congregation of the Index of Forbidden Books. See their criticisms in Gerhard Müller, "Die unbefleckte Empfängnis Mariens im Urteil päpstlicher Ratgeber 1848–1852," *Zeitschrift für Kirchengeschichte* 78 (1967): 300–39 at 313 (Cossa) and 325–26 (Tizzani). Hermann Josef Pottmeyer, too, has a rather dim view of Perrone's theology in general: "In spite of his clear effort to deepen the theology of the Church, Perrone's ecclesiology still remains determined by an over-emphasis on the dimension of authority." *Unfehlbarkeit und Souveränität*, 283–98, at 298. Perrone's understanding of the "sense of the faithful" left something to be desired, however. It is clear from Perrone's treatment in *De immaculato B.V. Mariae conceptu an dogmatico decreto definiri possit* that he attributed great importance to the "sense of the faithful" in advocating for the definition of Mary's immaculate conception, but I have not been able to find further use of it in the editions of his *Praelectiones theologicae*, vol. 8: *Tractatus de locis theologicis* Pars prima and Pars secunda after 1847. If anywhere, one would expect to find it incorporated into his treat-

Pius IX and the Definition of the Immaculate Conception (1854)

After centuries of papal encouragement, early in his papacy Pius IX moved to advance the status of the doctrine. However, he did so cautiously by engaging cardinals, bishops, theologians, and eventually the faithful in the process of consultation—a multilayered process that spanned seven years.[54] In June of 1848 Pius appointed a commission of twenty cardinals, officials of the Roman Curia, heads of religious orders, and prestigious theologians to advise him on the definability of the doctrine. In the main, the responses were affirmative, but some expressed reservations about whether the doctrine qualified as belonging to the deposit of revealed doctrines of the faith. In addition, many questioned whether a definition was opportune under the existing circumstances, and some suggested means short of an *ex cathedra* definition.[55] Special attention should be given to the report of the Conventual Franciscan Giovanni Battista Tonini who argued for the definition because of the existing devotion to it among the faithful. He pointed to the infallibility of the whole Church in matters of belief. The positive position of the Council of Trent, the

---

ment of the "authoritative witnesses." Was the argument from the "sense of the faith" only applicable when Perrone needed it to make a point about the immaculate conception? Why did he not employ it in his treatment of *De traditione*?

54. The documentation was gathered in ten volumes and entitled *Pareri dell'Episcopato cattolico, di capitoli, di congregazioni, di università, di personaggi ragguardevoli ecc. sulla definizione dogmatica dell'Immacolato Concepimento della B. V. Maria: rassegnati alla Santità di Pio IX. P. M. in occasione della sua enciclica data Gaeta il 2 febr. 1849* (Roma: Tipografia della Civiltà Cattolica, 1851–54). On the occasion of the fiftieth anniversary of the definition, Vincenzo Sardi published a two-volume collection entitled *La solenne definizione del dogma dell'Immacolato Concepimento di Maria Santissima: Atti e documenti publicati nel cinquacessimo anniversario della stessa definizione* (Rome: Tipografia Vaticana, 1904–5). Most authors reference the more accessible Sardi collection.

55. See the detailed discussion by Gerhard Müller, "Die unbefleckte Empfängnis Mariens im Urteil päpstlicher Ratgeber 1848–1852," *Zeitschrift für Kirchengeschichte* 78 (1967): 300–39, at 300–18; Juan Alfaro, "La fórmula definitoria de la Inmaculada Concepción," in ibid., 201–75, at 221–32; and René Laurentin, "L'action du Saint-Siège par rapport au problème de l'Immaculée Conception," in *Virgo Immaculata: Acta Congressus Mariologici-Mariani, Romae anno MCMLIV celebrati*, vol. 2: *Acta Magisterii ecclesiastici de Immaculata B. V. M. Conceptione* (Rome: Academia Mariana Internationalis, 1956), 1–98, at 79–80. A partial English translation by Charles E. Sheedy and Edward S. Shea can be found in *The Dogma of the Immaculate Conception: History and Significance*, ed. Edward D. O'Connor (Notre Dame, IN: University of Notre Dame Press, 1958), 271–324.

teaching of many popes, and the belief of the faithful all pointed to the definability of the doctrine.[56]

In December the pope appointed another commission to address the same issues as the Roman Commission. The Preparatory Congregation consisted of fourteen members drawn from the cardinals (eight), bishops (one), curial officials (two), and theologians (three) to examine whether the doctrine should be defined and by what means.[57] Again, the result was a positive response as to the definability of the doctrine, while the means of making the pronouncement was left open.[58] Following the advice of the Preparatory Congregation, in February 1849, Pius IX addressed the encyclical *Ubi primum* to the bishops of the universal church, their clergy, and the faithful, inquiring about the status of the doctrine: did the churches accept Mary's immaculate conception, and how was this belief supported in practice and by piety? He wrote:

> Moreover, we strongly desire that as quickly as possible you take it upon yourselves to make known to us the quality of devotion whereby your clergy and your faithful people venerate the conception of the Immaculate Virgin and the degree to which they desire that the matter be decided by the Apostolic See.[59]

In September 1850, Pius added three new members to the Roman Commission. Their reports were generally not favorable to the question

---

56. See Müller, "Die unbefleckte Empfängnis Mariens," 307–8. Müller characterizes this argument as "weighty." Bishop Domenico Angelini of Leuca also emphasized the importance of the agreement of the faithful as an argument favoring its definability. See Müller, ibid., 317.

57. Eventually the commission was expanded to include two additional theologians.

58. See Müller, "Die unbefleckte Empfängnis Mariens," 318–23 and Laurentin, "L'action du Saint-Siège par rapport au problème de l'Immaculée Conception," 80.

59. "Optamus autem vehementer, ut maiore qua fieri potest celeritate Nobis significare velitis, qua devotione vester Clerus, Populusque fidelis erga Immaculatam Virginis Conceptionem sit animatus, et quo desiderio flagret, ut eiusmodi res ab Apostolica Sede decernatur." Quoted in J. Robert Dionne, *The Papacy and the Church: A Study of Praxis and Reception in Ecumenical Perspective* (New York: Philosophical Library, 1987), 456. According to G. Müller, Antonio Rosmini Serbati had suggested this action to the Preparatory Congregation, even though he was not a member. See "Die unbefleckte Empfängnis Mariens," 319.

of the doctrine's definability or to its opportuneness.[60] In July 1851, Pius appointed three new consultors on the question, who were unanimous in affirming it.[61] Then, in August he appointed three more members who supported the possibility of a papal definition. [62] However, at the end of January 1852, a negative voice was still raised. At this late date, Bishop Andrea Maria Frattini, the rector of the Roman College, forcefully expressed his reservations about the definability of the doctrine.[63] It should be clear, then, that the opinions expressed throughout the process were very mixed indeed. A slight majority favored definition, while a minority had reservations regarding the opportuneness of the definition. Nevertheless, a number of highly influential members of the commissions continued to raise objections to the definition, primarily on the grounds that it could not be shown to be revealed.[64]

But what were the results of the question put to the episcopacy in the encyclical *Ubi primus*? Here, the support was more pronounced than that of the official commissions. Of 603 dioceses consulted, 546 were favorable

---

60. These included Vincenzo Tizzani, Alessandro Macioti, and Mariano Spada, OP. See Müller, "Die unbefleckte Empfängnis Mariens," 325–33; and Alfaro, "La fórmula definitoria de la Inmaculada Concepción," 226–27 (Frattini) and 236–37 (Tizzani).

61. These included Giuseppe Angelini, Giovanni Battista Rosani, and Guglielmo Audisio. It should be noted, however, that Angelini's approval was somewhat qualified. See Müller, "Die unbefleckte Empfängnis Mariens," 329–31.

62. These included Antonio Fania da Rignano, OFM, Giovanni Perrone, SJ, and Carlo Passaglia, SJ.

63. See Müller, "Die unbefleckte Empfängnis Mariens," 333–35.

64. After an exhaustive examination of the process of the Roman and Neapolitan commissions and of the reports of their members, Gerhard Müller concluded: "Of the twenty reports that have come down to us, nine were written by members of religious Orders. Of these, eight were in favor of a definition. But one of these, the one by Cardinal Recanati, recommended only an indirect decision. Of the remaining eleven reports from the diocesan clergy, only three called unambiguously for a dogmatic definition: Audisio, Rosani, and Capalti. Four held that the doctrine of Mary's immaculate conception was not open to definition: Cossa, Tizzani, Macioti and Frattini, while Giuseppe Angelini approved only an indirect decision and Domenico Angelini, Caterini, and Bizzarri favored the definition as a 'pious opinion' and not a dogma, with Bizzarri and Caterini pointing out problems with the opportuneness of the definition. . . . Calculating the total, therefore, only eleven (or twelve if the reversal of opinion by Cossa [late in the process] is taken into consideration) of the twenty consultors counseled the Pope to go ahead with the process, which is what he decided to do." See "Die unbefleckte Empfängnis Mariens," 336–37.

to a Marian definition, while leaving the precise form of the definition for the pope to decide. About fifty-seven dioceses were opposed, but for a wide variety of reasons. The small disparity between these numbers, however, does not adequately reflect the force of the opposition by some bishops and dioceses. The most outspoken opponent was the archbishop of Paris, Marie Dominique Auguste Sibour (1848–57). The bishops of Germany, Switzerland, Austria, Hungary, Bohemia, and Moravia were also less supportive of the Marian definition, but mostly for the reason that the definition would awaken opposition in their countries. The definition was not really needed, some argued, but instead would make life for Catholics more difficult in many situations in central Europe where Protestants and Catholics often lived side by side.[65] Müller writes:

> For the most part theologians opposed the change of a "pious opinion" into a dogma. The bishops hardly questioned the basis of the teaching in the Bible and tradition. They started with the facts: the devotion of the clergy and the laity. In this way they stuck strictly to the papal inquiry. With the exception of a few bishops, discussion of fundamental problems was felt to be of little worth.[66]

65. Gerhard Müller canvassed the responses of the bishops of central Europe in "Die Immaculata Conceptio im Urteil der mitteleuropäischen Bischöfe: Zur Entstehung des mariologischen Dogmas von 1854," *Kerygma und Dogma* 14 (1968): 46–70. The responses were gathered in vols. 2–7 of *Pareri dell'Episcopato cattolico, di capitoli, di congregazioni, di università, di personaggi ragguardevoli sulla definizione dogmatica dell'Immacolato Concepimento della B. V. Maria* (Roma: Tipografia della Civiltà Cattolica, 1851–54), the principal resource Müller consulted. The chief spokesmen among those who posed objections to the definition were the bishops of Basel, Ermland, Regensburg, Munich-Freising, Münster, Cologne, Hildesheim, Salzburg, Bamberg, Breslau, Olmütz, Brünn, St. Gallen, Paderborn, Bohemia, and Moravia. Müller points out that although the bishops of Cologne, Munich-Freising, Würzburg, Fulda, Regensburg, Münster, and Speyer personally favored a definition, they reported resistance to it, sometimes among their pastors and sometimes among professors of faculties of theology. Finally, Müller draws our attention to the large number of dioceses in central Europe that simply did not reply to the pope's consultation: Vienna, Seckau, St. Pölten, Gurk, Freiburg, Augsburg, Eichstätt, and Kulm. Did their silence connote opposition? See also the treatment by Siegfried Gruber, "Der deutsche Episkopat zwischen Ubi primum (2. Februar 1849) und Ineffabilis Deus (8. Dezember 1854)," *Mariologie und katholisches Selbstbewusstsein. Ein Beitrag zur Vorgeschichte des Dogmas von 1854 in Deutschland* (Essen: Ludgerus Verlag Hubert Wingen, 1970), 26–54.

66. Müller, "Die Immaculata Conceptio im Urteil der mitteleuropäischen Bischöfe," 68.

Suffice it for our purposes to note that the climate among the bishops of central Europe was less than enthusiastic about the definition of the immaculate conception. Nevertheless, even those bishops opposed to a definition attested to the fervor of Marian devotion among their clergy and people. The feast of Mary's Immaculate Conception was celebrated in their dioceses, and there was general acceptance of the "pious opinion" that the Mother of God had been conceived immaculately, without however specifying in any detail the theological content of this opinion. In general, in central Europe there was no groundswell for a Marian definition.[67]

At this point, Pius engaged Perrone to propose a draft of a text for the definition, which he submitted on March 26, 1851.[68] In May 1852, the pope named five theologians, including Carlo Passaglia, to a special commission to review the process up to that time. The commission completed its work at the end of August 1853. Everything was ready for proceeding to proximate preparations for the text of the definition. Passaglia submitted two alternate texts, *In mysterio*[69] and *Quemadmodum ecclesia*,[70] while five other texts were discussed between September 2 and late November 1854.[71] Even as the date determined for the definition approached, meetings and consultations continued to be held and the exact form of the definition had still not been decided. As the bishops began to arrive in Rome for the definition, they had opportunities to examine the proposed text and to comment on it. This is how Juan Alfaro characterized the final days before the definition:

67. Nor was the lack of enthusiasm limited to central Europe. Müller has also pointed out opposition to the definition in dioceses in northern Italy, viz., Milan, Bergamo, Como, Crema, Lodi, Mantua, Cremona, Brescia, and Pavia. See Müller, "Die Immaculata Conceptio im Urteil der mitteleuropäischen Bischöfe," 68.

68. The schema was entitled *Deus omnipotens* and can be found in Sardi, *La solenne definizione del dogma dell'Immacolato Concepimento*, vol. 2, 22–38. Cited by Laurentin, "L'action du Saint-Siège par rapport au problème de l'Immaculée Conception," 81, note 277.

69. Found in Sardi, ibid., 76–89. Cited by Laurentin, 83n289.

70. Found in Sardi, ibid. Cited by Alfaro, "La fórmula definitoria de la Inmaculada Concepción," 244–46.

71. Found in Sardi, ibid, *Sapientissimus*, 103–18; *Deus cuius viae*, 125–42; *Deus cuius viae*, 151–67; *Ineffabilis*, 177–94; and *Ineffabilis*, 259–74. Cited by Laurentin, 83n291. These schemas are discussed by Alfaro, "La fórmula definitoria de la Inmaculada Concepción," 246–48.

Although the definition of the immaculate conception was not the result of an ecumenical council, not only did Pius IX want to know beforehand the opinion of the Catholic episcopate concerning the definability of the Marian privilege, but in November 1854 he gave the text of the bull of definition to the bishops and cardinals in Rome so that they could in all liberty offer observations judged appropriate. Approximately one hundred bishops were convened four times between November 20 and 24 in the Grand Ducal Aula of the Vatican, with Cardinals Caterini, Brunelli and Santucci presiding and in the presence of theological consultants, to examine the text of the bull paragraph by paragraph. Their observations were acknowledged by Pacifici and Cannella. Some sent their observations in writing directly to the Pope. The text of the bull was also given to the cardinals assembled in Rome for the solemnity of the definition and who numbered about fifty. Their observations were committed to writing and delivered to the Pope. The analysis of the proposed corrections submitted by the bishops and cardinals and their influence on the final redaction of the bull of definition cast no little light on the precise meaning of the dogmatic definition.[72]

On this long and complex process, René Laurentin passed the following judgment.

It is evident from these few facts just how much time and attention were given to the preparation of the definition, how much agreement on various levels was brought to it, how many exchanges of points of view and how many face-to-face exchanges were held, how the charism of infallibility, far from being some form of illuminism or an irrational impulse, was active at the heart of a labor of determining the meaning of a traditional object of the faith.[73]

Roger Aubert, too, in his study of the role of the Belgian hierarchy in the definition, came to the following positive conclusion:

In pronouncing this solemn definition, it appears quite clearly how the pope decided not to act arbitrarily and according to his own personal

72. Alfaro, "La fórmula definitoria de la Inmaculada Concepción," 248–49. Alfaro presents several of these views on pages 249–55.

73. Laurentin, "L'action du Saint-Siège par rapport au problème de l'Immaculée Conception," 82.

lights, but only after he had ascertained that he was in full communion with the faith of the Church as expressed in the conviction of the bishops as privileged witnesses did he act. Then, after having inquired from the bishops their opinion as to the doctrine's foundation, he again took into account their observations on the form that the bull should take.[74]

What is not clear from the process of consultation is how exactly the faithful were consulted on the matter. It appears that the bishops consulted with their clergy, sometimes with their cathedral chapters, and sometimes too with university faculties in their dioceses, but did not consult the faithful directly. Still, the faithful were engaged in the process by the public prayers that the pope asked the bishops to initiate in their dioceses in preparation for a possible definition. Many had already been involved by concurring in the petitions that had been submitted to Rome requesting the definition of Mary's immaculate conception. It is clear that the faithful were not excluded from the process and were to some extent kept informed. Still, the process left much to be desired from the perspective of the direct participation of the faithful in it. As we shall see in the next chapter, the direct participation of the faithful was about to be encouraged by Cardinal Newman in England.

In the end, Pius IX proclaimed Mary's immaculate conception with the following formula of definition:

> To the glory of the holy and undivided Trinity, to the honor and renown of the Virgin Mother of God, the exaltation of the Catholic faith and the increase of Christian religion; by the authority of our Lord Jesus Christ, of the blessed apostles Peter and Paul, and our own authority, we declare, pronounce and define: the doctrine which holds that the most Blessed Virgin Mary was, from the first moment of her conception, by the singular grace and privilege of almighty God and in view of the merits of Christ Jesus the Savior of the human race, preserved

---

74. "L'Épiscopat belge et la proclamation du dogme de l'Immaculée Conception en 1854," *Ephemerides Theologicae Lovaniensis* 31 (1955): 63–99, at 92. Reprinted in *Virgo Immaculata: Acta Congressus Mariologici-Mariani, Romae anno MCMLIV celebrati*, vol. 2: *Acta Magisterii ecclesiastici de Immaculata B. V. M. Conceptione* (Rome: Academic Mariana Internationalis, 1956), 276–309.

immune from all stain of original sin, is revealed by God and, therefore, firmly and constantly to be believed by all the faithful.[75]

The long, complicated, and contentious history of this dogma thereby came to its official conclusion for Catholics, only to begin the process of reception by Catholics, the cool distancing by the Orthodox churches, and rejection by the ecclesial communities of the Reformation.

Meaning of the Dogma of Mary's Immaculate Conception

Contemporary theologians are keenly aware that once they have established which truths have been taught by the church as dogma, they must then elaborate what the dogmas mean in the corporate life of the church and in the life of the individual believer. Dogmas have been formulated in specific terms and categories of thought as true reflections of the human experience of God and God's dealings with humankind. This means that the human resources of thought and language must be employed to express some of the inexhaustible richness of the self-revelation of God.[76] Revelation does not drop from heaven like a meteor, as it were, but comes in a way that respects our human conditions of knowing and our being embedded in history. The truths of revelation are true in themselves, of course, but they also constitute meaning for those who receive divine revelation.[77] The recipients or believers do not determine the truth of

---

75. *The Christian Faith in the Doctrinal Documents of the Catholic Church*, ed. J. Neuner and J. Dupuis, rev. ed. (Staten Island, NY: Alba House, 1982), 204.

76. Here is how Karl Rahner expresses this important insight: "Christian faith at any particular historical period needs theological opinion in order to be given appropriate expression; no theology can be made up of the defined propositions of the Church's magisterium alone, for theology must be explained and explanation necessarily requires the use of concepts, assumptions and contexts of meaning which are subject to change." See "The One Christ and the Universality of Salvation," *Theological Investigations*, vol.16, trans. David Morland (New York: Crossroad,1983), 199–224, at 199, but similar statements can be found scattered throughout his voluminous writings.

77. On the question of meaning, see Bernard Lonergan, "Meaning," *Method in Theology* (New York: Herder and Herder, 1972), 57–99 and "Dimensions of Meaning," *Collection*, vol. 4 of *Collected Works of Bernard Lonergan* (Toronto: University of Toronto Press, 1993) 232–43; Gerhard Sauter, *The Question of Meaning: A Theological and Philosophical Orientation*, trans. Geoffrey W. Bromiley (Grand Rapids, MI: Wm. B. Eerdmans, 1995).

a revealed content, only the triune God can do that, but there is really no revelation where there is no one to either receive or believe it. To dogmatize revelation, therefore, locates the truth in conjunction with an event that declares its truth at an identifiable moment: the definition of an ecumenical council, the authoritative teaching of a pontiff, or the consensus of the faithful and their pastors. Once the various branches of theology and the other human sciences have done their work determining the fact that a dogma exists, the task still remains for theologians, scholars from other branches of learning, and the mutual activity of the faithful and their pastors to determine how a doctrine impacts the life of the church. To determine the meaning of a revealed truth is an ecclesial activity that never ceases. Belief for the Christian is always searching for how the revealed truth imparts its original and its emerging meaning at this historical moment.[78] To conclude, we now turn our attention to the task of establishing the meaning of the immaculate conception and the role of the "sense of the faithful" in determining it.

Catholics face a triple task in determining the meaning of Mary's immaculate conception. On the one hand, they must make sense of it for themselves in light of the difficulties the doctrine of original sin poses today. What is original sin and what does a Catholic believe when he speaks of original sin? The Catholic is in a different individual, social, and cultural context than when original sin tended to dominate the understanding of Christian identity. How will she rethink and reclaim a view of original sin within the context of Vatican II's emphasis on God's universal saving will? Second, how can today's Catholic Church reconnect with Orthodox Christians who acknowledge Mary's holiness but in a way different from the Catholic formulation? Finally, how can Catholics build on genuine Marian piety in the ecclesial communities of the Reformation

---

78. Sara Butler has presented the clearest explanation of what Pius IX taught and what he did not teach in *Ineffabilis Deus*—that is, its original content and its meaning at the moment of its definition. See her "The Immaculate Conception: Why Was It Defined as a Dogma? And What Was Defined?" in *Studying Mary: The Virgin Mary in Anglican and Roman Catholic Theology and Devotion. The ARCIC Working Papers*, ed. Adelbert Denaux and Nicholas Sagovsky (New York: T&T Clark, 2007), 147–64. An earlier, less extensive version of the essay appeared as "The Immaculate Conception in Anglican-Roman Catholic Dialogue," *Ephemerides Mariologicae* 54 (2004): 447–60. Butler's essay deserves careful study.

that accept the witness of the New Testament to Mary and the teachings of the earliest ecumenical councils on Mary?

Contemporary theologians exhibit a wide diversity of meanings of original sin, and this variety can bewilder the ordinary believer. It would not be germane to our topic to examine and pass judgment on these many understandings.[79] Just as the church over the centuries had to refine Augustine's understanding of original sin, especially at the Council of Trent, advances in understanding what it means to be a person, how the human species has evolved, and what contemporary science tells us about cosmology and the age of the universe have forced theologians to reexamine what the church has inherited with the doctrine of original sin. In a way, these probing questions have forced us to return to what is essential in the doctrine.

Today, the theologian is inclined to state that original sin points more to the priority of the mystery of grace and God's will to share the divine life with the whole of humankind and to place less emphasis on human fallibility and sinfulness. Sin is the context within which the triune God shares the divine life with men and women of all times, circumstances, and cultures. Sin has complicated God's plan for universal salvation, but it has not annulled it. God's plan to share the divine life without limit is still God's original plan. The appearance of sin has distorted our vision of the plan and our ability to fathom and accept God's plan, but God has not substituted a second plan when the first one failed through the emergence of sin. Augustine saw clearly the devastating effects of sin on our creaturely relationship with God. What he did not see so clearly was the total faithfulness of God to the original plan. In the person of

---

79. For an explanation of theories of original sin up to 1975, see Brian O. McDermott, "The Theology of Original Sin: Recent Developments," *Theological Studies* 38 (1977): 478–512. For more recent developments, see Siegfried Wiedenhofer, "The Main Forms of Contemporary Theology of Original Sin," *Communio* 18 (1981): 514–29; Christophe Boureux and Christoph Theobald, eds., *Original Sin: A Code of Fallibility*, Concilium 2004, no. 1 (London: SCM, 2004); *Unheilvolles Erbe? Zur Theologie der Erbsünde*, ed. Helmut Hoping and Michael Schulz, Quaestiones Disputatae 231 (Freiburg: Herder, 2009); Matthew Levering, "Original Sin," *Engaging the Doctrine of Creation: Cosmos, Creatures, and the Wise and Good Creator* (Grand Rapids, MI: Baker Academic, 2017): 227–71; and James P. O'Sullivan, "Catholics Re-examining Original Sin in Light of Evolutionary Science: The State of the Question," *New Blackfriars* 99 (2018): 653–74.

the eternal Word become incarnate, God would pour forth even more profligately God's very life, thereby wiping out the deviations of sin and defeating evil.[80]

Whereas Christians for too many centuries have been preoccupied by the power of sin, the church of the Second Vatican Council was open to the possibility of the saving will of God for all men and women since the emergence of the species. This theory of a universal salvific will of God recaptured the universalistic vision of the first generations of Christians as expressed in the New Testament.[81] According to the Fourth Gospel,

---

80. The priority of grace points to another problem of interpreting the doctrine of original sin—the question of justification and the moment it occurs for the saved. Karl Rahner has devoted special attention to this question and has shown that even before the moment baptism is administered (or the words of absolution are uttered by the priest in the sacrament of reconciliation), the individual has already been embraced by God's grace. The offer of grace is not a mere possibility for the unjustified, but is a really graced moment for that person. The sacrament of baptism (and penance) is another real element of the act of justification, but it does not indicate the point at which justification occurs for the first time and absolutely. The offer of grace and graced human response bring justification to expression, but they also "ordinarily" call for "sacramental expression" in baptism or reconciliation. In the matter of the person born with original sin, then, the church does not claim the absence of grace entirely. Given his understanding of the process of justification, Rahner envisions an *a pari* situation between Mary's immaculate conception and the conception of each human being under the sign of the concrete offer of grace by God. The two situations, however, are not identical (*eadem*) but they are also not unrelated to each other either. According to Rahner, Mary is the "most perfectly redeemed" of humankind and no other individual can claim this singular situation, but that does not isolate Mary from the rest of humankind. She remains firmly embedded in human life and history, "the human condition," as it were. Mary's singularity is derived from the uniqueness of her role in the history of salvation as the woman who has freely consented to bear the eternal Word—with all the weight of what that decision implies. But we must also claim that every justified person must do the same thing in her or his unique act of will and individual situation (*a pari* and not *eadem*). For an explanation of Rahner's thought on this matter, see Jacek Bolewski, *Der reine Anfang: Die Dialektik der Erbsünde in marianischer Perspektive nach Karl Rahner* (Frankfurt: Josef Knecht, 1991): "Dialektik der Erbsünde," 92–217 (three chapters) and "Erbsünde und marianische Wahrheit," 218–89 (two chapters). See also Dominik Matuscheck, *Konkrete Dogmatik: Die Mariologie Karl Rahners*, Innsbrucker theologische Studien 87 (Innsbruck: Tyrolia Verlag, 2012): 315–32.

81. Vatican II referred explicitly to God's universal will in the Constitution on the Sacred Liturgy (art. 5), the Dogmatic Constitution on the Church (arts. 16-17), and in the Decree on the Church's Missionary Activity (art. 3), but the council's hope for human

Jesus says, "And when I am lifted up from the earth, I will draw everyone to myself" (John 12:32). In Romans, Paul teaches that "through one righteous act acquittal and life came to all" (5:18). Two late first-century disciples of Paul teach that "the grace of God has appeared, saving all" (Titus 2:11), and "God our savior . . . wills everyone to be saved and to come to knowledge of the truth" (1 Tim. 2:3-4).[82] John Duns Scotus saw that the purpose of the incarnation of the word of God, the second person of the blessed Trinity, was to bring to completion the Father's plan to share the divine life with all humankind.[83] If this is true, then it makes more sense

---

salvation and its anticipated joy in it are implied throughout its decrees and declarations. This hopeful optimism vis-à-vis salvation might even be considered a leitmotiv of the entire council. Paul VI later adopted it in his apostolic exhortation "On Evangelization in the Modern World": "The Church is deeply aware of her duty to preach salvation to all. Knowing that the Gospel message is not reserved to a small group of the initiated, the privileged or the elect, but is destined for everyone" (no. 57). In his encyclical "Mission of the Redeemer," John Paul II too reasserted the teaching of Vatican II on the possibility of the salvation of all, but his real concern was to balance this universal call with the missionary mandate of the church to proclaim the Gospel and to call all to explicit faith in Christ (nos. 9–11). Finally, the *Catechism of the Catholic Church* refers to the teaching often and on central points of Catholic teaching. See §§ 74, 851, 1058, 1256, 1261, 1821, and 2822. As for theological opinion, Rahner made the teaching a central tenet of his theology. In particular, see Rahner's "The One Christ and the Universality of Salvation," *Theological Investigations* 16, trans. David Morland (New York: Seabury, 1979), 199–224, for his clearest exposition, but many other references from Rahner could also be cited.

82. See the treatment by Gerhard Lohfink, *Is This All There Is? On Resurrection and Eternal Life*, trans. Linda M. Maloney (Collegeville, MN: Liturgical Press, 2018), 168–69.

83. The position of Scotus (c. 1265–1308) is usually referred to as his theory of the absolute primacy or predestination of Christ. It seeks to enunciate the insight that the Word would have become incarnate even if humans had not sinned. It was the intention of the trinitarian persons from all eternity to create the cosmos in the image of the Son and to bring it to perfection in the Son and through the Spirit. See Dominic Unger, "Franciscan Christology: Absolute and Universal Primacy of Christ," *Franciscan Studies* 2 (1942): 428–74. The theory is often called "the Franciscan thesis" because it has generally been espoused by the Franciscan School of Theology in contrast with the views of St. Anselm and St. Thomas Aquinas. Recently, Daniel P. Horan has shown that the insight had been developed earlier by the German Benedictine abbot Rupert of Deutz (c. 1075–1130) and especially by the English secular cleric, and later bishop of Lincoln, Robert Grosseteste (c. 1168–1253). It is not clear whether Robert Grosseteste knew of Rupert's position before he developed it himself, nor is it certain that Scotus knew of Grosseteste's thesis. However, since Grosseteste has been the first teacher of the Franciscans at Oxford, it is

for Catholics today to speak in the first place of the mystery of grace than of the fact of original sin: "Where sin increased, grace overflowed all the more" (Rom 5:20). Christ is the "new" Adam, not as the replacement of the "first" Adam but as the prototype of the divine-human relationship that God has never abandoned but that Adam had failed to realize. The plan, however, still stands until it comes to its God-appointed completion: "So that God may be all in all" (1 Cor 15:28).[84]

Theologians like Joseph Ratzinger and more recently Gerhard Lohfink and Ludwig Weimer have turned to the biblical teaching of the holy remnant to make sense of Mary and her immaculate conception. What do they mean by this?

---

likely that Scotus, who had studied there later as a young friar, had heard of Grosseteste's ideas. None of this is intended to diminish the contribution of Scotus, who developed the insight in his theology to a degree not matched by either Rupert or Grosseteste. As a result, the "Franciscan" thesis enjoys the presumption of validity as an explanation of salvation at least equal to that of St. Thomas. See Daniel P. Horan, "Revisiting the Incarnation: Why the 'Franciscan Thesis' Is Not So Franciscan and Why It Does Not Really Matter," *The Cord* 59 (2009): 371–90 and idem, "How Original Was Scotus on the Incarnation? Reconsidering the History of the Absolute Predestination of Christ in the Light of Robert Grosseteste," *The Heythrop Journal* 52 (2011): 374–91, that includes an abundance of bibliographical references to the thought of Scotus (94n).

84. The Scotistic thesis rests upon the priority of those passages in the deutero-Pauline hymns in Ephesians 1:3-10 and Colossians 1:12-20 that refer to God's "plan" and "decree" (*oikonomia* and *prothesis*) and to God choosing (*eklegomai*) and predestining (*prooridzein*: "to know with a view toward God's plan," the same verb Paul uses in Romans 8:29) humankind to fulfillment. In both hymns we also find references to the forgiveness of sin and redemption through Christ's blood, but these ideas are incorporated to provide a complete picture of salvation. They, too, are essential to the tradition coming from the earliest Christians, but they complement the primary insight of salvation of God's favor or grace and do not alone constitute it. The Christian story of salvation is incomplete without mention of sin and its removal, as well as Christ's sacrificial love, but their mention does not constitute the primordial words or insight about salvation. Christianity will always be determined by the tension constituted by these two paradigms, and the meaning of salvation for any given period in the history of humankind will depend on which is given priority. What message does humankind need to hear today? Which paradigm correlates best with how men and women see themselves and their place in the cosmos? The answer to that question will also determine what we mean by Mary's immaculate conception. Was it primarily preservation from sin, in answer to Augustine's and Anselm's questions (Paradigm B), or predestination to grace, in the Scotistic view (Paradigm A)?

As early as 1977, Ratzinger pointed to the power of the biblical category of a "type" to explain both original sin and the immaculate conception.[85] According to this theory, God had never entirely rejected the people of Israel because a holy and faithful remnant continued to observe the covenant.[86] They might be few, and some are even insignificant socially speaking, but they continue to cherish God's Torah and Israel's institutions. This was the case right up to Mary of Nazareth, who together with others like her parents, her spouse Joseph, Elizabeth, Zechariah and John the Baptist, Simeon and the prophetess Anna, and surely many anonymous others as well, constituted the most recent expression of Israel's holy and faithful remnant. When the archangel Gabriel visited Mary to enlist her participation in God's plan for the incarnation of the eternal Word, the offer did not happen in a vacuum or to a totally isolated individual.

---

85. "One must observe that the concept 'fact' cannot be applied, in a strictly positivistic sense at any rate, to original sin. For original sin itself is not a fact in a positivistic sense, observable like the fact that Goethe was born on August 28, 1749. Original sin is a 'fact,' a reality of a different order, known only through typology. The basic text, Romans 5, is a typological interpretation of the Old Testament. Original sin became recognizable in the type Adam, and in his recurrence at the turning points of history. Its affirmation rests upon the typological identification of every single man and woman with humankind as such, with the average human, with men and women from the beginning on. Original sin was not handed on in the tradition (and previously communicated) from the beginning as a fact. It has been identified in a theological (reflex) manner through typological scriptural exegesis. To have missed this truth was perhaps the principal error of the neoscholastic doctrine on original sin. The moment this error was introduced, in whatever degree, in conjunction with the total lack of understanding of typological identification, it led to the questioning of original sin, the impossibility of thinking or talking about it. This being so, it is also clear that freedom from original sin cannot be communicated as a fact; it is only to be recognized by theology, and in no other way." The reader should note Ratzinger's use of a double typology at work here: original sin and freedom from original sin. See "The Marian Belief of the Church," *Daughter Zion: Meditations on the Church's Marian Belief*, trans. John M. McDermott (San Francisco: Ignatius Press, 1983), 66–67. I have altered the translation slightly.

86. On the biblical idea of a holy remnant, see Heinrich Gross, "Remnant," in *Encyclopedia of Biblical Theology: The Complete Sacramentum Verbi*, ed. Johannes B. Bauer (New York: Crossroad, 1981), 741–43; François Dreyfus, "Remnant," in *Dictionary of Biblical Theology*, ed. Xavier Léon-Dufour, rev. ed. (New York: Seabury, 1973), 484–86; Walther Günther and Hartmut Krienke, "Remnant, Leave," in *The New International Dictionary of New Testament Theology*, vol. 3, ed. Colin Brown (Grand Rapids, MI: Zondervan, 1978), 247–54; and Joachim Jeremias, "Der Gedanke des 'Heiligen Restes' im Spätjudentum und in der Verkündigung Jesu," *Zeitschrift für die neutestamentliche Wissenschaft* 42 (1949): 184–94.

Mary had been nourished by others and her fiat expressed the yearning of others. When Mary consented to conceive the eternal Word, she did so as the type or representative of the holy remnant throughout Israel's history, from Abraham and Sarah to Mary and her contemporaries among the holy remnant. Here is how Ratzinger develops his argument:

> One need not search very far for a typological identification grounding Mary's freedom from original sin. The Epistle to the Ephesians describes the new Israel, the bride, as "holy," "Immaculate," "luminously beautiful," "without spot, wrinkle, or the like" (5:27). Patristic theology further developed this image of the *Ecclesia immaculata* in passages of lyrical beauty. Consequently, from the very beginning there is a doctrine of the *Immaculata* in Scripture and especially in the Fathers, even if it concerns the *Ecclesia immaculata*. Here the doctrine of the *Immaculata*, like the whole of later Mariology, is first anticipated as ecclesiology. The image of the Church, virgin and mother, is *secondarily* transferred to Mary, not vice versa. So if the dogma of the immaculate conception transferred to the concrete figure of Mary those assertions which primarily belong to the antithesis new-old Israel, and are in this sense a typologically developed ecclesiology, this means that Mary is presented as the beginning and the personal concreteness of the Church. It entails the conviction that the rebirth of the old Israel into the new Israel, of which the Epistle to the Ephesians spoke, achieves in Mary its concrete accomplishment. It proclaims that this new Israel (which is simultaneously the true old Israel, the holy remnant preserved by the grace of God) is not only an idea, but a person. God does not act with abstractions or concepts; the *type*, of which the ecclesiology of the New Testament and the Fathers speak, exists as a *person*.[87]

But Ratzinger has not yet arrived at the point he is ultimately trying to make. How, in fact, are the typologies expressed in original sin and in Mary's immaculate conception correlated? This takes place where faith and theology have always situated it—at the core of Mary's personhood in the free acceptance of the will of God for her.

> The essence of sin can only be understood in an anthropology of relation, not by looking at an isolated human being. Such an anthropology is even more essential in the case of grace. We could therefore describe

---

87. *Daughter Zion*, 67–68.

original sin as a statement about God's evaluation of man; evaluation not as something external, but as a revealing of the very depths of his interior being. It is the collapse of what man is, both in his origin from God and in himself, the contradiction between the will of the Creator and man's empirical being.

This contradiction between God's "is" and man's "is not" is lacking in the case of Mary, and consequently God's judgment about her is pure "Yes," just as she herself stands before him as a pure "Yes." This correspondence of God's "Yes" with Mary's being as "Yes" is the freedom from original sin. Preservation from original sin, therefore, signifies no exceptional achievement; on the contrary, it signifies that Mary reserves no area of being, life, and will for herself as a private possession: instead, precisely in the total dispossession of self, in giving herself to God, she comes to the true possession of self. Grace as dispossession becomes response as appropriation.[88]

The doctrine of the *Immaculata* testifies accordingly that God's grace was powerful enough to awaken a response, that grace and freedom, grace and being oneself, renunciation and fulfillment are only apparent contradictories; in reality one conditions the other and grants it its very existence.[89]

We see how Ratzinger achieves a contemporary understanding of original sin and of Mary's immaculate conception by using the category of typology and by a double application of the category. Moreover, he does so by developing this typology in the contemporary contexts of personalism and intersubjectivity—that is, the meaningful relations that constitute what it means to be a person among other humans and with God as fully personal reality. Ratzinger's typological understanding of Mary's freedom from original sin is presented in terms of the Christian teaching about grace. In this context, Ratzinger redefines original sin as the absence of grace and thus the inability to be truly human.[90]

---

88. Ibid., 69–70.

89. Ibid., 71.

90. For another recent attempt to present Mary's freedom from original sin in terms of the dynamic of grace and human freedom as constituting human personhood, see Gisbert Greshake, *Maria-Ecclesia. Perspektiven einer marianisch grundierten Theologie und Kirchenpraxis* (Regensburg: F. Pustet, 2014), 246–57 ["Erbsündenfreiheit Marias"] and 259–83 ["Neuere Interpretationen"].

For their part, Gerhard Lohfink and Ludwig Weimer prefer to develop the notion of the holy remnant of Israel in an entirely historical way.[91] The relationship of faithfulness and unfaithfulness to the covenant can be plotted along a historical graph. We read about its low and high moments in the Old Testament histories, theologies, and lives of the prophets.[92] In the New Testament, it is St. Paul in particular who recounts and summarizes this checkered history of Israel's fidelity and disobedience.[93] In this understanding, God's plan of salvation is never completely overwhelmed by human sin but is kept alive with the holy remnant, culminating in the Virgin Mary. God has nurtured the holy remnant so that through its members the eternal Word might enter human history as the *raison d'être* of creation, history, and the entire cosmos in all its bewildering complexity and extraordinary beauty. Lohfink and Weimer summarize their insight by extending Mary's immaculate conception to Israel itself. Israel's infidelity has not meant the cessation of the covenant with God but its reaffirmation and transformation in the life, death, and resurrection of Jesus the true Israelite, emerging as it does out of the holy remnant and Mary of Nazareth in particular.[94] This means that both Jewish and Christian thinkers must wrestle with the implications of this theology for those who adhere to other religions or to none. Jesus is Universal Savior or not a savior at all. Again, we find ourselves at the point of departure of the fundamental insight of the Second Vatican Council with its vision of universal hope of salvation.

And what about the second imperative Catholics face: how does a contemporary Catholic understanding relate to that of the Orthodox churches? Is there any possibility of the two churches coming to an agreement on Mary between themselves? The churches of the East have maintained a broader perspective in insisting on Mary's perfect holiness (*panhagia*), even while rejecting the West's understanding of original sin. The East's theology of original sin does not focus on the issue of inherited guilt (hamartiology) but understands original sin as a heuristic concept,

91. See *Maria—nicht ohne Israel: Eine neue Sicht der Lehre von der Unbefleckten Empfängnis* (Freiburg: Herder, 2008).

92. See Lohfink and Weimer, "Gottes Gegenaktion: der Kampf gegen die Erbsünde in Israel," *Maria—nicht ohne Israel*, 105–217.

93. See Lohfink and Weimer, "Paulinische Theologie in Röm 1-8," *Maria*, 99–104.

94. See Lohfink and Weimer, "Maria: das Inbild des erlösten Israel," *Maria*, 218–395.

or theologoumenon, that clarifies what it means to be a human being (anthropology). In the East's view, the fact that Mary also stands under the condition of original sin safeguards her identity with all men and women. According to the explanation of Kallistos Ware:

> It is easy to appreciate why, on the Augustinian understanding of original sin, the doctrine of the Immaculate Conception seemed appropriate and even necessary to many western theologians. How, it was asked, could Mary be at once God's chosen vessel and a guilty object of His just anger? But on the less somber and less guilt-ridden eastern view of the fall no such difficulty arises; the doctrine of the Immaculate Conception is rendered unnecessary. The Blessed Virgin, although sinless, was still subject to physical pain and bodily death; and therefore, on the eastern understanding of original sin, while holy and pure from her mother's womb, she was exempt from the consequences of the fall. She participates organically in descent from Adam, but by the grace of God and through her own unremitting struggle against sin she was guarded from all personal impurity. . . . What is here in question . . . is a difference, not in the Roman Catholic and Orthodox attitudes towards Mary, but in our respective doctrines of original sin.[95]

Catholics can learn from the expansive vision of the Eastern view of Mary, the all holy one among God's creatures. Apropos of this insight, John Paul II has written: "The negative formulation of the Marian privilege, which resulted from the earlier controversies about original sin that arose in the West, must always be complemented by the positive expres-

---

95. "The Mother of God in Orthodox Theology and Devotion," in *Mary's Place in Christian Dialogue: Occasional Papers of the Ecumenical Society of the Blessed Virgin Mary, 1970–1980*, ed. Alberic Stacpoole (Middlegreen, Slough: St. Paul Publications, 1982), 169–81, at 177–78. Particularly helpful is Myrrha Lot-Borodine's "Le dogme de l'Immaculée Conception à la lumière de l'Église d'Orient," *Irénikon* 67 (1994): 328–44, who emphasized the difference in theological anthropology between East and West and hence their different understandings of original sin. In particular, Lot-Borodine stressed the eastern concern to safeguard Mary's continuity with all the holy ones ("saints" or justified persons) before the life, ministry, death, and resurrection of Jesus. Also helpful are Virginia M. Kimball, "The Immaculate Conception in the Ecumenical Dialogue with Orthodoxy: How the Term *Theosis* Can Inform Convergence," *Marian Studies* 55 (2004): 212–44 and Manfred Hauke, "The Immaculate Conception of Mary in the Greek Fathers and in an Ecumenical Context," *Chicago Studies* 45 (2006): 327–46.

sion of Mary's holiness more explicitly stressed in the Eastern tradition."[96] When Catholics today experience a certain theological confusion about the precise meaning of the doctrine of original sin, they can be reassured by the orthodox doctrine of Mary, the all holy one, or in John Paul II's expression, the perfectly holy one.[97] It is important for Catholics today to contextualize Mary's preservation from original sin by situating her sinlessness in the context of her whole existence as living entirely for God. Only in this way can Catholics rediscover their solidarity with Mary in the human struggle to overcome the power of sin and evil and so live in a genuinely human way after the pattern of Christian discipleship.[98]

96. *Theotókos: Woman, Mother, Disciple*, vol. 5 of his *Catechesis on Mary, Mother of God* (Boston, MA: Pauline Books & Media, 2000), 100–13, at 101, the pope's catechesis for June 12, 1996. Later, in his catechesis for November 12, 1997, the pope wrote: "There remain some disagreements regarding the dogmas of the immaculate conception and the assumption, even if these truths were first expounded by certain Eastern theologians. . . . These disagreements, however, are perhaps more a question of formulation than of content and must never make us forget our common belief in Mary's divine motherhood, her perpetual virginity, her perfect holiness and her maternal intercession with her Son." Ibid., 259.

97. For his part, too, Rahner stressed Mary's status as the exemplar of what it is to be a "perfect Christian"—that is, as the one who was "redeemed in the most perfect manner" ("Darum ist Maria die in vollkommenster Weise Erlöste"). Like Myrrha Lot-Borodine and Kallistos Ware, who carefully summarized the whole Eastern tradition for readers who are not too familiar with the nuances of that tradition, Rahner also situated Mary in the endless historical stream of women and men in whom God was working out the divine plan of salvation. See Rahner, "The Fundamental Idea of Mariology," *Mary, Mother of the Lord*, trans. W. J. O'Hara (New York: Herder, 1963), 32–41 and idem, "Le principe fondamentale de la théologie mariale," *Recherches de science religieuse* 42 (1954): 481–522. This important early work by Rahner has only recently been translated into English by Sarah Jane Boss and Philip Endean. See "The Fundamental Principle of Marian Theology," *Maria: A Journal of Marian Studies* 1/1 (August 2000): 86–122. On Rahner's fundamental Marian principle, see Dominik Matuschek, *Konkrete Dogmatik: Die Mariologie Karl Rahners*, 239–41 ["'auf die volkommenste Weise Erlöste'—Das mariologische Grundprinzip"]. In their recent book, Gerhard Lohfink and Ludwig Weimer, too, are committed to treating Mary in the context of salvation history rather than in isolating her by reason of her "privileges."

98. Very helpful in this regard are the observations of the German theologian Marion Wagner, "Ballast oder Hilfe? Zum Verständnis und zur Bedeutung der Mariendogmen heute," in *Maria zu lieben: Moderne Rede über eine biblische Frau*, ed. Stefanie Aurelia Spendel and Marion Wagner (Regensburg: F. Pustet, 1999), 11–22 and idem, "Auf sich

Finally, how might Catholics better explain what the immaculate conception means for them in the context of the Marian piety of the churches of the Reformation? While great strides have been made in the ecumenical dialogues in this area, disagreements still exist. The Lutheran and Catholic dialogue in the United States and the bilateral working group of the German National Bishops' Conference and the church leadership of the United Evangelical Lutheran Church of Germany have advanced ecumenical discussion of Mary by situating it in the broader context of the communion of the saints.[99] In these dialogues, Mary is no longer considered in isolation from all the saved but as herself among the saved. Her immaculate conception is seen less as a personal privilege and more as a complementary expression of what it is to be saved. Mary's preservation from sin is an integral part of God's *one plan* (or economy) to save all men and women from their sins. Preservation from sin and freeing from sin are mutually complementary dimensions of the divine will to save all humankind. The efficacy of Mary's being preserved from all sin redounds to the efficacy of God saving humankind from their sins, while the fact that in Christ men and women are saved from their sins is a concrete expression of God's *one salvific will*. There is no longer any need to play the one expression off against the other. According to this vision, the

---

beruhen lassen ohne Widerspruch? Zur Problematik und Bedeutung der beiden jüngsten Mariendogmen," *Trierer theologische Zeitschrift* 112 (2003): 197–207. Many other contemporary Catholic authors could be cited in this regard as well.

99. See "The Common Statement: The One Mediator, the Saints, and Mary" in *The One Mediator, the Saints, and Mary*, Lutherans and Catholics in Dialogue 8, ed. H. George Anderson, J. Francis Stafford, and Joseph A. Burgess (Minneapolis, MN: Augsburg Fortress, 1992), 21–132 and the Bilateral Working Group of the German National Bishops' Conference and the Church Leadership of the United Evangelical Lutheran Church of Germany, *Communio Sanctorum: The Church as the Communion of Saints*, trans. Mark W. Jeske, Michael Root, and Daniel R. Smith (Collegeville, MN: Liturgical Press, 2004), 1–91. Mention should also be made of the outstanding document *Mary in the Plan of God and in the Communion of Saints*, by the French Catholic, Lutheran and Reformed pastors and scholars who comprise the Groupe des Dombes, trans. Matthew J. O'Connell (New York: Paulist Press, 2002). On the Groupe des Dombes, see Bernard Sesboüé, "Groupe des Dombes," in *Dictionary of the Ecumenical Movement*, ed. Nicholas Lossky et al. (2nd ed.; Geneva: WCC Publications, 2002), 503–5 and Catherine E. Clifford's "Editor's Introduction," *For the Communion of the Churches: The Contribution of the Groupe des Dombes* (Grand Rapids, MI: Wm. B. Eerdmans, 2010), 1–11.

mystery of grace is given priority over the undeniable existence of sin, yet without losing sight of the reality of the tragically destructive power of evil. This change in the general perspective regarding the communion of the saints and Mary's place in it accounts for such irenic statements as the following:

> Sound reasons remain, now as before, which make Mary appear as a figure *between* the churches. These reasons are not always theological in nature, but—in spite of all clarifications—very often anchored in the area of emotions and confessional traditions. If a convergence is to be achieved, both Catholics and Lutherans need to show respect and understanding for the motives, concerns, and historical conditioning of the other. They must also summon the courage and freedom from prejudice to overcome all those barriers that do not need, for the sake of the faith, to remain in place (no. 263).[100]

And

> Lutheran Christians should, for the sake of the same goal of the unity of the faith, honor the efforts of the Catholic side to establish the place of Mary christologically and ecclesiologically. They are invited to consider that for Catholic thought the Mother of Christ is the embodiment of the event of justification by grace alone and through faith. It is from that conception that the Marian dogmas of the nineteenth and twentieth centuries are derived: If God elects a person in such a way as Mary, then Christian thought realizes that such a calling seizes that person totally—it begins in the first moment of that person's existence and never abandons that person. As far as the invocation and veneration of the Mother of God is concerned, there are no other rules or standards than those that are prescribed for all the saints. For Mary belongs, albeit as the most distinguished member, completely and fully in their communion (no. 267).[101]

Such sentiments need to be developed ecumenically by the churches by continuing to emphasize the unity of Mary, the saints, and all the saved

---

100. *Communio Sanctorum: The Church as the Communion of Saints*, 87.
101. Ibid., 87–88.

within the theological perspective of the priority of God's preordained plan to save all humankind.[102]

The contribution of the "sense of the faithful" in the area of Mary's immaculate conception is open-ended and incomplete. It is still needed in the areas of ecumenical convergence among Catholic, Orthodox, and Reformed Christians on the role and significance of Mary in Christian revelation and on the burning issue of "salvation outside the church," the role of other religions as embraced by God's salvific act, and the meaning and implications of the Trinity's universal saving will for humankind. These issues are thorny and by no means is it entirely clear to Christians how they will ultimately be resolved, but they represent an occasion of growth for the churches as they dialogue with humankind. Perhaps only at this point of convergence of the questions and insights regarding the divine salvific plan or "economy" will a fuller meaning of Mary's immaculate conception emerge beyond the explicit terms of the definition. In this ecumenical and interreligious effort, the exercise of the role of the "sense of the faith" will continue to be indispensable if the dogma is to yield fruit.

---

102. In this context, the emphasis of the Groupe des Dombes's *Mary in the Plan of God and in the Communion of the Saints* on Ephesians 1:4 (see nos. 268 and 270) and 1:6 deserves attention. The document boldly emphasizes the cosmic and universal salvific view of Ephesians and perceptively understands the connection of Mary's immaculate conception with this mystery. It writes: "The Catholic doctrine of the Immaculate Conception maintains that redemptive grace reached Mary at the very first instant of her existence. Although the doctrine is not formally attested in the scriptures, it is to be understood in the light of God's plan in the history of salvation. . . . If Mary was 'filled with grace' in a unique way, it was in order to bear witness to the fact that we in our turn are touched by the superabundant gift of grace that God has bestowed on us in his beloved Son (see Eph. 1:6). This vision transcends all logical necessity; it belongs to the realm of divine excess" (no. 274). The Groupe des Dombes grasps the bonds of relationality and reciprocity binding the Marian dogma of the immaculate conception with the more overarching biblical view of God's one plan of predestination. This insight demands further unpacking by theologians and greater application in the pastoral life of the churches.

Chapter Four

John Henry Newman and the Testing of the "Sense of the Faithful" in the Crucible of Controversy

Giovanni Perrone had perceived the importance of the "sense of the faithful" for determining revealed doctrine. He understood it to be a privileged source of revealed truth that one could turn to when Scripture and other witnesses did not provide adequate evidence to define a dogma of the faith. But Perrone also saw the "sense of the faithful" as the expression of the living tradition of the church and not just as a warrant of the church's infallibility. This enabled him to move beyond Melchior Cano's understanding of the "universal consent of the faithful" as an "authoritative witness" of the Christian faith, or *locus theologicus*. John Henry Newman (1801–90) built on these solid advances but also contributed to the fact that the "sense of the faithful" would no longer remain merely a fine point of technical theology known only to scholars and clerics. Newman moved the "sense of the faithful" into the very life of the church where practical and theoretical decisions are made. This shift cost him dearly and would cast a shadow over him in the eyes of Roman authorities and the Catholic hierarchy in England. Newman's insight into the "sense of the faithful" would be forged in the crucible of positions that made him suspect in the Catholic Church. Only his elevation as a cardinal late in life (1879) would dispel the shadows during Newman's life. Though doubts remained about Newman's theology and personal holiness for years after his death, these were laid to rest by his beatification by Benedict XVI in 2010 and his canonization by Pope Francis in 2019.[1]

The *Rambler* Commentary of May 1859

In 1845, Newman entered the Catholic Church and published his influential *An Essay on the Development of Christian Doctrine*.[2] This pioneering work introduced genuinely new ideas on the understanding of revelation. Instead of being a repository of doctrine fixed once and for all at the beginning of Christianity, revelation grows and develops, not by the extraneous addition of new doctrines but by the inner unfolding of the truth of revelation. It would no longer be necessary to maintain that the whole of Christian doctrine was consciously in place from the beginning. Instead, in the course of history the church comes to an ever greater grasp of revealed truth. Newman's extensive study of the fathers of the church and of the subsequent history of Christian doctrine had made him recep-

---

1. The following literature has been helpful in understanding Newman and his contribution: John T. Ford, "Newman on 'Sensus Fidelium' and Mariology," *Marian Studies* 28 (1977): 120–45; idem, "John Henry Newman as Contextual Theologian," *Newman Studies Journal* 2/2 (Fall 2005): 60–76; Jan H. Walgrave, "Newman's 'On Consulting the Faithful in Matters of Doctrine,'" in *The Teaching Authority of Believers*, Concilium 180, ed. Johannes B. Metz and Edward Schillebeeckx (Edinburgh: T&T Clark, 1985), 23–30; Edward Jeremy Miller, *John Henry Newman on the Idea of the Church* (Shepherdstown, WV: Patmos, 1987); idem, "Newman's *Sensus Fidelium* and Papal Fundamentalism," in *The Struggle over the Past: Fundamentalism in the Modern World*, Annual Publication of the College Theology Society 1989, vol. 35, ed. William M. Shea (Lanham, MD: University Press of America, 1993), 289–304; idem, "Newman on the Voice of the Laity: Lessons for Today's Church," *Newman Studies Journal* 3/2 (Fall 2006): 16–31; Ian Ker, "Newman, the Councils, and Vatican II," *Communio* 28 (2001): 708–28; Lawrence J. King, "Newman and Gasser on Infallibility: Vatican I and Vatican II," *Newman Studies Journal* 8/1 (Spring 2011): 27–39; and Hermann Geissler, "The Witness of the Faithful in Matters of Doctrine according to John Henry Newman," The International Centre of Newman Friends, available online at http://www.newmanfriendsinternational.org/newman/wp-content/uploads/2012/06/on-consulting-english1.pdf.

2. Rev. ed.; London: Longmans, Green, and Co., 1878. On the circumstances of Newman's conversion and the concomitant publication of *An Essay on the Development of Christian Doctrine*, see the discussion by Ian Ker, *John Henry Newman: A Biography* (Oxford: Clarendon Press, 1988). See also William J. Kelly, "Newman, John Henry" in *Bibliographical Dictionary of Christian Theologians*, ed. Patrick W. Carey and Joseph T. Lienhard (Peabody, MA: Hendrickson Publishers, 2002), 378–80.

tive to the ideas of development and change.[3] Such ideas, however, were suspect in the Catholicism of his day, which much preferred a fixed and static understanding of revelation. Change and development meant risk and danger. They also implied inadequacy, and the nineteenth-century church saw itself as fully equipped from the beginning by its founder.

But the incident that above all cast doubts regarding Newman was his short tenure as editor of the journal the *Rambler*.[4] Founded in 1848 by a lay convert to Catholicism, it had the aim "to re-habilitate Catholic thought in a non-Catholic world, and it did so by combining standards of scholarship previously unknown in Catholic journalism with attitudes critical of ecclesiastical authority which had become equally uncustomary."[5] From the beginning, the *Rambler* assumed an independent stance and expressed mild criticism when needed. The critical tone of some articles and book reviews brought its editor, Richard Simpson, to the attention of the English Catholic hierarchy, who thought it best to discontinue its publication.[6] Newman was brought into the conversation

3. See the discussion of Newman's *An Essay on the Development of Christian Doctrine* by Owen Chadwick, *From Bossuet to Newman* (2nd ed.; London: Cambridge University Press, 1987); Nicholas Lash, *Change in Focus: A Study of Doctrinal Change and Continuity* (London: Sheed and Ward, 1973) and idem, *Newman on Development: The Search for an Explanation in History* (Shepherdstown, WV: Patmos, 1975); and Jan H. Walgrave, *Unfolding Revelation: The Nature of Doctrinal Development* (Philadelphia: Westminster Press, 1972), 293–314 ["The English Contribution: J. H. Newman"].

4. On the personal circumstances of Newman's life in 1859 and the conditions surrounding his assuming the editorship of the *Rambler*, as well as the reaction of the English hierarchy to the May and July issues and Newman's being reported to Rome because of his "On Consulting the Faithful in Matters of Doctrine," see the discussion by Ian Ker, *John Henry Newman: A Biography* (Oxford: Clarendon Press, 1988), 470–89.

5. This is the description offered by John Coulson in his "Introduction" to Newman's *On Consulting the Faithful in Matters of Doctrine* (Kansas City, MO: Sheed and Ward, 1961), 1–49, at 2.

6. Simpson, a layman and a convert to Catholicism, was assisted by Sir John Acton, another convert whose opinions were influenced by his famous teacher, the German Catholic historian Ignaz von Döllinger of the University of Munich. The controversy that precipitated the confrontation between Simpson and the hierarchy revolved around a book review Döllinger had written in which he both praised St. Augustine as the greatest doctor of the West but also pointed to the fact that Jansenism drew inspiration from some emphases of Augustine's thought. At the time, Jansenism was not a mere bookish theological dispute but a real existential threat to Christians' spiritual lives and inner freedom. The English bishops took great umbrage at Döllinger's claim.

as a possible way of salvaging the journal. After careful thought, Newman agreed to act as editor, and he assumed responsibility for the May 1859 issue.

Most of the contents of this issue avoided criticism or anything that could be construed as opposition to the hierarchy. However, in a commentary on "Contemporary Events," Newman expressed his disappointment that the bishops had not engaged the laity on recent proposals by the Royal Commission on elementary education. Newman felt that the laity should be consulted on practical matters of this sort that touched their lives and their responsibilities.[7] In the notice he mentioned that he assumed "that their Lordships really desire to know the opinion of the laity on subjects in which the laity are especially concerned. If even in the preparation of a dogmatic definition the faithful are consulted, as lately in the instance of the Immaculate Conception, it is at least as natural to anticipate such an act of kind feeling and sympathy in great practical questions."[8] The bishops were stung by the criticism and regarded the statement as offensive. What did Newman mean that the laity should be "consulted"? Newman, who had been brought in to resolve the doubts surrounding the *Rambler,* only compounded the problem. He had to resign as editor and the *Rambler* was discontinued. In the July issue, the last under Newman's editorship, he included his now famous essay "On Consulting the Faithful in Matters of Doctrine," in which he carefully laid out his ideas on consultation of the laity and on the "consensus of the faithful" (*consensus fidelium*). One of the preeminent historians of his day, Newman drew heavily from the history of the early church in support of his contention.[9]

---

7. On Newman's pioneering ideas about the role of the laity in the church, I have benefitted from Richard J. Penaskovic, "Open to the Spirit: The Notion of the Laity in the Writings of J. H. Newman," a doctoral dissertation submitted to the Ludwig-Maximilians University, Munich, 1972. It covers the span of Newman's writings as an Anglican and a Catholic, and even addresses Newman's ideas about the "sense of the faithful."

8. Quoted by Coulson, "Introduction," 8.

9. Regarding "On Consulting the Faithful in Matters of Doctrine," Ker observed that "What he did not know was that it was to elicit from him his first original theological work as a Catholic, which marked the beginning of a theology of the Church that was to develop slowly but surely during the next two decades." *John Henry Newman: A Biography*, 478.

The *Rambler* Article of July 1859

The article is only fifty-four printed pages and is replete with references to patristic sources, particularly from the fourth century, that helped Newman arrive at his opinion and frame the argument. In the first section he begins by explaining the expression he had used that in the recent process of defining Mary's immaculate conception, the faithful had been "consulted." He points to the fact that two questions are involved in the statement. First, is it doctrinally correct to insist that the faithful be listened to in preparation for a doctrinal definition? And second, is this appeal to the faithful rightly called "consultation"?

Newman makes the important distinction that consultation can be used to express a fact or as calling for a judgment: "But the English word 'consult,' in its popular and ordinary use, is not so precise and narrow in its meaning;[10] it is doubtless a word expressive of trust and deference, but not of submission. It includes the idea of inquiring into a matter of *fact*, as well as asking a judgment."[11] He answers his own question by saying that Rome's recent consultation of the faithful was to determine the "fact" of their belief, not its theological understanding. "Doubtless their advice, their opinion, their judgment on the question of definition is not asked; but the matter of fact, viz. their belief, *is* sought for, as a testimony to that apostolical tradition, on which alone any doctrine whatsoever can

---

10. Newman is contrasting the "popular usage" here with the "technical usage" of the term as a theologian might use it. In fact, he goes out of his way to stress the point that a journal like the *Rambler* must run the risk of creating some unclarity since it is not intended to present theology in technical language. The laity would be deprived of the catechesis proper to their state, level of education, questions, problems, and interests, if the exactitude of a scholastic disputation or of a scholarly theological article was called into service. The laity would be left helpless in their ignorance in matters of the faith and the church would gravely suffer from this state. In concluding this opening section of "On Consulting the Faithful in Matters of Doctrine," he writes: "Without deciding whether or not it is advisable to introduce points of theology into popular works, and especially whether it is advisable for laymen to do so, still, if this actually *is* done, we are not to expect in them that perfect accuracy of expression which is demanded in a Latin treatise or a lecture *ex cathedra*; and if there be a want of this exactness, we must not at once think it proceeds from self-will and undutifulness in the writers." "On Consulting the Faithful in Matters of Doctrine," 62.

11. "On Consulting the Faithful in Matters of Doctrine," 54. Newman's emphasis.

be defined."[12] It is clear that in answer to his second question, Newman defends the process of consulting the faithful with regard to a truth of the faith that they believe—they are among the resources and authoritative witnesses (*loci theologici*) of the faith.[13] He continues: "[T]he *fidelium sensus* and *consensus* is a branch of evidence which it is natural or necessary for the Church to regard and consult, before she proceeds to any definition, from its intrinsic cogency; and by consequence, that it ever has been so regarded and consulted."[14]

After clarifying the issue that "to consult" can have a technical theological meaning and another meaning in popular parlance, Newman dedicates his second section of "On Consulting the Faithful in Matters of Doctrine" to an examination of Giovanni Perrone's presentation of the "sense of the faithful." What does Perrone understand by the "sense of the faithful" and have the faithful been consulted regarding the faith according to him? Newman tells us of the time he spent in Rome in 1847 with Perrone, who generously met with him and shared the results of his research on the "sense of the faithful."[15] He then tells us that after he returned to England, he was able to obtain a copy of Perrone's recently published book and study it carefully.[16] Newman passes in review what he has learned from Perrone's study.

Two points in particular emerge that have shaped Newman's own thought. First, he draws on Perrone's use of the term *conspiratio* ("breathing in unison") to explain the "sense of the faithful." In matters of faith that are not clearly attested to in Scripture or in the authoritative witnesses, something can be learned from the efforts of the bishops, of the fathers,

---

12. Ibid., 54–55. Newman's emphasis.

13. To consult the laity, then, is like consulting the liturgical practice of the church: "We may 'consult' the liturgies or the rites of the Church; not that they speak, not that [they] can take any part whatever in the definition, for they are documents or customs; but they are witnesses to the antiquity or universality of the doctrines which they contain, and about which they are 'consulted.'" See "On Consulting the Faithful in Matters of Doctrine," 55.

14. "On Consulting the Faithful in Matters of Doctrine," 55.

15. For the background and historical context of Newman's stay in Rome after his conversion, see C. Michael Shea, "From Implicit and Explicit Reason to Inference and Assent: The Significance of John Henry Newman's Seminary Studies in Rome," *Journal of Theological Studies* 67 (2016): 143–71.

16. See "On Consulting the Faithful in Matters of Doctrine," 64–65. See the discussion of the meeting of Newman and Perrone by Owen Chadwick, *From Bossuet to Newman*, 167–69.

doctors, and theologians of the church, and by the faithful laity. In these instances, e.g., the doctrine of Mary's immaculate conception according to Perrone, a process of "breathing in unison" among the bishops, theologians, and the laity resulted in the conviction that a teaching under examination or a faith-filled practice or claim can be held as divinely revealed truth.[17] What is important here is that no one source alone and in isolation from the others can arrive at this faith-conviction. Their mutual interaction constitutes this "breathing in unison." Newman approvingly cites the following formula from Pius IX's definition in 1854 used to express the apostolicity of the doctrine: "Divine words, tradition that is to be venerated, the constant *sensus* of the church, [and] the singular *conspiratio* of catholic bishops and the faithful."[18] Then he continues in his own words: "*Conspiratio*; the two, the Church teaching and the Church taught, are put together, as one twofold testimony, illustrating each other, and never to be divided."[19] Newman never called into question the responsibility of the bishops to define the faith, but they might have to

---

17. In addition to the doctrine of the immaculate conception, Perrone also examined the role of the laity in calling for a defense of the faith-conviction that the blessed—e.g., martyrs, confessors, the apostles, etc.—enter into the beatific vision immediately after death and before the Lord's Parousia. There is no need for these giants of the faith to wait until after the Lord's Parousia for their reward of the beatific vision. See Perrone, *De Immaculato B. V. Mariae Conceptu an dogmatico decreto definiri possit*, 147–48. Newman reviews Perrone's treatment on pages 69–70. On the positions of John XXII and Benedict XII regarding the beatific vision, see Decima Douie, "John XXII and the Beatific Vision," *Dominican Studies* 3 (1950): 154–75. A third controversy that Newman mentions very briefly was when the faithful sided with the Benedictine monk Paschasius Radbertus's understanding of the real presence (more realist in the sense of the role of the physical elements of the Eucharist) in his disagreement with his fellow monk Ratramnus (more figurative-symbolic in terms of what the Eucharist represents in mystery). See "On Consulting the Faithful in Matters of Doctrine," 104. On this controversy, see David N. Power, *The Eucharistic Mystery: Revitalizing the Tradition* (New York: Crossroad, 1992), 209–12 ["Presence in Truth and in Mystery"].

18. [He sets down] "divina eloquia, veneranda traditio, perpetuus Ecclesiae sensus, singularis catholicorum Antistitum ac *fidelium* conspiratio." Quoted by Newman, "On Consulting the Faithful in Matters of Doctrine," 71.

19. "On Consulting the Faithful in Matters of Doctrine," 71. Hermann Geissler has commented on this point thus: "Newman repeatedly speaks in this context of the *conspiratio pastorum et fidelium*, which is not to be seen only as cooperation of pastors and faithful, but also as mutual encouragement and sharing of the Spirit." See "The Witness of the Faithful in Matters of Doctrine according to John Henry Newman," 13.

draw upon the faith-convictions, devotions, customs, and practices of the faithful in fulfilling their responsibility. And secondly, Newman accepts Perrone's understanding of the "faithful," which distinguishes them from the pastors in the church and thus means the "laity." The "sense of the faithful" for Newman, then, does not mean all believers in the church, without regard for their position, but only the laity.[20] The distinction is important to Newman if his understanding of *conspiratio* among bishops, theologians, and the lay faithful is to make sense. Newman's meaning also distinguishes it from the teaching of Vatican II on the "sense of the faith," where the idea includes every baptized person in the church, the ordinary faithful and the members of the hierarchy.[21] We will examine this teaching of Vatican II at greater length in chapter 9. In the next section, Newman spells out more clearly how the *conspiratio* functions.

Newman begins the third section by telling the reader that he intends to include an example of the "sense of the faithful" that Perrone did not consider but that Newman regards as important for correctly understanding the notion. The example will embroil Newman yet more deeply in his conflict with the English hierarchy.

During his years as an Anglican, Newman had studied the Arian controversy in detail and written the monograph *The Arians of the Fourth Century*.[22] He was struck by the fact that the bishops wavered in their loyalty to Nicaea's teaching about the Son as "having the same nature"

---

20. As Newman says of Perrone's explanation, "Let it be observed, he not only joins together the *pastores* and *fideles*, but contrasts them; I mean (for it will bear on what is to follow), the 'faithful' do not *include* the 'pastors.'" See "On Consulting the Faithful in Matters of Doctrine," 65.

21. Ian Ker provides a different interpretation, however. According to Ker, "Newman, like *Lumen Gentium* (as we shall see) equivocated, or rather sometimes spoke scriptural and patristic language and sometimes the language of a clerical, institutional Church. . . .[Newman's] thought and language seem to coincide remarkably with that of article 12 of *Lumen Gentium*, which, since it breathes the same air as that of Newman's theological world, may reasonably be used to interpret Newman's words." See Ker's "Newman on the *Consensus Fidelium* as 'The Voice of the Infallible Church,'" in *Newman and the Word*, ed. Terrence Merrigan and Ian T. Ker (Grand Rapids, MI: Wm. B. Eerdmans, 2000) 69-89, at 74.

22. The first and second editions were published in 1833 and 1842 (London: J. G. & F. Rivington). After his conversion to Catholicism, Newman issued a third edition in 1871. The book has been an enormous publication success, with new editions and numerous reprintings up to the present (Hansebooks 2019).

as the Father (*homoousios*). Especially during the second phase of the controversy, when one synod of bishops rapidly followed another and the bishops went out of their way to find compromise formulas to appease the emperor, it was the lay faithful who remained true to Nicaea's teaching.[23] Though Newman argues that the bishops did not *à la limite* abandon the orthodox faith, they were far from staunch pastors and were in fact unreliable teachers. Their lack of loyalty was corrected instead by the vast majority of lay believers. The corporate "sense of the faith" of the laity maintained the church in the truth. Though the laity did not define the faith in this instance, their fidelity indicated a firm grasp of the truth of Nicaea's teaching on the full and equal divinity of the Son. The nub of Newman's argument comes to expression in the following quotation.

> It is not a little remarkable, that, though, historically speaking, the fourth century is the age of doctors . . . nevertheless in that very day the divine tradition committed to the infallible Church was proclaimed and maintained far more by the faithful than by the Episcopate.
>
> Here, of course, I must explain:—in saying this, then, undoubtedly I am not denying that the great body of the Bishops were in their internal belief orthodox; nor that there were numbers of clergy who stood by the laity, and acted as their centres and guides; nor that the laity actually

23. This confusing period has been told best by Michel Meslin, *Les Ariens d'Occident (335–430)* (Paris: Éditions du Seuil, 1967). See my review in *Revue d'histoire et de philosophie religieuses* 51 (1971): 169–74 for a summary of its contents. My unpublished doctoral dissertation at the University of Strasbourg, France, "The *De Trinitate* of Hilary of Poitiers and Arianism: Its Place, Argumentation, and Contribution during the Trinitarian Controversy of the Fourth Century" examined these turbulent years. Arianism has been the subject of much scholarly research in the past forty-five years. Some examples of recent scholarship on Arianism include Thomas A. Kopecek, *A History of Neo-Arianism*, 2 vols. (Cambridge, MA: Philadelphia Patristic Foundation, 1979); Hanns Christof Brennecke, *Hilarius von Poitiers und die Bischofsopposition gegen Konstantius II. Untersuchungen zur dritten Phase des arianischen Streites (337–361)* (Berlin and New York: Walter de Gruyter, 1984); idem, *Studien zur Geschichte der Homöer. Der Osten bis zum Ende der homöischen Reichskirche* (Tübingen: J. C. B. Mohr [Paul Siebeck], 1988); R. P. C. Hanson, *The Search for the Christian Doctrine of God: The Arian Controversy 318–381* (Edinburgh: T&T Clark, 1988); Michel R. Barnes and Daniel H. Williams, eds., *Arianism after Arius: Essays on the Development of the Fourth Century Trinitarian Conflicts* (Edinburgh: T&T Clark, 1993); and Rowan Williams, *Arius: Heresy and Tradition*, rev. ed (Grand Rapids, MI: Wm. B. Eerdmans, 2002).

received their faith, in the first instance, from the Bishops and clergy; nor that some portions of the laity were ignorant, and other portions at length corrupted by the Arian teachers, who got possession of the sees and ordained an heretical clergy;—but I mean still, that in that time of immense confusion the divine dogma of our Lord's divinity was proclaimed, enforced, maintained, and (humanly speaking) preserved, far more by the "Ecclesia docta" [those in the church who are taught] than by the "Ecclesia docens" [those in the church who teach]; that the body of the episcopate was unfaithful to its commission, while the body of the laity was faithful to its baptism; that at one time the Pope, at other times the patriarchal, metropolitan, and other great sees, at other times general councils,[24] said what they should not have said, or did what obscured and compromised revealed truth; while, on the other hand, it was the Christian people who, under Providence, were the ecclesiastical strength of Athanasius, Hilary, Eusebius of Vercellae, and other great solitary confessors, who would have failed without them.

I see, then, in the Arian history a palmary example of a state of the Church, during which, in order to know the tradition of the Apostles, we must have recourse to the faithful. . . . For I argue that, unless they had been catechized as St. Hilary says, in the orthodox faith from the time of their baptism, they never could have had that horror, which they show, of the heterodox Arian doctrine. Their voice, then, is the voice of tradition; and the instance comes to us with still greater emphasis, when we consider—1. that it occurs in the very beginning of the history of the "Ecclesia docens," for there can scarcely be said to be any history of her teaching till the age of martyrs was over; 2. that the doctrine in controversy was so momentous, being the very foundation of the Christian system; 3. that the state of controversy and disorder lasted over the long space of sixty years; and 4. that it involved serious persecutions, in life, limb, and property, to the faithful whose loyal perseverance decided it.

It seems, then, as striking an instance as I could take in fulfillment of Father Perrone's statement, that the voice of tradition may in certain cases express itself, not by Councils, nor Fathers, nor Bishops, but the "communis fidelium sensus."[25]

---

24. Newman does not mean the ecumenical councils of Nicaea and Constantinople I, but those regional and supra-regional synods that met in the years from 326 (Antioch) to 379 (Antioch).

25. "On Consulting the Faithful in Matters of Doctrine," 75–77.

Newman does not claim that a situation such as the Arian controversy is the norm,[26] but there are dangerous situations in the life of the church when the *consensus fidelium* does function. The *conspiratio* of bishops, theologians, and lay faithful is more than a pious idea, for there are situations of peril to the faith or of grave ignorance of it, when one group supplements a lack in the faith-conviction of the others.[27] And so he adds the following important caveat: "Though the laity be but the reflection or echo of the clergy in matters of faith, yet there is something in the 'pastorum et fidelium *conspiratio* [the *breathing in unison* of the bishops and the faithful]' which is not in the pastors alone."[28] We sense how hard Newman is struggling with the idea of the "sense of the faith" among the ordinary faithful. He is trying to find a way to express the importance of both the bishops and the laity, while also insisting on the mutuality of their places and roles in the church. The image of *conspiratio*, of "breathing in unison" like the two lungs in a human body, is his vehicle for doing so.[29]

26. Newman is quite clear about this situation: "As to the particular doctrine to which I have here been directing my view, and the passage in history by which I have been illustrating it, I am not supposing that such times as the Arian will ever come again. . . . And perhaps this is the reason why the 'consensus fidelium' has, in the minds of many, fallen into the background. Yet each constituent portion of the Church has its proper functions, and no portion can safely be neglected." "On Consulting the Faithful in Matters of Doctrine," 103. Leo Scheffczyk, who holds Newman in great esteem, respectfully disagrees with his claim that a similar situation will not arise for the church again in the future. Scheffczyk writes: "(Today we can no longer hold this to be certain.) Newman also believes that this is why the sense of the faith has receded into the background in his time. But, in principle, such a rule of faith can never entirely lose its meaning and effectiveness." See "*Sensus fidelium*—Witness on the Part of the Community," *Communio* 15 (1988): 182–98, at 185.

27. According to Newman, "The strength of one makes up in a particular case for the deficiency of another, and the strength of the 'sensus communis fidelium' can make up (*e.g.*) for the silence of the Fathers." "On Consulting the Faithful in Matters of Doctrine," 66.

28. "On Consulting the Faithful in Matters of Doctrine," 103–4. In his otherwise reliable presentation of Newman's "On Consulting the Faithful in Matters of Doctrine," Avery Dulles does not mention this defining characteristic of the "sense of the faithful" for Newman, and so fails to fully appreciate Newman's contribution. See *John Henry Newman* (2nd ed.; New York: Continuum, 2009), 105–8 and 158–59.

29. Among theologians who wrote after Vatican II, Jean-Marie Roger Tillard favored the image of a *conspiratio* as a way of understanding the "sense of the faithful" in his earliest writing on the topic. See "*Sensus Fidelium*," *One in Christ* 11 (1975): 2–29.

Characteristics of the "Sense of the Faithful" according to Newman

At the beginning of section 3, before examining the relevance of the Arian controversy for the understanding of the "sense of the faithful," Newman lists five characteristics of the notion that he will expand on in his historical presentation. In addition to his notion of the "consensus of the faithful" as a *conspiratio* among bishops, theologians, and the faithful, these points are his clearest expression of how he understands the concept. He already examined the first one in presenting the results of Perrone's scholarly efforts, namely, "as a testimony to the fact of the apostolical dogma." The following four points, though, move beyond the "sense of the faithful" as a simple "testimony to the fact" of a doctrine of the faith and express instead the "sense of the faithful" as contributing positively to the understanding of the faith. He writes that the "*consensus* is to be regarded . . . as a sort of instinct or *phronema*, deep in the bosom of the mystical body of Christ; as a direction of the Holy Ghost; as an answer to its prayer; as a jealousy of error, which it at once feels as a scandal." Let us examine each of these characteristics in turn.

Newman's use of the word "instinct" is drawn from Möhler by way of Perrone. In his *Symbolism*, Möhler had written:

> It is taught, that the Divine Spirit, to which are entrusted the guidance and vivification of the Church, becomes, in its union with the human spirit in the Church, a peculiarly Christian *tact* (ein eigenthümlich christlicher Tact) a deep sure-guiding *feeling* (sicher führendes Gefühl) which, as it abides in truth, leads also into all truth. By a confiding attachment to the perpetuated apostleship, by education in the Church, by hearing, learning, and living within her pale, by the reception of the higher principle, which renders her eternally fruitful, a deep interior *sense* is formed (wird ein tief innerlicher Sinn gebildet) that alone is fitted for the perception and acceptance of the written Word, because it entirely coincides with the *sense* (Sinn), in which the sacred scriptures themselves were composed.[30]

---

30. *Symbolism: Exposition of the Doctrinal Differences between Catholics and Protestants as Evidenced by Their Symbolical Writings*, chapter 38: "The Church as Teacher and Instructress. Tradition. The Church as Judge in Matters of Faith," trans. James Burton Robertson (New York: Crossroad Publishing, 1997), 277.

When we compare the other translations with the original German text, we note that where the French speaks of "un instinct" and the Italian of "un istinto," Möhler himself did not use the German word "Instinkt." But Newman, who clearly followed Perrone's French quotation of *Symbolism* at this point, referred to the "consensus of the faithful" as an "instinct."[31] Newman further qualifies this "instinct" with the Greek term *phronema*, whereas Möhler does not.[32]

The word "instinct," then, poses problems of interpretation for the reader, since it can be understood as a less-than-rational or even emotional response to sense knowing. But this is not how Newman uses the term. Newman envisions "instinct" as a dimension of a more global grasp of reality. Though the cognitive content of the "instinct" is not yet fully formed, it is real knowledge. This would seem to be why Newman at this point introduces the Greek term *phronema* in apposition with the vaguer English word "instinct." Clearly, Newman has borrowed *phronema* from the epistemological vocabulary that deals with cognition and knowledge.[33] The laity, then, perceive the faith in a spontaneous grasp that is open to further, more technical or refined definition, but which does not suffer from the lack of real cognitive content. The laity "know" the content of their faith-convictions. The "consensus of the faithful" is an "intuitive spiritual perception" of the faith.

31. Terrence Merrigan has shown how on pages 143 and 179 in his *The Arians of the Fourth Century* Newman had already spoken of an "intuitive spiritual perception in scripturally informed and deeply religious minds" and how the notion of "intuition" was an important element of his epistemology. See *Clear Heads and Holy Hearts: The Religious and Theological Ideal of John Henry Newman* (Louvain: Peeters Press, 1991), 235. In his more mature thought, Newman understood more broadly what Perrone referred to as "an instinct."

32. Commenting on Newman's use of "phronema" at this point, Coulson remarks: "The *phronema*, that instinct deep within the mystical body, is obviously a counterpart to the *phronesis* or illative sense which, in the individual, is that power to make a real, as opposed to a notional, assent in judgments of faith and conscience." Coulson, "Introduction," 23.

33. Möhler had already referred to Eusebius's use of the Greek expression *ekklēsiastikon phronēma* in the *Historia Ecclesiae* V, 27. See Möhler's footnote to his statement, "This general sense, this ecclesiastical consciousness (dies kirchliche Bewusstsein) is tradition, in the subjective sense of the word." In fact, Möhler goes on to equate this phrase with *ecclesiasticae intelligentiae* and *secundum ecclesiastici et catholici sensus normam*—with understanding (*intelligentia*) and sense or meaning (*sensus*).

Newman's third point is that the "consensus of the faithful" is under the direction of the Holy Spirit. In support he cites St. John Fisher, bishop of Rochester (1469–1535), who wrote of the Holy Spirit as guiding the church "not by force of precept but by a certain unspoken consensus both of the people and the clergy, in such a way that it is received by reason of all these unspoken prayers before we read that it has been confirmed by any decree of councils."[34] The "consensus of the faithful" first takes place at the level of the prayerful receptivity of the whole church and the direct active guidance of the Holy Spirit. The "consensus of the faithful" is a gift, the divine gift of the Spirit of truth. Before an act of ecclesiastical definition, however necessary and important, the church really possesses the truth of revelation as a response to its prayers.[35]

Finally, Newman makes another personal contribution to understanding the "consensus of the faithful" by drawing on a point he had earlier made in the lecture entitled "The Movement of 1833 Foreign to the National Church" in *Certain Difficulties Felt by Anglicans in Catholic Teaching*. In that essay he had drawn on the human body's own spontaneous rejection of something foreign to it as dangerous, while now he shows that the same is true of "the body of the church." Quoting himself, he writes:

> It is the property of life to be impatient of any foreign substance in the body to which it belongs. It will be sovereign in its own domain, and it conflicts with what it cannot assimilate into itself, and *is irritated and disordered* till it has expelled it.[36]

---

34. "Nulla praeceptorum vi, sed consensu quodam tacito tam populi quam cleri, quasi tacitis omnium suffragiis recepta fuit, priusquam ullo conciliorum decreto legimus eam fuisse firmatam." Cited by Newman, "On Consulting the Faithful in Matters of Doctrine," 74.

35. Newman insists on the importance of prayer and the "consensus of the faithful." In particular, he points out how the prayerful wishes of the faithful contributed to the definition of Mary's immaculate conception. He relies here on Denis Pétau's explanation of the relationship of prayer to the pope's act of definition in "On Consulting the Faithful in Matters of Doctrine," 74.

36. See "On Consulting the Faithful in Matters of Doctrine," 74. Newman's emphasis. The lecture can be found in *Certain Difficulties Felt by Anglicans in Catholic Teaching* (new ed.; London: Longman, Green, and Co., 1895), 33–66, at 52.

He then draws the parallel with the church as a body:

> The religious life of a people is of a certain quality and direction, and these are tested by the mode in which it encounters the various opinions, customs, and institutions which are submitted to it. . . . [S]ubmit your heretical and Catholic principle to the action of the multitude, and you will be able to pronounce at once whether it is imbued with Catholic truth or with heretical falsehood.[37]

This, then, is what Newman means by the experience of scandal on the part of the faithful when false claims are made and the faithful consequently exhibit a "jealousy of error." The spontaneity of the human body in rejecting a foreign irritant provides the analogue to the action of the faithful of Christ's body when they reject error. In the presence of error, the body of the church protects itself by distancing itself from the false claim. There is no premeditation here, no minute analysis of the claim, no marshaling of counterarguments, only the unquestioned rejection of its claim to truth. It conflicts with the teaching of the church as the faithful sense it.

The Validity of Newman's View of Arianism and His Understanding of the "Sense of the Faithful"

In recent years Newman's reading of Arianism and its effects in the great church of the fourth century have been questioned. Did Newman exaggerate the fidelity of the laity? Did he misrepresent the failure of the bishops? Does his historiography of the Arian controversy invalidate his claims regarding the "sense of the faithful"? How attached is his view of the "sense of the faithful" to his presentation of the historical facts?

Michael Slusser has criticized Newman on three counts.[38] First, he thinks that Newman advanced a romanticized view of the laity's fidelity. It is simply not possible to maintain the validity of Newman's argument from the historical data he relies on. Newman is convinced that the laity were faithful while the bishops by and large compromised the truth, so he

---

37. Ibid., 74–75. See *Certain Difficulties Felt by Anglicans in Catholic Teaching*, 55.

38. See Michael Slusser, "Does Newman's 'On Consulting the Faithful in Matters of Doctrine' Rest upon a Mistake?" *Horizons* 20 (1993): 234–40.

forces the evidence to prove his point. His reconstruction of the situation forces the evidence into the Procrustean bed he has prepared. Second, Slusser questions whether Newman correctly interpreted the relationship between the bishops and the faithful at the time. In a word, Newman was too eager to separate them into two groups and thereby misses the more profound unity of the local church in the fourth century.[39] And third, Newman has overestimated the value of the orthodoxy of doctrines at the time. Much more characteristic of the church in the fourth century was the concreteness of the lived experience of the faith over the abstract value of isolated creedal statements. At the time, Christians did not unduly separate what they believed from the way they lived and expressed their belief in their liturgical, moral, and devotional conduct. There was far greater unity among the various elements of the faith in the fourth century than Newman credited to the church.

David P. Long agrees by and large with Slusser's reading of Newman's flawed historiography, and he faults Newman for his cloudy reasoning.[40] Newman seems to get lost at times regarding what he is trying to assert and the proofs he brings forward. But Newman is clear on three points. First, he wants to advance the education of the Catholic laity as a value for the church in England as a whole. Second, he wants to coax the bishops into acknowledging the expertise of the laity in matters that directly concern them and the connection between their concerns and the faith. And third, Newman has discerned the theological depth of the laity's apprehension of the value of the devotional life and its contribution to understanding the faith. The formulation of faith-convictions cannot ultimately be neatly separated from the richness of faith as lived ecclesial experience. According to Long, "Newman may well have been on the right track when he emphasized the liturgical and devotional elements of the lay faithful over dogmatic pronouncements."[41]

---

39. We need to remember that the model for the church at the time was closer to communion ecclesiology (*communio*). The juridical elements and accents that would emerge in the West over time were not yet dominant.

40. "Newman's historiography included significant weaknesses that hampered his arguments. Perhaps he was trying too hard to find the perfect parallel for his nineteenth-century situation and so used the historical developments of the fourth-century Church as a 'proof text.'" See "John Henry Newman and the Consultation of the Faithful," *Newman Studies Journal* 10 (2013): 18–31, at 31.

41. "John Henry Newman and the Consultation of the Faithful," 31.

Conclusion

The criticisms of Slusser and Long have been useful in helping us focus on Newman's enduring contribution to the meaning of the "sense of the faithful" in the church. I would point to the following factors. First, the "sense of the faithful" is the result of the "breathing in unison" of the bishops and the faithful. Neither agent can function without the other, even though their contributions will differ. Second, there is something indispensable to the understanding of the faith that only the faithful contribute. Their contribution is not accessory or derivative. Third, this contribution is truly active. The distinction between the "teaching church" as active and giving and the "learning church" as passive and receptive is no longer viable. Fourth, the "sense of the faithful" is a genuine act of cognition, not something on the fringes of reason. It includes spontaneous prereflective elements, the imagination, analogy, logic, concrete experience, and judgment.[42] The epistemology of the church must take this form of knowing into consideration in formulating, defining, and defending the faith. And fifth, the Christian life is organic, whole, and unified. In the church, a believer's social and interpersonal experience, devotional and sacramental life, liturgical practice, morality, the demands of justice, and the call to holiness are all dimensions of a unified whole—the Christian experience. Despite certain ambiguities, the richness of Newman's contributions to the "sense of the faithful" clearly and undeniably emerge.[43]

42. In their different ways, the epistemologies of Rahner (transcendental knowledge and the nature of mystery) and Bernard Lonergan (transcendental method and insight) can be helpful here for understanding the "sense of the faith" as true knowing. It is simply not possible for me to pursue this point now in the discussion of the "sense of the faith," but I will return to these issues in the final chapter.

43. Hubert Hammans expressed the indispensable contribution of Newman to the "sense of the faith" in the following memorable words: "Without Newman's influence, what later theologians would say about the *sensus fidei* is unthinkable." *Die neueren katholischen Erklärungen der Dogmenentwicklung* (Essen: Ludgerus-Verlag Hubert Wingen, 1965), 242–62, at 244.

Chapter Five

The "Sense of the Faith" in the Nineteenth Century: Gains and Losses

During the final years of the nineteenth century appreciation for the "sense of the faithful" changed in the church. Matthias Joseph Scheeben represented cautious continuity with John Henry Newman's positive estimation of the "sense of the faith," while Johann Baptist Franzelin subordinated it to the role of the hierarchy. Finally, with Vatican I the "sense of the faithful" was largely eclipsed by the definition of papal infallibility. There was little room for it in the post-Vatican I church. This chapter narrates and explains these major changes in the church's appreciation of an emerging concept.

Johann Baptist Franzelin, SJ (1816–86)

Johann Baptist Franzelin was born in 1816 in Aldein, Tirol, then part of the Austro-Hungarian Empire. He entered the Society of Jesus in 1834, studied theology at the Roman College between 1845 and 1848 and Louvain in 1848–49, and finally assumed the chair of Dogmatic Theology at the Roman College in 1857. He influenced the preparations for the First Vatican Council (1869–70) and prepared a draft of the Dogmatic Constitution on the Catholic Faith. In 1876, Pius IX named him a cardinal.[1]

---

1. For the biographical facts regarding Franzelin, I have relied on Leo Scheffczyk, "Johann Baptist Franzelin (1816–1886)," in *Katholische Theologen Deutschlands im 19.*

Franzelin's *Tractatus de divina traditione et scriptura* (Treatise on Divine Tradition and Scripture) was published in 1870 and is generally considered his most enduring contribution to theology. Written for his students at the Roman College, this textbook influenced how future theologians for many years viewed tradition and the relationship of Scripture to tradition.[2] In it, Franzelin supported and advanced the idea of tradition as living and reflecting the very life and message of the church over the authoritative repetition of the doctrines of the church. For this reason Franzelin devoted special attention to the constitutive role of the church in proclaiming revelation. According to Scheffczyk:

> [For Franzelin] the problematic of tradition was concretely connected with the event of revelation in faith, in word and in the proclamation of the Church. Positively, it should be remarked that Franzelin did not understand revelation in an overly intellectualistic way, as only the handing on of theoretical truths and propositions. God's speaking is understood in the way the Old Testament understood it, and in the way modern theology understands it, as a unity of speaking and acting. . . . For Franzelin, then, the summit of revelation is the incarnation of the Son and (as modern theologians would phrase it) the Christ-event as the speech act (*Tatwort*) of God. This word in act and event finds its continuation in the Church of Jesus Christ. . . . In the entirety of its life and its history, the Church becomes a form of the interpretation of revelation and thereby a form of tradition.[3]

Jahrhundert, 3 vols., ed. Heinrich Fries and Georg Schwaiger (Munich: Kösel-Verlag, 1975), 2:345–67. See also William J. Kelly, "Franzelin, Johann Baptist" in *Biographical Dictionary of Christian Theologians*, ed. Patrick W. Carey and Joseph T. Lienhard (Peabody, MA: Hendrickson Publishers, 2002), 202–3.

2. According to Scheffczyk, Franzelin's theological method was closer to the spirit of the historical studies of Denis Pétau (1583–1652) and Louis de Thomassin (1619–95). He was widely read in the fathers of the church, especially the Greek fathers, and he drew on them liberally. Even though he gave wide berth to the use of speculative reason in elaborating the faith, Franzelin cannot be enlisted as a proponent of what was to emerge in the last third of the nineteenth century as "neoscholasticism." See "Johann Baptist Franzelin," 348–50. This, too, is the judgment of Walter Kasper, who wrote that Franzelin "was only influenced by it to a very limited degree. The definitive change came with the pontificate of Leo XIII, who in 1879 appointed avowed Thomists to various chairs of theology." See *Die Lehre von der Tradition in der Römischen Schule* in *Gesammelte Schriften*, vol. 1, ed. George Augustine and Klaus Krämer (Freiburg: Herder, 2011), 80 [16].

3. "Johann Baptist Franzelin," 361–62.

Franzelin rejected what at the time was generally regarded as Trent's theory of the relationship of Scripture to tradition—namely, that materially some truths of Christianity were contained in Scripture, while others were found only in tradition. According to the theory, Christian revelation was found "partly in Scripture" and "partly in tradition."[4] Franzelin understood their relationship more organically. Scheffczyk writes:

> Tradition is not to be thought of as independent of Scripture. It is in its essence the tradition of Scripture. . . . It follows that the relationship of Scripture and tradition is determined by the fact that truths that are not formally found in Scripture do not emerge without connection to Scripture and are to be understood as a development of Scripture.[5]

But while Franzelin is to be congratulated for reframing the question of tradition and Scripture, the same cannot be said for his understanding of the "consensus of the faithful" (*consensus fidelium*),[6] a topic he takes up in the textbook. Here, unfortunately, Franzelin represents a narrowing of the perspective on the "sense of the faithful" compared to the thought of Giovanni Perrone and John Henry Newman.[7]

---

4. This was not, in fact, the teaching of Trent. For how this theory emerged after the council, see the studies by Josef Rupert Geiselmann, "Das Missverständnis über das Verhältnis von Schrift und Tradition und seine Überwindung in der katholischen Theologie," *Una Sancta* 11 (1956): 131–50; idem, "Das Konzil von Trient über das Verhältnis der Heiligen Schrift und der nichtgeschriebenen Tradition," in *Die mündliche Überlieferung. Beiträge zum Begriff der Tradition*, ed. Michael Schmaus (Munich: Max Hueber Verlag, 1957), 123–206; and idem, "Scripture, Tradition, and the Church: An Ecumenical Problem," in *Christianity Divided: Protestant and Roman Catholic Theological Issues*, ed. Daniel A. Callahan, Heiko A. Oberman, and Daniel J. O'Hanlon (New York: Sheed and Ward, 1961), 39–72, especially at 39–43 ["Obstacles to the New Knowledge"].

5. "Johann Baptist Franzelin," 362–63. Peter Walter, too, writes approvingly of Franzelin, commenting that "tradition appears as a living process in which the whole Church participates and not just the pastors. It is realized in being proclaimed, in the witness of faith lived out, and in the liturgy and dogma." See *Johann Baptist Franzelin (1816–1886), Jesuit, Theologe, Kardinal: ein Lebensbild* (Bolzano/Bozen: Verlagsanstalt Athesia, 1987), 40. I wish to thank Dr. John P. Galvin for sharing this resource with me.

6. This is the expression Franzelin preferred, not the "sense of the faithful."

7. For Franzelin's views on the magisterium in general, see T. Howland Sanks, *Authority in the Church: A Study in Changing Paradigms* (Missoula, MT: Scholars' Press, 1974), 41–61.

In part 1 of the *Tractatus*, Franzelin deals with tradition and it is here that he discusses the "consensus of the faithful." On the relationship of the "consensus of the faithful" to tradition, Franzelin formulates the following thesis:

> The knowledge and the profession of the faith are always preserved from error by the Spirit of truth and are found in the consent of the whole assembly of believers through the authoritative magisterium of apostolic succession. Therefore, whether understood of believers individually or of the people as a whole, it is not a capacity for teaching with authority but *the duty of learning*. Nevertheless, the "catholic understanding" of the Christian people and their consensus regarding the dogmas of the Christian faith must be considered one of the criteria of divine tradition.[8]

The thesis is traditional inasmuch as it upholds the fact and the importance of the "consensus of the faithful" taught in these terms at least since the fifteenth century. But it is also restrictive insofar as it limits the role of the faithful to listening to their pastors and learning Christian truth from them. Franzelin makes this clear when he characterizes the infallibility of the "consensus of the faithful" as "passive," not "active" like that of the bishops. The infallibility of the faithful is mediated through the office of the bishops. In his explanation, Franzelin makes greater room for the indispensable role of apostolic succession as the means of communicating Christian truth in the church, and that clearly represents a positive contribution by him.

Another important element of Franzelin's explanation is his insistence on "faith as obedience," but he does not mean the richness of St. Paul's understanding of obedience. To Paul, faith is "hearing" God's revelation and welcoming it joyfully.[9] This is true for all believers, both for those

---

8. "Conscientia ac professio fidei in toto consentiente fidelium coetu a Spiritu veritatis per magisterium authenticum successionis apostolicae semper conservatur ab errore immunis. Licet ergo sive singulis de plebe fidelium sive plebibus integris non sit facultas authenticae docendi sed officium discendi, totius tamen populi christiani 'catholicus sensus' et consensus in dogmate christianae fidei censeri debet unum ex criteriis divinae traditionis." *Tractatus de divina traditione et scriptura*, 94. My italics. All translations of Franzelin's Latin text are mine.

9. See H.-J. Hermisson and Eduard Lohse, *Faith*, trans. Douglas Stott (Nashville, TN: Abingdon, 1981). As Jürgen Becker has written: "Faith is accordingly obedience in the sense that it acknowledges for itself what Christ is for faith. Faith is obedience in that it corresponds to the appeal, 'Be reconciled to God' (2 Cor. 5:20), and does not reject reconciliation. The obedient one is in this case not the recipient of a command but the one

who preach the faith and have received it obediently from the Lord, and those who receive the apostles' preaching in "obedient hearing" (*hypakoē pisteōs*). For Paul, it is not the moral overtone of obedience as a virtue that is prominent, but the religious act of "hearing" in all its biblical richness. But Franzelin has narrowed the act of believing in a way that will limit the possibility of any active role of understanding and appropriating the faith by believers. Thus, although Franzelin acknowledges the consensus of the whole church in continuity with past witnesses, he has limited the role of the faithful to something purely passive.[10]

In his historical treatment of the "consensus of the faithful," Franzelin mentions Tertullian (160–220), Gregory of Nazianzen (330–389), Augustine (354–430), and Vincent of Lérins (died mid-fifth century) from the past, as well as Pope Pius IX's more recent recourse to the faithful to ascertain their belief in Mary's immaculate conception. His historical treatment is more open to the role of the faithful in witnessing to Christian truth, and he characterizes this consensus as "certain and clear" (*certum et clarum*). For all that, the role of the laity in the "consensus of the faithful" is not concerned with more technical, theological considerations of the faith, since this is the responsibility of the bishops and the theologically learned. Instead, the contribution of the faithful pertains to their witness to the constant practice and customs in the church as these touch on the faith:

> Likewise, it is clear that the sort of consensus to which the Christian people are called . . . pertains to the explicit knowledge of believers

---

who answers out of insight into the salvific gift of God in Christ." *Paul: Apostle to the Gentiles*, trans. O. C. Dean (Louisville, KY: Westminster John Knox Press, 1993), 413. On this important dimension of faith for St. Paul, see Gerhard Schneider, "*hypakoē* obedience; *hypakouō* obey, be obedient," in *Exegetical Dictionary of the New Testament*, 3 vols., ed. Horst Balz and Gerhard Schneider (Grand Rapids, MI: Wm. B. Eerdmans, 1993), 3:394–95; Giuseppe Segalla, "L'obbedienza di fede' (Rm 1,5; 16:26) tema della Lettera ai Romani?" *Rivista Biblica* 36 (1988): 329–42; and James D. G. Dunn, *The Theology of Paul the Apostle* (Grand Rapids, MI: Wm. B. Eerdmans, 1998), 634–42 ["Faith and 'the law of faith'"].

10. Franzelin reiterates his position in his Scholion 1, where he writes: "It is a fact that whatever the Church universal believes by faith, that is, by reason of the promise and the institution of Christ, is infallibly true. Therefore, it is *the same universal Church that is the subject of such infallibility in believing*, and which is called *passive* by customary usage. (Quidquid ergo universalis Ecclesia fide credit, id ex promissione et institutione Christi constat infallibiliter verum esse. Huius igitur *infallibilitatis in credendo*, quae *passiva* dici solet, *subiectum est ipsamet Ecclesia universalis*.)" My italics.

and to what is definitely contained in public and constant practice and custom. As regards other, rather subtle doctrines, what consensus can be shown among the vast majority of the faithful who only believe implicitly what their pastors and the doctors in the faith believe regarding them?[11]

In a corollary, Franzelin shows his familiarity with John Henry Newman's "On Consulting the Faithful in Matters of Doctrine" as it appeared in the July 1859 issue of the *Rambler*.[12] He concedes that at times in its history, the hierarchy failed to provide the leadership expected of it, but he softens his criticism of the bishops during the controversy. He writes:

> Indeed it can happen that even if many bishops, and even entire ecclesiastical provinces, depart from the faith, yet the greater part of the flock of faithful will remain constant in its orthodox profession of the faith and keep communion and consent with apostolic succession, by retaining consent and communion with the center of unity, that is, with the see of Peter. Nevertheless, with the assistance of the Holy Spirit, it is not possible that the universal episcopate should fail and not remain the organ for conserving tradition by means of the ordinary external magisterium, by which the same Spirit continues and preserves communion and faith of the Catholic people.[13]

Like Newman, Franzelin points to the importance of the faithful during the Arian crisis, but he blunts his criticism of the bishops during the crisis,

---

11. "Pariter manifestum est, ad huiusmodi plebis christianae consensum appellari . . . quae vel in explicita fidelium cognitione versantur vel certe in publica et constanti aliqua praxi et consuetudine continentur; quis enim posset demonstrari consensus in doctrinis aliis subtilioribus, quae a multidudine fidelium implicite solum creduntur in fide pastorum et doctorum." *Tractatus de divina traditione et scriptura*, 102.

12. Franzelin was not aware that Newman was the author of the article, since it had appeared anonymously.

13. "Potest quidem accidere, ut Episcopi etiam multi etiam intergrarum provinciarum a fide deficiant, et tamen maior pars gregum fidelium in orthodoxa professione constans praeferat communionem et consensionem cum successione apostolica, quae permanet in consensu et communione cum centro unitatis i.e. cum Sede Petri; non tamen potest fieri ut deficiat universus Episcopatus, et ut hic non maneat sub assistentia Spiritus Sancti organon conservandae traditionis, per quod ut per magisterium ordinarium externum idem Spiritus communionem et fidem catholici populi contineat et conservet." *Tractatus de divina traditione et scriptura*, 103–4.

distancing himself from Newman's harsher judgment. Instead, he corrects Newman by writing: "Everything that this same anonymous author of the article demonstrates is that at this very time 'the teaching church was the active instrument of the Church's infallibility.' "[14]

It should be clear that Franzelin cannot bring himself to agree with Newman's reading of the Arian crisis. He misreads Newman in order to support his distinction of an active infallibility (*infallibilitas activa*) and a passive infallibility (*infallibilitas passiva*). But this distinction does not correspond exactly to Newman's distinction between a "teaching church" (*ecclesia docens*) and a "church taught" (*ecclesia docta*). Newman's distinction does not exclude an active role of the faithful. As we saw in chapter 4, the distinction places the hierarchy and the faithful in a meaningful reciprocal relationship to one another.

There is an unresolved tension in Franzelin's treatment of the "consensus of the faithful." His development of a more satisfactory understanding of tradition as the living witness of the church remains an enduring contribution to theology. To his credit, he remains faithful to the claim that the whole church is the subject of what it professes, teaches, and believes. The whole church testifies infallibly to Christian revelation.[15] And yet there is also for Franzelin a major difference regarding the contributions of the hierarchy and the faithful in arriving at this truth. Fatefully, Franzelin goes too far in exaggerating the difference between these two roles with his distinction between "active" and "passive" infallibility. His German student Matthias Joseph Scheeben will not make the same mistake. But the influence and prestige enjoyed by Cardinal Franzelin will go far in relegating the role of the faithful to its "obedience" to the hierarchy.[16] The ultramontane currents then in the air in Rome were on the ascendant.[17]

---

14. The reference is to "On Consulting the Faithful in Matters of Doctrine," 86.

15. Kasper calls the understanding of the "sense of the faithful" simply a *locus theologicus*, "the view of baroque scholasticism." See *Die Lehre von der Tradition in der Römischen Schule*, 482 [315].

16. The influence of Franzelin can be seen in the numerous approving references to his work among theologians, e.g., in the comments of Johannes Beumer, "Glaubenssinn der Kirche?" *Trierer theologische Zeitschrift* 61 (1952): 129–42, at 130–31, 139.

17. On ultramontanism, see John W. O'Malley, "The Ultramontane Movement," *Vatican I: The Council and the Making of the Ultramontane Church* (Cambridge, MA: Belknap Press, 2018), 55–95.

Matthias Joseph Scheeben (1835–88)

Eugen Paul aptly captures the contradiction that emerges from Scheeben's genius and the subsequent neglect of his valuable contributions to theology.[18] Paul compares Scheeben to a majestic mountain that everyone admires but few dare to climb. Often recommended to the attention of theologians, Scheeben, sadly, continues to be largely unread and neglected.[19] And yet he has so much to offer the contemporary reader, including the "sense of the faith."

Scheeben was born in 1835 near Bonn, the oldest of eight children. After studies in Cologne, he decided on the priesthood and was sent to Rome to study at the Roman College, where Carlo Passaglia, Clemens Schrader, and Johann Baptist Franzelin were among his teachers. After ordination in 1858, Scheeben began to teach moral theology and then dogma at the diocesan seminary in Cologne, where he remained until his premature death in 1888. Though he never aspired to a professorship at one of Germany's prestigious universities, Scheeben's theological output was as impressive as that of any university professor, encompassing popular works as well as dozens of scholarly articles and several books.[20]

18. See "Matthias Joseph Scheeben (1835–1888)" in *Katholische Theologen Deutschlands*, 3 vols., ed. Heinrich Fries and Georg Schwaiger (Munich: Kösel, 1975), 2:386–408. Also by Eugen Paul, *Denkweg und Denkform der Theologie von Matthias Joseph Scheeben* (Munich: Max Hueber, 1970) and *Matthias Scheeben*, Wegbereiter heutiger Theologie, no. 9 (Graz: Styria, 1976). See also D. Thomas Hughson, "Scheeben, Matthias Joseph" in *Biographical Dictionary of Christian Theologians*, ed. Patrick W. Carey and Joseph T. Lienhard, 448–49.

19. Theologians have debated the place of Scheeben in the theological spectrum of his day. Some have argued that he was an uncritical adherent of the newly emerging neoscholastic synthesis. Others have claimed that he was a faithful representative of the Roman School of Giovanni Perrone, Carlo Passaglia, Clemens Schrader, and Johannes B. Franzelin and as such somewhat hostile to the more critical German theology represented by the universities of Tübingen and Munich. Neither of these alternatives does justice to the independence of mind and theological creativity he demonstrated time and again. Scheeben neither belonged to any theological school or movement of his day nor was he the leader of a new school. He simply went his own way, fashioning a powerful synthesis of patristic sources, admiration for the best of theological thought of his day, his own pastoral sensitivity and love of the church, combined with his keen ability to create a workable synthesis. The foundation for this synthesis can be found in his starting points in the Trinity and the incarnation.

20. On the life, writings, and career of Scheeben, I have benefited from Aidan Nichols, "Introducing Scheeben," *Romance and System: The Theological Synthesis of Matthias Joseph*

Scheeben was an indefatigable writer who devoted much of his time to editing and writing for scholarly and more popular Catholic journals. This activity included studies on the interpretation of Vatican I and the issues it raised in ecclesiology, papal primacy, and infallibility, articles on the notion of the supernatural, faith and reason, theology and philosophy, and the theology of grace. He also contributed in-depth studies from the history of theology, as well as articles on contemporary authors and current theological movements. Scheeben's pioneering study *Nature and Grace* appeared in 1861, followed by his immensely popular *Mysteries of Christianity* in 1865. Both were later translated into English and several other modern languages.[21] His treatment of the Virgin Mary in the fifth volume of his *Handbook of Catholic Dogmatics* has also been translated into English and appeared as *Mariology* in two volumes.[22] The principal source for understanding Scheeben's teaching about the "sense of the faithful" is his *Handbook of Catholic Dogmatics*.[23]

Scheeben (Denver, CO: Augustine Institute, 2010), 1–19 and Ulrich Sander, *Ekklesiologisches Wissen: Kirche als Autorität. Die "Theologische Erkenntnislehre" Matthias Joseph Scheebens als antimodernistische Theologie der Moderne* (Frankfurt: Josef Knecht, 1997), 6–39 ["Matthias Joseph Scheeben (1835–1888): Werk und Wirkung"].

21. Both were translated by Cyril Vollert (St. Louis, MO: B. Herder, 1954 and 1946 respectively). Scheeben's popular spiritual writings include *The Glories of Divine Grace: A Fervent Exhortation to All to Preserve and Grow in Sanctifying Grace* (1863), German edition reprinted in 1949 [17th printing] and translated into English by Patrick Shaughnessy (Rockford, IL: Tan Books, 2000), as well as his popular writings on the Blessed Mother, especially the *Marienblüthen aus dem Garten der heiligen Väter und christlichen Dichter zur Verherrlichung des ohne Makel empfangenen Gottesmutter* (Schaffhausen, 1860).

22. Trans. by T. L. M. J. Geukers (St. Louis, MO: B. Herder, 1940). Scheeben's *Mariology* formed a part of his treatment of Christology in vol. 5, part 2, of the *Handbook* that was published originally in 1880. Because of his scholarly theological treatment of Mary, Scheeben is regarded as one of the great Mariologists in modern Catholic theology.

23. Recently, Michael J. Miller has undertaken a translation of Scheeben's *Handbook of Catholic Dogmatics*. At the time of this writing, volumes 1 and 5 have been published by Emmaus Academic, 2019–2021. When I researched Scheeben for this chapter, there was no English translation of the *Handbook*, except for Scheeben's *Mariology*, mentioned above. Consequently, I worked with the original German text and below have provided my own translations of the appropriate sections that deal with revelation, faith, the "sense of the faith," and the roles of the pope and bishops, theologians, and the ordinary faithful. I have opted to employ my own translation, while giving the reference where Miller's translation of the same passage can be found.

Scheeben did not live long enough to complete his crowning theological achievement, the *Handbook of Catholic Dogmatics*.[24] It was to comprise six volumes, but only five were completed, including treatments on a theory of theological knowledge, the triune God, creation and sin, Christology and redemption, and the doctrine of grace. Treatments on the church, the sacraments, and Christian eschatology were never written. Of primary pertinence to our topic is the first volume, the *Theologische Erkenntnislehre* (Theological Epistemology).[25]

Before Scheeben, introductory volumes on the uniqueness of faith and theological cognition were primarily apologetical in approach and tone. Since Scheeben timed the book's appearance to coincide with the sixth centenary of the deaths of Thomas Aquinas and Bonaventure in 1874, he poured special effort into constructing a "theory of theological knowledge." The celebration of Vatican I in 1869–1870 and its teaching on faith also contributed to the originality and the timeliness of the volume.[26]

The dogmatic tradition in Catholic theology relies heavily on human reason, which is enlisted to study and better understand Christian beliefs singly and in their relationships among themselves. Scheeben was profoundly influenced by the teaching of Vatican I regarding the nexus

---

24. The *Handbuch der katholischen Dogmatik* appeared in Scheeben's *Gesammelte Schriften*, 8 vols., ed. Martin Grabmann (2nd ed.; Freiburg: Herder, 1948).

25. It is volume 3 of Scheeben's *Gesammelte Schriften*.

26. The originality of the *Handbook of Catholic Dogmatics* can be seen in the way Scheeben organized the material. The following brief synopsis of the contents of the first volume demonstrates Scheeben's creativity. The *Handbook* is divided into two sections. Part 1 is entitled "The Objective Principles of Theological Knowledge" and consists of five subdivisions: (1) divine revelation as the originating principle of theological knowledge (§§1–6); (2) the objective mediation and valid proclamation of revelation in general, or the nature and organism of apostolic preaching and teaching (§§7–15); (3) Scripture as the original source of faith (§§16–20) and the oral apostolic deposit, or apostolic tradition more narrowly considered (§21); (4) the church's tradition or the testimony of the apostolic deposit as channel of the faith and of theological knowledge (§§22–27); and (5) the valid proclamation of the word of God in the teaching apostolate, or the church's regulation of the faith and theological knowledge (§§28–37). Part 2 is entitled "Theological Knowledge Considered in Itself" and consists of only one general section that is divided into two subsections: (1) the Christian and Catholic faith (§§38–46) and (2) the understanding of faith and theological knowledge (§§47–55). The treatment concludes with an independent section or excursus on the history of theology (§§56–60).

among the mysteries of the Christian faith and the ability of one mystery to illuminate another and so afford the mind real human access to these mysteries.[27] The human theological endeavor of growing in understanding the faith depended on this conciliar teaching with its roots in the Catholic appreciation of the role of analogy.[28] Scheeben laid the foundations for such knowledge precisely in his first volume of the *Handbook of Catholic Dogmatics.*[29]

In his *Handbook of Catholic Dogmatics*, Scheeben examined the supernaturality of revelation and its expression in the divine mysteries.[30] He preferred to refer to the "teaching apostolate" (*Lehrapostolat*) of the pope and bishops rather than the "teaching office" (*Lehramt*), and he viewed this apostolate or ministry as something that is organic and ecclesially

27. See Vatican I, Dogmatic Constitution on the Catholic Faith, chapter 4, "On Faith and Reason." Norman P. Tanner, ed., *Decrees of the Ecumenical Councils*, vol. 2 (Washington, DC: Georgetown University Press, 1990), 808.

28. On analogy, see David Burrell, *Analogy and Philosophical Language* (New Haven, CT; Yale University Press, 1975); David Tracy, *The Analogical Imagination: Christian Theology and the Culture of Pluralism* (New York: Crossroad, 1981); and Elizabeth A. Johnson, "The Right Way to Speak about God? Pannenberg on Analogy," *Theological Studies* 43 (1982): 673–92.

29. Matthias Joseph Scheeben, *Gesammelte Schriften*, vol. 3, ed. Martin Grabmann (2nd ed.; Freiburg: Herder, 1948). The *Handbook of Catholic Dogmatics* comprises 491 pages of German text in the *Complete Works* of Scheeben's writings published in 1948. The English translation by Michael J. Miller is 659 pages in two volumes (2019). In terms of content, Scheeben's contribution was a substantial one.

30. I have found the following treatments of Scheeben's theology helpful in elaborating my own synthesis of his contributions, especially to a criteriology of the faith and the "sense of the faithful" in particular. Peter Fernekess, *Der Glaubenssinn der Gläubigen in der Traditionslehre bei M. J. Scheeben* (Landau in der Pfalz, 1974); Marko Mišerda, "Scheebens Beitrag zur 'Sensus-Fidelium'-Diskussion," *Subjektivität im Glauben. Eine theologisch-methodologische Untersuchung zur Diskussion über den "Glaubens-Sinn" in der katholischen Theologie des 19. Jahrhunderts* (Bern: Peter Lang, 1996), 431–529; Ulrich Sander, *Ekklesiologisches Wissen: Kirche als Autorität. Die "Theologische Erkenntnislehre" Matthias Joseph Scheebens als antimodernistische Theologie der Moderne* (Frankfurt: Josef Knecht, 1997), especially chapters 4 ("Implicit Ecclesiology: Church and Difference and Identity in the Theology of M. J. Scheeben") and 5 ("Explicit Ecclesiology: Church as an Authority in Judging the Faith in M. J. Scheeben"); and Aidan Nichols, *Romance and System: The Theological Synthesis of Matthias Joseph Scheeben* (Denver, CO: Augustine Institute, 2010), especially chapters 2 ("The Nature of Faith"), 3 ("The Character of Theology"), and 7 ("Revelation and Its Transmission").

articulated. This is the context in which Scheeben situates his discussion of the "sense of the faith."

Scripture as the written deposit of the faith is given priority, but only when it is properly understood. Scheeben refers to Scripture as a "source" of belief, while the oral apostolic deposit is called a "channel" of the faith. Traditions that are written down or that can be documented must be understood within the broader context of the "living tradition" of the church. The apostolic deposit is open to authoritative judgment rendered by popes and ecumenical councils. There is genuine progress in the teaching of the church and its dogmas. The Catholic teaching on faith stresses its divine character that comes to expression in the word of God, but also its transcendence since it is directed toward God as essentially invisible and supernatural. The divine and transcendent quality of faith, however, does not exclude genuine knowledge as part of faith itself. Catholic faith, moreover, makes room for the authority and authenticity of ecclesiastical teaching. There is a place for understanding the faith (*intellectus fidei*), and this is the role of theology. [31]

Scheeben discusses the "sense of the faithful" in §13, which is entitled "The Continuation of the Organization of the Teaching Apostolate. The Organic Connection of the Teaching Body with the Body of Believers in the Catholic Church." Already in the opening paragraph, Scheeben indicates his characteristic terms and lines of argument. He writes:

> Just as the body of teachers depends on the living and reciprocal action with those subsidiary organs that it brings forth, so too are these teachers in the most intimate organic relationship with the body of believers (*corpus fidelium*) that it has established and built up, and which it holds together and leads—the community of the faithful. Together with these, according to the will and disposition of Christ, it constitutes an organic body, the whole body of those who preserve and represent Christian truth itself, namely, the community of the Church. Even though the body of believers does not participate in the official teaching function itself, but acts in a receptive way vis-à-vis the body of teachers, nonetheless the body of believers does not have a mechanical and purely passive relationship toward them. On the contrary, since the faith of the body of believers, given its supernatural character, is every bit as direct as the

---

31. On the nature of theology, see Avery Dulles's *The Craft of Theology: From Symbol to System* (expanded ed.; New York: Crossroad, 1995).

teaching of the body of teachers and stands under the direct influence of the Holy Spirit, so can and should the confession of belief by the body of believers in its own way serve to represent, proclaim, and testify to Christian truth. In this way it enters into such reciprocity of action with the proclamation of doctrine on the part of the body of teachers, that, even though the faithful are led and determined by their teachers, this very body of the faithful, by supporting and strengthening their teachers, exercises its own (distinctive) influence on them (no. 168).[32]

Scheeben is unambiguous about the mutuality of relationships between the faithful and their bishops based on the organic character of the church as a "community of believers" and "the body of believers." Secondly, he grounds the legitimacy of the contributions of the faithful in proclaiming and witnessing to the faith in the influence of the Holy Spirit, who is free to act directly on the faithful. Scheeben's language respects the role of the bishops as teachers and leaders, but the respect of the faithful for them does not preclude the fact that the teachers, too, need the support of their faithful—a support that goes beyond a merely "automatic" and "passive" obedience on the part of the faithful. They have a distinctive, active role in confirming the teaching of the bishops.

Scheeben takes up the mutuality of the relationship of these two witnesses—the bishops and the faithful—in a lengthy and careful explanation in numbers 170–72. He writes:

Three points emerge from this organic connection of the body of teachers with the body of believers in the community of the Church. First, the very idea of the teaching of Christ assumes the double forms of representation and witness. On the one hand, it takes the form of official, authentic, and authoritative doctrine and proclamation, while on the other, it takes the form of private, believing confession. Both forms together can be grasped with the help of the idea of authentic witness. In the first case, it is an authentic witnessing in the proper sense, that is, as the juridically public and proper (episcopal) task of teaching others as established and equipped by the Holy Spirit, while in the second case, it is an authentic witness more broadly speaking, that is, in the

---

32. *Theologische Erkenntnislehre*, 97; *Theological Epistemology*, 133. Scheeben regularly and frequently employed italics to highlight various ideas in the *Theologische Erkenntnislehre*. In reproducing these texts, I have chosen not to follow this practice, but to allow the translation to speak for itself.

sense of a truly public declaration and so a genuine proclamation that results from the prompting of the Holy Spirit. The first case appears as a reverberation and continual resounding of the word of God, as a constant address by God to men and women in the Church, while the second is rather an echo of the word of God, but still an echo that is also inspired by the Spirit of God, so that it, too, in its way is to be considered as the reverberation and the continual resounding of the word of God (no. 170).

On the other hand, the second form of testifying (to Christian truth) shows itself to be the echo of the teaching of the body of teachers, pointing to the content of their teaching, so too in its own way it confirms their effectiveness. The confession of the body of believers has its own force not simply because of the activity of the body of teachers, who have brought it about, but because of the direct action of the Holy Spirit on believers. It possesses an inner, relatively independent power to the very extent that the unanimous confession of the whole body of believers also represents an infallible witness of the Holy Spirit. Without this infallibility the very point of the infallibility of the body of teachers would be completely frustrated and the connection between the body of teachers and the body of believers would be open to being completely disrupted. Yes, the proper force of the testimony of the whole (body of believers) even has the special advantage that the action of the Holy Spirit is more clearly manifested in the marvels the Spirit works through them with his constant presence and activity. It is clearer than all that the body of bishops teach alone (no. 171).

Finally, the third form, that of the clearly existing confession of the totality of believers, insofar as it is a relatively independent witness of the Holy Spirit, can occasionally precede temporally and logically a given manifestation of the body of teachers and in this way acts as a point of reference that influences the later decision of the body of teachers. It can thereby influence an action of the body of teachers. Even so, it should be evident that neither the authority of the body of teachers nor its teaching is merely the product of or the reflection of the force of this witness, nor is this witness the only proximate or ordinary means by which the body of teachers receives its orientation regarding a doctrine to be presented. The body of teachers is and remains not only an independent judge of the faith, but also the independent authentic witness of the truth to and for the people, insofar as it presents to them the truth it has received in the power of Christ from its predecessors. Recourse to the witness of the faith as already in the possession of the people is therefore always of secondary assistance; it is not the first rule or source of the teaching of the body of teachers (no. 172).[33]

For Scheeben the principles of the organic character and mutuality of proclamation emerge clearly. The body of teachers cannot be played off against the body of the faithful. Each group has its dignity and its role to exercise, but not at the expense of the other. Where Franzelin subordinates the body of believers (the *ecclesia discens*) to the bishops as official teachers (the *ecclesia docens*), Scheeben prefers to stress their being in relationship with each other. For all that, Scheeben is quite clear that the bishops and their official teaching ministry have priority when it comes to teaching with authority or defining the faith. The ministry of the bishops possesses the three attributes of being public, authentic, and authoritative in character by reason of their apostolic office.[34] Even though the office of bishop is indispensable in the church and is invested with great authority, it must not be isolated from the life of the broader church, and from the faithful in particular, who also have an indispensable role to play in constituting the rich life of the church.

The second point to be noted is the importance of the role of the Holy Spirit active in both the body of teachers and the body of believers. Though the Spirit empowers each group to witness differently, Scheeben is clear that the Spirit acts "directly" on the members of each body. Though Scheeben's pneumatology might appear rather rudimentary by later standards, its presence in his thought is unmistakable. The place and role of the Spirit enriches both Scheeben's ecclesiology and his epistemology of revelation and faith.[35]

---

33. *Theologische Erkenntnislehre*, 98–99; *Theological Epistemology*, 134–36.

34. Scheeben discusses these three attributes in §8 entitled "A Closer Examination of and the Intrinsic Grounding of the Catholic View of the Transmission of Revelation and Its Proclamation by Apostolic Preaching." See *Theologische Erkenntnislehre*, 46–59. The three attributes are treated in nos. 68–74. See *Theologische Erkenntnislehre*, 47–50. I want to point out Scheeben's conclusion in no. 74: "The best and simplest expression for [this ministry] is the *apostolate* [*Apostolat*] or the *teaching apostolate* [*Lehrapostolat*], which is at any rate more meaningful than the [usual] German expression *teaching office* [*Lehramt*]."

35. Eberhard Schockenhoff also judges Scheeben very positively in the historical section of his important contribution on the *sensus fidelium* "Der Glaubenssinn des Volkes Gottes als ethisches Erkenntniskriterium? Zur Nicht-Rezeption kirchlicher Lehraussagen

In conclusion, the important roles played by the fathers of the church and by the most important theologians and theological schools in witnessing to and in contributing to the proclamation of Christian faith should be noted. Scheeben writes at some length of their positive contribution, acknowledging it as willed and guided by the Holy Spirit.

> After the fundamental center and the main conduit of tradition, namely the Apostolic See, there are other channels within the river of the common tradition, themselves under divine influence, namely individuals who by reason of their personal endowments and outstanding contributions, might be called secondary conduits and channels of the faith. Granted that they do not act with juridical authority, nonetheless they represent the faith both in fact and with moral authority. Their collective and constant witness should be, and in fact is accepted as the completely reliable exponent of the tradition in its entirety. As I have already shown (§12, IV), the Fathers and great teachers (of the past) are the extraordinary helpers of the body of teachers par excellence, and this by divine dispensation at various times and places, even though in themselves they are only helpers. Still, within the body of teachers and their ordinary helpers they occupy a central place. By nature and grace they are in a position to more clearly and comprehensively envision the content of revelation and tradition itself as regards the past and the present. Through their words and writings they cast their light as widely as possible and thereby exercise a very broad influence on the doctrine and faith and find general acceptance and approval. What these organs in fact taught in general and with constancy was either factually and explicitly taught by the whole body of teachers during their lifetimes, or in consideration of the perfection of their knowledge and by the guidance of divine providence and the natural influence they exercised in the Church, their teaching was later perceived by the body of teachers to be the genuine expression of their own teaching, a teaching implicitly and habitually held by the body of teachers. This is how their meaning, in part communicated by these privileged organs, entered into the general consciousness (of the Church). In this way the teaching of these thinkers represents ecclesiastical tradition not only inasmuch as they are a reliable historical witness or a reflection of the tradition at that time, but insofar as they represent the true and complete understanding of the faith (*intellectus fidei*). As

über die Sexualmoral durch die Gläubigen," *Theologie und Philosophie* 91 (2016): 321–62, at 343–46 ["Der Beitrag des Kölner Dogmatikers Matthias J. Scheeben"].

the bearers of this teaching their eyes have been enlightened by the Holy Spirit, through which the whole Church has come to possess the true and full understanding of the meaning of the deposit of faith and in which it possesses and guards that very faith (no. 341).[36]

This lengthy quotation speaks for itself. It makes abundantly clear that the indispensable role of the bishops never bypasses the contributions of theologians and other thinkers in the church, not to mention the convictions of the faithful at large regarding the content of the Christian faith.

Scheeben shows himself to be an important witness to the existence of the "sense of the faith" in the church. The roles and contributions of the faithful and of theologians and theological schools in the church contribute to the mission of the church to understand the revelation of Christ and to proclaim it effectively. The pope and the bishops are never isolated from the rest of the church but in Scheeben's eyes are in fact assisted in their ministry of teaching with authority by the faithful and theologians. Even though Scheeben's formulation of the "sense of the faith" is carefully circumscribed by his general ecclesiology and his very high regard for the authority of the pope and the bishops, he still managed to find ample room for a meaningful presentation of the "sense of the faith" and the assistance of theologians in understanding and formulating the faith for more effective proclamation.[37] Unfortunately, the general lack

---

36. *Theologische Erkenntnislehre*, 166; *Theological Epistemology*, 231–32. On the role played by the witness of the fathers of the church and on the problems which this patristic witness poses, see Michael Fiedrowicz, "Das Väterargument," *Theologie der Kirchenväter: Grundlagen frühchristlicher Glaubensreflexion* (2nd ed.; Freiburg: Herder, 2010), 255–90. See also Robert M. Grant, "The Appeal to the Early Fathers," *Journal of Theological Studies* 11 (1960): 13–24; Michel Fédou, *The Fathers of the Church in Christian Theology*, trans. Peggy Manning Meyer (Washington, DC: Catholic University of America Press, 2019); and Norbert Brox, "Zur Berufung auf 'Väter' des Glaubens," *Das Frühchristentum: Schriften zur historischen Theologie*, ed. Franz Dünzl, Alfons Fürst, and Ferdinand R. Prostmeier (Freiburg: Herder, 2000), 271–96.

37. Hermann Josef Pottmeyer has shown how Scheeben's understanding of the roles of pope, the bishops, and the faithful at large deepened over the years. In his earlier formulations, Scheeben was primarily interested in defending the papacy against the liberalism of his day—that is, the tendencies in society to accommodate or, in some ecclesiastical circles, to subordinate the church and its mission to the secular, civil order. The "early" Scheeben appears more focused on buttressing the jurisdiction of the pope and bishops, whereas the "later" Scheeben of the *Theologische Erkenntnislehre* exhibits greater balance and deeper respect for the organic and reciprocal character of the roles of the pope, the

of familiarity with his thought in the church at large, the favor shown by Leo XIII (1878–1903) to the scholastic method of teaching theology, especially in the church's seminaries, and the influence of the teaching of Vatican I regarding papal infallibility largely curtailed its influence.

Vatican I (1869–70)

It is commonly assumed that one of the chief purposes in convoking Vatican Council I was to define the pope's infallibility. However, at the time the council was convoked by Pius IX and during the preparations for the council, this goal was not clearly enunciated.[38] Pius IX encountered conflicting opinions in the Roman Curia regarding a council, and so he delayed his decision for two years before announcing on June 16, 1867, his intention

---

bishops, and the faithful. If the "early" Scheeben envisioned the bishops as subordinate to the pope, the "later" Scheeben grew to appreciate the place of the bishops in the constitution of the church as well as the role played by the faithful in understanding and witnessing to the apostolic tradition. See Pottmeyer, *Unfehlbarkeit und Souveränität. Die päpstliche Unfehlbarkeit im System der ultramontanen Ekklesiologie des 19. Jahrhunderts*, Tübinger Theologische Studien 5 (Mainz: Matthias-Grünewald, 1975): 264–78 for the "early" and 381–88 for the "later" Scheeben. Pottmeyer concluded his treatment of Scheeben with the following appreciation: "Even though Scheeben remained under the spell of ultramontane theology regarding the primacy of the pope's teaching authority in the Church, still, more than any other theologian of this tendency, he introduced an opening for an ecclesiology of communion, especially as regards the Church's proclamation of the faith. Regrettably, he was not able to develop these ideas in [what would have been] his volume on ecclesiology [in the *Handbook of Catholic Dogmatics*]. Still, in principle he was able to overcome the then dominant tendency to present the Church's proclamation of the gospel in predominantly juridical categories." Ibid., 388.

38. On the background and the unfolding of Vatican I, see Roger Aubert, "The Vatican Council," in *History of the Church*, vol. 8: *The Church in the Age of Liberalism*, ed. Hubert Jedin and John Dolan, trans. Peter Becker (New York: Crossroad, 1981), 315–30; Cuthbert Butler, "Preparations for the Council," *The Vatican Council 1869–1870, Based on Bishop Ullathorne's Letters*, Fontana Library edition ed. Christopher Butler (London: Collins and Harvill, 1962) 63–76. See John W. O'Malley, *Vatican I: The Council and the Making of the Ultramontane Church* (Cambridge, MA: Belknap Press, 2018). On the ecclesiological movements, principal figures, political forces, and differing theological positions in the years immediately preceding Vatican I that contributed to the agenda of the council, see John W. O'Malley, "The Eve of the Council," *Vatican I: The Council and the Making of the Ultramontane Church*, 96–132. Richard F. Costigan has studied a number of influential Gallican and ultramontane authors in his *The Consensus of the Church and Papal Infallibility: A Study in the Background of Vatican I* (Washington, DC: Catholic University of America Press, 2005).

to hold an ecumenical council. But even then the pope did not officially convoke the council until a year later, on June 29, 1868. It was not until January 21, 1870, that the assembled bishops in Rome were finally presented with the draft of a constitution on the church entitled *Supremi pastoris*, a document that did not contain any reference to the pope's infallibility.[39] The proposed constitution consisted of fifteen chapters that treated the church in the most general way.[40] Only chapter 11 handled the question of the primacy of the Roman pontiff, while chapter 9 dealt with the infallibility of the church, but not explicitly with the infallibility of the pope.[41]

Background

Neither Pius IX nor the cardinals, bishops, and theologians who had prepared the drafts of *Supremi pastoris* were inclined to force the issue of the pope's infallibility. Instead, they preferred to allow it to surface among the conciliar bishops themselves. During the early months of the council, the bishops started to concentrate on papal infallibility.[42] On March 7, a

---

39. *Supremi pastoris*, its twenty-one canons and *adnotationes* can be found in Johannes D. Mansi, *Sacrorum conciliorum nova et amplissima collectio*, vols. 49–53 (reprint; Graz: Akademische Druck und Verlagsanstalt, 1961), 51:539–636. *Supremi pastoris* had been preceded by a twelve-page proposed document entitled *De Ecclesia Christi: Expositio doctrinae et errorum futuri concilii patribus exhibenda*. See Mansi, *Sacrorum conciliorum nova et amplissima collectio*, 51:539–53. According to Gustave Thils, this document still contained a reference to the infallibility of the whole church, a reference that was later removed to focus the attention of the council exclusively on the infallibility of the bishops and of the pope. "L'Infaillibilité de l'Église dans la Constitution 'Pastor aeternus' du Ier Concile du Vatican," in *L'infaillibilité de l'Église: Journées oecuméniques de Chevetogne, 25-29 Septembre 1961* (Abbaye de Chevetogne: Éditions de Chevetogne, 1963), 147–82, at 151.

40. An outline of *Supremi pastoris* can be found in John W. O'Malley, *Vatican I: The Council and the Making of the Ultramontane Church*, 183–84. Throughout this section on Vatican I, I am indebted to Antoine Chavasse's careful examination of the notion of the infallibility of the church at Vatican I in his "L'ecclésiologie au Concile du Vatican: L'infaillibilité de l'Église," in *L'Ecclésiologie au XIXe siècle*, Unam Sanctam 34 (Paris: Cerf, 1960): 233–45.

41. On this point, so important for the present study, Chavasse wrote: "I wish then to examine whether the Council ever envisaged restricting the infallibility of the Church to the Pope. It is true that this interpretation has been suggested, but it is tendentious and misunderstands the real history of the Council." Ibid., 234.

42. See Mansi, *Sacrorum conciliorum nova et amplissima collectio*, 51:639–77 for an account of how the movement to define the pope's infallibility emerged from the floor of the council.

new text on the infallibility of the pope was submitted to the bishops as an addendum to chapter 11 of *Supremi pastoris*. Still, by the end of March it appeared that the rather complete treatment of the church represented by *Supremi pastoris*, or something like it, would eventually become the teaching of the council.[43] Unfortunately, this was not to be the end result. As the proceedings unfolded, the division among the bishops became so pronounced that it could no longer be bridged.[44] Time and energy were being consumed by their differences, so much so that the issues of papal primacy and infallibility completely absorbed the bishops' attention. There was little enthusiasm left for deciding the divisive issues with the help of a general ecclesiology. Primacy and infallibility became at this point the issues of the council in their own right. When a second draft of the constitution on the church, entitled *Tametsi Deus*, was prepared by the theological advisor Joseph Kleutgen, SJ, the bishops and Pius IX himself showed little interest in it.[45]

It appears, then, that at the outset the council vaguely intended to address a backlog of ecclesiological issues and tensions that had surfaced

43. According to Klaus Schatz, "It is certain that within that overall framework most of them [the bishops] accepted papal infallibility and considered the time more or less ripe for its definition. But that does not mean that within this overall theme of 'strengthening the principle of authority' infallibility necessarily had to become the dominant topic of the council to the point that everything else was made secondary. In the minds of most of the bishops it was one theme within a larger horizon, but by no means the central issue." *Papal Primacy: From Its Origins to the Present*, trans. John A. Otto and Linda M. Maloney (Collegeville, MN: Liturgical Press, 1996), 155.

44. Outside the General Congregations of the bishops, the Coordinating Committee and the Deputation on the Faith (*Deputatio de fide*) continued to revise chapter 11 and its addendum in light of the comments of the bishops. A point that continued to preoccupy and even divide the bishops pertained to who the subject of infallibility was. Were the bishops, in communion with the pope of course, in their own right infallible teachers? Or were they infallible teachers only to the extent that their teaching was an expression of the pope's own teaching? As the bishops continued to discuss such distinctions, three groups emerged: (1) those who were "committed infallibilists," i.e., the ultramontane bishops, (2) those who opposed a definition if it compromised the legitimate role of the bishops to teach infallibly, and (3) a group of bishops who only held that defining papal infallibility was "inopportune" given the current circumstances in church-state relations and in regard to relations with the other Christian churches. The last two groups constituted the minority position.

45. This decision was very unfortunate, because according to Antoine Chavasse and Gustave Thils, the document was theologically balanced and could have paved the way for a more satisfactory ecclesiology after the council.

since the Council of Constance (1414–18) but that had not been adequately addressed up to then. Some of the issues that called for redress included the sacramental character of the office of bishop, the divine right of the episcopate and its relationship to the see of Rome, the conciliarity of the church in the light of the teaching of the Council of Constance, and the tensions that had arisen in the two preceding centuries between national hierarchies and their secular rulers and governments exemplified in Gallicanism in France, Febronianism in Germany, and Josephinism in Austria and Hungary.[46]

The lack of clarity regarding the purpose of the council and the inability of the bishops to pursue this goal left the council vulnerable to extrinsic forces that rendered the council somewhat incoherent and ineffective. These included the growing conflict between France and Prussia that resulted in the outbreak of war between them and, in Italy, the march on Rome by the troops of the Risorgimento.[47] As a result, the bishops were forced to content themselves with the two truncated constitutions, *Dei Filius* on faith and revelation and *Pastor aeternus* on the pope's primacy and infallibility. They had to abandon any broader ecclesiological interests and the real need of the church for a fuller and more balanced ecclesiology. These contingent historical factors—lack of clarity on the council's goal, poor carrying to term of a definite purpose, and unfavorable political conditions—only deepened the ecclesiological imbalances that Vatican I had inherited and that it would bequeath to Vatican II. In a word, Vatican I was, like a number of ecumenical councils before it,

---

46. On Gallicanism, see Cuthbert Butler, "Gallicanism," *The Vatican Council 1869–1870*, 27–38, and Alistair Mason, "Gallicanism," in *The Oxford Companion to Christian Thought*, ed. Adrian Hastings, Alistair Mason, and Hugh Pyper (New York: Oxford, 2000), 259. Febronianism originated in Germany with Johann N. von Hontheim, Auxiliary Bishop of Trier, whose *De statu ecclesiae et legitima potestate Romani pontificis* (On the State of the Church and the Legitimte Authority of the Roman Pontiff) appeared in 1763 under the pen name of Justinus Febronius. On Gallicanism, Febronianism, and Josephinism, see John W. O'Malley, *Vatican I: The Council and the Making of the Ultramontane Church*, 26–34.

47. The Risorgimento and King Victor Emmanuel II of the Kingdom of Piedmont-Sardinia intended to unite the fractured regions and states of Renaissance Italy, including the Papal States, in a single modern nation that we know today as the Italian Republic. On the Risorgimento, see Roger Aubert, "The Beginning of the Risorgimento in Italy," in *History of the Church*, vol. 7: *The Church between Revolution and Restoration*, ed. Hubert Jedin and John Dolan, trans. Peter Becker (New York: Crossroad, 1981), 310–29 and idem, "The Roman Question," in *History of the Church*, ed. Hubert Jedin and John Dolan, 8:248–55.

largely ineffectual. It is true that Vatican I was immensely consequential for the life of the Catholic Church for the next ninety years, but by not attending to the problems and tensions it inherited, Vatican I was largely a failure and even compounded these problems.[48]

Two Problems of Interpretation

This is not the occasion to study in detail the teaching of Vatican I on the infallibility of the pope, or to rehearse the positions and machinations of the ultramontane party and of the minority bishops. Two points must suffice for the present study: the council's reference to the "infallibility the divine redeemer willed his Church to enjoy in defining doctrine concerning faith and morals" and the controversial phrase in the definition that "such definitions of the Roman Pontiff are of themselves, and not by the consent of the Church, irreformable."[49] How do these two conciliar statements comport with the "sense of the faith" as taught by Vatican II?[50]

---

48. This statement should not shock anyone. Other ecumenical councils, e.g., the so-called reforming councils of Lateran IV (1215) and Lateran V (1512–17) are generally acknowledged by scholars to have been failures at reforming a church very much in need of it. John W. O'Malley offers a more benign assessment of Vatican I in his *Vatican I: The Making of the Ultramontane Church*.

49. The definition reads as follows: "[W]e teach and define as divinely revealed dogma that when the Roman pontiff speaks *ex cathedra*, that is, when, in the exercise of his office as shepherd and teacher of all Christians, in virtue of his supreme apostolic authority, he defines a doctrine concerning faith or morals to be held by the whole Church, he possesses, by the divine assistance promised him in Peter, that infallibility which the divine Redeemer willed his Church to enjoy in defining doctrine concerning faith or morals. Therefore, such definitions of the Roman Pontiff are of themselves, and not by the consent of the Church, irreformable. (Docemus et divinitus revelatum dogma esse definimus: Romanum pontificem, cum ex cathedra loquitur, id est, cum omnium christianorum pastoris et doctoris munere fungens, pro suprema sua apostolica auctoritate doctrinam de fide vel moribus ab universa ecclesia tenendam definit, per assistentiam divinam, ipsi in beato Petro promissam, ea infallibilitate pollere, qua divinus Redemptor ecclesiam suam in definienda doctrina de fide vel moribus instructam esse voluit; ideoque eiusmodi Romani pontificis definitiones ex sese, non autem ex consensu ecclesiae irreformabiles esse.)" See Tanner, *Decrees of the Ecumenical Councils*, 2:816.

50. On Vatican I's teaching about the pope's infallibility and the larger issue of the relationship of this specific teaching to the generally assumed teaching of the "infallibility in believing" of the whole church, see the treatments of Robert W. Smucker, *Sensus Fidei. Der Glaubenssinn in seiner vorkonziliaren Entwicklungsgeschichte und in den Dokumenten*

We have seen that the nineteenth century was important for clarifying and solidifying the acceptance of the "sense of the faithful." The notion of the infallibility of the whole church in believing was therefore not totally absent from Vatican I. *Supremi pastoris* had introduced the topic of infallibility in general and some bishops advanced the infallibility of the whole church in their discussions of the more specific infallibility of the pope in defining a dogma. In their minds, these two forms did not exclude one another. In fact, the infallibility of the whole church in believing provided the proper context for the more limited exercise of the teaching office, especially when invoked by the pope teaching *ex cathedra*.[51] But this broad ecclesial view of infallibility could hardly be said to be characteristic of the ecclesiology of the majority of the bishops at Vatican I. In their mind, infallibility increasingly had to do with the definitions of an ecumenical council and of the pope teaching *ex cathedra* outside of a council—in a word, of the hierarchy as constituting the "teaching Church" (*ecclesia docens*).

Gustave Thils has examined the understanding of infallibility at Vatican I and has shown how the more general notion of "infallibility in believing" (*infallibilitas in credendo*) belonged to the theological world of ideas of the bishops. The bishops never denied this general notion of infallibility, but it was also no longer the focus of their attention. As we have seen above, the majority bishops increasingly became captivated by the idea of defining papal infallibility and, moreover, they were being called by the Coordinating Commission to concentrate on the papal exercise of

---

des Zweiten Vatikanischen Konzils (Regensburg: S. Roderer, 1998), 77–96 ["Das Erste Vatikanische Konzil und der *sensus Ecclesiae* (1869–1870)"], and Christoph Ohly, *Sensus fidei fidelium. Zur Einordnung des Glaubenssinnes aller Gläubigen in die Communio-Struktur der Kirche im geschichtlichen Spiegel dogmatisch-kanonistischer Erkenntnisse und der Aussagen des II. Vatikanum* (St. Ottilien: EOS, 1999), 112–18 ["Das I. Vatikanische Konzil (1869–1870)"]. Both of these studies stress the fact that the narrowing of the focus of Vatican I on papal infallibility never fully eclipsed the teaching that the whole church also exercises a certain "infallibility in believing."

51. This is the thesis of Margaret O'Gara in her magisterial study of the French bishops of the minority at Vatican I. See "The Central Emphasis: The Ecclesial Character of Infallibility," *Triumph in Defeat: Infallibility, Vatican I, and the French Minority Bishops* (Washington, DC: Catholic University of America Press, 1988), 221–55.

infallibility.[52] In the course of the debates at the General Congregations, as the plenary working sessions were called, bishops from several countries rose to defend the teaching that had become generally accepted in the church.[53] Furthermore, the drafts *Supremi pastoris*, *Tametsi Deus*, and the Official Report (*Relatio*) of Bishop Vinzenz Gasser of Brixen explaining the definition of the terms of infallibility and of the conditions of its exercise did not preclude this teaching.[54] Papal infallibility,

---

52. See G. Thils, "L'Infaillibilité de l'Église dans la Constitution '*Pastor aeternus*' du Ier Concile du Vatican," in *L'Infaillibilité de l'Église*. *Journées oecuméniques de Chevetogne 25–29 Septembre 1961* (Chevetogne: Éditions de Chevetogne, 1962), 147–82, here at 151–59. See also idem, "L'infaillibilité de l'Église '*in credendo*' et '*in docendo*,'" *Salesianum* 24 (1962): 298–336 and *L'infaillibilité du peuple chrétien "in credendo": notes de théologie posttridentine* (Paris: Desclée de Brouwer, 1963). In a lecture addressed to a group of pastors from the Reformed Church in what was then East Germany, Otfried Müller of the Catholic Faculty of Theology of the University of Erfurt, offered a clear and non-defensive explanation of the teaching of Vatican I on infallibility. Müller goes out of his way to clear up common misunderstandings as to what Vatican I taught. See his "Die päpstliche Unfehlbarkeit nach den Aussagen des Ersten und Zweiten Vatikanischen Konzils. Eine ökumenische Darstellung," in *Sapienter ordinare: Festgabe für Erich Kleineidam*, ed. Fritz Hoffmann, Leo Scheffczyk, and Konrad Feiereis (Leipzig: St. Benno-Verlag, 1969), 339–70, especially section 3, 348–57.

53. See the description by John W. O'Malley, *Vatican I: The Council and the Making of the Ultramontane Church*, 117.

54. Bishop Gasser used different formulations in his official report when referring to "infallibility in defining" and the possession of the deposit of faith by the entire church in the act of believing. In the first case, Gasser maintained that just as the bishops at an ecumenical council exercise infallibility by their judgments of defining a truth and excluding its error (in the anathema), so too does this "infallibility in defining" extend to the pope when he defines a truth of the faith. In this case, the phrase "that infallibility which the divine Redeemer willed his Church to enjoy" can only refer to the infallibility of the hierarchical magisterium. This is how Gasser argues on the question of the primary and secondary objects of the infallible magisterium. See Mansi, *Sacrorum conciliorum nova et amplissima collectio*, 52:1226–27, quoted in *The Gift of Infallibility*, 76–78. But this is not everything that Gasser maintained. Earlier in his official report, when he was dealing with the question of whether the pope in defining needed the explicit consent of the body of bishops, he used a different expression, one that includes the then-regnant opinion that the church as a whole is infallible or unerring in its belief. Here he writes: "We also believe that the assent of the Church will not be lacking to his definitions since it is not able to happen that the body of bishops be separated from its head, *and since the Church universal is not able to fail.*" The phrase that I have italicized is completely faith-

like the exercise of infallibility by the body of bishops, did not exclude the exercise of "infallibility in believing" by the faithful. Though it may have been relegated to the sidelines by the passion surrounding the definition of the pope's infallibility *ex cathedra*, the "infallibility of the whole body of Christians" (*infallibilitas universitatis christianorum*) remained secure in Catholic doctrine and theology.

If my interpretation is correct, it brings up the even thornier question of the meaning of Vatican I's claim that the pope's infallible definitions are "irreformable of themselves, and not by the consent of the Church." What can this possibly mean if the consent of the entire church cannot be lacking, according to the then-accepted understanding of infallibility? Are we involved here in a vicious circle of reasoning? What role does the "sense of the faithful" play in constituting the truth of an infallible teaching of the church? Is it only an expression of the virtue of obedience or does it go deeper than that?

The expression that infallible definitions are "irreformable of themselves, and not by the consent of the Church" stems from the order of law and not from the order of the act of faith and its understanding. Christians are expected to think deeply about the faith, assimilating it and its categories and internally appropriating it. This exclusionary phrase was one last attempt by the majority bishops at Vatican I to put Gallicanism behind the church once and for all. The French bishops at Vatican I, and *a pari* the German bishops, could hardly be accused of classical Gallicanism or Febronianism. Such ecclesiological theory has ceased to play any effective role in the relations between the French hierarchy and Rome for over a century and a half.[55] Louis XIV had revoked the so-called Gallican Articles in 1693 and Gallican ecclesiology had long ceased being taught in French seminaries. The article that was especially offensive to

---

ful to the teaching of the church's "infallibility in believing." Neither Bishop Gasser nor the majority of bishops at Vatican I, not even those who belonged to the majority party favoring the definition of the pope's infallibility, had the intention of repudiating what by then was the general teaching of the church that the church *qua* church is infallible.

55. In the words of John W. O'Malley, "Long before the council, however, classic Gallicanism had virtually disappeared, replaced by a much attenuated version that basically wanted to preserve, in the face of the more aggressive ultramontane claims . . . the traditional role of bishops." *Vatican I: The Council and the Making of the Ultramontane Church*, 5.

ultramontane bishops at Vatican I was article 4 that held that the consent of the church was required before a papal judgment became irreformable. It read: "Although the Pope has the chief voice in questions of faith, and his decrees apply to all churches and to each particular church, yet his decision is not unalterable unless the consent of the Church is given."[56]

In his Official Report, Bishop Gasser strove to make clear that the pope in the exercise of his infallible magisterium was subject to no conditions, antecedent or consequent. The pope was entirely free to determine the meaning of an article of the faith as long as it belonged to the apostolic deposit of faith. The pope did not need the approval of the bishops to go forward with a definition, nor did he need the approval of the bishops in an ecumenical council afterward. The consent of the bishops in these cases would have constituted a juridical requirement to be met by the pope. Vatican I taught that no such "juridical approbation" was needed in order for the pope to exercise his teaching authority infallibly. But the teaching did not mean that the pope was not required to teach what in fact the church as a whole actually believed—"the consensus (or agreement) of the faith." This second use of "consensus" hardly means "juridical approbation." This is how Bishop Gasser expressed it:

> Finally we do not separate the Pope, even minimally, from the consent of the Church, as long as that consent is not laid down as a condition which is either antecedent or consequent. We are not able to separate the Pope from the consent of the Church because this consent is never able to be lacking to him. Indeed, since we believe that the Pope is infallible through the divine assistance, by that very fact we also believe that the assent of the Church will not be lacking to his definitions since

---

56. "In fidei quaestionibus praecipue Summi Pontificis esse partes, eiusque decreta ad omnes et singulas ecclesias pertinere, nec tamen irreformabile esse judicium nisi Ecclesiae consensus acceperit." See Henry Bettenson and Chris Maunder, ed., *Documents of the Christian Church* (3rd ed.; New York: Oxford University Press, 1999), 285–86. The articles were quoted and condemned by Alexander VIII in his constitution *Inter multiplices*, March 19, 1682. See Henricus Denzinger and Adolfus Schönmetzer, eds., *Enchiridion symbolorum, definitionum et declarationum de rebus fidei et morum*, 33rd ed. (Freiburg: Herder, 1965), nos. 2281–85. Bishop Gasser himself referred to the fourth Gallican article in his Official Report. See Mansi, *Sacrorum conciliorum nova et amplissim collectio*, 52:1218; *The Gift of Infallibility*, 53–54.

it is not able to happen that the body of bishops be separated from its head, and since the Church universal is not able to fail.[57]

Moreover, Gasser also made it abundantly clear that although the pope cannot be held to any external juridical conditions, he is held morally to follow all the ordinary means that are usually employed to determine the meaning of a truth of the apostolic deposit.[58]

The question can legitimately be asked as to how the phrase that definitions of the Roman pontiff are "[1] irreformable of themselves and [2] not by the consent of the Church" found its place in the definition of the pope's infallibility. Only the phrase "irreformable of themselves" was in the formulation submitted to the bishops by the Deputation on the Faith on July 9.[59] The phrase "and not by the consent of the Church" was added after Gasser had given his Official Report. That is why Gasser never addressed the problematic formulation in his report of July 11. It was not to be found among the seventy-nine suggested amendments or questions addressed by him on behalf of the Deputation of the Faith. The problematic phrase "and not by the consent of the Church" was incorporated into the final text between July 11 and 16, without the bishops having had the opportunity to discuss its merits or demerits.[60]

---

57. Mansi, *Sacrorum conciliorum nova et amplissima collectio*, 52:1213–14; *The Gift of Infallibility*, 44. The reader should take note of all the elements of infallibility mentioned by Bishop Gasser, including the "Church universal," i.e., all believers in the church.

58. See Mansi, *Sacrorum conciliorum nova et amplissima collectio*, 52:1213. Ulrich Horst has shown how for centuries Thomists defended the necessity of serious study and broad consultation by a pope who was contemplating a definition of the faith outside the context of an ecumenical council. See *The Dominicans and the Pope: Papal Teaching Authority in the Medieval and Early Modern Thomist Tradition*, trans. James D. Mixson (Notre Dame, IN: University of Notre Dame Press, 2006).

59. The bishops were already familiar with the phrase "irreformable of themselves" as part of the formulation of the definition. It had been included in the text they received on May 9. See the helpful chart listing side by side the various formulations of the definition in Cuthbert Butler, *The Vatican Council 1869–1870*, 385.

60. On the circumstances surrounding the hasty insertion of the phrase "of themselves and not by the consent of the Church," see the discussion by John W. O'Malley, *Vatican I: The Council and the Making of the Ultramontane Church*, 214–22 ["The Final Days"]. According to Georges Dejaifve, "The phrase was in fact a last-minute addition to the decree, and was adopted without discussion by the majority of the Fathers on the 16th

Given the unusual circumstances surrounding the last-minute inter-polation of the phrase "and not by the consent of the Church," Catholics in particular need to recall the principle of ecclesiastical law that unnec-essary conditions are not to be unduly imposed on the consciences of Catholics in following the law. In this case it is imperative to point out that the term "consensus" here is to be construed as narrowly as possible—that is, as the *juridical term* that it is and not as an expression of the richer history of the word "consensus" in Catholic doctrine and theology.[61] This tradition was never rejected by Vatican I.

The Aftermath of Vatican I

Of course, practically speaking, the teaching of the infallibility of the whole church in believing was so overshadowed by the proclamation of the infallibility of the pope in defining a dogma *ex cathedra* that little or no theological reflection was dedicated to the "sense of the faithful"

July, only two days before the promulgation. And it must be frankly admitted that it is precisely this addition that has caused a proper understanding of the decree to be such a difficult matter for so many, whereas the document as a whole is sufficiently clear in its general tenor to be correctly understood by any attentive reader." " '*Ex sese, non autem ex consensu ecclesiae*,' " *Eastern Churches Quarterly* 14 (1961–62): 360–78, at 360. Bishop Gasser himself was opposed to the incorporation of this phrase in the formula of definition, but the Deputation on the Faith insisted on it. See his comments from July 16 regarding the additions to the final version of the definition in Mansi, *Sacrorum conciliorum nova et amplissima collectio*, 52:1314–17. These comments are not included in *The Gift of Infallibility*.

61. There is no reason why the widespread misinterpretation of the problematic phrase about "consent" should be perpetuated any longer. It should not be allowed to continue to burden the discussion of the office of the pope with fellow Christians from the Orthodox churches and the churches and ecclesial communities that have emerged from the Ref-ormation. It envisioned a danger that is no longer a threat—Gallicanism. The teachings of Vatican II on the college of bishops united with the pope as head of the college and that the church is a communion of local churches have moved us permanently beyond this outmoded problem. See article 25 of the Dogmatic Constitution on the Church for the council's attempt to find a balance between the teaching of Vatican I on the pope's teaching authority and that of the college of bishops together with the pope as head of the college. Vatican II re-receives the teaching of Vatican I by placing it in the broader context of an episcopal collegiality that includes the office and ministry of primacy in order to advance and guarantee the college's mission.

in the period immediately following Vatican I.[62] Even though Vatican I never officially intended to alter the balance of factors that expressed the infallibility of the church itself,[63] the subsequent interpretation of the teaching of Vatican I did in fact lead to such neglect.[64]

The bishops were increasingly seen as executors of the pope's will and collaborators in *his* mission rather than their proper participation in the apostolic mission. Theologians, too, were seen primarily as providing scriptural and dogmatic proofs for what the papal magisterium taught.

62. Dario Vitali has outlined the negative effects of Vatican I's teaching by showing how the theme of the "sense of the faithful" virtually disappeared from the neoscholastic manuals of theology written after the council. See *Sensus fidelium: Una funzione ecclesiale di intelligenza della fede* (Brescia: Morcelliana, 1993), 74–82. In the same chapter, "Il contesto teologico del *sensus fidelium*," Vitali explains just how difficult it was for Vatican II to restore the richer theology of a living tradition in which all the faithful participated, especially for the Dogmatic Constitution on the Church and the Dogmatic Constitution on Divine Revelation. See ibid., 82–94.

63. On the teaching of the bishops at Vatican I regarding the infallibility of what is called the "ordinary magisterium of the bishops," see Marc Caudron, "Magistère ordinaire et infaillibilité pontificale d'après la Constitution *Dei Filius*," *Ephemerides theologicae Lovanienses* 36 (1960): 393–431 and Bernard Sesboüé in "Le magistère ordinaire et universel et le magistère romain," *Revue d'éthique et de théologie morale "Le Supplément"* no. 219 (December 2001): 43–51. Unfortunately, the extension of an independently exercised ordinary papal magisterium proceeded unabated under Paul VI, John Paul II, and Benedict XVI. This drift is unnecessary and dangerous, introducing confusion into the genuine teaching of both Vatican I and Vatican II regarding the ordinary universal magisterium of the bishops. On this neuralgic issue, see the many contributions of Richard R. Gaillardetz, especially his "The Ordinary Universal Magisterium: Unresolved Questions," *Theological Studies* 63 (2002): 447–71 and "Engaging Magisterial Activism Today," *Horizons* 39 (2012): 230–51.

64. Caudron and Sesboüé point to the commentary by J.-M.-A. Vacant, *Le magistère ordinaire de l'Église et ses organes* (Paris: Delhomme et Briguet, 1887) as the source of the extension of the ordinary episcopal magisterium to the pope's ordinary teachings as well. Whereas Vatican I always understood the pope to be a member of the body of bishops who taught infallibly in the course of their ordinary magisterium, Vacant and others illegitimately extended this authority to the popes apart from the body of the bishops and when they taught a matter consistently and over a longer period of time. In sympathy with this line of reasoning, see P. Nau, "Le magistère pontifical ordinaire, lieu théologique," *Revue Thomiste* 56 (1956): 389–412 and a host of theologians before Vatican II. For references to such theologians, see M. Caudron, "Magistère ordinaire et infaillibilité pontificale d'après la Constitution *Dei Filius*," 393–94nn1–9.

As for the general faithful, they were expected to obediently accept and profess what the pope and the bishops taught them. None of this was officially taught by Vatican I but the force of its teaching regarding papal primacy and infallibility quickly led to such misconstruals. Vatican I did not teach that the pope should issue *ex cathedra* definitions with regularity or as convenience dictated. The papal exercise of infallible teaching was envisioned as something rare, usually when an article of faith was misunderstood and entailed danger to the belief of the faithful, as clearly circumscribed by definite conditions for its use, and as exercised by what had become the standard practice in the church—namely, the consultation of the bishops, theologians, the principal theological schools, Catholic universities, the superiors of religious orders, and the faithful at large.

With its clear teaching about the "sense of the faith" in article 12 of the Dogmatic Constitution on the Church, Vatican II has gone far in addressing the tensions that remained from Vatican I.[65] It will be evident to many that much still needs to be done to redress these imbalances by the complete reception of this teaching of Vatican II.

---

65. On Vatican II's reception of Vatican I's teaching on infallibility and the changes it introduced in its understanding into the life of the church, see Heinrich Fries, "*Ex sese, non ex consensu ecclesiae*," in *Volk Gottes. Zum Kirchenverständnis der katholischen, evangelischen und anglikanischen Theologie: Festgabe für Josef Höfer*, ed. Remigius Bäumer and Heimo Dolch (Freiburg: Herder, 1967), 480–500.

Chapter Six

The Growing Conviction of a Theology of the "Sense of the Faith" in the Twentieth Century

If the nineteenth century laid the foundations for understanding the traditional teaching of the "infallibility in believing" of the whole church in terms of a doctrine of the "sense of the faith," then the twentieth century solidified and authorized this teaching. What factors played a role in accomplishing this feat?

First, we must point to the continued interest by theologians and popes in the church as more than a "perfect society"—the limited view of the church that emerged out of the Enlightenment and the European restoration movements following the French Revolution (1789-1799). Little by little the notions of the church as the mystical body of Christ and the people of God began to predominate, abetted especially by a growing liturgical movement. Second, the collapse of the political order, with Europe in ruins after the First World War (1914-1918) and the disruptions of the Russian Revolution (1917-1923), forced the Roman hierarchy to admit the limits of the efforts of its clergy and the members of religious orders. If the church was to accomplish its mission, it would have to enlist the help of the laity. At least up to Vatican II, the answer was found in the movement called "Catholic Action."[1] The laity had to be mobilized by the

---

1. See Dennis J. Geaney, "Catholic Action," in *New Catholic Encyclopedia*, vol. 3 (New York: McGraw-Hill Book Company 1967), 262–63 and Erwin Iserloh, in *History of the*

bishops and encouraged by the pope to be active evangelizers in the name of the church. Only in this way could the church redirect and sanctify family life, the factory and workplace, education, the arts, economics, and politics. Human well-being and human flourishing depended on the efforts of all Catholics to the extent that they were officially engaged in the mission of the church and not as isolated individuals. Third, the disillusionment that set in in the aftermath of the Holocaust and World War II (1939-1945) dictated that only an integrated approach to healing the ills of the modern world could be successful. Only an ecumenical council that addressed all the major issues—church, religions, ecumenism, human freedom and dignity, the conditions of modernity—could hope to be successful. This was the vision of Pope John XXIII (1958–63), who introduced it with the encyclicals *Mater et Magistra* (1961)[2] and *Pacem in terris* (1963)[3] and brought it to fruition by convoking the Second Vatican Council in 1962.

Leadership at the top proved indispensable to the task. But there was also important leadership from below in the efforts of individual theologians and in the various important group movements that urged the church forward—the liturgical movement, of course, but also a renewal in biblical studies and methodology, an appreciation of the category of history and the importance of critical historiography, a modest renaissance in theology, the emergence of secular institutes and new religious communities, and a growing commitment to ecumenism. The purpose of this and the following chapter is to study those theologians who, in the face of these circumstances, contributed to this growth and to the reemergence of the category of the "sense of the faith," in the shadow of Vatican I.

Francisco Marín-Sola, OP (1873–1932)

In light of what was said in the last chapter concerning how Vatican I tended to submerge the fragile existence of the "sense of the faith" in

---

Church, vol. 10: *The Church in the Modern Age*, ed. Hubert Jedin, Konrad Repken, and John Dolan, trans. Anselm Biggs (New York: Crossroad, 1980), 307–10 ["Catholic Action"].

2. In *The Papal Encyclicals 1958–1981*, ed. Claudia Carlen (Ann Arbor, MI: Pierian Press, 1990), 59–90.

3. In ibid., 107–29.

the late nineteenth and early twentieth centuries, it is hardly surprising that theologians did not continue to build on the firm foundations laid by Cardinal Newman and Matthias Joseph Scheeben. An exception was the Spanish Dominican Francisco Marín-Sola, who published his *La evolución homogénea del dogma católico* (The Homogeneous Evolution of Catholic Dogma) in Spanish in 1923.[4] The work was based on a series of articles Marín-Sola had written for the scholarly journal *La Ciencia Tomista* between 1911 and 1922 in which he proposed a theory of the homogeneous development of Christian dogma.[5] The importance of the work was immediately evident and an expanded version in French appeared the following year.[6]

In chapter 4, entitled "The Different Paths of the Evolution of Dogma," Marín-Sola distinguishes the speculative from the affective or experiential way of arriving at the content of Christian dogma, and refers to the "sense of the faith" by employing such expressions as "le sens de la foi," "le sens chrétien," "le sentiment de l'Église entière," and "*sentire cum Ecclesia.*" It is precisely in his treatment of the affective way of arriving at dogma that Marín-Sola discusses the "sense of the faith."

---

4. A second edition was printed in 1952 by the Biblioteca de Autores Cristianos (Madrid) and is still available. This edition contains an introduction by Emilio Sauras that introduces the author, the work, and its connection with "la nouvelle théologie."

5. See Francis D. Nealy for a brief biography and a statement of the contribution of Francisco Marín-Sola to Thomism in the twentieth century and on Marín-Sola's theory of the development of dogma in particular in *New Catholic Encyclopedia*, 2nd ed. (Detroit: Gale Group, 2003), 9:166–67.

6. *L'Évolution homogène du dogme catholique*, 2 vols., translated by Basile Cambou (Fribourg, CH: Imprimerie et Librairie de l'Oeuvre de Saint-Paul). In a word, Marín-Sola's theory proposes the homogeneous development of dogma by discursive reasoning from virtually revealed truths in the sources of revelation. The process of development results in truths capable of being defined by the hierarchical church. For reactions to Marín-Sola's theory, see Karl Rahner and Karl Lehmann, *Mysterium Salutis: Grundriss heilsgeschichtlicher Dogmatik*, ed. Johannes Feiner and Magnus Löhrer, vol. 1 (Einsiedeln: Benziger, 1965), 727–76 ["Das Problem der Dogmenentwicklung"], at 753–56; Herbert Hammans, "Das virtuell Geoffenbarte ist definierbar: Tuyaerts, Marin-Sola" and "Die Kritik an der Theorie Marin-Solas," *Die neueren katholischen Erklärungen der Dogmenentwicklung* (Essen: Ludgerus, 1965), 129–46 and 147–63 respectively; and Edward Schillebeeckx, "The Development of the Apostolic Faith into the Dogma of the Church," *Revelation and Theology*, vol. 1, trans. N. D. Smith (New York: Sheed and Ward, 1967), 63–92, at 69–81 ["In the Modern Period"].

The basis for Marín-Sola's claim was to be found in Thomas Aquinas's teaching.[7] He writes: "This is the way of the heart, of the will, of piety or of feeling; the way of experience and of mysticism that St. Thomas often speaks about and which he calls 'the mode of connaturality,' 'a certain affinity,' '[knowledge] similar to experience,' '[understanding] perceived by contact,' and other such formulas."[8] Marín-Sola then relates the affective way of knowing to Thomas's understanding of human "habits" (*habitus*), that is, as stable dispositions and orientations of human acts. He writes:

> The believer, and especially the saint, interiorly possess a *new sense*, the sense of Christ according to Saint Paul ("We have the mind of Christ" according to 1 Corinthians 2:16), which we can call *the sense of faith* and *the eyes of faith*. . . . All Christians possess within themselves the supernatural dispositions (*habitus*) of faith, that is, the real beginning of the divine life. Among the faithful, many possess sanctifying grace, charity, and the infused virtues and gifts of the Holy Spirit. . . . The whole ensemble of supernatural "habits," especially the gifts of wisdom, understanding, and knowledge, are objective supernatural realities, a *second nature* as it were. This occurs at the deepest level of our being and permits us occasionally to discern the revealed deposit and to unravel many supernatural truths really implicit in them by a way that is connatural, intuitive, and, as it were, experiential. . . . This is what constitutes the "sense of the faith" or "Christian understanding," by means of which we often know or have intimations of certain truths contained implicitly in the deposit of revelation, and all this without the need for logical demonstration.[9]

Marín-Sola then goes on to cite twenty-seven passages from the writings of Aquinas in defense of his understanding of Thomas's affective, con-

---

7. Marín-Sola appears to have been inspired solely by Thomas Aquinas's thought, since he never mentions Möhler, Newman, or Scheeben in his development of the "sense of the faith."

8. "C'est la voie du coeur, de la volonté, de la piété ou du sentiment' voie expérimentale, mystique, dont parle souvent saint Thomas, qu'il appelle la voie '*per modum connaturalitatis,*' '*per quamdam affinitatem,*' '*quasi experimentalis,*' '*per contactum*' ou autres formules semblables." *L'évolution homogène du dogme catholique*, §216; 1:353. This passage and future quotations from Marín-Sola are my translations.

9. *L'Évolution homogène du dogme catholique*, §§218; 1:356–58. Italics are in the original text.

natural, or experiential way of coming to knowledge of the divine truths of Christian revelation.[10]

Later in his treatment, Marín-Sola develops the argument of the importance and the indispensability of the "sense of the faith" in the life of the church with the following insightful comments:

> In truth, a large number of propositions that have been infallibly defined or condemned by the Church and that appear so clear to us today and that are even easy to prove from Holy Scripture or by theological reason, owe this clarity and facility to the vivacity and the universality of our Christian "sense" (*sens*). Very often it was this "sense" that first discovered them, even if theological reason quickly intervened to confirm them and the Church, with the assistance of the Holy Spirit, defined them. Nevertheless they would perhaps never have been known or defined without the assistance of this "sense of the faith."[11]

> As long as this "sense of the faith" is found only among a few isolated faithful, and even if they are saints, or is found only in a part of the Church, its theological value is weak indeed. But as soon as it generally spreads and becomes the common patrimony of the bishops, theologians, and the faithful, it constitutes in itself, and even before being defined, an argument equal in value to that of the most evident theological reasoning. As a result, one or the other—either certain *reason* or the certain and universal *"sense"* (*sentiment*) of the Christian society—is for the Church a sufficient criterion to be included as a doctrine in the deposit of revealed truth and for its candidacy as a defined dogma (*sa définibilité*).[12]

The heart of Marín-Sola's justification of the efficacy of the "sense of the faith" in the church is his treatment of the gifts of the Holy Spirit as

---

10. See ibid., §219; 1:358–62. On connatural knowledge in Aquinas, see Jacques Maritain, "On Knowledge through Connaturality," *The Range of Reason* (New York: Charles Scribner's Sons, 1952), 22–29, who points to mystical, poetic, and moral experience as three basic forms of connatural knowledge. See also Thomas Ryan, "Revisiting Affective Knowledge and Connaturality in Aquinas," *Theological Studies* 66 (2005): 49–68 and Susan K. Wood's President's Address "The *Sensus Fidelium*: Discerning the Path of Faith," *Catholic Theological Society of America Proceedings* 70 (2015): 72–83.

11. *L'Évolution homogène du dogma catholique*, 1:368 (§220).

12. Ibid., 1:370 (§220).

taught by Thomas Aquinas.[13] The affective way that underpins the "sense of the faith" enjoys a certain preeminence vis-à-vis the speculative way of systematic theology because it directly attains the Divine itself. Equipped with sanctifying grace, supernatural charity, and the virtues, the believer is further endowed with gifts by the Holy Spirit that assist him or her with perceiving, understanding, and living out the truth of Christian revelation.[14]

In this process of believing, understanding, and appropriating the faith, the "gifts of the Holy Spirit" are key. Thomas highlights knowledge (*scientia*), understanding (*intellectus*), and wisdom (*sapientia*) as gifts (*dona*) and not their subsequent counterparts as virtues (*virtutes*) of the

13. Jesús Sancho Bielsa also relies heavily on Thomas Aquinas for his understanding of the "sense of the faith." See *Infalibilidad del Pueblo de Dios: "Sensus Fidei" e infalibilidad orgánica de la Iglesia en la Constitución "Lumen Gentium" del Concilio Vaticano II* (Pamplona: Ediciones Universidad de Navarra, S.A., 1979), 235–57 ["Naturaleza del "sensus fidei"]. See also idem, "Santo Tomás y el '*sensus fidei*' del Concilio Vaticano II," in *Prospettive teologiche moderne. Atti dell' VIII Congresso Tomistico Internazionale*, vol. 4 (Vatican City: Libreria Editrice Vaticana, 1981), 381–89.

14. Surprisingly, before the early twelfth century theologians had shown little interest in a theology of the virtues and the gifts of the Holy Spirit and their relationship to one another. The situation began to change with Anselm of Laon (ca. 1050–1117), Peter Lombard (ca. 1095–1169), and Philip the Chancellor (ca. 1160–1236). Subsequent scholastic writers extended the treatment of the virtues and gifts, but it was really with Thomas Aquinas that the first comprehensive treatment appeared. See Edward D. O'Connor, "The Fathers of the Church" and "Scholastic Thought before St. Thomas," *Summa theologiae*, vol. 24: *The Gifts of the Spirit (1a2ae. 68-70)*, Blackfriars edition of the *Summa theologiae* (New York: McGraw-Hill, 1974 [reprint of the 1964 edition]), 88–98 and 99–109 respectively. Aquinas's teaching about "stable dispositions" (*habitus*), "virtues" (*virtutes*), and "gifts" (*dona*) is rich and nuanced. For explanations of the nature of each and their interrelationships, see Brian Davies, *The Thought of Thomas Aquinas* (Oxford: Clarendon Press, 1992), 225–26 ["Dispositions"], 239–44 ["Virtues"], and 293–96 ["The Object of Charity"]; Bonnie Kent, "Habits and Virtues," in *Aquinas's Summa Theologiae: Critical Essays*, ed. Brian Davies (Lanham, MD: Rowman and Littlefield, 2006), 223–44; and Servais Pinckaers, *The Sources of Christian Ethics*, trans. Mary Thomas Noble (Washington, DC: Catholic University of America Press, 1995), 221–29 ["The Structure of St. Thomas's Moral Theology"] and 178–81 ["The Evangelical Law as the Head of the Body of Moral Teaching"] with special attention to the diagram on 179. For a contemporary retrieval of Aquinas's teaching as applied to moral theology, see Charles E. Bouchard, "Recovering the Gifts of the Holy Spirit in Moral Theology," *Theological Studies* 63 (2002): 539–58.

intellect.[15] The human intellectual virtues are ordered to specific acts of knowledge, understanding, and wisdom, whereas the Holy Spirit's gifts aim at the Divine in itself and open the believer to the very "principles" of divine truth.[16] The gifts as stable dispositions (*habitus*) imparted by the Holy Spirit open the believer to an elemental grasp or perception of divine truth before conscious reflection, so that we can say that the gifts of knowledge, understanding, and wisdom are real appropriations of truth, not preliminary or intermediate stages on the way of arriving at truth. At the level of the gifts the believer knows, understands, and lives out divine truth by intuition or connaturality (*sensus*) and not by discursive reason, argumentation, or demonstration, however important these are in their own orders of operation. The divine gifts of knowledge, understanding,

15. According to *Summa Theologica 1a2ae,* question 68, article 8 ("Whether the Virtues Are More Excellent Than the Gifts?"), Aquinas writes: "There are three kinds of virtues: for some are theological, some intellectual, and some moral. The theological virtues are those whereby man's mind is united to God; the intellectual virtues are those whereby reason itself is perfected; and the moral virtues are those which perfect the powers of appetite in obedience to reason. On the other hand the gifts of the Holy Spirit dispose all the powers of the soul to be amenable to the Divine motion. Accordingly, the gifts seem to be compared to the theological virtues, by which man is united to the Holy Spirit his mover, in the same way as the moral virtues are compared to the intellectual virtues, which perfect the reason, the moving principle of the moral virtues. Wherefore as the intellectual virtues are more excellent than the moral virtues and control them, so the theological virtues are more excellent than the gifts of the Holy Spirit and regulate them. . . . But if we compare the gifts to the other virtues, intellectual and moral, then the gifts have the precedence over the virtues. Because the gifts perfect the soul's powers in relation to the Holy Spirit their mover; whereas the virtues perfect, either the reason itself, or the other powers in relation to reason. And it is evident that the more exalted the mover, the more excellent the disposition whereby the thing moved requires they be disposed. Therefore the gifts are more perfect than the virtues." *The Summa Theologica of St. Thomas Aquinas,* American edition in 3 vols., trans. by the Fathers of the English Dominican Province (New York: Benziger Brothers, 1947), 1:885. I have emended the translation slightly. For a helpful guide to Thomas Aquinas's understanding of virtue in terms of the whole of his theology itself and as understood and developed in the course of the history of Thomistic thought and Dominican schools of theology, and in terms of the use and misuse of Aquinas in contemporary theologies of virtue ethics, see Thomas F. O'Meara, "Virtues in the Theology of Thomas Aquinas," *Theological Studies* 58 (1997): 254–85.

16. In Thomas's system, "principles" (*principia*) are more fundamental than actions perfected by virtues. *Principia* have a claim to priority.

and wisdom impart an immediacy of knowing and acting that precede subsequent virtuous acts of human reason and judgment.[17] Here is how Marín-Sola expresses it:

> In the matter of how the implicit truths of the revealed deposit of faith are penetrated, what differentiates the speculative way from the mystical is that the former only has study and reasoning at its disposal, whereas the latter also possesses grace and the gifts of the Holy Spirit that permit the believer to grasp in an experiential way a number of truths that are hidden from, or even completely ignored by, speculation or that are attained only after hard intellectual work. . . . Thanks to the gift of understanding and the gifts of wisdom, knowledge, and counsel, in the case of the connatural penetration of the truths of the faith, the mystic can employ these gifts when it is necessary to judge—connaturally— divine and created realities, as well as human acts.[18]

It should be clear, then, how central the thought of Thomas Aquinas is for Marín-Sola in his formulation of the "sense of the faith," especially Aquinas's theory of the way of connaturality and his treatment of the gifts of the Holy Spirit.[19]

---

17. On the development of Thomas's thought regarding the gifts of the Holy Spirit from his early *Commentary on the Sentences* (1252–57, with revisions in 1259) to the *Summa theologiae 1a2ae* (ca. 1269) and the full flowering in the *Summa theologiae 2a2ae* (1271–72), see Edward D. O'Connor, "The Evolution of St. Thomas's Thought on the Gifts," *Summa theologiae*, vol. 24, 110–30.

18. Ibid., 1:373 (§220). Marín-Sola then goes on to quote as his authority Thomas Aquinas, *Summa theologiae* 2a–2ae, q. 8, art. 6 ["Whether the Gift of Understanding Is Distinct from the Other Gifts"]: "Accordingly on the part of the things proposed to faith for belief, two things are requisite on our part: first that they be penetrated or grasped by the intellect, and this belongs to the gift of understanding (*ad donum intellectus*). Secondly, it is necessary that man should judge these things aright, that he should esteem that he ought to adhere to these things, and to withdraw from their opposites: and this judgment, with regard to divine things belongs to the gift of wisdom (*ad donum sapientiae*), but with regard to created things, belongs to the gift of knowledge (*ad donum scientiae*), and as to its application to individual actions, belongs to the gift of counsel (*ad donum consilii*)." *The Summa Theologica of St. Thomas Aquinas*, 2:1208.

19. Although Thomas's theology of the virtues is the focus of Thomas F. O'Meara, he does not fail to mention, at least in passing, the importance of gifts in Aquinas: "Aquinas's

Another important point that Marín-Sola makes is the process of the emergence of the "sense of the faith." Insight into the content of the deposit of revealed doctrine might begin with a single believer who then communicates his or her perception to others until it becomes the general conviction of the faithful. The process might take a long time, but the emergence of the revealed truth is well on its way to becoming a dogma in the end defined by the magisterium. He writes of this process:

> [Long before a doctrine becomes conscious to the speculative theologian] it often happens that a holy person, a simple member of the faithful who enjoys a lively and simple piety, has sensed (*senti*) or anticipated (*pressenti*) the development of a doctrine, and then has communicated it to other believers, who in turn have accepted it as an expression of their own understanding (*sentiment*) or of their own faith. Finally, this understanding reaches such a point of general acceptance that it becomes the general understanding (*sentiment commun*) of the whole of Christian society. This is what constitutes the "sense of the faith" or "Christian understanding."[20]

Marín-Sola also insists on the universality of the "sense of the faithful." All the faithful are involved in the process of understanding the faith, from the saint or mystic, to the ordinary Christian struggling to be a good believer, and even the sinner living on the fringes of the church. No one is excluded by Marín-Sola, and this fact deserves our attention. Though he usually writes glowingly of the role of the saint in the process of arriving at the "sense of the faith," he is also clear that sinners and, as we might say today, non-practicing and even alienated Christians, have their role to play in the process as well. Apropos of this he writes:

---

theology does not begin with human virtues nor does it end with them. It proceeds from two vital sources, the total personality and divine grace, and it ends in the instinctual gifts of the Spirit." See "Virtues in the Theology of Thomas Aquinas," 279.

20. Ibid., 1:357–58. Despite the fact that Marín-Sola sees this process of gradual growth of the consciousness in the church of a doctrine of the faith, he does not advert to the historical character of the process or invest the historicity of Christian faith with special value. In this regard, he shared this blindness with the vast majority of his contemporaries. Later in the twentieth century theologians will discover the importance of historicity for the faith and its understanding, but writing in the second and third decade of the century, Marín-Sola had not yet arrived at it.

> The "sense of the faith" reaches its *perfection* only in those in whom faith, grace, charity and the gifts [of the Holy Spirit] are found and without which there is no genuine experience of divine realities. Nevertheless, it can be said that it is found in all the faithful, even if imperfectly, and even in a transitory way in the believer who is in the state of mortal sin.[21]

This, too, is an important contribution from Marín-Sola, and a point that some commentators on the "sense of the faithful" pass over in silence or even exclude as a possibility.

In spite of Marín-Sola's admirable witness to the "sense of the faith" in the early twentieth century, there are still unresolved tendencies in his treatment. First of all, Marín-Sola remains ambiguous about the place of the "sense of the faith" in the church. The ultimate goal of a dogma is for it to be defined by the magisterium, that is, by the bishops and/or by the pope. The contributory roles of the faithful in arriving at a revealed truth and of theologians in explaining it in terms of the sources of the faith are, in the end, mere stages along the path to official definition by the hierarchy, which is the real goal in the development of dogma. But does this do justice to the "sense of the faithful" in the church's life? If a doctrine is not defined by the magisterium, does this negate the real influence of the doctrine in the church's life? Must everything that Christians believe be defined? Is this even possible? Is this healthy for the church? Is indeterminacy always harmful?

Marín-Sola also restricts infallibility to the hierarchical magisterium of the bishops and the pope. Unlike earlier authors who spoke of the infallibility of the whole church, Marín-Sola does not refer to the contribution of the faithful to this ecclesial infallibility. He is clear that the role of the faithful is indispensable in the process of coming to know the truths of the deposit and to their eventual definition, but he is ambivalent about how this role participates in the greater infallibility of the church as a whole. Though he never demeans the role of the faithful as the church learning (*ecclesia discens*) vis-à-vis the hierarchical church teaching (*ecclesia*

---

21. Ibid., 383–84. Italics are in the original text. Earlier, too, he wrote: "[The doctrines of the faith] might perhaps never have been known or have never been defined without the help of this sense of the faith (*ce sens de la foi*) that is so remarkable in the saints, but which is also found in every just soul, and even to a certain extent, in each Christian." Ibid., 1:368.

docens), he appears to hold the faithful in a subordinate place. Inescapably and unfortunately, Marín-Sola implies that the "sense of the faith" is something derivative and secondary. This impression continues to bedevil the discussion of the "sense of the faith" even to our day.

Mannes Dominikus Koster, OP (1901–81)

The contribution to the "sense of the faith" by Francisco Marín-Sola was significant, but because it was tucked away in a much longer speculative treatment of the nature of dogma and its development, it had little direct impact on the question of the "sense of the faith" in general. That changed with the multiple writings on the topic by the German Dominican Mannes D. Koster who returned to the topic several times during his long career, applying it to the sacrament of confirmation, to the dogma of Mary's assumption into heaven, and to theological method.[22]

Koster's first foray into the "sense of the faith" was a short article entitled "Theologie, Theologien und Glaubenssinn," in which he pointed to it as a neglected resource in the church's theological tradition:

> The organ that opens the believing people [of God] to progress in understanding the faith is the "sense of the faith," the *sensus fidelium*. . . . There is an order that has always obtained, namely, the content of faith

---

22. The literature on M. D. Koster is not copious. See Karl Adam, "Ekkesiologie im Werden? Kritische Bemerkungen zu M. D. Kosters Kritik an den ekklesiologischen Versuchen der Gegenwart," *Theologische Quartalschrift* 122 (1941): 145–66; Yves Congar, "D'une 'Ecclésiologie en gestation' à Lumen Gentium Chap. I et II," in *Freiburger Zeitschrift für Philosophie und Theologie* 18/1-2 (1971) [=*Kirche im Wachstum des Glaubens: Festgabe Mannes Dominikus Koster zum 70. Geburtstag*, ed. Otto Hermann Pesch and Hans-Dietrich Langer (Freiburg, Switzerland, 1971)]: 366–77; Michael Schmaus, "Eine Anmerkung zum Problem der Demokratisierung im Bereich der kirchlichen Lehrunfehlbarkeit," in *Kirche im Wachstum des Glaubens*, ed. O. H. Pesch and H.-D. Langer, 255–65; Leonhard Hell, "Koster, Dominikus Mannes" in *Lexikon für Theologie und Kirche*, vol. 6 (3rd ed.; Freiburg: Herder, 1997), col. 405; Hartmut Westermann, "Ecclesia ab Abel? Zur Auseinandersetzung zwischen Karl B. Adam und Mannes D. Koster," *Theologische Quartalschrift* 195 (2015): 57–74; and especially Piotr Napiwodzki, *Eine Ekklesiologie im Werden: Mannes Dominikus Koster und sein Beitrag zum theologischen Verständnis der Kirche*. Dissertation zur Erlangung des Doktortitels an der Theologischen Fakultät der Universität Freiburg Schweiz, 2005. Available at https://doc.rero.ch/record/5056/files/1_NapidodzkiP.pdf.

is present first of all, and only then is it proclaimed, believed, and lastly understood by moving either from life itself to faith or from methodical scrutiny or theology.[23]

Next, Koster turned to the two forms that the "sense of the faith" takes, but without sacrificing the underlying unity of the process. There is a "sense of the faith of the faithful" and a "sense of the faith of the bishops." Each of these forms operates out of its proper goal as intended by God: the "sense of the faith of the faithful" with a view to believing spontaneously and intuitively what the sources of revelation propose and incorporating them into the Christian life as a whole, while the "sense of the faith of the bishops" has been entrusted with teaching officially and judging definitively with the responsibility of doing so "infallibly." In Koster's words:

> The organ of the teaching Church (the *sensus pastorum*) is also the same "sense of the faithful," except for the fact that the teaching Church possesses the charism of infallibility. Thus, the "sense of the faith" of the magisterium judges infallibly both theological understanding and the "sense of the faith" of the believing People [of God].[24]

This formulation might suggest a division in the ecclesial "sense of the faithful," but that would be a misreading of Koster. He makes it clear that the two forms are intrinsically ordered to each other and that underlying both is a fundamental unity. He writes:

> The "sense of the faith" of the whole Church and of the individual Christian is one and leads to the consciousness of everything that is to be believed. Nevertheless, the whole believing Church comes to this

23. "Das Organ des gläubigen Volkes für den Fortschritt in der Glaubenskenntnis ist der 'Glaubenssinn', der *sensus fidelium*. . . . Denn das ist die Urordnung, die hier obwaltet: Zuerst ist da der Glaubensgegenstand, dann wird er verkündet, dann geglaubt, dann aufgefasst, entweder nur zum Leben aus dem Glauben oder auch zum methodischen Durchdenken, zur Theologie." Koster, "Theologie, Theologien und Glaubenssinn," *Theologie und Seelsorge* 35 (1943): 82–90, at 87–88.

24. "Das Organ der lehrenden Kirche ist auch wieder nur der 'Glaubenssinn', der *sensus pastorum*, jedoch in Hinordnung auf das Charisma der Unfehlbarkeit. Und daher urteilt der 'Glaubenssinn' des Lehramtes unfehlbar über die theologische Vernunft wie über den Galubenssinn des gläubigen Volkes." Ibid., 87.

consciousness, to which both the laity and the clergy belong. All those ordained, including the bishops, are members of the Church but with a view to a diversity of functions which pertain to the ordained and the non-ordained for the good of the Church. But this does not in any way necessitate a separation of the "sense of the faith" of the ordained and the non-ordained. The "sense of the faith" is one in the whole Church.[25]

With this initial contribution, Koster provided the basic elements of his understanding of the "sense of the faith."

Koster returned to the topic is his article "Der Glaubenssinn der Hirten und Gläubigen."[26] The "sense of the faith" is akin to an

ability, a feeling, an eye, and a sense for each and every thing that falls within the ambit of the holy faith. . . . The word "sense" is associated with a person's inclination to enthusiastically grasp something and her or his openness to the spirit, much as one knows what is fitting and

25. "Vielmehr ist es der eine gleiche 'Glaubenssinn' der ganzen Kirche und der einzelnen Christenmenschen, der zur Bewusstmachung der von allen im Glauben angenommenen Dinge führt. Allerdings geschieht diese Bewusstwerdung bei der gesamten glaubenden Kirche, zu der wie die Laien so auch der Klerus, d. h. alle Geweihten bis zum Bischof der Gesamtkirche hinauf gehören, in Hinordnung auf die verschiedenen Funktionen, die den Geweihten und den Nichtgeweihten zugunsten der Kirche obliegen. Doch bedingt das in gar keiner Weise einen Unterschied des 'Glaubensinnes' bei den Geweihten und Nichtgeweihten. Der 'Glaubenssinn' ist einer in der ganzen Kirche." Ibid., 90.

26. The first two sections of this article had appeared in *Die Neue Ordnung* 3 (1949): 226-43, with the titles "'The Nature of the 'Sense of the Faith'" and "'The Way the 'Sense of the Faith' is Known." But Koster had added two further sections to the earlier article to complete his presentation, namely, "The 'Sense of the Faith' and the Transmission of the Faith" and "The 'Sense of the Faith' and the Magisterium." It is this longer form that we will examine in order to explain Koster's full understanding of the "sense of the faith." It appeared in *Volk Gottes im Wachstum des Glaubens: Himmelfahrt Mariens und Glaubenssinn* (Heidelberg: F. H. Kerle, 1950). Mention should also be made of Koster's use of the "sense of the faith" in a treatment of the sacrament of confirmation, *Die Firmung im Glaubenssinn der Kirche* (Münster: Verlag Regensberg, 1948). See pages 111-27 ["Das Wachstum des Glaubenssinnes"] and 176-79 ["Der Glaubenssinn und die Wandlungen der Firmhandlung"]. Also from 1948 and reprinted in *Volk Gottes im Wachstum des Glaubens*, 11-57, is an article on Mary's bodily assumption into heaven. It represents Koster's contribution to the then-lively discussion that was taking place among theologians regarding the meaning of Mary's assumption and whether it could even be defined. See *Die Neue Ordnung* 2 (1948): 60-85.

peculiar in a particular case, and so strives for it, and as it were has a firm and constant orientation toward it.[27]

Koster bases his understanding of the "sense of the faith" on Thomas Aquinas's discussion of faith as both a virtue and a gift of the Holy Spirit. Although the believer has the "capacity to believe" (Glaubenskraft), it must come to realization as a "virtue" (*virtus*) or "stable disposition" (*habitus*), and as a "gift" (*donum*).

Like Marín-Sola, Koster too relies on Aquinas's teaching in the *Summa Theologiae* I-II, question 68 ("On the Gifts") and II-II, questions 8 ("On the Gift of Understanding"), 9 ("On the Gift of Knowledge"), and 45 ("On the Gift of Wisdom"). God's gifts to the believer are necessary for the human being if she or he is to attain the divine life in its fullness. In this dynamic, virtues as stable dispositions (*habitus*) are ordered to the gifts. There is no duplication involved, for the gifts are the crowning of the virtues. The "sense of the faith" operates on the level of the mind's grasp of divine truth, and so the intellectual virtues of knowing, understanding, and wisdom must be perfected by their corresponding gifts of knowing, understanding, and wisdom. Thus, moral and intellectual virtues are directed toward an intermediate act, while the gifts attain their object, God, immediately. This teaching of Aquinas is why Koster stresses the fact that knowing, understanding, and wisdom play a major role in constituting the "sense of the faith" of the faithful and of the bishops.

---

27. "Es bedeutet soviel wie Vermögen, Gespür, Auge, Sinn für alles und jedes einzelne, was in den Bereich des heiligen Glaubens fällt. . . . Das Wort 'Sinn' meint . . . die mit Lust und Neigung verbundene Empfänglichkeit und Auffassungsfähigkeit des Geistes, wie sie auf das ihm Zukömmliche und Eigentümliche im einzelnen geht, nach ihm strebt und so gleichsam eine feste Richtung einschlägt und beibehält." "Der Glaubenssinn der Hirten und Gläubigen," 62. Koster points to the frequent use of the word *Sinn* ("sense") by Goethe and to the fact that it is a common expression in ordinary German parlance. The term *Sinn*, then, is non-technical in German and only the addition of the more precise field, *Glauben* ("faith"), distinguishes it from other uses as a technical theological term. Koster further points out that *Glaubenssinn* as a technical term is characterized by five dimensions. It is a *receptivity* (die Empfänglichkeit) for a particular truth of the faith, an *orientation* toward it (das Hinstreben), the *capacity* (das Vermögen) to grasp it, and most importantly the *disposition* (die Neigung) to act on it and a *vigilant readiness* (das wache und offene Auge für jedes einselne) to perceive it. Only when all five operations are present can we speak of the "sense of the faith" in its fullness. See ibid., 63–64.

Knowing, understanding, and wisdom are intellectual virtues and are in need of being elevated by the gifts that correspond to them.[28]

Koster then reaffirms the teaching that the "sense of the faith" is radically one, even though it is manifested differently in the lay faithful and in the pope and the bishops. In so teaching, Koster draws the following three conclusions: (1) the unity of the "sense of the faithful" precedes in dignity the role of theology in elaborating the "sense of the faith"; (2) despite the underlying unity of the "sense of the faithful" and the "sense of the pastors," each form has its own task to perform; and (3) that no form can aggrandize the task of the other without loss to the irreducible unity of the "sense of the faith."

In the second part, Koster tries to clarify the different epistemological tasks of the faithful and their pastors, something that the magisterium

---

28. Koster points to the importance of the "sense of the faith" in the magisterium. (1) At the twenty-first session of Trent, the council introduced its teaching that the laity were not bound to receive the Eucharist under both forms of consecrated bread and wine, even though Scripture itself is quite clear regarding Jesus's command to do so, the bishops speak of "the Spirit of wisdom and understanding, the Spirit of counsel and piety" and the "custom of the Church" as directing their decision. See Norman P. Tanner, *Decrees of the Ecumenical Councils*, 2 vols. (Washington, DC: Georgetown University Press, 1990), 2:726. (2) At session 3 of Vatican I, at the conclusion of its teaching on faith and reason in chapter 3, we read: "May understanding, knowledge and wisdom increase as ages and centuries roll along, and greatly and vigorously flourish, in each and all, in the individual and the whole Church, but this only in its own proper kind, that is to say, in the same doctrine, the same sense, and the same understanding." See Tanner, ibid., 809. (3) Pius XII spoke of Christ as "He who imparts the light of faith to believers; it is he who enriches pastors and teachers and above all his vicar on earth with the supernatural gifts of knowledge, understanding and wisdom, so that they may loyally preserve the treasury of faith, defend it vigorously, and explain and confirm it with reverence and devotion." *Mystici corporis*, art. 50. See *AAS* 35 (1943), 216 and *The Papal Encyclicals 1939–1958*, ed. Claudia Carlen (Ann Arbor, MI: Pierian Press, 1990), 47. He also cites Colossians 1:9, Philippians 1:9, and Ephesians 1:17-18 as providing scriptural evidence for the "sense of the faith." It would seem that Koster is reading more into these sources than they can bear. Koster does not neglect the evidence from history and lists Jerome, Basil, Vincent of Lérins, John Cassian, and Augustine as patristic sources of the teaching. William of Auxerre, Alexander of Hales, Bonaventure, Albert the Great, and Thomas Aquinas represent the high Middle Ages. Finally, he mentions Melchior Cano, Francisco Suárez, Juan Martínez de Ripalda and Juan de Lugo from the time after Trent, and Giovanni Perrone and John Henry Newman in the nineteenth century.

had neglected to do up to this point. Koster informs the reader that he intends to follow the thought of Thomas Aquinas on this matter. He begins with Thomas's teaching of the priority of the believer's "capacity to believe" (Glaubenskraft) before all attempts to state, teach, or define the contents of faith. God must first equip a person to believe, and this process includes two elements. The first is the gift of the "light of faith" (*lumen fidei*) or the very ability of a person to perceive divine truth. It equips the believer to recognize what God has revealed and what has not been revealed.[29] The second is the dynamic orientation of each person toward divine truth.[30] Without the "capacity to believe," the so-called gifts of the Holy Spirit would make no sense. The "capacity to believe," however, is too general to arrive at accurate knowledge of divine truth. The believer is oriented toward the truth, but without clearly perceiving it.[31] Our human orientation toward the divine is too diffuse to identify the divine in any detailed way and thus prone to misidentify it. As Koster remarks in explanation:

> The "capacity to believe" cannot exclude false conjectures about matters of faith, even though such conjectures agree with and affirm the latter and what is properly related to it. But the "capacity to believe" cannot preclude the possibility that it might affirm the opposite of what faith calls for—a situation that is impossible when we know something

---

29. According to Thomas, "The light of faith makes us see what we believe. For just as, by the habits of the other virtues, we see what is becoming to us in respect of that habit, so, by the habit of faith, the human mind is directed to assent to such things as are becoming to a right faith, and not to assent to others." *Summa theologiae* II-II, q. 1, art. 4, ad 3. *The Summa Theologica of St. Thomas Aquinas*, American edition, 2:1172.

30. As Koster says: "The capacity to believe is the necessary receptivity toward each and every object of faith. It has the character of a graced equipping of the believer. (Die Glaubenskraft ist daher notwendig die Empfänglichkeit für jeden einzelnen Glaubensgegenstand und für alle insgesamt. Ihr kommt der Charakter einer gnadenhaften Ertüchtigung zu.)" "Der Glaubenssinn der Hirten und Gläubigen," 75.

31. Koster characterizes this orientation thus: "[The believer's awareness of what is revealed or not revealed] does not happen consciously and rationally, as is the case with the reasons of credibility, but by way of a 'natural inclination' for matters of faith that is completely spontaneous and beyond his or her consciousness. (Das geschieht nicht bewusst und rationell, nach Art der Glaubwürdigkeitslehre, sondern durch eine 'naturhafte Hinneigung' ganz spontaner und überbewusster Art zu den Dingen des Glaubens.)" Ibid., 76.

by demonstration from principles. Among other reasons, here is the great weakness of the "capacity to believe" that excludes it from being considered the "sense of the faith" in the full meaning of that term.[32]

Though indispensable for faith, the "capacity to believe" itself is in need of the additional gifts of knowledge, understanding, and wisdom. Koster completes this section by considering Thomas's teaching on the nature and role of these three gifts. Only the complementarity these gifts provide can account for the "sense of the faith" in its full meaning.[33]

Koster begins with the gift of knowledge. Its primary task is to help the "capacity to believe" discern what God has revealed to us and in such a way as to do so correctly and with certitude.[34] But the gift of knowledge is not intended for the faithful alone but for the pope and the bishops as well. According to Thomas, "Knowledge is a gift and is common to all holy persons."[35] The universality of the gift of knowledge is what ultimately constitutes the "sense of the faith" as twofold—namely, the "sense of the faithful" at large and the "sense of the bishops or pastors" with their unique responsibility. Koster makes it very clear that the pope's and the bishops' infallible teaching office does not preclude the special gift of knowledge but rather demands it. But just as this gift assists the bishops in meeting their task in the church, it also assists the faithful at large in coming to the "correct and certain" knowledge of what pertains to divine

32. "Vermag die Glaubenskraft nicht vor falschen Mutmassungen über Glaubensdinge zu bewahren, obgleich sie mit jenen darin übereinkommt, dass sie durchaus bejaht, was ihr eigentümlich und verwandt ist. Sie kann nicht verhindern, das Gegenteil von dem zu denken, was zu glauben ist, ein Umstand, der beim Wissen unmöglich ist. Dass ist die eine grosse Schwäche der Glaubenskraft, die neben andern es verhindert, das sie Glaubenssinn im Vollsinne ist." Ibid., 75–76.

33. Though Marín-Sola had already pointed out the importance of these three gifts, as we saw above, Koster gives special attention to them in terms of their role in bringing about the "sense of the faith."

34. This is the whole point of Thomas's teaching of the indispensability of the gift of knowledge, which he treats in the four articles of question 9. See *The Summa Theologica of St. Thomas Aquinas*, American edition, 2:1210-1213.

35. *Summa theologiae* II-II, q. 9, art. 1, ad 2. See *The Summa Theologica of St. Thomas Aquinas*, American edition, 2:1211. A better translation here would read, "Knowledge is a [special] gift and is common to all the saints, i.e., all Christians or all the justified."

revelation often well in advance of the bishops and theologians.[36] Koster then cites examples from history where the magisterium in fact turned to the "sense of the faithful" at large before teaching something with authority and even infallibly.

The second special gift is understanding.[37] It is inadequate merely "to know" a truth contained in the so-called deposit of the faith. The faithful also need to have some "understanding" of the truth. The gift of understanding adds insight and a deeper penetration into the nature of a given revealed truth. Revelation does not come to the believer as disembodied but in various forms and expressions: narratives, tales, songs and hymns, prophecies and visionary experiences, learned discourses, dogmatic definitions, sermons and catecheses, symbols that are spoken and symbolic actions, pictures, icons, mosaics, stained glass or other representations, expressions of piety, prayers, and practices. The list could be extended indefinitely. Some of these expressions of revealed truth are more or less adequate to the task of expressing divine truth, but many are inadequate, flawed, or time-conditioned. That is why the field of the gift of understanding is so vast and why this gift is necessary. Understanding enables the believer to see through any errors, any distortions and perversions of the truth, the pretenses of those who belittle the faith, philosophical and historical counterarguments, or whatever objections are made contrary to divine truth. The gift of understanding sustains the believer in the face of all of them.

Though the pope and the bishops and the faithful at large receive the gift of understanding, each receives it for a different purpose. The pope and the bishops need the gift of understanding to penetrate more directly the meaning of the revealed truth in order to present it more clearly, to defend it against error, to correct misunderstandings, to modify or eliminate misleading expressions of the truth, to test various devotions and pious practices, and to define revealed truth when it is gravely threatened

36. As Koster remarks: "By reason of the gift of knowledge the faithful are entirely capable of discerning with certitude and correctly whether something pertains to the faith or not, and so is a candidate for definition or not, and this without any positive influence from the magisterium and in given circumstances even do so long before their pastors and teachers." "Der Glaubenssinn der Hirten und Gläubigen," 81.

37. Thomas treats the gift of understanding in the *Summa theologiae* II-II, q. 8 in 8 articles.

or when the faithful call for a definition. To accomplish this task, however, the pope and the bishops need to penetrate divine truth more deeply, especially by adverting to the inner connections among divinely revealed truths—one truth elucidating, amplifying, and confirming the other truths in the unity of the deposit of the faith. In other words, in order to defend the faith, the bishops must also grow in the deeper penetration of the truth of the Christian faith.

The faithful, too, must grow in their understanding of the faith by themselves receiving this gift from the Holy Spirit. The growth in understanding the faith on the part of the faithful is no less important than the growth of their pastors. It, too, constitutes the fullness of the reality we call the "sense of the faith," even though it is exercised differently. It is this gift that has enabled the faithful to hold fast to certain truths, sometimes for centuries, when the theologians differed among themselves as to whether the truth belonged to the deposit of faith or when the bishops hesitated to teach a revealed truth with greater explicitness. This constancy of belief by the faithful is of equal value to the deposit of revelation, as is the teaching function of the pastors. But it is lived out and expressed differently.[38] Throughout his presentation of the gift of understanding, Koster has been at pains to express that everyone in the church must become as attentive to the indispensability of this special gift as they are committed to employing the ordinary human means of arriving at divine truth. Study and critical reason are not to be excluded, of course, but they must also make way for the Holy Spirit's gift of understanding, and the church needs to grow in its appreciation of this gift.

Finally, Koster turns to the special gift of wisdom. Here, too, as with the gifts of knowledge and understanding, he sees wisdom bringing the "capacity to believe" to completion as the "sense of the faith." As the gifts of knowledge and understanding perfect the believer's intellect, wisdom addresses the affective component of faith.[39] Apropos of wisdom, he writes:

38. Koster remarks: "Finally, the fact cannot be argued away that there are individuals who precisely as believing Christians bring to perfection either the understanding of Scripture or some clarifications of the truths of the faith that have not been admitted up to this point, and which the ecclesial magisterium eventually accepts and acknowledges as its own." "Der Glaubenssinn der Hirten und Gläubigen," 87.

39. Koster follows Thomas's treatment of this special gift in *Summa theologiae* II-II, q. 45 in 6 articles, with special attention to art. 2.

Given its affective affinity with God and because God's gracious gift of love is bestowed on believers, the proper task of wisdom is to judge the divine matters of faith. . . . Just as our [human] senses make present to us and, as it were, give sensible things a body for us, so too does [wisdom] bring us to the fullness of the "sense of the faith." The gift of wisdom is the real cause why holy matters of faith are often honored, celebrated, appreciated and valued, even before they are proposed to us to be believed. Wisdom orders human activity and our affective life in such a way that it far outstrips our limitations. It is the sensibility (*Gespür*) we have for everything that pertains to God as our salvation, and the reason why we hold them in such high reverence.[40]

The special field of wisdom is the wide range of cult and devotion in the church.[41] Precisely in these matters, the faithful at large enjoy a certain preeminence, while the pope, bishops, and theologians join with them in their capacity as believers. The gift of wisdom often orientates the faithful toward the truths of the faith but as first felt, lived, and experienced before they are taught or defined. The history of the development of dogma in the church attests to this phenomenon again and again. Because this is the case with the gift of wisdom among the faithful, Koster remarks: "The Church's magisterium is not free to either regard or disregard such a wit-

40. "Der Glaubenssinn der Hirten und Gläubign," 88. I have translated the German *Gespür* as "sensibility," but it could just as easily be rendered "instinct" or "intuition." The advantage of "sensibility" is that it retains the connotations of "feeling" and "sensing" characteristic of Thomas Aquinas's epistemology. To Aquinas, knowing is always based on the senses and the act of abstracting truth from what the senses provide the intellect. Such notions are retained and transmitted by the German verb *spüren* (to feel, to sense), and for that reason I have preferred "sensibility" as the most appropriate translation.

41. As we will see in chapter 9, Vatican II has extended the area of wisdom's contribution beyond that of cult and devotion to include the fields of individual and social morality, social phenomena, culture, the arts, and custom. But even restricting ourselves to Koster's observation, we need to remember the adage *lex orandi, lex credendi*—the objects of our prayer and worship are just other expressions of what we believe concretely. Perhaps another way of formulating the insight of this pregnant adage is that the language of prayer and worship is first-order speech and precedes the second-order language of the creeds, the articles of faith, and the church's dogmas. The latter are always rooted in the former, which enjoy a certain priority and preeminence.

ness [on the part of the faithful at large]. Rather, it is virtually obligated to take it into consideration."[42]

Next, Koster considers the role of the "sense of the faith" in the process of the transmission of the faith. In this theological context, too, the unitary "sense of the faith" is expressed in two forms, each operating without detriment to the other. Koster distinguishes three senses in which the transmission of the faith takes place. The first meaning points to the divine revelation that God has entrusted to the church as an undivided whole, and which has come down to the church as Scripture and tradition. But this divinely entrusted faith can also be considered in its individual expressions, and as such in a twofold way. It can encompass a truth of revelation that the church formerly has not consciously acknowledged but which it is now becoming aware of and learning about, or a truth that the church has already become increasingly conscious of and which it now expressly acknowledges. These forms and stages of the emergence of the faith as a process of handing on the faith show the active side of tradition. This growing consciousness might at first take the forms of concrete practices on the part of the faithful or as judgments on the part of the pastors of the church that are not yet definitive but are slowly moving in that direction. In a final stage, these gradually emerging convictions and beliefs can be the object of a definition by the church's pastors. Still, it is important to note how these stages are related to one another throughout the traditionary process. The pope and bishops do not define a truth of the faith without any reliance on the lived faith of the faithful, while the faithful welcome the definition of their pastors when this occurs. Both forms of the "sense of the faith"—that of the faithful and that of the pastors—are intertwined and influence each other.[43]

Koster reminds us that the human learning process takes place piecemeal and in stages. Truth, even divine truth as communicated to human beings, emerges slowly and over time, one insight at a time.[44] The church grows in its grasp of the truth in this partial way and yet is never devoid of the truth of what is revealed. Even though at times it might be the body

---

42. "Das Lehramt der Kirche ist daher nicht frei, ein solches Zeugnis zu sehen oder zu übersehen, sondern geradezu gezwungen, es zu berücksichtigen." Ibid., 89.

43. Ibid., 94–97.

44. Ibid., 97.

of the faithful who transmits the now partially perceived truth, while at other times it is the pastors who assume the initiative, still it is the whole church who is the beneficiary.[45] Apropos, Koster writes:

> It is unambiguously clear then that the Church must have an organ by which it is gradually introduced to the objective faith of tradition. As shown earlier, this organ is the "sense of the faith" of the pastors and of the faithful. . . . When it is recalled just how the Church arrives at the knowledge of tradition, then it is clear that this occurs only by way of the "sense of the faith."[46]

What, then, is the role and value of theological activity in the church, in light of Koster's emphasizing the coordinate activity of pastors and faithful in determining and expressing Christian truth? Is there any room for the theologian?

We have seen how the concrete forms and practices of an emerging doctrine are often expressed in terms that can also hide the full content they seek to express. That is the limitation of human language and the unruliness of the profusion of human experiences. Here the theologian can be of service to both the faithful and the pastors. The specialist can help to exclude misunderstandings and to offer better reasons to support what the faithful and the pastors understand in their respective realms of activity. To the "correct and certain" function of the faithful and on the way to the "infallible" teaching of the pastors, the theologian brings her or his critical faculty in pursuit of a better understanding of Christian truth. Koster characterizes this function as operating within the realm of "probability." The theologian offers arguments from the historical sources, from a comparison of the various doctrines among themselves, and from more acute theological speculation to clarify and advance the emerging teaching, but this important service only operates at the level

---

45. Ibid., 97–98.

46. Ibid., 98. By way of explanation, Koster adds: "Beyond a doubt this is mystery, but such that the Spirit's bringing the Church to the knowledge of objective tradition happens in just this way and brings it to expression by a means that is connatural [to it as mystery]. . . .The 'sense of the faith' of the Church is always the judge of its own activity, that is to say, the one 'sense of the faith' of the pastors is the infallible judge, whereas the one 'sense of the faith' of the body of the faithful is the 'more certain' judge only." Ibid., 99.

of what is "more probable," not what is "more certain" (the "sense of the faith" of the body of the faithful) or "infallible" (the "sense of the faith" of the pastors).[47]

According to Koster, there is no doubt that theological activity contributes to the church's growing in the truth of Christian revelation and that he defends this activity. Nonetheless, he also judges theologians severely when they see their role as above that of the body of believers and occupying an intermediate state between the faithful and the pastors. Their more critical understanding of the theological issues at stake does not displace the indispensable role of the "sense of the faith" of the ordinary faithful, but must humbly put itself in its service.[48]

Next, Koster considers certain objections to, and problems with, his understanding of the "sense of the faith." Here the uniqueness of Koster's understanding emerges with even greater clarity. Koster inquires regarding the relationship of the teaching of the fathers of the church and of theologians in the church to that of the "sense of the faith." Though some theologians tended to see the unanimity of the fathers and of theologians as constituting an infallible witness, Koster is clear that only the pastors of the church are an infallible source of teaching, while the fathers and theologians must be ranked with the "sense of the faith" of the body of believers. This is true for Augustine and Thomas Aquinas just as it is of any other theologian in the church. The activity of theologians in the church must be understood as a part of the "sense of the faith" of the ordinary faithful and not that of the pastors. Theologians and the ordinary faithful differ from one another in terms of the gifts of the Holy Spirit given to each group: theologians enjoy a greater degree of the gift of

47. Throughout this section Koster references the teaching of Matthias J. Scheeben in idem, *Handbuch der katholischen Dogmatik*, vol. 1: *Erkenntnislehre*, ed. Martin Grabmann (2nd ed.; Freiburg: Herder, 1948), nos. 200, 318, and 607; and *Handbook of Catholic Dogmatics*, vol. 1, Part 1 trans. Michael J. Miller (Steubenville, OH: Emmaus Academic, 2019), 151, 220–21, and 382.

48. "Der Glaubenssinn der Hirten und Gläubigen," 99–105. Koster's criticism of theologians who tried to exaggerate their activity at the expense of the contributions of the faithful elicited some misunderstanding of his true position. He was falsely accused of a lack of appreciation of the theologian's task and vocation in the church. In fact, he says quite clearly: "Whoever understands the stress of the role of the 'sense of the faith' as a justification to demote the role of theology [in the process] errs." Ibid., 104.

understanding, while the faithful are distinguished by the Spirit's gift of wisdom. Nevertheless, both groups still belong to the "sense of the faith" of the body of the faithful and not of that of the pastors.[49]

The final issue Koster examines in this long essay deals with the "sense of the faith" and the definition of a dogma. What roles do the "sense of the faith" of the faithful and of the pastors play in the process and how are these roles related to each other? Koster distinguishes the two phases of such definitions by the church: the preparatory phase during which the doctrine begins to emerge and is solidified, and the final phase of its definition by the pastors and its reception in the church. Koster illustrates the first phase by considering two examples from the history of dogmas: the definition of the fate of the just prior to the general judgment by Benedict XII in 1336 and the definition of Mary's immaculate conception by Pius IX in 1854. In both of these cases the faithful played an essential role in the process of their definition.[50]

Finally, Koster considers the "sense of the faithful" in the period following a definition, or that period of time in which the church grows in its faith. Koster points to three areas in which such growth occurs. The first envisions growth and deepening in the understanding of what has been defined and its place in the deposit of the faith. Such growth helps the church avoid the twin dangers of undervaluing what has been defined and of misunderstanding it. The positive role of growing in the faith and more deeply appropriating it is primary for Koster, but it does not eliminate completely the need to guard the truth of the faith in order to

---

49. Ibid., 105–113. After clarifying the mutual roles of the pastors and of the rest of the faithful, including the fathers of the church as theologians and of the other doctors and great theologians of the church, Koster continues with an examination of the contribution of each to the growing and deepening doctrinal heritage of the church throughout history. He highlights the trinitarian, christological, and Marian dogmas of the first five centuries, growth in the understanding of grace and human freedom, the iconoclastic controversy, the growing contribution of theologians from the Carolingian period onward, the eucharistic controversies of early scholasticism, the fate of the deceased before the Parousia, continuing devotion to Mary and the Marian doctrines derived from such devotion, the important contribution of theologians to the formulation of the *filioque* clause, sacramental theology, the papal office, and the doctrine of justification, to name just a few. See ibid., 113–22.

50. Ibid., 122–36 ["Glaubenssinn und zu erfolgende Lehrentscheidung"].

avoid falling into error—the negative role. The second area is growth in love and greater unity in love in the church. Christian truth for Koster is never detached from the church as a communion of love. What is believed must enrich the communal life of the church, or what Koster calls the church as household or family. And the third area is growth in Christian maturity: the definition of the faith should lead all Christians to more committed action. For Koster, faith leads to a deeper understanding of Christian truth and greater efforts to incarnate the truth in action. It is the Holy Spirit who in stirring up the "sense of the faith" of all inspires and instills deeper understanding, greater mutual love, and mature action in each Christian and in the whole household of the church.[51]

Reflections on Koster

A criticism of Koster's theology of the "sense of the faith" is his understanding of infallibility. As we have seen, many theologians before him pointed to the positive role the faithful played in attesting to Christian revelation. They accorded the faithful participation in infallibility in believing—a real infallibility of what they believed that is a constitutive dimension of revelation. Though the faithful do not teach infallibly in an official capacity by reason of apostolic office, they truly play their part in the broader infallibility of the universal church. By restricting infallibility exclusively to the pope and pastors of the church, Koster has impoverished the notion itself. The infallibility of the pope and bishops runs the risk of being isolated in the life of the church, open to an overly juridical interpretation of an infallible office rather than the richer notion of an infallible church consisting of the pastors and all the faithful.

Another criticism is that Koster remained a prisoner to a propositional understanding of revelation and he did not sufficiently appreciate the richness and depth of tradition. In the end, Vatican II would develop these ideas, as we will see in chapter 11.

In conclusion, the contribution of Mannes Koster to the emerging importance of the "sense of the faith" in the life of the church can hardly be overstated. Before him no other theologian had dedicated as much systematic attention to the topic or had treated it with the theological rigor that he brought to the discussion. Even to this day, his contribution

---

51. Ibid., 136–43 ["Glaubenssinn und erfolgte Lehrentscheidung"].

is widely unacknowledged, and those who have commented on him have often misunderstood him or criticized him unfairly.[52]

Regarding Koster's contributions to an understanding of the "sense of the faith" and its eventual acceptance at Vatican II, the German Dominican stressed the underlying unity of the "sense of the faith" and the reciprocity of the two roles that constitute it. The "sense of the faith" of the pastors informs and guides the "sense of the faith" of the faithful at large without reducing their contribution to merely listening to, obeying, and implementing what the pastors teach. The pastors, in turn, must listen to the genuine faith insights of the baptized faithful who have a real contri-

---

52. One of the first to criticize Koster was Johannes Beumer, SJ (1901–89), who taught for many years at the Jesuit Faculty of Theology of Sankt Georgen in Frankfurt, Germany. Beumer did not accept Koster's distinction between a "sense of the faith" of the pastors and of the faithful, but instead proposed a distinction between the "sense of the faith" in an objective sense and the "sense of the faith" in a subjective sense. Beumer's language and sentiments were closer to J. B. Franzelin's theology of active and passive infallibility, as well as the clear distinction between a teaching church (the pope and bishops) and a learning church (the faithful at large). Beumer also accused Koster of lacking a real appreciation for the role of theologians, whom he saw as denigrated by Koster in favor of the faithful at large. See "Glaubenssinn der Kirche?" *Trierer Theologische Zeitschrift* 61 (1952): 129–42. In a second article, Beumer criticized Koster for conceding too much importance to the practices, devotions, and beliefs of the faithful when it came to more technical doctrinal questions. How could the faithful be expected to contribute on matters that clearly exceeded their competencies? See idem, "Glaubenssinn der Kirche als Quelle einer Definition," *Theologie und Glaube* 45 (1955): 250–60. Other criticisms were expressed by Sophronius Classen, OFM, "Wachstum des Glaubens," *Wissenschaft und Weisheit* 15 (1952): 144–49. Francis X. Lawlor, SJ, wrote a mostly positive review of Koster's book in which he admirably and carefully explained the relationship between the "sense of the faith" of the faithful and that of the pastors when the faithful have factually provided the impetus for a later dogma and were followed by the pastors. In the end, however, he basically subordinated the faithful to the hierarchy by restricting their influence and situating all authority of teaching to the pope and the bishops, quoting the recent encyclical *Humani generis* (August 12, 1950), article 34: "This deposit of faith our divine Redeemer has given for authentic interpretation not to each of the faithful, not even to theologians, but *only* to the teaching authority of the Church." My emphasis. See *Theological Studies* 12 (1951): 254–57. This perceptive review demonstrates precisely the delicate and sensitive nature of the issues involved and indeed the daring of Koster's contribution. More recently, see Leonard Fic, *Il "sensus fidei" nel pensiero di M. D. Koster e nel Vaticano II* (Rome: Pontifical University of St. Thomas in Urbe, 1995), who continues the tendency mostly to see problems with Koster's thought.

bution to make to what the church believes and teaches. Sometimes the pastors lead in a deeper understanding of the faith, while at other times it is the faithful or the theologians among them who provide the leadership.

Second, Koster is very clear in his division of the labor of each group. The faithful offer a "correct and certain" understanding of the faith, but they do not teach infallibly. The pastors, too, sometimes teach in a "correct and certain" manner, while at other times they and they alone are equipped by Christ and the Holy Spirit to teach and interpret in an infallible way. In Koster's view, there is both overlap and division of responsibilities.

Third, in Aquinas's teaching about the stable habits or dispositions, virtues, gifts of the Holy Spirit, and the nature of connatural knowledge, Koster drew on a reasonable Thomistic theory of faculty analysis to support his theological claim. Though his attempt to prove this theory in the explicit teachings of Trent, Vatican I, and Pius XII is not successful, this fact does not overturn the teaching of Aquinas on the matter. A commentator is free to accept or reject this general Thomistic theory, but Koster has at least offered us a well-rounded answer to what the "sense of the faith" is.

Fourth, with his pronounced stress on Thomas Aquinas's teaching about the relationship among virtues, stable dispositions ("habits"), and the gifts of the Holy Spirit, Koster showed an early appreciation of the pneumatological dimension of the church's life. Koster pointed in the direction that the "sense of the faith" is first and foremost a gift and that the Holy Spirit is its source.

In the end, the strengths outweigh the weaknesses in Koster's presentation of the "sense of the faith," and the preconciliar church owed him a debt of gratitude. Because of Koster's contributions, the church had its first truly systematic presentation of the nature, role, and importance of the "sense of the faith." As we will see below, other theologians built on the solid foundations laid by Koster, even if they developed the idea of "the sense of the faith" in ways that did not adopt all of Koster's ideas.

Chapter Seven

Consolidation of the Theology of the "Sense of the Faith" in the Twentieth Century

After the foundations laid by Mannes D. Koster in particular, theological reflection on the "sense of the faith" continued with a number of theologians whose ideas helped prepare for the incorporation of the teaching in the documents of Vatican II. I propose to consider two major French theologians who clearly contributed to the advancement of the "sense of the faith." In the case of Yves Congar, the development emerged from his wrestling with fundamental questions about the church—its nature, mission, and ministry. Clément Dillenschneider, on the other hand, interacted with the discussion surrounding the definition of the dogma of Mary's bodily assumption into heaven, which Pius XII proposed to define. As was the case earlier with Pius IX's definition of the immaculate conception, the possibility of a new definition involved fundamental issues of the nature of dogma, its relationship to the witness of Scripture and the historical sources, and the possibility of development.[1] Apparently, these fundamental issues had not been adequately addressed by theological efforts a century earlier. Both of these influences, that of theologians wrestling with basic theological questions and that of the

---

1. In the next chapter I will examine the dogma in greater detail, in particular its rootedness in the history of liturgy and the meaning of the dogma for Catholics today.

definition of Mary's assumption, ultimately contributed to the teaching of Vatican II on the "sense of the faith."

Yves Congar, OP (1904–95)

In 1951, the French Dominican theologian Yves Congar published an influential article on the prophetic role of the laity in the church that included observations on what he referred to variously as the *sensus fidelium*, the *consensus fidelium*, the *sensus fidei*, the *sensus catholicus*, and the *sensus ecclesiae*. The article was subsequently incorporated as a chapter in his groundbreaking book *Lay People in the Church: A Study for a Theology of Laity*, published in French in 1953 just two years after the article had originally appeared.[2] With this book, Congar became one of the most important advocates for the "sense of the faithful."[3]

---

2. Yves Congar, "Le peuple fidèle et la fonction prophétique de l'Église, *Irénikon* 24 (1951), 289–312 and 440–66. The material in other chapters, too, had been the object of Congar's attention before they appeared in *Lay People in the Church: A Study for a Theology of Laity*, trans. Donald Attwater (1st ed.; London: Geoffrey Chapman, 1957; rev. ed.; Westminster, MD: Newman Press, 1965). Congar pointed out that his articles "Sacerdoce et laïcat dans l'Église," in both *Vie Intellectuelle* 14 (1946): 6–39 and in *Masses Ouvrières* 18 (1946): 19–56, as well as his "Pour une théologie du laïcat," *Études* (January 1948): 42–54 and (February 1948): 194–218, were preliminary studies of chapters that later appeared in *Lay People in the Church*.

3. Still, it should be mentioned that Congar was no blind defender of the "sense of the faithful." In the course of his treatment, he points out the limits of the notion as well: "Too much must not be attributed to the *sensus fidelium*, not only in view of the hierarchy's prerogatives . . . but in itself. History tells us of the widespread failures of faith in the Christian people: in the East of the seventh century in [the] face of Islam, in England and the Scandinavian countries in the face of the Protestant Reformation, in unhealthy enthusiasms here and superstitious devotions there, and so on. The treatise on theological criteria sets out to determine certain limits, certain rules or conditions within which the infallibility of the *sensus fidelium* is or is not certainly operative, as it tries to do so also in respect of the Fathers, for they too were sometimes mistaken. . . . [T]he final ecclesiological principles must be looked for in the theology of the missions of Christ and of the Holy Spirit, with their duality and unity. If it be right that the *sensus fidelium* or *sensus catholicus* is a power of adhesion and discernment in the body of the faithful, it is also and conjointly a sense of oneness and fellowship in which an essential element is an obedient attitude towards apostolical authority living in the episcopal body." *Lay People in the Church*, 288–89.

Even though Congar was familiar with the thought of Mannes Koster on the "sense of the faith" and regarding his ecclesiology in general, Congar was more directly influenced by the ideas of Johann Adam Möhler and John Henry Newman, with an occasional nod toward Matthias Joseph Scheeben.[4] Paramount in his approach was the adoption of the threefold offices of Christ that he shares with his church (often referred to as the *tria munera*). Christ is the priest, the prophet, and the king or shepherd in his church, roles that are shared with the ordained and the faithful in general, though in different ways. Congar was familiar with the earlier study of the trilogy of christological offices by the German moral theologian Josef Fuchs, published in 1941.[5] He adopted this framework instead of the then-customary twofold division of ecclesiastical office into two quite separable powers of "orders" and "jurisdiction" as more adequate

---

4. Helpful studies on the thought and influence of Yves Congar include Charles Mac-Donald, *Church and World in the Plan of God: Aspects of History and Eschatology in the Thought of Père Yves Congar OP* (Frankfurt: Peter Lang, 1982); Aidan Nichols, *Yves Congar* (London: Geoffrey Chapman, 1989); Cornelis Th. M. van Vliet, *Communio sacramentalis: das Kirchenverständnis von Yves Congar—genetisch und systematisch betrachtet* (Mainz: Matthias-Grünewald, 1995); André Vauchez, ed., *Cardinal Yves Congar 1904–1995: Actes du colloque réuni à Rome les 3-4 juin 1996* (Paris: Cerf, 1999); Étienne Fouilloux, "Friar Yves, Cardinal Congar, Dominican: Itinerary of a Theologian," *U. S. Catholic Historian* 17 (1999): 63–90; Elizabeth T. Groppe, *Yves Congar's Theology of the Holy Spirit* (New York: Oxford University Press, 2004); and Gabriel Flynn, ed., *Yves Congar: Theologian of the Church* (Louvain: Peeters, 2005). The reader should also consult Congar's notebooks from Vatican II and his memoirs: *Le concile au jour le jour* (Paris: Cerf, 1963); *Le concile au jour le jour. Deuxième session* (Paris: Cerf, 1964); *Le concile au jour le jour. Troisième session* (Paris: Cerf, 1965); *Le concile au jour le jour. Quatrième session* (Paris: Cerf, 1966); *Journal of a Theologian (1946–1956)*, ed. Étienne Fouilloux, trans. Denis Minns (Hindmarsh, SA: ATF Theology, 2015); and *My Journal of the Council*, ed. Éric Mahieu, trans. Mary John Ronayne and Mary Cecily Boulding, E.T. ed. Denis Minns (Collegeville, MN: Liturgical Press, 2012). Finally, various interviews of Congar contain helpful information and insights: Jean Puyo, *Une vie pour la vérité: Jean Puyo interroge le Père Congar* (Paris: Centurion, 1975), and Bernard Lauret, ed., *Fifty Years of Catholic Theology: Conversations with Yves Congar*, trans. John Bowden (Philadelphia, PA: Fortress, 1988).

5. Congar even translated Fuchs's doctoral dissertation *Magisterium, Ministerium, Regimen. Vom Ursprung einer ekklesiologischen Trilogie* (Cologne, 1941) into French as "Origines d'une trilogie ecclésiologique à l'époque rationaliste de la théologie" in *Revue des sciences philosophiques et théologiques* 53 (1969): 185–211.

to understanding office and mission in the church.[6] As we will see in chapter 9, the framework of Christ's three offices was largely incorporated into the documents of Vatican II as well as official postconciliar sources.[7]

In part 2 of *Lay People in the Church*, Congar developed the three offices of Christ and showed how the lay faithful also truly participate in them. It is in the chapter entitled "The Laity and the Church's Prophetical Function" that Congar elaborated on the "sense of the faithful" in particular, and he begins by clearly delineating what he means by prophecy:

> Prophecy is equivalent to magisterium or the teaching function. But the word is wider than this, and therefore less precise: it includes activities of knowledge or expression which do not come under the head of magisterium or teaching. In its widest extension the prophetical function of the Church includes all the work of the Holy Spirit in her whereby, in her present state of pilgrimage . . . she knows God and his purpose of grace, and makes them known to others. Thus understood, the prophetical function includes mystical knowledge or foretelling of the future and prophetical explanation of events in time, as well as teaching in its ordinary sense. In this chapter the rather vague word "prophecy" is taken in its fullest extent . . . so that due attention may be given to the part taken by the laity in the Church's teaching function. That is the heart of the matter where these questions are concerned.[8]

After demarcating the field, Congar indicates how both Old and New Testament teach that the people as a whole are the recipients of God's promises, truth, and revelation, and he concludes:

6. Congar applies Christ's priestly function to the whole church in the chapter entitled "The Laity and the Church's Priestly Function" and Christ's ruling or directing function in the chapter entitled "The Laity and the Church's Kingly Function" in the revised edition of *Lay People in the Church*, 121–233 and 234–70 respectively.

7. The three offices are used in the revised rite of baptism to characterize the dignity of being a Christian. See the prayer for the anointing after baptism: "The God of power and Father of our Lord Jesus Christ has freed you from sin and brought you to new life through water and the Holy Spirit. He now anoints you with the chrism of salvation, so that, united with his people, you may remain forever a member of Christ who is Priest, Prophet, and King." National Conference of Catholic Bishops/International Commission on English in the Liturgy, *The Rites of the Catholic Church*, vol. 1 (Collegeville, MN: Liturgical Press, 1990), 208 [Christian Initiation of Adults] and 388 [Baptism for Children].

8. *Lay People in the Church*, 271.

In many passages of the liturgical, patristic and theological tradition these things are repeated and synthesized: the anointing that makes men [and women] Christians also makes them prophets; all have the Spirit of God within them, and so are not like a flock of silly sheep, whose understanding is all in the shepherd who looks after them. Rather are they all united to their Shepherd through whose Spirit they are endowed with understanding and discernment.[9]

The fact that such a prophetic function on the part of all believers exists in the church is clear in Congar's presentation of the sources of the "sense of the faithful" in history and from his enthusiastic support of it. Just how does Congar understand the notion? How does the "sense of the faithful" fit into his understanding of the church? It is precisely this question that opens up an inquiry into how the "sense of the faithful" functions in Congar's ecclesiology.[10] Let us examine Congar's explanation in *Lay People in the Church* and his subsequent reservations and revisions of this underlying ecclesiology after the council.

---

9. Ibid., 273. The role of the Holy Spirit, the pneumatological element in Congar's theology, should be noted.

10. In his treatment in *Tradition and Traditions*, Congar employs both expressions, the "sense of the faith" and the "sense of the faithful" indiscriminately. He writes:

"Often the Fathers of the council [of Trent] gave their decisions on some such ground as: 'Et hic est sensus Ecclesiae', 'talis est consensus Ecclesiae perpetuus', 'consensus totius Ecclesiae fuit et est', 'communis consensus Ecclesiae est'. Analogous expressions are to be found in contemporary theologians such as Melchior Cano and Martin Perez de Ayala, whose names rightly figure in the history of the treatise on Tradition. The formula 'secundum sensum quem tenuit et tenet Ecclesia' has become a *topos* in conciliar or papal declarations.

"This early evidence makes it clear that tradition does not separate a subjective sense, a kind of instinct of faith, from the objective content; it does not recognize any autonomy in the mystical and subjective instinct for the things of God as opposed to the means God has chosen for his self-revelation to men: revelation, the Church, the doctors and saints.

"The subjective sense, a kind of Catholic instinct where faith is concerned, is of great interest to modern writers who would prefer to call it the *sensus fidelium, sensus fidei,* the sense of faith. These authors have been apt to concentrate on the psychological and subjective aspects of knowledge." *Tradition and Traditions: An Historical Essay and a Theological Essay*, trans. Thomas Rainborough (New York: Macmillan, 1966), 316–17. I have tried to reflect this use of *sensus fidelium* and *sensus fidei* by Congar by employing both expressions in my exposition of his thought.

The framework of the three offices of Christ clearly provides the orga-nizing principle for Congar's presentation of ministries in the church.[11] But which principles act as the most general foundations of his entire ecclesiology? Any organizing principles need to be studied against the adequacy and correctness of the most general ecclesiological principles. A careful reading of *Lay People in the Church* reveals two sets of such general principles, each consisting of two acts that are ordered to one another.

The first of these double principles of ecclesiology for Congar includes his distinction between the "structure of the Church" and the "life of the Church."[12] Structure points to what was given to the church by Christ and his Spirit as constitutive of the church. Structure includes the sacraments, the "deposit of the faith," and the hierarchy. These constitute the church as given by Christ and therefore are inalienable. From the perspective of structure, humankind receives the church as gift and grace; it does not construct it. Ecclesial structure does not come about either by human willing and striv-ing or by human effort and building. But the church cannot exist simply as structure; it demands another principle, that of life. This principle lays equal claim to constituting the church, especially because it assures the accom-plishment of the church's mission and the achievement of its purpose. This vast realm includes the believing person's concrete vocation, the nature and qualities of the church's communities, the variety of theological schools, the liturgies and spiritualities of the church, and many other factors too numer-ous to mention. The following quotation from Congar indicates the nature of each principle considered separately and as mutually ordered to each other.

> We believe the whole question can be clarified by the distinction between structure and life. . . . [D]isasters happen whenever one gratuitously passes from the plane of life to that of structure. By *structure* we under-stand the principles which, because they come from Christ, representing

11. It should now be clear why the modest contributions of Ferdinand Walter and George Phillips, studied above in chapter 2, would become so important for understanding the identity of the Christian and the nature of Christian ministry at a later time. Congar drew on this influence via Josef Fuchs's dissertation.

12. On the distinction, see Cornelis van Vliet, *Communio sacramentalis*, 110–19 ["Die Be-griffe 'Struktur' und 'Leben' der Kirche"], who examines the distinction primarily in Congar's *Vraie et fausse réforme dans l'Église* (1st ed., Paris: Cerf, 1950; 2nd ed., 1967). This distinction is then taken up again and further developed by Congar in his *Lay People in the Church*. Paul Philibert's English translation *True and False Reform in the Church* is a partial translation of the 2nd ed., which unfortunately omits part 3, "The Reformation and Protestantism."

with him and in his name the generative causes of the Church, are the things in her, as her *pars formalis* [the formal element], that constitute men [and women] as Christ's Church. These are essentially the deposit of faith, the deposit of the sacraments of faith and the apostolical powers whereby the one and the other are transmitted. Therein resides the Church's essence. By *life* we understand the activity which men [and women], made Church by the said principles, exercise in order that the Church may fulfil her mission and attain her end, which is, throughout time and space, to make of men [and women] and a reconciled world the community-temple of God.

The Church is constructed hierarchically; the life through which she fulfils her mission presupposes the co-operation of the faithful.[13]

The second set of double reciprocal principles is concerned with the hierarchy and the community, or in other words, the hierarchical and the collegial principle.[14] The second principle builds on that of structure and life, but is more limited in scope. According to this principle, the church is endowed with divine powers that are invested in individuals—bishops and the clergy who assist them. Their power and authority, however, can achieve its goal only with the cooperation and the collaboration of all the faithful in the church. According to this principle, the hierarchy truly needs the lay faithful, and the laity truly enact the church. Moreover, each acts in accordance with its own divinely assigned area of responsibility or competence. The competence of the hierarchy is directed to the church's inner life,[15] that of the lay faithful to the world and secular activity.[16]

13. Ibid., 262. Other expressions of the fundamental ecclesiological principle of structure and life can be found on pages 51, 224–27, 247, 258–59, 262–66, 273, 279, 281, and 328.

14. See van Vliet, *Communio sacramentalis*, 119–34 ["'Hierarchie' und 'Gemeinschaft' als zwei aufeinander bezogene Prinzipien der Kirche"].

15. Congar writes: "There is an institution to the service of the Church by way of appointment. . . . It suffices for us to grasp, as part of the 'datum' that theology has to interpret and 'construct', the truth that there is in the Christian economy another modality, title, source of priestly quality besides those of baptism. There is a ministerial or hierarchical priesthood. . . . The hierarchical priesthood is not simply a function instituted by men to meet the requirements of good order and of the theological competence of ministers; it is a matter of a hierarchical rank which entails 'sacred capacities'. These powers are to consecrate the eucharist, to forgive sins and to minister the sacraments; other powers are joined with these, in respect of teaching and ruling. The divinely instituted hierarchy consists of the episcopate, the presbyterate and the diaconate." *Lay People in the Church*, 147–48.

16. Congar works out the secular vocation of the layperson primarily in the chapter entitled "In the World and Not of the World," where his dependence on Thomas Aquinas's

Nevertheless, according to Congar, there is no dichotomy in this assignment of competences and there are even spheres where the members of one group overlap the area of the other. The church cannot realize its vocation without engaging the world, and yet the church cannot usurp the reason for which the world was created. On the other hand, the world and the laity who are its primary agents cannot come to completion without the church as intermediary. The church and the world are mutually ordered to each other, and yet the church and the world enjoy autonomy in their own spheres and rightly resist unlawful encroachment from each other. Apropos, Congar writes:

> One can speak of an "Adamic function" of creation and a "Christic function" of redemption, provided that the connexion of the first with the second is made clear, and that they are not referred respectively to the laity and the clergy: creational tasks ("Adamic function") are more especially the business of the laity, but their final meaning is in Christ and they do not prevent lay people from having their part in the redemptive function and duties of the Church. . . . In any case, the creational function or vocation of the laity is itself in one sense a function or vocation of the Church, or at the very least in the Church.[17]

Neither sphere is superior to the other, since both are divinely willed, and the incarnation of the Word forestalls any attempt to separate the Church ultimately from the world. This interface of competences precludes a spirit of rivalry between them and instead calls forth a spirit of interdependence and collaboration.

According to this second double principle, therefore, an ordained believer is not removed from the world and from taking responsibility for it, just as the lay believer is not restricted entirely to the world and excluded from meaningful activity in the church. Congar even dedicated

---

defense of the autonomy of the natural order and of the relationship of secondary causes to God as primary cause is clearly stated and explained. Congar writes: "We have learned that though the work of the world is not the last end, neither is it *solely a means*; subordinate to the absolute end, it partakes of the character of means, but also of *intermediate end*, having its *own* value in its order. Accordingly it is appropriate that our commitment to it—in complete subordination to our supreme commitment to the faith—should be real and valid in its order too. We are engaged neither as to sheer means nor as to absolute end, but as to an intermediate end." See *Lay People in the Church*, 400–51, at 421.

17. *Lay People in the Church*, 432.

the lion's share of the chapter entitled "The Laity and the Church's Apostolic Function" to the ecclesial movement known as "Catholic Action" in order to work out these interdependencies and the tensions between them that necessarily result from their overlapping competences.[18] The layperson, then, cannot be excluded from direct activity and responsibility in the church, and should even be invited by the hierarchy to serve there and be welcomed by them. And yet, according to the second double principle, the lay faithful enjoy a true authority in the church that is not, however, based on apostolic competence directly but as shared with those who do enjoy proper apostolic authority. This is true so that the church can fulfill its mission—a mission that cannot be achieved without the lay faithful. The tensions and mutualities that emerge from this discussion of competences point to how difficult and delicate it is to realize their mutual coordination in the concrete life of the church.[19] We tend

---

18. Ibid., 362–99.

19. Congar was a genius when it came to the history of ideas and how they were realized in both secular and ecclesiastical history. He was virtually peerless in his mastery of the literature and his ability to draw the connections between what happened in history and what its significance was in theology and for the faith. He demonstrated this ability in such works as *Vraie et fausse réforme dans l'Église* (1st ed., Paris: Cerf, 1950; rev. ed., 1968); *L'ecclésiologie du haut moyen age: de Saint Grégoire le Grand à la désunion entre Byzance et Rome* (Paris: Cerf, 1968); *L'Église de Saint Augustin à l'époque moderne* (Paris: Cerf, 1970); and countless articles too numerous to list. This ability to relate his vast historical knowledge to theological issues is also characteristic of whole sections of his *Lay People in the Church*. However, when it came to systematically organizing and explaining the underlying ideas, Congar was not always successful. He was not a systematic theologian in the sense of a Thomas Aquinas or his contemporaries Karl Rahner and Bernard Lonergan. He had flashes of insight that would greatly enrich a systematic ecclesiology, but he had difficulty, it seems to me, in bringing these insights to clear and convincing expression. And yet, none of his theological contemporaries could match the extent of his contributions to the teachings of Vatican II. His influence in this sphere was unparalleled, which is not to deny other thinkers at Vatican II, e.g., Gerard Philips, their rightful contributions. I suggest that it was the depth and the detail of his knowledge of the history of the Catholic tradition that endowed him so generously in this regard. But this wealth of ideas also helps to explain the hermeneutical difficulties the postconciliar church has had in arriving at straightforward interpretations of the documents of Vatican II. There is simply too much to order and digest, and the framers of the documents and the bishops who approved them were unable to do so. We in the postconciliar period are left with an unending task of understanding and exposition. A recent outstanding contribution in this regard is Ormond Rush, *The Vision of Vatican II: Its Fundamental Principles* (Collegeville, MN: Liturgical Press, 2019).

to think in binary terms, whereas Congar invites us to think in terms of reciprocity and mutual relations without surrendering the primacy of various competences.

Applied to the notions of the "sense of the faithful," Congar's masterful historical presentation, the creativity of his two double principles of ecclesiology, and his championing of the framework of the three offices of Christ as the best organizing principle for ecclesiology and for the ministry greatly enriched thinking on the "sense of the faithful" in the preconciliar church after the appearance of *Lay People in the Church*.[20] It

---

20. After the council, Congar had second thoughts about his earlier treatment in *Lay People in the Church*. In a talk commemorating the 750th anniversary of the establishment of the Dominican Order in Poland and subsequently published as "Mon cheminement dans la théologie du laïcat et des ministères," he remarked: "In [*Lay People in the Church*] I put a reasoned construction on the data by distributing two titles of participation or two fashions of participating in the priesthood, kingship, and prophetic office of Christ: one title referring to the dignity or quality of existence common to all Christians, the other to the authority, and thus superiority, that characterizes instituted ministers. I now wonder whether this is a happy mode of procedure. . . . The inappropriate element in my procedure of 1953 was perhaps to distinguish too nicely. The risk I ran was to define the ministerial priesthood purely in itself, along a line of thought which extended the Scholasticism of the twelfth and thirteenth centuries. . . . That position is not tenable, neither in consideration of God's actuating power, nor in relation to a necessary pneumatology, nor in the face of the rediscovery of the charism[s] and the variety of ministries whereby God builds up the Church [174–75]." Congar goes on to rethink the hierarchical element in terms of a broader and more fundamental evaluation of ministries in the church: "As to terminology, it is worth noticing that the decisive coupling is not 'priesthood/laity' . . . but rather 'ministries/modes of community service' [176]. . . . It would then be necessary to substitute for the linear scheme a scheme where the community appears as the enveloping reality *within which* the ministries, even the instituted sacramental ministries, are placed as *modes of service* of what the community is called to be and do" [178]. See "Mon cheminement dans la théologie du laïcat et des ministères," *Ministères et communion ecclésiale* (Paris: Cerf, 1971), 9–30, and translated as "My Path-Findings in the Theology of Laity and Ministries," *The Jurist* 32 (1972): 169–88. On Congar's ecclesiological changes of view after Vatican II, see Rémi Chéno, "Les *retractationes* d'Yves Congar sur le rôle de l'Esprit Saint dans les institutions ecclésiales," *Revue des sciences philosophiques et théologiques* 91 (2007): 265–84. It is important to note that Congar does not reject the hierarchical element in his double principle but recasts it in a wider and more satisfactory relation to the communal or collegial element and to the more fundamental element of ministries in the church. A helpful guide to the content and reasoning of Congar's *Lay People in the Church* is Joseph Famerée's *L'ecclésiologie d'Yves Congar avant Vatican II: histoire*

was practically a foregone conclusion that this teaching would appear in some form or other in subsequent theological treatises and eventually in the teachings of Vatican II. Congar's approach introduced the possibility of flexibility and change, as well as the element of historicity into his theology of the church in a way that was hardly encountered elsewhere among Catholic ecclesiologists of the time. Congar's eminent stature during and after the council, and his continuing contributions to the theme of the "sense of the faithful" and other related subjects,[21] help to explain the explosion of literature on the topic after Vatican II.[22]

Congar developed his understanding of the "sense of the faith" from his deep study of and familiarity with the church's tradition and its doctrinal expression. His ideas do not seem to have been directly influenced by the widespread discussion among theologians at the time regarding the doctrine of Mary's bodily assumption into heaven. This was not true in the case of Congar's Redemptorist French compatriot, Clément Dillenschneider.

---

et Église. Analyse et reprise critique (Louvain: Leuven University Press, 1992), 167–218. Pages 204–18 contain helpful critical remarks by Famerée and other ecclesiologists on the limitations of Congar's thought in light of the advances of Vatican II. These pages, too, contain Congar's own admissions of the inadequacies of his ecclesiology before Vatican II and some suggestions for improving and deepening it. Also worthy of attention is A. N. Williams, "Congar's Theology of the Laity," in *Yves Congar*, ed. Gabriel Flynn, 135–59.

21. Congar returned to the subject in a concise but helpful treatment in *Tradition and Traditions*, 314–38 ["The 'Ecclesia' as the Subject of Tradition"]. For Congar's studies on other, though related, subjects, see "A Semantic History of the Term 'Magisterium,'" in *The Magisterium and Morality*, Readings in Moral Theology 3, ed. Charles E. Curran and Richard A. McCormick (New York: Paulist, 1982), 297–313; idem, "A Brief History of the Forms of the Magisterium and Its Relations with Scholars," in ibid., 314–31; idem, "Magisterium, Theologians, the Faithful, and the Faith," *Doctrine and Life* 31 (1981): 548–64; idem, "Reception as an Ecclesiological Reality," in *Election and Consensus in the Church*, Concilium 77, ed. Giuseppe Alberigo and Anton Weiler (New York: Herder and Herder, 1972), 43–68; and idem, "The 'Hierarchy of Truths,'" *Diversity and Communion*, trans. John Bowden (Mystic, CT: Twenty-Third Publications, 1985), 126–33.

22. We will have occasion in chapter 9 to observe Congar's contributions to advancing the "sense of the faithful" during Vatican II. His efforts were usually behind the scenes, as he tried to explain the meaning and import of the teaching to the bishops and to interested audiences, and as he worked on drafts of the texts of the Dogmatic Constitution on the Church and the Dogmatic Constitution on Divine Revelation.

Clément Dillenschneider, CSSR (1890–1969)

Like Francisco Marín-Sola, Clément Dillenschneider was concerned
with the idea of the development of dogma: what is it and what factors
govern and explain it? Moreover, like Mannes Koster, Dillenschneider
was motivated by the development in the area of the modern Catholic
Marian dogmas in particular. They were problematic because they often
lacked a clear foundation in Scripture and the historical sources and because of the divided opinion of theologians regarding them. Nevertheless,
these dogmas were important because their foundation was most clearly
expressed in other sources, such as the liturgical feasts and the devotional life of the church. The theological discussion surrounding Mary's
assumption opened up possible advances in understanding doctrinal
development and the "sense of the faith." By his efforts, Dillenschneider
made important contributions in the fields of the development of dogma,
the understanding of the Marian dogmas, and the role of the "sense of
the faith" in the church.

Born in Dabo, France (Moselle/Lorraine), Dillenschneider taught for
most of his life in the Redemptorist House of Studies in Echternach in
neighboring Luxembourg, until its relocation in Ostwald, Alsace. He
distinguished himself with his many writings on mariological themes,
which led him to investigate further the issue of dogmatic development.
He was an early participant in the Mariological Society of France and was
much sought after as a lecturer in this field. He concentrated on the topics
of the Blessed Virgin's mediatorial role and her bodily assumption into
heaven.[23] In 1954, he published *Le sens de la foi et le progrès dogmatique
du mystère marial* (The Sense of the Faith and the Dogmatic Progress of
the Marian Mystery), a title that clearly indicates his triple interest in the
development of dogma, the special role of the "sense of the faith" in this
evolution, and the growth in the church's understanding of the doctrines

---

23. The sources for the life and the contribution of Dillenschneider are sparse. There
is no entry for him in the 3rd edition of the *Lexikon für Theologie und Kirche* or in the
New Catholic Encyclopedia. However, short biographies and the list of his writings can be
found in the issues of *Ephemerides Mariologicae* 20 (1970): 245–51 (M. Benzerath) and
Marianum 32 (1970): 366–68 (O. Gregorio) in which his death was announced. He was
awarded the medal of a Chevalier de la Légion d'Honneur by his grateful countrymen for
his contributions in spreading French culture and scholarship worldwide.

relating to the Blessed Virgin's role in salvation history.[24] It should be noted at the outset that Dillenschneider's book is no mere summary of the positions of others up to this point but a real advance in the understanding of the "sense of the faith" (*le sens de la foi*).

In the first part of *Le sens de la foi et le progrès dogmatique du mystère marial*, Dillenschneider considers the possibility of a development of dogmas in Catholic theology, the nature of development, and some theories regarding it.[25] In the second part he examines the traces in history of the role of the "sense of the faith" in arriving at the knowledge of Mary's virginity and motherhood, the immaculate conception and Mary's holiness, and her assumption into heaven.[26] It is only in the third part of the book, however, that Dillenschneider elaborates systematically what he means by the "sense of the faith."[27]

Dillenschneider begins auspiciously with a consideration of the role of the Holy Spirit in the church's perception of the faith. The Holy Spirit is indispensable for grasping and elaborating the content of Christian revelation. After showing the error of the former position that the fathers of the church were "inspired" when it came to truths not directly revealed in Scripture, Dillenschneider explains how the Holy Spirit in fact brings the church to a growing perception of the fullness of revelation—by a movement from lesser to greater understanding.[28] All in the

---

24. *Le sens de la foi et le progrès dogmatique du mystère marial*, Bibliotheca Mariana Moderni Aevi Textus et Disquisitiones, no. 2 (Rome: Academia Mariana Internationalis, 1954).

25. *Le sens de la foi*, "La place du sens de la foi dans l'explicitation dogmatique du mystère marial (Partie méthodologique)," 1–115.

26. Ibid., "Les manifestations du sens de la foi dans la Tradition vivante des doctrines mariales évoluées et maintenant définies (Partie historique)," 117–262.

27. Ibid., "Nature et valeur du sens de la foi dans l'explicitation dogmatique du mystère marial (Partie critériologique)," 263–374.

28. *Le sens de la foi*, 281–83. Dillenschneider refers to the article of Gustave Bardy, "L'inspiration des Pères de l'Église," *Recherches de science religieuse* 40 (1952): 7–26 and to Joseph de Ghellinck's study in *Le mouvement théologique du XIIe siècle. Sa préparation lointaine avant et autour Pierre Lombard, ses rapports avec les initiatives des canonistes: études, recherches et documents* (2nd ed.; Bruges: Éditions "De Tempel," 1948), 475–77 for an explanation of the widespread theory that the fathers and theologians of the church up to the twelfth century were divinely "inspired" in the advances they made in understanding and formulating doctrine. According to Bardy, these men spoke of their inspiration by the Holy Spirit in a way analogous to the Spirit's inspiring Scripture.

church are involved in this growth in understanding: the pope and the bishops, theologians, and the ordinary faithful. The result, according to Dillenschneider, is not a new revelation or the perfect formulation of a dogma that was only implicitly taught until it was finally defined. The dogmatic definition of an implicitly revealed truth like Mary's immaculate conception or her assumption remains implicit and so is different from a truth that is explicitly revealed in Scripture.[29] Here is how Dillenschneider expresses his understanding of what might be called second-order Marian dogmas:

> In gradually enlightening the Church regarding the virtual riches of
> a primitive Marian revealed truth, the Holy Spirit does not transform

---

This was especially true of the advances in doctrine at the Councils of Nicaea, Constantinople, Ephesus, and Chalcedon. Since no theory of development was available to them, many bishops, fathers, and theologians saw the hand of the Holy Spirit in leading them to move beyond the literal meaning of Scripture. Joseph Ratzinger brings up this, to us unaccustomed, question in his "On the Interpretation of the Tridentine Decree on Tradition," in *Revelation and Tradition*, Quaestiones Disputatae 17, trans. W. J. O'Hara (New York: Herder and Herder, 1966), 50–68, at 57. Dillenschneider also explains and rejects the theories of later theologians who tried to move beyond the inspiration theory of dogma but who were too quick to see "new revelations" in later dogmas. In particular, Dillenschneider studies Jean Gerson (1363–1423), Anthony of Cordova (†1578), and Paul of Saint Catherine (seventeenth century), theologians who were all too ready to speak in these exaggerated terms. See *Le sens de la foi*, 284–87. It is important to remember that the notion of revelation was hardly developed by theologians at this stage. Its technical meaning only began to emerge under the pressure of the Enlightenment that challenged the necessity of revealed truth in the face of God's magnificent gift of human reason to his creatures. Why would God set limits to human reason and establish two orders of knowledge? The problem would bedevil Catholic theologians until the teaching of Vatican I on the nature and necessity of revelation. The collapse of the availability of the theory of continued inspiration for explaining the church's growth in understanding revealed truth helps explain why theologians began to elaborate the idea of the development of doctrine, an idea that was unheard of up to this point. I will discuss the idea of revelation at greater length in chapter 11. On the development of dogma, see Michael Seewald, *Dogma im Wandel: Wie Glaubenslehren sich entwickeln* (Freiburg: Herder, 2018).

29. Dillenschneider shows this in the case of Francisco Suárez. Though Suárez was to be praised for excluding "new revelations" by bishops and theologians, he still went too far in speaking of the full flowering of an implicitly revealed truth into an explicit one. This goes too far in Dillenschneider's judgment, since an implicit doctrine can never become an explicit one.

these virtual truths directly into explicitly revealed truth for us. He leaves them in the state of being implicitly revealed, even as he makes their content explicit to our understanding. Mary's immaculate conception and her glorious assumption, even after their definition by the magisterium and under the illuminating assistance of the Holy Spirit, remain implicitly revealed truths, even though their content has been infallibly unfolded so that the Church might understand them. After their definition they are authoritatively explicit Marian dogmas. Nevertheless, such dogmas do not become explicitly revealed truth, since an explicitly revealed truth never becomes explicitly revealed by the mere fact of its having been brought to the explicitly conscious level of understanding.[30]

The role of the Holy Spirit throughout the process of revelation and its understanding is clearly stated. It seems to me, too, that Dillenschneider's theory of the development of dogma that is careful to distinguish between explicit and implicit dogmas can be of great ecumenical pertinence.[31]

---

30. "L'Esprit Saint, en éclairant peu à peu l'Église sur les richesses virtuelles au donné marial primitif ne transformera pas, même pour nous simplement, ces virtualités en révélé explicite. Il les laissera dans l'état où elles sont de révélé implicite, mais il en explicitera le contenu à notre entendement. L'Immaculée Conception de Marie et son Assomption glorieuse, même après leur définition par le Magistère sous l'assistance illuminatrice de l'Esprit Saint, resteront du révélé implicite, mais dont le contenu aura été infailliblement désenveloppé à l'intelligence de l'Église. Elles sont désormais des dogmes marials authentiquement explicités; elles ne sont pas devenue pour autant du révélé explicite; car le révélé *explicité* ne devient jamais du fait de son explicitation du révélé *explicite.*" *Le sens de la foi*, 290. My translation.

31. That is why I spoke above of first-order dogmas and second-order dogmas, terms that are perhaps more helpful today than their more scholastically inspired terms "explicit" and "implicit" dogmas. Though Dillenschneider does not speak of a "hierarchy of truths," this teaching of Vatican II is pertinent here. All dogmas are authoritative, but not all have the same importance or weight. Some are more fundamental or central than others that depend upon them for their proper understanding. Viewing the immaculate conception and Mary's assumption as second-order dogmas might help alleviate some of the tension Christians issuing from the Reformation feel vis-à-vis Roman Catholic mariological teaching and practice. On the teaching of a "hierarchy of truths" at Vatican II, see "The Decree on Ecumenism (*Unitatis redintegratio*)," art. 11 in *The Decrees of the Ecumenical Councils*, 2 vols., ed. Norman Tanner (Washington, DC: Georgetown University Press, 1990), 2:914–15. For helpful commentary and explanations of the concept, see George Tavard, "'*Hierarchia veritatum*': A Preliminary Investigation," *Theological Studies* 32

The next step in his argument in defense of the "sense of the faith" is the liturgy and the devotional life of Christians as a privileged area in which the faithful at large express their understanding of Christian revelation. He writes, "Among the factors that account for the growing explicitness of a revealed truth the liturgy occupies a special place."[32] Although this role has been neglected too often by theologians in the past, today there is growing appreciation of the theological axiom that "the law of prayer is the law of belief" (*lex orandi, lex credendi*) and its pertinence to the "sense of the faith." Just what does this axiom purport to say and what is its authority when it comes to determining the truths of the Christian faith? Dillenschneider takes great pains to provide the clarifications needed to avoid misusing the axiom.[33]

(1971): 278–89; Yves Congar, "The 'Hierarchy of Truths,'" *Diversity and Communion*, trans. John Bowden (Mystic, CT: Twenty-Third Publications, 1985), 126–33; Denis Carroll, "*Hierarchia veritatum*: A Theological and Pastoral Insight of the Second Vatican Council," *Irish Theological Quarterly* 44 (1977): 125–33; William Henn, "The Hierarchy of Truths Twenty Years Later," *Theological Studies* 48 (1987): 439–71; idem, "The Hierarchy of Truths and Christian Unity," *Ephemerides theologicae Lovanienses* 66 (1990): 111–42; and Bernd J. Hilberath in *Herders theologischer Kommentar zum Zweiten Vatikanischen Konzil*, 5 vols., ed. Peter Hünermann and Bernd J. Hilberath (Freiburg: Herder, 2005), 3:150–57 [*UR*, art. 11,3].

32. "Parmi les facteurs d'explicitation du donné révélé la liturgie tient une place à part." *Le sens de la foi*, 293.

33. See *Le sens de la foi*, 294–300. Dillenschneider explains how the axiom originated in the continued discussion of the need for God's grace in the years immediately following the death of St. Augustine. In the so-called *Indiculus* of the layman Prosper of Aquitaine (ca. 390–465), the author attempted to refute the assertions of those later Pelagians who largely conceded Augustine's theology of grace except for the very first movements of faith. According to these "semi-Pelagians," men and women are capable of taking the first steps toward saving faith (the *initium fidei*) and only then does God respond with the graces necessary for a lifetime of faith. Among the arguments he cited, Prosper drew on the sacramental practice of the church in support of Augustine's positions. In chapter 8 of the *Indiculus*, Prosper pointed to the prayers of the priest at liturgy as encapsulating the very belief of the church. He writes: "Let us examine the sacred words of the prayers the priests say. Let us examine these sacred words which were handed down from the apostles throughout the world and which are uniformly used in every Catholic church, and thus find in the prayers of the liturgy the confirmation for the law of our faith (*quae ab apostolis tradita in toto mundo atque in omni ecclesia catholica uniformiter celebrantur, ut legem credendi lex statuat supplicandi*)." See *Enchiridion symbolorum, definitionum et declarationum de rebus fidei et morum*, 33rd ed., ed. Henricus Denzinger and Adolfus Schönmetzer (Rome: Herder, 1965), no. 246. English translation from *The Church*

First of all, Dillenschneider points out how the axiom assisted Pius IX and Pius XII in their definitions of Mary's immaculate conception and bodily assumption. In his encyclical *Mediator Dei*, Pius XII pointed to the importance of the liturgy as a source of the faith. In particular, Dillenschneider quotes the following words from the encyclical: "The worship [the Church] offers to God, all good and great . . . is a continuous profession of Catholic faith. . . . The entire liturgy, therefore, has the Catholic faith for its content, inasmuch as it bears public witness to the faith of the Church."[34] Nevertheless, for Dillenschneider the axiom the

_____

Teaches: Documents of the Church in English Translation, trans. John F. Clarkson, SJ, John H. Edwards, SJ, William J. Kelly, SJ, and John J. Welch, SJ (Rockford, IL: Tan Books and Publishers, 1973), 224 [= no. 541]. At its origin, the axiom referred to a specific teaching on the absolute necessity of grace for salvation. However, when the *Indiculus* was later incorporated into the body of the teachings of Pope Celestine I (422–32) as the *Capitula Coelestina*, its teaching gained the authority of a papal teaching and began to be extended to other situations where liturgical and sacramental practice were seen to determine the content of the faith. Prosper's *Indiculus* became so identified with Celestine's *Capitula* that it took the efforts of Maïeul J. Cappuyns, OSB, to reinstate the correct authorship of Prosper. See Cappuyns's "L'Origine des capitula pseudo-célestiniens contre le semi-pélagianisme" in *Revue Bénédictine* 41 (1929): 136–70. The original formulation *legem credendi lex statuat supplicandi* was eventually simplified in the more aphoristic formula *lex orandi, lex credendi*. That the influence of this axiom has only grown since Dillenschneider is exemplified by the role it has played in the emergence of liturgical theology as contrasted with the scholastic theology of the sacraments before Vatican II that concentrated almost exclusively on the issues of their institution by Christ, their number, the matter and form of the sacraments, and their causality. See the valuable discussion by Aidan Kavanagh in *On Liturgical Theology* (New York: Pueblo Publishing, 1984), 91–93, 134–35, and 150; Edward J. Kilmartin, "Theology as Theology of the Liturgy," *Christian Liturgy: Theology and Practice* (Kansas City, MO: Sheed and Ward, 1988), 93–99; and Kevin W. Irwin, "Liturgical Theology" in *The New Dictionary of Sacramental Worship*, ed. Peter E. Fink (Collegeville, MN: Liturgical Press, 1990), 721–33, at 722–23 ["Historical Overview"].

34. *Le sens de la foi*, 297–98, quoting *Mediator Dei*, para. 47. See Claudia Carlen, *The Papal Encyclicals 1939–1958* (Ann Arbor, MI: Pierian Press, 1990), 128. The citation by Dillenschneider is very brief and we should note that he omitted an important idea Pius XII included in the section indicated by the second ellipsis, namely: "In the sacred liturgy we profess the Catholic faith explicitly and openly, not only by the celebration of the mysteries, and by offering the holy sacrifice and administering the sacraments, but also by saying and singing the credo or Symbol of the faith—it is indeed the sign and badge, as it were, of the Christian—along with other texts, and likewise by reading the holy scripture, written under the inspiration of the Holy Spirit." Pius XII appears to stress the role of authoritative written sources proclaimed in the liturgy for a correct understanding of the axiom

"law of prayer is the law of belief" has a determinate content. He speaks of three criteria that determine the meaning and the use of the axiom: the content must be a dogma, the precise object of the liturgical feast must be clear, and it must be universal.[35] What does he mean by these criteria?

The first criterion is the most important because it indicates that a revealed truth must be enshrined in the liturgy that is celebrated. A historical event alone or a long-cherished local or national feast are not adequate to apply the axiom. Dillenschneider gives the example of the feast of Mary's presentation in the temple. Its antiquity and focus of interest do not rest on a truth that belongs to the deposit of Christian revelation and that breaks open and extends that truth to the church at large. The same is true of Marian memorials that are circumscribed by their history, e.g., the Blessed Mother's appearance at Lourdes or Our Lady of the Rosary (October 7).[36] These, and many other examples, might strengthen the faith of Christians but they are not adequate for grounding a revealed truth and so do not measure up to the axiom that "the law of prayer is the law of belief." What is true of a mere historical fact or of a devotional practice does not meet the standard of a criterion of belief.

In a later chapter Dillenschneider probes this criterion more deeply.[37] He explains that a dogmatic truth not explicitly stated in Scripture can nonetheless become a dogma because it is founded on a more basic truth

---

"the law of prayer is the law of belief." Dillenschneider, however, considers the consciously formulated expressions of the faith within the liturgy to be secondary and locates them within the primary horizon of the liturgy in its entirety as the privileged expression of divine mystery. On the inexhaustibly rich notion of mystery, see Philip Gleeson, "Mystery," in *The New Dictionary of Theology*, ed. Joseph A. Komonchak, Mary Collins, and Dermot A. Lane (Wilmington, DE: Michael Glazier, 1987), 688–92.

35. See *Le sens de la foi*, 300–302. Dillenschneider applies these criteria to the dogmas of Mary's immaculate conception and her bodily assumption on 302–5 and 305–16 respectively. Christoph Ohly examines the contribution of Dillenschneider and the importance of these three criteria in particular in his *Sensus Fidei Fidelium: Zur Einordnung des Glaubenssinnes aller Gläubigen in die Communio-Struktur der Kirche im geschichtlichen Spiegel dogmatisch-kanonischer Erkenntnisse und der Aussagen des II. Vaticanum* (St. Ottilien: Eos Verlag, 1999), 145–50.

36. Formerly known as Our Lady of Victory, the liturgical celebration was thought to attest to the intercessory power of prayer to Mary and the power of praying the rosary in particular, which resulted in the victory of Lepanto in 1571.

37. See "Le sens de la foi dans la conscience de l'Église, facteur d'explicitation du donné marial," *Le sens de la foi*, 317–41.

that is in Scripture. Mary's immaculate conception is another statement regarding Mary's place and role in salvation history that is based on the more fundamental truth of Mary as the Mother of God. It renders more explicit the content of what it is for Mary to be the Mother of God, not just in other terms but as a valid dogmatic expression in itself. Yet, in the case of Mary's immaculate conception and her assumption into heaven, these dogmas do not reach the level of explicitness of the revealed truth that grounds them. On the one hand they do not add new content to the deposit of revealed truth, but open up for believers the fuller content of a revealed truth. Here is how Dillenschneider expresses it:

> For the sense of the faithful to have dogmatic character it is enough that their intuitions are related to a truth that is connected with an obvious truth of revelation. And so it suffices that the faithful by their devotion and their lived faith implicitly attest to the fact that the privileges of the immaculate conception and the assumption correspond to the concrete revealed truth of Mary's mission as the worthy Mother of Christ. . . . Under the circumstances their intuitions did not err but were based on a veritable dogmatic foundation.[38]

The second criterion reinforces the first by insisting that the object of prayer and cult must be certain.[39] The magisterium does not define something that does not clearly pertain to the faith, and it might take many centuries of reflection by theologians and successive popes before such clarity is reached, or it might simply never happen. Dillenschneider considers the case of Julian of Eclanum's challenge to Augustine's defense of the need that parents have their infants baptized because of original sin.[40] He also examines Nestorius's tampering with Mary's title as the

---

38. "Mais pour que le sens chrétien ait caractère dogmatique il suffit que ses intuitions portent sur une vérité qui est en connexion avec un donné révélé obvie. Ainsi suffisait-il que les fidèles attestent implicitement par leur dévotion et leur foi vécue que les privilèges de l'Immaculée Conception et de l'Assomption conviennent au donné révélé concret de la mission de Marie comme digne Mère du Christ. . . . Leurs intuitions donc ne s'égaraient pas en l'occurrence; elles s'appuyaient sur un véritable fondement dogmatique." *Le sens de la foi*, 328–29. Note that here Dillenschneider employed the term "le sens chrétien" in place of "le sens des fidèles" as equivalent to it.

39. See ibid., 301.

40. On Julian of Eclanum (c. 385–455), see Vittorino Grossi, *Patrology*, vol. 4: *The Golden Age of Latin Patristic Literature from the Council of Nicea to the Council of Chalcedon*, ed.

Mother of God by substituting the clearer, less problematic title of Mother of Christ for it.[41] Each of these cases can be approached from the deeper theological issues they embody, but according to Dillenschneider the faithful get right to the nub of the doctrine by spontaneously supporting the traditional practice of infant baptism as intrinsically meaningful in the one case and by accepting nothing less than the full title that Mary is the Mother of God on the other. Theological niceties will eventually catch up with what the faithful believe, but in a critical situation of belief, it was the "sense of the faith" that carried the day and spurred the bishops to decide these matters by authoritative teaching.[42]

Finally, the third criterion demands that the feast or "cult" (*cultus*) under consideration be accepted universally.[43] Is the feast limited to one religious order (e.g., the Franciscans following Duns Scotus who defended Mary's immaculate conception as compared to the Dominicans who followed Thomas Aquinas's rejection of the doctrine) or to one nation or geographical area of the church (e.g., Our Lady of Knock, Ireland) or is it celebrated universally? This criterion is met when a feast is extended to the whole church, as Clement XI did in 1708 in the case of Mary's immaculate conception.[44] According to Dillenschneider:

Angelo Di Berardino, trans. Placid Solari (Westminster, MD: Christian Classics, 1986), 487–92 ["Julian of Eclanum"] and Peter Brown, "Julian of Eclanum," *Augustine of Hippo: A Biography* (new ed.; Berkeley, CA: University of California Press, 2000), 383–99.

41. Patriarch of Constantinople, Nestorius (c. 385–451) was condemned at the Council of Ephesus (431). He had preached that Mary was the Mother of Christ (*Christotokos*) and that the title Mother of God (*Theotokos*) was misleading and led to error. Nestorianism, the heresy that in fact divided Christ into two subjects and not just two natures, was named after him. That the condemnation of Nestorius for heretical teaching was entirely justified is now no longer accepted by all scholars of the period. See Manlio Simonetti, "Nestorius—Nestorianism" in *Encyclopedia of the Early Church*, 2 vols., ed. Angelo Di Berardino, trans. Adrian Walford (New York: Oxford University Press, 1992), 2:594.

42. See ibid., 329–31. To cite a more recent example, what is the status of Pope Paul VI's declaration that Mary is the mother of the church? How have the faithful reacted to it? Is it a lively part of the Catholic imagination or consciousness? What theological problems still surround the title? Will the claim ever be substantiated theologically?

43. See ibid., 301 and 331–33.

44. But even in this instance, Clement XI's action extended only to the Latin Rite of the Catholic Church. The feast of Mary's Immaculate Conception was incorporated into the liturgical calendar only of the West where it is obligatory, and even to this day is not included in the calendar of the Eastern Rite churches of the Catholic Church.

The "sense of the faith" of an individual Christian, however holy he or she might be, does not carry any dogmatic weight. . . . The fact that the "sense of the faith" on any given question is manifest among large segments of the Christian people cannot leave the theologian indifferent to their belief. Nevertheless, it cannot serve as a criterion of certitude. . . . On the subject of an implicit revealed truth, as long as it remains limited to a few isolated believers however holy they may be, or even to a notable part of the Church, it cannot function as a sufficient criterion of the revealed character of this truth. Everything changes if the "sense of the faith" becomes universal, when it has become unanimous in the whole Church, among pastors and faithful, and when the entire believing Church is in the grasp of this truth.[45]

In conclusion, it can be said that Dillenschneider's contribution to the acceptance of the "sense of the faith" in the pre-Vatican II church was an important one. Though his contributions were not pioneering like those of Mannes D. Koster, he advanced the acceptance of the concept more broadly in the church (1) by focusing on the role of the Holy Spirit in arriving at a fuller understanding of truth in the church, (2) by situating the "sense of the faith" in the context of the growth or development of dogma, (3) by stating clearly that doctrinal development does not add anything new to the deposit of faith but contributes by offering a better, more explicit expression of an implied truth, (4) by championing the correct understanding and use of the long-held but often neglected theological axiom "the law of prayer is the law of belief," and (5) by presenting the criteria that explained how such doctrinal growth takes place.

After studying the contributions of Francisco Marín-Sola, Mannes D. Koster, Yves Congar, and Clément Dillenschneider, it is now time to examine the role of the "sense of the faith" and how it culminated in Pius XII's definition of Mary's assumption into heaven.

---

45. "Le sens chrétien individuel d'un fidèle, ce dernier fût-il un saint, n'a de soi aucune portée dogmatique. . . . Que si sur une question donnée le "sensus fidei" se manifeste dans de larges couches du peuple chrétien, ce phénomène ne devra sans doute pas laisser le théologien indifférent; tel quel, il ne saurait servir comme critère de certitude. . . . En tout cas, aussi longtemps qu'il ne se manifeste au sujet d'une vérité révélé implicite que chez quelques fidèles isolés, si saints soient-ils, ou même dans une partie notable de l'Église, il ne peut être retenu comme critère suffisant du caractère révélé de cette vérité. Tout change si ce sens s'est universalisé, au point d'être devenu unanime dans l'Église entière, pasteurs et fidèles, et que toute l'Église croyante en est saisie." See ibid., 331–32.

Chapter Eight

The "Sense of the Faith" and the Dogmatic Definition of Mary's Assumption into Heaven

The "sense of the faith" was to play an important role in Pius XII's efforts to define Mary's assumption into heaven, as it had done earlier with Pius IX's definition of Mary's immaculate conception. The fact that twice in recent Catholic history the papal magisterium had drawn on the argument from the belief and witness of all believers, including the ordinary faithful, in pronouncing on a Marian dogma was to count heavily in the theological debate at Vatican II on the necessity, role, and nature of the "sense of the faith." In the years after World War II, there was renewed interest in the "sense of the faith" and considerable theological debate among theologians whether this "sense" justified another Marian definition that was not clearly attested to in Scripture. Should Pius XII issue a definition and under what conditions? This chapter will examine the role of the "sense of the faith" in the most recent Marian dogma. It will study (1) the emergence of the Marian feasts and the role of the liturgy and popular devotion in their development, (2) the theological debate surrounding the definability in the 1940s of Mary's assumption, (3) the definition itself, and (4) its meaning.

Already at the First Vatican Council there were calls for Pius IX to define the dogma of Mary's assumption. The pope resisted these calls to bring to completion his definition of Mary's immaculate conception with another Marian definition.[1] The time was not auspicious politically and Pius IX was not at all certain that the moment was ripe theologically for another definition. The matters surrounding this Marian doctrine demanded further study. Most theologians, for instance, characterized the doctrine as an opinion worthy of respectful acceptance (*pia sententia*) instead of a position close to the deposit of faith (*proxima fidei*), and far from a doctrine clearly of the faith (*de fide*). Under the political and theological circumstances, could the pope realistically proceed posthaste with a definition? Wisely, he opted not to do so.

Still, the requests for the pope to define the assumption poured into the Vatican. Successive popes did not respond positively to these petitions and filed them away in the archives of the Holy Office. In 1942, however, Pius XII (1939–58) acceded to their publication.[2] It is not clear why the pope decided at the height of World War II that the time had come to address the matter. Did Pius XII see a possible Marian definition as an indispensable element in the reconstruction of society on solid Christian foundations after the war and a way to put the affairs of the church back into good order? And why a papal Marian definition and not the teaching of an ecumenical council?[3] The gravity of the situation after the war would certainly have justified a pastoral council. Whatever the reasons, the gesture had the effect of putting the question of Mary's assumption front and center of the church's concerns.

The history of the dogma of Mary's assumption bears certain similarities to that of the immaculate conception that we considered in chapter 3. Both doctrines experienced times of clarity mixed with periods of

---

1. Georg Söll, *Mariologie*, Handbuch der Dogmengeschichte, vol. 3, fascicle 4 (Freiburg: Herder, 1978), 215–33, at 217 ["Die assumptionistischen Bewegungen und die Definition der Himmelaufnahme Mariens 1950"].

2. See Wilhelm Hentrich and Rudolfo Gualtero de Moos, eds., *Petitiones de Assumptione corporea B. V. Mariae in caelum definienda ad Sanctam Sedem delatae: propositae secundum ordinem hierarchicum dogmaticum, geographicum, chronologicum ad consensum ecclesiae manifestandum*, 2 vols. (Vatican City: Typis Polyglottis Vaticanis, 1942).

3. On the question of Pius XII's interest in the possibility of convoking an ecumenical council, see G. Caprile, "Pie XII et un nouveau projet de concile oecuménique," *Documentation catholique* 64 (1967): cols. 49–68.

theological questioning and devotional neglect.[4] Here, too, the liturgical celebration of Mary's glorification preceded and reinforced its eventual doctrinal clarification. The history of the emergence of the Marian feasts is highly instructive in this regard.

The Emergence of the Feast of the Assumption

From the History of the Liturgy

From its very beginning, Christianity was a religion that celebrated its belief that God had intervened definitively in the life and ministry, the death and resurrection of Jesus of Nazareth. Every Sunday was the occasion for Christians to gather to commemorate the Lord's resurrection. The Old Testament Scriptures were proclaimed, Jesus's teachings were recounted, the apostles' teachings were recalled together with a growing body of apostolic letters and writings, and the Eucharist was celebrated—all within an eschatological context of keenly anticipating the Lord's coming again to his people.[5]

In time, the horizons of the liturgy were expanded to include the Lord's life and ministry and focused attention on his incarnation and manifestation to the world. In this way the church came to celebrate the feast of Christmas commemorating Jesus's birth,[6] a reconceived celebration of the Epiphany to include Jesus's birth,[7] and the so-called *Hypapante*

---

4. The detailed study of the assumption by Simon Claude Mimouni, *Dormition et Assomption de Marie: histoire des traditions anciennes*, Théologie historique 98 (Paris: Beauchesne, 1995) is dedicated to this issue. In English, Stephen J. Shoemaker has taken up the issue especially concerning the early apocryphal writings in his *Ancient Traditions of the Virgin Mary's Dormition and Assumption*, Oxford Early Christian Studies (New York: Oxford University Press, 2002) together with his numerous contributions since 2002. See the twenty-five entries in Shoemaker's *Mary in Early Christian Faith and Devotion* (New Haven, CT: Yale University Press, 2016) for these references, 281–82.

5. See Justin Martyr, *Apology* I, 65–66. On the celebration of the Eucharist in the first centuries, see Paul F. Bradshaw, *Eucharistic Origins*, Alcuin Club Collections 80 (London: SPCK, 2004 and [reprint] Eugene, OR: Wipf & Stock, 2012).

6. In Rome at the end of the third century. See Ignazio M. Calabuig, "The Liturgical Cult of Mary in the East and West," in *Handbook of Liturgical Studies*, vol. 5: *Liturgical Time and Space*, ed. Anscar J. Chupungco (Collegeville, MN: Liturgical Press, 2000), 219–97, at 238–44.

7. In Bethlehem in the late fourth century.

or the meeting of Jesus and Simeon at the presentation of Jesus in the temple.[8] In all three memorials Mary, too, was commemorated, but entirely from the perspective of her role in the salvation effected by her son. She played the supporting role of the woman who conceived the savior and gave him to Israel. Gradually, however, Mary's contribution to the incarnation received increased attention. This is the case with the Sunday before Christmas that highlighted Mary's active role in consenting to the conception of her son.[9] Only somewhat later, together with the emerging veneration of the martyrs and other holy men and women, did feasts begin to emerge that focused on Mary herself.[10]

Principal among these feasts was the celebration of Mary as "Mother of God." This title originated years before the Council of Ephesus taught that Mary was indeed the Mother of God, but it assumed even greater impetus after the council.[11] It was first celebrated in Jerusalem on August 15 from

8. In Jerusalem in the late fourth century.

9. In Cappadocia around 375 it was celebrated in December, while in Antioch and Egypt, it was celebrated in January during the fifth century.

10. See Pierre Jounel, "The Veneration of the Saints," in *The Church at Prayer*, vol. 4: *The Liturgy and Time*, ed. Aimé G. Martimort, trans. Matthew J. O'Connell (New ed.; Collegeville, MN: Liturgical Press, 1986), 108–29 and Philippe Rouillard, "The Cult of Saints in the East and West," in *Handbook for Liturgical Studies*, vol. 5: *Liturgical Time and Space*, ed. Anscar J. Chupungco, 299–316.

11. Until recently, the prevailing thesis among historians held that devotion to Mary, and in particular under the title of "Mother of God," emerged shortly before the Council of Ephesus in 431. The council's definition of Mary as the "Mother of God" not only condemned Nestorius's rejection of the title and its claim as an innovation, but it also became the impetus for Marian devotion which had been absent in the church until then. The fifth century, according to this thesis, launched the cultic veneration of Mary, grounded as it now was in the teaching of Ephesus. Today, however, scholars are persuaded that Marian devotion had been present for decades in the church and that Mary as "Mother of God" in particular "was part of the religious landscape of the eastern Mediterranean world at least fifty years before the Council of Ephesus. Thus it is increasingly difficult, if not impossible, to conceive of the Christological deliberations of Ephesus as sealed off from the broader concerns about Mary generated by her nascent cult." See Stephen J. Shoemaker, "The Cult of the Virgin in the Fourth Century: A Fresh Look at Some Old and New Sources," in *The Origins of the Cult of the Virgin Mary*, ed. Chris Maunder (London: Burns and Oates, 2008), 71–87, at 72. Shoemaker has developed his thesis further in his recent *Mary in Early Christian Faith and Devotion* (New Haven, CT: Yale University Press,

the early fifth century.[12] In the sixth century the feast began to be called the "Dormition of Mary" and the "Assumption of Mary."[13] Around 600 AD, the emperor Maurice extended the feast to the empire in the East. In the West, the feast was introduced in Rome in the mid-seventh century under the growing influence of Greek-speaking clergy and congregations there. One of these Greek popes was Sergius I (687–701), who adorned

---

2016). See also Sarah Jane Boss, "The Title Theotokos," in *Mary: the Complete Resource*, ed. S. J. Boss (New York: Oxford University Press, 2007), 50–55.

12. According to Stephen J. Shoemaker, "By the early fifth century, Jerusalem's calendar included an annual commemoration of the Memory of Mary on 15 August." *Mary in Early Christian Faith and Devotion*, 181. Apropos of this feast, Ignazio M. Calabuig has written: "This was, then, a celebration of the divine, virginal, and saving motherhood of Mary. There is nothing that would allow us to think that this was a commemoration of her death or assumption or that it was a feast for the dedication of a church." See "The Liturgical Cult of Mary in the East and West," in *Handbook for Liturgical Studies*, ed. Anscar J. Chupungco, 5:219–97, at 253. In Constantinople, a feast honoring Mary's divine maternity and virginity was celebrated on December 26, years before the arrival of Nestorius in the capital.

13. On the distinctions among the Greek and Latin terms *koimēsis/dormitio* ("dormition"), *metastasis/transitus* ("the passing over"), and *analēpsis/assumptio* ("assumption"), see the discussion of these terms by Simon Claude Mimouni in the "Introduction" to *Dormition et assomption de Marie*, 1–36 at 7–13 ["Le problème de la terminologie: la 'dormition' et 'l'assomption'"] and 13–21 ["Le problème de la doctrine: la 'dormition' et l'assomption'"]. Mimouni has shown how these expressions need to be seen against a hermeneutical grid that includes the following four possibilities: dormition without resurrection, dormition and assumption, the assumption including resurrection, and the assumption without resurrection. Dormition, *transitus*, and assumption can occur separately and independent of each other, but need not necessarily exclude one another. The phrases demand understanding in their own proper context, mainly liturgical. Because this is the case in the oldest documents, there is much room for confusion. According to Mimouni, the origins of belief regarding Mary's final status were the claims and celebrations of her peaceful "falling asleep" or dormition. Soon, however, statements appeared that Mary had been "assumed," but not as claims that competed with her "dormition." The mystery of who Mary was is expressed in either phrase or in both. True to its own spirit, the East has preferred the more open and circumspect "dormition," but not necessarily by denying a real "assumption." In point of fact, the term "assumption" arose in the East, but was eventually co-opted by the West together with the West's emphasis on the corporeal glorification of Mary. In his introduction, Brian E. Daley points out that a fourth term can also be found in the Greek homiletic tradition, *metathesis* or "transferral," a term that Mimouni does not include in his grid. See *On the Dormition of Mary: Early Patristic Homilies*, trans. Brian E. Daley (Crestwood, NY: St. Vladimir's Seminary Press, 1998), 27.

the feast with a procession, a liturgical feature from the East.[14] From that time forward the "Dormition of Mary" was considered the principal Marian feast, and it is of theological interest that this very feast became the point around which Marian doctrine converged.[15] Other feasts honoring Mary soon emerged celebrating first her birth, then her conception by St. Anne, and finally her presentation in the temple.[16]

14. Pope Sergius, whose family was from Antioch, Syria, hailed from Sicily. This fact points to the influence of the liturgy of the East on the Roman Church during the second half of the seventh century and explains the growing Marian devotion in Rome. Eamon Duffy has pointed out the extensive influence of the East in Rome at this time. Greek influence eventually predominated in the upper circles of the Roman Church with the election of Pope Theodore I (642–49) and lasted through the papacy of Zacharias (741–52). With very few exceptions, the popes during this period of approximately a hundred years were Greek-speaking expatriates whose families had settled in Sicily or southern Italy and who had brought with them the liturgical and devotional traditions from Syria and Palestine. Some of the factors that encouraged such emigration to Italy and Sicily included the disruption of Christians caused by the growth of Islam in their native countries and the turmoil in the Eastern church due to the iconoclast controversy that raged from about 725 to 787 (the year of the holding of the seventh ecumenical council, Nicaea II) and again from 814 to 843. See Eamon Duffy, *Saints and Sinners: A History of the Popes* (New Haven, CT: Yale University Press, 1997), 57–68 ["The Byzantine Captivity of the Papacy"].

15. By the 770s the name was changed to the "Assumption of Mary." See *Le sacramentaire grégorien: ses principales formes d'après les plus anciens manuscrits*, vol. 1, ed. Jean Deshusses, Spicilegium Friburgense 12 (Fribourg, CH: Universitätsverlag, 1971), 262. Cited by Pierre Jounel who notes that this title "was already in general use at Rome." See "The Veneration of Mary," in *The Church at Prayer*, ed. Aimé G. Martimort, 4:130–50, at 135.

16. On the history of the emergence of the Marian feasts, René Laurentin has remarked: "Hence two types of celebrations can be distinguished in this period. The first come from the deeper movement of the liturgy and are biblical and Christological. The others grow out of popular devotion and . . . these celebrations will later be extensively refined. In them the mystery of Mary as a person is brought into much bolder relief. . . . The feasts of the first type originated before Ephesus, whereas the others bear the mark of this council and its aftermath. In this development the dynamic element is the angelic salutation. The dogmatic root is Mary's role in the Incarnation and the title *Theotokos* which in its every aspect is the object of untiring meditation and celebration." *A Short Treatise on the Virgin Mary*, trans. Charles Neumann (Washington, NJ: AMI Press, 1991), 82. See further Pierre Jounel, "The Veneration of Mary," in *The Church at Prayer*, ed. Aimé G. Martimort, 4:130–50, and Kilian McDonnell, "The Marian Liturgical Tradition," in *The One Mediator, the Saints, and Mary*, Lutherans and Catholics in Dialogue 8, ed. H. George Anderson, J. Francis Stafford, and Joseph A. Burgess (Minneapolis, MN: Augsburg Fortress, 1992), 177–91.

Various dynamics surrounded the Marian feasts. One factor was the emergence of apocryphal stories about Jesus and eventually, too, about Mary. Here one can point to the influence of the so-called *Protevangelium of James* on the church's growing conviction of Mary's perpetual virginity.[17] The same can be said of the pious legends recounting Mary's death and glorification as she was surrounded by the twelve apostles and choirs of angels.[18] They

17. The original title of this apocryphon was the "Birth of Mary: Revelation of James," but the title *Protevangelium*, the title assigned to the work in the sixteenth century, has prevailed. An English translation by A. J. B. Higgins can be found in *New Testament Apocrypha*, vol. 1: *Gospels and Related Writings*, edited originally by Edgar Hennecke and in an updated edition by Wilhelm Schneemelcher (Philadelphia: Westminster Press, 1963), 374–88. See the introduction by Oscar Cullmann, ibid., 370–74. Another frequently cited source is J. K. Elliott, *The Apocryphal New Testament: A Collection of Apocryphal Christian Literature in an English Translation Based on M. R. James* (Oxford: Clarendon Press, 1993 [reprinted 2009]), 47–57 [introduction, editions, synopses, modern translations, and general bibliography] and 57–67 [text].

18. These are collectively referred to as accounts of "the passage of Mary" or the *transitus Mariae*. R. L. P. Milburn has provided helpful quotations in English from these legends in "The Historical Background of the Doctrine of the Assumption," *Early Christian Interpretations of History* (London: Adam and Charles Black, 1954), 161–92, at 163–71. They have been studied in detail by Antoine Wenger, *Assomption de la T. S. Vierge dans la tradition byzantine du VIe au Xe siècle*, Archives de l'Orient Chrétien 5 (Paris: Institut Français des Études Byzantines, 1955); Édouard Cothenet, "Marie dans les Apocryphes," in *Maria: Études sur la Sainte Vierge*, vol. 6 (1961), ed. Hubert du Manoir (Paris: Beauchesne, 1949–1971), 71–156; and Michel van Esbroeck, "Les textes littéraires sur l'assomption avant le Xe siècle," *Les Actes apocryphes des Apôtres: Christianisme et monde païen* (Geneva: Labor et Fides, 1981), 265–88. For the state of research up to 1983, see the helpful summary by Michael O'Carroll "Assumption Apocrypha," in *Theotokos: A Theological Encyclopedia of the Blessed Virgin Mary*, rev. ed. with Supplement (Wilmington, DE: Michael Glazier, 1983), 58–61, with an extensive bibliography. More recent studies include Stephen J. Shoemaker, *Ancient Traditions of the Virgin Mary's Dormition and Assumption*, Oxford Early Christian Studies (New York: Oxford University Press, 2002); Enrico Norelli, *Marie des apocryphes: enquête sur la mère de Jésus dans le christianisme antique*, Christianismes antiques (Geneva: Labor et Fides, 2009); and Simon Claude Mimouni, *Les traditions anciennes sur la Dormition et l'Assomption de Marie: études littéraires, historiques et doctrinales*, Supplements to *Vigiliae Christianae*, 104 (Leiden: Brill, 2011). The date for the appearance of the earliest *Transitus Mariae* is from the fifth century AD or earlier (A. Wenger) to the second half of the sixth century (S. C. Mimouni). According to Brian E. Daley, in a homily delivered at a synod of bishops in Nisibis, Syria, in 489, the Syrian Jacob of Serug had spoken of Mary's burial on the Mount of Olives, her summoning the patriarchs and prophets to share eternal life with her, and the solemn reception of her

remain historically unreliable sources that nonetheless exercised a powerful influence on the Christian Marian imagination.[19]

There was also the formative role of pastoral preaching in the context of these feasts, sermons that drew out the underlying belief in Mary's assumption in their hearers and in this way refined their faith and advanced the doctrine. In the remainder of this section, I will concentrate on these sermons and their theological contributions, and on the interplay of the basic faith of the people and the deepening of their faith by the piety and rich theology of preachers. It is important to note that neither element taken alone can account for the growth in the belief in Mary's assumption. Both are required in mutual interplay and enrichment.

Theological and Pastoral Reflection

Brian E. Daley has translated these sermons preached by Eastern bishops and monks and studied their contents and approach to an understanding of Mary.[20] The authors he has studied include John of Thessalonica (bishop from ca. 605 to ca. 630) in Greece, Theoteknos of Livias (late sixth to

---

soul by Christ who crowns her as queen. Daley then adds: "It is interesting to note that neither Ps.-Dionysius nor Jacob of Serug suggests that Mary's body shared in her glorification; in Jacob's homily, her body apparently joins those of her ancestors in the realms of the dead, to await resurrection." See "Introduction," *On the Dormition of Mary,* 8–9.

19. The problems created by these stories about Mary's glorification were already anticipated by Bishop Epiphanius of Salamis around 377. In his *Panarion,* he twice commented on the state of ignorance regarding Mary's final fate. Epiphanius envisions three possibilities: Mary died a natural death, Mary suffered a martyr's death (see Luke 2:35 with its reference to the sword that would pierce her heart), or Mary did not die but has been transported to a special place where she awaits her son's Parousia. It is clear, then, that in some circles Mary's final fate was an object of lively inquiry, and this approximately sixty years before Ephesus's definition. See Brian E. Daley, *On the Dormition of Mary: Early Patristic Homilies* (Crestwood, NY: St. Vladimir's Seminary Press, 1998), 5–6 for the references to Epiphanius's *Panarion* and a translation of the pertinent passages. As these early intuitions about Mary's final moments were translated into highly developed accounts of an assumption and glorification, these very details would impede the progress of more sober theological reflection on the mystery. Their intention might have been commendable, but their effect slowed a widespread acceptance of the theological truth they were trying to communicate. That meaning would always have to be fleshed out and separated from any underlying fanciful representations.

20. *On the Dormition of Mary: Early Patristic Homilies,* Popular Patristic Series, no. 18 (Crestwood, NY: St. Vladimir's Seminary Press, 1998).

seventh century) in Palestine, Pseudo-Modestus of Jerusalem (possibly late seventh century), Andrew of Gortyna (660–740) in Crete, Germanus of Constantinople (bishop from 715 to 730), and the monks John of Damascus (ca. 675–753) in Palestine, and Theodore (759–826), abbot of the Studios monastery in Constantinople. The breadth of the geography and the dating of these works from the sixth to the ninth centuries should be noted. All are from the East and we have nothing comparable from Western bishops and theologians of the same period.

At the end of his study of these twelve sermons, Daley drew the following general conclusions. First, while the authors acknowledge that Mary died, was buried, and was raised from the tomb to heavenly glory within a few days of her burial, as the broad ecclesiastical tradition maintained, the texts are characterized by what Daley calls a "cultivated vagueness about the event being celebrated."[21] This accounts for the widespread use of euphemisms employed to speak of the event: dormition or peaceful "falling asleep," her passage into glory as "transferral" or "change of state," a "crossing over" or a "change of dwelling." The homilists "emphasize the mysterious, ineffable character of what Christians discern as Mary's end, and suggest that if the liturgy itself did not call for some attempt at explanation, it might be more reverent, as well as more practicable, to 'choose silence over words.' "[22]

Second, the liturgical context enjoys a certain priority over doctrinal or apologetic issues. The sermons were delivered at the vigil celebrated throughout the night before the feast or at the Mass of the feast, sometimes at sites in Jerusalem that were associated with Mary's life, death, and burial. Daley writes:

> There are clear allusions, too, in these homilies to the ceremonies that, by the eighth century, surrounded the preacher's efforts: to processions, to the veneration of Mary's tomb . . . or of an icon of the scene of her burial, all as part of the imaginative and celebratory process by which the congregation is called to witness the events of Mary's "passage" for itself. . . . The meaning of this liturgically celebrated Mystery, in fact, in the view of several of these preachers, is that it justifies the Church's wider cult of Mary as a living means of access to God.[23]

---

21. "Introduction," *On the Dormition of Mary*, 27.
22. Ibid., 28.
23. Ibid., 29.

Third, though the preachers do sometimes draw on elements of the apocryphal narratives, they exercise caution in employing them. These narrative elements never occupy center stage in the homilies, but provide useful rhetorical support. According to Daley: "None of these homilies makes the simple recounting of the aprocryphal dormition narrative its central focus, but rather treats the story both as the reason and model for the present liturgical celebration and as the starting-point for theological reflection."[24]

Fourth, the sermons serve the primary function of providing a theological deepening of the topic of Mary's death and glorification. In Daley's words: "It is . . . *theological reflection* which is, in various ways, the central project of all these Marian sermons."[25] Pride of place is given to reflecting on the implications of Mary's title of "Mother of God," on the flesh that she gave to her son and shared with him, on her perfect virginity, on her obedience in contrast to Eve's disobedience, on her intercessory role, and not on fixing an authoritative narrative of the events associated with Mary's final days or on determining the exact dogmatic content of the belief that was being celebrated on the feast of Mary's dormition. As Daley wrote:

> The reason is not simply that extraordinary honor is appropriate for one who has played such a central role in the Christian story of salvation—though the appeal to what is "fitting" certainly plays an important role in these preachers' theological argument. At a more profound level, all of them see the reason for Mary's present glorification in the eschatological inclusivity of Christ's Paschal Mystery itself. . . . Mary is the first to experience the full transformation of body and spirit—the "divinization" of what is human—that is promised to everyone who becomes "one body" with [Christ] in faith and baptism. . . . So for every Christian who hopes in Christ, death becomes a "falling-asleep" rather than an experience of terror and demonic subjugation.[26]

Fifth, the highly rhetorical style employed by the homilists of this period is not mere decorative show but serves in its turn the broader purpose of elucidating the meaning of Mary's dormition that had been celebrated in the East now for a century or more. The modest use of nar-

---

24. Ibid., 30.
25. Ibid., 30. Author's italics.
26. Ibid., 31–32.

rative, the deployment of the many tools of rhetoric, the intercalation of hymns, litanies, and praises to Mary in the text, but especially the effort at theological reflection, are engaged to explain why Christians honor Mary with the title of "Mother of God" and with the liturgical celebration of her dormition. According to Daley,

> Far from being Scriptural commentaries, theological tracts or moral exhortations, all of the works we have been discussing are festal pieces, examples of Christian epideictic or "show" oratory, whose whole purpose is to delight and to engage a devout public. . . . Like all *encomia* in earlier classical oratory, the purpose of an ancient hymn was to bestow glory on a divine figure, in the context of a ritual celebration, and to draw the hearers into the attitude of joy, wonder and dependent trust that is at the heart of worship. . . . These homilies are not simply narrations or meditations . . . but appeals to their hearers to participate in the Dormition feast, as a new and culminating manifestation of the glory of the Mother of God.[27]

I submit that these five elements of the sermons on Mary's dormition from the sixth to the eighth centuries help to enlighten the process itself that is referred to as the "sense of the faithful." What is unfolding is a community celebration of a liturgical feast that involves the people and their leaders, be they bishops or abbots. As such it includes stories, hymns, emotional acclamations, processions, long night vigils, communal fasting, public preaching, and sometimes the very geography where the liturgy was being celebrated—all culminating in the Eucharist. Every element nourishes and deepens the faith of the community and moves it over time to a greater appreciation of the feast and a deeper perception of its meaning. Note, however, that it is all of the elements that constitute the "sense of the faith" of Mary's dormition/assumption, not as isolated from each other but as mutually contributing to and enriching the faith of all. No one element, whether the authority of the bishop/abbot, the structure of the liturgy and its constitutive elements, the emotional expressions of the love for Mary and her son, or the emerging awareness of the content of the mystery being celebrated alone constitutes "the sense of the faith." The full conviction of Mary's assumption was not reached with the preaching of these sermons and the celebration of these rites and their

---

27. Ibid., 33–34.

liturgy, but a crucial moment in the elaboration of the church's belief in Mary's fulfillment had been experienced, and as such this experience was destined to increase in the convictions of Christians in East and West.[28] In the case of the West, it would result in a dogmatic definition, while in the East it would become solidified in the liturgy, the theology, and the piety of the church.[29]

The Church of the West

At this point we need to turn our attention to how the process unfolded in the Western church. Here progress was more hesitant since the West lagged behind the East in its reflection on Mary. According to Josef Rupert Geiselmann, "the belief in Mary's bodily assumption into heaven was very widespread in the western Church and this faith rested primarily on the apocryphal narratives of Mary's passing"—a fact that would work against its complete acceptance, especially among certain theologians.[30] One of these theologians was the Benedictine Ambrose Autpert (730–84), the first Latin writer to address Mary's assumption in a fragment of a sermon that has come down to us.[31] Though he is effusive in praising the Virgin Mary and is convinced that she reigns with her son in heaven, he is hesitant to claim that Mary has been assumed bodily into heaven. Such hesitation was to sow the seeds of exaggerated caution among Western thinkers for centuries.[32]

---

28. Speaking about the church in the West, Pierre Jounel summed up this devotion in the following words: "The feast of the Assumption remained the most popular of the feasts celebrated in Mary's honor. Many churches were named after it, and many parishes and religious institutes placed under the patronage of Mary assumed into glory." "The Veneration of Mary," in *The Church at Prayer*, 4:135.

29. The case of Pius XII's declaration of Mary's assumption was founded on a process much like the one I have just described.

30. J. R. Geiselmann, "Die betende Kirche und das Dogma von der leiblichen Aufnahme Mariens in den Himmel," *Geist und Leben* 24 (1951): 356–80, at 369.

31. On Ambrose Autpert, see Michael O'Carroll, "Ambrose Autpert," in *Theotokos*, 22–23 and Luigi Gambero, *Mary in the Middle Ages: The Blessed Virgin Mary in the Thought of Medieval Latin Theologians*, trans. Thomas Buffer (San Francisco: Ignatius Press, 2005), 43–50.

32. See PL 89:1275c–1276d for a fragment of a sermon attributed to Ambrose. In a longer sermon, this time attributed pseudonymously to Augustine, we read: "Many people are indeed disturbed because her body was not found on earth, nor is her corporeal as-

Somewhat later, in a text actually from the ninth-century theologian Paschasius Radbertus of Corbie (785–865), the West's hesitation regarding Mary's bodily assumption was openly expressed in the letter *"Cogitis me."*[33] Radbertus wrote:

> We know neither how, nor when, nor by which holy people that most holy body was taken from that place, nor where it was placed, just as we do not know whether it rose, although some wish to sustain that she, having been resuscitated, was clothed in blessed immortality together with Christ in heaven. . . . The fact is that we do not know what to think of all this. However, we hold that it is best to entrust everything to God, for whom nothing is impossible, rather than wanting to define boldly what we cannot prove.[34]

---

sumption found in catholic history, as it is read in the apocrypha. Besides, neither is it proper for anyone to investigate rashly on the condition of her body who, without doubt, has been raised above the heavens and reigns together with Christ. For men it must be sufficient to know that the Virgin is truly believed to be the Queen of Heaven, because she gave birth to the King of Angels. . . . It is therefore indispensable that man does not reveal, falsely rather than openly, what God wished to remain hidden. Therefore, on the Assumption of the Virgin, all that remains is to uphold the truth of this thought [that] according to the teaching of the Apostle [Paul] we believe that the Virgin was assumed above the angels, 'although not knowing whether in the body, or out of the body (see 2 Corinthians 12:2).'" See Pseudo-Augustine, *Sermo* 208 [PL 39, 2129–34, at 2130]. Translation from Brian K. Reynolds, *Gateway to Heaven: Marian Doctrine and Devotion, Image and Typology in the Patristic and Medieval Periods* (Hyde Park, NY: New City, 2012), 1:311–12. Translation slightly emended.

33. This letter was eventually incorporated into the collection of letters by Jerome. See J.-P. Migne, *Patrologia Latina* 30, cols. 122–42, where it became Jerome's Letter 9, "To Paula and Eustochium, on the Assumption of the Blessed Virgin Mary." Modern authors no longer attribute it to Jerome and so do not include it in their collections and translations of his works. On the identification of Paschasius Radbertus as the true author of *Cogitis me*, see Henri Barré, "La lettre du Ps.-Jérôme sur l'Assomption est-elle antérieure à Paschase Radbert?," *Revue Bénédictine* 68 (1958): 203–26. See also Albert Ripberger, *Der Pseudo-Hieronymus-Brief IX, "Cogitis me": ein erster marianischer Traktat des Mittlealters von Paschasius Radbert*, Spicilegium Friburgense 9 (Fribourg, CH: Universitätsverlag, 1962), 3–45. The text of Paschasius Radbert's (= Pseudo-Jerome's) letter can be found on pages 57–113.

34. See Brian R. Reynolds, *Gateway to Heaven*, 313 for a discussion of Paschasius Radbertus and for the translation.

The effect of these writings by Ambrose Autpert and Paschasius Radbertus on the West's full acceptance of the doctrine of Mary's bodily assumption can hardly be exaggerated. The inclusion of Radbertus's ideas in the readings of the Divine Office had the effect over several centuries of impeding the acceptance of the feast in monastic circles and among the laity who attended these liturgical services and were instructed by the monks.

The West's hesitancy regarding the assumption only began to be reversed with the appearance of another pseudonymous work, this time attributed to Augustine.[35] Since the authority of Augustine was preeminent in the church of the early and late Middle Ages, the dissemination of this document went a long way in dispelling doubt about the doctrine and in promoting its acceptance by monks and nuns, theologians, bishops, and the laity. The champion of the acceptance of Mary's assumption in the West was an anonymous author from the end of the eleventh century![36]

Three points of the anonymous author's argumentation should be noted. First, he never mentions or draws on the apocryphal legends of Mary's assumption into heaven. Clearly, he understands their dubious, distracting, and often contradictory statements about the arrival of all twelve apostles, the hosts of angels in attendance, and Michael the archangel's role in conducting Mary to heaven as a drawback to theologically securing the doctrine. Second, he is forthright in admitting that Mary's assumption cannot rest on the authority of any direct scriptural reference. This inconvenience does not exclude the role of reason (*ratio*), however, in arguing to the doctrine. Reason, properly deployed, carries its own weight (*auctoritas*). Finally, the means that reason employs is an argument from the "fittingness" (*convenientia*) that Mary's divine son should bring her to heaven after her death in order to preserve from decay her body—the body that had conceived him and given birth to him. What could be more fitting?

35. See J.-P. Migne, *Patrologia latina* 40, cols. 1141–48.

36. See the study of Giuseppe Quadrio, *Il trattato "De Assumptione Beatae Mariae Virginis" dello Pseudo-Agostino e il suo influsso nella Teologia Assunzionistica Latina*, Analecta Gregoriana 52 (Rome: Gregorian University Press, 1951) and the review by Karl Rahner, *Zeitschrif für katholische Theologie* 75 (1953): 234–35, who questions Quadrio's early dating of the work [viz., the early part of the tenth century].

The doctrine was far from assured in the West, but it now was on more solid footing and its acceptance progressed little by little.[37] Concretely, the readings from Pseudo-Augustine's *Liber de assumptione beatae Mariae Virginis* (A Treatment of the Assumption of the Blessed Virgin Mary) replaced the skeptical reading from Radbertus in the Divine Office celebrated by monks and monastic women. In this way, liturgical reform positively influenced the acceptance of the doctrine by theologians and the faithful at large. Pope Pius V crowned these efforts with his revisions of the Divine Office (1568) and the Roman Missal (1570) for the celebration of Mary's assumption. While theologians continued to harbor doubts about the status of the assumption as a dogma of Christian revelation in the strict sense, they did not reject outright the propriety of celebrating the feast liturgically or of praying to Mary as glorious queen and intercessor. As for the laity, they continued to grow in their devotion to Mary assumed into heaven, especially under the growing influence of Marian devotions in the seventeenth and eighteenth centuries,[38] and Pius IX's definition of Mary's immaculate conception in 1854.

The Debate of Mary's Assumption

The definition of Mary's immaculate conception did not answer the methodological questions regarding Marian doctrine that theologians continued to pose in the years following 1854. Even before the possibility of a papal definition of Mary's assumption emerged in the 1940s, theologians sought to clarify the object of a dogmatic definition and the conditions for its definition. Can a truth that is not clearly attested in Scripture and the historical sources be defined, and if so, under what conditions? That is why Johannes Ernst of the University of Regensburg challenged the

---

37. For the continuing history of the growth in the acceptance of the doctrine of Mary's assumption, see Martin Jugie, "La doctrine de l'Assomption dans l'Église latine de la fin du IXe siècle à nos jours," *La mort et l'assomption de la Sainte Vierge: Étude historico-doctrinale*, Studi e testi 114 (Vatican City: Biblioteca Apostolica Vaticana, 1944): 360–500, and Brian K. Reynolds, *Gateway to Heaven*, 318–29 [twelfth and thirteenth centuries in the West, including Albert the Great, Thomas Aquinas, and Bonaventure].

38. See René Laurentin, *A Short Treatise on the Virgin Mary*, trans. Charles Neumann (Washington, NJ: AMI Press, 1991), 127–34 ["The Marian Movement of the 17th and 18th Centuries"].

definability of Mary's assumption in a book and in a series of articles from 1924 to 1930.[39]

Two highly respected scholars in particular rehearsed the principal reasons against a definition. Joseph Coppens of the University of Louvain, Belgium, severely criticized the biblical sources that some scholars pointed to as at least implicitly teaching the doctrine.[40] Coppens did not stop at pointing out the scriptural weakness of such arguments, but extended his remarks to include much broader theological difficulties such a definition would entail.[41] In a word, a definition by the pope would include the widest possible claim that the assumption belongs to the apostolic deposit of revealed truth. Does the church have the right to make such a claim in addition to the simple assertion that Mary has been assumed into heaven? Coppens maintained that the church had historically and wisely refrained from a dogmatic definition. He reviewed the arguments submitted by some theologians that the assumption is virtually or formally implied in other dogmas of the church and thereby contained in the deposit of faith. Coppens alerted his readers to the danger in such speculative procedures of compromising the character of theology as a science, a position the church has had to strenuously defend in the light of Enlightenment thought and the development of the specialization of

---

39. See *Die leibliche Himmelfahrt Mariä: historisch-dogmatisch nach ihrer Definierbarkeit beleuchtet* (Regensburg: Verlag Manz, 1921); and idem, "Der pseudo-augustinische Traktat 'de assumptione beatae Mariae' über die leibliche Himmelfahrt der seligsten Jungfrau," *Theologisch-praktische Quartalschrift* 77 (1924): 449–55; idem, "Die leibliche Himmelfahrt Mariä und der Glaube der Kirche," *Theologisch-praktische Quartalschrift* 78 (1925): 34–45 and 260–73; idem, "Über die Definierbarkeit der Lehre von der leibliche Himmelfahrt Mariä noch einmal," *Theologisch-praktische Quartalschrift* 80 (1927): 532–44; idem, "Um die Definierbarkeit der leiblichen Himmelfahrt Mariä," *Bonner-Zeitschrift für Theologie und Seelsorge* 4 (1927): 322–36; and idem, "Neues zur Kontroverse über die Definierbarkeit der Himmelfahrt Mariä," *Bonner-Zeitschrift für Theologie und Seelsorge* 6 (1929): 289–304 and 7 (1930): 16–31.

40. See his "La définibilité de l'Assomption," *Ephemerides theologicae Lovanienses* 23 (1947): 5–35, at 15–20.

41. At the very outset of his article, Coppens makes it clear that he accepts the fact of Mary's assumption and generally accepts the Marian piety of the Catholic Church. As a Catholic, he is no skeptic or opponent of Mary's assumption, and, should it eventually be defined, he would accept the teaching. His principal concern in the article is determining whether it can be defined with methodological rigor from a theological point of view. He thinks not.

the branches of knowledge in the nineteenth and twentieth centuries. Does the church really want to downplay the role of positive theology and historical research? To do so would represent a retreat from the world of facts and instead would take refuge in theological abstractions. If positive theology cannot produce a kernel of historical fact regarding Mary's assumption, is it wise for the church to put trust in theologians' speculations that the doctrine is contained implicitly in other doctrines? What kind of substantiation would a papal definition provide? How secure would the new dogma be?

Next, Berthold Altaner, the highly respected professor of patrology at the University of Würzburg, Germany, issued a detailed three-part article in which he, too, called into question whether Mary's assumption could be defined.[42] Given his area of expertise, Altaner concentrated on the weakness of the argument from history and on an examination of the massive study of the question by Martin Jugie that had appeared in 1944.[43] In the third part of the article, Altaner expressed his grave reservations regarding the argument from the "sense of the faithful," an argument that he characterized as a classic example of the fallacy of *petitio principii*—the logical error by which someone attempts to prove something by assuming the very truth of what he is trying to prove. The procedure is circular reasoning, not a proof. And Altaner was equally brutal in his criticism of the arguments drawn from the appropriateness of Mary's assumption that drew on other Marian dogmas or doctrines based on reason, the so-called arguments for fittingness. However helpful such arguments might be in offering explanations of the faith, they utterly fail to convince when it comes to offering solid grounds that justify a dogmatic definition. No amount of speculative reasoning can establish "the fact of a belief" that cannot be found in Scripture or the early historical sources.

The reservations of Coppens and Altaner were thoughtful and attracted serious scholarly attention. Although they called into question the possibility of a definition of Mary's assumption in principle, they did not prevent the definition.

---

42. See "Zur Frage der Definibilität der Assumptio B. M. V.," *Theologische Revue* 44 (1948): cols. 129–40; *Theologische Revue* 45 (1949): cols. 129–42; and *Theologische Revue* 46 (1950): cols. 5–20.

43. *La mort et l'assomption de la sainte Vierge: Étude historico-doctrinale*. Studi e testi 114 (Vatican City: Biblioteca Apostolica Vaticana, 1944).

The Definition of Mary's Assumption

On May 1, 1946, Pius XII addressed the encyclical *Deiparae Virginis Mariae* to the bishops of the Catholic Church inquiring as to their belief in Mary's assumption as well as that of their clergy and faithful, and whether they wished the doctrine to be defined.[44] In this respect the processes invoked by Pius IX and Pius XII were very similar. Both popes acknowledged the need to consult the church as widely as possible. And yet the processes differed somewhat. As we saw above in chapter 3, Pius IX relied heavily on the decisions of his predecessors, established numerous commissions to study the matter, and consulted the bishops and the ordinary faithful. In this way, the pope invoked legitimate ecclesiastical authority, engaged theological expertise, and sought to discover whether there was consensus on the matter in the church. All in all, a balanced approach.

The process pursued by Pius XII differed in several significant respects. It operated under the pressure of the petitionary process by acceding to the publication of the findings.[45] As scholars have pointed out, these petitions generally cited dubious sources for the definition. They did not add anything new to the long-standing theological discussion and did not clarify the unanswered questions about Mary's assumption. The petitions lacked theological heft.[46] Moreover, official opposition to the definition of the assumption was rather muted compared to a century earlier regarding the immaculate conception.[47] Most of the bishops who opposed the definition did so because they found the historical moment inopportune. At a time when Roman Catholic relations with the churches of the Ref-

44. It appeared first in *Il Monitore Ecclesiastico*, fascicle 7–12 (1946), 97–98 and later in *Acta Apostolicae Sedis* 42 (1950): 782–83. E.T. in *The Papal Encyclicals 1939–1958*, ed. Claudia Carlen (Ann Arbor, MI: Pierian Press, 1990), 109–10.

45. On the petitionary movement, see Martin Jugie, *La mort et l'Assomption de la sainte Vierge: Étude historico-doctrinale* (Vatican City: Biblioteca Apostolica Vaticana, 1944), 488–96 ["Bref aperçu sur le mouvement pétitionniste de la définition et son importance théologique"].

46. See Clément Dillenschneider, *Le sens de la foi et le progrès dogmatique du mystère marial* (Rome: Academia Mariana Internationalis, 1954), 219–20, where Dillenschneider was concerned primarily about the problem of pressure tactics exerted by the petitionary movement.

47. The most enthusiastic support for a definition was among the churches of Italy, Spain and Portugal, the Near East, and Central and South America.

ormation and the Eastern churches were showing signs of improvement, a definition would only further complicate these relations. The response was in general very positive and the pope entrusted the preparation of the draft of the definition to a commission composed of Cardinal Alfredo Ottaviani, prefect of the Holy Office, and nine eminent theologians.[48]

On October 30, 1950, Pius XII convened the College of Cardinals and about seven hundred bishops to present the matter one last time to them before issuing a definition. The definition was set for November 1. The pope could have chosen the feast of the Assumption, or even the Immaculate Conception or some other Marian feast, but he chose the feast of All Saints instead.

The apostolic constitution *Munificentissimus Deus* is a long and cumbersome document.[49] The definition itself is preceded by sixteen pages of mariological sources and history. Although there are no formal divisions in the text, three can easily be discerned. The first twelve paragraphs speak of the intimate connection between Mary's immaculate conception and her ultimate glorification. Mary's assumption flows naturally from her maternity, virginity, and perfect holiness. Just as her beginning is marked by God's favor, so too is the completion of her life marked by the favor of her assumption.[50] The pope mentions the positive results of his efforts to ascertain the belief of the bishops, their clergy, and the faithful regarding Mary's assumption.[51] The second section is the longest and draws on arguments from authority and, in the absence of any directly scriptural reference to the belief, also builds on the fittingness (*convenientia*) of Mary's assumption in the nexus of other Marian doctrines. The authorities include the witness of the liturgy, liturgical books and

---

48. Michael O'Carroll gives the names in "Munificentissimus Deus" in *Theotokos*, 259–60.

49. See *Acta Apostolicae Sedis* 42 (1950): 753–92 and the English translation in *American Ecclesiastical Review* 124 (1951): 1–17.

50. This section speaks of Mary's "privileges" and "prerogatives" eight times. It is clear that the document exemplifies a mariology based on these "privileges." The effect of such a mariology is to distance Mary from the rest of the communion of saints, while many mariologies written after Vatican II have tried to close this gap by resituating Mary in the communion of saints.

51. The pope alludes to the constant stream of petitions requesting a dogmatic definition of Mary's assumption.

sacramentaries; important fathers of the church, especially John of Damascus and Germanus of Constantinople; and the value of a typological use of Scripture they, and other writers, often employed. Finally, there is a long list of doctors of the church and eminent theologians who have espoused the doctrine.[52] It should be noted that *Munificentissimus Deus* nowhere alludes to the *Protoevangelium of James* or to the legendary reports of Mary's death surrounded by the apostles and the transporting of her mortal remains to heavenly glory. The effect of these many witnesses and sources is to show that the "various testimonies, indications, and signs of this common belief of the Church are evident from remote times down through the course of the centuries" (no. 13). The definition, then, is based on cumulative evidence from various sources.[53]

Finally, in the brief third section, we find the definition itself, which is introduced by an important paragraph that situates the dogma in the faith of the whole church. Just as we have seen in so many other situations, the faith is never separated from the believing community.

> The universal Church, within which dwells the Spirit of truth who infallibly directs it towards an ever more perfect knowledge of the revealed truths, has expressed its own belief many times over the course of the centuries, and since the bishops of the entire world have almost unanimously petitioned that the truth of the bodily assumption of the Blessed Virgin Mary into heaven should be defined a dogma of divine and Catholic faith—this truth which is based on the sacred writings, which is thoroughly rooted in the minds of the faithful, which has been approved in ecclesiastical worship from the most remote times, which is completely in harmony with the other revealed truths, and which has been expounded and explained magnificently in the work, the science, and the wisdom of the theologians (no. 41).[54]

52. These include Amadeus of Lausanne, Anthony of Padua, Albert the Great, Thomas Aquinas, Bonaventure, Bernardine of Siena, Robert Bellarmine, Francis de Sales, Alphonsus Liguori, Peter Canisius, and Francisco Suárez.

53. The definition does not rely on theories of development of doctrine or on speculation arrived at from syllogistic arguments. Thereby, it avoided giving approval to theories of the development of doctrine and gave scant comfort to theological schools, usually neoscholastic, that argued from premises that arrived at new doctrines from formal or virtual implication.

54. *AAS* 42 (1950) 789; *American Ecclesiastical Review* 124 (1951): 15–16.

The definition that follows is presented with the full teaching authority of the pope but not without consensus shown in the general acceptance of the doctrine by the bishops, the ordinary faithful, and theologians. The constitution does not employ the phrase the "sense of the faith," but it contains all the elements of this "sense of the faith" as later taught by Vatican II.

Finally, what did Pius XII define and what is not included in the definition? In the formula used for the definition of the dogma, Pius XII taught the following:

> By the authority of our Lord Jesus Christ, of the blessed apostles Peter and Paul, and by our own authority, we proclaim, declare and define as a dogma revealed by God: the Immaculate Mother of God, Mary ever Virgin, when the course of her earthly life was finished, was taken up body and soul into the glory of heaven (no. 44).[55]

The formula of definition is so concise that it is possible to read too much into it or not enough.[56]

First, Mary is identified by pointing to attributes and roles drawn from salvation history recorded in the Scriptures: she is mother and virgin. Other attributes and roles are drawn from the theological tradition regarding her: she is the Immaculate One and the Mother of God. The statement implies an intrinsic relationship of her sinlessness, her virginity, and her divine maternity, but does not spell it out. Second, these attributes and roles are ascribed to Mary of Nazareth who is a historical personage. She can be located in the historical record of Israel and humanity. She is not a mythological figure. Third, as with any other human being, the days of her life were numbered and her life came to its appointed end. The text does not directly answer the controverted question regarding whether Mary was subjected to the normal process of dying. The believer is free

---

55. *AAS* 42 (1950) 791; *American Ecclesiastical* Review 124 (1951): 17.

56. The finest exposition on the teaching of *Munificentissimus Deus* is Liam G. Walsh, "The Definition of the Dogma of the Assumption of Mary into Heavenly Glory," in *Studying Mary: The Virgin Mary in Anglican and Roman Catholic Theology and Devotion: The ARCIC Papers*, ed. Adelbert Denaux and Nicholas Sagovsky (London and New York: T&T Clark, 2007), 165–92. I have learned enormously from Walsh's presentation and cannot do justice to it in so short a résumé. Moreover, the summary I give is in my own words and any limitations are entirely my own.

to identify with Mary who like us died, but the formulation also leaves open the possibility claimed by others that Mary completed her life in another, preternatural way.[57] Fourth, the definition envisions the whole of who Mary is. From an anthropological point of view, in the entirety of who she is humanly speaking ("body and soul"), Mary has passed from time-bound existence to totally fulfilled existence.[58] Fifth, the action by which this is accomplished is in the passive voice: Mary "was assumed." She is not the initiator of the action but the recipient. Her risen son is the implied agent. Mary's assumption is yet another "divine gift." And finally, the condition of her coming to fulfillment is called "heavenly glory." The glory that is spoken of is the realm of the triune God. In the Old and the New Testaments, "glory" indicates the divine.[59] There is no statement about a "place" and its "conditions" called "heaven." The

57. Some theologians claimed that Mary, without the intervention of death, had been glorified immediately, as would be the case for those believers who were living at the end of the world (see 1 Thess. 4:15-17 and 1 Cor. 15:52). This is the position of the so-called immortalists, who claim that Mary was granted the privilege of being spared the act of dying. It should be noted that these theologians do not share the more positive theology of dying developed by Karl Rahner and others. See Rahner, *On the Theology of Death* (New York: Herder and Herder, 1972), which first appeared as a long article in the *Zeitschrift für katholische Theologie* 79 (1957): 1–44.

58. The observations of Liam G. Walsh on the terms "taken up body and soul" in the definition are especially helpful. Walsh carefully examines the meaning of the words "body," "soul," and "spirit" as found in the Scriptures and in philosophy. He explains each concept in itself and in relationship to the others. See "The Definition of the Dogma of the Assumption of Mary into Heavenly Glory," 187–90.

59. The biblical notion glory is prominent and rich in meaning in both Old and New Testaments. Not only is it a quality of the divine, but God's creatures are invited to share in this glory. See any of the standard dictionaries that deal with basic biblical categories, e.g., *Theological Dictionary of the New Testament*, ed. Gerhard Kittel and Gerhard Friedrich, trans. Geoffrey W. Bromiley (Grand Rapids, MI: Wm. B. Eerdmans, 1964), 2:242–55; *Theological Dictionary of the Old Testament*, ed. G. Johannes Botterweck and Helmer Ringgren, trans. John T. Willis, Geoffrey W. Bromiley, and David E. Green (Grand Rapids, MI: Wm. B. Eerdmans, 1978), 3:335–41; *The New International Dictionary of New Testament Theology*, ed. Colin Brown (Grand Rapids, MI: Zondervan, 1976), 2:44–52; *Exegetical Dictionary of the New Testament*, ed. Horst Balz and Gerhard Schneider (Grand Rapids, MI: Wm. B. Eerdmans,1990), 1:344–48; *Encyclopedia of Biblical Theology: The Complete Sacramentum Verbi*, ed. Johannes B. Bauer (New York: Crossroad, 1981) 295–98; and *Dictionary of Biblical Theology*, ed. Xavier Léon-Dufour, rev. ed. (New York: Seabury, 1973), 202–5.

word "heavenly" modifies "glory" and indicates divine transcendence unambiguously. Properly speaking, then, Catholics should not speak of Mary's assumption into heaven, since she is taken up into "glory." It is also inaccurate to speak of her "bodily" or corporal assumption, if it lends credence to an understanding that Mary could be understood in terms of two adequately divisible components, "body" and "soul." Mary's assumption involves all that she is—anthropologically (from the point of view of what human science and a perennial Christian philosophy teach about being human) and eschatologically (from the point of view of the creative and redemptive orders of faith).[60] Finally, nothing is said directly about Mary as "Queen of Heaven" or about any mediatorial role she plays with respect to the salvation wrought by her son or in response to the intercessory prayers of believers. These dimensions are not excluded, of course, but neither are they explicit or implied objects of the definition.[61]

How might a contemporary Catholic explain the meaning of Mary's assumption in light of the complex history of Marian liturgies; the attempts of countless bishops, monks, and theologians to plumb the depths of Marian devotion; the teaching of popes culminating in the definition of 1950; and against the backdrop of the standard Catholic eschatological synthesis of the time?

The Meaning of the Dogma of Mary's Assumption

The current chapter has tried to show that Mary's assumption is, in fact, a dogma of the faith and that the whole church has been involved in

---

60. There is no doubt that behind the terms of the definition stands the Catholic synthesis on eschatological matters that had been developed over the centuries and that were an unquestioned part of the neoscholastic synthesis that reigned in Catholic universities and seminaries. This synthesis was certainly in place in 1950 and officially up until Vatican II, though theologians in France, Belgium, the Netherlands, and Germany were already calling various elements of the synthesis into question. For a straighforward presentation of this synthesis, see Stephen Yates, *Between Death and Resurrection: A Critical Response to Recent Catholic Debate Concerning the Intermediate State* (London: Bloomsbury Academic, 2017).

61. See also the fine treatment by Karl-Heinz Menke, *Fleisch geworden aus Maria: Die Geschichte Israels und der Marienglaube der Kirche* (Regensburg: F. Pustet, 1999), 151–64 ["Der von der Sünde und deren Folgen unberührte Tod Marias"].

discovering and elaborating it. But the task of determining the meaning of the dogma still awaits our attention. Is it possible that the whole church is also involved in discovering its meaning in changed times and circumstances? How might the "sense of the faith" be deployed in the continuing search for the meaning of Mary's assumption for the church?

Theologians have developed their ideas on the meaning of Mary's assumption in three areas. First, they have pointed out the context of doxology in which Pius XII spoke. It should be noted again that in choosing November 1 as the date for issuing his definition the pope established a hermeneutical context for its understanding. The setting of the feast of All Saints immediately situates Mary in the mystery of the communion of the saints. It does not set her above or outside their communion, but in their very midst. Perhaps in an unintended way, this context nonetheless modifies the otherwise dominant tenor of Mary's privileges.

Already in 1977, Joseph Ratzinger developed the insight that the definition was noteworthy by reason of its highly doxological character. He wrote:

> One would have to pay attention to the dogma's historical development and the factors in its formulation. This would show that the decisive driving force behind the declaration was veneration for Mary, that the dogma, so to speak, owes its origin, impetus, and goal more to an act of homage than to its content. . . . This dogma was intended to be an act of veneration, the highest form of Marian praise. What the East achieves in the form of liturgy, hymns, and rites, took place in the West through the form of a dogmatic proclamation, which was intended to be, so to speak, a most solemn form of hymnology. This is how it should be understood. It distinguishes the last two Marian dogmas in a certain respect from the earlier form of ecclesial confessions, even though the doxological element always played a more or less accentuated role.[62]

---

62. *Daughter Zion: Meditations on the Church's Marian Belief*, trans. John M. McDermott (San Francisco: Ignatius Press, 1983 [originally published in German in 1977]), 73. Note the doxological character of Pius XII's words introducing the formula of definition: "For which reason, after we have poured forth prayers of supplication again and again to God, and have called upon the Spirit of Truth, for the glory of Almighty God who has lavished his special affection on the Virgin Mary, for the honor of her Son, the immortal King of the ages and the Victor over sin and death, for the increase of the glory of that same august Mother, and for the joy and exultation of the entire Church; by the authority of Our Lord

Ratzinger would go even further in characterizing the nature of Pius XII's dogma as veneration by adding:

> We can also say that the formula of the assumption makes explicit what veneration presupposes. Every veneration involves the predicate *Sanctus* (*Sancta*) and has as its presupposition life with the Lord; it only has meaning if the object of veneration is alive and has attained the goal. To that extent one could say that the dogma of the Assumption is simply the highest degree of canonization, in which the predicate "saint" is recognized in the most strict sense, i.e., being wholly and undividedly in eschatological fulfillment. Here we see the fundamental biblical context which supports the whole declaration . . . that the gospel itself prophesies and requires veneration for Mary: "Behold, from henceforth all generations will call me blessed" (Lk 1:48).[63]

In reorienting the definition of Mary's assumption in terms of the doxology the church offers to God, Ratzinger has succeeded in adding needed nuance and balance to the meaning of the dogma.[64]

The second point theologians have been at pains to stress includes some rather basic anthropological considerations. These include the inadequacy of understanding death as the separation of the soul from the body. To the extent that such ideas of death presuppose that some "thing" called the "soul" can be separated from some other "thing" called the "body" in the human person, they are philosophically simplistic. They certainly misrepresent Thomas Aquinas's understanding of the

---

Jesus Christ, of the blessed apostles Peter and Paul, and by our own authority, we pronounce, declare, and define it to be a divinely revealed dogma: that the immaculate Mother of God, the ever Virgin Mary, having completed the course of her earthly live, was assumed body and soul into heavenly glory." *American Ecclesiastical Review* 124 (1951): 1–17, at 17.

63. *Daughter Zion*, 74.

64. Angelus Häussling, "Wie Maria verehren? Erwägungen eines Liturgiewissenschaftlers anlässlich einer Feststellung Joseph Ratzingers," in *Theologie und Leben: Festgabe für Georg Söll zum 70. Geburtstag*, ed. Anton Bodem and Alois M. Kothgasser (Rome: LAS, 1983), 231–41, follows Ratzinger's lead. Franz Courth, "Mariens leibliche Verherrlichung: Zu einem Entwurf von J. Ratzinger," *Trierer theologische Zeitschrift* 88 (1979): 34–42, is critical of Ratzinger for downplaying the corporal character of the assumption. Anton Ziegenaus, "Die leibliche Aufnahme Mariens in den Himmel im Spannungsfeld heutiger theologischer Strömungen: die Frage nach der Rezeption des Dogmas," *Forum katholische Theologie* 1 (1985): 1–19, criticizes Ratzinger's doxological interpretation as minimalist.

human person as an underlying unity of two mutually ordered "principles" (*principia*) that constitute the person. From this perspective, the "body" represents the whole of the person from the point of view of how that person expresses herself to the world and to other persons especially. On the other hand, the "soul" represents the whole of the person from the point of view of the world of spirit, which is also an anthropological constant in a Judaeo-Christian understanding of human being. The one person is inextricably material and spiritual, and either principle of this relational duality can express the whole of who the person is as long as the other principle is not denied or ignored. When, therefore, Pius XII declared that Mary "was assumed, body and soul," there can be no intention to divide her into two component "parts" that in principle can be separated from each other. Even after death, the person is indivisibly somatic ("body") and spiritual ("soul" or "spirit"). No modern Catholic theologian has been more insistent on the radically indivisible unity of the human person than Karl Rahner. In numerous contexts, he never wavered from defending this unity.[65] But this unavoidable anthropological teaching has inescapable eschatological implications. And that brings us to the third series of statements as they apply to Mary's assumption.

In an illuminating article on Karl Rahner's understanding of Mary's assumption, the Polish Jesuit Jacek Bolewski carefully examined the stages of development in Rahner's eschatology, in particular in connection with his evolving ideas in mariology.[66] Rahner refined his positions both on Mary and on eschatology over more than thirty years of reflection. He did this in dialogue with a controversial idea developed by others that he at first rejected. Only with time did he come to see how the newer insight presented a key to understanding death, and Mary's death and glorification in particular. What was this revolutionary idea?

---

65. See the articles cited below in footnote 70. Already in 1959, Rahner had provided a clear, though brief, explanation of the relationship of the soul and the body in terms of their unity and their difference as exemplifying the unity in difference between the economies of creation and redemption. See "The Order of Redemption within the Order of Creation," *The Christian Commitment: Essays in Pastoral Theology*, trans. Cecily Hastings (New York: Sheed and Ward, 1963), 38–74, at 44–46.

66. "Das Assumptio-Dogma und seine Bedeutung für die Eschatologie nach Karl Rahner," *Collectanea Theologica* 58 (1988): 89–152.

In 1950, the same year Pius XII declared Mary's assumption, the German-Swiss Catholic theologian Otto Karrer proposed the theory that when a person died he or she also was immediately raised from the dead, which meant the total glorification of the person in the event of dying itself.[67] There is no need for an intermediate state—that is, the state in which a person exists between dying and his or her being glorified with all the saved in the resurrection of the dead. There is no need for a general judgment associated with the end of the world, since the latter occurs for the individual in one's personal particular judgment. There is also no need for a state or condition called "purgatory," since any further final preparation of the person for the beatific vision is also an intrinsic factor of the dying of the saved person. Karrer's thesis also addressed the neuralgic issue that the "spiritual (immortal) soul" was in a state of separation from the "material body," since there was no need for such separation.[68] Karrer reconceived all these eschatological elements of the Catholic understanding of life after death. The act of dying, the

67. The first reference appeared in the issue for November 26, 1950, of the *Neue Züricher Zeitung*, page 6. A second reference appeared as "Rückblick auf die marianische Kontroverse" the following year in the journal *Schweizer Rundschau* 50 (1951): 664. Karrer returned to the topic with "Über unsterbliche Seele und Auferstehung," *Anima* 3 (1953): 332–36. These references are from theologians who cited them at the time. I have not been able to consult them firsthand. On Otto Karrer, see Victor Conzemius, "Otto Karrer (1888–1976): Theological Forerunner of *Aggiornamento*," *The Catholic Historical Review* 75 (1989): 55–72.

68. Rahner explained the relationship of the "separated soul" to matter in *On the Theology of Death*, trans. Charles H. Henkey (New York: Herder and Herder, 1972 [reprint of the 1965 edition]), 16–26 ["Death as the Separation of Body and Soul"]. Rahner pointed out the philosophical and theological difficulties with the traditional understanding of the "separated soul" and tried to obviate them with his theory that with death the "separated soul" does not lose all relationship to the matter of the universe but that it assumes an even wider relationship to matter, his so-called pan-cosmic theory. Though Rahner would eventually abandon this theory, it showed the growing dissatisfaction among the theologians of his day with the theology of the "separated soul" and Rahner's attempt to deal with it creatively. Originally, Rahner developed his theology of death in conjunction with his class notes for his mariology course at the University of Innsbruck, Austria. It was a lengthy excursus for the research he was doing on Mary's assumption and was first published in the journal *Synopsis* 3 (1949): 87–112. Rahner later published an expanded version of the excursus in *Zeitschrift für katholische Theologie* 79 (1957): 1–44. This is the version that became volume 2 of the Quaestiones Disputatae series.

intermediate state, purgatory, and judgment were reimagined as facets of a single though complex event. But Karrer's theory seemed to challenge the privilege Mary enjoyed in her assumption, since now what was said of her could, *mutatis mutandis*, be said of all the saved. What is to be said of this daring theory and has it been received by Catholic theologians?

Rahner read Karrer's theory when it was published but refrained from incorporating it into the mariological ideas he continued to develop. Instead, in lectures and articles he examined the underlying anthropological issues and all the elements of traditional Catholic eschatological teaching at a deeper level.[69] Over the years, most German Catholic theologians came to accept Karrer's suggestions in some form or other.[70] In

---

69. Principal among the studies before and during Vatican II are Rahner's "The Resurrection of the Body," *Theological Investigations*, vol. 2, trans. Karl-H. Kruger (Baltimore, MD: Helicon, 1963), 203–16 (originally published in 1953); "The Life of the Dead," *Theological Investigations*, vol. 4, trans. Kevin Smyth (Baltimore, MD: Helicon, 1966), 347–54 (originally published in 1959); the enormously influential "The Hermeneutics of Eschatological Assertions," ibid., 323–46 (originally published in 1960); and "The Unity of Spirit and Matter in the Christian Understanding of the Faith," *Theological Investigations*, vol. 6, trans. Karl-H. and Boniface Kruger (Baltimore, MD: Helicon, 1969), 153–77 (originally published in 1963). Among the studies after the council are "The Body in the Order of Salvation," *Theological Investigations*, vol. 17, trans. Margaret Kohl (New York: Crossroad, 1981), 71–89 (originally published in 1967); " 'The Intermediate State,' " ibid., 114–24 (originally published in Spanish in 1972 and in German in 1975); "Eschatology," *Foundations of Christian Faith: An Introduction to the Idea of Christianity*, trans. William V. Dych (New York: Crossroad, 1978), 431–47 (originally published in 1976); and "Purgatory," *Theological Investigations*, vol. 19, trans. Edward Quinn (New York: Crossroad, 1983), 181–93 (originally published in 1980).

70. In 1979, the Congregation for the Doctrine of the Faith issued a brief instruction entitled "Letter on Certain Questions concerning Eschatology." It wished "to recall what the Church teaches in the name of Christ, especially concerning what happens between the death of the Christian and the general resurrection," and was clearly a response to the growing movement in theology to rethink death, the intermediate state, and the individual believer's resurrection. In the sixth point, it remarked: "In teaching her doctrine about man's destiny after death, the Church excludes any explanation that would deprive the Assumption of the Virgin Mary of its unique meaning, namely the fact that the bodily glorification of the Virgin is an anticipation of the glorification that is the destiny of all the other elect." See *The Christian Faith in the Doctrinal Documents of the Catholic Church*, ed. J. Neuner and J. Dupuis, rev. ed. (Staten Island, NY: Alba House, 1982), no. 2317 (page 692). Gisbert Greshake's and Gerhard Lohfink's *Naherwartung, Auferstehung, Unsterblichkeit: Untersuchungen zur christlichen Eschatologie* had appeared in 1974 and in 1976 Rahner's *Foundations of Christian Faith* in which he wrote: "The Assumption of

the end, Rahner, too, accepted the theory that the resurrection of the person also coincides with the person's death.[71] Today, the theory of "resurrection in death" has a considerable following among European Catholic theologians.[72]

Two Roman Catholic theologians who have addressed the theory of "resurrection in death" for the past fifty years are Gisbert Greshake and Joseph Ratzinger. Greshake in particular has exerted enormous influence on this question, rallying two generations of German theologians to support some form of "resurrection in death."[73] At every step, however, he has

---

the Blessed Virgin, body and soul, into heaven says nothing else about Mary but what we also profess about ourselves in an article of faith in the Apostles' Creed: the resurrection of the flesh and eternal life" (page 388).

71. In Rahner's *Foundations of Christian Faith: An Introduction to the Idea of Christianity*, trans. William V. Dych (New York: Crossroad, 1978), he wrote: "It is at least a possible opinion in Evangelical Theology that the fulfillment of the single and whole person does not necessarily take place on a temporal axis which is our own, but rather that it takes place for a person with his death and in his own eschatology" (388). See the detailed analysis of Rahner's contribution by Matthias Remenyi, *Auferstehung denken: Anwege, Grenzen und Modelle personaleschatologischer Theoriebildung* (Freiburg: Herder, 2016), 457–503 ["Die Assumptio Mariae und ihre Interpretation durch Karl Rahner"].

72. Some form of "resurrection in death" is the common opinion among German-speaking theologians, with Leo Scheffczyk, Anton Ziegenaus, and Manfred Hauke representing an influential minority opinion. The theory has even gained a following among some French-speaking, Italian, and Spanish theologians, but to a lesser degree than in Germany, Switzerland, and Austria. With a few exceptions, English-speaking theologians in North America, Australia, Great Britain, and Ireland have hesitated to accept the theory. Stephen Yates has written an admirably clear and balanced discussion of the thorny philosophical and theological issues involved in speaking about life after death and the so-called intermediate state. He has carefully described and compared the traditional Catholic position and the more recent theory of "resurrection in death" as espoused by Catholic theologians, noting both the differences between them and the continuing problems that bedevil each position. See *Between Death and Resurrection: A Critical Response to Recent Catholic Debate concerning the Intermediate State* (London: Bloomsbury Academic, 2017).

73. See Greshake and Gerhard Lohfink, *Naherwartung—Auferstehung—Unsterblichkeit: Untersuchungen zur christlichen Eschatologie*, Quaestiones Disputatae 71 (5th ed.; Freiburg: Herder, 1986); idem, with Jacob Kremer, *Resurrectio mortuorum: Zum theologischen Verständnis der leiblichen Auferstehung* (Darmstadt: Wissenschaftliche Buchgesellschaft, 1986); idem, "Auferstehung im Tod. Ein parteiischer Rückblick," *Theologie und Philosophie* 73 (1998): 537–57; and idem, *Leben—stärker als der Tod: Von der christlichen Hoffnung* (Freiburg: Herder, 2008).

been challenged by Ratzinger, who for his part has moved Greshake to a more nuanced position and broadened his own view to include elements of Greshake's theology.[74] Central to the issue has been coming to terms with the nature of the "soul" and its relationship to the "body." Greshake has concentrated on the indispensable "corporality" (*Leiblichkeit*) of the human person and thus the need to avoid isolating the soul as in the standard theory of the separated soul after death. Ratzinger on the other hand has reinterpreted the "soul" in terms of the radical "relatedness" (*Bezogenheit*) of the human person. To be a person is to be in "relation" (*Beziehung*) to God and to others. To Ratzinger, "soul" always bespeaks what he calls "relationality" (*Beziehungsfähigkeit*).

What about the idea of "resurrection"? According to Greshake, resurrection is a single moment that includes the individual person's death and what Scripture and the creeds refer to as the general resurrection at the end of history. To Greshake, both are two moments of a single event, one that coincides with a person's dying and the other an anticipation of eschatological completion for humanity, history, and the cosmos at "the end of time." Ratzinger, however, still defends a distinct salvific event at the end, even while conceding a real resurrection of the person in death as the coming to fruition of the person's dying and rising with Christ in baptism or for non-Christians by some expression of what Christians understand as faith. Ratzinger has never surrendered his defense of the difference and the unity of individual and general eschatology.[75] What,

---

74. Ratzinger developed and refined his position in a series of articles beginning with "Jenseits des Todes," *Internationale katholische Zeitschrift* 1 (1972): 231–44; followed by "Zwischen Tod und Auferstehung," *Internationale katholische Zeitschrift* 9 (1980): 209–23; and in *Dogmatic Theology*, vol. 9: *Eschatology: Death and Eternal Life*, trans. Michael Waldstein (Washington, DC: Catholic University Press, 1988). Ratzinger developed his understanding of the human soul with "Zum Personverständnis in der Theologie," *Dogma und Verkündigung* (Munich: Erich Wewel, 1973), 205–23; in "Zur Theologie des Todes," ibid., 281–94; in "Auferstehung und ewiges Leben," ibid., 301–14; in "Resurrection of the Body. B. Theological," in *Sacramentum Mundi: An Encyclopedia of Theology*, 6 vols., ed. Karl Rahner (New York: Herder and Herder, 1970), 5:340–42; and in "The Immortality of the Soul and the Resurrection of the Dead," *Eschatology: Death and Eternal Life*, 104–61. See Karl-Heinz Menke, *Das unterscheidend Christliche: Beiträge zur Bestimmung seiner Einzigkeit* (Regensburg: F. Pustet, 2015), 492–505.

75. Bernard P. Prusak, too, defends a double resurrection of the saved person in "Bodily Resurrection in Catholic Perspectives," *Theological Studies* 61 (2000): 64–105, at 103–4.

then, are the implications of these two approaches for a Catholic understanding of Mary's assumption?

The answer is, I think, in the interconnections of both Greshake's and Ratzinger's concerns in eschatology, but as applied to Mary. For Greshake, Mary's assumption is her personal fulfillment in the event of her "resurrection in death," just as it is for every saved person. What distinguishes Mary's assumption and resurrection in death is the singularity of who she is in salvation history. Mary is the Mother of the Lord and the personification of the church (the church-in-person), the Lord's ecclesial body.[76] For Greshake, the general resurrection is anticipated for Mary in her dying. His eschatology, then, is inspired by the "fulfilled eschatology" of the Fourth Gospel. For Ratzinger, on the other hand, Mary's assumption is truly identical with her "dying into resurrection," but her death is not coterminous with the general resurrection of the dead. Ratzinger continues to insist on the in-built tension of much of New Testament eschatology (Mark, Matthew, Luke, Paul, Peter), between "already" and "not yet." Nonetheless, for Ratzinger, this "eschatological tension" no longer comes to expression with the help of the theological construct (theologoumenon) of the "separated soul." For Ratzinger, the "soul" now expresses the glorified person's ontology of being-in-relation (*Bezogenheit*) to God and all created reality, and that comes to expression in the glorified person's body or corporality (*Leiblichkeit*).[77]

Terrence P. Ehrman has recently presented the discussion between Greshake and Ratzinger on the understanding of the soul in Catholic theology and on the theory of "resurrection in death" in "Joseph Ratzinger's Debates with Gisbert Greshake: An Argument for the Resurrection of Matter," *Modern Theology* 36 (2020): 239–58. Ehrman's article is an important presentation of the European context of the discussion over the past sixty years. It is to be hoped that Gerhard Lohfink's recent exposition and cogent defense of contemporary German theology of the last things will garner a more appreciative audience among English-speaking readers. See his *Is This All There Is? On Resurrection and Eternal Life*, trans. Linda M. Maloney (Collegeville, MN: Liturgical Press, 2018).

76. See *Maria-Ecclesia. Perspektiven einer marianisch grundierten Theologie und Kirchenpraxis* (Regensburg: F. Pustet, 2014), where Greshake envisions Mary in terms of a theory of "corporate personality." See 421–23 ["Zum Begriff einer 'corporate personality'"] in particular.

77. For some recent literature on the continuing discussion regarding "resurrection in death," see Ulrich Lüke, "Auferstehung—Im Tod? Am jüngsten Tag?" in *Auferstehung der Toten. Ein Hoffnungsentwurf im Blick heutiger Wissenschaften*, ed. Hans Kessler (Darmstadt:

In Rahner, Mary's assumption points to the exemplarity of her dying into glory. Her death confirms her symbolic character because of the uniqueness of her role in the history of salvation. Rahner expressed this role in the following words: "Mary is also the highest and the most radical instance of the realization of salvation, of the fruit of salvation, and of the reception of salvation."[78] The metaphor of her assumption retains its power and meaning according to Rahner, since metaphors and symbols can never be completely displaced by logical categories. The imagination and discursive reason complement one another and both are needed for understanding revelation.[79]

Wissenschaftliche Buchgesellschaft, 2004), 234–51; Josef Wohlmuth, *Mysterium der Verwandlung. Eine Eschatologie aus katholischer Perspektive im Gespräch mit jüdischem Denken der Gegenwart* (Paderborn: F. Schöningh, 2005); Alexander Lahl, *Hoffnung auf ewiges Leben: Entscheidung und Auferstehung im Tod* (Freiburg: Herder, 2009); Thomas Schärtl, "'Vita mutatur, non tollitur'. Zur Metaphysik des Auferstehungsgedankens," in *Worauf es letzlich ankommt. Interdisziplinäre Zugänge zur Eschatologie*, ed. Tobias Kläden, Quaestiones Disputatae 265 (Freiburg: Herder, 2014), 125–49; and Matthias Remenyi, *Auferstehung denken. Anwege, Grenzen und Modelle personaleschatologischer Theoriebildung* (Freiburg: Herder, 2016). Peter Carnley speaks of "Platonizing ideas" on the resurrection of the dead that found their way into Paul's own eschatological thought and formulations. Carnley has examined Middle Platonism with a view to rehabilitating some form of the "immortal soul" (Wis 3:1-9) as acceptable on biblical authority. Carnley opens up new perspectives on New Testament and later eschatology. See "Paul and Stoicism," "The Resurrection of the Body," and "A Little More Platonic Light," in *The Reconstruction of Resurrection Belief* (Eugene, OR: Cascade Books, 2019), 73–99, 242–68, and 269–88, respectively.

78. See *Foundations of Christian Faith*, 387. In a series of sermons delivered in the course of the Marian Year of 1954, Rahner elaborated on this insight as follows: "If Christianity is the radiating influence of one's own grace in unselfish service for the salvation of others, Mary is the most perfect instance of what it means to be a Christian, for it was the salvation of us all, Jesus Christ our Lord, whom she conceived by the consent of her faith and in the physical reality of her divine motherhood. . . . Viewed in this light, Mary is clearly the perfect Christian and an actual typical expression of what redemption itself in its most perfect form actually means." *Mary Mother of the Lord: Theological Meditations*, trans. W. J. O'Hara (London: The Catholic Book Club, 1963), 37. In addition to these two formulations, perhaps Rahner's most appropriate expression can be found in his as yet untranslated "Assumptio-Arbeit" from 1950, where he calls Mary "die am vollkommensten Erlöste"—"the most perfectly redeemed." See *Karl Rahner Sämtliche Werke*, vol. 9, ed. Regina Pacis Meyer, 367.

79. As important as it was for Rahner to critically rethink the many ideas found in the Catholic understanding of eschatology, the reader today must also heed Rahner's equally important warning that Christian eschatology is best presented in the guise of the symbols in which it comes to expression. Contemporary eschatological theology challenges us to

Other theologians have pointed in the same direction as Rahner. Otto Semmelroth spoke of Mary as the archetype of the church, where church stands for the community of all the redeemed of the whole of history.[80]

---

rethink the content of the symbols, but in the end we must always return to them and employ them with a kind of learned naiveté. In his classic contribution, Rahner wrote: "And here of course one will not be so naïve as to think that the thing had once been thought of without images but that this lofty concept had then been clothed in 'imagery' for the sake of the weaker brethren. Thought is always image as well, because there is no concept without imagination. . . . It is never a matter of aiming at a language devoid of imagery and hence when dealing with eschatological assertions of trying to rid oneself of the picturesque diction to reach a sphere where the thing itself appears as it is in itself in its pure objectivity: there is no way of discarding imagery, the indirect allusion, the mere convergence of diverse elements." See "The Hermeneutics of Eschatological Assertions," *Theological Investigations*, trans. Kevin Smyth (Baltimore, MD: Helicon Press, 1966), 4:323–46, at 344. There is a power of expression in metaphors and symbols that cannot be completely captured in purely logical or abstract terms. The exclusive use of such terms can be unsatisfactory without being complemented and challenged by the nuances and connotations that only symbolic language can supply. There is no reason to banish from eschatology all references to such images as the end of the world or the Parousia of Christ. In this way, too, Mary's assumption is a powerful symbol of what Christians hope for all humankind.

80. See *Mary, Archetype of the Church*, trans. Maria von Eroes and John Devlin (New York: Sheed and Ward, 1963). Neither Semmelroth nor Greshake mention that early in the twelfth century, Francis of Assisi, in his "Salutation of the Blessed Virgin Mary," wrote: "Hail, O Lady, Holy Queen, Mary, holy Mother of God, *who are the Virgin made Church*, chosen by the most Holy Father in heaven whom he consecrated with his most holy beloved Son and with the Holy Spirit the Paraclete, in whom there was and is all fullness of grace and every good. (Ave Domina, sancta Regina, sancta Dei Genetrix Maria, *quae es virgo ecclesia facta* et electa a sanctissimo Patre de caelo, quam consecravit cum sanctissimo dilecto Filio suo et Spiritu Sancto Paraclito, in qua fuit et est omnis plenitudo gratiae et omne bonum.)" See *Francis of Assisi: Early Documents*, vol. 1: *The Saint*, ed. Regis J. Armstrong, J. A. Wayne Hellmann, and William J. Short (New York: New City Press, 1999), 163, and *Opuscula Sancti Patris Francisci Assiensis*, ed. Cajetan Esser (Grottaferrata [Roma]: Ad Claras Aquas, 1978), 300. Francis was not a theologian, so where did this insight about Mary as the "Virgin made Church" come from? He does not say that Mary is a type of the church (as St. Ambrose did before him) but that the Virgin Mary has "become (*facta*) Church." What does he mean by this bold claim? Did Francis intuit the connection between the message of Christ speaking to him from the cross of San Damiano, "Repair the Church" and the person of the Virgin Mary? Does Francis's profound sense of the church and his devotion to Mary explain the connection he drew between Mary and the church? Was it an expression of a theology of the heart rather than a product of theological reasoning? Was it Francis's "sense of the faith"? Or was the claim characteristic of popular Marian piety of the time, at least in certain circles? At

Donal Flanagan sought to highlight Mary's assumption as the "type" (*typos*) of the glorification of the redeemed humanity of the deceased and thereby reintegrate the assumption into Catholic eschatology.[81] Many contemporary theologians build on this ecclesial insight and portray Mary as the perfect disciple of her son, the only Savior of humankind.[82] In article 62 of *Lumen Gentium* Vatican II acknowledged the titles of Mary as "advocate, benefactress, helper and mediatrix,"[83] but hesitated to call Mary outright the "Mother of the Church." The bishops feared that the title might be misunderstood as separating Mary from the other members of the church of which she is the preeminent one.[84] Finally, as we saw above,

---

any rate, the passage deserved to be included in the references to chapter 8, "The Blessed Virgin Mary, Mother of God, in the Mystery of Christ and the Church," of the Dogmatic Constitution on the Church of Vatican II, but those who drafted the text seem not to have been aware of its existence.

81. See "Eschatology and the Assumption," in *The Problem of Eschatology*, Concilium, vol. 41, ed. Edward Schillebeeckx and Boniface Willems (New York: Paulist Press, 1969): 135–46.

82. Typical of this literature is Patrick J. Beardsley, "Mary the Perfect Disciple: A Paradigm for Mariology," *Theological Studies* 41 (1980): 461–504; Brian E. Daley, "Woman of Many Names: Mary in Orthodox and Catholic Theology," *Theological Studies* 71 (2010): 846–69; and Elizabeth A. Johnson, *Truly Our Sister: A Theology of Mary in the Communion of Saints* (New York: Continuum, 2003).

83. Because Popes Leo XIII, Pius X, Pius XI, and Pius XII had employed these designations for Mary, the bishops at Vatican II agreed to apply them to Mary, not as strictly dogmatic formulations but as expressions of the deeply Marian convictions of the faithful.

84. See The Dogmatic Constitution on the Church, numbers 60–65 ["The Blessed Virgin and the Church"]. The discussions at Vatican II on whether Mary should be treated in a separate document or as a chapter in the Dogmatic Constitution on the Church were among the most acerbic at the council. In the end, a scant majority of bishops voted to speak of Mary in terms of the mystery of the church. The vote on October 29, 1963, was 1,114 for incorporation in the schema on the church and 1,074 for two independent schemas. Outside the sessions in St. Peter's, the fallout was sometimes bitter and recriminatory. See Alberto Melloni, in *History of Vatican II*, vol. 3: *The Mature Council, Second Period and Intersession, September 1963–September 1964*, ed. Giuseppe Alberigo and Joseph A. Komonchak (Maryknoll, NY: Orbis, 2000), 95–98 ["The Marian Question"]. On the discussion surrounding the title of Mary, Mother of the Church, see Evangelista Vilanova, ibid., 367–72 ["The Text on the Blessed Virgin"] and 425–28 ["The Chapter on the Blessed Virgin"] and Joseph A. Komonchak, *History of Vatican II*, vol. 4: *Church as Communion, Third Period and Intersession, September 1964–September 1965*, ed. Giuseppe Alberigo and Joseph A. Komonchak (Maryknoll, NY: Orbis, 2003), 52–62 ["Chapter VIII"] and Luis Antonio G. Tagle, ibid., 446–48 ["The Declaration of Mary as Mother of the Church"].

Gisbert Greshake has recently proposed Mary as the human embodiment of the church as the community of the saved. Do these insights, derived from the past seventy years, diminish the church's veneration for Mary or overshadow her indispensable role in the history of salvation? Many in the Catholic tradition do not think so.

What, then, is the meaning of Mary's assumption? First, the doxological definition does not describe the circumstances of Mary's dying.[85] The dogma does claim, however, that Mary has been raised to glory as a sign of her participation in the resurrection of her son. It does not insist on the exact identity of Mary's earthly or physical corporeal elements but claims that she participates fully in the glorified state of the redeemed. According to Paul, the glorified body is characterized by identity in difference. The glorified person now participates in all her human and personal dimensions in the glorified existence of the risen Lord.[86] As such, Mary's assumption can also be understood as the sign of our glorification with the risen Christ in our own deaths, of the place of creation in God's plan for the universe, and of the hope that expresses this belief and sustains a truly human life for all. Mary's assumption celebrates the victory of her son's resurrection and of the church's claim that humankind is called to

---

85. This is why the tradition of the church, beginning with the critical observations of Epiphanius of Salamis late in the fourth century, has not encouraged impertinent curiosity regarding any empirical details surrounding Mary's death and glorification. According to Epiphanius: "If anyone holds that we are mistaken, let him simply follow the indications of Scripture, in which is found no mention of Mary's death, whether she died or did not die, whether she was buried or was not buried. . . . As far as I am concerned, I dare not speak out, but I maintain a meditative silence. . . . I do not say that she remained untouched by death, nor can I confirm whether she died. In fact, Scripture has remained above the human mind and has left this point in uncertainty." *Panarion* 78, 11, quoted by Reynolds, *Gateway to Heaven*, 1:298. Mary's assumption is neither pure legend nor unadulterated history. It reveals what really happened to Mary to someone who has the "eyes" to see its truth.

86. This is why Paul writes: "How are the dead raised? With what kind of body will they come back? . . . It is sown corruptible; it is raised incorruptible. It is sown dishonorable; it is raised glorious. It is sown weak; it is raised powerful. It is sown a natural body; it is raised a spiritual body. If there is a natural body, there is also a spiritual one. . . . For that which is corruptible must clothe itself with incorruptibility, and that which is mortal must clothe itself with immortality. . . . Thanks be to God who gives us the victory through our Lord Jesus Christ" (1 Cor 15:35, 42-44, 53, 57). See Pierre Benoit, "Resurrection: At the End of Time or Immediately after Death?" in *Immortality and Resurrection*, Concilium 60, ed. Pierre Benoît and Roland Murphy (New York: Herder and Herder, 1970), 103–14.

participate fully in this mystery.[87] Mary's assumption unmasks the lie that life is meaningless and that the powers of destruction will ultimately overwhelm humankind. It gives us the confidence to accept all the dimensions of our humanity and to face death with serene acceptance instead of defiant resistance. It points to reason and meaning as the values that govern human life and the cosmos in the face of all efforts to enthrone brute power, violence, and absurdity. It indicates the victory of God's justice over our efforts to thwart it, and it points to loving mercy as the power that governs the universe. Because we can say without fear of contradiction that all this is true of Mary, we can say that it is true of all the saved.[88]

A Continuing Task

Seventy years after its definition, the terms for understanding the dogma of Mary's assumption have certainly changed, and the case can even be made that the dogma has been greatly enriched because of the advances in theological reflection on eschatology. What has been the role of the "sense of the faith" in this ongoing process?

Today, to participate in the reformed Rite of Christian Burial (formerly called a Funeral Mass or a Requiem Mass) is to sense that a profound change in religious sensibility has occurred. The prayers in the liturgy

---

87. *Munificentissimus Deus* attempts to express such goals when, shortly before the formal definition, it states: "And so we may hope that those who meditate upon the glorious example Mary offers us may be more and more convinced of the value of a human life entirely devoted to carrying out the heavenly Father's will and to bringing good to others. Thus, while the illusory teachings of materialism and the corruption of morals that follows from these teachings threaten to extinguish the light of virtue and to ruin the lives of men by exciting discord among them, in this magnificent way all may see clearly to what a lofty goal our bodies and souls are destined. Finally it is our hope that belief in Mary's bodily assumption into heaven will make our belief in our own resurrection stronger and render it more effective." *American Ecclesiastical Review* 124 (1951): 16.

88. The theology of the assumption developed here does not concentrate on its character as a "privilege" of Mary, singling her out from the faithful and from all the redeemed. It understands language of Marian "privileges" as signaling the church's great love for Mary, but also as a linguistic expression that must not be used to separate Mary from the throng of those redeemed by her son.

exhibit new accents.[89] In general, they address the deceased with personal terms such as our "brother" and "sister."[90] Some still speak of a future "day of resurrection," but others leave open the possibility of the deceased already receiving "the fullness of eternal joy" and entering into "the kingdom of [the Lord]." Others speak of sharing "in the wondrous victory of Christ" and of receiving "the joys of eternal happiness." Less preoccupied with the sins of the departed and their residue in the deceased person and in society, the positive tone of these prayers fosters a more open view about the fate of the deceased. As a result, the ordinary Catholic today thinks and speaks more hopefully about the fate of the deceased person. And yet, if you asked that same Catholic about details of the resurrection of the dead, or the last judgment, or the end of the world, or the state of purgatory, he or she would probably be unable to offer much insight or communicate a sense of certainty on these questions.

There is a serious gap between the understanding of theologians and that of the ordinary faithful on the eschatological articles of the faith. The effort to communicate newer insights regarding eschatology and the dogma of Mary's assumption is hardly evident in the Catholic Church. Nor do priests and deacons incorporate the newer insights in their preaching, even though some hear of them at today's theological faculties.[91] The ordinary process governing the "sense of the faith"—namely, the active collaboration of theologians and educators, bishops and their clergy, and the ordinary faithful—is largely neglected today. But ignoring the task can only lead to problems in this area, and that is dangerous.[92]

---

89. See *The Roman Missal*, English translation according to the Amended Third Latin Typical Edition (Vatican City: Libreria Editrice Vaticana, 2008), International Commission on English in the Liturgy (2010).

90. Unfortunately, the misleading reference to "soul" is used in other prayers.

91. Dermot A. Lane's informative and balanced treatment in *Keeping Hope Alive: Stirrings in Christian Theology* (New York: Paulist Press, 1996) has been available for a quarter of a century already, but seems not to have made the transition from the classroom to the pulpit.

92. Humans are rightly concerned about life after death and the fate of humanity and the universe, and it is precisely here where courageous restraint is called for. The language of eschatology is governed by hope. Its language should be modest and able to cope with ambiguity. It employs symbols and cannot be understood in a crassly literal way. Eschatological language is suggestive and thrives on religious metaphors. It is not omniscient but is deeply religious and not superficially curious. For helpful reflection on these difficult

The effort of Pope Francis to engage the "sense of the faithful" needs to include the church's eschatology. Though eschatology is often considered an esoteric area of theology, it is really an area of the pastoral ministry that for Catholics constantly intersects with human life and the destiny of the species, as well as with the practice of venerating the saints, and Mary above all.[93] Continued reflection, in the spirit of the "sense of the faith," on the doctrine of Mary's assumption and its connection with Christian eschatology can only be a blessing in the church and for the process of evangelization.[94] The "sense of the faith" on these important but elusive eschatological issues is an inescapable imperative of the present and the future. The teaching of Vatican II, which we will examine in detail below, not only explains the truth of past doctrines and practices, it also points the way to the importance of the "sense of the faith" here and now in the church.[95] The understanding of Mary's assumption is far from finished.

---

themes, see Emmanuel Falque, *The Metamorphosis of Finitude: An Essay on Birth and Resurrection*, trans. George Hughes (New York: Fordham University Press, 2012), and *The Guide to Gethsemane: Anxiety, Suffering, Death*, trans. George Hughes (New York: Fordham University Press, 2019).

93. To ignore these issues or relegate them to pastoral insignificance can only lead to the strange aberrations that often result in human religious behavior, such as fascination with the occult, the emergence of New Age spiritual practices, flirtation with heterodox ideas of reincarnation and the transmigration of souls, consulting mediums, among others. Lohfink addresses these concerns in "Part One: What People Think," *Is This All There Is?*, 1–56.

94. This is the reason I have gone into this topic at such length and with attention to the details and nuances of Mary's assumption and its intimate connection with the church's eschatological teaching. This theological and doctrinal information simply must be shared pastorally with the contemporary church at large in order to more fruitfully engage the "sense of the faithful" and find our way to an eschatology that truly speaks to humankind's longing for the meaning of the whole.

95. After examining how the Catholic Church has changed certain long-accepted traditions, including the social practice of slavery, restricting people's freedom to practice their religion in accord with their consciences, the absolute necessity of baptism for salvation, including the baptism of infants, and until recently the Church's toleration of capital punishment, Francis A. Sullivan has forcefully pointed out the continuing need of the "sense of the faith" in the life of the Church to address other issues that have not been adequately posed and answered, e.g., the wisdom of continuing to insist on clerical celibacy in the Roman Catholic Church. See his "Catholic Tradition and Traditions," in *The Crisis of Authority in Catholic Modernity*, ed. Michael J. Lacey and Francis Oakley (New York: Oxford University Press, 2011) 113-32, especially 131-32.

Chapter Nine

The "Sense of the Faith" and Vatican II

W hen Pope John XXIII called for a new ecumenical council on January 25, 1959, the "sense of the faith" was an ambiguous teaching in Roman Catholic theology. The fact that two popes had relied on something like a "sense of the faithful" for their Marian definitions could not be simply dismissed, however. In fact, in a series of articles published during Vatican II, the mariologist Tommaso M. Bartolomei accepted the role of the "sense of the faith" in the church's increased awareness of the contents of revelation. He defended the use of the "sense of the faith" in the recent definitions of Mary's immaculate conception and assumption. However, upon closer examination, Bartolomei understood the "sense of the faith" in the circumscribed way of Johann Baptist Franzelin. Positing the distinction between a "teaching" and a "learning" church, Bartolomei defined the "sense of the faith" as "the supernatural intuition of the believer, originating in the power of faith and the gifts of the Holy Spirit, by which the believer, in communion with the Church, is endowed with the habit of penetrating, discerning, and appreciating the virtually revealed truths proposed by the Magisterium."[1] Before Bartolomei, the authors of

---

1. "Il 'senso della fede' è dunque l'intuizione soprannaturale del credente, scaturiente dalla potenza della fede e dei doni dello Spirito S., per cui, in comunione con la Chiesa, egli è abilitato a penetrare, discernere e apprezzare le virtualità del dato rivelato, proposto

the theological manuals written in the first half of the twentieth century had often failed to include this teaching in their discussions,[2] and theologians who acknowledged something like a "sense of the faithful" often held divergent views on its meaning and scope.[3]

It is rather surprising, then, that the earliest drafts of a document on the church included this ambiguous and controverted idea. A handful of bishops and theological faculties had mentioned the "sense of the faith" and called for its clarification. In fact, there was never a time during the conciliar process when the "sense of the faith" was simply absent or en-

---

dal Magistero." See "Natura, realtà, genesi e valore del 'Sensus fidei' nell'esplicitazione delle virtualità dei dommi," *Asprenas: Rivista di teologia* 10 (1963): 269–94, at 270. The teaching of Vatican II, as we will see, develops a more dynamic and inclusive meaning of the "sense of the faith." The other two articles in the series by Bartolomei are "L'influsso del 'Senso della Fede' nell'esplicitazione del domga dell'Immacolata Concezione della B. Vergine degna Madre di Dio," *Marianum* 25 (1963): 297–346 and "L'influsso del 'senso della fede' nell'esplicitazione del domma dell'Assunzione corporale di Maria," *Ephemerides Mariologicae* 14 (1964): 5–38.

2. In his *Manuale theologiae dogmaticae*, vol. 1: *De revelatione christiana, de ecclesia Christi, de fontibus revelationis* (1st ed., 1925; rev. ed., Paris: Apud Berche et Pagis, 1949), Canon Jean Marie Hervé's presentation is characteristic of many others in the nineteenth- and twentieth-century manuals of theology. Hervé never uses the expressions *sensus fidei* or *sensus fidelium* but he does not suppress what had become the common Catholic teaching—that there is such a thing as "passive infallibility" and that it plays a role in the church. This role, however, is regarded as very restricted. He writes: "(1) The subject of [passive] infallibility is the universal Church itself, which cannot err in believing and in embracing the Catholic truth. (2) This truth is beyond a doubt catholic: for if the universal Church could err in its faith, it would no longer be indefectible; it would no longer be the unique and necessary way of salvation; it would thereby cease to be the true Church of Christ. This infallibility depends on [the] active infallibility [of the pope and bishops], just as an effect depends on its cause, since the 'purpose of the society of those who believe is to preserve as spotless the truth of what it teaches regarding faith and morals'" (470–71). My translation. Hervé's understanding of "active and passive infallibility" shows that he accepted a clearly limited role of the laity in holding and attesting to the truth of Christian revelation.

3. See Johannes Beumer, "Glaubenssinn der Kirche?," *Trierer theologische Zeitschrift* 61 (1952): 129–42; and idem, "Glaubenssinn der Kirche als Quelle einer Definition," *Theologie und Glaube* 45 (1955): 250–60; Máximo Peinador, "El 'sensus fidei' y el progreso dogmático en el misterio marial," *Ephemerides Mariologicae* 6 (1956): 463–73; and Claudio García Extremeño, "El *sentido de la fe*, criterio de la tradición," *La Ciencia Tomista* 87 (1960): 569–605.

tirely forgotten. The history of the period from 1959 to 1965 is interesting in terms of the council's efforts to clarify the meaning of the "sense of the faith," to situate it in terms of its place in the life of faith and in theology, and to find the appropriate place in the documents of Vatican II to incorporate this teaching. In this chapter I propose to address these questions of the meaning and importance of the "sense of the faith" and to follow its genesis and development at the council.[4]

Preparatory Phase of Vatican II (January 1959 to Fall of 1962)

In 1959 and early 1960, the Preparatory Commission established by John XXIII contacted the universal episcopate, the major superiors of religious congregations, the heads of Roman congregations, and ecclesiastical faculties throughout the world in order to determine which topics the council should treat.[5] The topic of the "sense of the faith" was not on the minds of many, but neither was it entirely absent. Bishops Jean-Julien Weber of Strasbourg, France; Walter P. Kellenberg of Rockville Center, New York; Lorenz Jäger of Paderborn, Germany; Arturo Tabera Araoz of Albacete, Spain; and Antoni Pawlowski of Włocławek, Poland; as well as the Major Superior Giuseppe A. De Palma, SCJ, called for clarifications.[6]

More numerous were the bishops who inquired about the implications for the place of the laity in an ecclesiology that was based on the church as the mystical body of Christ. The theology of the mystical body implied the dignity of each of the faithful and an active role to be exercised by them. It was evident to many bishops that Pius XII's encyclical *Mystici*

4. On the entire period of the emergence of the "sense of the faith" as a possible theme of the council to its inclusion in the final text in *Lumen Gentium*, see Jesús Sancho Bielsa, "El Concilio Vaticano II y la formulación del 'Sensus Fidei,'" *Infalibilidad del Pueblo de Dios: "Sensus Fidei" e infalibilidad orgánica de la Iglesia en la Constitución "Lumen Gentium" del Concilio Vaticano II* (Pamplona: Ediciones Universidad de Navarra, S.A., 1979), 91–144.

5. See Étienne Fouilloux, "The Antepreparatory Phase: The Slow Emergence from Inertia (January, 1959–October, 1962)," in *History of Vatican II*, vol. 1: *Announcing and Preparing Vatican Council II, Toward a New Era in Catholicism*, ed. Giuseppe Alberigo and Joseph A. Komonchak (Maryknoll, NY: Orbis Books, 1995), 55–166.

6. In this section I rely heavily on the detailed research of Robert W. Schmucker, "Der Sensus Fidei in den Dokumenten des Zweiten Vatikanischen Konzils," *Sensus Fidei: Der Glaubenssinn in seiner vorkonziliaren Entwicklungsgeschichte und in den Dokumenten des Zweiten Vatikanischen Konzils* (Regensburg: S. Roderer Verlag, 1998), 120–219, at 122–23.

corporis involved practical implications for the relationship of the hierarchical element of the church and the vast majority of the faithful in the
church.[7] How could the slumbering power of the laity be awakened and
unleashed for the spread of the faith? It was clear to many that the answer
to this question could not bypass deeper reflection on the dignity and
the role of the lay faithful. How might the "sense of the faith" contribute
to such a clarification?[8]

Finally, a third area of reflection that intersected with the "sense of the
faith" was the reawakening of the traditional teaching of the infallibility of the church as a whole. Was this value lost when infallibility was
restricted to the pope and the bishops? What is the relationship between
"infallibility in teaching" (*infallibilitas in docendo*) and "infallibility in
believing" (*infallibilitas in credendo*), and how are these two modes of
infallibility related to each other?[9] In a word, the "sense of the faith"
and its implications was an important theme in the background as the
church prepared for the council.

In the second phase of the preparations for the council, a Preparatory
Theological Commission was charged with collating the thousands of
requests and suggestions of those contacted and incorporating them
into documents the council might consider.[10] Since many of the sugges-

---

7. See *Acta Apostolicae Sedis* 35 (1943), 193–248 for the Latin text. For an English
translation, see "On the Mystical Body of Christ," in *The Papal Encyclicals 1939-1958*,
ed. Claudia Carlen (Ann Arbor, MI: Pierian Press, 1990), 37–63.

8. Many bishops could be cited in this regard, as well as the Pontifical Urban Faculty,
and the theological faculties of Lille and Lyons, France, and Maynooth, Ireland. See Robert
W. Schmucker, *Sensus Fidei*, 124–25; Jesús Sancho Bielsa, "El misterio de la Iglesia y la
infalibilidad," *Infalibilidad del Pueblo de Dios*, 17–90; Bielsa, "Infalibilidad orgánica de la
Iglesia," ibid., 271-87; and ibid., 178–90 ["Infalibilidad del pueblo de Dios"].

9. Such were the concerns of Bishops Raffaele Calabria of Otranto, Italy; Walter P. Kellenberg of Rockville Center, New York; Francis Simons of Indore, India; and the faculties
of the Pontifical Gregorian University and the Pontifical Faculty Marianum in Rome, and
the Institut de Théologie Catholique of Paris. See Schmucker, *Sensus Fidei*, 127.

10. See the following treatments for the history of this period. Joseph A. Komonchak,
"The Struggle for the Council during the Preparation of Vatican II (1960–1962)," in *His-
tory of Vatican II*, vol. 1: 167–356 and Alberto Melloni, "The Beginning of the Second
Period: The Great Debate on the Church," *History of Vatican II*, vol. 3: *The Mature Council,
Second Period and Intersession, September 1963–September 1964*, ed. Giuseppe Alberigo
and Joseph A. Komonchak (Maryknoll, NY: Orbis Books, 2000), 1–115.

tions had to do with the church, the commission proposed a schema that comprised eleven chapters.[11] This document, *Aeternus Unigeniti Pater*, was the preliminary text for what would eventually become the Dogmatic Constitution on the Church.

Chapter 8, "On Authority and Obedience in the Church," took up the question of the origin, nature, and exercise of authority in the church. While urging the leaders in the church to exercise their authority responsibly (arts. 36–37), it also admonished the faithful to obey and show respect for legitimate ecclesiastical authority by avoiding harmful criticism (art. 38). In a final article, it broached the issue of public opinion in the church (art. 39). *Aeternus Unigeniti Pater* mentions the "sense of the faith" in order to distinguish it from public opinion:

> In the Church of Jesus Christ, it is well known that there exists a certain supernatural sense of the faith among the entire Christian people that is always good and that it is the foundation of the special and indefectible character of the Catholic Church. It has its origin from above and consists of the consensus of the faithful and the bishops in matters of faith and morals and is directed by the authoritative magisterium. Finally, it is awakened by the Holy Spirit who assists the magisterium in presenting Catholic teaching, and it is also active in the faithful so that they might obediently accept, correctly understand, and more deeply penetrate the doctrine proposed to them. In this way, the divine salvific mission of the Church is greatly advanced.
>
> Public opinion, however, is something that takes place in the order of action, as a certain spontaneous and vital reaction of the faithful to whatever takes place in individual communities or in the Universal Church.

---

11. The chapters bear the following headings: (1) On the Nature of the Church Militant, (2) On the Members of the Church Militant and the Necessity of the Church for Salvation, (3) On the Episcopacy as the Highest Degree of the Sacrament of Order and the Priesthood, (4) On Residential Bishops, (5) On the States of Acquiring Evangelical Perfection, (6) On the Laity, (7) On the Magisterium of the Church, (8) On Authority and Obedience in the Church, (9) On Relations between the Church and the State and Religious Tolerance, (10) On the Necessity of the Church of Announcing the Gospel to All Peoples and throughout the World, (11) On Ecumenism. For the text, see *Acta et documenta Concilio Oecumenico Vaticano II* (Vatican City: Typis Polyglottis Vaticanis, 1969), Series II (Praeparatoria), vol. III, Pars I, 135–204.

. . . The pastors of the Church must indeed be diligent and fair-minded in judging matters that are proposed by everyone and especially by those who possess expertise. Nevertheless, the opinion is to be rejected that Church leaders must always and obligatorily consult public opinion, or that they must decide and dispose of matters in accord with the mind of the majority of the faithful (art. 39).[12]

This long passage evinces a certain confusion by speaking about the theological teaching on the "sense of the faith" that had emerged in the nineteenth and twentieth centuries in the context of calls for the legitimate role of public opinion in the church. The latter had only recently emerged in the secular societies of the period. One detects some anxiety on the question of public opinion in the church.[13] At the same time the text defends the existence and role of the "sense of the faith" in the church

---

12. "Est quidem in Ecclesia Christi, ut bene notum est, quidam supernaturalis sensus fidei populi universi christiani, qui semper bonus est et indefectibilem peculiaremque proprietatem constituit catholicae Ecclesiae: ex alto provenit, et nihil aliud est nisi consensus fidelium et pastorum in rebus fidei et morum, authentico magisterio gubernatus. Ultimam exsuscitatur a Spiritu Sancto, qui, dum eidem magisterio adest in catholica doctrina proponenda, idem in fidelibus operatur ut doctrinam propositam oboedienti animo accipiant, recte intelligant, et profundius scrutentur; eodem plurimum divina missio salvifica Ecclesiae adiuvatur. Alia vero est opinio publica, quae in ordine agendi versatur, et est spontanea et vitalis quaedam reactio fidelium ad ea omnia quae, sive in singulis communitatibus, sive in universali Ecclesia eveniunt. . . . Pastores Ecclesiae satagere quidem debent ut aequo animo causas ab omnibus, et a rerum peritis praesertim, prolatas iudicent; sed reprobanda est omnino illorum sententia, qui tenent praepositos in Ecclesia publicam opinionem neceessario et semper consulere debere, vel ad mentem maioris partis fidelium omnia diiudicare et disponere." *Acta et documenta Concilio Oecumenico Vaticano II* (Vatican City: Typis Polyglottis Vaticanis, 1969), Series II (Praeparatoria), vol. 3, pars I, 175. My translation.

13. A footnote to the paragraph on the "sense of the faith" makes the following remark: "The intention of the paragraph is not to state everything that could be proposed on the nature of the "sense of the faith" of the Christian people, but only that which is necessary to clearly distinguish it from what is called 'public opinion,' and which is the issue dealt with here. (Intentio paragraphi non est proponendi omnia quae proponi possunt de natura sensus fidei populi christiani, sed ea tantum quae necessaria sunt ut clare distinguatur a 'publica opinione,' sic dicta, quae circa agenda versatur.)" *Acta et documenta Concilio Oecumenico Vaticano II*, Series II (Praeparatoria), vol. 3, pars 1, 176. My translation. For a more positive evaluation of the role of public opinion in the church, see Dario Vitali, "*Sensus fidelium* e opinione publica nella Chiesa," *Gregorianum* 82 (2001): 689–717.

as a basic theological reality. Article 39 tries to keep these two ideas apart, but is not entirely successful.

Nevertheless, some of the hallmarks of the final teaching of Vatican II are already evident: (1) the "sense of the faith" pertains to all the faithful, including the bishops ("the entire Christian people"); (2) it is a supernatural reality given by the Holy Spirit; (3) that explains why the church is indefectible; (4) that it is manifest in the consensus of both the bishops and the faithful; (5) that the bishops take the lead in teaching with authority; and (6) that the faithful have a positive role in elaborating the meaning and pertinence of church teaching.

But here, too, the text betrays certain ambiguities: what is the nature of the "consensus" that is spoken of? What does the term "indefectible" refer to?[14] How do the faithful arrive at a deeper understanding of the faith and how do they make it known to the bishops? Do the bishops always take the initiative? How is the "obedience" of the faithful related to their role in advancing the meaning of church doctrine?[15] Is the role of the lay faithful rooted in a theological reality and what is it? In a word, the reader senses that the passage is tentative and that the "sense of the faith" needs to be explained at greater depth.

First Session (Fall 1962) and Intersession (December 1962 to September 1963)

Some 2,200 bishops from throughout the Catholic world gathered in St. Peter's Basilica on October 11, 1962, for the opening Mass and Pope John XXIII's address to the council fathers. After several days dedicated to organizational matters and the election of presidents of the various commissions, the fourth General Congregation, as a plenary session of the bishops was called, met on October 22 to discuss the first schema the bishops would consider, "On the Sacred Liturgy" (*De sacra liturgia*). The bishops continued to work productively on this schema up through

---

14. Cardinal Paul Émile Léger of Montreal, Canada, asked that the text better reflect the teaching that infallibility is a gift to the whole church and not simply a charism of the pope and bishops. See Schmucker, *Sensus Fidei*, 147n79.

15. Cardinal Franz König of Vienna, Austria, suggested that the text should refer to the positive contribution of the faithful in arriving at the development of dogma. See Schmucker, *Sensus Fidei*, 147n79.

November 14, when the first preliminary vote was taken. It was overwhelmingly affirmative. The bishops then turned their attention to the more contentious schema "On the Sources of Revelation" (*De fontibus revelationis*). These discussions took place through November 21. The bishops were not satisfied with the approach of the schema as proposed and it was remanded to the Theological Commission for further reworking. Then, in the General Congregations on November 23, 24, and 26, the bishops considered the schema "On the Means of Social Communication" in the church (*De instrumentis communicationis socialis*). Since the schema was uncontroversial, the bishops concluded their discussions rather quickly and from November 26 to 30 turned their attention to the schema "On the Unity of the Church" (*De ecclesiae unitate*). Finally, on December 1, the bishops were free to consider *Aeternus Unigeniti Pater*, the schema on the church. The discussions continued until December 7, the eve of the end of the first session of the council on December 8, 1962.[16]

By the end of the first session of the council, the bishops had begun to have a clearer sense of their responsibility for the whole church. The collegiality they were experiencing at the council itself imparted a deeper understanding of their role as bishops and they began to appreciate the richness of their pastoral experiences and insights. In the wake of the bitterly divisive discussions of the Preparatory Commission's document "On the Sources of Revelation," the bishops became impatient with the endless wrangling over disputed theological minutiae and concluded that another document was needed.[17] More importantly, they realized that they needed

---

16. See the discussion of these schemas by Mathijs Lamberigts, "The Liturgy Debate," 107–66, Giuseppe Ruggieri, "The First Doctrinal Clash," 233–66, Lamberigts, "The Discussion of the Modern Media," 267–79, and Ruggieri, "Beyond an Ecclesiology of Polemics: The Debate on the Church," 281–357 in *History of Vatican II*, vol. 2: *The Formation of the Council's Identity: First Period and Intersession, October 1962–September 1963*, ed. Giuseppe Alberigo and Joseph A. Komonchak (Maryknoll, NY: Orbis Books, 1997).

17. On the controversy on the sources of revelation during the first session and the aftermath of the controversy, see the discussion below on articles 8 and 10 in particular. See also Joseph Ratzinger, *Theological Highlights of Vatican II* (New York: Paulist Press, 1966), 40–48 ["Early Debate on Revelation"] and Jared Wicks, "Vatican II on Revelation: Behind the Scenes," *Investigating Vatican II: Its Theologians, Ecumenical Turn, and Biblical Commitment* (Washington, DC: Catholic University of America Press, 2018), 80–97. See also the discussion of articles 8 and 10 of *Dei verbum* below and the literature cited there.

to develop the teaching on revelation in a way that would help the church state its belief on Scripture and tradition for the contemporary church and proclaim the faith more effectively to the world. As the discussion on the Preparatory Commission's document on the church advanced, the bishops quickly came to the conclusion that it, too, needed to be rewritten in light of the same pastoral concerns. How could they speak about the church in a way that would be true to its doctrinal claims and also invite men and women of the mid-twentieth century to consider the church's offer of truth and salvation? The bishops' rejection of *Aeternus Unigeniti Pater* led to the formation of a subcommission entrusted with the task of presenting a new text on the church for the bishops' consideration.[18]

During the intersession of 1962–1963, several working groups produced substitute drafts of the document on the church.[19] But already in October and November, Professor Gérard Philips of the University of Louvain had been writing an alternate text to *Aeternus Unigeniti Pater*.[20] Philips's text had several advantages over the others. Since it did not completely reject *Aeternus Unigeniti Pater* but improved it in the light of comments made by the bishops, it represented a middle course on many of the sensitive issues. This advantage later argued for its acceptance by the bishops. Moreover, rather than expressing the views of any national group of theologians, Philips composed it in consultation with a wider group of theologians from several countries. Already in mid-January 1963, then, a revised version was ready for submission when the subcommission met in Rome on February 21, 1963. All of the other alternative drafts had

---

18. This subcommission on the church consisted of Cardinal Michael Browne, OP; Cardinal Paul Émile Léger; Cardinal Franz König; Archbishop Pietro Parente of Perugia, Italy; Bishop André Marie Charue of Namur, Belgium; Archbishop Gabriele Marie Garrone of Toulouse, France; and Bishop Joseph Schröffer of Eichstätt, Germany. These seven were joined by Marie-Rosaire Gagnebet, OP; André Naud, P.S.S.; Pierre Lafortune, Karl Rahner, SJ; Carlo Balič, OFM; Gérard Philips, Jean Daniélou, SJ; and Gustave Thils. In short order Yves Congar, OP; Heribert Schauf; and Charles Moeller joined as theological experts.

19. Jan Grootaers presents these various drafts in *History of Vatican II*, ed. G. Alberigo and J. A. Komonchak, 2:399–404 ["The Range of Available Texts"].

20. Giuseppe Alberigo has included a detailed step-by-step history of the emergence of *Lumen Gentium* in "Chronology of the Drafting of the Dogmatic Constitution *Lumen Gentium*" in *Constitutionis Dogmaticae Lumen Gentium: Synopsis Historica*, ed. Giuseppe Alberigo and Franca Magistretti (Bologna: Istituto per le Scienze Religiose, 1975), xxiii-xxv.

too many drawbacks or had been submitted too late for consideration.[21] The intrinsic qualities of the text, as well as the accommodating personal manner of Philips as its spokesman, meant that Philips's draft became the working document when the bishops reassembled for the second session in October 1963.[22] It is important to note this fact, because in this way the reference to the "sense of the faith" in the original document, but more importantly the significant value it represents in the life of the church, was preserved in the text and became the occasion of the bishops refining the notion by further observations and suggestions. Hidden away originally in another context, that of the limits of public opinion in the church, the teaching was able to survive.

As the process of reworking Philips's draft progressed during the intersession, greater attention was dedicated to the chapter on the laity. At the meeting on May 25, 1963, according the Jan Grootaers: "The principal subjects discussed were, once again, the definition of a *lay person*, the Christian people's sense of the faith, the idea of the universal priesthood, the significance of the 'profane' world, and the relations of the laity with the hierarchy."[23] Changing the context of the discussion of the "sense of the faith" from a chapter on authority and obedience in the church in the original document to the chapter on the laity in the reworked draft was auspicious for the future of the teaching. The new context proved more congenial for deepening the meaning of the "sense of the faith." The same

---

21. These included drafts by Archbishop Pietro Parente; Bishop Léon-Arthur Elchinger of Strasbourg, France; Bishop Jean de Cambourg of Clermont, France; Bishop Francisco Barbado y Vieja of Salamanca, Spain; Bishop Isaac Ghattas of Thebes, Egypt; Cardinal Maurice Feltin of Paris; a schema from a group of German theologians and bishops; and a schema from the hierarchy of Chile. See Jan Grootaers, *History of Vatican II*, ed. G. Alberigo and J. A. Komonchak, 2:399–400, for a brief description of these drafts.

22. On the personal advantages of Philips as a theologian and as a human being, see the comments of Grootaers, *History of Vatican II*, 2:401–2. The few changes that demanded attention were the necessary clarifications on the notion of the layperson in the church and the status of religious life and the call to perfection. How were the laity called to perfection in a manner equal in dignity to, though different from, religious men and women in the church? The questions at stake were how can one both defend the call of everyone to holiness without denigrating the state of evangelical life of vowed religious, and how to speak about religious life without denigrating the life of the "ordinary" lay Christian. Two different, though complementary, values were at stake here: the rich and noble heritage of vowed religious life and the innate dignity of every baptized person in the church.

23. *History of Vatican II*, 2:407–8.

can also be said of introducing the topic of the universal priesthood in the chapter.[24] This traditional but long-neglected teaching in Catholicism was to become the soil that nourished the "sense of the faith."[25]

With the passage of time, and especially because of the criticism of the Reformers in the sixteenth century, the Catholic Church downplayed the priesthood of all the faithful by its one-sided defense of the ordained priesthood. This led to widespread neglect of the traditional teaching, so that it had to be rediscovered by Catholic scholars in the twentieth century.[26] The papal magisterium, too, cautiously reintroduced the priesthood of all believers. In his encyclical *Mediator Dei*, Pius XII warned against misunderstandings and certain aberrations that attributed a joint power of

24. See Bielsa, *Infalibilidad del pueblo de Dios*, 156–65 ["Condición sacerdotal de la Iglesia"] and 166–72 ["Sacerdocio común y *sensus fidei*"].

25. Laurence Ryan has outlined the history of the notion of the priesthood of all the faithful in the early church and shown how virtually all of the important writers of this period drew on the scriptural teaching of the priesthood of all believers, including Justin, Clement of Alexandria, Origen, Tertullian, Cyril of Jerusalem, Athanasius, Cyril of Alexandria, Gregory of Nyssa, Gregory of Nazianzen, John Chrysostom, Ambrose, Augustine, Jerome, Leo I, Gregory I, and Prosper of Aquitaine. See his "Patristic Teaching on the Priesthood of the Faithful," *Irish Theological Quarterly* 29 (1962): 25–51. Three years later, Ryan followed this study with an examination of the teaching in the theological literature before Vatican II and at the council. See his "Vatican II and the Priesthood of the Laity," *Irish Theological Quarterly* 32 (1965): 93–115. The literature on this important topic since the council is vast, but mention should be made of the informative and balanced treatment by Jean-Pierre Torrell, *A Priestly People: Baptismal Priesthood and Priestly Ministry*, trans. Peter Heinegg (New York: Paulist Press, 2013).

26. Catholic scholars who wrote about the priesthood of the faithful in the 1930s and 1940s include Bernard Botte (1934), "L'idée du sacerdoce des fidèles dans la tradition" and Bernard Capelle (1934), "Le sacerdoce des fidèles: synthèse et conclusion," in *La participation active des fidèles au culte. 16e Semaine Liturgique, Louvain, 1933* in *Cours et conférences des Semaines Liturgiques*, vol. 11 (Louvain: Abbaye du Mont-César, 1934): 21–28 and 69–74 respectively; Engelbert Niebecker (1936), *Das allgemeine Priestertum der Gläubigen* (Paderborn: F. Schöningh); Gustave Thils (1938), "Le pouvoir cultuel du baptisé," *Ephemerides theologicae Lovaniensis* 15:683–89; Lucien Cerfaux (1939), "Regale Sacerdotium," *Revue des sciences philosophiques et théologiques* 28:5–39; Bernard Capelle (1940), "Problèmes du 'sacerdoce royale' des fidèles," *Questions liturgiques et paroissiales*, 81–93 and 141–50; Paul Dabin (1941), *Le sacerdoce royal des fidèles dans les livres saints* (Paris: Bloud et Gay); Yves Congar (1946), "Sacerdoce et laïcat dans l'Église," *Vie Intellectuelle* 14:6–39; Peter Ketter (1947), "Das allgemeine Priestertum der Gläubigen nach dem 1. Petrusbrief," *Trierer theologische Zeitschrift* 56:43–51, and Paul F. Palmer (1947), "The Lay Priesthood: Real or Metaphorical?" *Theological Studies* 8:574–613.

consecration to the laity when the priest consecrated the bread and wine at Mass or that spoke of a certain "concelebration" by the laity. Nevertheless, the pope went on to acknowledge that the laity did in fact exercise their priestly character as the priestly people of God when he wrote:

> By the waters of baptism, as by common right, Christians are made members of the Mystical Body of Christ the Priest, and by the 'character' which is imprinted on their souls, they are appointed to give worship to God. Thus they participate, according to their condition, in the priesthood of Christ. . . . The people unite their hearts in praise, impetration, expiation and thanksgiving with prayers or the intention of the priest, even of the High Priest himself, so that in the one and same offering of the victim and according to a visible sacerdotal rite, they may be presented to God the Father. . . . Now the sacrifice of the New Law signifies that the supreme worship by which the principal offerer himself, who is Christ, and, in union with him and through him, all the members of the Mystical Body pay God the honor and reverence that are due to him.[27]

The pope addressed this topic with even greater conviction and terminological precision, but still cautiously, in his allocution "*Magnificate Dominum*" in 1954. He writes:

> At any rate, it should not be denied or called into question that the faithful enjoy a certain "priesthood" [quoddam habere "sacerdotium"] and one must not underestimate or ignore it. For in his First Letter, the Prince of the Apostles addresses the faithful in these words: "You, however, are a chosen race, a royal priesthood, a holy nation, a purchased people" (1 Pet. 2:9); and just before this, he asserts that the faithful possess "a holy priesthood to offer spiritual sacrifices acceptable to God through Jesus Christ" (verse 5). But whatever the full and proper meaning of this honorable title and its reality is, it must be firmly held that the [priesthood of the] faithful is indeed exalted and mysterious, and differs not only in degree, but in essence also [non gradu tantum, sed etiam essentia differre], from [that] priesthood fully and properly so called, which is found in the power of effectuating the sacrifice of

---

27. See *Acta Apostolicae Sedis* 37 (1947): 521–95 at 556. E.T. *The Papal Encyclicals 1939–1958*, ed., Claudia Carlen (Ann Arbor, MI: Pierian Press, 1990), 119–54, at 135.

Christ himself and in acting together with the person of Christ, the High Priest.[28]

In light of the rediscovery of the priesthood of all the faithful by the papacy, it would have been unthinkable that no reference to it would be made in *Aeternus Unigeniti Pater*. Roman theologians might assign it a modest place in the document, but it simply could not be ignored.

Already in *Aeternus Unigeniti Pater*, therefore, the church as the people of God was characterized with the words of First Peter 2:9 as "a chosen race, a royal priesthood, a holy nation." In the prologue itself of *Aeternus Unigeniti Pater,* we read the following:

> For it has pleased the Father that the redeemed not be comprised of individuals who are saved without any condition or connection between them but as those who quite simply have been called into his presence from the multitude of nations to constitute a new chosen race, a kingly priesthood, a holy people, in a word, a new Israel (art. 1).[29]

Every subsequent version would include a reference to the teaching regarding the priestly character of the people. This teaching could provide a better context for the church as the holy, royal, and priestly people of God, as was Israel according to the covenant with Moses on Sinai (Exod 19:6).[30]

---

28. See See *Acta Apostolicae Sedis* 46 (1954), 669. My translation. Pius XII clearly wanted to admit the full import of the covenantal prerogatives of First Peter as they apply to the church, while avoiding collapsing one priesthood (that of the ordained) entirely into the other (the priesthood that the laity truly enjoy). The pope was not entirely successful in his efforts at balancing these two realities and so left to others the task of sorting out their relationship. Vatican II represented a clear advance on this matter but hardly arrived at a fully satisfactory formulation.

29. "Complacuit enim Patri non ut redempti, quavis habitudine connexioneque seclusa, coram se plane singuli sanctificandi consisterent, sed ut ex multitudine advocati, novum genus electum, regale sacerdotium, gentem sanctam, novum scilicet Israel constituerent." *Acta et documenta Concilio Oecumenico Vaticano II*, Ser. II, vol. 3, pars 1: 135. My translation.

30. As the principal architect behind the various iterations of the Dogmatic Constitution on the Church, Philips was thoroughly aware of the exegetical and theological literature on the priesthood of the faithful. Already in 1954 Philips had discussed the topic in the original French edition of his *The Role of the Laity in the Church*, trans. John R. Gilbert and James W. Moudry (Chicago: Fides Publishers, 1955), 57–60 ["The Universal Priesthood

And yet, references to the "priestly" character of this people could not but cause some confusion regarding its interpretation. Surely the meaning of "priesthood" as applied to the lay faithful could not be the same when applied to the ordained in the church. Clarifications were needed.

Another way to indicate that the church is the people of God was to spell out its participation in the three offices or *munera* of Christ. Just as Christ is prophet, priest, and king, so do all those who belong to him as his body and as his people exercise these roles or offices.[31] Thus, in the new text we read the following:

> Together with Christ who has conquered the prince of this world and whom to serve is to reign, the faithful rule in the freedom of the sons of God, and who by denying themselves and living a holy life oppose the sway of sin in themselves and in others (#9). Therefore, in their own way participating in the priestly, prophetic, and kingly office of Christ, they observe the new and greatest commandment, of love namely, by which we love our neighbor with the same love with which he first loved us, and especially our least brothers and sisters, in whom he willed that he be acknowledged in a special way (#10). The whole Church, which offers God the fruit of lips that confess his name (see Hebrews 13:15), and who are indefectible in believing, also show forth this special property in the supernatural "sense of the faith" of the whole Christian people (#11). This "sense of the faith," by which all are rendered docile to God (see John 6:45), emerges out of their consensus on matters of faith and morals "from the bishops to the last of the lay faithful," as St. Augustine says (#12). Awakened by the Spirit of truth, this same "sense of the faith" is found in the written word of God and as handed down with his assistance, and is guided and sustained by the magisterium. Those who believe actively embrace it, advance in a more profound understanding of the truth of the faith, and apply it more faithfully in their lives (#13).[32]

---

of the Faithful"]. Philips's important book was quickly translated into English, Italian, Spanish, and German, and was widely read throughout the Catholic Church in the 1950s. The idea was hardly a novelty when Vatican II was convoked.

31. See Bielsa, *Infalibilidad del pueblo de Dios*, 149–56 ["La novedad de Cristo"].

32. "Christifideles cum Christo, qui principem huius mundi devicit et cui servire regnare est, in libertate filiorum Dei regnant et sui abnegatione vitaque sancta regnum peccati in seipsis (cf. Romans 6:12) et in aliis impugnant (#9). Munus Christi igitur sacerdotale,

Second Session (Fall 1963)

When the bishops reassembled for the second session of the council at the end of September 1963, they were in possession of a text that consisted of the following four chapters: (1) The Mystery of the Church, (2) The Hierarchical Constitution of the Church and the Episcopate in Particular, (3) The People of God and the Laity in Particular, and (4) The Call to Holiness in the Church. Mention of the "sense of the faith" continued to be an integral part of the revised document that was now incorporated in chapter 3. However, on July 4, the Coordinating Commission had proposed an emendation of the division of the draft that involved two significant changes for the ecclesiology of Vatican II. The first introduced a separate chapter on the people of God, while the laity would be treated in a chapter of their own. The new second chapter would treat at greater length the images of the church found in chapter 1. It was hoped that this change would accentuate the prominence of the biblical image of the people of God. The new chapter would treat what was common to each person in the church and corroborate the dignity of each person before various roles were assigned or the differences in the states of life in the church came to expression.[33] The second significant step meant that the

---

prpheticum et regale quodammodo participantes, mandatum eius novum et maximum observant, caritatem videlicet, qua proximos amamus ea dilectione qua Ipse prius dilexit nos, praesertim minimos fratres, in quibus vult peculiari modo Se agnosci (#10). Ecclesia tota, quae Deo offert fructum labiorum confitentium nomini Eius (cf. Hebrews 13:15), et in credendo indefectibilis est, hanc suam peculiarem proprietatem etiam in supernaturali sensu fidei universi populi christiani manifestat (#11). Hic sensus fidei, quo omnes sunt docibiles Dei (cf. John 6:45), coalescit ipsorum consensu de rebus fidei et morum, 'ab Episcopis usque ad extremos laicos fideles,' ut dicit S. Augustinus (#12). A Spiritu veritatis excitatus, idem sensus fidei verbo Dei scripto et tradito sub Eius assistentia inhaeret, et a Magisterio ducitur ac sustentatur, cui credentes active respondent, veritatem fidei profundius perspiciendo, et in vita fidelius applicando (#13)." My translation.

33. Differences due to the assignment of place, tasks, and special vocations in the church would be considered in subsequent chapters. In a related move, the subcommission was moving toward a statement that would make clear that all Christians were called to holiness before each one ultimately decided on what form that decision would take concretely: the lay state, the clerical state, or the vowed life under a rule. In this matter, too, but for different reasons, the subcommission was first interested in determining what was held in common in the church before introducing differentiations among the

discussion of the hierarchy in the church, so preponderant in the church of the West since the Gregorian reforms of the eleventh century, was modified with a view to achieving a better balance of authority and participation in mission in the church. The outline of this revised draft now was: (1) The Mystery of the Church, (2) The People of God in General, (3) The Hierarchical Constitution of the Church, (4) The Laity in Particular, and (5) The Call to Holiness in the Church.[34] In the new division of chapters, the development of the theme of the "sense of the faith" was now divided between chapters 2 and 4. I propose to examine these two statements by the council and explain their meaning in light of the growing acceptance of the "sense of the faith" by the bishops.

In their discussions at the plenary sessions at the start of the second session, the bishops generally judged that the new text and the new division of chapters corresponded to the lines of thought they had indicated at the end of the first session. The period from September 30 to October 31 had been set aside for discussion of the revised text of the Constitution on the Church, or *Lumen Gentium* as it was now called, a text that still did not include important themes that were to be added later in the

---

members. It should be noted that this decision freed the council from making statements about the superiority of any state of holiness vis-à-vis the others. This move, too, reinforced the tendency of the council to concentrate on those factors that united members in the church over those that created distinctions. As such, this logic was in harmony with the parallel move to see how everyone in the church shared responsibility for the revelation Christ had entrusted to it.

34. Yves Congar indicates that the proposed draft of the new chapter "On the People of God" was completed on September 7, 1963, in Malines, Belgium, just before the opening of the second session of the council. See *My Journal of the Council*, trans. Mary John Ronayne and Mary Cecily Boulding and ed. Denis Minns (Collegeville, MN: Liturgical Press, 2012), 313. However, according to Congar, it was only at a meeting of the Coordinating Commission in Rome on October 9, that agreement was finally reached about the new chapter as well as about including another chapter on Mary in the proposed constitution and submitting these proposals to the full body of bishops for their approval. In the words of Congar: "It was a great and important meeting from the point of view of the future orientation of things. What has been played out this evening was, partly, the opening towards human beings (*De populo Dei*) and the soundness of a mariology cured of its maximalist canker." See *My Journal of the Council*, 356–59, at 359.

process of its evolution.[35] A month was a considerable amount of time for the bishops to discuss, clarify, and come to consensus on the text. The bishops decided to accept the recommendation of the Coordinating Commission that a new second chapter on the people of God be written and separated from the discussion on the laity in the church. The context better indicated that the "sense of the faith" is an endowment of all the faithful whatever their place or rank in the church and called for a more general presentation of the theme. No longer restricted to a chapter dedicated to the theme of the laity in the church, the "sense of the faith" could now emerge more clearly as a dimension of every believer. Since the new chapter was now to include the theme of the "sense of the faith" and who participated in it, this discussion is of special interest to us.

Several bishops spoke in favor of the "sense of the faith" and offered helpful clarifications of its nature. Among these were Pedro Cantero Cuadrado of Huelva, Spain; Gúrpide Beope of Bilbao, Spain; and Émile de Smedt of Bruges, Belgium. Cantero Cuadrado stressed the internal action of the Holy Spirit who influenced each of the faithful in accepting the Christian faith. He referred to this action as an "intuition" and

---

35. Even the revised draft of the council's teaching on the church continued to undergo further development in the second session and during the intersession of 1963–1964. In this way chapters on the pilgrim state of the church, the place of consecrated life under a rule, and the Blessed Virgin Mary in the communion of saints and her symbolic role in the church would eventually emerge through the processes of separating them as themes from other contexts and adding them to the document. At other times the development emerged because of the *modi* (emendations) submitted by the bishops as they voted on the text. In other situations, the bishops deemed that certain topics were too important for a cursory treatment in the document on the church and deserved treatment of their own in a separate document. The Decree on Ecumenism (*Unitatis redintegratio*), the Declarations on the Relations of the Church to Non-Christian Religions (*Nostra aetate*) and On Religious Liberty (*Dignitatis humanae*), and the Pastoral Constitution on the Church in the Modern World (*Gaudium et spes*) are four such cases. In yet other situations, the bishops felt the pressure of certain constituents in the church to at least say something constructive, something that would provide direction in the future. Examples here are the Decree on the Ministry and Life of Priests (*Presbyterorum ordinis*) together with the Decree on the Training of Priests (*Optatam totius*) and the Decree on the Up-to-Date Renewal of Religious Life (*Perfectae caritatis*). Finally, the theological *periti* at the council also added to the final version of *Lumen Gentium* by a judicious change in the text's wording that was accepted by the bishops, sometimes without having the opportunity to discuss it further. The process of producing the text simply moved on inexorably!

a kind of "taste" for Christian truth that permitted the faithful to have a "presentiment" of what was still hidden in the deposit of the faith. He wanted to stress the active role of the faithful in arriving at and witnessing to Christian truth. To Cuadrado the "sense of the faith" is an active and dynamic element in the church, intimately connected with the authority of the bishops as teachers of the faith but also exhibiting a certain independence of the lay faithful in the process of the church arriving at the fullness of Christian truth.[36]

Bishop Beope, too, stressed the active role of the faithful in understanding the faith and he compared the "sense of the faith" of believers to "consciousness."

> The "sense of the faith" is given to everyone by the Holy Spirit who is, as it were, the soul of the Church. It can be compared to consciousness. The Church has a consciousness of truths [of the faith] and this consciousness includes more elements than human knowledge itself is aware of. The People of God and Christ's faithful have a consciousness of some truth, without yet knowing how it can be explained theologically. The immaculate conception is a good example of this. . . . The whole believing Church is not merely passive but is active in handing on the deposit of faith, yet never apart from the ecclesiastical magisterium. The faithful not only receive from the magisterium but the whole People of God exerts a positive influence on the magisterium.[37]

36. "Hic 'sensus fidei' efformatur influxu Spiritus Sancti, tum actione externa praedicationis magisterii Ecclesiae . . . , tum actione interna et immediata eiusdem Spiritus veritatis in animis omnium fidelium . . . , quibus etiam fideles possunt acquire profundiorem perspicientiam, intuitionem et quasi saporem veritatum fidei, immo etiam veritatem in deposito revelationis absconditam quandoque praesentire." Quoted by Schmucker, *Sensus Fidei*, 172n148. In the judgment of Schmucker, "Bishop Cantero Cuadrado attributes to the 'sense of the faith' a far-reaching function in the Church that is characterized by a clearer accent on the dynamism of the 'sense of the faith.'" Ibid.

37. "Sensus fidei per Spiritum Sanctum qui est veluti anima Ecclesiae, omnibus datur. Potest compari conscientiae. Ecclesia habet conscientiam veritatum et haec conscientia plura elementa quam scientia ipsa habet. Sic populus Dei et Christi fideles habent conscientiam alicuius veritatis cuius enucleatio scientifica ipsis non patet. Sic v.g. in casu Immaculatae Conceptionis. . . . Tota enim Ecclesia credens non solum est passiva sed etiam activa in tradendo deposito fidei, utique nunquam sine magisterio ecclesiastico. Fideles enim non tantum a magisterio accipiunt, sed etiam datur influxus positivus fidei totius populi Dei in magisterium." Quoted by Schmucker, *Sensus Fidei*, 173n150. My translation.

Finally, Bishop de Smedt stressed the active role of the faithful in determining the "sense of the faith" but in particular he wanted to make its exercise more concrete by associating it with the participation of the faithful in the prophetic role of Christ:

> The lay faithful themselves . . . by their supernatural "sense of the faith," play an active role in coming to a subsequent understanding of Christian teaching, always remaining subject to the magisterium and serving as an instrument of the prophetic office of Christ, who helps his Church avoid erring regarding the truth and helps them come to a deeper understanding and a more faithful application of it in their lives. All of this can be found in the draft of the schema, but without its mentioning the office of Christ the prophet and so in a manner that suffers from being too abstract.[38]

Not all the bishops supported the active role of the "sense of the faith" by the faithful. Some insisted on its subordinate place vis-à-vis the pope and the bishops. Cardinals Giuseppe Siri of Genoa, Italy; Ernesto Ruffini of Palermo, Sicily; and Archbishop Raffaele Calabría of Benevento, Italy, staunchly defended the traditional distinction between the "teaching Church" and the "learning Church," in which the magisterium is active and the faithful passively receive revealed truth from the pope and bishops. Quite simply, the faithful do not contribute to determining the content or the understanding of the deposit of faith. The church is infallible because the bishops teach infallibly and the faithful believe what the pope and bishops teach them with authority. The meaning of the "sense of the faith" is quite restricted and simply points to the firm and constant witness of the faithful insofar as they are and have been obedient to the teachings of the pope and bishops.[39] In this way, a handful of bishops at

---

38. "Laici . . . in subsequenti intellectione doctrinae ipsi suo supernaturali sensu fidei habent partem activam, magisterio ecclesiastico subordinatam, tanquam organum Christi prophetae qui Ecclesiam suam adiuvat ne a veritate declinet eamque profundius intelligat et in vita fidelius applicet. Haec omnia dicuntur in schemate . . . sed ibi exponuntur sine relatione cum munere prophetico Christi et modo nimis abstracto." Quoted by Schmucker, *Sensus Fidei*, 174n151. My translation.

39. According to Cardinal Ruffini: "Sensus fidelium magni faciendus est—et re in definitionibus dogmaticis magni fit—non quia in fidelibus a Deo directe efficiatur vel a Spiritu Sancto excitetur, sed quia talis sensus doctrinam, a magisterio infallibili Ecclesiae

Vatican II held to an understanding of the "sense of the faith" that had never advanced beyond the most restrictive interpretation of the teaching of Johann Baptist Franzelin and as influenced by a one-sided teaching on papal infallibility interpreted by certain ultramontane theologians after Vatican I.

Real progress in understanding the "sense of the faith" was made during the second session of the council. On the debit side, however, mention must be made of continued conceptual imprecision of the term itself, of how the "sense of the faith" is to be determined, of whether or not all sectors of the church are to be consulted and the degree of obligation in consulting them, and the "sense of the faith" as a criteriological norm for determining the content of the faith and practice of the church. All of these ambiguities would emerge in the postconciliar church and render its acceptance and implementation problematic. Nevertheless, it can be claimed that by the end of the second session, the "sense of the faith" among all the members of the church and at all levels in the church was a teaching that few among the bishops at Vatican II called into question. Further helpful clarifications were still to be made at the council itself, and we now turn our attention to these efforts.

Intersession (December 1963 to September 1964) and Third Session (Fall 1964)

Even before the end of the second session, the subcommission on the church met on November 13 and December 3 to work on the proposed new chapter on the people of God. Congar informs us of the difficulty in forging a coherent text from the bits and pieces taken from *Aeternus Unigeniti Pater*, the comments of the bishops during the General Congregations or their written submissions, and the pet suggestions coming from various theologians, suggestions that often contributed little to craft-

---

fidelibus per saecula traditam et peculiari Dei providentia immunem ab errore servatam, patefacit. . . . Infallibilitas activa residet in Ecclesia docente seu in magisterio authentico et vivo, quod unice pertinet ad Romanum Pontificem et ad episcopos sub Romano Pontifice et una cum illo, doctrinam divinitus revelatam proponentes ac definientes; infallibilitas autem passiva, seu in credendo, stat in Ecclesia discente, quae doctrinam revelatam a magisterio authentico et vivo submisse accipit." Quoted by Schmucker, *Sensus Fidei*, 176nn158 and 156.

ing a unified text.[40] The subcommission met again in Rome on January 31 and February 1 to write the new chapter 2 on the people of God. But other urgent issues of the constitution were surfacing, issues that would practically monopolize the attention of the bishops and theologians far more than chapter 2: the collegiality of the bishops and how it relates to the pope's primacy, not to mention a proposed text on the Virgin Mary and the unresolved question of whether the text should be included as a chapter in the Dogmatic Constitution on the Church or be issued as a separate document. The Theological Commission met in Rome on March 2 and 5 and completed the text of the new chapter 2 on the people of God. On March 10 and 12, the final text of chapter 4 on the laity was completed.

The council reconvened for its third session on September 15, 1964. On September 17, on behalf of the Theological Commission, Archbishop Gabriel Garrone of Toulouse, France, presented the Official Report, or *relatio*, of chapter 2 to the assembled bishops. Archbishop Garrone stressed the following points: Many bishops had requested that the theme of the people of God in the Dogmatic Constitution on the Church be expanded in order to point out its place in time and history; to make it clear that the church as a whole consists of all the faithful and as such pertains to the finality of the church, while the hierarchy is a means ordered to that end and in service to it; to better bring to light that the unity of the church comes to perfection in the diversity of services and roles (*munera*) and in the diversity of the particular churches, traditions, and cultures; to employ a better locution than the term "membership" when speaking of the relationship of non-Catholic Christians to the church; and to emphasize that the missionary task of the church continues throughout history and involves all the faithful.

Garrone explained how the new chapter emerged from reworking statements made in earlier chapters together with some entirely new

---

40. In response to the meeting on December 3, Congar wrote in his journal: "As we worked on the text in detail, it became painfully clear how much both the *De Ecclesia*, and this chapter *De Populo Dei* in particular, have suffered from never having been THOUGHT THROUGH. Bits have been taken from here and there. . . . [T]hat does not produce A TEXT! Philips satisfied all requests . . . , adding 'something' on the Eucharist here, 'something' on the mission there, 'something' on the diversity of cultures somewhere else. . . . What is lacking is ONE idea that controls and arranges the whole." See *My Journal of the Council*, 463.

ideas. The process of redaction has resulted in an introductory paragraph (art. 9), three paragraphs that constitute the first part and that treat the prerogatives of the whole people of God as enumerated by the First Letter of Peter: its priestly quality pertaining to the church's cultic activity (art. 10) and sacramental life (art. 11) as well as its activity of announcing the Gospel (art. 12). The second part of chapter 2 takes up several issues that elucidate how the church is apostolic and truly catholic, and that incorporate all those human values and customs that characterize humankind in all its rich variety (art. 13). Some of humankind enjoy all the means that the Father has willed for human fulfillment (art. 14), while others enjoy only partial participation in the means willed by God—namely, faith, the sacraments, Scripture, and the order of bishops with Peter (art. 15). Other men and women who do not profess the Christian faith are not thereby excluded from the people of God but participate in it because of their relationship to God's covenant or because of the presence of God's grace in their hearts (art. 16). These insights help to better explain the missionary task of the church in bringing all women and men into an explicit acceptance of Christ the Head of humankind (art. 17). Finally, Garrone concluded with a brief comment on each paragraph of chapter 2, in particular by pointing out new elements that have been incorporated into the previous text in the process of redaction.[41] In regard to the discussion of the "sense of the faith" in the official report, Garrone summarized the presentation as follows:

> Regarding the "sense of the faith" and charisms among the Christian people, it is clearly a matter of two distinct realities. The first point concerns the "sense of the faith" of the whole people, and its meaning is explained more adequately and profoundly [12,1]. The other deals

---

41. See *Acta Synodalia Sacrosancti Concilii Oecumenici Vaticani II* (Vatican City: Typis Polyglottis Vaticanis, 1970–1978), III/1: 500–504. The summary presented by Archbishop Garrone, though it hardly does justice to the richness and detail of the actual text, does succeed in communicating the difficulty the authors encountered in responding to the requests and demands of the bishops in a coherent way. The two sections of chapter 2 show very clearly how the council tried to make some principal points, while also trying to introduce important ideas and teachings without being entirely successful in integrating them in the text as a whole. This creates the impression that some ecclesiological ideas have only been partially elaborated.

with the distribution of the gifts of the Holy Spirit. These are described more fully and accurately as regards their character and positive goal, and also regarding the authority of those who have been entrusted with responsibility for them in the Church [12,2].[42]

On the following day, September 18, a vote was taken on the new chapter on the people of God and it was overwhelmingly approved. There were no new objections to the teaching on the "sense of the faith." A final vote on the whole constitution was taken on November 19 and the document was proclaimed by Paul VI on November 21. What, then, did Vatican II teach about the "sense of the faith"?

Lumen Gentium, Article 12

We have looked at the emergence of the teaching on the "sense of the faith" in *Aeternus Unigeniti Pater* and in all the subsequent versions of Vatican II's Constitution on the Church. We have also seen how the contexts in which it was taught changed (first, public opinion and second, the laity) and how its meaning was deepened by its being associated more intimately with the notion of the people of God and with the three offices (*munera*) of Christ. It is now time to examine the text of *Lumen Gentium* in which the teaching comes to expression. Here, then, is the final text of Vatican II:

> The holy people of God also shares in the prophetic office of Christ by spreading its living witness abroad especially by a life of faith and charity and by offering to God a sacrifice of praise, the fruit of the lips of those who confess his name (see Hebrews 13:15). The universal body of the faithful who have been anointed by the Holy One (see 1 John 2:20 and 27), cannot err in believing, and they give evidence of this unique property which is theirs by means of the supernatural "sense of the faith" of the entire people, when "from the bishops to the least of

---

42. "De sensu fidei et charismatibus in populo christiano. Manifeste agitur de duabus rebus distinctis. Prima est sensus fidei totius populi, qui sensus uberius et penitus explicatur. Altera est diffusio donorum Spiritus Sancti, quae plenius et accuratius describuntur, indicatis eorum indole et fine positivo, indicato quoque munere Praepositorum Ecclesiae circa illa." Ibid., III/1: 503. My translation.

the believing laity" [quoting St. Augustine] they show their universal consensus on matters of faith and morals. Indeed, by this very sense of the faith which the Spirit of truth stirs up and nourishes in them, the people of God receives not merely human words but the very word of God (see 1 Thessalonians 2:13), "the faith that was once handed over to the saints" (Jude 3). The believing faithful do so under the leadership of the sacred teaching authority [of the pope and bishops] to which they trustingly defer and by adhering indefectibly to it [the word of God]. By judging correctly, they more profoundly enter into it [the faith] and apply it more comprehensively to life.[43]

The passage is rich and dense with meaning. I propose to examine the individual elements of the "sense of the faith" taught in article 12,1. Each item adds an important element to a proper understanding of the "sense of the faith." The council's presentation of the theme is built up cumulatively, so that the many mutual elements of its formulation together constitute a profound spiritual reality of the Christian faith.

First of all, the "sense of the faith" is a gift from God to God's holy people. The text speaks of the people's "sharing" (*participat*) in the work of Christ. From the history of the Christian teaching on grace we know that such "sharing" points to the theological reality of God communicating the divine life to creatures endowed with freedom and reason.[44] Grace is not a "thing" or "something quantitative" that God communicates to creatures but is God's self-communication. Grace is a relationship that God freely

43. "Populus Dei sanctus de munere quoque prophetico Christi participat, vivum eius testimonium maxime per vitam fidei ac caritatis diffundendo, et Deo hostiam laudis offerendo, fructum labiorum confitentium nomini eius (cf. Heb 13:15). Universitas fidelium, qui unctionem habent a sancto (cf. 1 Jn 2:20 et 27), in credendo falli nequit, atque hanc suam peculiarem proprietatem mediante supernaturali sensu fidei totius populi manifestat, cum 'ab episcopis usque ad extremos laicos fideles' universalem suum consensum de rebus fidei et morum exhibet. Illo enim sensu fidei, qui a Spiritu veritatis excitatur et sustentatur, populus Dei sub ductu sacri magisterii, cui fideliter obsequens, iam non verbum hominum, sed vere accipit verbum Dei (cf. 1 Th 2:13), 'semel traditae sanctis fidei' (Ju 3), indefectibiliter adhaeret, recto iudicio in eam profundius penetrat eamque in vita plenius applicat." The Latin text can be found in *Decrees of the Ecumenical Councils*, vol. 2, ed. Norman P. Tanner (Washington, DC: Georgetown University Press, 1990), 858. The text presents a number of problems of interpretation to a translator, and so I have given my own translation. See appendix A for a comparison of several English translations.

44. See Roger Haight, *The Experience and Language of Grace* (New York: Paulist Press, 1979) for a short but helpful history of the word "grace" and the controversies surrounding it.

and with total love establishes with men and women. It is the fulfillment of the human vocation. The "sense of the faith" is a manifestation of humankind's being called into an intimate relationship with its God. That is why the opening sentence speaks of the "life of faith and charity" and of "a living witness." Grace, or "sharing," and faith are about life divinely communicated and humanly lived to the fullest. That is why the "sense of the faith" is later in the paragraph called "supernatural." It participates in the order of God's life and God's salvific will with respect to humankind.

Second, Vatican II points to the Trinity as the source of this supernatural "sharing." The Christian Scriptures, the historical sources, and the history of theology all point to the Holy Spirit as active in bestowing, eliciting, confirming, and perfecting the perception of truth by free rational creatures. God as Spirit is active in the event of the human being's coming to truth, whether it is the truth enunciated in creation or the truth of the mystery of divine life itself. The Holy Spirit is the source of truth whose agency is directly at work in imparting truth. Here, too, Vatican II sees truth in terms of gift and grace. It is never purely human accomplishment, but also never less than human accomplishment. God's truth is human fulfillment, and divine truth is communicated by the Holy triune Spirit.[45]

Third, faith-inspired knowing is real knowledge or cognition. This is the point of the council's speaking of the "sense" of the faith. The word "sense" or *sensus* is taken from the vocabulary of epistemology while remaining open to knowledge imparted by metaphor or figures of speech. In the case of the "sense of the faith" it is primarily practical, not speculative, knowledge.[46] The "sense of the faith" is centered on how faith is to be lived

45. Jos Moons has shown how the role of the Holy Spirit as bestower and sustainer of the "sense of the faith" in the believer became clearer in the successive versions of article 12 of the Dogmatic Constitution on the Church. See his " 'Aroused and Sustained by the Holy Spirit'? A Plea for a Pneumatological Reconsideraton of *Sensus Fidei* on the Basis of *Lumen Gentium* 12," *Gregorianum* 99 (2018): 271–91. Moons vigorously defends the thesis that as the years unfolded Vatican II came to a greater appreciation of the Holy Spirit in the church and thereby mitigated the tendency in the West to concentrate exclusively on the Son in the economy of salvation.

46. The cognition entailed by the "sense of the faith" does not exclude speculative knowledge, of course, but speculation employs abstract concepts, technical vocabulary, and discursive reasoning—epistemological means that are often beyond the competence of the ordinary faithful and often, too, beyond that of the ordinary clergy. I will return to this topic in chapter 11.

in truth and incorporated into the whole fabric of the life of the church. As the introductory words to article 12,1 say, it its directed "to a life of faith and charity. . . . [that] offers to God a sacrifice of praise, the tribute of lips that honor his name." That is why the believer is rendered "a living witness." It quietly, unobtrusively, and confidently embraces faith as lived. The "sense of the faith" might even be called "knowing by discipleship."

Fourth, Vatican II situates the "sense of the faith" in the people of God as a whole, or as the council says, in "the universal body of the faithful." The bishops even quote St. Augustine, who, though in an entirely different context than the council's teaching on the "sense of the faith," used the phrase "from the bishops to the last of the faithful" to stress its universality.[47] Everyone in the church is endowed with the supernatural "sense of the faith," and so no one is excluded. All believers taken as a totality and before any distinction among them as to office, responsibility, or vocation in the church constitute "the universal body of the faithful." The operative perspective here is that *we are all* the body of believers who have been entrusted with God's inexhaustible truth and with the responsibility to grow in our understanding of that truth so that we might proclaim it in ever-changing circumstances and to ever more hearers of that word.

Fifth, this universality means that the relations of those who constitute "the universal body of the faithful" are mutually inclusive. A vocabulary of subordination is inappropriate and misleading for the reality of the "sense of the faith" of all the faithful. As my translation of article 12,1 above indicated, the bishops do not speak of the ordinary faithful as

---

47. See *The Predestination of the Saints*, chapter 14, line 27, a late work by Augustine (428–429) opposing a moderate form of Pelagianism that accepted the doctrine of original sin as taught by Augustine. In the original context, Augustine was arguing for the acceptance of the book of Wisdom as canonical, since he wants to use its teaching to oppose the Pelagians. He writes: "The judgment of the book of Wisdom ought not to be repudiated, since for so long a course of years that book has deserved to be read in the Church of Christ, from the station of the readers of the Church of Christ, and to be heard by all Christians, from bishops downwards, even to the lowest lay believers, penitents, and catechumens." *A Select Library of the Nicene and Post-Nicene Fathers*, First Series, 14 vols., trans. Robert Ernest Wallis (New York: The Christian Literature Company, 1887), 5:511. St. Augustine, then, cannot be invoked as a direct witness of the council's teaching on the "sense of the faith" on the basis of this quotation.

being "faithfully obedient" to them, but rather that they show "respect" or "deference" in the faith to them.[48] Although it is entirely appropriate to speak about a division of labor in ascertaining and teaching the truth of God entrusted to the whole church, such vocabulary can never supplant the responsibility of everyone for the revelation God has entrusted to the whole church. In addition to the unity of the pope and bishops with the ordinary faithful in the church, there is the aspect of the mutuality of their insights into the faith with the understanding of the pope and the bishops.

Sixth, Vatican II retrieved the traditional Catholic teaching that the whole church is infallible in matters of Christian revelation. A number of scholars have pointed out a certain creeping infallibility, or as Congar said, a certain inflation of the idea of papal infallibility at the expense of the more traditional teaching on the infallibility of the church itself.[49] When *Aeternus Unigeniti Pater*, Gérard Philips's reworked text, and *Lumen Gentium* are compared with one another, I submit that the "infallibility

---

48. The two most commonly cited English translations, Norman P. Tanner's and Austin Flannery's, speak at this point of "being obedient to" or "obeying" the pope and the bishops. But that is not what the Latin text indicates. Instead of speaking of "*obedientia*" or "*obedire*," the Latin speaks of "*obsequens*," from the Latin verb "*obsequi*," which means "to pay homage to" or "to respect." Only the Walter M. Abbott edition gets it right when it speaks of "the lead of a sacred teaching authority to which it [the body of the faithful] loyally defers." *The Documents of Vatican II*, translation editor Joseph Gallagher (New York: Guild Press/America Press/Association Press, 1966), 30. It should be quite evident that caution needs to be observed on this point, since speaking of "obedience" can easily be understood as subservience on the part of the laity. Originally, *Aeternus Unigeniti Pater* said that the faithful "accept the doctrine proposed [to them] in an obedient spirit (ut doctrinam propositam obedienti animo accipiant)," but this was changed to the expression "under the guidance of the sacred magisterium to which it faithfully defers (sub ductu sacri magisterii cui fideliter obsequens)." The revised formulation, then, avoids any hint of subordination of the laity or any form of tutelage that would keep them in a state of subservient receptivity. We always need to be careful about the misleading consequences of overly casual references to "obedience."

49. "There has also been a veritable inflation of the category of infallibility, as if between what is infallibly true and error, there did not exist an immense field of partial truth, of probable certitude, of research and approximations in knowledge, and indeed of very precious truth that does not enjoy the guarantee of being risk-free and that comes with human finitude." See "Infaillibilité et indéfectibilité," *Revue des sciences philosophiques et théologiques* 54 (1970): 601–18, at 608.

of the whole Church" emerges clearly."[50] Let us look at each version and compare them to one another.

In *Aeternus Unigeniti Pater,* the reference is rather weak and only speaks of the "sense of the faith" as "an indefectible and unique mark of the Catholic Church," whereas Philips's reworked text speaks of it in much stronger terms. His text says: "The whole Church which offers to God the fruit of lips that confess his name, and which is indefectible in its belief, is also manifested in the supernatural 'sense of the faith' of the whole Christian people of God." Finally, though *Lumen Gentium* 12,1 does not directly employ the term "infallible," it does speak of the reality itself when it says that "the universal body of the faithful who have been anointed by the Holy One cannot err in believing (*in credendo falli nequit*)." The church is destined to proclaim the truth of the Gospel to the whole world and infallibility exists to assist the church in this mission. Infallibility stands for the eschatologically victorious salvific truth the church has been entrusted with and charged by Christ to bring to the world. Vatican II has retrieved the responsibility of all believers in the church for Christian revelation.

---

50. The First Vatican Council, in defining the infallibility which the pope enjoys as supreme pastor and teacher in the church and the conditions under which he can exercise it, never included a definition of the term "infallibility." Conciliar documents are not dogmatic treatises in theology. They work with concepts and themes that are generally accepted by theologians and other scholars (e.g., exegetes and historians), and this procedure offers greater flexibility and latitude in interpreting them. However, it can also lead to confusion on the one hand and to excessive claims as to their meaning on the other. Nonetheless, in its decree of definition, Vatican I pointed to a number of factors that need to be considered in coming to an understanding of the slippery term "infallibility." I would point to five such factors. The church is infallible because (1) it is entrusted with divine teachings that must be kept pure and uncontaminated (*salutaris Christi doctrina . . . sincera et pura conservaretur*); (2) the Catholic faith entrusted to the church must be beyond "failing utterly" (*fides non potest sentire defectum*); (3) the Catholic faith is grounded in "the Scriptures and apostolic traditions" (*quae sacris scripturis et apostolicis traditionibus consentanea*); (4) Christian faith exists for the salvation of all men and women (*ut excelso suo munere in omnium salutem fungerentur*); and (5) believers will be preserved from errors regarding the content and understanding of the faith (*ab erroris venenosa esca aversus . . . conservaretur*). See the "Constitutio dogmatica prima de ecclesia Christi, Caput IV: De Romani pontificis infallibili magisterio," *Decrees of the Ecumenical Councils*, ed. Norman P. Tanner (Washington, DC: Georgetown University Press, 1990), 2:815–16.

Lumen Gentium 12,1 also employs the term "indefectible" when it refers to the people of God "adhering indefectibly to [the word of God]." In an important article on the relationship of the terms "infallibility" and "indefectibility" to one another, Congar argued cogently that the notion of "indefectibility" was perhaps more appropriate to the role of the whole body of the faithful in possessing and proclaiming the truth of the Gospel throughout history than the hotly disputed and often misunderstood notion of "infallibility."[51] In the fresh perspective of chapter 2 of *Lumen Gentium*, the council was in a better position to recast the traditional Catholic teaching of the "infallibility of all who believe" into the terms of the church's "indefectibility" (*indefectibilitas*). Congar, who had worked closely with Philips and the Subcommission on the Church, saw distinct advantages in recasting "infallibility" in terms of "indefectibility." He argued that "infallibility" tended to become absorbed in abstract theories of truth and understanding, whereas "indefectibility" came closer to rendering the biblical understanding of truth as the eschatological goal toward which the church is always moving throughout history. Indefectibility allows for the partial groping of the human mind in the presence of the mystery of divine truth that will only be truly known when the believer is fully united with God in beatitude. Such an approach is respectful of the historical limitations of human knowing and the historicity of its formulation. Though perhaps humbler as a term and more modest in its claims than the term infallibility, indefectibility is perfectly appropriate to the church's "sure and certain" knowledge of revealed truth.

Seventh, Vatican II teaches that the supernatural anointing of each believer by the Holy Spirit as a "sense of the faith" (*sensus fidei*) leads to a "consensus in the faith" (*consensus fidei*): "The universal body of the faithful . . . give evidence of this unique property by means of the supernatural 'sense of the faith' of the whole people when . . . they show their universal consensus on matters of faith and morals."[52] In other words,

---

51. "Infaillibilité et indéfectibilité," *Revue des sciences philosohiques et théologiques* 54 (1970): 601–18.

52. Every version of the document of Vatican II on the church, from *Aeternus Unigeniti Pater* to *Lumen Gentium* referred to "consensus" in conjunction with its teaching on the "sense of the faith." On the notion of consensus and its meaning in the light of various contemporary philosophical theories of truth, especially the theory of consensus, see Peter Scharr, *Consensus fidelium: Zur Unfehlbarkeit der Kirche aus der Perspektive einer Konsenstheorie der Wahrheit* (Würzburg: Echter, 1962).

Vatican II points to the unitive function of the "sense of the faith." Christians are not left isolated from one another in their faith but are invited to share that faith with each other. This consensus, however, is not primarily the result of their efforts to constitute it, but is a gift of the Holy Spirit to all believers. Consensus is achieved in believing with others that some teaching is true or that some practice incarnates what is interiorly believed. That is why the terms the "sense of the faith" (*sensus fidei*), the "sense of the faithful" (*sensus fidelium*), and the "consensus of the faithful" (*consensus fidelium*) are used interchangeably so often in the literature.

But the meaning of consensus and the means of determining it can prove very elusive.[53] Consensus among human beings is ultimately not quantifiable. At best, numbers and percentages can only hint at the underlying social or ecclesial agreement.[54] And yet, numbers and percentages are necessary indices.[55] They point toward consensus but never grasp it entirely or explain it adequately. Consensus is arrived at when the faithful

---

53. On the topic of consensus in general, and on ecclesial consensus in particular, see Peter Scharr, *Consensus fidelium. Zur Unfehlbarkeit der Kirche aus der Perspektive einer Konsenstheorie der Wahrheit* (Würzburg: Echter, 1992). See also Hermann Josef Sieben, "Consensus, unanimitas, und maior pars auf Konzilien, von der Alten Kirche bis zum Ersten Vaticanum," *Theologie und Philosophie* 67 (1992): 192–229.

54. In his doctoral dissertation on the "sense of the faith," Dominik Burghardt attempted an explanation of the thorny and slippery notion of consensus as it relates to "consensus in the faith." He writes: "The *consensus fidelium* is not governed by a principle based on the majority as though consensus were a matter of 'quantity,' but it is a principle of identity that is based on the category of 'quality.' The *consensus fidelium* is not authentic because it primarily expresses the opinion of the majority of believers, but because the faithful, whatever their status, express an understanding that is in harmony with and that concretizes the faith of the Church from its very origin, with the result that it is received in principle by the whole Church. The *consensus fidelium* cannot be empirically determined by a vote taken at a given point in time, but is by its nature spontaneous and beyond human control because the *sensus fidei* grows as a supernatural gift of grace." One can palpably sense in Burghardt's strained formulation how difficult the notion of consensus is when we are speaking about a consensus of the faith. The *consensus fidelium* eludes human manipulation, and all the faithful can only surrender to it when it takes hold of them. It is not a matter of percentages but a matter of self-recognition and self-realization (that is, identity and authenticity). See *Institution Glaubenssinn: die Bedeutung des 'sensus fidei' im kirchlichen Verfassusngsrecht und für die Interpretation kanonischer Gesetze* (Paderborn: Bonifatius Verlag, 2002), 189–90.

55. See ibid., 178–85 ["Konsenserhebung durch Statistik?"].

and their leaders in the faith, the pope and the bishops, acknowledge it. If one of these two constitutive groups does not admit that the consensus is ripe, then it has not yet been reached. It might, however, be incipient or well advanced. Only the patient and prayerful process of communicating on an issue and of respectfully debating it will ultimately result in both groups acknowledging that the consensus is already present as a gift of the Spirit. Some urge that ecclesial consensus emerges best in a culture of communication in the church:[56] communication that is free, open, in-formed, and mutually respectful. Others point to the role of discernment in arriving at consensus, a role that the postconciliar church is coming to acknowledge more and more.[57] In this respect, too, the growing emphasis on the synodality of the church as taught by Vatican II holds out promise of greater success for arriving at and recognizing consensus on the faith of the church.[58]

Eighth, *Lumen Gentium* 12 rejects a merely static understanding of the "sense of the faith." The earliest expression of growth in the faith appeared already in *Aeternus Unigeniti Pater* as the rather direct statement that the Holy Spirit gave a supernatural "sense of the faith" to the faithful "so that they might correctly understand doctrine and study it in greater depth (ut doctrinam . . . recte intelligant et profundius scrutentur)." In Philips's redacted text the teaching was expanded to say that the faithful "perceived the truth of faith at a deeper level and by applying it faithfully to life (. . . veritatem fidei profundius perspiciendo et in vita fidelius applicando)." The final redaction of *Lumen Gentium* 12 goes even further in teaching that the faithful "by judging correctly, more profoundly enter into it [the faith] and apply it more comprehensively to life (recto iudicio in eam profundius penetrat eamque in vita plenius applicat)." To the bishops

---

56. I am indebted to Professor Michael Root of The Catholic University of America for this insight and his suggestive locution of a "culture of communication."

57. On the process of discernment and its role in arriving at consensus, see Amanda C. Osheim, *A Ministry of Discernment: The Bishop and the Sense of the Faithful* (Collegeville, MN: Liturgical Press, 2016).

58. See Scharr, *Consensus fidelium*, 185–88 ["Die Ortskirche als Ort der Wahrheitsfind-ung"] on the role of the local church in achieving consensus, and Ormond Rush, "The Church Local and Universal and the Communion of the Faithful," in *A Realist's Church: Essays in Honor of Joseph A. Komonchak*, ed. Christopher D. Denny, Patrick J. Hayes, and Nicholas K. Rademacher (Maryknoll, NY: Orbis Books, 2015), 117–30.

at Vatican II the understanding of the faith is something dynamic. The church is never simply fixed in its understanding of the faith. Dynamism and movement beyond a static understanding of the content of revelation do not contradict or threaten the truth-character of the Christian faith. The faith grows in understanding but without rejecting the true insights of the past. And yet the present moment in human historicity is not simply identifiable with the past. The present is truly a new moment and an opportunity for growth in understanding, even of the faith.

Ninth, the final text associates the participation of the whole church by way of the bestowal on all of the "supernatural sense of the faith" with the prophetic office (*munus*) of Christ.[59] Earlier versions by Philips and the Subcommission on the Church had mentioned all three of Christ's offices (*munera*)—the priestly, the prophetic, and the kingly—together when it taught the "sense of the faith" and the participation of all in it. The final version, however, speaks only about the prophetic office at this

---

59. The prophetic office of Christ envisions him as the one who proclaims the living and effective word of God. It is based on the Hebrew understanding of the "word" or *dabhar* of God. In the Hebrew mind "words produce realities." They do more than simply reflect internal mental states and epistemic understanding. Words are laden with power, and so exercise causation. The classic scriptural text is Isaiah 55:10-11. Examples include promises and vows, blessings and curses, prophecies of events, the exposing of human thoughts and intentions, treaties and their obligations, etc. If this is true of human words, how much the more is it true of divine words. The Old Testament prophets spoke God's power-laden oracles of weal and woe and thereby shaped Israel's history. Jesus as prophet speaks the power-laden words of God and so directs the course of history. In Jesus's wake, the church, too, in its "prophetic office" is entrusted with power. In the Spirit, it speaks the word of God and does not merely reflect on it. In certain critical and limited circumstances, the church determines reality by speaking God's word. When the "sense of the faith" is an expression of Christ's prophetic office, the whole church in all its members participates in and exercises its prophetic responsibility to shape reality according to the form and will of Christ. The literature on the word of God is extensive. A few resources include John L. McKenzie, "The Word of God in the Old Testament," *Myths and Realities: Studies in Biblical Theology* (Milwaukee, WI: Bruce, 1963), 37–58; Bruce Vawter, "History and the Word," *Catholic Biblical Quarterly* 29 (1967): 512–23; Jerome Kodell, "'The Word of God Grew.' The Ecclesial Tendency of *Logos* in Acts 1, 7; 12, 24; 19, 20," *Biblica* 55 (1974): 505–19; and J. Bergman, H. Lutzmann, and W. H. Schmidt, "*dābhar*," in *Theological Dictionary of the Old Testament*, 15 vols., ed. G. J. Botterweck and H. Ringgren, trans. J. T. Willis, G. W. Bromiley, and D. E. Green (Grand Rapids, MI: Wm. B. Eerdmans, 1978), 3:84–125.

point. Unfortunately, this move tends to obscure the underlying unity of the threefold offices in which all participate. The text does not relate the three offices to each other, with the result that each appears isolated from the other two,[60] even though it makes clear that the faithful participate in all three offices.[61] But is the "sense of the faith" limited to the prophetic office of Christ as participated in by all the faithful? Given the indivisibility of the three offices in Christ, is the same true of its participated form in all the faithful? Does the "sense of the faith" come to expression in the priestly and kingly offices of the faithful as well? The answer is not clear in the text.[62] But what does appear clear is that the teaching of Vatican II on the "sense of the faith" is unthinkable apart from these mutually enriching themes: the church is the people of God and this people participates in and exercises the three offices of Christ the preacher or prophet, Christ the priest or sanctifier, and Christ the king or leader.

60. See Anthony Ekpo, "The *Sensus Fidelium* and the Threefold Office of Christ: A Reinterpretation of *Lumen Gentium* No. 12," *Theological Studies* 76 (2015): 330–46. For a comprehensive examination of the prophetic office in the documents of Vatican II, see Norbert Weis, *Das prophetische Amt der Laien in der Kirche. Eine rechtstheologische Untersuchung anhand dreier Dokumente des Zweiten Vatikanischen Konzils*. Analecta Gregoriana 225 (Rome: Gregorian University Press, 1981).

61. Even *Aeternus Unigeniti Pater* was clear on this point. Thus, in chapter 1 on the Nature of the Church Militant, we read about the analogy between the christological mystery of one person in two natures as extended to the church: "For just as in the Incarnate Word the human nature is the living instrument of the same divine nature, acting in behalf of our salvation and that of the whole world and continuing to so act in heaven, so too the society of the Church is adorned with the charisms of the preacher, of the priest, and of the king, in service of the building up of the body of Christ in the Spirit of Christ (Etenim sicut in Verbo Incarnato natura humana ut vivum instrumentum divinae eiusdem naturae, pro nostra et totius mundi salute inserviit et in coelis inservire perseverat, ita Ecclesiae societas praeconis, sacerdotis, regis charismatibus exornatur, ut Spiritui Christi in aedificatione Corporis Christi serviat)" (art. 6). My translation. It seems that from the earliest stages of the production of what would eventually emerge as the Dogmatic Constitution on the Church, the three offices of Christ himself and as participated in by the church were never far from sight.

62. See the cautions I expressed in my article "The *Sensus Fidelium*: Old Questions, New Challenges," in *Learning from All the Faithful: A Contemporary Theology of the Sensus Fidei*, ed. Bradford E. Hinze and Peter C. Phan (Eugene, OR: Pickwick Publications, 2016), 125–42, at 130–31 ["The Threefold Office of Christ"].

Lumen Gentium, Article 35

Because the council decided to add a separate chapter on the people of God to the Dogmatic Constitution on the Church, the treatment of the "sense of the faith" was divided between the new chapter on the people of God (chapter 2) and the original chapter on the people of God and the laity. Commentators have concentrated on the general teaching of article 12,1 to the neglect of the complementary statements of article 35. These statements deserve to be considered in their own right, and we now turn to them.

Chapter 4 of Philips's new text draws on material developed in chapter 6 of *Aeternus Unigeniti Pater*.[63] The first thing we note when we read this chapter in its original context is its stress on the rightful participation of all the faithful in the church's mission.

> Called to be the People of God and constituted as the one body of Christ under one head, everyone, as living members who have received the favor of the Creator and the grace of the Redeemer, is obliged to spend all their energy in working for the growth of the Church and for its continued increase in holiness. Although the Lord himself has sanctified some to be pastors and teachers in the work of ministry, he has done so that the faithful might not be like capricious children but

---

63. According to Alberto Melloni, Gérard Philips had been entrusted by the Preparatory Commission to write chapter 6, "On the Laity," of *Aeternus Unigeniti Pater*. ("What was still at this point chapter III was the child of an initial revision of the chapter on the laity from the preparatory phase and had kept almost everything from that chapter, which Philips himself had written.") See "The Beginning of the Second Period: The Great Debate on the Church," in *History of Vatican II*, vol. 3: *The Mature Council, Second Period and Intersession, September 1963–September 1964*, ed. Giuseppe Alberigo and Joseph A. Komonchak (Maryknoll, NY: Orbis Books, 2000), 80. As one of the leading Catholic authorities of the day on the topic of the laity, Philips was familiar with the positive but limited steps taken by Popes Pius XI and Pius XII in particular on enhancing the value of the laity in the church and plumbing the sources of the earlier theology of the priestly character of the laity in the church. This explains why later during the council, Philips was able to draw liberally upon what *Aeternus Unigeniti Pater* had already said. Now, however, in light of what some bishops were saying in their speeches and written submissions, and what the theological experts on the various subcommissions were advocating, Philips was able to deftly rewrite the text in such a way as to both build on and move beyond what he had already written in *Aeternus Unigeniti Pater*.

The "Sense of the Faith" and Vatican II   255

in the measure each has received that they might work for the building up of the body until all reach the maturity of the fullness of Christ (see Ephesians 4:11-6). Therefore, the pastors have not been appointed to assume the full burden of the Church's mission, but rather that all the faithful whom they lead might make their contribution, each in his own way and in her proper place in the body, and so cooperate in the common task to be accomplished. There is, in fact, only one vocation of the whole organic body.[64]

It should be noted that even though the governing biblical image of the church in this section is still the Body of Christ, the biblical image of the people of God has also been introduced. The rest of the chapter develops the theme of the participation of all in the one mission of the church with the help of the categories of the threefold office of Christ. We saw above that chapter 2 spread the discussion of the three offices of priest, prophet, and king/leader among separate articles. Chapter 4 does so as well. Article 34 treats the priestly office, while article 35 deals with the prophetic office, and article 36 elaborates on the office of leadership.[65] In its own right, however, article 35 makes an important contribution to the council's teaching on the "sense of the faith" in several ways.

Article 35 is divided into four paragraphs and reads as follows:

> Christ is the great prophet who proclaimed the reign of the Father by the witness of his life and by the power of his word, and he continues to accomplish his prophetic office until the full revelation of his glory.

64. "Ad Populum Dei evocati et in uno Corpore Christi sub uno Capiti constituti, quicumque sunt, ut viva membra ad Ecclesiae incrementum eiusque continuam sanctificationem vires suas omnes, a beneficio Creatoris et a gratia Redemptoris acceptas, conferre tenentur. Ipse autem Dominus quosdam in Ecclesia pastores et doctores ad opus ministerii sanctificavit, ut fideles, non tamquam parvuli fluctuantes, sed secundum operationen in mensuram uniuscuisque membri augmentum Corporis faciant, donec perveniant omnes ad aetatem plenitudinis Christi (cf. Eph. 4:11-16). Pastores ergo instituti non sunt ut totum onus in se suscipiant, sed ut omnes fideles, quos regunt, eo adducant ut suo modo et ordine ad commune opus explendum cooperentur. Una est enim totius organici Corporis vocatio." *Acta et Documenta Concilio Oecumenico Vaticano II Apparando*, Series II, 3/1 (Vatican City: Typis Polyglottis Vaticanis, 1969), 154–55. My translation.

65. Chapters 2 and 4 both fail to relate the three offices to each other and thus create the conditions for underestimating them.

He does this not only through the hierarchy who teach with authority in his name but also through the lay faithful whom he has appointed his witnesses and whom he has equipped with the sense of faith and the gift of his word (see Acts 2:17-18; Revelation 19:10). Through the lay faithful he demonstrates the power of the gospel in the daily life of family and society. The lay faithful show themselves to be sons and daughters of the promise when they are strong in faith and hope and when they redeem the present moment (see Ephesians 5:16 and Colossians 4:5) and so patiently await the economy of future glory (see Romans 8:25). They should not bury this hope in the depths of their souls but as men and women who are constantly being converted and waging war "against the rulers of the world's darkness and the spirits of iniquity" (Ephesians 6:12) show forth their hope in the humanly constructed systems of secular life.

As the sacraments of the new law nourish the life and the apostolate of the faithful by prefiguring the new heavens and the new earth (see Revelation 21:1), so do the lay faithful prove themselves to be true heralds of their belief in the things to be hoped for (see Hebrews 11:1) They only need to ceaselessly join their daily life to the confession of the faith. Such evangelization is a proclamation of Christ when it comes to expression in the witness of daily life and in the spoken word. It acquires specific and proper effectiveness when it is realized in the ordinary circumstances of secular life.

That state of life that is sanctified by its own sacrament, the life of matrimony and of the family, shines forth in this very precious office. Where the Christian religion pervades the entire institution of life and increasingly transforms it day by day, that is where the apostolate of the lay faithful is to be seen as an outstanding school of the practice of the faith. That is where husband and wife discover their proper vocation and where they offer each other and their children the witness of their faith and of the love of Christ. Christian family life boldly proclaims the power of the reign of God as both present reality and as the hope of blessed life to come. By their example and their witness the married lay faithful accuse the world of sin and offer guidance to those who seek the truth.

Even when they are occupied in temporal affairs the laity still can and must engage in the valuable task of evangelizing the world. But if the situation should arise that there are not enough ordained ministers [to meet the needs of the faithful], or that in times of persecution [of the church] by the State, the lay faithful may provide certain sacred actions and they receive the appropriate authorization to perform these actions.[66] Indeed, while many of the lay faithful expend all their energy in apostolic work, it is incumbent on all to cooperate in the expansion and the growth of the reign of Christ in the world. That is why the lay faithful are encouraged to dedicate themselves assiduously to growing in their knowledge of revealed truth and to insistently entreat God to bestow on them the gift of wisdom.[67]

First, the Dogmatic Constitution on the Church makes it unmistakably clear that all Christians are called to share in the ministry of the word of the church. That is undoubtedly the point of the text's repeated use of technical vocabulary when speaking of this office. By the very fact that one is baptized and invested with the dignity of being a "believer in Christ" (a *christifidelis*), Christians are *eo ipso* "appointed witnesses" (*testes constituit*), "true heralds" (*validi praecones*) of the faith, and "evangelists" who proclaim the gospel (*actio ad evangelizandum mundum exercere*). The document does not use such vocabulary lightly or inappropriately. Such calls to all believers are to be taken in the spirit of the full denotation of these terms. They are not empty tropes or pious platitudes but actual challenges to all the faithful to "persist in proclaiming the word [the gospel], whether it is convenient or inconvenient" (2 Tim 4:2) and

66. This sentence concludes with a cryptic phrase, *pro facultate supplent*, that is translated variously. Most translate it rather innocuously as "in so far as they can" (Tanner), "to the best of their ability," (Flannery), and "suivant leurs moyens" (Philips). I doubt that the juxtaposition of the Latin terms *"facultas"* and *"supplere"* (as in the well-known phrase *ecclesia supplet*) is mere happenstance here. My translation picks up on the underlying idea of ecclesiastical authorization needed for certain ecclesial actions and claims that these are directly mediated to the lay minister by the church as needed in a situation of the lack of clergy or in an emergency, for example. On this important question and its fascinating implications, see Louis Ligier, " 'Lay Ministries' and Their Foundations in the Documents of Vatican II," in *Vatican II: Assessment and Perspectives Twenty-Five Years After (1962–1987)*, 3 vols., ed. René Latourelle (New York: Paulist Press, 1989), 2:160–76. This matter is not the focus of our attention at the moment, and so we must leave it for another time.

67. My translation. The Latin text can be found in *Decrees of the Ecumenical Councils*, vol. 2, ed. Norman P. Tanner (Washington, DC: Georgetown University Press, 1990), 877–78. See appendix B for the Latin text and a comparison of my translation with other English translations.

"to be ready to give an explanation for your hope" (1 Pet 3:15).[68] The council has abandoned the centuries-old construct of a "teaching" and a "learning" church, of those who are really "active" and those who are merely "passive" in the church.

Second, the principal area of the faith for which the lay faithful have responsibility includes the intersection of the faith and family life in particular and then the whole domain of secular activity: politics; the economy and finances; labor and its conditions; education; the ever-expanding fields of modern science, technology, and ecology; medicine and the healing and caring professions; literature and the arts; leisure and entertainment. The Dogmatic Constitution on the Church challenges the lay faithful to become fully involved in all the areas of human living and thriving and to refuse to dichotomize the multiplicity of secular activities from one another. Instead, everyone is challenged to work at interrelating all the dimensions of human and social well-being, guided by their faith. Such a task is never finished. In this regard, too, it must be remembered

---

68. The ramifications of this conciliar teaching are enormous. First, the faithful are not to be discouraged or muzzled by the hierarchy in fulfilling this prophetic task. Second, the faithful are personally responsible for growing in their faith by taking advantage of all the available means (e.g., pursuing studies beyond the rudiments of the faith, establishing informal or even formal study groups that include mixed groups of Catholics, Orthodox Christians, and Christians originating in the Reformation, engaging with others in prayer groups or pursuing *lectio divina*, ecumenical and interreligious efforts on behalf of social justice and human dignity, becoming involved in efforts to advance peace and resolve conflicts). Third, the hierarchy are responsible for seeing to it that the faithful have opportunities to grow in the knowledge of their faith by providing institutes of learning and study programs at various levels of proficiency, as well as regular forums for open discussion and consultation on social issues of the day and matters of belief among their fellow Christian disciples. This task might very well necessitate initiatives from bishops and their priests (presbyters), together with their diocesan and parochial pastoral councils in allocating financial resources to meet this imperative task. Fourth, communities of men and women religious might consider how they can assist the lay faithful and the bishops in meeting this urgent need, perhaps by making some of their personnel, property, and financial resources available to the church for this purpose. This suggestion might be the occasion of a refounding of some orders and maybe the founding of new orders or secular institutes, perhaps of mixed membership, e.g., vowed religious and dedicated laity, or of dedicated men and women, or of Catholics, Orthodox Christians, and Reformed Christians.

that the members of the hierarchy do not cease to be citizens of the world and members of their families of origin, and that they, too, have a right to be heard on this vast array of secular affairs. They should, in fact, be keenly interested in all these matters, while always taking precautions that they do not invoke their rightful ecclesiastical authority to unduly interfere in secular matters and family life.

Third, article 35 takes up the issue of growth in understanding the faith initiated in article 12,1. Here, as earlier, the text is not too specific about how such growth comes about.[69] Nevertheless, the principle still obtains: "The lay faithful are encouraged to dedicate themselves assiduously to growing in their knowledge of revealed truth." The life world and life experience of the lay faithful are indispensable for the full understanding and living out of the faith. It is incumbent upon all in the church to become increasingly conscious of the implications of their life experience for their faith and to take responsibility for relating them to each other. The commentary of Peter Hünermann on article 35,1 is worth quoting here:

> When we remember that in *Lumen gentium* the Church is referred to primarily as a "messianic people," then the Constitution's emphasis on its prophetic character makes greater sense. The People of God does not merely repeat what their shepherds have taught them as the deposit of faith, nor do they merely restate the deposit's meaning as they have received it. The People of God propose the witness of Jesus innovatively and concretely and in this way show themselves to be a prophetic people, in spite of their human frailty and sinfulness. This is the context in which the Council explicitly teaches that the glorified Lord himself has equipped the laity with the "sense of the faith" and the gift of his word. The "sense of the faith" points to the fact that, once they have turned to the living God and have been incorporated into the community of the Church, all who believe are intimately familiar with and understand the faith. As they direct and shape their lives by

---

69. The bishops missed an important opportunity here to spell out in greater detail how growth in understanding the faith might come about. Moreover, article 35 never mentions the Holy Spirit, whereas article 12 went out of its way to highlight the role the Spirit plays in bringing the faithful to knowledge of the faith and how to live it out. The silence of article 35 regarding the Spirit indicates the tentativeness of *Lumen Gentium's* pneumatology. I will address this issue at greater length in chapter 11.

the faith, they too, as the community of believers, lead it and contribute to its orientation.[70]

This imperative can be met individually but more often it is accomplished interpersonally, collectively, and communally. In this vast conversation, the lay Christian must give equal attention to the demands of his or her faith, of course, but not at the expense of participation in the realms of family and secular concerns.

The Presence of the "Sense of the Faith" in *Dei Verbum*, Articles 8 and 10

In early treatments of Vatican II's teaching on the "sense of the faith," scholars focused their attention on articles 12 and 35 of the Dogmatic Constitution on the Church. Because articles 8 and 10 of the Dogmatic Constitution on Divine Revelation do not explicitly use the phrases the "sense of the faith" or the "sense of the faithful," their rich contribution to this teaching had been passed over in silence. More recently, the pertinence of *Dei Verbum* for the ecclesiology of Vatican II has been noted by several commentators, including the authors of the International Theological Commission's *Sensus Fidei in the Life of the Church*.[71] What do articles 8 and 10 teach about the "sense of the faith" of the faithful?

The document that eventually became Vatican II's *Dei Verbum* had a troubled and even somewhat turbulent history.[72] Originally entitled

---

70. See *Herders Theologischer Kommentar zum Zweiten Vatikanischen Konzil*, 5 vols., ed. Peter Hünermann and Bernd Jochen Hilberath (Freiburg: Herder, 2004), 2:473.

71. Robert Schmucker has shown the consonance of *Dei Verbum* with the teaching of *Lumen Gentium* on the "sense of the faithful," and particularly in regard to its dynamic character. See *Sensus Fidei*, 280–83. See also *Sensus Fidei in the Life of the Church* (London: Catholic Truth Society, 2014), articles 46, 67, and 82. It may also be accessed at https://www.vatican.va/roman_curia/congregations/cfaith/cti_documents /rc_cti_20140610_sensus-fidei_en.html.

72. On the vagaries of the composition of *Dei Verbum* and the often heated controversies surrounding the issues treated in this schema, see Joseph A. Komonchak, "The Struggle for the Council during the Preparation of Vatican II (1960–1962)," in *History of Vatican II*, vol. 1, ed. Giuseppe Alberigo and Joseph A. Komonchak (Maryknoll, NY: Orbis Books, 1995), 167–356, at 272–85 ["The Word of God"]; Giuseppe Ruggieri, "The

"On the Sources of Revelation" (*De fontibus revelationis*), it consisted of five chapters and elicited impassioned support from some bishops and fierce opposition from others. The schema was issued by the Theological Commission charged by John XXIII to prepare texts for consideration by the bishops at Vatican II. Why was it so controversial and even bitterly divisive?

To some, *De fontibus revelationis* incarnated the most narrow focus possible on the sources of revelation characteristic of certain Roman schools, while dismissing or ignoring the latest historical research on the teaching of Trent.[73] At the same time, it showed a total lack of sympathy

---

First Doctrinal Clash," in *History of Vatican II*, vol. 2, ed. Giuseppe Alberigo and Joseph A. Komonchak (Maryknoll, NY: Orbis Books, 1997), 233–66; Jan Grootaers, "The Drama Continues between the Acts: The 'Second Preparation' and Its Opponents," in ibid., 359–514, at 385–91 ["The Schema on Revelation"]; Evangelista Vilanova, "The Intersession (1963–1964)," in *History of Vatican II*, vol. 3, ed. Giuseppe Alberigo and Joseph A. Komonchak (Maryknoll, NY: Orbis Books, 2000), 347–490, at 372–77 ["The Commission for the Schema on Revelation"] and 428–30 ["The Schema on Revelation"]; Hanjo Sauer, "The Doctrinal and the Pastoral: The Text on Divine Revelation," in *History of Vatican II*, vol. 4, ed. Giuseppe Alberigo and Joseph A. Komonchak (Maryknoll, NY: Orbis Books, 2003), 195–231; Christoph Theobald, "The Church under the Word of God," in *History of Vatican II*, vol. 5, ed. Giuseppe Alberigo and Joseph A. Komonchak (Maryknoll, NY: Orbis Books, 2006), 275–362. For commentaries on *Dei Verbum*, see Joseph A. Ratzinger, Alois Grillmeier, and Béda Rigaux in *Commentary on the Documents of Vatican II*, vol. 3, ed. Herbert Vorgrimler (New York: Herder and Herder, 1969), 155–272; Helmut Hoping, "Theologischer Kommentar zur Dogmatischen Konstitution über die göttliche Offenbarung *Dei Verbum*," in *Herders Theologischer Kommentar zum Zweiten Vatikanischen Konzil*, vol. 3, ed. Peter Hünermann and Bernd Jochen Hilberath (Freiburg: Herder, 2005), 695–831; and Christoph Theobald, "La constitution dogmatique sur la révélation divine *Dei Verbum*," *La réception du concile Vatican II*, vol. 1: *Accéder à la source* (Paris: Cerf, 2009), 701–69.

73. The Tübingen scholar Josef Rupert Geiselmann had written monographs and articles showing that Trent never intended a theory of the sources of revelation that understood "part" of the content to be contained in Scripture and "part" found only in tradition. To Geiselmann, Trent's teaching was more subtle inasmuch as it spoke of the "source" of revelation in the singular (*fons*) and not in the plural (*fontes*). Also, when Trent did speak of "scripture" and "tradition," it connected them to each other by the simple particle "and" (*et*) and not by what most post-tridentine authors understood as *partim . . . partim*—revealed truth is "partly in scripture" and "partly in tradition." The *partim . . . partim* understanding led to a theory of two separate sources of revelation among

for the position held by the churches of the Reformation. Then, too, it was captive to the wrangling over theological minutiae of a deeply entrenched neoscholastic method and showed little interest in reframing the church's teaching in pastoral terms. It was also vehemently opposed to giving any quarter to the newer methods of exegesis that had emerged among non-Catholic biblical scholars and that were increasingly practiced by Roman Catholics as well. Consequently, it operated out of an archaic and even naive understanding of the "historical facts" communicated by Scripture. Two worlds of biblical interpretation were locked in mortal combat. Moreover, the bishops in council grew increasingly responsive to the demands of ecumenism—a goal of the council set by John XXIII. Finally, the fact that the church had never fully addressed what it meant by

---

Catholics. Many Catholic theologians drew the conclusion that tradition as a separate source was materially more comprehensive than Scripture, an understanding that contributed to a diminution in the appreciation of Scripture. Two other consequences of this mistaken theory included the denial that Scripture contained all the essential doctrines necessary for belief (the material sufficiency of Scripture) and the growing influence of the magisterium of the church, especially the papal magisterium, in determining the content of revealed dogmas and their interpretation. Moreover, if the magisterium was the "proximate rule of what was contained in tradition," then it was also the "proximate rule of the meaning of scripture." These theories led to the isolation of the magisterium from the equally legitimate roles of theologians in the church and from the contribution of the understanding of the faith by the faithful (the *sensus fidelium*). See J. R. Geiselmann, *Lebendiger Glaube aus geheiligter Überlieferung: Der Grundgedanke der Theologie Johann Adam Möhlers und der katholischen Tübinger Schule* (Mainz: Matthias-Grünewald, 1942); idem, "Das Missverständnis über das Verhältnis von Schrift und Tradition und seine Überwindung in der katholischen Theologie," *Una Sancta* 11 (1956): 131–50; idem, "Das Konzil von Trient über das Verhältnis der heiligen Schrift und der nicht geschriebenen Tradition" in *Die mündliche Überlieferung: Beiträge zum Begriff der Tradition*, ed. Michael Schmaus (Munich: Max Hueber Verlag, 1957), 133–67; idem, "Scripture, Tradition, and the Church: An Ecumenical Problem," in *Christianity Divided: Protestant and Roman Catholic Theological Issues*, ed. Daniel A. Callahan, Heiko A. Oberman, and Daniel J. O'Hanlon (New York: Sheed & Ward, 1961), 39–72; and idem, *Die heilige Schrift und die Tradition* (Freiburg: Herder, 1962); E.T. *The Meaning of Tradition*, trans. W. J. O'Hara (New York: Herder and Herder, 1966). Joseph Ratzinger criticized Geiselmann's interpretation and offered another in "On the Interpretation of the Tridentine Decree on Tradition," in *Revelation and Tradition*, Quaestiones Disputatae, no. 17, trans. W. J. O'Hara (New York: Herder and Herder, 1966), 50–68.

"divine revelation," even though it had expended a great deal of energy in defining "revealed truths," only complicated matters further.[74] As regards the issue of the "sense of the faith," it is pertinent to note that the role of the "sense of the faith" did in fact arise in this highly charged controversy. Why, then, is there no mention of it in the final text?

After the failure of the first draft of *De fontibus revelationis* in November 1962, John XXIII created a Mixed Commission to prepare a new text. This commission consisted of members from the Theological Commission and the Secretariat for Christian Unity.[75] The hope was that in this way the legitimate concern for ecumenism that was gaining strength at the council would not be ignored and that the text would profit from a broader theological base. It did not hurt that the president of the Secretariat for Christian Unity, Cardinal Augustin Bea, SJ, had been a longtime professor of Scripture at the Biblical Institute of the Gregorian University in Rome. He was sure to represent the legitimate interests of Scripture scholars who had fought long and hard to introduce some of the newer methods of biblical exegesis and interpretation into the discussions. The results of the reworking of the draft, however, pleased no one in the end.[76] A new initiative was needed and that was the challenge Paul VI issued at the end of the second session of the council. The pope indicated that the topic of revelation would be treated by the bishops during the third session. This meant that the failure of the Mixed Commission's draft had to be addressed. The bulk of the work of producing a viable conciliar text was done during the intersession between the second and third sessions of the council.

74. I will address the nature of revelation in greater detail in chapter 11.

75. On the composition of the Mixed Commission, see Evangelista Vilanova, "The Intersession (1963–1964)," in *History of Vatican II*, vol. 3, ed. Giuseppe Alberigo and Joseph A. Komonchak, 372–77 ["The Commission for the Schema on Revelation"].

76. According to Ratzinger, "no one was very happy with the new draft. It was too inadequate and vague, recognizable at first sight as a product of resignation." See "Dogmatic Constitution on Divine Revelation: Origin and Background," in *Commentary on the Documents of Vatican II*, vol. 3, ed. Herbert Vorgrimler (New York: Herder and Herder, 1969), 155–66, at 161.

The result of this effort at producing a better text was Form D of the schema,[77] distributed to the bishops on April 22, 1963.[78] In the concluding paragraph of chapter 1, "On Revelation Itself," we read:

> It is clear therefore that, in the all-wise plan of God, sacred scripture, sacred tradition, and the magisterium of the Church are so connected and associated with each other that one cannot exist without the others. Together these three efficaciously confer the salvation of souls in their own way, and do so with the support and concurrence of the sense of the faithful (art. 10).[79]

77. I am following the list of the texts of what would eventually become *Dei Verbum* as established by Alois Grillmeier and followed by Ratzinger. See *Commentary on the Documents of Vatican II*, ed. H. Vorgrimler, vol. 3:165–66. On the various texts of the schema on revelation, see Bernard-Dominique Dupuy, "Historique de la Constitution," in *La révélation divine*, 2 vols., ed. B.-D. Dupuy (Paris: Cerf, 1968), 1:61–117; Johannes Feiner, "La contribution du Secrétariat pour l'Unité des Chrétiens à la Constitution dogmatique sur la Révélation divine," in *La révélation divine*, 1:119–55; Charles Moeller, "Le texte du chapitre II dans la seconde période du Concile (Sessions II, III et IV)," in *La révélation divine*, 1:305–43; Riccardo Burigana, *La Bibbia nel Concilio. La redazione della costituzione "Dei Verbum" del Vaticano II* (Bologna: Il Mulino,1998); and Hanjo Sauer, "Die dogmatische Konstitution über die göttliche Offenbarung *Dei Verbum*," in *Vierzig Jahre II. Vatikanum. Zur Wirkungsgeschichte der Konzilstexte*, ed. Franz X. Bischof and Stephan Leimgruber (Würzburg: Echter, 2004), 232–51.

78. It can be found in *Acta Synodalia Sacrosancti Concilii Oecumenici Vaticani II*, III/3, 782–91. This is the "textus prior" that Archbishop Ermengildus Florit of Florence contrasted with the "textus emendatus" or Form E in his official report to the bishops on changes that were incorporated into the text. See *Acta Synodalia Sacrosancti Concilii Oecumenici Vaticani II*, III/3, 69–82 for the text and explanations of the individual changes in chapters 1 and 2 of *Dei Verbum*. See ibid., 131–40 for Archbishop Florit's detailed Official Report (*Relatio*) on chapters 1 and 2 of *Dei Verbum*, given on September 30, 1964. These *Relationes* are important for understanding the role of the "sense of the faith" in *Dei Verbum*, for it is here that references to the "sense of the faith" can be found. The fact that Archbishop Florit had been a professor of New Testament exegesis at the Pontifical Lateran University before being named archbishop of Florence helped him in his role of mediating between the bishops of the minority and those of the majority at Vatican II. He was seen to be an "honest broker" who understood and could represent both groups with fairness.

79. "Patet igitur S. Scripturam, S. Traditionem ac Ecclesiae Magisterium, iuxta sapientissimum Dei consilium, ita inter se connecti et consociari, ut unum sine aliis consistere non possit. Tria simul ad animarum salutem suo modo efficaciter conferunt; sensu quoquo fidelium subordinate concurrente." *Acta Synodalia Sacrosancti Concilii Oecumenici Vaticani II*, III/3, 81. My translation. Schmucker has pointed out how only Ángel Temiño Sáiz, bishop of Orense, Spain, mentioned the "sense of the faithful" in conjunction with

However, when we turn to Form E, there is no longer any mention of the "sense of the faithful."[80] The Official Report provided the following explanation of the change in the text:

> The final words "with the support and concurrence of the sense of the faithful" are omitted because four episcopal conferences and several Fathers find fault with it for different reasons.[81] Moreover, these words are no longer needed since the first sentence states that the revealed deposit has been committed to the whole Church and by that very fact clearly refers to the importance of the "sense of the faithful." For this reason, moreover, an entire paragraph has been dedicated to it in the schema *De Ecclesia*, art. 12, page 13, lines 6–20.[82]

It should be amply clear that the authors of *Dei Verbum* understood the appropriateness of referring to the "sense of the faithful" at this point in the document and that even after the removal of an explicit reference to it, the idea left its traces and effects on the text. That this is the case, and that chapter 2 of *Dei Verbum* can rightly be cited as supporting the "sense of the faithful," can be shown by examining the elements of the idea of the "sense of the faithful" in the text.[83]

In article 8,2 we read:

---

the discussion of the draft presented to the bishops and discussed in November 1962. See *Acta Synodalia Sacrosancti Concilii Oecumenici Vaticani II*, I/3, 147. See *Sensus Fidei*, 236.

80. "It is clear, therefore, that in the all-wise plan of God, sacred tradition, sacred scripture, and the magisterium of the Church are so connected and interrelated that one cannot exist without the others, but together all, and each in its own way, efficaciously confer the salvation of souls. (Patet igitur S. Traditionem, S. Scripturam et Ecclesiae Magisterium, iuxta sapientissimum Dei consilium, ita inter se connecti et consociari, ut unum sine aliis non consistat, omniaque simul, singula suo modo ad animarum salutem efficaciter conferant)." Ibid. My translation.

81. See *Acta Synodalia Sacrosancti Concilii Oecumenici Vaticani II*, III/3, 792–919 for the sources of these observations.

82. "Omittuntur autem ultima verba: sensu quoque fidelium subordinate concurrente, quae diversimode a quattuor conferentiis Episcopalibus et a nonnullis aliis Patribus impro-bantur. . . . De cetero illa verba inutilia redduntur post additam primam periodum, ubi, eo ipso de momento sensus fidelium ex professo dicitur; cui praeterea integra dedicatur paragraphus in Schemate De Ecclesia, n. 12, p. 13, linn. 6–20." Ibid., 88. My translation.

83. This is case for article 8 of *Dei Verbum*, which some scholars mention, but I con-tend that it is also the case for article 10, where elements of the "sense of the faithful" can also be found.

This tradition that comes from the apostles grows in the Church with the assistance of the Holy Spirit. For comprehension of the realities and the words that are handed on grows when the faithful contemplate and study what has been placed in their hearts (see Luke 2, 19 and 51), when they plumb with their minds the depths of the spiritual realities they experience, and when they accept the sure charism of truth that comes from the preaching of the bishops in apostolic succession. And so, as the ages succeed one another, the Church continues to move into the fullness of divine truth, until the words of God come to fulfillment in her.[84]

The same teaching on the "sense of the faith" that we saw in articles 12 and 35 of *Lumen Gentium* is expressed here, too, in *Dei Verbum*, article 8.[85]

No commentator on this article has captured its meaning and relevance more perceptively than Joseph Ratzinger when he wrote:

The second paragraph of our text points out the dynamic character of tradition, thus arousing lively opposition on the part of the Canadian Cardinal Léger. It states that tradition, which stems from the Apostles, develops under the assistance of the Holy Spirit in the Church, i.e. that there is a growing understanding of the words and realities that have been handed down to us. Again, three factors of this growth are

84. "Haec quae est ab apostolis traditio sub assistentia Spiritus Sancti in ecclesia proficit: crescit enim tam rerum quam verborum traditorum perceptio, tum ex contemplatione et studio credentium, qui ea conferunt in corde suo (cf. Lc 2, 19 et 51), tum ex intima spiritualium rerum quam experiuntur intelligentia, tum ex praeconio eorum qui cum episcopatus successione charisma veritatis certum acceperunt. Ecclesia, scilicet, volventibus saeculis, ad plenitudinem divinae veritatis iugiter tendit, donec in ipsa consummentur verba Dei." Norman P. Tanner, ed., *Decrees of the Ecumenical Councils*, vol. 2 (Washington, DC: Georgetown University Press, 1990), 974. My translation.

85. This is also the judgment of Robert Schmucker, who writes: "The Constitution *Dei verbum* adopts the fundamental statements of *Lumen gentium* and contextualizes them in some detail in an effort to ponder how progress in the understanding of revelation comes about. In the final analysis, such progress always happens only in the mutuality of the magisterium and the faithful. When the whole Church remains in the truth, it is then possible for her to strive for the fullness of divine truth. The infallible faith of the whole Church is the foundation for every member of the Church, each in her own way and in her assigned place, to strive for an ever deeper understanding of the faith." *Sensus Fidei*, 281–83. Schmucker treats the teaching of *Dei Verbum* 8,2 in greater detail than I can do in this chapter.

listed: contemplation and study on the part of believers; inner understanding, which comes from spiritual experience; and the proclamation
by the teaching office. The final point is made that the Church and its
understanding of revelation is moving forward towards the fullness
of the divine work in the Church in the *eschaton*. It is important that
the progress of the word in the time of the Church is not seen simply
as a function of the hierarchy, but is anchored in the whole life of the
Church; through it, we hear in what is said what is unsaid. The whole
spiritual experience of the Church, its believing, praying and loving
intercourse with the Lord and his word, causes our understanding of
the original truth to grow and in the today of faith extracts anew from
the yesterday of its historical origin what was meant for all time and
yet can be understood only in the changing ages and in the particular
way of each. In this process of understanding, which is the concrete way
in which tradition proceeds in the Church, the work of the teaching
office is one component (and, because of its nature, a critical one, not
a productive one), but it is not the whole.[86]

I know of no other explanation that captures the "sense of the faith" at
the organ of tradition as accurately as Ratzinger does.

We might wish that the final text of *Dei Verbum* had spoken explicitly
of the "sense of the faithful," but the fact that it did not does not preclude our acknowledging the presence of the idea itself in article 10.[87]

---

86. *Commentary on the Documents of Vatican II*, vol. 3 (New York: Herder and Herder,
1969), 186.

87. In his Official Report (*relatio*) on chapters 1 and 2 of *Dei Verbum*, Archbishop
Florit made a number of astute comments that confirm my analysis. In a footnote to his
commentary "On the relationship of the revealed deposit as passed on by tradition and
scripture to the whole Church and to the magisterium," the archbishop remarked that
"whereas the former formulation referred only to the magisterium, the new text speaks
[more inclusively] of the whole Church as well as the magisterium (Denique quidnam
de relatione depositi revelati ad totam Ecclesiam . . . —in praecedenti schemate: ad
Magisterium solummodo; in novo: ad totam Ecclesiam et Magisterium)." My translation.
And in the body of the commentary, we read the following: "Since the revealed deposit
is a divine gift to the whole Church, it follows that it is incumbent on the whole Church
to preserve it, to abide in it, and to transmit the same to every generation. And so, it
follows that this deposit governs and supports the life of the Church, just as it in turn
is supported by the life of the Church in which it completely participates. Therefore, it
experiences that process as dynamic, which the general sense of the faithful accounts for

In summary, the teaching of Vatican II on the "sense of the faith" or the "sense of the faithful" permeates the council's teaching on the meaning of revelation and tradition. The absence of the technical term the "sense of the faithful" in *Dei Verbum* does not invalidate this claim.[88]

Conclusions on the Teaching of Vatican II on the "Sense of the Faith"

We have seen that the theme of the "sense of the faith" was considered at every stage of Vatican II. It was not a burning issue at the council and only a small minority of bishops called for it to be included in the documents of Vatican II, but it survived every phase of the writing and editing of the Dogmatic Constitution on the Church. The overwhelming majority of bishops voted for it and, we should assume, saw it as fitting into the larger context of the church they wanted to emerge out of Vatican II.

In terms of the thesis of John W. O'Malley regarding the council as a whole, the "sense of the faith of the faithful" was another strand in the fabric woven by Vatican II in its effort to shape new language and employ

---

and from which it flows and constitutes the criterion for knowing inexhaustible divine revealed truth. . . . For it is the responsibility of the magisterium to define truth that is to be held *de fide* if such truth is to be juridically imposed as a matter of faith. Nevertheless, what is so defined already belongs to the substance of the faith of the universal Church, inasmuch as what the magisterium defines follows from it. (Cum Depositum revelatum donum sit divinum toti Ecclesiae factum, totius Ecclesiae consequenter officium incumbit illud conservandi, eidem inhaerendi, idem que cunctis generationibus transmittendi. Exinde provenit quod hoc Depositum, sicut Ecclesiae vitam regit et portat, ita a vita Ecclesiae portatur de eaque prorsus participat: ac propterea illum dynamicum experitu processum, ratione cuius communis fidelium sensus, exinde profluens, criterium cognoscendae veritatis divinitus revelatae non semel efficiatur. . . . Veritas enim quae tamquam de fide tenenda a Magisterio definitur si iuridice ob illam definitionem credenda imponitur, substantialiter tamen iam fidem universae Ecclesiae attigerat: propterea quod definitionem a Magisterio est consecuta.)" *Acta Sacrosancti Concilii Oecumenici Vaticani II*, III/3, 139. My translation.

88. At the end of his treatment of chapter 2 of *Dei Verbum*, Schmucker summarizes his understanding with these words: "The Constitution on Divine Revelation maintains what the Constitution on the Church also claims, that the duty of guarding the deposit of the faith is entrusted to the whole people of God. In this context, *Dei Verbum* treats the content of the "sense of the faith" but without explicitly naming it." *Sensus Fidei*, 293.

new literary forms to express its insights, and so forge a unified style of the council. According to O'Malley:

> A style choice is an identity choice, a choice in this instance about the kind of institution the council wanted the church to be. The fathers chose to praise the positive aspects of Catholicism and establish the church's identity on that basis rather than by making Catholicism look good by making others look bad. In this way and in others the style shift expressed and promoted a shift in values and priorities. The shift in style as proposed in Vatican II thus entailed changing behavioral patterns, but the change in those patterns, as in the adoption of dialogue as a preferred mode of discourse, was not a technique or strategy but an outward expression of the adoption of an inner pattern of values. Style, sometimes misunderstood as merely an ornament of speech, an outer garment adorning a thought, is really the ultimate expression of meaning. The "what" of speech and the "how" of speech are inseparable.[89]

> Although the words can be divided into categories like horizontal-words, equality-words, reciprocity-words, interiority-words, change-words, empowerment-words, and others, they evince an emotional kinship among themselves and, along with the literary genre in which they are encased, imbue Vatican II with a literary unity unique among councils. In this way they express an overall orientation and a coherence in values and outlook that markedly contrast with those of previous councils and, indeed, with most official ecclesiastical documents up to that point. Vatican II [was] a language event.[90]

I submit that the terms the "sense of the faith," the "sense of the faithful," and the "consensus of the faithful," together with the language of the "people of God," "the priesthood of all the faithful," and the "prophetic office of Christ," are parts of the whole of the council's "new" vocabulary, literary genres, and search for the church's self-understanding. But this very phenomenon of novelty at Vatican II points us in the right direction for situating the place and importance of the "sense of the faith" in the council's teaching. To wrestle with the "sense of the faith" in isolation

---

89. John W. O'Malley, *What Happened at Vatican II* (Cambridge, MA: Belknap Press, 2008), 305–6.

90. Ibid., 306.

from all the other central contributions at the council is to doom it to insignificance, and this would be a tragic loss for the church.

Many students of Vatican II have remarked on the vagueness of the council's teaching about the "sense of the faith" and the "consensus of the faithful." This epistemological situation has created doubt about the viability and applicability of the teaching. Much of the theological literature after the council has tried to address these issues. In fact, with the passing of time the conviction of the importance of Vatican II's teaching on the "sense of the faith" has grown, and theologians have succeeded in introducing needed clarifications.[91] I believe that theologians and commentators have largely received the council's teaching on the "sense of the faith." Little by little the teaching is gaining a foothold in the larger church as well.

It has become increasingly clear in the past twenty-five years in particular that the absence of official forums in the church at which important social, ecclesial, moral, and pastoral matters can be candidly discussed urgently needs to be addressed.[92] Without such means and

91. I have surveyed the copious literature on the "sense of the faith" in two long articles: "*Sensus fidei*: Theological Reflection Since Vatican II (1965–1989)," *Heythrop Journal* 34 (1993): 41–59 and 123–36, and "*Sensus fidei*: Recent Theological Reflection (1990–2001)," *Heythrop Journal* 46 (2005): 450–75 and 47 (2006): 38–54. I hope to bring these surveys up to date by canvassing the literature from 2002 to the present in a future article.

92. Some of the more significant literature on this important topic include Sabine Demel, "Dringender Handlungsbedarf. Der Glaubenssinn des Gottesvolkes und seine rechtliche Umsetzung," *Herder Korrespondenz* 58 (2004): 618–23; Georg Bier, "Wir sind Kirche. Der Glaubenssinn der Gottesvolkes in kirchenrechtlicher Sicht," in *Rezeption des Zweiten Vatikanischen Konzils in Theologie und Kirchenrecht heute. Festschrift für Klaus Lüdicke zur Vollendung seines 65. Lebensjahres*, ed. Dominicus Meier, Peter Platen, Heinrich J. F. Reinhardt, and Frank Sanders (Essen: Ludgerus Verlag, 2008), 73–97; Pamela McCann, "The *Sensus fidei* and Canon Law," *Studia Canonica* 44 (2010): 211–58; Myriam Wijlens, "Sensus fidelium—Authority: Protecting and Promoting the Ecclesiology of Vatican II with the Assistance of Institutions?" in *Believing in Community: Ecumenical Reflections on the Church*, ed. Peter De Mey, Pieter De Witte, and Gerard Mannion (Leuven: Peeters, 2013), 207–28; Anthony Ekpo, "Canon Law and the Agents of the *Sensus Fidelium*: A Theological and Canonical Exploration," *The Canonist* 4/1 (2013): 65–86; and idem, "From *Sensus Fidei* to *Sensus Legis*: Reconciling Faith and Law in the Church," *The Canonist* 4/2 (2013): 157–68; idem, *The Breath of the Spirit in the Church: The* Sensus Fidelium *and Canon Law* (Strathfield, NSW, Australia: St Pauls, 2014); Judith Hahn, "Lehramt und Glaubenssinn. Kirchenrechtliche Überlegungen zu einem spannungsreichen

ecclesial structures, and absent guarantees of their right to exist in law, the "sense of the faith of the faithful" cannot contribute to determining the church's understanding of important matters, according to the mind of the bishops at Vatican II. Attention to questions of structure will guarantee that the "sense of the faith of the faithful" will be a real force in the church and not a dead letter. In the next chapter, I will examine how Vatican II's teaching on the "sense of the faith" has been received officially and what needs to be done to secure this important teaching of Vatican II.

Verhältnis—aus aktuellen Anlass," in *Glaube in Gemeinschaft. Autorität und Rezeption in der Kirche*, ed. Markus Knapp and Thomas Söding (Freiburg: Herder, 2014), 182–212; and Helen Costigane, "Sensus Fidelium and Canon Law: Sense and Sensitivity?" *New Blackfriars* 98 (2017): 157–70.

Chapter Ten

Official Reception
of the "Sense of the Faith"

The Second Vatican Council was formally adjourned by Pope Paul VI on December 8, 1965. This solemn act of concluding the council, however, does not mean the end of the council as a process. Other official acts must follow the council to bring it to completion: the promulgation of the decisions or decrees of the council, the implementation of these decisions, and its reception by the church. Since the councils of Trent and Vatican I in particular, the element of reception of a council has been largely ignored. Scholars such as Alois Grillmeier, SJ, and Yves Congar, OP, however, recalled the role and the importance of the process of the reception of a council.[1] The present chapter will consider only one indispensable dimension of the reception of Vatican II's teaching on the "sense of the faith"—namely, its official reception in the Codes of Canon Law of the Latin and the Eastern churches, its importance and role in the

---

1. Grillmeier's first contribution appeared in conjunction with a collection of studies in *The Ecumenical Review* for 1970 on the Council of Chalcedon. This landmark council had been celebrated 1,500 years earlier in 451 and had been the subject of a collection of scholarly studies edited by A. Grillmeier and H. Bacht as *Das Konzil von Chalkedon* in 3 volumes (Würzburg: Echter, 1951–1954). The fifteenth centenary of Chalcedon provoked keen interest in the ecumenical councils of the early church and accounts for Grillmeier's discovery of the idea of the reception of a council.

statements of the popes since Vatican II, its inclusion in the *Catechism of the Catholic Church*, and recent statements of the International Theological Commission on the topic.[2]

What Is Reception?

In a helpful article on reception, the Greek Orthodox theologian John Zizioulas pointed out that, based on his personal experience, the topic first emerged at meetings of the Faith and Order Commission of the World Council of Churches in Oxford, England, in 1965 and Bad Gastein, Austria, in 1966.[3] He wrote:

> [These meetings] brought together Church historians and patristic scholars to discuss the Councils in the Ancient Church. It emerged then that reception is an important part of conciliarity. But it also emerged that we know very little about the meaning and especially the theological content of this term, a fact that called for further reflection.
>
> As time went on the idea of reception began to enter into the ecumenical vocabulary officially and in a decisive way. It was, I remember, in Louvain, at the meeting of Faith and Order Commission in 1972 that an attempt was made to make use of this idea in a decisive way. As time went on the idea of reception became more and more the object of attention both theologically and practically in the ecumenical movement. Reception is now a subject we cannot ignore.[4]

Building on these modest origins described by Zizioulas, a small handful of contributions to reception began to appear in the 1970s, and by the

---

2. I have examined the reception of the "sense of the faith" in my articles that have surveyed the theological literature after Vatican II. These should be consulted for a broader view of the discussion of the issue, problems in interpreting the "sense of the faith," and the general consensus among theologians regarding its importance and its role in the life of the church. However, to date I have not examined the "sense of the faith" in the documents of the magisterium as I attempt to do in this chapter.

3. "The Theological Problem of 'Reception,'" *Centro Pro Unione Bulletin* no. 26 (1984): 3–6 and reprinted in *One in Christ* 21 (1985): 187–93.

4. "The Theological Problem of 'Reception,'" *One in Christ* 21 (1985): 188.

1980s the literature was rapidly expanding.[5] The first to do so was Yves Congar who, already in 1972, had published his "Reception as an Ecclesiological Reality" in the influential and widely read journal *Concilium*, and with this one stroke ended the long neglect of this important topic of the faith.[6] Congar wanted to expand the understanding of reception beyond the juridical confines of how the decisions and teachings of the bishops in council to include how decisions would lead to a genuine enrichment of the life of the church in a broader way. He also wanted to go beyond the scholastic understanding of reception as the obedience of the faithful to the bishops as official teachers. The result of Congar's initiative on reception was a much broader understanding of the idea that traced it through the ecumenical councils and regional synods, the emergence of the canon of Scripture, the use of synodal letters among bishops for centuries, liturgical matters including the determination of a calendar of feasts and commemorations, the veneration of saints by establishing a canon of saints, and finally matters of church law and discipline. Congar was able to show that a phenomenon like reception or consensus among the local churches was a fact of the church's life. Reception did not represent an innovation or a dangerous form of conciliarist or Gallican theology but the normal way in which the apostolicity of the church's teaching and practices came to expression and were shared by the churches.

After Congar, numerous scholars were able to build on the solid and positive foundations he had established. One of these was John Zizioulas. In a short but significant contribution, Zizioulas added a number of

5. I have counted over 200 books, articles, entries in encyclopedias, and treatments in ecclesiological treatises that have appeared since 1968. Works that can be profitably consulted include *Glaube als Zustimmung: Zur Interpretation kirchlicher Rezeptionsvorgänge*, Quaestiones Disputatae 131, ed. Wolfgang Beinert (Freiburg: Herder, 1991); *Reception and Communion among Churches*, ed. Hervé Legrand, Julio Manzanarez, and Antonio García y García (Washington, DC: Canon Law Department of Catholic University of America, 1997); Gilles Routhier, *La réception d'un concile*, Cogitatio Fidei 174 (Paris: Cerf, 1993); and Ormond Rush, *The Reception of Doctrine: An Appropriation of Hans Robert Jauss' Reception Aesthetics and Literary Hermeneutics* (Rome: Gregorian University Press, 1997).

6. A slightly more detailed version had originally appeared as "La 'réception' comme réalité ecclésiologique" in *Revue des sciences philosophiques et théologiques* 56 (1972): 369–403, but it received much greater attention with its appearance in *Concilium* in English, German, Italian, Spanish, Portuguese, and Dutch.

important theological considerations that extended Congar's pioneering ideas. Zizioulas addresses what might otherwise be passed over in silence because it is so rudimentary to the faith.[7] Thus, he pointed out that what the church has received is first and foremost the divine love of the triune God: "The Church exists in order to give what she has received as the love of God for the world."[8] This gift of God takes the form of the "gospel" as the good news of this divine love for the world, a gospel that proclaims "a *Creed* which she confesses to be a true statement of the acts of God in the history of his people and Man, that is, of the way God so loved the world as to give his only Son for it."[9] In turn, the gospel and its creedal formulation must not obscure the fact that it represents a person and not merely ideas: "The Church does not receive and perpetuate ideas or doctrines as such, but life and love, the very life and love of God for Man."[10] Finally, then, at the very center of the church's life stands the fact of reception and this in two senses. First, the church offers itself to the world in order that the gospel of God's love for the world will be received by the world. Second, as a communion of local churches, these very churches must receive each other and in this way constitute the one church of God. For Zizioulas, reception is realized in the Spirit as an event of communion that comes to expression in concrete communities who celebrate the Eucharist in the unity of the ministry of the local bishop (*episkopē*) but that is open to the ministry of all the other local bishops and is thereby universal. Finally, because the church is identified by the oneness of the gospel it proclaims, it can do so only in the context of the local culture and its forms of expression. The church, as the embodiment of receiving and being received by God and the world, can do so only within the diversity of the world's cultures. There is no supra-historical or universalizing culture that is the context of reception in the radical sense intended by Zizioulas. The church comes to realization as local churches enfleshed by culture.

Though tantalizing in its brevity, Zizioulas's contribution rendered an indispensable service to those who wrote after the appearance of his

---

7. "Theological Problem of 'Reception,'" 187–93.

8. Ibid., 190.

9. Ibid.

10. Ibid., 191.

article by reducing reception to its ultimate theological principles. Reception is not some secondary topic in theology or in ecclesiology but a theme at the very heart of the Christian faith: the church and the world receive all from a loving God who calls everyone and everything to receive divine love and share it with others, who are themselves in turn called to receive it from them and extend it to others. In a word, reception is the very rule of life both in the cosmos and in the "world of belief."

With the solid base provided by Zizioulas, it is possible to move on to other fruitful aspects of the notion of reception. The literature is replete with historical studies of the councils and synods of the church, of the mutual exchange of doctrinal formulas; of liturgical rituals and practices, and of the sacraments; of ecclesiastical discipline; of canonical legislation and processes; of matters of institutional order, forms of the ministry, and the exercise of authority; of gifts of the Spirit and the rich spiritual and contemplative treasures of each local church and rite; of the exemplary, courageous, and saintly women and men of the multitude of local churches; of the clarity and challenge of the moral teaching espoused by each church; of ecumenical polity, collaboration, and cooperation among the churches and ecclesial communities; of the mutually supportive leaders of the churches; of the pastoral insights and strengths that have emerged among the churches over the centuries; and finally of the numerous carefully crafted bilateral, multilateral, and international ecumenical statements and agreements that have emerged from the ecumenical movement since the conclusion of Vatican II. This vast and rich literature is available for all to consult and mine as it confirms and encapsulates the fundamental principles outlined briefly yet clearly by Zizioulas. Now we, too, can proceed with an examination of reception in the areas I indicated at the start of this chapter.

The Revised Code of Canon Law (1983) and the Code of the Canons of the Eastern Churches (1990)

An aspect of the reception of the "sense of the faith" that has received considerable attention has been the question of why the 1983 Code did not refer to the "sense of the faith" or the "sense of the faithful" explicitly. This silence has often been understood as an expression of the ambiguity of this teaching of Vatican II itself and also of how awkwardly such a notion fits into the legal framework of a code of laws. Since it was the intention of the pope as the supreme legislator of the church to reframe the church's laws in light of the teaching of Vatican II,[11] some have even inferred that the absence of the term indicates that John Paul II had serious reservations about it.[12] Whatever reasons John Paul II had for not including an explicit reference to the "sense of the faith" in the Code, some history of how the Code of 1983 emerged is necessary for understanding it.

The Emergence of a Lex Ecclesiae Fundamentalis

When John XXIII announced the Second Vatican Council, he also indicated the need to reformulate the church's Code of Canon Law. It would be necessary to reframe the canons of the church in light of the teachings of the council. The Roman Catholic Church, however, consists of a Latin church and an Eastern church, each with its own code of laws. As Vatican II was drawing to its conclusion, Paul VI began to entertain the idea that the church should have a basic statement of the nature of the church and its mission. Such a statement could undergird the codes of the churches of the East and the West vis-à-vis one another. Outside the church, too, it could serve as a statement of the basic principles of how the church presented itself to other national states. These countries had already formulated their constitutions or were in the process of doing so, after the realignment of nations that took place after the Second World War and with the dismantling of the colonial system in the 1950s and 1960s.[13]

---

11. See John Paul II, Apostolic Constitution *Sacrae disciplinae leges* (January 25, 1983) in *Code of Canon Law, Latin-English Edition: New English Translation* (Washington, DC: Canon Law Society of America, 2017), xxvii–xxxii.

12. Commentators have sometimes asked such leading questions as: Does the council's teaching on the "sense of the faith" confuse the matter of how the pope and the bishops teach with authority? Does the teaching imply a limitation on papal teaching as taught by Vatican I and reiterated by Vatican II? Does the notion smack of democratizing tendencies in the church after Vatican II that have no place in the Catholic Church? Wouldn't advancing the "sense of the faith" inevitably implant the modern and inappropriate idea that the Catholic faithful should be polled for their views on matters of faith and morals? Wouldn't it politicize the faith and how the church arrives at its doctrinal and pastoral determinations? In my opinion, these questions are really invidious because they misunderstand the meaning of the teaching of Vatican II and try to sow doubts about it.

13. The formulation of a "charter" for the recently founded United Nations (1945) was also an impetus for the Roman Catholic Church to clearly state for all the world to read how it understood itself in terms they could understand.

Not many Catholics were aware of this project of writing a charter of the church. Nevertheless, it occupied a great deal of time of canonists from mid-1965 until 1982, when the final product was presented to John Paul II.[14] The bishops were kept apprised of the project and their support was sought at the First General Synod of Bishops in 1967, the First Extraordinary Synod of Bishops in 1969, and the Second General Synod of Bishops in 1971. There are three editions of the *Lex Ecclesiae Fundamentalis (LEF)*: a *textus prior* in 1968, a *textus emendatus* in 1970, and a final *schema postremus* in 1982.[15] The history of the editions shows that the "sense of the faithful" was mentioned explicitly in the various versions and rewritings of the *textus prior* and *emendatus*. It did not appear in the final version, however.

In both the *textus prior* and *textus emendatus*, the church is referred to as the "People of God" and the ministry of teaching is related to the prophetic role of Christ in which all the faithful (*christifideles*) participate, some of whom are ordained while the vast majority are not. The teaching is drawn practically verbatim from article 12 of *Lumen Gentium*, and the "sense of the faith" is mentioned explicitly.[16] The language is lively and concrete. By the emergence of the final version, the *schema postremus*, the tenor has changed completely. There is no mention of the church as the people of God, or of the prophetic ministry of the church, or of the "infallibility in belief" of the faithful, or of the "sense of the faith" of all the faithful and their pastors. Canon 59 refers to the lay faithful as those

14. On the history, interpretation, and documentation of the *Lex Ecclesiae Fundamentalis*, I have relied heavily on Daniel Cenalmor Palanca, *La Ley Fundamental de la Iglesia: Historia y análisis de un proyecto legislativo* (Pamplona: Ediciones Universidad de Navarra, 1991). See also Thomas J. Green, "*Lex fundamentalis*: The Law Within," in *Proceedings of the Canon Law Society of America* 67 (2005): 21–76 and Winfried Aymans, "Das Projekt einer *Lex Ecclesiae Fundamentalis*," in *Handbuch des katholischen Kirchenrechts*, ed. J. Listl, H. Müller, and H. Schmitz (Regensburg: F. Pustet, 1983), 65–71.

15. For the texts, see Pontificia Commissio Codici Iuris Canonici Recognoscendo, *Schema Lex Ecclesiae Fundamentalis cum relatione* (Rome: Typis Polyglottis Vaticanis, 1969); idem, *Schema Lex Ecclesiae Fundamentalis: Textus emendatus cum relatione de ipso schemate deque emendationibus receptis* (Rome: Typis Polyglottis Vaticanis, 1971); and *Schema Lex Ecclesiae Fundamentalis: Codex recognitus* (Rome: Typis Polyglottis Vaticanis, 1976). The *textus prior* and the *schema postremus* can be found in Daniel Cenalmor Palanca, *La Ley Fundamental de la Iglesia*, Appendices III and IV.

16. See canon 55, with three paragraphs, in the *textus prior*, and canon 55, with two paragraphs, for the *textus emendatus*.

who "manifest their universal adherence to what the church teaches under the guidance of the sacred magisterium."[17] The language is no longer that of Vatican II, but has reverted to the dry and lifeless terminology of neoscholasticism before Vatican II. How is the radical change in the language and the perspective of the final draft to be accounted for? We will see the same process unfold during the preparation of the text of the new Code of Canon Law.

The Revision of the Code of Canon Law

At the same time that canonists, theologians, bishops, and cardinals were working on the *Lex Ecclesiae Fundamentalis*, many others were working on a revision of the Code of Canon Law for the Latin church and writing a Code for the Eastern churches. The Pontifical Commission for the Revision of the Code of Canon Law began its work in earnest on November 20, 1965, a few days before the conclusion of Vatican II.[18] As with *LEF*, the bishops gathered for the First Ordinary General Assembly of the Synod of Bishops in 1967 were informed about the process and approved ten principles formulated by the commission that would govern the revision.[19] The universal episcopate was consulted throughout the process and the bishops who had assembled for the Fifth Ordinary General Assembly of the Synod of Bishops in 1980 were consulted on the progress that had been made up to that time. Clearly, the process of studying, consulting, and drafting the new Code was intensive and world-wide. The final text was submitted to John Paul II on October 29, 1981. The Code of Canon Law for the Latin church has been favorably received in general, it seems,

17. See Daniel Cenalmor Palanca, *La Ley Fundamental de la Iglesia*, canon 59, p. 492.

18. I have relied on John A. Alesandro, "General Introduction," in *The Code of Canon Law: A Text and a Commentary*, ed. James A. Coriden, Thomas J. Green, and Donald E. Heintschel (New York: Paulist Press, 1985), where the author outlines the process of revision, 1–22, at 4–8 ["The Process of Revision"], and Carlo Fantappiè, *Storia del diritto canonico e delle istituzioni della Chiesa* (Bologna: Il Mulino, 2011), 286–94 ["La svolta constituzionale del Concilio Vaticano II"], 294–99 ["La difficile transizione: dal Concilio ai Codici"], and 299–309 ["Il Codice Latino del 1983 e il Codice delle Chiese Orientali del 1990"].

19. According to John A. Alesandro, "One of the main purposes of the ten principles was to guarantee harmony between the Church's revised law and the conciliar documents." These principles can be found in "General Introduction," *Code of Canon Law*, 6.

but of course one would not expect that a document of this scope would escape all calls for improvement. The ambiguity of the Code in regard to "the sense of the faith" is a point at issue.

The final text of the Code does not explicitly mention the teaching function of all the faithful. The earlier drafts, too, fail to mention the "sense of the faith" in conjunction with the role of all the baptized in fulfilling the teaching function entrusted to each believer in baptism. At most, it could be said that the appropriate passages contain traces and hints of the conciliar teaching, and many canonists and theologians have called for these passages to be revised to explicitly mention the "sense of the faith." In this way, the council's teaching on the responsibility of all the faithful for the church's witness to Christian revelation would be clearly expressed. The text of the Code needs to be clear on this central conviction of the bishops at Vatican II. Silence on this matter simply leads to continued neglect of this central, albeit to some, inconvenient teaching. The persistent neglect of the teaching continues to promote an unhealthy imbalance in the church.[20] Many canonists have pointed to various canons where this imbalance can be redressed. I want to point to two canons in particular.

Book 3 of the Code treats the teaching function of the church and this is where one would expect to find a clear statement of the universal responsibility in the church for its teaching—its content, confession, and

---

20. Just as Vatican II had to address the ecclesiological imbalance between papal primacy and episcopal collegiality in the church after Vatican I, the post-Vatican II church needs to address a new imbalance that has been provoked by the council's clear empowerment of the laity and their equal responsibility for the whole life of the church—its teaching and witnessing to Christian truth (*munus docendi*), its mission of sanctifying the world (*munus sanctificandi*), and its co-responsibility in leadership (*munus regendi*). Vatican II has called forth just such a vision of the church. By necessity, it had to leave the details of implementing its vision to the bishops and the faithful after the council. This vision is not served by maintaining silence on the "sense of the faith" of all the faithful, and by not implementing the concrete changes in polity that will advance it. Instead, in the face of its own legitimate concern to defend its authority in a world where authority itself is often under attack, the pope and the bishops have maneuvered themselves into a position in which the equal claims of the faithful have been neglected. They have failed to see that their greatest ally is in a situation where all in the church "conspire" or "breathe together" in fulfilling the same mission and task. This has contributed to the debilitating imbalance that the church now faces.

transmission. After defending the right of the church to teach Christian truth in freedom and its right to teach even truths of the moral and social order that defend the human person and her or his salvation (cc. 747–748), and after canon 749 defends the rights of the pope and the bishops to teach and define divine revelation with authority, the Code finally addresses the role of the faithful in fulfilling the teaching function.

> A person must believe with divine and Catholic faith all those things contained in the word of God, written or handed on, that is, in the one deposit of faith entrusted to the Church, and at the same time proposed as divinely revealed either by the solemn magisterium of the Church or by its ordinary and universal magisterium which is manifested by the common adherence of the Christian faithful under the leadership of the sacred magisterium; therefore all are bound to avoid any doctrines whatsoever contrary to them (c. 750, §1).[21]

An attentive reading of this canon reveals an overly cautious and hesitant expression of the teaching of Vatican II. First of all, it makes clear that the deposit of faith is "entrusted to the Church," which can only mean the whole church. Here, only the church in its entirety adequately expresses the meaning of "Church" in canon 750. The second phrase that deserves attention is the mention of Christian revelation being "manifested by the common adherence of the Christian faithful under the leadership of the sacred magisterium." This, too, can only mean the whole church, the entire people of God, since revelation is not present where the Christian faithful withhold their adherence or where the pastors do not teach with the fullness of their authority. Both elements, the faithful and the pope and the bishops, together constitute the "sense of the faithful." It would have been clearer here if the Code had simply mentioned the gift of the Spirit to each and every believer in the form of the "sense of the faith," or the gift to all in the "consensus of the faithful." The substance of the teaching of Vatican II is present in canon 750, but its clarity, and hence its full implementation, has been dimmed. This lack of clarity and conviction is what has created the sense of imbalance regarding the teaching function of the whole church. Only a clear insertion of the teaching of article 12

---

21. *Code of Canon Law, Latin-English Edition: New English Translation* (Washington, DC: Canon Law Society of America, 2017), 246.

of *Lumen Gentium* on the "sense of the faith" can remedy this situation and thereby open up the concrete means by which all in the church will be able to participate in the teaching function.

The second area where the Code could have been more faithful to Vatican II concerns its treatment of the obligations and rights of all the Christian faithful in canon 212. Paragraph 3 of this canon quotes article 37 of *Lumen Gentium* and says the following:

> To the degree that their knowledge, competence, and excellence are well founded, [the Christian faithful] have the right and even at times the duty to inform their sacred pastors of *their judgment on matters which pertain to the good of the Church* and to communicate their judgment to the rest of the Christian faithful, without prejudice to the integrity of the faith and morals, with respect for their pastors, and conscious of the advantage for all and the dignity of each person.[22]

The German canonist Dominik Burghardt has correctly pointed out the confusion caused by the formulation of the canon in terms of "competence" (*pro scientia, competentia et praestantia quibus pollent*). The faithful, whatever their status in the church, do not base their "judgments" (*sententiae*) on their human competence alone but primarily on the gift of truth by the Spirit—the "sense of the faith" as taught by Vatican II. Burghardt writes:

---

22. "Pro scientia, competentia et praestantia quibus pollent, ipsis ius est, immo et aliquando officium, ut sententiam suam de his quae ad bonum Ecclesiae pertinent sacris Pastoribus mainfestent eamque, salva fidei morumque integritate ac reverentia erga Pastores, attentisque communi utilitate et personarum dignitate, ceteris christifidelibus notam faciant." *Code of Canon Law, New English Translation*, 63. I have given my own translation of canon 212. I find the translation in the new English version deficient. The earlier English translation is closer at points to what I have tried to express with my translation. See *Code of Canon Law: A Text and Commentary*, 146. My principal objection is to the translation of *sententia* as "opinion," in both the earlier and the new English translation of the Code. "Opinion" is much too weak and misleading. *Sententia* also connotes "meaning," "purpose," "judgment," and "decision." In light of what I indicated in chapter 9 of the council's decision to change the context of the "sense of the faith" from the discussion of public opinion to the responsibility for teaching (*munus docendi*) in the revised text of Gérard Philips, the mistranslation of *sententia* as "opinion" seems particularly egregious.

It is not "knowledge, competence and excellence" on the part of believers that primarily entitles them to express their judgments, but the fact that they are bearers of the "sense of the faith" that gives them the "right to be heard." The fact that not every Christian can claim knowledge, competence, and excellence means that the danger of crassly misunderstanding the meaning of the paragraph needs to be guarded against. On the one hand, it creates confusion by incorporating constitutional elitism into the law, and on the other, it transposes intra-ecclesial dialogue into a realm governed by purely secular principles. The "sense of the faith," on the other hand, does not depend on secular qualifications but on the intensity of lived communion with God and the Church. Its incorporation would have avoided such misunderstandings and would have imparted to the canon a clearly theological figuration. Moreover, the complementarity of the office of the magisterium and the "sense of the faith" of the faithful, as well as the obligation to obey and the "right to be heard" would have found appropriate expression.[23]

The formulation of canon 212, §3 seems to miss the whole point of the "sense of the faith" and so demands reformulation.[24]

The Contribution of the Code of Canons of the Eastern Churches
Unlike the Code of Canon Law for the Latin church, the Code of Canons of the Eastern churches contains two explicit references to the "sense of

---

23. *Institution Glaubenssinn. Die Bedeutung des sensus fidei im kirchlichen Verfassungsrecht und für die Interpretation kanonischer Gesetze* (Paderborn: Bonifatius Verlag, 2002), 179–80. It is not that human knowledge, competence, and even excellence are not to be welcomed in the church and that Christians who possess these desirable qualities are not to be encouraged to make these gifts available to the church, but the fact that they are not the most secure basis for the teaching function in the church. Canon 212, §3 needed to draw on the teaching of *Lumen Gentium* 12 and 35, as well as article 37.

24. The only point at which the *New Commentary on the Code of Canon Law* refers to the "sense of the faith" is in Robert J. Kaslyn's commentary on canon 212. Kaslyn does not state clearly that the canon is based on *Lumen Gentium* 12, but instead invokes the teaching of Vatican II to maintain the balance between the ordinary faithful and their pastors when the former express their opinions to their leaders, and when differences of opinion can threaten the *communio* of the church. To his credit, however, Kaslyn offers a very positive reading of "the 'knowledge, competence, and prestige' of the faithful who express opinions," seeing in these qualities real contributions to the church's understanding of the faith. See *New Commentary on the Code of Canon Law*, ed. John P. Beal, James A. Coriden and Thomas J. Green (New York: Paulist Press, 2000), 265–67, at 266.

the faith." They are in canons 603 and 604, and appear in chapter 1 of the section that deals with the Ecclesiastical Magisterium (Title XV).[25] Although canons 603 and 604 fall within the treatment of "The Teaching Function of the Church in General," they seem to be dominated by the theme of the official ecclesiastical magisterium, so that the participation in the teaching function by the ordinary faithful, according to Vatican II, does not emerge with sufficient clarity. Neither canon makes any reference to articles 12 or 35 of *Lumen Gentium* in the footnotes citing their sources. As we will see, however, this is not really a shortchanging of Vatican II in the teaching of the Eastern Code.[26]

Canon 603 refers to the Pastoral Constitution on the Church in the Modern World, article 62, which deals with the relationship of the Christian faith to culture. Paragraph 2 in particular urges greater openness on the part of the church to more contemporary forms of literature and the arts, in order to elevate human life and values through the collaboration of the church and the cultures in which it lives and operates. When the canon is read against the contents of the whole of article 62, it offers a pertinent and powerful insight on the scope of the "sense of the faith," yet in a way different from *Lumen Gentium* 12.

Canon 604 also approaches the teaching of Vatican II on the "sense of the faith" from a different perspective and so helps to deepen how the postconciliar church understands the teaching. This canon refers to the multiplicity of the particular churches in the universal church as something fundamentally positive, but that can also be challenging, given "the varieties of doctrinal enunciations in the various churches."[27] The footnote

25. The two codes are organized differently. Whereas the Code of the Latin church has seven general sections, called "Books," that are further divided into "titles" and "chapters," the Code of the Eastern Churches simply has thirty different sections, called "titles," that follow thematically one after the other. These "titles" are further divided into "chapters" and "articles."

26. Dominik Burghardt, too, has interpreted these canons positively, even though they do not reference *Lumen Gentium* 12. He writes: "Even though LG 12 is not what supports the formulation of canons 603 and 604, nevertheless we can identify the use of the notion of the *sensus fidei* in these canons with what the Council meant by the expression 'sense of the faith.'" *Institution Glaubenssinn*, 202.

27. *Code of Canons of the Eastern Churches, Latin-English Edition*, prepared under the Auspices of the Canon Law Society of America (Washington, DC: Canon Law Society of America, 2001), 235.

refers to the Decree on the Catholic Eastern Churches, article 2, which states: "There is a remarkable interchange between them [the various churches or rites], so that the variety within the Church not only does no harm to its unity, but rather makes it manifest."[28] And, as canon 604 states: "The Catholicity of the Church is brought into better light through legitimate diversity."[29] Moreover, this insight is extended to the other churches and ecclesial communities that have issued from the Reformation, when the footnote also references the Decree on Ecumenism, article 4.[30] In both instances cited in the footnote to canon 604, these conciliar documents do not mention the "sense of the faith" explicitly, but the Code of Canons of the Eastern Churches has discerned its implied teaching there.[31]

The Latin church, then, could be enriched by the clarity of the teaching of the Eastern churches on the "sense of the faith." Will it dare to clarify its espousal of Vatican II on this point in reformulating and improving its treatment of the topic in the Code of Canon Law in the future?[32]

---

28. *Orientalium ecclesiarum*, 2. See Norman P. Tanner, *Decrees of the Ecumenical Councils*, vol. 2 (Washington, DC: Georgetown University Press, 1990), 900.

29. *Code of Canons of the Eastern Churches*, 235.

30. See Tanner, *Decrees of the Ecumenical Councils*, 2:911–12.

31. In his commentary on the Code of Canons of the Eastern Churches, George Nedungatt strangely does not mention the appearance of the term the "sense of the faith" in canons 603–604. He talks around this important term of Vatican II, but never explicitly adverts to it. See *A Guide to the Eastern Code: A Commentary on the Code of Canons of the Eastern Churches*, ed. George Nedungatt (Rome: Pontificio Istituto Orientale, 2002), 457–62.

32. Many canonists have made suggestions for which canons are prime candidates for mention of the "sense of the faith" in the Code. See Eugenio Corecco, "Aspects of the Reception of Vatican II in the Code of Canon Law," in *The Reception of Vatican II*, ed. Giuseppe Alberigo, Jean-Pierre Jossua, and Joseph A. Komonchak (Washington, DC: Catholic University of America Press, 1987), 249–96; Rinaldo Bertolino, "*Sensus Fidei*, Charismen und Recht im Volk Gottes," *Archiv für katholisches Kirchenrecht* 163 (1994): 28–73; Christoph Ohly, "Systematische Erwägungen zur ekklesiologisch-verfassungsrechtlichen Einbindung des 'sensus fidei fidelium' in das Wesen und die Sendung der Kirche," *Sensus fidelium. Zur Einordnung des Glaubenssinnes aller Gläubigen in die Communio-Struktur der Kirche im geschichtlichen Spiegel dogmatisch-kanonistischer Erkenntnisse und der Aussagen des II. Vatikanum* (St. Ottilien: EOS Verlag, 1999), 273–346; and Burghardt, *Institution Glaubenssinn*, 172–204 ["*Sensus fidei* und Kodifikation"] and 336–44 ["Ergebnisse und Ausblick"], to name only a few of the more prominent contributions.

The Papal Magisterium since Vatican II

John Paul II (1978–2005)

Pope John Paul II introduced the "sense of the faith" into his first encyclical "The Redeemer of Man" (*Redemptor hominis*) and returned several times to the notion over the course of his long papacy.[33] It might prove instructive to see how John Paul understood the "sense of the faith" and what its function was in his writings.

John Paul II was elected pope on October 15, 1978, and issued his first encyclical on March 4, 1979. "The Redeemer of Man" is programmatic in character and attempts to set the tone for a new papacy. The mystery of redemption is central to John Paul's vision: God redeems humankind in the Son and invites the church to cooperate in this mission. Chapter 3, "Redeemed Man and His Situation in the Modern World," is markedly anthropocentric in approach and draws heavily on Vatican II's Pastoral Constitution on the Church in the Modern World.[34] The new pope was keenly aware of the threatened human condition at the height of the Cold War and he was conscious of the dangerous ideas propagated by the purveyors of late modernity. Chapter 4, "The Church's Mission and Man's Destiny," is John Paul's first attempt to spell out his understanding of how the church is called to address these issues. In number 19 the pope

---

33. In 1973 the Congregation for the Doctrine of the Faith mentioned the "sense of the faith" in its *Declaration in Defense of the Catholic Doctrine on the Church against Certain Errors of the Present Day (Mysterium Ecclesiae)* on the matter of infallibility. See *Acta Apostolicae Sedis* 65 (1973), 396–408, at 399. Though he is not mentioned by name, in 1970 Hans Küng had denied the doctrine in his *Infallible? An Inquiry*, trans. Edward Quinn (Garden City, NY: Doubleday & Company, 1971) and provoked a world-wide discussion and reconsideration of the teaching of Vatican I and Vatican II. The Congregation for the Doctrine of the Faith approached the church's infallibility from the widest possible angle, speaking about the infallibility of the whole church (article 2: "The Infallibility of the Universal Church") before addressing the special role of the magisterium (article 3: "The Infallibility of the Church's Magisterium"). Thus, after rehearsing the teaching of *Lumen Gentium* 12, the declaration goes on to say: "Without a doubt the faithful, who in their own manner share in Christ's prophetic office, in many ways contribute towards increasing the understanding of faith in the Church" (no. 2). *Declaration in Defense of the Catholic Doctrine on the Church against Certain Errors of the Present Day* (Washington, DC: Publications Office United States Catholic Conference, 1973), 4.

34. John Paul quotes or references *Gaudium et Spes* twelve times.

turns to what will become characteristic of his thought throughout his papacy: "The Church as Responsible for the Truth." It is precisely here that John Paul introduces the teaching of Vatican II on the "sense of the faith." He writes:

> In the light of the sacred teaching of the Second Vatican Council, the Church thus appears before us as the social subject of responsibility for divine truth. . . . Fidelity must be a constitutive quality of the Church's faith, both when she is teaching it and when she is professing it. . . . Christ himself, concerned for this fidelity to divine truth, promised the Church the special assistance of the Spirit of truth, gave the gift of infallibility to those whom he entrusted with the mandate of transmitting and teaching the truth . . . and he furthermore endowed the whole of the People of God with a special sense of the faith (no. 19).[35]

At this point, the pope situates the church's mission of witnessing to God's truth in the context of the teaching of Vatican II that the church is called to participate in Christ's own mission as prophet. He writes:

> Increasing care must be taken that the various forms of catechesis and its various fields . . . should give evidence of the universal sharing by the whole of the People of God in the prophetic office of Christ himself. Linked with this fact, the Church's responsibility for divine truth must be increasingly shared in various ways by all. . . . The present-day Church, guided by a sense of responsibility for truth, must persevere in fidelity to her own nature, which involves the prophetic mission that comes from Christ himself: 'As the Father has sent me, even so I send you. . . . Receive the Holy Spirit' (John 20:21-22).[36]

Right from the start, then, John Paul demonstrated his commitment to the council's teaching on the "sense of the faith." His phrasing of the teaching is cautious, but he cannot deny its place in the church's self-understanding after Vatican II. In light of this, the fact that he will return to it in five other encyclicals or apostolic exhortations is not surprising.

---

35. *Acta Apostolicae Sedis* [*AAS*] 71 (1979): 257–324, at 305–6; *The Redeemer of Man* (Boston, MA: Pauline Books & Media, 1979), 43–44.

36. *AAS* 71 (1979) 309; *Redeemer of Man*, 46.

Furthermore, the pope's appreciation of the "sense of the faith" will continue to grow over the years.

John Paul demonstrated a predilection for the themes of marriage and the family and he turned to them two years later in his apostolic exhortation "The Role of the Christian Family in the Modern World" (*Familiaris Consortio*). He begins with an investigation into the situation of the present-day family and its problems, an investigation that demands discernment. This is the context in which he introduces his next inquiry into the "sense of the faith." In number 5 he writes:

> The discernment effected by the Church becomes the offering of an orientation in order that the entire truth and the full dignity of marriage and the family may be preserved and realized.
>
> This discernment is accomplished through the sense of [the] faith, which is a gift that the Spirit gives to all the faithful, and is therefore a work of the whole Church according to the diversity of the various gifts and charisms that, together with and according to the responsibility proper to each one, work together for a more profound understanding and activation of the word of God. The Church, therefore, does not accomplish this discernment only through the pastors, who teach in the name and with the power of Christ, but also through the laity. . . . The laity, moreover, by reason of their particular vocation have the specific role of interpreting the history of the world in the light of Christ, in as much as they are called to illuminate and organize temporal realities according to the plan of God, creator and redeemer.[37]
>
> Christian spouses and parents can and should offer their unique and irreplaceable contribution to the elaboration of an authentic evangelical discernment in the various situations and cultures in which men and women live their marriage and their family life. They are qualified for this role by their charism or specific gift, the gift of the sacrament of matrimony.[38]

These three paragraphs demonstrate John Paul's acceptance of the doctrine of the council on the "sense of the faith" and his application of it to an urgent issue that the church and society in general both face—the

---

37. *AAS* 74 (1982) 81–191, at 85–86; *The Role of the Christian Family in the Modern World* (Boston, MA: Pauline Books & Media, 1981), 15–16.

38. *AAS* 74 (1982) 86; *Role of the Christian Family in the Modern World*, 16.

fragility of the family. He does two things admirably: he points to the uniqueness of the role the laity play regarding an urgent pastoral problem, and he connects the council's teaching on charisms to its teaching on the "sense of the faith." In this instance, the two are intimately intertwined.

The pope attempts to dispel possible misunderstandings of the "sense of the faith." First, he clearly distinguishes the "sense of the faith" from public opinion in the church and from specialized knowledge or expertise. He writes:

> Following Christ, the Church seeks the truth, which is not always the same as the majority opinion. She listens to conscience and not to power, and in this way she defends the poor and the downtrodden. The Church values sociological and statistical research, when it proves helpful in understanding the historical context in which pastoral action has to be developed and when it leads to a better understanding of the truth. Such research alone, however, is not to be considered in itself an expression of the sense of [the] faith.[39]

The "sense of the faithful" is a supernatural gift of the Spirit to all who believe and should not be confused with public opinion, however useful it might be on its own terms.

Second, the pope touches on the issue of the role of the pastors of the church with regard to the "sense of the faith" of the faithful. He points to three legitimate roles the pastors play in the exercise of their apostolic ministry as it pertains to the "sense of the faith." He writes:

> The pastors must promote the sense of the faith in all the faithful, must examine and authoritatively judge the genuineness of its expressions, and educate the faithful in an ever more mature evangelical discernment.[40]

Though I would have liked John Paul to have also explicitly admonished the pastors to carefully and respectfully listen to the insights of the faithful, as the Decree on the Ministry and Life of Priests says in article 9, it must

---

39. Ibid.
40. Ibid.

be said that this duty is implied in his insistence on the importance of the experience of the lay faithful in the areas of marriage and family life.[41]

John Paul's teaching in *Familiaris Consortio* is the longest and most detailed treatment he offered in the course of his papacy. His subsequent references were shorter but sometimes added subtle details to his teaching.

In his apostolic exhortation "The Lay Members of Christ's Faithful People" (*Christifideles laici*), John Paul stressed the teaching of Vatican II that all in the church participate in the three offices of Christ (no. 14). In connection with the prophetic office, he once again resumed the teaching of Vatican II on the "sense of the faith" of the faithful, referencing articles 12 and 35 of *Lumen Gentium* explicitly.[42] In his encyclical "The Splendor of Truth" (*Veritatis splendor*), number 109, he summarized the conciliar teaching, but with special reference to the contribution of theologians, including lay theologians.[43] In this regard, he stressed the contribution that critical theological reflection on moral and pastoral matters adds to the church's understanding of the faith.

In his encyclical "The Gospel of Life" (*Evangelium vitae*), John Paul strove to address the full range of issues regarding the dignity and the sanctity of life and the obligations that flow from it. No papal document had gone into such detail on a matter whose gravity emerged in the twentieth century in the wake of two horrific world wars, the Holocaust and other genocides, the flagrant disregard of the rights of noncombatants in war, a pervasive existential anxiety in the face of possible nuclear annihilation, and increased access to the means of preventing conception, terminating life in the womb, and medically terminating life at the end stages. The pope characterized these and other practices as constituting "the culture of death (no. 12)."[44] But how could he make his case? The

---

41. See *Decrees of the Ecumenical Councils*, vol. 2, ed. Norman P. Tanner, 1,054, where we read: "[Presbyters] are to test the spirits to see whether they are of God, discern with a sense of faith the manifold gifts (*charismata*), both exalted and ordinary, that the laity have, acknowledge them gladly and foster them with care."

42. See *AAS* 81 (1989), 393–521, at 411–12; *The Lay Members of Christ's Faithful People* (Boston,MA: Pauline Books & Media, 1988), 30–34.

43. See *AAS* 85 (1993), 1134–1228, at 1218–19; *The Splendor of Truth* (Boston, MA: Pauline Books & Media, 1993), 131–32.

44. See *AAS* 87 (1995), 401–522, at 409; *The Gospel of Life* (Boston, MA: Pauline Books & Media, 1995), 27.

sources of revelation do not seem to offer a clear-cut prohibition in all situations. This is the context in which the pope introduces the "sense of the faith" as a possible explanation. He writes:

> In effect, the absolute inviolability of innocent human life is a moral truth clearly taught by sacred scripture, constantly upheld by the Church's tradition and consistently proposed by her magisterium. This constant teaching is the evident result of that "supernatural sense of the faith" which, inspired and sustained by the Holy Spirit, safeguards the People of God from error when "it shows universal agreement in matters of faith and morals" (no. 57).[45]

The conviction of the living tradition of the church and of the "sense of the faith" that guides the tradition gives John Paul II the courage to teach that "by the authority which Christ conferred upon Peter and his successors, and in communion with the bishops of the Catholic Church, *I confirm that the direct and voluntary killing of an innocent human being is always gravely immoral*" (no. 57).[46] The pope's teaching does not answer every question as to the extent of the teaching and its binding force in every case, but John Paul has clearly set the Catholic Church on a definite path—an unquestioned commitment to safeguard and defend all human life within a context that takes all "life issues" into account. According to the pope's argumentation, this takes place within the context of a living tradition, of the "sense of the faith," and of the mutual contribution (*conspiratio*) of the pope and the bishops as pastors together with the living faith of the ordinary faithful.

Finally, and somewhat surprisingly, John Paul invoked the "sense of the faith" in his encyclical "On Commitment to Ecumenism" (*Ut Unum Sint*). The pope was an ardent supporter of Vatican II's commitment to ecumenism. But those who saw the ecumenical movement as weakening and blurring the faith of the church tried to use the pope's efforts to set boundaries to experiments in the church to curtail ecumenism as well. They also employed the pope's reminders to the pastors and the faithful of the full range of the church's teachings as though he was calling the council's ecumenical commitment into question. The encyclical intended

---

45. See *AAS* 87 (1995), 464–65; *Gospel of Life*, 92.
46. See AAS 87 (1995), 465; *Gospel of* Life, 92.

to reaffirm John Paul's commitment to ecumenism and to reassure the leaders of the other churches and ecclesial communities that his intra-ecclesial efforts at "correcting the course" in the Catholic Church did not call his ultimate commitment to ecumenism into question.

Against this historical backdrop, John Paul wanted to challenge the church to continue courageously along the path of accepting and assimilating the results of the various accords that had been reached. How were they to be received by the churches? This is the context of the pope's turning once again to the fruitfulness of the insight offered by the "sense of the faith" as taught by Vatican II. He writes:

> While dialogue continues on new subjects or develops at deeper levels, a new task lies before us: that of receiving the results already achieved. These cannot remain the statements of bilateral commissions but must become a common heritage. For this to come about and for the bonds of communion to be thus strengthened, a serious examination needs to be made, which, by different ways and means and at various levels of responsibility, must involve the whole People of God. We are in fact dealing with issues which frequently are matters of faith, and these require universal consent, extending from the bishops to the lay faithful, all of whom have received the anointing of the Holy Spirit. It is the same Spirit who assists the magisterium and awakens the *sensus fidei*.
>
> Consequently, for the outcome of dialogue to be received, there is needed a broad and precise critical process which analyzes the results and rigorously tests their consistency with the tradition of faith received from the apostles and lived out in the community of believers gathered around the bishop, their legitimate pastor (no. 80).[47]

What is surprising about the use of the "sense of the faith" by John Paul II is the extent to which he employed the teaching and his creativity in extending its use to other contexts of thought and practice in the church and among the churches. While it is true that he often invoked the teaching with caution, he also employed it boldly and creatively.[48]

---

47. See *AAS* 87 (1995), 921–82, at 969–70; *On Commitment to Ecumenism* (Boston, MA: Pauline Books & Media, 1995), 89–90. The Latin expression was retained in the English translation.

48. Pope Benedict XVI (2005–13) did not directly address the issue of the "sense of the faith" in his encyclicals. His reservation regarding the teaching came to expression

Pope Francis (2013–)

Pope Francis issued his apostolic exhortation "The Joy of the Gospel" (*Evangelii Gaudium*) within a few months of assuming the papacy. Francis used the exhortation to summarize and promote the work of the Thirteenth Ordinary General Assembly of the Synod of Bishops, which dealt with the topic of the new evangelization that had also preoccupied his predecessors Paul VI, John Paul II, and Benedict XVI. His long apostolic exhortation lays out in detail the pope's program for his papacy within the context of the work of evangelization. It is to be marked by the centrality of the gospel and the joy that it inspires in humankind. A spirit of hope and joy pervades the exhortation and is evident on every page. Francis shows unbounded confidence in the teachings of Vatican II and wants to go out of his way to unleash their transformative power. We see this in the case of the "sense of the faith" as well. Not only does he pick up the threads of John Paul's teaching, but he encourages the church to move boldly into the future.

Francis speaks about the "sense of the faith" at two points in his exhortation. In the section entitled "The Entire People of God Proclaims the Gospel," the pope concentrates on the teaching of Vatican II that everyone is called to proclaim the gospel. He reiterates the traditional theological position that the church is infallible because of the primacy of "infallibility

---

in his early writings as a theologian and he did not seem to change his opinion over time. In his 1967 commentary on article 10 of the Constitution on Divine Revelation, he wrote: "It is to be regarded as a fortunate decision of the Council that, in emphasizing the share of the laity in the work of keeping the word pure, it did not become involved with the theory of the consensus of faith, which, in connection with the dogmas of 1854 and 1950, resulted in the acceptance of the view that the whole Church has a share in the making manifest of the word. For there is still too much that needs clarification in this theory before it can be regarded as a safe expression of this particular point. It is difficult here to regard entirely as unjustified the doubts of the Tübingen dogmatic theologian J. E. Kuhn, who feared that the theory of the consensus of faith would favour arbitrary and secondary traditions." See "The Transmission of Divine Revelation," in *Commentary on the Documents of Vatican II*, ed. Herbert Vorgrimler (New York: Herder and Herder, 1969), 181–98, at 196. A few years earlier, in 1964, in the first of his annually published reports on Vatican II, Ratzinger wrote: "There is much talk today in theological circles of the Church's 'sense of faith' as a source of dogma. Such a source is not always fully trustworthy. Who can determine what this 'sense of faith' is?" *Theological Highlights of Vatican II*, trans. Henry Traub (New York: Paulist Press, 1966), 52.

in belief" (*infallibilitas in credendo*). Absent are the repeated and tiresome cautions about those in the church who teach with authority and those who are led in the faith by their pastors so often encountered in previous magisterial statements. In the past, the distinction often served as a caution and restraint on the ordinary faithful and their role in witnessing to and elaborating the faith. Francis does not deny the distinction of responsibilities but neither does he dwell on it obsessively. He wants to breathe new life into the teaching and unleash its potential, and he does not hesitate to introduce some unaccustomed theological vocabulary to advance this goal. He writes:

> In all the baptized, from first to last, the sanctifying power of the Spirit is at work, impelling us to evangelization. The people of God is holy thanks to this anointing, which makes it infallible *in credendo*. This means that it does not err in faith, even though it may not find words to explain the faith. The Spirit guides it in truth and leads it to salvation. As part of his mysterious love for humanity, God furnishes the totality of the faithful with an *instinct of faith—sensus fidei—*which helps them to discern what is truly of God. The presence of the Spirit gives Christians a certain connaturality with divine realities, and a wisdom which enables them to grasp those realities intuitively, even when they lack the wherewithal to give them precise expression (no. 119).[49]

Later he takes up the theme again but now in the context of the poor and their special role in the people of God. He writes:

> For the Church, the option for the poor is primarily a theological category rather than a cultural, sociological, political, or philosophical one. God shows the poor "his first mercy." This divine preference has consequences for the faith life of all Christians. . . . That is why I want a Church which is poor and for the poor. They have much to teach us. Not only do they share in the *sensus fidei*, but in their difficulties they know the suffering Christ. We need to let ourselves be evangelized by them. . . . We are called to find Christ in them, to lend our voice to their causes, but also to be their friends, to listen to them, to speak for

---

49. See *AAS* 105 (2013), 1019–1137, at 1069–70; *The Joy of the Gospel* (Boston, MA: Pauline Books & Media, 2013), 83–84.

them, and to embrace the mysterious wisdom which God wishes to share with us through them (no. 198).[50]

The "wisdom" that the poor have to share with the people of God is not a theme that is ordinarily mentioned in connection with the "sense of the faith." Pope Francis has espoused the contribution of the liberation theology of his native Central and South America, especially as enunciated in the documents of the Conference of Latin American Bishops at Medellín, Colombia (1968), Puebla, Mexico (1979), and Aparecida, Brazil (2007) and offered it to the universal church as a valid development of the teachings of Vatican II. In this surprising way, he has breathed new life into the council's teaching regarding the "sense of the faith." As his pontificate unfolds, one must wait and see what new challenges emerge in this regard.

The *Catechism of the Catholic Church*

The Second Extraordinary Synod of Bishops, convened in 1985 to assess the reception of Vatican II twenty years after the council, discussed the benefits of formulating a catechism for the universal church. The *Roman Catechism* had been written to address the issue of how best to present the content of the Catholic faith and how to evangelize in the light of the situation of the church in the sixteenth century and the teachings of Trent.[51] Some bishops at the synod wondered whether such a catechism could address some of the confusion in the postconciliar period about what Vatican II had actually taught and assist the church in the process of evangelization, a topic that was becoming a central concern to Paul VI and John Paul II.[52] The proposal was accepted by the participants and a commission of twelve cardinals and bishops was set up to coordinate the effort. Cardinal Joseph Ratzinger, the prefect of the Congregation for the Doctrine of the Faith, chaired the commission. Seven bishops

---

50. *AAS* 105 (2013), 1103; *Joy of the Gospel*, 136–37.

51. See Berard L. Marthaler, "Four Pillars of Catechesis: The Catechism of the Council of Trent," *The Catechism Yesterday and Today: The Evolution of a Genre* (Collegeville, MN: Liturgical Press, 1995), 33–41.

52. See Marthaler, "The Dutch Catechism: Harbinger of a New Genre," *The Catechism Yesterday and Today*, 121–31.

from Europe, South America, North America, and the Middle East were chosen to write the text under the editorship of the Dominican professor Christoph Schönborn of the University of Fribourg, Switzerland. The Coordinating Commission kept the bishops of the universal church informed throughout the process and invited suggestions from them. In the end, the commission sifted through twenty-four thousand suggestions for improving the text. It took seven years and ten versions to complete the task.[53] John Paul II issued the *Catechism of the Catholic Church* (*CCC*) on October 11, 1992. A revised second edition that incorporated John Paul's teaching in *Evangelium vitae* was published in 1997.

More important than this historical data on the origin of the *CCC* and how it was composed is the question: For whom was it composed? Obviously, from a certain point of view it is intended for the whole church and all its members. Nevertheless, the principle that governed its composition was that it was intended for the universal episcopate. The bishops are the ones who must decide how to use the *CCC* for their national conferences and their dioceses. No single catechism could possibly take into consideration all the languages, societies, and cultures in the church and respond to each one's unique situation. That is why the Coordinating Commission and Pope John Paul II addressed the *CCC* to the bishops to use in their own national, regional, and local circumstances. John Paul's apostolic constitution *Fidei depositum* approving the *CCC* states unequivocally:

> This catechism is given to [the church's pastors and the Christian faithful] that it may be a sure and authentic reference text for teaching catholic doctrine and particularly for preparing local catechisms.[54]

> This catechism is not intended to replace the local catechisms duly approved by the ecclesiastical authorities, the diocesan bishops and the Episcopal Conferences, especially if they have been approved by the Apostolic See. It is meant to encourage and assist in the writing of

---

53. On the details of the editorial process, see Marthaler, "The *Catechism of the Catholic Church*: The Old and the New," *The Catechism Yesterday and Today*, 143–57.

54. John Paul II, *Fidei depositum* (October 11, 1992) in *Catechism of the Catholic Church* (2nd ed., Washington, DC: United States Catholic Conference, 1997), 5. See also "The Aim and Intended Readership of This Catechism," *Catechism of the Catholic Church*, numbers 11–12.

> new local catechisms, which take into account various situations and cultures, while carefully preserving the unity of faith and fidelity to catholic doctrine.[55]

It should be clear, then, that the *CCC* is intended as a resource in the church to be consulted on the doctrinal content of the Catholic faith and the church's sacramental, liturgical, moral, and prayer life. It is not designed to serve as a universal text for catechizing the faithful. That is the task of catechisms prepared for local, regional, and national use. Such catechisms should be encouraged by the bishops, with the *CCC* offering guidance to their authors. Given this scope of the *CCC*, what does it say about the "sense of the faith"?

The *CCC* is quite comprehensive in presenting the "sense of the faith." Before discussing the individual articles of the faith as presented in the church's Creed, the *CCC* treats the nature of revelation, its transmission, and the role of sacred Scripture in communicating Christian revelation. Precisely when it considers the transmission of the faith, the *CCC* examines what Vatican II meant by the "sense of the faith." First, it presents the teaching regarding the supernatural character of the gift and its appreciation by all who believe. The Holy Spirit is identified as the source and constant animator of those who believe (nos. 91–93) and as the one who assists in their growth in understanding the faith (nos. 94–95).[56] In other words, the *CCC*'s teaching regarding the "sense of the faith" is ample, even-handed, and clear. The *CCC* later takes up this general teaching on the "sense of the faith" when it turns its attention to the people of God, where it speaks explicitly of the priestly, prophetic, and royal roles of the whole people of God (see nos. 783–786), and under the prophetic role explicitly speaks of the "sense of the faith" (see no. 785, which draws on LG 12 directly). Also, when considering the teaching office of the pope and bishops, the *CCC* mentions the mutual contribution (*conspiratio*) of the bishops and the faithful in believing and teaching infallibly:

---

55. *Catechism of the Catholic Church*, 6.

56. The footnotes reference *Lumen Gentium* 12, *Dei Verbum* 8 and 10, as well as *Gaudium et spes* 23 and 24, and *Unitatis redintegratio* 4. Only the absence of *Lumen Gentium* 35 catches the reader's attention.

In order to preserve the Church in the purity of the faith handed on by the apostles, Christ who is the Truth willed to confer on her a share in his own infallibility. By a "supernatural sense of faith" the People of God, under the guidance of the Church's living magisterium, "unfailingly adheres to this faith" (no. 889).[57]

The *CCC* does not dwell anxiously on the role played by the pope and the bishops in teaching and defining the faith, but shows admirable restraint when speaking about the mutual contribution of the pope and the bishops and the ordinary faithful.

Given the prominent and balanced place accorded the "sense of the faith" in the *CCC*, the question emerges once again as to why the teaching continues to play so insignificant a role in the postconciliar church even to this day. Why are the faithful largely ignorant of this teaching and of their rightful place as genuine witnesses to the truth of Christian revelation? Why do the bishops speak so rarely about the "sense of the faith" of the church and why do they fail to encourage it? The teaching in the *CCC* hardly justifies such silence and neglect.

The Role Played by the Congregation for the Doctrine of the Faith

The Congregation for the Doctrine of the Faith (CDF) needs little introduction. Formerly known as the Congregation of the Holy Office, it succeeded to the Congregation for the Holy Inquisition and was reorganized and renamed by Paul VI after Vatican II.[58] The new name was intended to indicate a profound change in its mission and how to carry it out. In a word, it was hoped that the CDF, though still expected to defend the orthodoxy of doctrinal teaching in the church, would promote

---

57. *Catechism of the Catholic Church*, 235.

58. See Jérôme Hamer, "In Service of the Magisterium: The Evolution of a Congregation," *The Jurist* 37 (1977): 340–57 and Barnabas M. Ahern, "Doctrine of the Faith, Congregation for the" in *New Catholic Encyclopedia*, vol. 17: *Supplement: Change in the Church* (New York: McGraw-Hill, 1979), 192–93. See the motu proprio of Paul VI *Integrae servandae* in *AAS* 57 (1965): 952–55 and the apostolic constitution *Regimini Ecclesiae* in *AAS* 59 (1967): 897–99 for the changes introduced after Vatican II, and the apostolic constitution of John Paul II *Pastor Bonus*, arts. 48–55 in *AAS* 80 (1988): 873–74.

the doctrine of the faith by proactively assisting theologians in their indispensable task in the church. In this regard, it was hoped that less attention would be dedicated to pursuing theologians who deviated from the church's teaching and more effort expended in helping and guiding theologians in fulfilling their charge. It must frankly be admitted that the new charge for the CDF has rarely been met in the postconciliar era and that the former spirit of surveillance still has priority. This is certainly the case regarding the CDF's "Instruction on the Ecclesial Vocation of the Theologian" (*Donum veritatis*).[59] Unfortunately, instead of exuding a spirit of fraternal guidance and support of the theologian today, it is often harsh in its judgments and unhelpful in the guidance it offers. It demonstrates a spirit of suspicion vis-à-vis the theologian and his or her contributions to the church.[60] Nevertheless, it demands our consideration because of the frequency with which it refers to the "sense of the faith" and the suspicion it sometimes shows regarding it.

The "sense of the faith" is mentioned in each of the four sections that constitute *Donum veritatis*. In section 1, "The Truth, God's Gift to His People," *Lumen Gentium* 12 is approvingly quoted in support of the Vatican II teaching that indeed it is the whole church that is endowed with infallibility: "The whole body of the faithful who have an anointing that comes from the Holy One (cf. 1 Jn. 2:20, 27) cannot err in matters of belief" (no. 4).[61] Then, in section 2, "The Vocation of the Theologian," in a positive and helpful, though surprisingly very terse presentation of this vocation in the church, the document indicates the importance of the "sense of the faith" as "a sure rule for guiding his reflections and help-ing him assess the correctness of his conclusions" (no. 8).[62] The text, of course, does not claim authority for the individual positions and state-ments of theologians, but it does situate their work within the supportive

59. Washington, DC: Office for Publishing and Promotion Services, United States Catholic Conference, 1990. Also printed in *Origins* 20/8 (July 5, 1990): 117–26.

60. For the reaction of British, Canadian, American, German, and French theologians, see the collection *Streitgespräch um Theologie und Lehramt: Die Instruktion über die kirchliche Berufung des Theologen in der Diskussion*, ed. Peter Hünermann and Dietmar Mieth (Frankfurt: J. Knecht, 1991).

61. *Instruction on the Ecclesial Vocation of the Theologian* (Washington, DC: United States Catholic Conference, 1990), 5–6.

62. Ibid., 8.

embrace of the church's "supernatural sense of the faith" as in general operative when theologians are responsibly engaged by their ecclesial task. According to *Donum veritatis*, the theologian "responds to the dynamism found in the faith itself" and "theology also arises from love and love's dynamism. In the act of faith, man knows God's goodness and begins to love him. Love, however, is ever desirous of a better knowledge of the beloved" (no. 7).[63] *Donum veritatis* presents a noble and challenging calling to the theologian as a responsible and mature believer who is engaged by the church at its very center.

It is surprising then to find so little resonance of the theologian's contribution to the church in section 3, "The Magisterium of the Church's Pastors." The tone suddenly turns cautionary, as though the pope and the bishops are in competition with theologians who must be treated warily. According to number 14, the magisterium "must protect God's people from the danger of deviations and confusion, guaranteeing them the objective possibility of professing the authentic faith free from error, at all times and in diverse situations."[64] Or again, in number 20, "The pastoral task of the magisterium is one of vigilance. It seeks to ensure that the people of God remain in the truth which sets free."[65] Where has the respect for and appreciation of the vocation of the theologian disappeared to? Where is the confidence in the "supernatural sense of the faith" that the Holy Spirit unceasingly pours forth into the church, its faithful, theologians, and pastoral leaders alike?

This same tone is further intensified in section 4, "The Magisterium and Theology."[66] Though the section begins auspiciously by claiming, "This service to the ecclesial community brings the theologian and the magisterium into a reciprocal relationship. The latter authentically teaches the doctrine of the apostles. And, benefiting from the work of theologians, it . . . promotes, with the authority received from Jesus Christ, new and

---

63. Ibid.

64. Ibid., 11.

65. Ibid., 14.

66. This section is almost as long as the other three sections of *Donum veritatis* combined, with its lengthy treatment of "dissent," now not viewed as something that can offer the possibility of clarifying the church's proclamation and of possibly improving the formulation of its doctrines, but as dangerous and as a threat to the pope's and the bishops' authority.

deeper comprehension, clarification and application of revealed doctrine" (no. 21).[67] But the spirit of open collaboration does not last very long. Instead, cautions and restrictions on the theologian's research, writing, and teaching are multiplied. When, finally, *Donum veritatis* refers to the "sense of the faith" in section 4, it spreads more confusion than light on its nature. The following long quotation creates confusion by conflating disparate ideas that Vatican II was very careful to distinguish.

> Dissent sometimes also appeals to a kind of sociological argumentation which holds that the opinion of a large number of Christians would be a direct and adequate expression of the "supernatural sense of the faith."
>
> Actually, opinions of the faithful cannot be purely and simply identified with the *sensus fidei*. The sense of the faith is a property of theological faith; and as God's gift which enables one to adhere personally to the truth, it cannot err. This personal faith is also the faith of the church, since God has given guardianship of the word to the church. Consequently, what the believer believes is what the church believes. The *sensus fidei* implies then by its nature a profound agreement of spirit and heart with the church, *sentire cum ecclesia*.
>
> Although theological faith as such then cannot err, the believer can still have erroneous opinions since all his thoughts do not spring from faith. Not all the ideas which circulate among the people of God are compatible with the faith. This is all the more so given that people can be swayed by a public opinion influenced by modern communications media. Not without reason did the Second Vatican Council emphasize the indissoluble bond between the *sensus fidei* and the guidance of God's people by the magisterium of the pastors. These two realities cannot be separated. Magisterial interventions serve to guarantee the church's unity in the truth of the Lord. They aid her to "abide in the truth" in face of the arbitrary character of changeable opinions and are an expression of obedience to the word of God (no. 35).[68]

Despite many positive statements of the importance of the "sense of the faith" in the teaching of Vatican II in *Donum veritatis*, in the end one is left with the impression that the "sense of the faith" is a confused and possibly even a dangerous idea. The believer is better off leaving teaching

---

67. *Instruction on the Ecclesial Vocation of the Theologian*, 15.
68. Ibid., 22–23.

to the pope and the bishops, since the insights of the ordinary faithful, and even of the more educated theologian, can be reduced to "opinion." This is clearly a selling short of the authentic teaching of Vatican II in articles 12 and 35 of *Lumen Gentium* and articles 8 and 10 of *Dei Verbum*. A vague reference to "having the mind of the Church (*sentire cum ecclesia*)"[69] does not measure up to the clear teaching of Vatican II regarding the "sense of the faith." There is no wonder that the members of the International Theological Commission discerned the urgent need to study these matters in greater depth. And that brings us precisely to their efforts in the wake of the confusion sown by *Donum veritatis*.

The Contribution of the International Theological Commission

In recent years the International Theological Commission (ITC) has issued two book-length documents in which the "sense of the faith" has played an important role and one in which it was the actual topic of the document.[70] These documents have positively advanced the acceptance of the "sense of the faith" in the wider church and, even though they are not official statements of the magisterium, they deserve to be examined in the context of this chapter because of the unique bonds between the ITC and the CDF.

The ITC emerged as a fruit of Vatican II. The idea originated with the bishops at the First Ordinary General Assembly of Bishops in 1967. Paul VI instituted the commission in 1969 to build on the positive experience of the fruitful collaboration of bishops and theologians at the council.[71]

---

69. See the article "Sentire ecclesiam" by the young Joseph Ratzinger, *Geist und Leben* 36 (1963): 321–26.

70. These documents include *Theology Today: Perspectives, Principles, and Criteria* (Washington, DC: The Catholic University of America Press, 2012); *Sensus Fidei in the Life of the Church* (London: Catholic Truth Society, 2014); and *Synodality in the Life and Mission of the Church* (March 2, 2018), www.vatican.va/roman_curia/congreations/cfaith /cti_documents/rc_cti_20180302_sinodalita_en.html#.

71. There are thirty members of the ITC who are appointed for a period of five years, and whose appointment can be extended for a second five-year period. Ordinarily, at the end of one quinquennium, half the members are changed. This rotation system leads to both continuity and the addition of fresh blood in the body. Nowadays, the members are drawn from the diocesan and regular clergy, from religious societies of men and women, and from the laity, female and male. In recent years, representatives of Eastern Catholic

The pope hoped that a commission of theologians from around the world would help enrich theological discussion in the church and make available studies that would contribute to the quality of theological research in the church. Even though the ITC is not a direct instrument of the church's magisterial authority, it collaborates with it very closely. The prefect of the CDF is the *ex officio* president of the ITC. After consulting the episcopal conferences regarding worthy theologians, he recommends members to the pope who nominates them. Often, the pope and the CDF recommend the topics to be studied, but the ITC itself enjoys broad independence to propose topics that the members deem worthy of their study and attention. The studies are not designed to produce new scholarly results or to directly engage the most creative or challenging theological currents of the day but to frame the topic under consideration in such a way as to dispassionately expose the *status quaestionis* on a given topic. According to one member of the ITC, its work "focuses on the clarification of urgent doctrinal principles rather than on precise points of doctrinal practice."[72] Cardinal Joseph Ratzinger characterized the work of the ITC

Churches have been included. A general secretary, appointed by the president of the commission, assigns the members to one of three subcommissions that work on different theological subjects over the five-year period. If a topic is not finished at the end of a quinquennium, or is judged not yet ripe for publication, its study may be extended for a further five years. The full body of the commission meets once a year, but the three groups are free to meet more frequently, if necessary. Scholars share the results of their study with each other in the form of research papers. A document produced by a subcommission is voted on by the entire membership of the ITC. In some cases, a simple majority of the votes is sought and the document is issued *in forma generica*, i.e., approval only of the principal ideas of the document. In other situations, it receives an absolute majority and is issued *in forma specifica*, i.e., approval of the entire text, including its ideas, wording, and presentation. It is then submitted to the president. A document of the ITC is published only after it has received the *imprimatur* of the president, who then submits it to the pope for his approval. The ITC is regulated by John Paul II's *motu proprio "Tredecim anni,"* issued on August 6, 1982. See *Acta Apostolicae Sedis* 74 (1982): 1201–5. An English translation is available on the Vatican's website.

72. Barnabas M. Ahern, "International Theological Commission," *New Catholic Encyclopedia*, vol. 17: *Supplement: Change in the Church* (New York: McGraw-Hill, 1979), 297–98, at 297. According to Carl J. Peter, another member of the commission: "Although it has been criticized for various reasons, the specific function of the ITC has been clearly defined, viz., to keep the Church's teaching office abreast of developments in theology throughout the whole world. The strictly theological contributions it has made result from a method involving simultaneous commitment to critical inquiry and to the truth-

in the following way: "The special contribution of the Commission is to gain a hearing for the common voice of theology amid all the diversities that exist. For notwithstanding the legitimate pluralism of theological cultures in the Church, the unity of theology must remain and empower theologians to offer some common account of their subject."[73]

To date, the ITC has issued twenty-nine documents on a wide range of topics.[74] The character of these studies has changed over the fifty years of the ITC's existence. Some have been in the form of theses, but others have offered more extensive treatments of their subjects. Some treatments have included commentaries by individual members of the commission, while most have not. In more recent years, the studies have assumed the form of well-rounded but concise treatments of a given subject. This is the case especially for the three studies that have addressed the topic of the "sense of the faith" either directly or by way of inclusion, and to which we now turn.

Theology Today: Perspectives, Principles, and Criteria (2012)

Twenty-two years after the CDF's controversial "Instruction on the Ecclesial Vocation of the Theologian," the ITC issued its own examination of the theme. It has proven to be a welcome contribution in the opinion of many theologians. *Theology Today* is the product of two different subcommissions that worked between 2004 and 2012.[75] I think it can justly be claimed that what theologians might have hoped for in the "Instruction

---

claims of Roman Catholic teaching." See "International Theological Commission," *New Catholic Encyclopedia*, vol. 18: *Supplement 1978–1988* (Palatine, IL: Jack Heraty & Associates, 1989), 205–6, at 206.

73. "Foreward," *International Theological Commission: Texts and Documents 1969–1985*, ed. Michael Sharkey (San Francisco: Ignatius Press, 1989), vii–viii, at viii.

74. Google International Theological Commission, List of the Documents of the International Theological Commission. The documents appear in most modern languages, but are published in journals that are often difficult for the general public to access. Copies in hard print tend to be difficult to access, but the Libreria Editrice Vaticana makes a twenty-seven-volume Logos Edition in English available in digital format.

75. *Theology Today: Perspectives, Principles, and Criteria* (Washington, DC: The Catholic University of America Press, 2012). Paul McPartlan of The Catholic University of America presided over the second subcommission that brought the project to completion, while four members served on both subcommissions. For commentaries, see Thomas Söding, "Im Denkgebäude der katholischen Kirche. Eine kurze Einführung in das Dokument der Theologenkommission," in *Die Rolle der Theologie in der Kirche. Die Debatte über das Dokument der Theologenkommission*, ed, Thomas Söding, Quaestiones Disputatae 268

on the Ecclesial Vocation of the Theologian" has been positively realized in *Theology Today*.

Chapter 1 of *Theology Today*, "Listening to the Word of God," builds on the teaching of Vatican II that theology is grounded in God's self-revelation to humankind. According to *Dei Verbum*, the word of God enjoys primacy in expressing the church's faith[76] and in theology's effort to understand and express its faith.[77] By examining God's revelation in Scripture, theology demonstrates its quality as a genuinely rational human enterprise. The word of God impels men and women as its recipients to a deeper understanding of its contents.[78]

Chapter 2, "Abiding in the Communion of the Church," is the heart of *Theology Today*, because it relates a contemporary understanding of Catholic theology to the church as communion (*communio*). All the elements make sense because they emerge out of Vatican II's teaching on communion and converge on this teaching. Communion explains why the ecclesial elements that might otherwise account for debilitating conflicts in the church are able to be reconciled: Scripture versus apostolic tradition; the theologian versus the whole body of believers; the theologian's authority versus that of the pope and the bishops; the individual theologian's specialization, school of thought, or narrow focus versus the balance provided by the guild of theologians; and finally, the church versus the world. In each instance, *Theology Today* calls for mutuality and collaboration. Here, too, is where *Theology Today* introduces the "sense of the faith," which enjoys a certain priority over the individual theologian's expertise and situates his or her calling in the life of the church.

(Freiburg: Herder, 2015): 72–90 and Lieven Boeve, "Creating Space for Catholic Theology? A Critical-Empathetic Reading of *Theology Today*," *Theological Studies* 74 (2013): 828–55.

76. A unique feature of *Theology Today* is that it has added a succinct summary of each major topic treated by formulating an applicable *criterion*. Thus, number 9 maintains that "[a] criterion of Catholic theology is recognition of the primacy of the Word of God." Taken as a whole, these criteria can help the theologian understand and exercise his or her craft.

77. "A criterion of Catholic theology is that it takes the faith of the Church as its source, context and norm" (no. 15).

78. "A criterion of Catholic theology is that, precisely as the science of faith, 'faith seeking understanding'. . . theology aims to understand in a rational and systematic manner the saving truth of God" (no. 19).

The *sensus fidelium* does not simply mean the majority opinion in a given time or culture, nor is it only a secondary affirmation of what is first taught by the magisterium. The *sensus fidelium* is the *sensus fidei* of the people of God as a whole who are obedient to the Word of God and are led in the ways of faith by their pastors. So the *sensus fidelium* is the sense of the faith that is deeply rooted in the people of God who receive, understand and live the Word of God in the Church (no. 34).

For theologians, the *sensus fidelium* is of great importance. It is not only an object of attention and respect, it is also a base and a *locus* for their work. On the one hand, theologians depend on the *sensus fidelium*, because the faith that they explore and explain lives in the people of God. It is clear, therefore, that theologians themselves must participate in the life of the Church to be truly aware of it. On the other hand, part of the particular service of theologians within the body of Christ is precisely to explicate the Church's faith as it is found in the Scriptures, the liturgy, creeds, dogmas, catechisms, and in the *sensus fidelium* itself. Theologians help to clarify and articulate the content of the *sensus fidelium*, recognizing and demonstrating that issues relating to the truth of faith can be complex, and that investigation of them must be precise. It falls to them also on occasion critically to examine expressions of popular piety, new currents of thought and movements within the Church, in the name of fidelity to the Apostolic Tradition (no. 35).[79]

Finally, chapter Three, "Giving an Account of the Truth of God," focuses on what the authors of *Theology Today* identify as a particularly vexing problem for Catholic theology and its self-understanding, the

79. *Theology Today*, 31–32. In number 36, the appropriate criterion reads: "Attention to the *sensus fidelium* is a criterion for Catholic theology. Theology should strive to discover and articulate accurately what the Catholic faithful actually believe." Ibid., 32. In number 38 there is another reference to the "sense of the faith": "Between bishops and theologians there should be a mutually respectful collaboration; in their obedient listening to the Word and faithful proclamation of it; in their attention to the *sensus fidelium* and service of the growth and maturing of faith; in their concern to transmit the Word to future generations, with respect for new questions and challenges; and in their hope-filled witness to the gifts already received; in all of this bishops and theologians have their respective roles in one common mission, from which the magisterium and theology each derive their own legitimacy and purpose. Theology investigates and articulates the faith of the Church, and the ecclesiastical magisterium proclaims that faith and authentically interprets it." Ibid., 33–34.

relationship of reason to faith and the inalienable rationality of faith. There have been times in the history of the church when the relationship was seen as harmonious, but that is no longer the case for modernity and especially for late modernity. Today, Catholic theology must defend and explicate its right to claim that faith is not irrational, that it is not pure mythology or emotionalism, but that by its use of critical reason it shares in the ideals of "science" and can rightly claim that it, too, is a "science."[80] Catholic theology respectfully engages the "hard" and "soft" sciences in its own quest to understand faith better and to bring its own contribution to late modernity in the face of strong currents to render truth entirely relative.[81]

Not only has *Theology Today* helped to calm the roiled waters stirred up by *Donum veritatis* and provided a positive and healthy vision of the place and role of the theologian in today's church, it has also advanced the understanding and importance of Vatican II's teaching on the "sense of the faith." From the perspective of this study, this is an important contribution to the postconciliar church.

Sensus Fidei in the Life of the Church (2014)

The ITC's recent *Sensus Fidei in the Life of the Church* is most welcome because of the seriousness with which it takes the "sense of the faith" and because it clearly advances the understanding of the teaching of Vatican

---

80. See the criterion in number 73: "A criterion of Catholic theology is that it should strive to give a scientifically and rationally argued presentation of the truths of the Christian faith. For this, it needs to make use of reason and it must acknowledge the strong relationship between faith and reason." Ibid., 61.

81. According to number 85, "A criterion of Catholic theology is that it attempts to integrate a plurality of enquiries and methods into the unified project of the *intellectus fidei*, and insists on the unity of truth and therefore on the fundamental unity of theology itself. Catholic theology recognizes the proper methods of other sciences and critically utilizes them in its own research. It does not isolate itself from critique and welcomes scientific dialogue." Ibid., 70. I think chapter 3's efforts at claiming that theology is "science" is its weakest section. The word "science" means something else entirely than *scientia* in former times. True, theology needs to identify itself in terms of its use of critical reason, but that task and goal is not the same as what is today commonly understood as "science." I think that *Theology Today* is on to something valuable, however, when in its concluding remarks (nos. 86–99) it speaks of theology in terms of *sapientia*—wisdom, or sapiential (connatural) knowledge. Unfortunately, this is not the occasion to pursue this insight.

II.[82] The subcommission responsible for the document composed it between 2009 and 2014. It consists of an introduction, four chapters, and a short conclusion. How, then, has the ITC contributed to the reception of the "sense of the faith"?

After summarizing the teaching of Vatican II (nos. 1–2), the introduction distinguishes the two basic meanings that underlie the "sense of the faith." One refers to the individual believer's discernment of the truth of faith. But since the believer participates in the faith as something communally shared in the church, the "sense of the faith" also points to this ecclesial instinct of faith of the church itself. It introduces a helpful distinction by coining two technical terms that express this difference: the *sensus fidei fidelis*, i.e., the understanding of each individual believer, and the *sensus fidei fidelium*, i.e., the ecclesial grasp of Christian revelation. This latter expresses what the council meant when it referred to the *consensus fidelium*, i.e., the consensus of all who accept divine revelation (no. 3). Next, the introduction dispels the false dichotomy of a "teaching church" and a "believing church," saying "the council taught that all the baptised participate in their own way in the three offices of Christ as prophet, priest and king. In particular, it taught that Christ fulfills his prophetic office not only by means of the hierarchy but also via the laity" (no. 4). To make such claims, however, does not address the many questions that remain regarding the meaning, the extent, the distinctions, the conditions of its exercise, and the discernment of the "sense of the faith." These are the tasks of the four chapters that constitute the remainder of the document (nos. 5–6).

As it did in its earlier *Theology Today: Perspectives, Principles, and Criteria*, chapter 1 establishes a firm foundation for the "sense of the faith"

---

82. London: Catholic Truth Society, 2014 and *Origins* 44 (2014–15), 133–55. Also available online at http://www.vatican.va/roman_curia/congregations/cfaith/cti_documents/rc_cti_20140610_sensus-fidei_en.html#_ftnref5. For commentaries, see Thomas Söding, "Der Sinn für Gott im Kirchenvolk. Eine Einführung in das Document der Internationalen Theologischen Kommission," in *Der Spürsinn des Gottesvolkes. Eine Diskussion mit der Internationalen Theologischen Kommission*, ed. Thomas Söding, Quaestiones Disputatae 281 (Freiburg: Herder, 2016), 77–103, and Gerard Mannion, "*Sensus Fidelium* and the International Theological Commission. Has Anything Changed between 2012 and 2014?" in *Learning from All the Faithful: A Contemporary Theology of the Sensus Fidei*, ed. Bradford E. Hinze and Peter C. Phan (Eugene, OR: Pickwick Publications, 2016), 69–88.

in the teaching of Scripture and the living tradition of the church. Even though Scripture never uses the technical term the "sense of the faith," the teaching of Vatican II is true to the Bible's vision of how the Spirit of truth is active in the whole church by anointing all with the infallibility of the faith itself (no. 7). Chapter 1 admirably summarizes the biblical teaching on faith as response to the word of God (nos. 8–10) by pointing to the personal and ecclesial dimensions of faith (nos. 11–12) and by showing the capacity of believers to know and witness to the truth (nos. 13–21). Then comes a lengthy exposition of the development of the "sense of the faith" and its place in the history of the church that covers the fathers of the church (nos. 23–26), some important medieval thinkers including Thomas Aquinas and Bonaventure, as well as concrete cases regarding the Eucharist, life after death of the individual believer, and Marian doctrine and devotion (nos. 27–28), and the challenge of the Reformation and the Catholic response to it (nos. 29–33). It concludes with somewhat more detailed discussions of the contributions of theologians in the nineteenth and twentieth centuries (nos. 34–43), before studying the contribution of Vatican II in the Dogmatic Constitution on the Church and the Dogmatic Constitution on Divine Revelation (nos. 44–46) and concluding with a paragraph on John Paul II's use of the teaching (no. 47).[83]

Chapter 2, though short, is important. It introduces the distinction of the "sense of the faith of the [individual] believer" (*sensus fidei fidelis*) from the "sense of the faith of all believers" who constitute the church (*sensus fidei fidelium*). The terminology helps the reader to better distinguish what is characteristic of the act of faith of each believer from what characterizes the faith of the entire body of believers. Chapter 2 deals only with the "sense of the faith of the believer," while chapter 3 will take up the "sense of the faith of all believers." What, then, does chapter 2 teach?

The members of the ITC are to be congratulated for developing the theology of the "sense of the faith." Up to this point, Vatican documents had largely only quoted Vatican II or applied its teaching in the context of some other issue to which the "sense of the faith" was germane. None

---

83. I have covered much of this material at greater length in this book, but I want to express my gratitude for the concern that *Sensus Fidei in the Life of the Church* has shown in bringing this rich history of the notion to the attention of such a broad readership.

had advanced the teaching or tried to develop it theologically. The effort of the ITC in *Sensus Fidei in the Life of the Church* is to be welcomed. Chapter 2 cites certain terms employed by many theologians up to this point, mentioning "a sort of spiritual instinct" of the truth (no. 49), a certain "flair" for the truth (no. 54), a "correct intuition" of the truth (no. 55), and the more technical term "connaturality" with truth (no. 50). Although it also mentions "a sort of perception (*aisthesis*)" (no. 49), unfortunately it does not develop this insight. The ITC had decided to concentrate on connaturality, on faith as a virtue, and on the gifts of the Holy Spirit that enable the Christian to live out his or her faith as the key elements of its explanation. This creates problems.

In chapter 6 above, we already examined how Francisco Marín-Sola had examined the "sense of the faith" and connaturality by drawing on Thomas Aquinas's theology of graced human "dispositions" (*habitus*). The ITC's *Sensus Fidei in the Life of the Church* also does so, but it presents its case differently. It begins instead with faith as a virtue and so interprets the "sense of the faith" in terms of the act of believing rather than as an act of understanding or interpreting the faith. By adopting Aquinas's understanding of believing, it embarks upon a technical discussion of faith—one that sees believing in highly intellectualistic terms. This tends to downplay the dimension of trust in the act of faith in favor of the dimension of the mind's grasp of truth. Also, the ITC's approach passes over the dialogical character of believing, where faith is understood in terms of an interpersonal dialogue between God and the believer. The stress of trust and dialogue creates a richer context for understanding faith, an alternative that, I would argue, better addresses contemporary humankind's struggle with faith as an act and as content.[84] The Thomistic framework preferred by the ITC is too constricting and creates problems of how to

---

84. Theologians refer to these as *fides qua* and *fides quae*, where the first refers to the act of total self-entrusting of the believer to God revealing and the second as the attempt on the part of the church and the believer to frame this experience in concrete terms. In other words, the believing person's act of self-giving points to claims that can be made about God and God's will for humankind and the cosmos. See Yves Congar, *Tradition and Traditions: An Historical Essay and a Theological Essay*, trans. Michael Naseby and Thomas Rainborough (New York: Macmillan, 1967), 314.

explain both the act of believing and communicating the faith.[85] The affective dimension of the "sense of the faith" that Marín-Sola perceived so clearly and that he featured so prominently in his explanation is totally absent. What remains is faith in a coolly intellectualist framework. It doesn't work, even though it emphasizes some very positive points about believing.[86] Today the average contemporary theologian, not to mention the ordinary believer, will not be excited by a narrowly Thomistic understanding of faith that is presented in isolation from broader perspectives.

Chapter 2 concludes with some valuable observations on how the "sense of the faith of the individual believer" is manifested in the church by discerning the coherence of a teaching or practice with the true faith in the communion of the church (nos. 61–63); by distinguishing between what is essential and what is secondary (no. 64); and by discerning the role of the particular historical and cultural contexts of the believer's witness to Christ (no. 65).

Chapter 3 introduces the ITC's second important distinction on the "sense of the faith," the individual believer's faith in the context of the whole people of God. The chapter advances our understanding of the

---

85. See my comments on "The 'Object' of Faith" and the literature cited there in my article "The *Sensus Fidelium*: Old Questions, New Challenges," in *Learning from* All *the Faithful: A Contemporary Theology of the* Sensus Fidei, ed. Bradford E. Hinze and Peter C. Phan (Eugene, OR: Pickwick Publications, 2016), 125–42, at 138–39.

86. The text reminds the reader of Aquinas's teaching that faith "enables the believer to participate in the knowledge God has of himself and of all things" (no. 53). This is a stunning insight from Aquinas, but unfortunately the text does not cite the appropriate references in Aquinas's writings. Also very welcome is the acknowledgment of the true understanding of the faith by non-Catholic believers too. In number 56 we read: "It follows that a certain type of *sensus fidei* can exist in 'the baptized who are honored by the name of Christian, but who do not profess the Catholic faith in its entirety' (cf. LG 15). The Catholic Church therefore needs to be attentive to what the Spirit may be saying to her by means of believers in the churches and ecclesial communities not fully in communion with her." *Sensus Fidei in the Life of the Church*, no. 34. Finally, number 59 encourages the pastors of the church to pay close attention to the faith insights of the ordinary faithful, when it says: "It [the *sensus fidei*] enables him or her to see more precisely the value and the limits of a given doctrine, and to propose ways of refining its formulation. That is why those who teach in the name of the Church should give full attention to the experience of believers, especially lay people, who strive to put the Church's teaching into practice in the areas of their own specific experience and competence." Ibid., no. 35.

"sense of the faith" and deserves careful study. Compared to the previous chapter, it is more positive in its view of the place of the "sense of the faith" in the life of the church and more balanced in its expressions, in particular by avoiding narrow or overly abstruse theological frameworks. Chapter 3 is central to the thought of *Sensus Fidei in the Life of the Church* and makes important contributions. When its ideas are followed to their logical conclusion, it changes everything in the relationships among the hierarchy of the pastors, the critical contributions of theologians, and the role of the ordinary faithful. I will return to this in my concluding remarks.

Chapter 3 first discusses the essential role the "sense of the faith" plays in its witness to and in the development of Christian faith and its practice. It demonstrates a refreshing openness to the historicity of the formulations of doctrine (no. 68) and to the dynamic character of the faith and its formulation in doctrine (nos. 69–71). It says, for instance:

> As she awaits the return of her Lord, the Church and her members are constantly confronted with new circumstances, with the progress of knowledge and culture, and with the challenges of human history, and they have to read the signs of the times, "to interpret them in the light of the divine Word" (DV 8), and to discern how they may enable revealed truth itself to be "more deeply penetrated, better understood and more deeply presented" (GS 44). In this process, the *sensus fidei fidelium* has an essential role to play. It is not only reactive but also proactive and interactive, as the Church and all its members make their pilgrim way in history. The *sensus fidei* is therefore not only retrospective but also prospective, and though less familiar, the prospective and proactive aspects of the *sensus fidei* are highly important. The *sensus fidei* gives an intuition as to the right way forward amid the uncertainties and ambiguities of history, and a capacity to listen discerningly to what human culture and the progress of the sciences are saying. It animates the life of faith and guides authentic Christian action (no. 70).[87]

It is fascinating to observe how the ITC at this point widens the scope of its consideration. First of all, it introduces another phrase that theologians developed to speak about the "sense of the faith," namely, the

---

87. Ibid., 40–41.

conspiratio pastorum et fidelium or "the mutual contribution of the pastors and the faithful" in elaborating the church's faith. But the ITC reminds us that this contribution on the part of the faithful has included more than only doctrine or dogma. It has also included the moral and the social teaching of the church (nos. 72–73). It is hard to imagine how the pastors could have developed the contributions of the church in these two areas of human action without the contributions, encouragement, and stimulus of the ordinary faithful. The rich social teaching of the papal magisterium is incomprehensible apart from the whole church's "sense of the faith." The generous credit that has been liberally given to popes, bishops, and moral theologians must be shared with the ordinary faithful. It is time that their inescapable contributions were acknowledged.[88]

In the next section, the document turns to the oft-mentioned tense relationship of the "sense of the faith" of the faithful with the hierarchy. One reads it on every page of *Donum veritatis*, among other sources, and even in chapter 2 of *Sensus Fidei in the Life of the Church*. It is what might be called the "tug-of-war" approach. Only one party can win the contest. Refreshingly, chapter 3 largely abandons this sterile viewpoint. Number 74 gets right to the point:

> In matters of faith the baptised cannot be passive. They have received the Spirit and are endowed as members of the body of the Lord with gifts and charisms "for the renewal and building up of the Church" (LG 12), so the magisterium has to be attentive to the *sensus fidelium*, the living voice of the people of God. Not only do they have the right to be heard, but their reaction to what is proposed as belonging to the faith of the Apostles must be taken seriously, because it is by the Church as a whole that the apostolic faith is borne in the power of the Spirit. The magisterium does not have sole responsibility for it. The magisterium should therefore refer to the sense of faith of the Church as a whole. The *sensus fidelium* can be an important factor in the development of doctrine, and it follows that the magisterium needs means by which to consult the faithful.[89]

88. See Joachim Wiemeyer, "Soziallehre der Kirche—als Ausdruck des Glaubenssinns des Gottesvolkes," in *Der Spürsinn des Gottesvolkes. Eine Diskussion mit der Internationalen Theologischen Kommission*, ed. Thomas Söding, Quaestiones Disputatae 281 (Freiburg: Herder, 2016), 331–49.

89. Ibid., 42–43.

And later, when treating the necessity of the reception of doctrine in the church (nos. 78–80), we read:

> There are occasions, however, when the reception of magisterial teaching by the faithful meets with difficulty and resistance, and appropriate action on both sides is required in such situations. The faithful must reflect on the teaching that has been given, making every effort to understand and accept it. . . . The magisterium must likewise reflect on the teaching that has been given and consider whether it needs clarification or reformulation in order to communicate more effectively the essential message. These mutual efforts in times of difficulty themselves express the communion that is essential to the life of the Church, and likewise a yearning for the grace of the Spirit who guides the Church "into all the truth" (Jn 16:13) (no. 80).[90]

I know of no other statements by recent popes, the CDF, or the ITC itself that insist so clearly on the indispensable role of the whole church, including *all* the ordinary faithful, in witnessing to and formulating the faith and praxis of the church as do these two paragraphs in *Sensus Fidei in the Life of the Church*. When, therefore, number 77 speaks of the role of the popes and the bishops' responsibility to judge the authenticity of the "sense of the faith" of the faithful, it is clearly moderated in light of chapter 3's holistic understanding of the "sense of the faith." The heretofore traditional "tug-of-war" has been changed into cooperation between the pastors and the faithful, a cooperation which of course is not (and cannot be) without a certain healthy tension among the pastors, theologians, and the ordinary faithful.[91]

In the third section of chapter 3, theologians are also reminded that they, too, depend on the "sense of the faithful" in meeting their role in the church:

90. Ibid., 45.

91. Number 76 makes it crystal clear that the pastors are always to be counted among the faithful: "Being responsible for ensuring the fidelity of the Church as a whole to the word of God, and for keeping the people of God faithful to the Gospel, the magisterium is responsible for nurturing and educating the *sensus fidelium*. Of course, those who exercise the magisterium, namely the pope and the bishops, are themselves, first of all, baptised members of the people of God, who participate by that very fact in the *sensus fidelium*." Ibid., 44. In such matters, tension can be life-giving, while an unremitting tug-of-war for superiority is self-defeating.

As a service towards the understanding of faith, theology endeavours, amid the *conspiratio* of the charisms and functions in the Church, to provide the Church with objective precision regarding the content of its faith, and it necessarily relies on the existence and correct exercise of the *sensus fidelium*. The latter is not just an object of attention for theologians, it constitutes a foundation and a locus for their work (no. 81).

This mutuality is spelled out in numbers 82–84. Just as the previous section dealt with the mutuality of the pastors and the faithful at large, so too a mutuality of roles and dependencies exist between the church's professional theologians and the faithful at large. Chapter 3 forges onward with its underlying perspective of mutuality and wholeness.

Finally, section 4 picks up and advances what chapter 2 said of the positive role and contributions of non-Catholic Christians and the ever-growing body of ecumenical documents to the understanding of the faith. It tries to clarify situations where some disagreements and tensions continue to exist among the churches (nos. 85–86), but here too the positive thrust of chapter 3 continues to be carried onward. All in all, this chapter represents a high point and climax in the "official literature" on the "sense of the faith." It deserves to be better known and studied carefully.

Chapter 4 develops several practical implications of the "sense of the faith": the dispositions needed for participating in the "sense of the faith" (nos. 88–105). These include participation in the life of the church, listening to the word of God, openness to reason, adherence to the magisterium, holiness, and working for the edification of the church. Problems in this section begin to crop up, however. The dispositions are not so much wrong as misdirected. The tenor in which they are expressed mirrors the narrowness of chapter 2, especially in the section that deals with the relation of the "sense of the faith" of the faithful with the "sense of the faith" of the pope and the bishops, and when the document treats popular religiosity (nos. 107–112) and public opinion in society and in the church (113–119).[92] Once again, the magisterium is given pride of place and the

---

92. It needs to be signaled that already in the Dogmatic Constitution on the Church, Vatican II clearly set aside any association of the "sense of the faithful" with public opinion in any form. Yet, again and again, especially in documents emanating from the Vatican, e.g., *Donum veritatis*, but also in the opinion of those who oppose the rightful place of the "sense of the faithful" in the church, suspicion is aroused that the "sense of the faithful" is

old game of tug-of-war reappears. The reader who has been excited by the balance and holism of chapter 3 feels abandoned. Why the reversion to the old stereotypes when chapter 3 has offered a more promising approach? The reader senses an impasse that the authors have not been able to bridge. Only with the final section on ways of consulting the faithful (nos. 120–126) does the trustful and promising approach of chapter 3 reappear.[93] In number 128 of the document's "Conclusion," we also read these more hopeful words:

> The *sensus fidei* is closely related to the "*infallibilitas in credendo*" that the Church as a whole has as a believing "subject" making its pilgrim way in history. Sustained by the Holy Spirit, it enables the witness that the Church gives and the discernment that the members of the Church must constantly make, both as individuals and as a community, of how best to live and act and speak in fidelity to the Lord. It is the instinct by which each and all "think with the Church," sharing one faith and one purpose. It is what unites pastors and people, and makes dialogue between them, based on their respective gifts and callings, both essential and fruitful for the Church (no. 128).[94]

By way of a general conclusion to *Sensus Fidei in the Life of the Church*, I want to reiterate the pioneering teaching of chapter 3. The first and only adequate witness to and source of the faith of the church is the "sense of the faith" of the church in its entirety—the *universitas fidelium* and the *tota ecclesia apostolica*—before any distinctions of status or function in

---

a form of public opinion in the church. This tactic is devious and needs to be unmasked and repudiated once and for all.

93. One can also point to a few other felicitous expressions that reassure the reader. For example, in number 119 we read: "Nevertheless, it is the whole people of God which, *in its inner unity*, confesses and lives the true faith. The magisterium and theology must work constantly to renew the presentation of the faith in different situations, confronting if necessary dominant notions of Christian truth with the actual truth of the Gospel, but it must be recalled that the experience of the Church shows that sometimes the truth of the faith has been conserved not by the efforts of theologians or the teaching of the majority of bishops but in the hearts of believers." Ibid., 59–60. My italics. Such a viewpoint, based on the fact of the "inner unity" of the people of God, clearly excludes factionalism and the dominance of a secular attitude of rivalry in the church.

94. Ibid., 63.

the church. The pope and the bishops in their special way give witness to it and depend on it. Theologians, too, in their special way give witness to it and depend on it. The vast number of the faithful in the church in their special way give witness to it and depend on it. The way of the magisterium is not superior to the insights and contributions of theologians and the ordinary faithful but is ordered to them. The way of theologians is not superior to that of the pope and the bishops and the ordinary faithful but is ordered to them. The way of the ordinary faithful is not superior to that of the pope and the bishops and the theologians but is ordered to them. Nothing is taught by the pope and bishops that is not also believed by all the faithful, which does not render the teaching authority of the pope and bishops superfluous. Nothing is taught by theologians that is not also believed by the teaching magisterium and all the faithful, which does not render the clarifying role of theologians superfluous. Nothing is believed by all the faithful which is not also believed by the pope and bishops and by theologians, which does not render the convincing witness of all the faithful superfluous. Only unity in the faith, mutuality of functions and contributions, and mutual dependence can express this deep insight. In a word, only a "mutual contribution (*conspiratio*) of the pastors and theologians and all believers" is an adequate expression of the truth. It is time to abandon any understanding or ecclesiological model that pits one group against the others. We cannot, then, pass over in silence the path-breaking implications of this insight, and we have chapter 3 of *Sensus Fidei in the Life of the Church* to thank for it. Henceforth the church's task will be trying to realize this exciting vision.

Synodality in the Life and Mission of the Church (2018)

The latest document issued by the ITC in 2018, *Synodality in the Life and Mission of the Church*, takes up a theme that has become central to the papacy of Pope Francis.[95] To the pope, synodality focuses in one term the vision of Vatican II for a renewed church, a participatory church, a

---

95. The official text is the Italian version, but an English translation has also been issued by the Vatican Press at www.vatican.va/roman_curia/congregations/cfaith/cti_documents/rc_cti_20180302_sinodalita_en.html#. On synodality, now see also Pope Francis's encyclical *Fratelli tutti: On Fraternity and Social Friendship* (Washington, DC: United States Conference of Catholic Bishops, 2020).

missionary church, a church that draws upon the strengths of the first Christian millennium when the churches of the East and West were one in life and in law. To be "together on the way" (*syn hodos*) also picks up on Vatican II's view of the church as "pilgrim Church" or church on its journey with Christ and the Spirit to the Father.[96] It is not the least bit surprising, then, that the ITC should take up this rich and unifying theme of Pope Francis's program for the church and dedicate an entire study to it. It is also not surprising that the "sense of the faith" should play a prominent role in effectuating synodality.

Synodality in the Life and Mission of the Church is comprised of four chapters: "Synodality in Scripture, in Tradition and in History" (chapter 1), "Towards a Theology of Synodality" (chapter 2), "Implementing Synodality: Synodal Subjects, Structures, Process and Events" (chapter 3), and "Conversation to Renew Synodality" (chapter 4). The "sense of the faith" appears in each chapter and points to the indispensable role it plays in the realization of a synodal church. Rather than examine the many paragraphs in which the "sense of the faith" is explicitly mentioned, it might prove more beneficial for our purposes to examine the wider themes the authors employ to develop synodality.[97] These include the role of charisms or gifts of the Spirit in the church,[98] the need for broad consultation[99] and discernment[100] in a synodal church. These three themes come up repeatedly throughout the document and frame the context for an understanding of synodality. They must also be seen in their relationship to each other and how they mutually elucidate each other and shed light on the "sense of the faith."

---

96. See *Synodality in the Life and Mission of the Church*, numbers 3–9 for helpful information and explanations of the terms "synod," "synodal," and related terms.

97. *Synodality in the Life and Mission of the Church* is a major theological document that deserves a careful and extensive exposition, but that is not possible in the current chapter. I must leave this task to others. However, I do wish to list the paragraphs in which references to the "sense of the faith" or the "sense of the faithful" are found. The reader can consult them as he or she wishes, but their sheer number speaks for itself. See numbers 9, 38, 56, 64, 72, 94, 100, 108, and 117.

98. See numbers 18, 22, 36, 53, 54, 61, 67, 72, 76, 79, 83, 104, 105, 106, 109, 114, 115, and 117.

99. See numbers 21, 55, 68, 73, 79, 84, 91, 94, 100, and 102.

100. See numbers 21, 68, 69, 70, 76, 94, 103, 111, 113, and 114.

Charisms are mentioned in the same article of the Dogmatic Constitution on the Church as is the "supernatural *sensus fidei* of the whole people." After treating the "sense of the faith" in article 12,1, the bishops turned their attention to the importance of "gifts" (*dona*), "special graces or gifts" (*gratiae speciales*), and especially "charisms whether outstanding or common insofar as they are widely diffused [in the Church])" (*charismata sive clarissima, sive etiam simpliciora et latius diffusa*) (article 12,2). The bishops at Vatican II saw the intimate connection between these two realities. To the credit of the members of the ITC, they have reminded us of this relationship.

"Charisms" or "spiritual gifts" or simply "gifts" appear again and again in *Synodality in the Life and Mission of the Church*. Whichever term is used, it points to the same reality—a gift from the Holy Spirit to an individual believer. Such gifts enrich and enliven the church and are distributed to all regardless of their status in the church: there is the charism of official leadership, the charism of critical reflection on the faith, and innumerable gifts of holiness, service, insight, prophecy, healing, ad hoc leadership, etc. of all the faithful. We cannot imagine a truly synodal church that is not richly endowed with charisms that the Spirit shares liberally with everyone in the church. A synodal church is a charismatic church.[101]

The second idea that *Synodality in the Life and Mission of the Church* returns to repeatedly is consultation. In the church, everyone's viewpoint and insights are important. Progress in the search for truth is found only in the richness of human experience and in the depths of the human heart. Everyone has an insight and must be listened to with respect. But consultation must have a fair and efficient process for gathering and sharing the wealth of information that emerges. A synodal church is a church that listens and welcomes the contributions of all.

But not all ideas, insights, and experiences are of equal weight. The faculty of deliberation must be engaged to arrive at a consensus on what is best for the church in new historical circumstances or in different local conditions. Not every option will lead to the common good. Not every route can be pursued. Discernment is a concrete process for receiving data, weighing information, and skillfully moving toward a decision that can be broadly shared and implemented. But discernment takes time and

---

101. On charisms, see Judith A. Merkle, *Beyond Our Lights and Shadows: Charism and Institution in the Church* (New York: Bloomsbury T&T Clark, 2016).

great patience. A synodal church is one that painstakingly and prayerfully discerns the truth.

The ITC includes a theme that was dear to the hearts of the bishops at Vatican II but that has been largely overshadowed in recent years—"the signs of the times."[102] What God is doing in the world and what is going forward in human affairs and history invite men and women to reflect on their significance for salvation and the completion of the cosmos, for human wholeness, and for overcoming the power of sin and division. What is happening in the full range of human activities is not irrational or mute but freighted with meaning and purpose. We, however, must engage these challenging and confusing situations, these puzzles and enigmas, these signs and symbols in an effort to make sense of them. A synodal church is a church that is fully engaged with the world, with human affairs, and with the vast array of cultures in all their diversity and richness.

A synodal church is like a courtly Renaissance dance, consisting of many intricate steps. There is no synodality where the "sense of the faith of the faithful" is not respected. There is no "sense of the faith of the faithful" where the faithful are not seen as endowed with many gifts and charisms. There is no synodal church where its members are not sensitive to the "signs of the times." There is no synodal church where the "sense of the faith of the faithful," nurtured by their charisms and attending to the "signs of the times," is not seriously consulted. There is no synodal church where the "sense of the faith of the faithful" does not engage in the demanding process of discernment of the truth. The ITC is to be congratulated for pointing out the presence and "compenetration" (*perichoresis*) of all these ecclesial elements.

Conclusion

In this chapter, we have examined the process of the official reception of the "sense of the faith" as taught by Vatican II in the Codes of the Canons of the Roman and the Eastern churches, in the *Catechism of the*

---

102. See numbers 75, 76, and 113. For mention of "the signs of the times" in the documents of Vatican II, see the Pastoral Constitution on the Church in the Modern World, articles 4 and 11. On "the signs of the times," see the recent article by Stefano Cucchetti, "Liberi nel discernimento dello Spirito. Lo Spirito e la storia nella teologia dei 'segni dei tempi,'" *La Scuola Cattolica* 147 (2019): 347–75.

Catholic Church, and in the statements of Popes John Paul II and Francis. Though the rarer statements of the Congregation for the Doctrine of the Faith have not ignored this teaching, they have also frequently expressed cautious reservations vis-à-vis the "sense of the faith." In the case of the more recent statements of the International Theological Commission, however, we have observed a growing acceptance of the teaching and a serious effort to understand it better and apply it to the life of the church.

Over the past fifty-five years, the pace of reception has been slow and cautious, and efforts to marginalize the "sense of the faithful" have been addressed. The efforts of Pope Francis especially and the recent studies undertaken by the ITC have focused the church's attention on the important role of the "sense of the faith" in the life of the church. Nevertheless, the faithful at large are still gravely deficient in awareness of the gift they have received in the "sense of the faith," and up to now the church has developed precious few opportunities for exercising this gift of the Holy Spirit. In a word, there has been clear progress in the reception of the *doctrine* of the "sense of the faith of the faithful," but efforts on the levels of *education and implementation* in the church have been woefully inadequate. There is still much to be done before it can be said that the Catholic Church has effectively received this key teaching of Vatican II.

Chapter Eleven

The "Sense of the Faith": Components of a Possible Synthesis

The preceding chapters have examined the historical circumstances that help to explain the emergence of what Vatican II taught regarding the "sense of the faith." They began with the roots of the teaching in the second Christian millennium and with some of the theories that theologians devised to justify it and explain its meaning. Various theories have attempted to understand the conciliar teaching in terms of human knowing, but no single theory has examined the "sense of the faith" comprehensively. The present chapter does not purport to present a fully fleshed-out understanding of the "sense of the faith" as knowledge, but it does strive to offer an understanding in terms of epistemological categories that emerged before, during, and after Vatican II to better understand this seminal teaching.

The "knowledge" presented by the "sense of the faith" is real but differs from the knowledge that is available on the basis of strictly discursive reasoning. By broadening the categories in which the "sense of the faith" operates, I hope that a more convincing theory of its meaning will emerge. Without a deeper understanding of these categories, it is not possible to really understand how the "sense of the faith" emerged before Vatican II and how it found its way into the council's teachings. No category studied below can alone explain the depth of the teaching, but taken together they can help us arrive at a possible synthesis of the many rich individual elements of an epistemology of the "sense of the faith." The various components of the synthesis I propose in this chapter emerged primarily out of the fertile theology connected with the *ressourcement* movement in the twentieth century before the council and the continued efforts of numerous theologians following Vatican II. It is time to examine in more detail these fruitful theological elements. It is my hope that individual readers will be able to arrive at their own synthesis on the basis of the components I hereby offer for consideration.

The Retrieval of Experience

Introductory Remarks

A good place to start our reflection on the kind of knowing that the "sense of the faith" represents is the category of experience, a rich and multi-faceted epistemological concept. Many philosophers and theologians have spoken about it and yet they rarely agree among themselves on what constitutes experience. I propose to draw on some of the elements that are often found in recent discussions regarding it. Experience-based knowing has often been neglected and the reason for this is an interesting and cautionary story.

Robert O. Johann has described why experience eventually came to be minimized by modernity. He wrote:

> The attitude of a good part of Western philosophy toward thought involves, I think, a kind of false intellectualism. Because the products of reflective thinking manifest a necessity and universality not to be found in the realm of concrete action and experience, it is held that thinking somehow or other provides access to a region that is higher and more real than that of ever-changing experience. Instead of seeing thought as the symbolic formulation of structures present in experience and therefore as derivative from experience, the intellectualist views experience as itself secondary to this "higher region," a contingent and wholly dispensable image of the changeless structures disclosed to thought. The experience of people and things is meant to serve simply as a springboard for the mind.[1]

---

1. "The Return to Experience," *Review of Metaphysics* 17 (1963–64): 319–39, at 319.

In this telling quotation, Johann has unmasked the prejudice toward experience manifested since the onset of the Enlightenment, a prejudice that fully blossomed with rationalism. Modern science, too, though it would rehabilitate the value of observing what is particular with its method of experimentation, also seems to underestimate experience in its particularity. It is focused on formulating general laws, theories, and hypotheses.

What is the case in philosophy and the modern sciences has also happened in the life of faith in the church. In 1547, at the Council of Trent, the bishops addressed the teaching about whether a Christian could obtain certainty about his or her justification. In rejecting such certainty, the bishops taught that "no one can know, by that assurance of faith which excludes all falsehood, that he has obtained the grace of God."[2] Theologians after the council stressed the teaching, which seemed to exclude all experience of grace and the confident claim that a person was justified.[3] Salvation was an object of hope, not knowledge, and the way to salvation

2. See the *Decree on Justification*, chapter 9: "Against the Vain Confidence of the Heretics" in *Decrees of the Ecumenical Councils*, vol. 2, ed. Norman P. Tanner (Washington, DC: Georgetown University Press, 1990), 674.

3. The role of "actual graces," too, greatly increased in the controversy on grace and freedom between the Dominican Domingo Báñez (1528–1604) and the Jesuit Luis de Molina (1536–1600). So divisive was the controversy that Pope Clement VIII established a commission to examine the positions of the two schools and to decide between them. However, the so-called *Congregatio de auxiliis* (1598–1607) was inconclusive. The exaggerated concentration on actual graces had the unfortunate effect of focusing the attention of theologians and spiritual writers exclusively on auxiliary graces (sufficient versus efficacious) as distinct from grace as a state of being (sanctifying grace). The result was that Catholics tended to be overly (one might almost say neurotically) concerned with "obtaining" these graces. For centuries the theology of grace suffered from being objectified and quantified in this unhealthy way. The theology of grace tended to be directed toward actions rather than stressing its character as a gift of divine adoption. Because of the danger of manipulating grace in an acts-oriented theology of grace, the Roman magisterium discouraged the experiential dimension of the life of grace. For the ordinary Catholic, the lack of clarity regarding one's state of grace led to the practice of frequent, and often weekly, recourse to the sacrament of reconciliation in the church before Vatican II. The reception of the Eucharist, too, tended to be understood in terms of it being a source of "actual graces." I can vividly remember how lively this teaching was in the pre-Vatican II church of my youth. See Karl Rahner, "Grace and Freedom," *Sacramentum Mundi: An Encyclopedia of Theology*, vol. 2, ed. Karl Rahner (New York: Herder and Herder, 1968), 424–27.

was through the reception of the Catholic sacraments. As a result, ecclesiastical authorities after Trent were suspicious of anything that smacked of the experiential in the life of faith. Religious experience was more and more considered to be outside the realm of conscious knowledge.[4]

The growth of mysticism in the Catholic Church during this period was also a serious challenge to the church, which distrusted mysticism's often intense emotionalism and graphic imagery. The Tridentine church strove to keep mysticism in check by limiting it to the chosen few and preferred instead spiritualities that were based on images of struggle and battle. It discouraged the faithful from speculating about their personal salvation and their degree of perfection but encouraged instead attitudes of conformity and obedience. Such actions tended over time to discourage Catholics from reflecting on their religious experience.

In the academic realm, too, theology succumbed to the influence of rationalism by exalting the mind over concrete experience. While steadfastly resisting the allure of Immanuel Kant's idealism and Georg W. F. Hegel's exaltation of absolute spirit, Catholicism as represented by Roman theologians was infatuated with a highly conceptualized understanding of reality. The idea was more real than extra-mental reality, and theologians became entangled in worlds formed from concepts. What little attention remained of extra-mental experience was finally banished by Rome in its struggle with modernism in the late nineteenth and early twentieth centuries.[5] Modernists like George Tyrrell (1861–1909) preferred to reflect on the concreteness of religious experience, often in opposition to the dogmas that had been fashioned from the conceptualistic framework inherited from René Descartes (1596–1650). As it was, experience was highly suspect in ecclesiastical and academic circles, and the conceptual-

---

4. On this thorny issue, see Piet Fransen, *The New Life of Grace*, trans. Georges Dupont (Tournai: Declée Company, 1969), 282–92 ["Is experiential knowledge of grace possible?"] and "Towards a Psychology of Divine Grace," *Intelligent Theology*, vol. 3 (Chicago: Franciscan Herald Press, 1969), 7–45.

5. On modernism, see John W. O'Malley, *What Happended at Vatican II* (Cambridge, MA: Belknap Press, 2008), 68–71, and Charles J. T. Talar, "'The Synthesis of All Heresies': 100 Years On," *Theological Studies* 68 (2007): 491–514. Allesandro Maggiolini deals explicitly with the question of the use of experience by modernist authors in his "Magisterial Teaching on Experience in the Twentieth Century: From the Modernist Crisis to the Second Vatican Council," *Communio* 23 (1996): 225–43.

ism of the nineteenth century, tinged as it was by the rationalism of the time, advanced unchecked in the church.

Because of the condemnations of modernism, many of the sharpest Catholic intellectuals took refuge in studies that reached back well before the emergence of the baroque theology of the seventeenth and eighteenth centuries and the neoscholasticism of the nineteenth and early twentieth centuries. The fields were ripe in the study of patristic writers of the church and of early and high scholastic authors. These fields included philosophy and theology, of course, but also the study of the liturgy and of earlier pastoral practices. Scripture posed special problems because of the delicacy of dealing with the word of God, but here, too, exegetes and biblical scholars worked patiently and cautiously. Scripture studies were also assisted by the continued discovery of ancient texts, such as the Dead Sea Scrolls (1947) and the codices at Nag Hammadi in Egypt (1945). These scholars sedulously avoided arousing the suspicion and ire of Vatican officials by advancing their research as unobtrusively as possible. They kept their eyes on the targets of their research and refrained from hastily drawing conclusions for the practical life of the church. In this way, *ressourcement* scholars were free to work and avoided condemnation by Rome.

The patience of these scholars was rewarded when in the 1940s, Pope Pius XII cautiously began to incorporate some of their findings in his path-breaking encyclicals *Mystici Corporis* on the Church (1943), *Divino afflante Spiritu* on Scripture and its interpretation (1943), and *Mediator Dei* on the liturgy (1947). He also undertook modest reforms of liturgical and sacramental practices. The darkest days of the Vatican's antimodernist campaign appeared to be over. When Pope John XXIII judged that the church was ready for the reform of an ecumenical council, these *ressourcement* scholars had produced a vast trove of useful knowledge that greatly enlarged the historical and theological material available to the church.[6] It was the perfect moment to convoke a reform council.

---

6. On the *ressourcement* movement, see the essays in *Ressourcement: A Movement for Renewal in Twentieth-Century Catholic Theology*, ed. Gabriel Flynn and Paul D. Murray (New York: Oxford University Press, 2012), especially "Part III: *Ressourcement* as a Threefold Programme of Renewal," 305–51.

How, then, did the category of experience come to enjoy renewed acceptance and prominence in the twentieth century? What factors or movements account for this?

Some Examples from History

At the beginning of his *Metaphysics*, Aristotle mentioned the epistemological importance of experience. He wrote:

> The animals other than man live by appearances and memories, and have but little of connected experience; but the human race lives also by art and reasonings. Now from memory experience is produced in men; for the several memories of the same thing produce finally the capacity for a single experience. And experience seems pretty much like science and art, but really science and art come to men *through* experience. . . . With a view to action experience seems in no respect inferior to art, and men of experience succeed even better than those who have theory without experience. . . . But yet we think that *knowledge* and *understanding* belong to art rather than experience, and we suppose artists to be wiser than men of experience (which implies that Wisdom depends in all cases rather on knowledge); and this because the former know the cause, but the latter do not. For men of experience know that the thing is so, but do not know why, while the others know the "why" and the cause. Hence we think also that the master-workers in each craft are more honorable and know in a truer sense and are wiser than the manual workers, because they know the causes of the things that are done.[7]

We see that Aristotle definitely makes a place for knowing by experience, even as he distinguishes it from a higher form of knowing in a specific area—art, which in turn is distinguished from a higher form of knowing in a more universal sense, science. In the Western tradition of epistemology, then, experience definitely has a place. Experience is practical knowledge; knowledge acquired from doing and acting; knowledge that is part of a continuum of different acts of cognition.

---

7. "Metaphysica," *The Basic Works of Aristotle*, ed. Richard McKeon (New York: Random House, 1941), 689–926, at 689–90. Italics in the original.

When we turn to the concrete life of the early church, we also find an important role for knowledge-based experience, but in this case explicitly religious experience. As part of the initiation of adult catechumens into the church, the process of election, preparation, and imparting of the sacraments included many impressive and even dramatic experiences: exorcisms, anointing with blessed oil, disrobing and being vested, plunging into deep water, further anointing with chrism, eating the blessed loaf and drinking from the one cup, singing of psalms and hymns, processing to the church with the other initiates, and joyful reunion with the whole community of believers.[8] The liturgy and its rites were designed to immerse the initiate in a powerful experience that involved the communication of knowledge of what salvation was and what it meant to be a member of God's church. In addition to the knowledge imparted by didactic means in the pre-baptismal catecheses (readings from Scripture, explanation of the articles of the creed, the delivery of the Our Father), it also included the experiential knowledge involved in the actual reception and celebration of the sacraments. The initiate was enveloped by the symbols of the church and learned about them by experiencing them. This was the place for the mystagogical catecheses that followed the pre-sacramental instructions.[9] During the octave of Easter the bishop imparted further understanding of the sacramental, liturgical, and ecclesial life of the neophyte by educing a more conscious knowledge out of the sacramental celebration itself. The bishop's explanations were meant to confirm the neophyte's experience and invite him or her to continue on the mystagogical way of self-surrender throughout life.[10]

---

8. On the catechumenate and the rites of initiation in the patristic period, see Edward J. Yarnold, *The Awe-inspiring Rites of Initiation: The Origins of the R.C.I.A.* (2nd ed.; Collegeville, MN: Liturgical Press, 1994), which also includes the *Catecheses* of Cyril of Jerusalem, Ambrose, John Chrysostom, and Theodore of Mopsuestia. See also Yarnold's "Initiation: Sacrament and Experience," in *Liturgy Reshaped*, ed. Kenneth Stevenson (London: SPCK, 1983), 17–31, and Maxwell E. Johnson, *The Rites of Christian Initiation: Their Evolution and Interpretation* (expanded ed.; Collegeville, MN: Liturgical Press, 2007).

9. On the notion of mystagogy, see Enrico Mazza, *Mystagogy: A Theology of Liturgy in the Patristic Age*, trans. Matthew J. O'Connell (New York: Pueblo Publishing, 1989).

10. The same was true of the mystagogical dimensions of the sacraments of reconciliation and orders, but unfortunately we cannot pursue them at this point. What a change in perspective on ordained ministry the contemporary church might gain if it looked at

In varying degrees of implementation and success, the church has always valued the knowledge of the faith that comes from experience. I have concentrated on the sacramental instances of such experiential knowledge, but the case could easily be made for other areas of the church's life. Today, this might include the professional, social, political, moral, spiritual, aesthetic, and doctrinal experience of everyone in the church. How, then, might we better understand the category of experience and the kind of knowledge it yields?

Closer Theological Examination of Experience

In his study of experience, the American philosopher John E. Smith was one of the first to remind theologians of the importance and utility of experience for understanding religious faith. Smith defined experience as "the many-sided product of complex encounters between what there is and a being capable of undergoing, enduring, taking note of, responding to, and expressing it. As a product, experience is a result of an ongoing process that takes time and has a temporal structure."[11] After Smith, very few theologians dismiss experience as secondary or derivative. They now see that faith and the life of the church passes through the process of experience and needs to continue to be in vital contact with it.

---

episcopal, presbyteral, and diaconal ordination from this experiential ministerial perspective rather than from the points of view of the degree of power and status the ordinand attains with each succeeding degree of orders. How might the mystagogical dimensions of ordination be better realized today? The symbolic elements are there already—the call to ministry, the prostration and invocation of the saints, consent of the community, imposition of hands of the ordaining bishop and presbyters, anointing with chrism, vesting with appropriate liturgical garb, and handing over of chalice and paten—and yet it often seems to miss the mark as a powerful ecclesial experience.

11. "The Recovery of Experience," *Experience and God* (New York: Oxford University Press, 1968), 21–45, at 23. Smith was also at pains to exclude the following errors regarding experience: "There have been, for example, narrow theories of experience that would confine it to the data supposedly disclosed through the senses, with the result that whatever fails to meet the qualifications of being a sensible datum is *ipso facto* excluded from experience. Furthermore, experience has in the past been understood as the passive reception of what is 'given' to a purely theoretical observer and the content of experience has been thus restricted to atomic data exclusive of relations, of tendencies, and of dimensions of meaning such as the aesthetic, the moral, and the religious." Ibid., 22.

One of those theologians was the French Dominican Jean-Pierre Jossua who began to emphasize the nexus of experience and faith in a series of articles in the early 1970s.[12] Jossua was able to draw on a current of thought in twentieth-century French Catholicism that stressed the importance of experience.[13] Jossua was primarily interested in relating the experience of faith to the language of Christian witness, proclamation, liturgical texts, and dogmatic formulations. To Jossua, Christian discourse was no longer capable of communicating the Christian message effectively. Recovering the category of experience and its richness offered the best opportunity to revitalize the Christian vocabulary of witness. In an effort to offer the Christian faith in a renewed form, Jossua teamed with Patrick Jacquemont and Bernard Quelquejeu to publish *Une foi exposée.*[14] While other local churches, e.g., the Netherlands and Germany, were producing new catechisms in the 1960s and 1970s, Jossua and his Dominican confreres pursued an experiment in rephrasing and reframing Christian vocabulary to better serve the uses to which language was applied. To them, experience was the key to success here.

By far the most influential theologian to analyze and apply the idea of experience to Catholic theology in recent years was the Belgian Dominican Edward Schillebeeckx (1914–2009). He wrote about it often and thereby forced other Catholic theologians to come to terms with its role in theology and in the life of the church. Philip Kennedy has examined Schillebeeckx's break with the intellectualist mindset he inherited from

---

12. See "Christian Experience and Communicating the Faith," in *The Crisis of Religious Language*, ed. Johann B. Metz and Jean-Pierre Jossua, Concilium 85 (New York: Herder and Herder, 1973), 57–69, and "Théologie et expérience chrétienne," in *Théologie, le service théologique dans l'Église. Mélanges offerts à Yves Congar pour ses soixante-dix ans*, Cogitatio Fidei 76 (Paris: Cerf, 1974), 113–29. Together with his confrere Bernard Quelquejeu, they would provide the entry on "Erfahrung" for the *Neues Handbuch theologischer Grundbegriffe*, vol. 1, ed. Peter Eicher (Expanded ed.; Munich: Kösel, 1991), 349–59.

13. See Jean Nabert, *L'expérience de la liberté* (Paris: Presses Universitaires de France, 1923); Robert Lenoble, *Essai sur la notion d'expérience* (Paris: J. Vrin, 1943); and Jean Mouroux, *L'expérience chrétienne: introduction à une théologie* (Paris: Aubier, 1952), translated into English by Geoffrey Lamb as *The Christian Experience: An Introduction to a Theology* (New York: Sheed and Ward, 1954).

14. Paris: Cerf, 1972.

his confrere, teacher, and mentor Dominic De Petter.[15] Schillebeeckx redirected his epistemology when, after Vatican II, he began to teach a course on hermeneutics at the University of Nijmegen, the Netherlands. At the heart of his intellectual conversion was the discovery of the category of experience, and no Catholic theologian has done more to develop it and hand it on. What are the main features of Schillebeeckx's teaching?[16]

First, concrete experiences invite us to relate them to former experiences if we are to understand them. In the ongoing process of receiving experiences, both reflection and interpretation act reciprocally on all our experiences and on each other. Thought is always mediated by a theory of interpretation that clarifies and refines our understanding.

> In experiencing we identify what is experienced, and we do this by classifying what we experience in terms of already known models and concepts and categories.[17]

> The irreducible elements of our experiences form a totality which already contains interpretation. We experience in the act of interpreting, without being able to draw a neat distinction between the element of experience and the element of interpretation.[18]

As we receive new experiences, we are repeatedly challenged to refine both our thinking and our theory of interpretation. The process never ends because we are constantly subject to new experiences.

---

15. See Philip Kennedy, "Schillebeeckx's Sources," *Schillebeeckx*, Outstanding Christian Thinkers Series (Collegeville, MN: Liturgical Press, 1993), 31–53. Kennedy writes how Schillebeeckx "changed from a largely abstract and theoretical perspective, to speaking about God in terms of human action. In other words, he changed from according a primacy to theories in his theological discussions to stressing that primacy ought to be accorded to human practices and actions which provoke reflection" (43). Kennedy wrote his doctoral dissertation on Schillebeeckx, *Deus Humanissimus: The Knowability of God in the Theology of Edward Schillebeeckx* (Fribourg, CH: University Press, 1993.)

16. The main sources for Schillebeeckx's teaching are "The Authority of New Experiences," *Christ: The Experience of Jesus as Lord*, trans. John Bowden (New York: Seabury Press, 1980 [published originally in Dutch in 1977]), 30–64; *Menschliche Erfahrung und Glaube an Jesus Christus: eine Rechenschaft* (Freiburg: Herder, 1979); and "Erfahrung und Glaube," in *Christlicher Glaube in moderner Gesellschaft* 25 (Freiburg: Herder, 1980), 73–116.

17. "Authority of New Experiences," 32.

18. Ibid., 33.

Consequently, experience is a richly nuanced totality in which experience, thought and interpretation run together in the same way as past, present and expectations of the future.[19]

Second, experiences and our attempts to understand them demand that we express them in words and not deal with them only as concepts locked away in our minds. As Schillebeeckx says: "A new experience is also a speech event. Speech is an ingredient of experience."[20] Language and speech, however, are social practices that we learn from participating in them. We do not create our own language *ab ovo*, but like experience itself, we speak of our experiences in the context of already existing speech acts.[21]

Third, the triad of experience, understanding, and interpretation overcomes the object-subject dichotomy inherited from Descartes.

The experience of ourselves and the world cannot be completely analyzed in terms of a difference between objective and subjective. . . . Man experiences actively, with his whole being and having, and contributions of object and subject can never be distinguished with complete exactitude.[22]

At least partially, there is something which is "given", which we cannot completely manipulate or change; in experience we have an offer of reality. On the other hand, it is not purely objective; for the experience is filled out and colored by the reminiscences and sensibilities, concepts and longings of the person who has the experience.[23]

Fourth, Schillebeeckx points to the indispensability of the resistance we encounter in our experiences. The fact that we cannot fully manipulate or control our experience is not an unfortunate drawback of experience that we need to overcome but an opening for what is novel and unanticipated. We only grow because of the refractoriness of life and our inability to control or manipulate the experiences life constantly throws at us. This feature assumes a dominant position in Schillebeeckx's synthesis and he

19. Ibid., 33.
20. Ibid., 32.
21. We will examine this idea in greater detail below.
22. "Authority of New Experiences," 32.
23. Ibid., 33.

devotes more and more attention to the negative experiences of life as his theological development progresses. Only by encountering negative experiences does (Christian) hope break through and redirect what is negative toward a positive value and outcome for us. Contrary to our assumptions, experiences of suffering and oppression hold the promise of newness and salvation. Liberation, joy, and wholeness are found only by working our way through life's negativities, not by avoiding them.

> Surprising, unexpected, new ways of perceiving are opened up in and through the resistance presented by reality. In this regard real experience only becomes productive when inherited insights are given critical consideration as a result of the resistance offered by reality, when something new is experienced or when what has already been experienced is suddenly seen in a different context. . . . People learn from failures—where their projects are blocked and they make a new attempt, in sensitive reverence for the resistance and thus for the orientation of reality.[24]

It is not Schillebeeckx's intention to glorify human limitations or to minimize the reality of pain or suffering, but he is trying to do justice to the dialectical character of all human striving. If we want to understand reality, it must be on the terms that reality dictates and not by prioritizing our unquestioned preconceptions, theories, dogmas, or projections. Experience opens us up to the rich, complex, and refractory nature of reality.[25]

The implications of the understanding of experience proposed by Jossua and Schillebeeckx are profound for understanding the faith and Christian life. I propose to unpack some of these implications in what follows. I hope that the centrality of the category of experience for the life of faith will become more evident and that the implications of experience for the "sense of the faith" will emerge with greater clarity. But before moving on, we need to pause for a brief moment to see how Vatican II adopted and employed the notion of experience in its documents.

---

24. Ibid., 35.

25. See also Mary Catherine Hilkert, "Discovery of the Living God: Revelation and Experience," in *The Praxis of Christian Experience: An Introduction to the Theology of Edward Schillebeeckx*, ed. Robert J. Schreiter and Mary C. Hilkert (San Francisco: Harper & Row, 1989), 35–51.

Experience and Vatican II

Terms for "experience" were definitely incorporated into the documents of Vatican II. Even though "experience" is not among the most significant terms of the council, the reality of experience was everywhere present there. The bishops gathered in Rome over four years underwent a profound experience of co-responsibility for the universal church and of collegiality among themselves and with the Bishop of Rome. I propose to examine two passages in which the term experience is employed in important theological contexts that show experience is a genuine resource in the church for growing in the understanding of revelation.

We have already considered the importance of article 8 of the Dogmatic Constitution on Divine Revelation in chapter 9. We saw that although the article does not use the phrase the "sense of the faith," it was reflecting on this teaching as already taught in article 12 of the Dogmatic Constitution on the Church from another angle.[26] This important article speaks about the growing understanding of the tradition entrusted to the church: with the assistance of the Holy Spirit, this understanding "increases" (*proficit*). Article 8 points to three ways in which this happens: through the contemplation and study of believers, through the "experience" of the realities of the faith by reason of the intimacy believers bring to their experience of the faith (*ex intima spiritualium rerum quam experiuntur intelligentia*), and by the active ministry of the word of the pope and bishops. In this context, the question of whether the word "experience" should be used was certainly considered. In his commentary on this article, Joseph Ratzinger, who was directly involved in writing the draft of chapter 2 of *Dei Verbum*, described the opposition of Cardinals Ernesto Ruffini and Paul-Émile Léger to the teaching of the dynamic character of tradition taught here. But Ruffini and several others also objected to the use of the verb "to experience" in the paragraph because of its suspicious connections with modernism and its condemnation by Pius X.[27] Nonetheless, the vast majority of bishops did not have difficulties with the word and supported its retention in the text.

The second instance can be found in article 46 of the Pastoral Constitution on the Church in the Modern World. This paragraph marks a

26. The Dogmatic Constitution on the Church had been approved by the bishops during the third session in 1964, before they approved the final text of *Dei Verbum*.

27. See *Commentary on the Documents of Vatican II*, vol. 3, ed. Herbert Vorgrimler (New York: Herder and Herder, 1969), 186–89.

transition from part 1 ("The Church and Humanity's Vocation") to part 2 ("Some Urgent Problems") and mentions in passing that "the Council now draws attention in the light of the gospel and of human experience to certain urgent contemporary needs." What is important in this context is the connection that the council establishes between "the gospel" (revelation) and "human experience" (the recipients of revelation and their mode of receiving it). They work together and not in isolation from one another. The commentary by the German Redemptorist Bernhard Häring, the most renowned moral theologian of his day and a *peritus* at the council, is illuminating. He writes:

> It is also said [in article 46] that the points of view of the gospel and of human experience have to be combined. It is clear that "the gospel" here does not mean a mere repetition of biblical statements but rather a light in which human experience finds its true meaning. What is in question, therefore, is a specifically Christian conception of the history of redemption. God's action still continues. *It becomes visible in human experience, when this is examined in the light of the gospel.* We are here approaching a new way of proclaiming the "law of nature" or the ordinances and the abiding operation of the Creator, expressly in the light of the gospel. In this way the natural moral law is viewed more realistically and historically, incorporated into the actual history of salvation, and in that way it is enriched and verified.[28]

Other passages in the Pastoral Constitution on the Church in the Modern World could be cited in support of the theological import of the use of experience at Vatican II, but what we have just considered will have to suffice. It should be clear that Vatican II judged experience to be an important factor in the life of faith of the Christian. What, then, are some of the implications of Vatican II's acceptance of the category of experience in the life of the church?

Historical Consciousness

Let us begin with a negative experience that everyone today encounters, whatever their personal, religious, social, or political circumstances might

---

28. See *Commentary on the Documents of Vatican II*, vol. 5, ed. Herbert Vorgrimler (New York: Herder and Herder, 1969), 228–29. Italics added.

be. It goes by the name "historical consciousness," and it profoundly impacts human cognition.

Before the nineteenth century, philosophers had little appreciation of the historical character of knowing.[29] In the West, antiquity understood knowledge to be governed by universal metaphysical principles discovered by the methods of induction and deduction. The Middle Ages advanced this metaphysical knowledge primarily with the help of a dialectical method of understanding in which logic played a dominant role. While Renaissance humanism began to explore richer forms of understanding mediated by literature and classical literary and rhetorical forms, the movement was cut short by the emergence of rationalism with the European Enlightenment. Rationalism sought clarity and absolute certainty at the expense of the richness and spontaneity of knowledge. The Romantic Movement in literature and philosophy strove to reorient thought in terms of an organic view of nature and the role of sentiment in knowing, but the allure of rationalism proved too powerful to resist. In the meanwhile, modern science emerged with its rigorous method of observation leading to the formulation of hypotheses and the constant need to reformulate these on the basis of more accurate observation and the gathering of more data. Accuracy of observation and the creativity of human imagination in formulating explanatory theory account for progress in understanding. [30]

29. Giambattista Vico (1668–1744) was the exception. See Karl Löwith, "Vico," *Meaning in History* (Chicago: University of Chicago Press, 1949), 115–36, and R. G. Collingwood, *The Idea of History* (New York: Oxford University Press, 1956), 63–71 ["Anti-Cartesianism: (i) Vico"].

30. See Thomas Kuhn, *The Structure of Scientific Revolutions* (2nd ed.; Chicago, IL: University of Chicago Press, 1970); Stephen Toulmin, "Intellectual Disciplines: Their Goals and Problems," *Human Understanding: The Collective Use and Evolution of Concepts* (Princeton, NJ: Princeton University Press, 1972), 145–99; Ian G. Barbour, *Myths, Models and Paradigms: A Comparative Study in Science and Religion* (San Francisco: Harper & Row, 1974), idem, *Religion in an Age of Science* (San Francisco: Harper, 1990); John Polkinghorne, *One World: The Interaction of Science and Theology* (Princeton, NJ: Princeton University Press, 1986), idem, *Reason and Reality: The Relationship between Science and Theology* (Philadelphia, PA: Trinity Press International, 1991), idem, *Faith, Science and Understanding* (New Haven, CT: Yale University Press, 2000); and John F. Haught, *Is Nature Enough?: Meaning and Truth in the Age of Science* (New York: Cambridge University Press, 2006).

In all of these movements, human cognition has proved incapable of escaping the effects of history. A sense of fallibility and vulnerability grew stronger and threatened the supposedly rock-solid foundations of rationalism, science, and bureaucratic social organization. Human beings are not entirely autonomous, but are subject to forces outside their control. In the twentieth century, continued archeological discoveries, theoretical mathematics (e.g., quantum physics), and modern biology and cosmology (e.g., the discovery of dark matter) greatly contributed to a sense of impotence as humans acquired more and more detailed knowledge of the universe even while finding it impossible to grasp its intrinsic meaning. The term "historical consciousness" has been coined to capture the overwhelming sense of human fallibility and vulnerability in the face of all these experiences.[31] We are overtaxed by the limitless data we must categorize, as well as by the vastness of the cosmos and the mind-boggling duration of the universe's existence. How can we make sense out of all this? How can we achieve genuine happiness as individuals and as societies?

Although historical consciousness views the human person against the negative experiences of fallibility and vulnerability, it also opens up the person to understand oneself as actively involved in the very construction of reality, the world, and value and meaning. Truth is not meant to be read mechanically off the page of the world and human relationships, as it were. The knowing subject is intimately involved in the process of understanding and shaping the world, its institutions, cultural artifacts, and technology. Historical consciousness points in the direction of human agency. In the act of knowing, the person both reads the antecedent meaning that it finds and that constitutes it. At first perceived as a threat, historical consciousness actually frees the knower to better enter into the process of understanding reality.[32]

---

31. According to Roger Haight, "Historical consciousness refers to the contemporary sense of being in history, the awareness that human beings have emerged out of a long and distant past and are moving toward an unknown future in this world. It also involves an expanded horizon of consciousness, a product of modernity, by which people are aware of the multiple histories of other peoples and their own interrelatedness with them and interdependence upon them. History implies change, and the relativity and contextuality of all human values and ideas." See "Sin and Grace" in *Systematic Theology: Roman Catholic Perspectives*, ed. Francis Schüssler Fiorenza and John P. Galvin (2nd ed.; Minneapolis, MN: Fortress Press, 2011), 375–430, at 419.

32. See Bernard J. Lonergan, "The Transition from a Classicist World-View to Historical-Mindedness," *A Second Collection*, ed. William F. J. Ryan and Bernard J. Tyrrell (Philadelphia, PA: Westminster Press, 1974), 1–9.

In terms of our discussion, historical consciousness affects our grasp of the quality of our knowledge and its certainty. But it also affects our understanding of the "sense of the faith" and its role in believing. Just as historical consciousness has affected our confidence in our ability to know reality and to collectively share this knowledge, it also poses unavoidable questions about our knowledge of the faith. Especially, however, historical consciousness poses questions about the degree of certainty in matters of faith. The confidence we have formerly claimed about the knowledge of the content of our faith and questions about infallibility and the role of ecclesiastical authority in determining this content have been seriously eroded by historical consciousness. The role of the magisterium and the greater participation of the ordinary faithful in determining the faith have been seriously challenged by historical consciousness. In such a situation, as we will see in greater detail below, the teaching authority of the bishops, the role played by theologians and other experts in human affairs, and the contribution of the ordinary faithful will need to rely on one another more than in the recent past. Historical consciousness challenges the church to a cooperative model of teaching and learning in the church rather than a competitive one.[33]

Questions and Human Being

We advance in understanding our faith by sharing what we do understand with one another. Nevertheless, in the life of faith, as in life in general, questions remain with us and the only way forward is to pursue them. Are the adherents of other religions saved, and if so, how? What does the real presence of Christ in the Eucharist mean today, given the competing epistemologies characteristic of our times? Why does the official church condemn certain forms of assisted conception? Is there a natural law that governs all times, conditions, and human beings? The list could be extended indefinitely. Is it wrong to ask such questions?

To ask questions is a normal and healthy human activity. Ask any parent about his or her children's incessant questioning. It's often annoying, but

33. For a complementary view of history and historicity as profoundly impacting the individual, society, and the church, see Ormond Rush, "Principle 13: Faith/History," *The Vision of Vatican II: Its Fundamental Principles* (Collegeville, MN: Liturgical Press, 2019), 165–87.

it is how children grow in understanding. Knowledge begins with questions, with the search for answers that impart the meaning we seek.[34] It should not be any different for the life of faith. But there are different kinds of questions, and the differences should be noted. There are questions of fact and questions of meaning; questions of method and existential questions; questions directed toward actions, and questions concerned with the operations of the mind.

Questions come to us spontaneously, unbidden. Some arouse mere curiosity in us, while others elicit anxiety, longing, a craving for clarity. Some questions elicit other questions and are posed in a meaningful series in which the answer to one question leads logically to another. Some answers bring the series of questions to an end, but many, particularly questions of meaning, do not. The series stretches on and on as the search for meaning, purpose, and direction continues.

One modern thinker who dedicated much thought to questions and their role was the Canadian Jesuit Bernard Lonergan (1904–84). He saw in the dynamism of our ability to pose questions a key to what it is to be human. Lonergan examined the conditions for asking questions, the character of these conditions, and their final purpose. In one of many summaries of his search, he wrote:

> The immanent source of transcendence in man is his detached, disinterested, unrestricted desire to know. As it is the origin of all his questions, it is the origin of the radical, further questions that take him beyond the defined limits of particular issues.[35]

> Every question is to be submitted to the process of intelligent grasp and critical reflection. Negatively, then, the unrestricted desire excludes the unintelligent and uncritical rejection of any question, and positively

---

34. According to Hans-Georg Gadamer, "The path to all knowledge leads through the question." *Truth and Method*, trans. Joel Weinsheimer and Donald G. Marshall (revised English ed.; New York: Crossroad, 1989), 363–64. On the role of questions in understanding, see *Truth and Method*, 362–79 ["The Hermeneutic Priority of the Question"] where Gadamer examines the logic of the question, the dialectic of question and answer, and the difference between fruitful and only apparent or pretended questions.

35. *Insight: A Study of Human Understanding* (New York: Philosophical Library, 1958), 636.

the unrestricted desire demands the intelligent and critical handling of every question.[36]

And earlier, in his treatment of judgment, Lonergan wrote:

> The questions we answer are few compared to the questions that await an answer. Knowing is a dynamic structure. If each judgment is a total increment consisting of many parts, still it is only a minute contribution towards the whole of knowledge. But, further, our knowing is dynamic in another sense. It is irretrievably habitual. For we can make but one judgment at a time, and one judgment cannot bring all we know into the light of actual knowing. . . . All we know is somehow with us; it is present and operative within our knowing; but it lurks behind the scenes and it reveals itself only in the exactitude with which each minor increment to our knowing is effected. The business of the human mind in this life seems to be, not contemplation of what we know, but relentless devotion to the task of adding increments to a merely habitual knowledge.[37]

It should be evident that the human being is a person whose destiny is to search for meaning and that the royal road thereto is to pose the right questions and answer them as best he or she can.

Such comments might seem anodyne in their generality, but they are anything but commonplace and ordinary. Many Catholics are uncomfortable with asking questions about their faith. They have been taught that it is the responsibility of the pope and the bishops to teach them with authority. They need only heed what the hierarchy teaches them. This, evidently, is a vast oversimplification of the rightful role of the hierarchy to teach. That role cannot exclude the role of asking questions in the search for understanding the faith and in the quest for the meaning of existence. Rightful ecclesiastical authority and being true to one's human nature by asking questions must be compatible with one another. For the Catholic, to ask questions in pursuit of truth, understanding, and meaning is the concrete way he or she is true to the faith and respectful of the rightful authority of the pope and bishops. The hierarchy has no right

36. Ibid., 638.
37. Ibid., 277–78.

to foreshorten the human process of learning and the normal process of growing in understanding the Christian faith.[38] Cooperation between the hierarchy and the faithful is the only way to achieve the goal.[39]

Applied to the issue of the meaning of the "sense of the faith," it should be evident that the "sense of the faith" will play an indispensable role in the individual Catholic's appropriation of the faith for the quality of the questions she or he will feel free to pursue. The same must also be true for the corporate body of the church. The freedom to engage in the process of question and answer in genuine pursuit of understanding is the ultimate justification for the "sense of the faith" in the church, never forgetting that the Holy Spirit accompanies the process throughout, both for the individual believer and for the body of believers.

Language and Symbol

A one-sided conceptual and rationalistic view of truth has meant the loss of the vitality of language and symbolic thought in philosophical and theological discourse. Theology after Vatican II has worked mightily to address this neglect.

Studies in linguistics have demonstrated the complex character of language and shown that language has a constitutive role in forming

---

38. Instead of speaking of a "teaching church" (*ecclesia docens*) and a "learning church" (*ecclesia discens*), I prefer to speak of a "searching church" (*ecclesia quaerens*). To fly, as it were, the church needs the two wings of questioning and learning—the wing of all the faithful and the wing of their legitimate pastors. But both wings must genuinely pose questions and learn from them.

39. It should be evident that there will often be tension between these two poles, but tension can be healthy and life-giving. There is no reason for the hierarchy to act contrary to human nature and the human vocation (Lonergan's "unrestricted desire to know"), just as there is no reason for the faithful to reject outright the legitimate role of offering guidance by the pope and bishops (the real authority of the magisterium). I prefer to pose the issue in terms of the right of the person to ask questions than in terms of a right to dissent from official Catholic teaching. I do not deny that there are situations when legitimate dissent is called for. I simply do not find the category helpful in most cases. I wish to acknowledge my debt to Avery Dulles's superb "Doubt in the Modern Church," *The Survival of Dogma* (Garden City, NY: Doubleday & Company, 1971), 137–51, from which I have long drawn inspiration. Here, too, I prefer the category of question to that of doubt, although it is clear that they are intimately connected to one another.

concepts and arriving at understanding. In other words, language is more than an instrument by which we communicate our ideas and understanding of reality or convey facts and data to one another. Philosophers like Martin Heidegger,[40] Hans-Georg Gadamer,[41] and Charles Taylor[42] have stressed the ontological character of language and speech. Without speech, we humans would not be able to think and reason. To understand and to speak are mutually dependent operations. Contemporary explanations of the nature of language and speech contradict the widely held instrumental view of language as a mere means of communicating our thoughts and ideas. According to the instrumental view, pre-linguistic ideas and understanding have priority. This is the error of conceptualism that we have already noted.

Charles Taylor speaks of the designative and expressive dimensions of language.[43] A theory of language based on designation sees language as the outer form or shell containing the content of what we humans think. Language is merely an instrument of thought, the means by which understanding and ideas are communicated. Taylor develops the expressive dimension of language which holds that language is more than what can be asserted or claimed. The real power of our assertions is itself dependent on our ability as humans to enter into the inexhaustible richness of reality and be affected by it. We not only "comprehend" reality, we also interact with it. We "feel" and "sense" reality as much as we "understand" it. Taylor shows how an expressive view of language opens out to those dimensions of language that elude us, that remain mysterious.[44] An expressive view

---

40. See "Language," *Poetry, Language, Thought,* trans. Albert Hofstadter (New York: Harper & Row, 1971), 189–210, and "The Way to Language," *Basic Writings from Being and Time (1927) to The Task of Thinking (1964)* (expanded ed.; San Francisco: Harper, 1993), 397–426.

41. See "The Ontological Shift of Hermeneutics Guided by Language," *Truth and Method,* 381–491.

42. See *The Language Animal: The Full Shape of the Human Linguistic Capacity* (Cambridge MA: Belknap Press, 2016) and the articles mentioned below.

43. "Language and Human Nature," *Philosophical Papers,* vol. 1: *Human Agency and Language* (New York: Cambridge University Press, 1985), 215–47.

44. See Charles Taylor, "Language Not Mysterious?" *Dilemmas and Connections: Selected Essays* (Cambridge, MA: Belknap Press, 2011), 39–55.

of language is also better equipped to encompass not only the verbal but also the symbolic character of language.

Drawing on the interpretations of Johann Gottfried Herder (1744–1803) and Wilhelm von Humboldt (1769–1859), Taylor emphasizes language as the interplay of five elements that constitute a multifaceted activity.[45] First, language opens the person to conscious reflection. We are not first conscious of our thoughts and their intelligible contents, and then in a subsequent act determine the appropriate vocabulary to state their content. Language is always already there inviting us into the world of reflection. Second, the mutuality of language and consciousness or reflection introduces us to the reality of the world that surrounds us as an intelligible world. Third, language is more than isolated words or terms that we mentally possess. Above all, language is speech and demands to be spoken. We organize our words in phrases and complete sentences that incorporate emerging patterns of grammar and syntax. Our sentences build on each other to fashion a claim, a question, an invocation, a petition, a command, or an argument. Fourth, our speaking is directed to conversation with other members of our species who are also endowed with speech and have the same urgency to communicate. Language is all about the sharing of meaning and mutually seeking fuller meaning. And finally, language takes place within a community of men and women who share the same language. Language is characteristic of a people or group of persons who communicate and converse with one another. Just as language reveals to each one of its participants what it is to be a "person endowed with thought," so a common language reveals the identity of the group to those who share the same language. As their language grows and is refined, the commitment of the group members to each other deepens and the bonds of mutuality are strengthened. Here is where intersubjective meaning is shared and "consensus" formed. Most importantly, Taylor points out how the "common meaning" that has emerged constitutes the group as a language group.[46]

How might Taylor's theory of language apply to the "sense of the faith" as taught by Vatican II? Does contemporary language theory help us understand the interpretative character of the "sense of the faith"?

---

45. See "Language and Human Nature," 227–34.

46. See "Interpretation and the Sciences of Man," *Philosophical Papers*, vol. 2: *Philosophy and the Human Sciences* (New York: Cambridge University Press, 1985), 15–57, at 32–40.

Charles Taylor's stress on the expressive quality of language can open us up to the rediscovery by many postconciliar theologians of the value of metaphor and symbols in understanding the faith. Already at Vatican II, the bishops were sensitive to words and expressions that touched minds and hearts. Such vocabulary could be put to the service of the pastoral needs of the church, of a more fruitful communication with the world beyond the church, and for arriving at greater ecumenical and interreligious understanding.[47] Something similar could be maintained with the council's use of metaphor and similes in speaking about the mystery of the church. Not everything can be reduced to clear concepts and the technical vocabulary that reproduces these ideas. Much about the faith eludes such dogmatic formulation. Think for a moment about the centrality of the metaphor of the kingdom or realm of God in Jesus's ministry.[48] The kingdom simply cannot be reduced to a definition.[49] Think, too, of the many images that the Dogmatic Constitution on the Church uses to speak about the church: the Body of Christ, a sheepfold, a cultivated field, a choice vineyard, the building of God, etc.[50] The same can be said for the importance that symbols have regained in the church.[51]

Symbols are not a poor substitute for clear and precise concepts that can be neatly arrayed in a definition. What if we thought of dogma as both clear and concise concepts and evocatively polyvalent symbols? A didactic definition might be of service in one context of understanding the faith (e.g., the Son as "consubstantial" with the Father), a symbol in a different context (e.g., the sacraments and eschatology). Is the language of Mary's assumption strictly didactic in nature or symbolic? If it is symbolic, is this less than didactic in quality or simply a different but equally valid form of expression that is more appropriate to this mystery given its unique

---

47. I noted this earlier in chapter 9 when pointing to the observations of John W. O'Malley on the speech patterns of Vatican II.

48. See the classic study by Rudolf Schnackenburg, *God's Rule and Kingdom*, trans. John Murray (New York: Herder and Herder, 1963).

49. See Norman Perrin, *Jesus and the Language of the Kingdom: Symbol and Metaphor in New Testament Interpretation* (Philadelphia, PA: Fortress Press, 1976).

50. See the Dogmatic Constitution on the Church, articles 6 and 7. The image of the people of God is treated separately in chapter 2, articles 9–17.

51. See Karl Rahner's classic article "The Theology of the Symbol," *Theological Investigations*, vol. 4, trans. Kevin Smyth (Baltimore, MD: Helicon Press, 1966), 221–52 and Avery Dulles, "The Symbolic Structure of Revelation," *Theological Studies* 41 (1980): 51–73.

character? Apropos of the "sense of the faith," might ordinary believers not be sensitive to the wide range of symbolic expression available to them? Are not the areas of devotion and liturgy in the church's life a rich vein of symbolic representation, as well as a fertile source of deeper understanding because of the advantage metaphoric expression lends them?[52]

Levels of Understanding

I have neither the space nor the competence to present an epistemology that can fully explain the kind of understanding that the "sense of the faith" entails. Nonetheless, many theologians have asked about the quality of knowing encompassed by the "sense of the faith." Is it knowing in the strict sense or a faint approximation to it? The question cannot be evaded.

Understanding involves various acts and degrees of explicitness. Most theologians advert to these differences, but do not always agree among themselves as to what they are. Many have used descriptive expressions to speak about the "sense of the faith," such as an "intuition," a "flair," a "taste," a "*conspiratio*," as we have seen in earlier chapters. But do these descriptions include real, solid knowledge? Is the "sense of the faith" epistemologically justified? I propose to examine the use of three Latin verbs that are traditionally used to express the type and quality of knowledge in men and women who "know" something. These verbs include *scire*, *intellegere*, and *sentire*. How do they differ from each other? Are they related among themselves? What is the connotation of each one?

According to Charlton T. Lewis and Charles Short, *scire* means "to know in the widest sense of the word; to understand, perceive; to have knowledge of or skill in any thing, etc." [53] In classical Latin, then, *scire* is used very broadly. It is derived from the Greek verb *skeiō* (*keiō*), meaning to split, divide, distinguish.[54] The substantive form *scientia* is derived from

---

52. On the hotly debated issue of the ordination of women to the priesthood, for example, might not the "sense of the faith" be better attuned to the symbol of "order" (*ordo* in Latin; *taxis* in Greek) in ecclesiastical ministry than to a theory of gender or gendered roles that probably cannot gain universal acceptance in the church?

53. Lewis and Short, "*scio*," in *A Latin Dictionary* (Oxford: Clarendon Press, 1879), 1643–44.

54. It is worth noting that these activities are closer to skills that can be mastered than to innate ideas or depth of insight. At an early stage, *scientia* is practical, not speculative, knowledge.

it and means "a knowing or being skilled in any thing, knowledge, science, skill, expertness."[55] *Scientia* was favored to express well-founded knowledge, knowledge based on solid evidence. In the philosophical tradition of Aristotle, it came to be associated with knowledge that was explained by the four classical causes (material, formal, efficient, and final) or because it flowed from unquestioned "principles" (*principia*). With the emergence of modern science, *scientia* became the term of choice to designate solid knowledge based on empirical evidence that could be carefully observed, categorized, and replicated by subsequent experiments.[56]

Intellegere enjoys a broad spectrum of meanings. Fundamentally, it denotes "to perceive, understand, comprehend," but in particular contexts it can mean (1) to have an accurate knowledge of or skill in a thing, (2) to distinguish, (3) to see, perceive, observe, (4) to comprehend or judge rightly regarding persons, and (5) to see, feel, or notice in a transferred sense. It is helpful to observe its etymology as a composite verb formed from the preposition *inter* and the action of *legere*. In a word, "intelligence" or "intellection" comes from the ability to "gather" (*legere* is from the Greek *legō*) scattered elements and make sense out of them by viewing them in relationship to each other (*inter*). To the Greek mind, this ability to meaningfully arrange what is haphazard leads to "speaking" or "speech"—*logos*.[57] The "word" then is "ordered speech"—words that have been taken out of their confused randomness and meaningfully ordered to produce specific content and communication.[58]

Finally, regarding *sentire*, Lewis and Short distinguish three areas where it is employed: (1) physical action, (2) mental activity, and (3) when it is used in a transferred sense. Physically, *sentire* means "to discern by the

---

55. *A Latin Dictionary*, 1642.

56. On modern science as method, see Bernard Lonergan, *Insight*, 423–30 ["Scientific Method and Philosophy"].

57. See A. Debrunner and H. Kleinknecht, "*legō, logos* etc." in *Theological Dictionary of the New Testament*, ed. Gerhard Kittel and Gerhard Friedrich, trans. and abridged in one volume by Geoffrey W. Bromiley (Grand Rapids, MI: Wm. B. Eerdmans, 1985), 505–7 ["In the Greek World" and "The Logos in the Greek and Hellenistic World"] and Thorleif Boman, *Hebrew Thought Compared with Greek*, trans. Jules L. Moreau (Philadelphia, PA: Westminster Press, 1960), 67–69 ["The Word in Greek Thought"].

58. Again, it is worth noting how at an early stage, *intellectus* is a practical skill. With time, the more speculative notes of understanding came to predominate.

senses; to feel, hear, see, etc.; to perceive."[59] Mentally, it approximates *intellegere* and means "to feel, perceive, observe, notice" as well as "to experience." Finally, in the transferred sense, it means "to think, deem, judge, opine, imagine, suppose." The substantive form corresponding to it is *sensus*.[60] How are we to understand this wealth of meanings and applications of *sentire*?

It is evident that the use of the predicate *sentire* is closely connected to what a person learns from carefully adverting to his or her senses of hearing, feeling, seeing, and smelling. There is meaningful content in what the person senses. Sense knowledge is not devoid of intelligible content. But sense knowledge also leads to imagining, judging, and deciding (the mental and transferred levels of signification). Like *scire* and *intellegere*, *sentire* is first and foremost practical knowledge, but it is not limited to that.

Are there any lessons to be learned from this brief lexical overview about the kind of knowledge expressed by the terms *sensus fidei*, *sensus fidelium*, *sensus catholicus*, and *sentire ecclesiam*?[61] First of all, it should be clear that these revered Latin expressions are more than vague "hunches," or "clues," or "intimations." They are real knowledge, albeit of a kind that is sentient-intellective, practical-speculative, and imaginative-conceptual. They have a composite character. The "sense of the faith" is never distant from its roots in lived "experience," but as experience questioned, contemplated, judged, and applied.

An unanticipated and surprising source for understanding the cognitive character of the "sense of the faith" is provided by the thirteenth-century saint Francis of Assisi. In his prayer before the crucifix of San Damiano, Francis uses the terms *sensus* and *cognitio* in the same breath. He writes: "Most High, glorious God, enlighten the darkness of my heart and give me true faith, certain hope, and perfect charity, sense and knowl-

59. See "*sentire*" in *A Latin Dictionary*, 1672–73.

60. See "*sensus*" in *A Latin Dictionary*, 1670–71.

61. For these phrases, see the comments by Yves Congar, *Lay People in the Church: A Study for a Theology of Laity*, trans. Donald Attwater, rev. ed. (Westminster, MD: The Newman Press, 1965), 288 and by Joseph Ratzinger, "*Sentire ecclesiam*," *Geist und Leben* 36 (1963): 321–26.

edge, Lord, that I may carry out your holy and true command."[62] After invoking divine illumination and the gift of the theological virtues, Francis adds "sense and knowledge"—sentiments that point to how God's will is to be put into practice. The two terms illuminate one another and move the believer to obey God's will. The petition for "sense" and "knowledge" is a request for knowledge that will lead to authentic religious praxis. As practical knowledge, and unlike theological discourse, its way of knowing is not discursive, formal, and reflexive. It doesn't examine its logical thought process or the complex questions it generates on another level of understanding. Instead, it homes in on how faith is to be lived in truth and incorporated into the whole fabric of a person's life and the life of the church. It embraces a faith lived quietly, confidently, and courageously, even in the face of questions, difficulties, and problems.

A Fuller Understanding of Revelation

The Second Vatican Council marked a watershed in the Catholic understanding of revelation. Before the council, revelation was understood in a largely static way—a fixed body or deposit of truths. After Vatican II, it emerged with accents of dynamism, historicity, personalism, and intersubjectivity. In the period after the council, theologians have consolidated and further advanced these remarkable gains.[63] Unfortunately, it is not possible here to review the surprising progress that was made between the submission of the original neoscholastic text "On the Sources of Revelation" (*De fontibus revelationis*) and the final product, the Dogmatic Constitution on Divine Revelation.[64] A brief overview of theological opinion

---

62. "Summe, gloriose Deus, illumina tenebras cordis mei et da mihi fidem rectam, spem certam et caritatem perfectam, sensum et cognitionem, Domine, ut faciam tuum sanctum et verax mandatum." *Opuscula sancti Patris Francisci Assisiensis*, ed. Kajetan Esser (Grottaferrata: Editiones Ad Claras Aquas, 1978), 224. The English translation is from *Francis of Assisi: Early Documents*, vol. 1: *The Saint*, ed. Regis J. Armstrong, J. A. Wayne Hellmann, and William J. Short (New York: New City Press, 1999), 40.

63. For a current treatment of revelation in the light of Vatican II, see Gerald O'Collins, *Revelation: Towards a Christian Interpretation of God's Self-Revelation in Jesus Christ* (New York: Oxford University Press, 2016).

64. See Rino Fisichella, "*Dei Verbum*. I. History," in *Dictionary of Fundamental Theology*, ed. René Latourelle and Rino Fisichella (New York: Crossroad, 1995), 214–18 and Ronald

on revelation before Vatican II, however, might be helpful for the purpose of comparing the teaching on revelation of Vatican I and Vatican II.

It would probably surprise the ordinary believer, and many theologians as well, to learn that the notion of revelation itself has been a neglected area of theology for centuries.[65] The church spoke of revelation, of course, and it had ideas as to what it meant, but these ideas were very broad and largely unexamined. Scripture and tradition were the sources of the truths God had revealed and these were contained in the "deposit of the faith." Strictly speaking, revelation pertained to truths that men and women could not arrive at by the use of their reason alone. God had to communicate them to humankind by the agency of the patriarchs, prophets, priests, and sages in the Old Testament and by Christ and the apostles in the New. These revealed truths were either about the actions God demanded of his people or were direct teachings from God that were communicated in formal statements or propositions.[66] History and historical events, prayers and spirituality (e.g., the psalms), the time-conditioned ritual life of Israel (e.g., Leviticus), and biblical literary forms (e.g., apocalyptic literature and imagery) were merely the context within which revealed doctrine itself ("faith and morals") came to expression.

In the patristic period and the Middle Ages, knowing and believing constituted a unity because each activity was intimately related to the

---

D. Witherup, *Scripture: Dei Verbum*, Rediscovering Vatican II (New York: Paulist Press, 2006). Jared Wicks provides a helpful view of the genesis and progress of *Dei Verbum* based on the diaries and reports of participants at the council in "Vatican II on Revelation—From behind the Scenes," *Theological Studies* 71 (2020): 637–50.

65. See John Baillie, *The Idea of Revelation in Recent Thought* (New York: Columbia University Press, 1956); Gabriel Moran, "The Question of Revelation," *Theology of Revelation* (New York: Herder and Herder, 1966), 22–37; Avery Dulles, *Revelation Theology: A History* (New York: Herder and Herder, 1970) and "From Images to Truth: Newman on Revelation and Faith," *Theological Studies* 51 (1990): 252–67; and John B. Webster, "Revelation, Concept of" in *The Blackwell Encyclopedia of Modern Christian Thought*, ed. Alister E. McGrath (Cambridge, MA: Blackwell, 1993), 557–61.

66. See Michaele Nicolau, "De revelatione," *Sacrae Theologiae Summa*, vol. 1 (Madrid: Biblioteca de autores cristianos, 1962), 84–179, for a representative presentation of the standard theology of revelation in the years before Vatican II. In the academic year 1963–64, we seminarians at the University of Innsbruck were still being taught this truncated version of the theology of revelation, even as the council was struggling with newer ideas and formulations.

other: one believed in order to know and one grew in knowledge in order to believe.[67] But by the time of the Enlightenment this synthesis had given way to two separate realms of knowing: one based on natural evidence, the other on divine authority.[68] Though the Bible continued to be the witness to the manifestation of divine glory, it was increasingly seen as the source of facts about God. According to Wolfgang Beinert, "The *truth* of God was converted into many *truths* that could be articulated in multiple sentences. They could not be changed or supplanted by other terms, and they were protected from the effects of history. Instead of understanding revelation as an epiphany, it now became a source of theoretical information."[69]

By the time of the introduction of neoscholasticism in the late nineteenth century, the richness of biblical revelation had been reduced to a fixed body of propositions of the faith (the "deposit of the faith") that the believer accepted because of the divine guarantee that supported them. Gone were the beauty and allusiveness of biblical imagery and poetry, the drama of biblical men and women struggling to know God and God's

67. Augustine expressed this classically with his formulation, "Understand that you might believe, believe that you might understand." Sermon 43, 7 and 9 in J.-P. Migne, *Patrologia Latina* 38, 257–58. Available online at https://www.augustinus.it/latino/discorsi /discorso_054_testo.htm.

68. Wolfgang Beinert points out that the introduction of an understanding of revelation into two separate and distinct orders of knowing was facilitated by a different understanding of the authority of the pope and the bishops that followed from the so-called Gregorian reform of the eleventh century. This change centralized ecclesiastical authority in the hands of the pope and stressed obedience to teaching emanating from Rome. With time, theological reflection on revelation was reduced to commenting on documents that increasingly originated with the papal magisterium. See "Die Reflexion über die Offenbarung in der Theologie- und Dogmengeschichte," in *Glaubenszugänge: Lehrbuch der Katholischen Dogmatik*, vol. 1, ed. Wolfgang Beinert (Paderborn: F. Schöningh, 1995), 61–65, at 62–63. Moreover, the terms "nature" and "the supernatural" were also henceforth ascribed to two separate spheres of activity, further obscuring their original unity-in-difference and promoting an extrinsic connection between them. See Karl Rahner, "Concerning the Relationship between Nature and Grace," *Theological Investigations*, vol. 1, trans. Cornelius Ernst (Baltimore, MD: Helicon Press, 1961), 297–317.

69. "Die *Wahrheit* Gottes wird in viele *Wahrheiten* umgemünzt, die man in ebenso vielen Sätzen artikulieren kann. Diese sind dann unveränderlich, terminologisch nicht überholbar, geschichtsenthoben. An die Stelle des epiphanischen tritt ein *instruktionstheo-retisches* Offenbarungsverständnis." *Glaubenszugäge*, vol. 1, 62. Author's italics.

ways and striving to be faithful to God, the grandeur of liturgy and its symbolism, the power of the prophetic experience of God's spirit, the miraculous world of God's wonders—in a word, all the facets of a real history of salvation. The Catholic theologian needs to advert to the fact that such an impoverished understanding of revelation was the heritage of Vatican I.[70] The new council would need to address this problem. As we shall see shortly, it did so, but left an ambiguous situation regarding revelation in its wake also.

With the development of historical-critical methods for the study of the Bible in the nineteenth century and their refinement and broad acceptance in the twentieth, Protestant and Catholic scholars alike were forced to come to terms with the meaning of revelation. For the most part, Protestants concentrated on the role of history in the process of revelation. Oscar Cullmann and Wolfhart Pannenberg and his circle of associates were able to draw effectively on this approach to history.[71] Catholics, on the other hand, devoted greater attention to the ecclesial and pastoral dimensions of revelation. Romano Guardini pursued the ways that the celebration of the liturgy could be reinvigorated.[72] Bernhard Häring, CSSR, attempted to reform a moral theology that, long under the sway of canonical categories, was largely juridical and insuf-

---

70. Traditionalism and fideism distracted the papacy in its struggle with rationalism, which claimed epistemic supremacy. This distraction further clouded the issue of the nature of revelation. Traditionalism and fideism denigrated the innate power of the mind, the one by insisting on the existence of a primordial primitive revelation of saving truths handed down from our proto-parents (Hugues de Lamennais), the other by claiming that only faith offered humankind access to saving truth (Louis Bautain).

71. See Oscar Cullmann, *Christus und die Zeit* (Zurich: Evangelischer Verlag, 1946), E.T. *Christ and Time*, trans. Floyd V. Filson (London: SCM Press, 1951); and *Offenbarung als Geschichte*, ed. Wolfhart Pannenberg (Göttingen: Vandenhoeck & Ruprecht, 1961), E.T. *Revelation as History*, trans. David Granskou (New York: Macmillan, 1968). Influential in the English-speaking world was G. Ernest Wright's *God Who Acts* (Chicago, IL: Henry Regnery, 1952). See H. Richard Niebuhr, *The Meaning of Revelation* (New York: Macmillan, 1941) for an early more personalist understanding.

72. See *Vom Geist der Liturgie* (Freiburg: Herder, 1918); E.T. *The Spirit of the Liturgy* (New York: Benziger, 1931); *Besinnung vor der Feier der Messe: erster und zweiter Teil* (3rd ed.; Mainz: Matthias-Grünewald, 1939); and E.T. *Meditations before Mass*, trans. Elinor Castendyk Briefs (Westminster, MD: The Newman Press, 1958).

ficiently scriptural.[73] Josef A. Jungmann, SJ, turned his attention to how preaching and catechetics could be improved by a deeper understanding of revelation itself.[74] In theological education, Henri de Lubac, SJ, asked how the nature-supernature divide could be healed and balance restored to the theological tract on grace.[75] And Karl Rahner, SJ, in an attempt to engage modernity in conversation, showed an openness to transcendental thought (primarily via Joseph Maréchal, SJ [1878-1944]) and German phenomenology (via Edmund Husserl [1859-1938] and Martin Heidegger [1889-1976]) in order to reinvigorate the Catholic theology of revelation.[76]

At Vatican II, it became obvious to the majority of bishops that the schema "On the Sources of Revelation" they found before them was woefully inadequate to the pastoral challenges they faced. To the neoscholastics, the question of the sources of revelation was preeminent. In the mind of the bishops, the text's neglect regarding the nature of revelation itself needed to be remedied. On the other hand, Vatican I had pronounced on revelation, and so they needed to take its teaching into account. But

---

73. See *Das Gesetz Christi: Moraltheologie dargestellt für Priester und Laien*, 3 vols. (Munich: Erich Wewel, 1954); E.T. *The Law of Christ: Moral Theology for Priests and Laity*, 3 vols., trans. Edwin G. Kaiser (Westminster, MD: The Newman Press, 1961–66).

74. See *Die Frohbotschaft und unsere Glaubensverkündigung* (Regensburg: F. Pustet, 1936); E.T. *The Good News Yesterday and Today*, abridged and trans. by William A. Huesman (New York: W. H. Sadlier, 1962).

75. See *Surnaturel: Études historiques* (Paris: Aubier-Montaigne, 1946); E.T. *The Mystery of the Supernatural*, trans. Rosemary Sheed (New York: Herder and Herder, 1967).

76. See Karl Rahner, *Hörer des Wortes: Zur Grundlegung einer Religionsphilosophie* (Munich: Verlag Kösel-Pustet, 1941); E.T. *Hearer of the Word: Laying the Foundation for a Philosophy of Religion*, trans. Joseph Donceel (New York: Continuum Publishing, 1994). In the years following Vatican II, Rahner further developed and widely propagated his understanding of revelation as the fulfillment of a universal orientation of humankind to God as the very meaning and goal of what it is to be human. This theology of a transcendental relationship to God as the human's end, given to all men and women without exception and with a view to God's gracious will to become human in Jesus of Nazareth, was the concrete formulation of the meaning of revelation for Rahner. The human transcendental orientation also was the context for Rahner's emphasis on the priority of pre-reflexive or pre-discursive knowledge. Many have followed Rahner on these views. See his *Foundations of Christian Faith: An Introduction to the Idea of Christianity*, trans. William V. Dych (New York: Seabury Press, 1978). For an appreciative critique of Rahner's philosophical grounding of his transcendental orientation, see Karen Kilby, *Karl Rahner: Theology and Philosophy* (New York: Routledge, 2004).

Vatican I had also pronounced on the gift of infallibility in the church and its concrete exercise by the pope when speaking *ex cathedra*. Papal infallibility, when exercised under quite specific conditions, seemed to involve an understanding of revelation in propositional terms and thereby risked understanding revelation too narrowly. Such an understanding would be a limitation in light of what revelation is in its full meaning, but it was a distinct advantage when it was a matter of the role of the pope and bishops in teaching with authority in the church. The dogma of papal infallibility drew clear lines of teaching authority, but how is the tension between revelation as more-than-propositional and infallibility to be resolved? Let us look at these issues more closely.

First of all, Vatican I did, in fact, teach a broader view of revelation than is generally acknowledged. In chapter 2 of the Dogmatic Constitution on the Catholic Faith, it taught that "[i]t was pleasing to his [God's] wisdom and goodness to reveal himself and the eternal laws of his will to the human race."[77] A sentence later, *Dei Filius* spoke of the culmination of revelation in the person of the Son, by quoting Hebrews 1:1-2: "In times past, God spoke in partial and various ways to our ancestors through the prophets; in these last days, he spoke to us through a son." However unduly concise its formulation of revelation, I do not think it is possible to accuse Vatican I of an exclusively propositional understanding of revelation. It can, however, be faulted for not thinking through the ramifications of its teaching.[78]

Vatican I had indeed understood revelation correctly, but it lost its focus on the nature of revelation by moving too hastily to the question of the magisterium, particularly the papal magisterium. Moreover, after the council the papal magisterium failed to address the problem associated with the narrow neoscholastic teaching on revelation as consisting of divinely revealed propositions. Pius IX and his successors hesitated before the task of deepening and securing the council's insight into revelation and opted instead to strengthen the papacy's hold over the deposit of the faith.

---

77. Tanner, *Decrees of the Ecumenical Councils*, vol. 2, 806.

78. For a clear and sympathetic presentation of Vatican I and II on revelation, see Heinrich Fries, "Revelation as a Theme of Two Councils," *Fundamental Theology*, trans. Robert J. Daly (Washington, DC: Catholic University of America Press, 1996), 367–81.

For its part, Vatican II is to be commended for receiving and fruitfully expanding Vatican I's teaching that revelation deals first and foremost with the mystery of God and God's salvific will. Revelation consists in both words and deeds that interact with each other in history, thus overcoming a narrowly propositional and ahistorical view of revelation.[79] Moreover, revelation culminates in the person of Jesus Christ as the locus of God's self-revelation and not in a deposit of timeless truths. Vatican II thus secured revelation as an event of the persons of the Trinity engaging humankind in interpersonal dialogue.[80] This was an extraordinary achievement of the council. But Vatican II, like Vatican I before it, was also unable to follow through on drawing out the implications of its teaching.[81] How is revelation handed on? What role do all the faithful exercise in its transmission and interpretation?

Here, unfortunately, Vatican II succumbed to half-measures. On the one hand, with its teaching on the "sense of the faith" it defended the role of all the faithful in expressing the content of revelation (LG 12 and 35), while it maintained the strict division between a teaching and a learning church (LG 25). Such irresolution emboldened an obstinate opposition in the church to redouble its efforts in defending an exalted papal magisterium at the expense of the responsibility of both the body of bishops and the body of the faithful for the faith and its integrity. Ill advised by theologians and curial officials who feared that Vatican II unduly limited the teaching authority of the pope, successive popes have tried to shore

---

79. "The pattern of this revelation unfolds through deeds and words which are intrinsically connected: the works performed by God in the history of salvation show forth and confirm the doctrine and realities signified by the words; the words, for their part, proclaim the works, and bring to light the mystery they contain." *Dei Verbum* 2. See also *Dei Verbum* 4. In this instance, I have chosen the translation by Austin Flannery. See *Vatican Council II: Constitutions, Decrees, Declaration; The Basic Sixteen Documents* (Collegeville, MN: Liturgical Press, 2014), 98.

80. See the Dogmatic Constitution on Divine Revelation, articles 2-4. For a reliable examination of Vatican II on revelation, see Ormond Rush, "Principle 7: Revelation/Faith," *The Vision of Vatican II*, 39–53. See also Richard R. Gaillardetz and Catherine E. Clifford, "A Theology of Divine Revelation," *Keys to the Council: Unlocking the Teaching of Vatican II* (Collegeville, MN: Liturgical Press, 2012), 31–38.

81. See Ronald D. Witherup, *Scripture: Dei Verbum*, 54–58 ["Compromise and Incompletion"].

up their teaching authority and even extend it.[82] The result has been the current malaise regarding teaching authority in the church.[83] Inside the Catholic Church, among the churches of the Reformation, and in the Eastern churches there is widespread unease with the Roman Catholic Church's official position on the papal magisterium.[84]

82. I refer to the Congregation for the Doctrine of the Faith's *Professio fidei* and the *Iusiurandum fidelitatis* (1989), the teaching of John Paul II in *Ordinatio sacerdotalis* (1994) and *Ad tuendam fidem* (1998), and the Congregation for the Doctrine of the Faith's "Responses to Some Questions Regarding Certain Aspects of the Doctrine of the Church" (2007). While many in the church have rallied behind these documents, none has been universally accepted by Catholic theologians and many of the faithful. The wise caution of John E. Thiel deserves to be recalled: "We should recognize that authority in the Church is often ambiguous and that that ambiguity reflects the mystery of the God to whom authority in the Church is responsible. . . . Even though, and perhaps because, the Church is blessed with an infallibility assured by the Spirit, it can fail to respect this wisdom, most often by extending its infallibility to places it does not reach. When the magisterium or theologians, for example, describe the teaching of the ordinary magisterium as 'non-infallible' or 'not-fallible,' do they not indirectly make infallibility the measure of all authority? These designations place authoritative teaching in a magisterial limbo between infallibility and fallibility, the discernment expressed in the teaching too uncertain in the Church to invoke the papal prerogative of infallibility and the Church too unused to the ambiguity of authority to convey in its language the fallible character of the authoritative discernment. Would it not be better for the magisterium to acknowledge the mysterious nature of discernment in the Church by speaking of the ambiguity, and yet valued authority, of the discernments expressed in its own ordinary teaching?" John E. Thiel, "Responsibility to the Spirit: Authority in the Catholic Tradition," *New Theology Review* 8, no. 3 (August 1995), 53–69, at 67.

83. See the essays edited by Richard R. Gaillardetz in *When the Magisterium Intervenes: The Magisterium and Theologians in Today's Church* (Collegeville, MN: Liturgical Press, 2012).

84. Until this malaise is satisfactorily addressed, the conciliar teaching on the co-responsibility of the bishops for teaching in the church and the role of the "sense of the faith of the faithful" will remain hollow and largely ineffectual. My first impulse is to argue that the impasse can only be surmounted by returning to the root of the problem, namely, Paul VI's teaching in *Humanae vitae* (1968), and the spate of Roman documents by John Paul II and the Congregation for the Doctrine of the Faith just mentioned whose clear intent has been to shore up only one interpretation of the extent of papal teaching authority and the manner of its exercise. On further reflection, I am not so sure of the validity of this tactic. It might, in fact, be better to trust in the abiding assistance of the Holy Spirit and allow the process of reception or non-reception to play itself out. Tensions and disagreements in the church are not a bad thing. What the papacy must defend at this time is the freedom of the faithful, theologians, and bishops to express their true convictions, while listening respectfully and with an open mind to the views of others.

In conclusion, I have tried to show how Vatican II bequeathed a richer theology of revelation by building on the valid insights of Vatican I, the beneficial results of the *ressourcement* movement in Catholic theology, and the contributions of the bishops and their theological advisors at Vatican II. In isolation, actions and words can be obscure, but together they facilitate insight and meaning. History, too, can be deeply ambiguous, while the idea of history as dialogue helps to give it a sense of direction. Finally, truth can seem so lofty, elusive, and unattainable, but when it is embodied in a person like ourselves, in Jesus Christ, we can seek it with greater confidence. The teaching of the Dogmatic Constitution on Divine Revelation on the mutuality of words and actions in revelation, on revelation as God's dialogue with humanity throughout history, and on the person of Jesus Christ as the perfect expression of divine revealed truth represent priceless advances on the doctrine of revelation.

An Emerging Understanding of Tradition

Tradition, too, has emerged today as a category that formerly received little explicit attention by theologians and the magisterium. None of the eight ecumenical councils held in the West between 1123 and 1418 mentions or treats tradition. The first to do so was Trent, which in its fourth session in 1546 used tradition to officially determine the canon of the books of the Old and New Testaments and to reject the opinions of the Reformers in excluding certain ecclesiastical customs and practices (*consuetudines, observationes, institutiones*).[85] The context of the teaching was decidedly practical and pastoral, not theoretical. Before Trent, the Council of Constance had addressed the errors of John Wycliffe (1320–84) and Jan Hus (1374-1415), who enumerated a variety of practices that they objected to in the church. At most one might discern the emergence of concern with what will come to be seen in the Roman church as traditions or traditional practices, but still not an overarching theological category called "tradition."[86] Nonetheless, given the polemical

---

85. Joseph Ratzinger has pointed out the spectrum of theological opinions on "traditions" at Trent. See "On the Interpretation of the Tridentine Decree on Tradition," in *Revelation and Tradition*, Quaestiones Disputatae 17, trans. W. J. O'Hara (New York: Herder and Herder, 1966), 50–68.

86. See Ratzinger, "Revelation and Tradition," in *Revelation and Tradition*, 26–49.

atmosphere among Catholics and Reformers after Trent, tradition began to loom large both as a badge of identity and a rallying cry of opposition. Two Christian identities emerged around a rather novel and untested theological category.

Since the retrieval of a broader understanding of tradition by Johann Adam Möhler in the nineteenth century and Yves Congar's advocacy for Möhler's views in the twentieth, the church has been remedying its neglect of the meaning of tradition. "Tradition" had been reduced to a mere function of providing the pope and the bishops with material contents for them as they addressed the growing doctrinal and moral issues Catholics faced. It would take an ecumenical council to break out of the narrow confines of the standard treatment of tradition among theologians.[87] Vatican II did so by courageously taking up the intertwined questions of the church and its mission, the value of the created order, human relationships including relations among Christians and relations with the world's religions, and the church's very life as expressed in revelation, Scripture, and tradition. The council addressed tradition in the Dogmatic Constitution on Divine Revelation.[88] We have already examined how Vatican II deepened its understanding of revelation, and now it is time to consider how tradition is related to it.

In general, Vatican II preferred concrete biblical language when referring to revelation. It spoke of the "word of God" and of the "gospel" rather than "revelation." "Words" are spoken and "good news" is proclaimed and preached. The "word of God" exists in the speaking, in the doing, in the declaring, in the preaching—and in the handing down or "traditioning." *Traditio*, and its Greek equivalent *paradosis*, is the act of "handing on,"

---

87. See Ormond Rush, "Principle 12: Scripture/Tradition," *The Vision of Vatican II: Its Fundamental Principles* (Collegeville, MN: Liturgical Press, 2019), 141–64.

88. See Richard R. Gaillardetz and Catherine E. Clifford, "A Theology of Tradition," *Keys to the Council*, 39–46. Recently, Gerald O'Collins has clearly presented the teaching of Vatican II and contextualized the council's teaching in light of what was also unfolding at the Fourth World Conference on Faith and Order in 1963 at Montreal, Canada. See his "The Background for Discussing Christian Tradition," *Tradition: Understanding Christian Tradition* (New York: Oxford University Press, 2018) 1-19. O'Collins's book is an important, comprehensive, and reliable contribution to the contemporary discussion of the meaning and place of tradition in the Catholic Church and in the other Churches and Christian ecclesial communities.

and only secondarily (and somewhat misleadingly) "the deposit of what has been handed down." The church is perpetuated by its Lord and the Lord's Spirit insofar as it acts to hand its entire self on in history. This is what theologians mean by "living tradition."

In an insightful article on tradition and its inherent tensions, Avery Dulles helpfully spelled out the underlying and interconnected issues associated with tradition.[89] Religions like Judaism and Christianity survive and thrive by embracing tradition on the one hand and expanding its meaning and its extent on the other. For Christianity, tradition not only guarantees its continuity but also assures its vitality. Tradition needs to be both clearly identifiable and definable, but also, within limits, flexible and open. The church exists in the concrete conditions of history as given in the here and now of existence. Here, once again, Vatican II was wise to acknowledge the historicity of the church's existence and of the means of communicating its saving message. The council was wise to see the need to reform how it celebrates its sacramental life liturgically, and it was wise to be receptive to symbols, terms, and categories that prepare it for survival, continued growth, and vitality.[90]

Tradition is a complex and tension-laden ecclesial reality that resists simplification and easy attempts to resolve its in-built stress points. Unfortunately, attempts by individuals and groups to resolve these tensions in too facile a manner have only made the task of working out the proper balance of continuity and change more elusive and divisive in the postconciliar church. In his article, Dulles offers us no simplistic description or definition of tradition. Instead, he speaks of what is known versus what can be further known, objective versus participatory knowledge,[91] conserva-

---

89. See "Vatican II and the Recovery of Tradition," *The Reshaping of Catholicism: Current Challenges in the Theology of Church* (San Francisco: Harper & Row, 1988), 75–92.

90. Deserving of mention above all in this regard is the church as people of God that has enhanced the dignity and co-responsibility of each and every member of the church. See Dario Vitale, *Popolo di Dio* (Assisi: Cittadella, 2013). Also, by introducing such theological categories as communion (*koinonia*), collegiality, and synodality, the council has helped to moderate excessive ecclesiastical centralization and bureaucratization by introducing a "shared model" of hierarchical authority.

91. On participatory knowledge, see also Peter Carnley, "The Nature of Faith," *Resurrection in Retrospect: A Critical Examination of the Theology of N. T. Wright* (Eugene, OR: Cascade Books, 2019), 158–80, at 168–70.

tion versus innovation or renovation, permanence versus adaptation, and stasis versus dynamism. To Dulles, "tradition" is not one alternative over the other but all tensively interacting with each other.

How does Dulles's approach compare with the statement of Lutherans and Catholics in the United States in their common statement *Scripture and Tradition*? In a technique that has been helpful in formulating their common statements, the Lutheran and Catholic contributors each first present their understanding of the topic enlightened by the best recent scholarship followed by a nuanced statement of their current position. The technique of balancing statements clears the ground for a declaration that both sides can share and that represents an advance over earlier, less nuanced expressions. In the case of Scripture and tradition, the Catholic members of the consultation draw on the Dogmatic Constitution on Divine Revelation's teachings. Taken together, the council's insights create a certain balance in the teaching that was not there before. They stress the unity of tradition and Scripture, which "form a single sacred deposit of the word of God, entrusted to the Church" (art. 10).[92] A certain preeminence is accorded Scripture as the word of God, while tradition hands on the word in its full purity through faithful preaching and teaching. The teaching authority of the pope and bishops is both acknowledged and modified when the council teaches that "this teaching function is not above the word of God but stands at its service" (art. 10).[93] Moreover, the task of the whole people of God in witnessing to the word is not forgotten: "What has been handed down from the apostles includes everything that helps the people of God to live a holy life and grow in faith. In this way the [whole] Church, in its teaching, life, and worship, perpetuates and hands on to every generation all that it is and all that it believes" (art. 8).[94] The delicate balance of elements in these formulations is inescapable—and necessary. No one item apart from the others makes

92. "Sacra traditio et sacra scriptura unum verbi Dei sacrum depositum constituunt ecclesiae commissum." Tanner, *Decrees of the Ecumenical Councils*, vol. 2, 975.

93. "Quod quidem magisterium non supra verbum Dei est, sed eidem ministrat." Ibid.

94. "Quod vero ab apostolis traditum est, ea omnia complectitur quae ad populi Dei vitam sancte ducendam fidemque augendam conferunt, sicque ecclesia, in sua doctrina, vita et cultu, perpetuat cunctisque generationibus transmittit omne quod ipsa est, omne quod credit." Tanner, *Decrees of the Ecumenical Councils*, vol. 2, 974. I have added the word "whole" in brackets to unambiguously make my point.

sense in and of itself. The living word of God, handing on the faith from one generation to the next, the living reality of faith as lived out, necessary but servant-like authority, and the task and responsibility of the whole body of believers—all of this, and not anything less, is "tradition." But these "elements" are nothing if not tensive.

The vocabulary of relationality can be helpful here. The "elements" enumerated above, taken from the teaching of Vatican II, cannot be isolated but ultimately are meaningful only insofar as they are related to one another.[95] They constitute each other. "Tradition" means the whole as mutually related and constituting the ecclesial parts. "Tradition" cannot mean one element of the church and of the faith that can be isolated from the others.

Finally, regarding the question that concerns us, tradition and the "sense of the faith" of the whole church are inextricably connected with one another. No competent Roman Catholic theologian would want to exclude the teaching responsibility of the pope and the bishops, but by the same token after Vatican II neither can the theologian exclude the responsibility and the inalienable role of the body of the church faithful in determining the faith of the church. That, I maintain, is the genuine

---

95. Joseph Ratzinger developed a rich anthropology of relationship in his understanding of human persons. For example, in his commentary on the biblical teaching of the account of creation, he wrote: "The image of God means, first of all, that human beings cannot be closed in on themselves. Human beings who attempt this betray themselves. To be the image of God implies relationality. It is the dynamic that sets the human being in motion toward a totally Other. Hence it means the capacity for relationship; it is the human capacity for God. . . . Therefore the image of God also means that human persons are beings of word and of love, beings moving toward Another, oriented to giving themselves to the Other and only truly receiving themselves back in real self-giving." *In the Beginning. . . : A Catholic Understanding of the Story of Creation and the Fall*, trans. Boniface Ramsey (Grand Rapids, MI: Wm. B. Eerdmans, 1995), 47–48. In the context of Christian eschatology, too, Ratzinger further develops his understanding of relationship as dialogical: God calling forth human potential through the dialogue of the incarnation, and human individuals truly realizing themselves in the dialogue with others and so realizing their vocation to become "persons." See *Dogmatic Theology*, vol. 9: *Eschatology: Death and Eternal Life*, trans. Michael Waldstein, ed. Aidan Nichols (Washington, DC: Catholic University of America Press, 1988), 155–57. I myself have developed the idea of relationality in my *Apostolicity Then and Now: An Ecumenical Church in a Postmodern World* (Collegeville, MN: Liturgical Press, 2004), 139–45 ["Return of the 'Other' and Relationality"].

teaching of the church regarding its infallibility, the infallibility of the whole Body of Christ. A deepened theology of tradition calls forth the teaching of the "sense of the faith of the faithful," and the "sense of the faith of the faithful" lends credibility to tradition.

Vatican II represents a needed correction of the course regarding Scripture and tradition. In my opinion, the council does not present an unambiguous and entirely consistent teaching on the nature of "tradition." Some of the former tensions between Scripture and tradition can still be found in the text, and the council has not clearly demarcated the limitations of the teaching authority of the pope and the bishops, not to mention how that authority is related to the equal responsibility for the faith of the whole body of the faithful.[96] The council's proposals are modest but still very important. Vatican II challenges the church to do better than the former "two-source theory" of revelation and a one-sided understanding of the magisterium.[97] I think the resources are available to us: the whole church as the searching people of God, the nature of faith as co-constituting the event of revelation, the role of the "sense of the faith of the faithful," and an understanding of relationality as constitutive of reality. But these ideas are hardly accepted universally in the church. The road ahead is still a long one. And that brings me to my final topic in this concluding chapter.

The Place of Pneumatology

The role of Christ in salvation history and in the continuing life and activity of the church has tended to overshadow the place and role of the

96. See Ronald D. Witherup, *Scripture: Dei Verbum*, 54–58 ["Compromise and Incompletion"] and Ormond Rush, *The Vision of Vatican II*, 163–64.

97. The treatments by John E. Thiel are well worth consulting: "Tradition and Authoritative Reasoning: A Nonfoundationalist Perspective," *Theological Studies* 56 (1995): 627–51; "Perspectives on Tradition," *Catholic Theological Society of America Proceedings* 54 (1999): 1–18; "The Analogy of Tradition: Method and Theological Judgment," *Theological Studies* 66 (2005): 358–80; "The Aesthetics of Tradition and the Styles of Theology," *Theological Studies* 75 (2014): 795–815; and *Senses of Tradition: Continuity and Development in Catholic Faith* (New York: Oxford University Press, 2000). See also the contributions in *Wie geschiet Tradition? Überlieferung im Lebensprozess der Kirche*, ed. Dietrich Wiederkehr, Quaestiones Disputatae 133 (Freiburg: Herder, 1991) and Walter Kasper, "Das Verhältnis von Schrift und Tradition. Eine pneumatologische Perspektive," *Theologie und Kirche*, vol. 2 (Mainz: Matthias-Grünewald, 1999), 51–83.

Holy Spirit in the economy of salvation. No pope, council, or responsible theologian has denied the importance of the Holy Spirit in the economy of salvation, of course, but neither has the theological tradition in the West highlighted or developed the Spirit's indispensable contribution very much.[98] Here, one must frankly speak of a "pneumatological deficit." Although there has always been an awareness of the role played by the Holy Spirit in the founding of the church at Pentecost, in the inspiration of Scripture, and in the deliberations and decisions of ecumenical councils and the elections of popes, the Spirit's role has generally been restricted to these few and far between highpoints in the church's life. On a day-to-day basis, Western Christians have tended to rely directly on the presence, power, and guidance of Christ, hardly adverting to the Holy Spirit.[99] At Vatican II, however, and mainly due to the contributions from the bishops of the Eastern churches, modest efforts were made to reflect more intentionally on the action of the Spirit and to incorporate the Spirit's contribution in the conciliar documents.[100] Since the council though, pneumatological reflection has been sporadic.[101] The question of

98. Yves Congar is one exception. See his *Tradition and Traditions: An Historical Essay and a Theological Essay*, trans. Michael Naseby and Thomas Rainborough (New York: Macmillan, 1967), 338–47 ["The Holy Spirit, the Transcendent Subject of Tradition: His Active Presence in the Church the Body of Christ"] and *I Believe in the Holy Spirit*, 3 vols., trans. David Smith (New York: Seabury Press, 1983).

99. The same cannot be said of the modern charismatic movement throughout the church, but this has tended to limit its influence to prayer, healing, and spirituality. For changes in the charismatic movement in recent years, see Kristina Cooper, "A Gift for the Common Good," *The Tablet* (January 23, 2021): 14–15. Cooper points out how the movement in the United Kingdom has become more involved in contributing to the mission and life of parishes and dioceses.

100. See the intervention by Archbishop Néophytos Edelby, *Acta synodalia sacrosancti Concilii Oecumenici Vaticani II* (Vatican City: Typis Polyglottis Vaticanis, 1970–1978), III/3: 306–8. See also Walter Kasper, "The Renewal of Pneumatology in Contemporary Catholic Life and Theology: Towards a Rapprochement between East and West," *That They May All Be One: The Call to Unity Today* (New York: Burns & Oates, 2004), 96–121.

101. Raymond E. Brown highlighted this claim in his "Diverse New Testament Views of the Spirit—A Preliminary Contribution of Exegesis to Doctrinal Reflection," *Biblical Exegesis and Church Doctrine* (New York: Paulist Press, 1985), 101–13. With his characteristic clarity, Brown pointed out that it is impossible to harmonize all the statements regarding the (Holy) Spirit in the Old and New Testaments. In light of Brown's exegetical and dogmatic cautions, the hierarchy needs to be open to the Spirit's movements throughout the church and not react too hastily or dismissively to the insights and initiatives of

the "sense of the faith" is certainly one ecclesiological issue that is ripe for further deepening by reflecting on the Spirit.[102] Discerning the truth of revelation and applying it to the life of faith as it is currently experienced cries out for more daring thought.[103] I propose to examine some of these efforts and to issue a challenge for even greater efforts.

We begin with what the Dogmatic Constitution on Divine Revelation says about the Spirit and revelation.[104] Article 8 concentrates on the growth in understanding the word of God in the church and twice points to the role the Spirit plays in this process.[105] Since we have already examined the council's teaching in chapter 9, there is no need to repeat it here. I only want to point out the close connection Vatican II draws between the action of the Spirit in leading the church into a deeper understanding and firmer possession of the truth and the role of the whole church in doing so.

> This tradition which comes from the apostles progresses in the Church under the assistance of the Holy Spirit. There is growth in understanding of what is handed on, both the words and the realities they

---

those who do not occupy hierarchical office. Also, see Karl Rahner, "Do Not Stifle the Spirit!," *Theological Investigations*, vol. 7, trans. David Bourke (New York: Herder and Herder, 1971), 72–87 and idem, "Observations on the Factor of the Charismatic in the Church," *Theological Investigations*, vol. 12, trans. David Bourke (New York: Seabury Press, 1974), 81–97.

102. See the pioneering work of Ormond Rush, "The Holy Spirit and the Church" and "The Holy Spirit and the Sense for the Faith" in *The Eyes of Faith: The Sense of the Faithful and the Church's Reception of Revelation* (Washington, DC: Catholic University of America Press, 2009), 37–62 and 63–87, and his more recent "The Prophetic Office in the Church: Pneumatological Perspectives on the *Sensus Fidelium*-Theology-Magisterium Relationship," in *When the Magisterium Intervenes*, ed. Richard R. Gaillardetz, 89–112. See also Thomas Söding, "Das Wehen des Geistes: Aspekte neutestamentlicher Pneumatologie" in *Atem des sprechenden Gottes: Einführung in die Lehre vom Heiligen Geist*, ed. Bernhard Nitsche (Regensburg: F. Pustet, 2003), 22–71 and Bernhard Nitsche, "Geistvergessenheit und die Wiederentdeckung des Heiligen Geistes im Zweiten Vatikanischen Konzil," ibid., 102–44.

103. See Richard Lennan and Nancy Pineda-Madrid, eds., *The Holy Spirit: Setting the World on Fire* (New York: Paulist Press, 2017) and the encouraging comments by Gerald O'Collins in his *Tradition: Understanding Christian Tradition*, 136-37.

104. See R. R. Gaillardetz and C. E. Clifford, "The Holy Spirit in the Church," *Keys to the Council*, 57–65.

105. The Holy Spirit is mentioned a total of twenty-four times in the constitution. See articles 2, 4, 5, 7, 8, 9, 10, 11, 17, 18, 19, 20, 21, and 23.

signify. This comes about through contemplation and study by believers, who "ponder these things in their hearts" (see Lk. 2:19 and 51); through the intimate understanding of spiritual things which they experience; and through the preaching of those who, on succeeding to the office of bishop, receive the sure charism of truth (art. 8).[106]

This important quotation makes it abundantly clear that it is the Holy Spirit who leads the whole church, both the ordinary faithful and their pastors, into a deeper grasp of the truth of revelation. In doing so, the text does not sharply distinguish the contributions of the ordinary faithful and their leaders. The Holy Spirit works through everyone in the church. The following paragraph picks up this train of thought and advances it.

> By this tradition comes the Church's knowledge of the full canon of biblical books; by this too the scripture itself comes to be more profoundly understood and to realize its power in the Church. In this way the God who spoke of old still maintains an uninterrupted conversation with the bride of his beloved Son. The Holy Spirit, too, is active, making the living voice of the gospel ring out in the Church, and through it in the world, leading those who believe into the whole truth, and making the message of Christ dwell in them in all its richness (see Col. 3:16) (art. 8).[107]

In his commentary on article 8, Joseph Ratzinger pointed specifically to its pneumatological character.

> In this context we can now finally see the pneumatological character of the idea of tradition. Tradition is ultimately based on the fact that the Christ event cannot be limited to the age of the historical Jesus, but continues in the presence of the Spirit. . . . Only if this pneumatic dimension is taken into consideration, can Christology be seen in its full New Testament breadth, and at the same time the scriptural equivalent of our modern problem of understanding become apparent. In this necessary correction of a Christocentric view that had become too narrowly incarnational the Council was able to learn much from the views of those fathers who stood in the tradition of the Eastern Church.[108]

---

106. Tanner, *Decrees of the Ecumenical* Councils, vol. 2, 974.

107. Ibid.

108. *Commentary on the Documents of Vatican II*, vol. 3, ed. Herbert Vorgrimler (New York: Herder and Herder, 1969), 189–90.

Both the conciliar text and Ratzinger's commentary point to the Spirit's enduring role in the church of leading it into the correct and appropriate understanding of revelation.

The next witness to Vatican II's discovery of the importance of the Holy Spirit in the life of the church is article 12 of the Dogmatic Constitution on the Church. We have already examined this passage in chapter 9, but now it is time to focus our attention on the pneumatology of article 12.[109]

Article 12 is divided into two paragraphs, each treating a topic that is related to the other. We have had opportunity to study the teaching regarding the "sense of the faith," but so far have not examined the second paragraph that expresses the council's teaching on charisms. It is interesting that the bishops did not divide the prophetic office of the people of God (paragraph 1) from the gifts (charisms) of the Holy Spirit necessary to live out their faith (paragraph 2), but saw the two statements as ordered to each other and elucidating one another. It is the Spirit who empowers the prophetic mission of the believer and crowns him or her with appropriate charisms.

> Moreover, the same Holy Spirit not only sanctifies and guides the people of God by means of the sacraments and the ministries and adorns it with virtues, he also apportions his gifts (*dona sua*) "to each individually as he wills" (1 Cor. 12:11), and among the faithful of every rank he distributes special graces (*gratias speciales*) by which he renders them fit and ready to undertake the various tasks and offices which help the renewal and the building up of the Church. . . . These charismatic

---

109. Recently, Jos Moons subjected article 12 of *Lumen gentium* to a careful analysis of the place and importance of the Holy Spirit in arousing and sustaining the "sense of the faith." He closely charted the changes in the various redactions of what eventually became the final version of LG 12 and showed (convincingly in my opinion) the gradual but cautious movement toward a more overtly pneumatological formulation and understanding of the role of the Holy Spirit as the source and sustaining power of the "sense of the faith of the faithful." See his "'Aroused and Sustained by the Holy Spirit'? A Plea for a Pneumatological Reconsideration of *Sensus Fidei* on the Basis of *Lumen Gentium* 12," *Gregorianum* 99 (2018): 271–91. The article merits serious attention. Among other lessons, Moons points out the hesitancy and inconsistencies in the various texts. In the end, we are left with conciliar texts that have clearly moved the question forward regarding the Holy Spirit's role in the economy of salvation, but also without having achieved full clarity or total conviction.

gifts (*quae charismata*), whether they be very outstanding or simpler and more widely diffused, are to be accepted with thanksgiving and consolation, since they are primarily suited to and useful for the needs of the Church.[110]

The final example of the growing awareness of the bishops at Vatican II of the importance of the role of the Holy Spirit in the church is found in the Decree on the Apostolate of the Laity. The history of this decree sheds light on the thesis of the growing awareness of pneumatology at Vatican II.[111] In general it reflects the ecclesiological themes developed at greater length in the Dogmatic Constitution on the Church, but as regards pneumatology, it definitely breaks new ground.

In October 1964, the bishops finally had the chance to discuss the text presented to them.[112] Several interventions addressed the question of the continuing role of the Holy Spirit in the church. Hanjo Sauer has presented summaries of these interventions in his contribution "The Council Discovers the Laity."[113] Two of these interventions caught my attention. Bishop Steven Leven, an auxiliary of San Antonio, Texas, defended the participation of the laity in the apostolate of the church.

> [He] thought the schema needed to explain even more clearly that the apostolate of the laity belongs to the very essence of the Church. This apostolate is the exercise of a gift that the Holy Spirit has entrusted to the Church. The right of the Church's authorities to guide and direct this apostolate does not include a right to suppress it and to exert such pressure on it that it is regarded as worthless.[114]

Bishop Heinrich Tenhumberg, auxiliary of Münster, Germany, spoke for eighty-three German and Scandinavian bishops. He pointed out that

---

110. Tanner, *Decrees of the Ecumenical Councils*, vol. 2, 858.

111. See Dolores R. Leckey, *The Laity and Christian Education: Apostolicam Actuositatem, Gravissimum Educationis*, Rediscovering Vatican II (New York: Paulist Press, 2006).

112. On the process, see the presentation "The Council Discovers the Laity" by Hanjo Sauer in *History of Vatican II*, vol. 4, ed. Giuseppe Alberigo and Joseph A. Komonchak (Maryknoll, NY: Orbis Books, 2003), 233–67.

113. *History of Vatican II*, vol. 4, 233–67.

114. Ibid., 248. The remarks of Bishop Leven can be found in *Acta Synodalia sacrosancti Concilii Oecumenici Vaticani II*, III/4:81–83.

[t]he explanations of the necessity of the lay apostolate were too much like external additions. . . . It would be better to speak, right from the beginning, about the Holy Spirit, in whom every apostolate has its source and foundation. In addition, the concept of apostolate was too much tied up with the hierarchy; it needed to be made clear that every apostolate has its own intrinsic value and special place.[115]

It appears that the commission working on the text of *Apostolicam actuositatem* took these and other observations to heart. In the final text presented to the bishops in 1965 for their approval, two important articles had been added.[116] In articles 3 and 4 we find an important development of the role of the Holy Spirit. Article 3 in particular forcefully reiterates the teaching of the Dogmatic Constitution on the Church regarding the participation of the faithful in the offices of Christ, the centrality of baptism and confirmation in sacramentally grounding their participation in the church's apostolate, and the role of the Holy Spirit in liberally bestowing charisms on the faithful to help them achieve the goal of the apostolate. Article 3 mentions the Holy Spirit no less than five times and harmoniously weaves its pneumatological statements into references to Christ the Head, Christ's mystical body, and Christ's role in assigning to the faithful their participation in the apostolate. This article is one of the most successful of the council's statements on the intrinsic relationship of Christology and pneumatology.

Article 4, also added in 1965, treats the theme of the spirituality proper to the laity. It is a long and somewhat rambling presentation, but it also advances the place and the importance of the Holy Spirit in realizing the indispensability of spirituality in the lay life and vocation, when it teaches:

---

115. Ibid., 249. See *Acta Synodalia sacrosancti Concilii Oecumenici Vaticani II*, III/4:91–94.

116. See the commentaries by Ferdinand Klostermann, in *Commentary on the Documents of Vatican II*, vol. 3, ed. Herbert Vorgrimler (New York: Herder and Herder, 1969), 315–22 and Guido Bausenhart, in *Herders theologischer Kommentar zum Zweiten Vatikanischen Konzil*, vol. 4, ed. Peter Hünermann and Bernd Jochen Hilberath (Freiburg: Herder, 2005), 51–59. On the process surrounding the final revision of the text and the vote on the text, see Mauro Velati, "Completing the Conciliar Agenda," in *History of Vatican II*, vol. 5, ed. Giuseppe Alberigo and Joseph A. Komonchak (Maryknoll, NY: Orbis Books, 2006), 185–273, at 264–73 ["The Laity: A Role in the Church?"].

This general way of the spiritual life will take on particular qualifications according to their state of married or family life, or celibacy or widowhood, their state of health, or their professional and social activities. Accordingly, they should perseveringly cultivate the qualities and gifts appropriate to their condition of life and should make use of the gifts [appropriate to each one (*propriis donis*)] which the Holy Spirit bestows.[117]

Though other instances could be cited, these four—the living and dynamic character of tradition, the centrality of the "sense of the faith," the indispensable role of charisms in Christian life and in the church, and the expanded teaching of the Decree on the Apostolate of the Laity—must suffice as indications of the modest attention to pneumatology introduced by the bishops at Vatican II.[118] There should now be no doubt about the indispensability of the Spirit for a life of faith. But has this clear teaching been received and implemented concretely in the church?

If we survey the theological literature of the last sixty years, the "pneumatological deficit" I spoke of becomes apparent. Though we can point to numerous studies on the Spirit, most of them are dedicated to understanding the person of the Spirit in the mystery of the Trinity. The application of the role of the Spirit in the church has been rare.[119] This fact has

117. Tanner, *Decrees of the Ecumenical Councils*, vol. 2, 984. I have slightly altered the translation by adding the phrase in backets that appears in the Latin text but which Tanner has inexplicably omitted. See also articles 23, 29, 30, and 33.

118. In addition to the texts just studied, some of the other contexts of the council's invocation of the Holy Spirit include the Dogmatic Constitution on the Church (articles 4, 7, 8, 9, 12, 13, 15, 17, 25, 32, 39, 40, 41, 42, 48, and 50); the Pastoral Constitution on the Church in the Modern World (articles 10, 11, 21, 38, 40, 43, and 44); the Decree on the Church's Missionary Activity (articles 2, 4, 7); and the Decree on Ecumenism (articles 1, 2, 3, 4, 7, 20, 21, and 24).

119. Just as theologians distinguish between the immanent Trinity and the economic Trinity, so too can we distinguish treatments of the Holy Spirit that concentrate on the person of the Spirit in the Trinity and those that examine the "mission of the Spirit" in the order or economy of salvation. The "pneumatological deficit" I am speaking of refers to this latter role or the "mission of the Spirit" in the church. With the exception of the moderately frequent references to the economic role of the Spirit in the Dogmatic Constitution on the Church, one really cannot point to a breakthrough of pneumatology at Vatican II. The perspective of the bishops remains overwhelmingly Christocentric, focusing on the ministry of Christ, the mysteries of Christ, and the influence of the glorified Christ. We

contributed to why there has been so little effort to inform the church at large of the existence, meaning, and ramifications of the council's teaching on the "sense of the faith." It has also contributed to the absence of any mention of the "sense of the faith" in the revised Code of Canon Law for the Latin church. There are still few meaningful regular means of consultation in place in the church for implementing the council's teaching. The "pneumatological deficit" has also contributed to the backpedaling on the meaning of the teaching in official documents that have been issued by Rome over the last sixty years. Whenever the topic has been broached, cautions have been raised immediately and the specter of "public opinion" in the church resurrected. The council's own modest efforts to strike a proper balance between the Christocentric and the pneumatological elements of the church continue to be unrealized. How, then, can this ecclesiological impasse be surmounted?

I have no omniscient bird's-eye view or magic wand that can remove the impasse. Concrete steps must be taken to include the ordinary faithful in inner-ecclesial discussions of faith and morals in society and in the church.[120] John Henry Newman had it right when he insisted that the laity should be consulted on matters that affect them. I submit that the best way to correct this imbalance is to make pastoral councils of parishes and other, more regular diocesan-wide consultations obligatory in the church. Bishops and pastors must make efforts to meet regularly with the faithful and show respect for their views, as well as for those of a broad spectrum of theologians. Episcopal conferences should also urge that their views be sought by Vatican dicasteries before these congregations issue world-wide directives. Perhaps, too, episcopal conferences need to examine their own internal and external procedures of consultation. All

---

are indebted to Ormond Rush for listing approximately ten books and articles in English, French, German, and Spanish on the economic role of the Spirit and in the church in particular. See "Principle 8: Christological/Pneumatological," *The Vision of Vatican II: Its Fundamental Principles* (Collegeville, MN: Liturgical Press, 2019), 54–80, at 61n26. See also the collection of papers edited by Doris Donnelly, Adelbert Denaux, and Joseph Famerée in *The Holy Spirit, the Church and Christian Unity: Proceedings of the Consultation Held at the Monastery of Bose, Italy (14–20 October 2002)* (Leuven: Peeters, 2005).

120. The International Theological Commission, in its *Sensus Fidei in the Life of the Church*, has made several helpful suggestions in articles 120–126 ["Ways of Consulting the Faithful"].

voices deserve to be respectfully heard and the members of the episcopal conference need to be assured real freedom of expression.

Without a receptive church, the "sense of the faith" intended by Vatican II will never be realized. To broaden the base of consultation in the church in the way I am suggesting need not diminish the true authority and the indispensable leadership of the church's pastors. If anything, the model of a "searching church" will begin to restore the confidence in the church that so many believers have lost in recent years and redress the sense of imbalance in the exercise of the magisterium. A receptive and searching church can reawaken the sense of universal responsibility that was so palpable in the years immediately following Vatican II and that filled the church with the hope of new possibilities—for itself and for humanity. It is imperative that the church in the twenty-first century recover this spirit. By fostering a deeper appreciation of the activity of the Holy Spirit, the "sense of the faith" can become a reality in the church, and the vision of Vatican II can be realized.

Conclusion

I was assigned to teach the course on the church in the spring semester of 1972 and I taught the course annually for the next forty years. Ecclesiology has been a focus of my theological interest over these many years. The topic of the "sense of the faith" came up in these lectures on the church and this teaching of Vatican II has always intrigued me. In my first years as a professor, the literature on the "sense of the faith" was rather sparse, but by the late 1970s I noticed a perceptible upswing in the amount of literature and I decided to follow it more closely.[1] In the 1980s and 1990s, the literature on the "sense of the faith" increased exponentially and the quality of its treatment also improved. A comment by Walter Kasper grabbed my attention. Already in 1970 Kasper had written: "[Article 12 of *Lumen Gentium*] maintains that the witness to the truth of the Gospel is not only the task of the magisterial office of the Church in the narrower sense, but is also the task of the whole People of God. The significance of this statement can hardly be exaggerated and we are far from having exhausted its consequences in principle and in practice."[2] I sensed a challenge in Kasper's words. The present book is my most sustained effort to bring the riches of this seminal teaching of Vatican II to a wider audience.

As the literature in general on the "sense of the faith" increased, one glaring lack remained the paucity of available sources of the doctrine in English. From the wide reading I had done on the teaching, I noticed

---

1. See the appended chronological bibliography for an aid in visualizing the astonishing growth of the literature on the "sense of the faith of the faithful" from 1940-2020.

2. "Zum Problem der Rechtgläubigkeit in der Kirche von morgen," in *Kirchliche Lehre— Skepsis der Gläubigen*, ed. F. Haarsma, W. Kasper, and F. X. Kaufmann (Freiburg: Herder, 1970), 44–45.

references to the sources in many footnotes. When I realized how helpful these sources were for me in better understanding the council's teaching, I resolved to bring these sources to the attention of anglophone readers. I have concentrated on providing these original sources and an English translation so readers will be in a better position to decide the import of the teaching for themselves. Scholars who have the requisite linguistic skills can decide for themselves as to the accuracy of my translations and the correctness of my interpretations, and I hope that this procedure has not been overly burdensome for the average reader. The effort to deal with the sources should help everyone in the process of coming to a better understanding of this rich, but often misunderstood, teaching.

I have tried to address the issue of the misunderstanding of the "sense of the faith" in some detail. I hope I have been successful. In general, there are two principal misunderstandings. The first confuses the "sense of the faith" with public opinion or with the result of polls regarding what Catholics or other Christians believe. Attempts to reduce the "sense of the faith" to polling results has introduced considerable confusion into understanding the meaning of the teaching.[3] However helpful polls might be in pinpointing difficulties regarding what Catholics believe on a given subject, the results still remain "superficial": they only deal with a surface understanding. Nonetheless, the collection and sifting of data among what Catholics actually believe or hold to be true is unavoidable and salutary in the process of arriving at truth.[4]

---

3. The *National Catholic Reporter* (September 6–19, 2019) carried the results of a 2019 poll conducted by the Pew Research Center that seemed to indicate a widespread lack of clarity and conviction regarding the Eucharist by Catholics. The "real presence" emerges with some regularity as a topic of polling among Catholics (2008, 2011). Such polls never achieve real clarity as to the content of eucharistic belief among Catholics. The matter is hidden deep in Catholic consciousness and the various options are expressed in terms and categories that are often ambiguous. That said, professional theologians, teachers, catechists, and parish RCIA directors should strive to find appropriate and effective ways of explaining the church's traditional belief. The tasks of clarifying religious meanings and communicating their content clearly and accurately is a never-ending task.

4. See Jerome P. Baggett, "Becoming Absence-Minded: Sociological Reflections on the Sensus Fidelium," *Catholic Theological Society of America Proceedings* 70 (2015): 1–26, and Neil Ormerod, "*Sensus Fidei* and Sociology: How Do We Find the Normative in the Empirical?" in *Learning from All the Faithful: A Contemporary Theology of the* Sensus Fidei, ed. Bradford E. Hinze and Peter C. Phan (Eugene, OR: Pickwick Publications, 2016): 89–102.

Far more important than polls is whether a consensus exists among believers regarding a doctrine and its meaning. The "sense of the faith" is directed toward grasping whether there is a consensus and then embracing it. But consensus is a complex and multilayered phenomenon. Unfortunately, theologians and the magisterium have paid too little attention to the nature and the conditions governing consensus. The Common Ground Initiative launched by the late Cardinal Joseph L. Bernardin (1928–96) was an attempt to explore consensus in the Catholic Church, but the ferocity of its opponents sadly cut short its path to success. Though the Common Ground Initiative continues as a movement, its promising beginnings have not yet yielded the hoped-for fruits. The role of consensus and the conditions for establishing it remain an underdeveloped theme, and I honestly do not see how the "sense of the faith" can find its place in the future without greater attention to this elusive dynamic. I urge younger Catholic philosophers and theologians to pursue this important yet neglected area of ecclesial life.

The second misunderstanding is, in fact, rather common and leads to widespread confusion in the church. It concerns the subjects of the universal "sense of the faith," or as it is commonly referred to, the "sense of the faithful." The difficulty here arises from the fact that in popular parlance the words "the faithful" can mean both the lay believers as distinct from the hierarchical members of the church or all believers regardless of their status, place, or calling in the church. Vatican II is, however, entirely clear that its teaching refers to *the whole church and all its members*. The "sense of the faith" is a gift of the Holy Spirit to *everyone in the church* that imparts the truth of the faith and its meaning for Christian life to *each and every member of the people of God*. Confusion arises when the words "the faithful" are mistakenly used to signify only a part of the members of the people of God—namely, the ordinary faithful. Article 12 of the Dogmatic Constitution on the Church goes out of its way to make crystal-clear who these "faithful" are: "The *universal body of the faithful* who have been anointed by the Holy One, cannot err in believing, and they give evidence of this unique property which is theirs by means of the supernatural sense of the faith of *the entire people*, when 'from the bishops to the least of the believing laity' they show *their universal consensus* on matters of faith and morals." Great care needs to be exercised grammatically in the use of the phrase the "sense of the faithful," or the increasingly common expression the "sense of the faith of the faithful," to ensure that the phrase is understood in the universal sense.[5]

The theme of infallibility has also arisen in the course of our journey through the history of the "sense of the faith." We saw how the latter term, the "sense of the faith," was based on the earlier insight into the "infallibility in belief" (*infallibilitas in credendo*) of the whole church. For authors like Thomas Netter, Antoninus of Florence, Melchior Cano, and others in the sixteenth and seventeenth centuries, the church itself was preserved from error regarding the faith and one need only inquire as to what the church believed to have assurance that what the individual accepted or understood as belonging to the contents of Christian belief was in fact true. It was only with the passing of time that, after the Council of Trent, infallibility became associated more or less exclusively with the exercise of teaching authority at the highest levels—the teachings of the councils and *ex cathedra* definitions of popes. And yet, even as the hierarchical exercise of teaching authority emerged as the expression of "the teaching church," the barely conscious memory of the broader understanding of infallibility as a quality of the entire church refused to be submerged entirely. Vestiges of it circulated at Vatican I only to reemerge at Vatican II some ninety years later. Far from being a matter that was settled once and for all by Vatican I, Vatican II's re-reception of the dogma has revealed fault lines in the teaching.

Vatican II did not repudiate Vatican I, but it definitely exposed unanswered questions that needed to be examined and clarified. Vatican II spoke of the "sense of the faith of [all] the faithful" as enjoying the guidance and protection of the Holy Spirit. Was it hinting at a certain priority of the infallibility of the church as a whole, without compromising the necessary exercise of infallibility by the pope and the bishops? But even as it pointed in this direction, Vatican II left many unanswered questions as to how the "global infallibility of the Church" and the "focused infallibility of the magisterium" interact with each other and are reflective of

---

5. The confusion caused is even greater when the "sense of the faithful" in the narrower sense of only ordinary believers in the church is combined with the "sense of the faith" as the result of polling Catholics as to what they believe. In this case, the confusion of terms is more or less total. Is there any wonder that many in the church are skeptical of the orthodoxy or the applicability of the teaching?

one reality. The post-Vatican II church has been experiencing a protracted experiment with the "co-existence" of these two "modes of infallibility" that are in search of their common goal. And so, as the church faces new and more complex problems, it is searching for a better *modus operandi* for coexisting and collaborating in the common effort of understanding the faith for our day and proclaiming it with conviction. While there have been misguided attempts to reinforce relatively recent authoritarian forms of teaching with authority, there are also hopeful signs of breaking free of these constrictive forms and adopting a new model of teaching with authority. The task is arduous but unavoidable. Infallibility is very much a live question in the church, a true *quaestio disputata*.

The nature of the "sense of the faith" as cognition has been another focus of this book. As we have seen, many thinkers have referred to it as an "intuition" of the truth, a "flair" or "sensitivity" for the truth, an "instinct" for the truth, a form of "connatural knowledge," and "sense knowledge." It should be evident that these designations for the cognitive nature of the "sense of the faith" vary considerably among themselves. An "intuition" is often assumed to be inferior to clear thinking and so is denigrated as cognition. A "flair" for the truth operates as a metaphor, not as a clear and convincing definition. And "sense knowledge" is just an initial stage en route to the real perspicacity of rigorous thought. Such perspectives are not open to an epistemology that sees knowledge in terms of "degrees of knowing." Is it possible that sense knowledge, intuition, and instinct are real forms of knowing that are open to more general or speculative forms of knowing?

Like many students of my generation, I had learned about objective knowledge in the physical sciences of course but also in philosophy. It was the ideal that we were urged to strive for. Objective knowledge is rigorous, critical, and logical thinking and it corresponds to much of what we know. From Avery Dulles, however, I learned of another form of cognition, "participatory knowledge." I know some things only by participating and sharing in their reality. I must invest myself to arrive at knowledge in this epistemological category. Participatory knowledge is founded on trust. I must trust in my mysterious power of knowing and I must trust in others as sources of truth. Self-surrender is the means to fulfill this basic human dimension of trust. Much of our personal knowledge belongs to this category, as does religious thought. To know about human and divine relationships, we must be willing to surrender ourselves to the Other, who then opens us to deeper realities otherwise inaccessible to us. Participatory knowledge has its own reasons and is a valuable way, epistemologically speaking, to discover aspects of truth and moral goodness that objective knowledge alone cannot plumb. Objective and participatory forms of knowledge are not opposed to one another but complement each other. Is it possible that the "sense of the faith" is one way to be open to dimensions of truth that are inaccessible to objective knowledge alone?

It seems to me that the field of epistemology is open to understanding knowledge in terms of a continuum of acts or stages or phases of cognition. Knowledge is multifaceted and multilayered with many linkages within its phases and stages. Logic yields one degree of knowing, abstraction with the help of metaphysical principles yields another, while connatural knowledge yields yet another. All are genuine acts of knowing, but no single epistemological act is the whole of knowing the truth. What is important is that each phase is open to completion by another. My forays in chapter 11 into the importance of experience, the role played by our questions, and the implications of language as constitutive of reality were intended to open the reader to the complementary nature of knowing and understanding. If, then, individual cognition is cumulative, moving from one phase of understanding to a more comprehensive one in a continuing series of complementary acts, then what would it look like when it is a community that is searching for understanding? How does the community of faith, the church, arrive at its grasp and understanding of revelation?

The teaching of Vatican II about the "sense of the faith of the faithful" makes sense in the context of the cumulative and complementary process I have limned. For example, the ordinary faithful discern that there are situations when a couple is morally free to use artificial means of contraception in good conscience. They bring their insight and grasp of the truth to their pastors for further reflection. Theologians and other professionals, too, add their contributions to the unfolding process of reflection. Or the pastors, bishops, and pope discern that capital punishment is morally wrong and that Catholics must oppose it. They bring their challenging insight of truth to the faithful for consideration. Theologians are invited to add their contributions to the process. In another scenario, theologians propose that the administration of the sacrament of the anointing of the sick by lay ministers in addition to the ordained clergy is permissible and propose the sacramental practice to their fellow believers, the ordinary faithful, who reflect on it and bring it to their pastors for further reflection. In each of these cases, when the church senses that it has achieved consensus on a matter, the pastors might discern that the matter warrants authoritative teaching, dogmatic definition, or inclusion in the Code of Canon Law. Each and every level of reflection in the church has its place and role to play in this complex epistemological process. The result of such communal discernment of the truth might take many years before it achieves full consensus. Along the way the ordinary faithful, theologians, and the pastors must allow time and space for the consensus to emerge and should encourage the free and honest exchange of insight into the faith and its practice.[6] This process, then, becomes the ordinary way for the exercise of the infallibility of the church.[7]

Finally, the problem of the widespread ignorance of the "sense of the faith of all the faithful" needs to be addressed and corrected. There are movements in the church that are striving to realize the vision of Vatican II, but the vast majority of Catholics do not know that the council has invited their active participation in the church's prophetic task. This is a matter of educating Catholics about the teaching and encouraging them to become actively involved. If more Catholics believed that their engagement was welcome in the church, I submit that the scandals rocking the church today would be less an occasion for leaving the church and more an incentive to all believers to tackle these problems. If more believers sensed that their engagement was welcome, more would feel free to share their questions, doubts, and positive insights with each other and with their pastors.

---

6. I agree with Ryan Marr, when he writes: "In many (most?) cases, authentic manifestations of the *sensus fidelium* can only be identified retrospectively. For now, we do our part by faithfully transmitting the tradition that has been handed down to us while at the same time discerning the signs of the times." See "John Henry Newman on Consulting the Faithful: An Idea in Need of Development," in *Learning from All the Faithful*, ed. Bradford E. Hinze and Peter C. Phan, 42–52, at 52.

7. Unfortunately, I have not been able to examine some of these issues at length and in sufficient detail in the present book. I hope to address these, and several other pressing ecclesiological concerns, in a follow-up book.

I am, of course, speaking about the "culture of communication" mentioned in chapter 9. The hierarchy fears an uncontrollable "free market of ideas," while the ordinary faithful are alienated by a sense of their unimportance and impotence. However indispensable open communication in the church is, it must be accompanied by juridically established procedures for sharing and exchanging ideas. This is a shockingly neglected area of ecclesial life today. Beyond national synods, which are always a possibility, there must be more regular, ordinary, and local opportunities of meeting and freely sharing concerns and ideas among leadership, professional staff, and the ordinary believer. The experience of communication must first be offered, tested, and perfected before moving on to more ambitious institutions for introducing needed change.

If there is to be a "culture of communication" in the church, two areas of membership must be addressed. Women in particular feel marginalized and alienated in the church. Special efforts must be made to include women in the dialogue and decision making. There are also the marginalized and the poor. Pope Francis has pointed out how these two groups are a source of wisdom and blessings in the church. The poor and the marginalized are commonly seen as those to whom the church must minister, instead of seeing them as privileged ministers of Christ who call the church to conversion and change and who have much wisdom to share. The poor and the marginalized must be invited into the "culture of communication" and given opportunities to speak to the church.

These concluding ideas and suggestions probably seem hopelessly naive and unattainable under current circumstances. I am quite aware of the resolve and hard work it will take to realize the vision of Vatican II of a church that truly lives out the "sense of the faith of all the faithful." I could expend more energy trying to develop a blueprint for such a church, but this task is better left to the people of God at large—its ordinary faithful with their varied and vast experience, its professionals with their highly honed competencies, and with the pope, the bishops, and deacons and presbyters with their authority and the pastoral wisdom of the centuries. The rest must be left to the presence of the glorified Christ in his church and to the power and enlightenment of the abiding Holy Spirit leading us and all humankind to the Father.

Appendix A

Lumen Gentium 12, 1: Latin Text and English Translations

Latin Text	John J. Burkhard, OFM Conv	Austin Flannery, OP	Norman P. Tanner, SJ
Populus Dei sanctus de munere quoque prophetico Christi participat, vivum eius testimonium maximae per vitam fidei ac caritatis diffundendo, et Deo hostiam laudis offerendo, fructum labiorum confitentium nomini eius. Universitas fidelium, qui unctionem habent a sancto, in credendo falli nequit, atque hanc suam peculiarem proprietatem	The holy people of God also shares in the prophetic office of Christ by spreading its living witness abroad especially by a life of faith and charity and by offering to God a sacrifice of praise, the fruit of lips of those who confess his name. The universal body of the faithful who have been anointed by the Holy One, cannot err in believing, and they give evidence of this unique property which is theirs by means of	The holy People of God shares also in Christ's prophetic office: it spreads abroad a living witness to him, especially by a life of faith and love and by offering to God a sacrifice of praise, the fruit of lips praising his name. The whole body of the faithful who have an anointing that comes from the holy one cannot err in matters of belief. This characteristic is shown in the supernatural appreciation of the faith of the whole people,	The holy people of God has a share, too, in the prophetic role of Christ, when it renders him a living witness, especially through a life of faith and charity, and when it offers to God a sacrifice of praise, the tribute of lips that honor his name. The universal body of the faithful who have received the anointing of the holy one, cannot be mistaken in belief. It displays this particular

mediante supernaturali sensu fidei totius populi manifestat, cum "ab episcopis usque ad extremos laicos fideles" universalem suum consensum de rebus fidei et morum exhibet. Illo enim sensu fidei, qui a Spiritu veritatis excitatur et sustentatur, populus Dei sub ductu sacri magisterii, cui fideliter obsequens, iam non verbum hominum, sed vere accipit verbum Dei, "semel traditae sanctis fidei," indefectibiliter adhaeret, recto iudicio in eam profundius penetrat eamque in vita plenius applicat.	the supernatural sense of the faith of the entire people, when "from the bishops to the least of the believing laity" they show their universal consensus on matters of faith and morals. Indeed, by this very sense of the faith which the Spirit of truth stirs up and nourishes in them, the people of God receives not merely human words but the very word of God, "the faith that was once handed over to the saints." The believing faithful do so under the leadership of the sacred teaching authority to which they trustingly defer and by adhering indefectibly to it [the word of God – J.B.]. By judging correctly, they more profoundly enter into it [the faith – J.B.] and apply it more comprehensively to life.	when, "from the bishops to the last of the faithful" they manifest a universal consent in matters of faith and morals. By this appreciation of the faith, aroused and sustained by the Spirit of truth, the People of God, guided by the sacred teaching authority, and obeying it, receives not the mere word of men, but truly the word of God, the faith once for all delivered to the saints. The People unfailingly adheres to this faith, penetrates it more deeply with right judgment, and applies it more fully in daily life.	quality through a supernatural sense of the faith in the whole people when "from the bishops to the last of the faithful laity," it expresses the consent of all in matters of faith and morals. Through this sense of faith which is aroused and sustained by the Spirit of truth, the people of God, under the guidance of the sacred magisterium to which it is faithfully obedient, receives no longer the words of human beings but truly the word of God; it adheres indefectibly to "the faith which was once for all delivered to the saints"; it penetrates more deeply into that same faith through right judgment and applies it more fully to life.

Lumen Gentium 35, 1 and 4: Latin Text and English Translations

Latin Text	John J. Burkhard, OFM Conv	Austin Flannery, OP	Norman P. Tanner, SJ
35,1	35,1	35,1	35,1
Christus, propheta magnus, qui et testimonio vitae et verbi virtute regnum proclamavit Patris, usque ad plenam manifestationem gloriae suum munus propheticum adimplet, non solum per hierarchiam, quae nomine et postestate eius docet, set etiam per laicos, quos ideo et testes constituit et sensu fidei et gratia verbi instruit (cf. Ac	Christ is the great prophet who proclaimed the reign of the Father by the witness of his life and by the power of his word, and he continues to accomplish his prophetic office until the full revelation of his glory. He does this not only through the hierarchy who teach with authority in his name but also through the lay faithful whom he has appointed his witnesses and	Christ is the great prophet who proclaimed the kingdom of the Father both by the testimony of his life and by the power of his word. Until the full manifestation of his glory, he fulfils this prophetic office, not only through the hierarchy who teach in his name and by his power, but also through the laity. He accordingly both establishes them as witnesses and provides them with an appreciation of the faith (*sensus*	Christ, the great prophet, who by the witness of his life and the power of his word, proclaimed the Father's kingdom, continues to carry out his prophetic task, until the full manifestation of his glory, not only through the hierarchy who teach in his name and by his power, but also through the laity whom he constitutes his witnesses and equips with an understanding

2:17-18; Ap 19:10), ut virtus evangelii in vita quotidiana, familiari et sociali eluceat. Ipsi se praebent ut filios repromissionis, si fortes in fide et spe praesens momentum redimunt (cf. Eph 5:16; Col 4:5) et futuram gloriam per patientiam exspectant (c. Rm 8:25). Hanc autem spem non in animi interioritate abscondant, sed conversione continua et colluctatione "adversus mundi rectores tenebrarum harum, contra spiritualia nequitiae" (Eph 6:12) etiam per vitae saecularis structuras exprimant.	whom he has equipped with the "sense of the faith" and the gift of his word (see Acts 2:17-18; Rev. 19:10). Through the lay faithful he demonstrates the power of the gospel in the daily life of family and society. The lay faithful show themselves to be sons and daughters of the promise when they are strong in faith and hope and when they redeem the present moment (see Eph. 5:16; Col. 4:5) and so patiently await the economy of future glory (see Rom. 8:25). They should not bury this hope in the depths of their souls but as men and women who are constantly being converted and waging war "against the rulers of the world's darkness and the spirits of iniquity" (Eph. 6:12) show forth their hope in the humanly constructed systems of secular life.	*fidei*) and the grace of the word (see Acts 2:17-18; Apoc 19:10) so that the power of the Gospel may shine out in daily family and social life. They show themselves to be children of the promise if, strong in faith and hope, they make the most of the present time (Eph 5:16; Col 4:5), and with patience await the future glory (see Rom 8:25). Let them not hide this hope then in the depths of their hearts, but rather express it through the structure of their secular lives in continual conversion and in wrestling "against the world rulers of this darkness, against the spiritual forces of iniquity" (Eph 6:12).	of the faith and a grace of speech (see Ac 2:17-18; Ap 19:10) precisely so that the power of the gospel may shine forth in the daily life of family and society. The laity show that they are children of the promise, if strong in faith and hope they make full use of the present moment (see Eph 5:16; Col 4:5) and await with patience the glory that is to come (see Rm 8:25). This hope, however is not to be hidden in the depths of their hearts. It has also to be expressed through the structures of secular life, through their continual conversion and their struggle "against the world rulers of the present darkness, against the spiritual hosts of wickedness" (Eph 6:12).

35,4	35,4	35,4	35,4
Proinde, laici, etiam quando curis temporalibus occupantur, pretiosam actionem ad evangelizandum mundum exercere possunt et debent. Quodsi quidam eorum, deficientibus sacris ministris, vel iisdem in regimine persecutionis impeditis, quaedam officia sacra pro facultate supplent; et si plures quidem ex eis totas vires suas in opere apostolico impendunt: universos tamen oportet ad dilatationem et incrementum regni Christi in mundi cooperari. Quapropter laici solerter in profundiorem cognitionem veritatis revelatae incumbant, et instanter a Deo sapientiae donum impetrent.	Even when they are occupied in temporal affairs the lay faithful still can and must engage in the valuable task of evangelizing the world. But if the situation should arise that there are not enough ordained ministers [to meet the needs of the faithful], or that in times of persecuion [of the church] by the State, the lay faithful may provide certain sacred actions and they receive the appropriate authorization to perform these actions. Indeed, while many of the lay faithful expend all their energy in apostolic work, it is incumbent on all to cooperate in the expansion and the growth of the reign of Christ in the world. That is why the lay faithful are encouraged to dedicate themselves assiduously to growing in their	Therefore, when occupied with temporal affairs, the laity can and must be involved in the precious work of evangelizing the world. When there is a shortage of sacred ministers or when government persecution prevents their functioning, some lay people make up for this by performing some sacred functions to the best of their ability; others, more numerous, are engaged full time in apostolic work. Nevertheless, it is the duty of all lay people to cooperate in spreading and building up the kingdom of Christ. The laity, consequently, have the duty to work hard to acquire a deeper knowledge of revealed truth and earnestly pray to God for the gift of wisdom.	Therefore, even when occupied with temporal cares, the laity can and must perform the valuable task of evangelising the world. Some lay people, when there is a shortage of sacred ministers or when these are impeded by a persecuting government, supply some of the sacred offices in so far as they can; a greater number are engaged totally in apostolic work. It is, however, the duty of all to work together for the extension and growth of the kingdom of Christ on earth. Consequently the laity have a duty to try diligently to deepen their knowledge of revealed truth and earnestly pray to God for the gift of wisdom.

	knowledge of revealed truth and to insistently entreat God to bestow on them the gift of wisdom.		

A Chronological Bibliography of the "Sense of the Faith" from 1940 to 2020

1939–1940

Laros, Matthias. "Laie und Lehramt in der Kirche." *Hochland* 37:45–54.

1943

Koster, Mannes D. "Theologie, Theologien und Glaubenssinn." *Theologie und Seelsorge* 35:82–90.

1948

Koster, Mannes D. *Die Firmung im Glaubenssinn der Kirche*. Münster: Verlag Regensberg.

_____. "Die Opportunität der feierlichen Definition der Himmelfahrt Mariens." *Neue Orientierung* 2:60–85. Reprinted in *Volk Gottes im Wachstum des Glaubens*, 11–57. See below for 1950.

1949

Koster, Mannes D. "Der Glaubenssinn der Hirten und Gläubigen." *Neue Orientierung* 3:265–98. Reprinted in *Volk Gottes im Wachstum des Glaubens*, 59–92. See below for 1950. Also reprinted in *Volk Gottes im Werden: Gesammelte Studien*, eds. H.-D. Langer and O. H. Pesch. Wahlberger Studien der Albertus-Magnus-Akademie, 7. Mainz: Matthias-Grünewald, 1971, 131–50.

1950

Koster, Mannes D. *Volk Gottes im Wachstum des Glaubens. Himmelfahrt Mariens und Glaubenssinn*. Heidelberg: F. H. Kerle.

1951

Congar, Yves. "Le peuple fidèle et la fonction prophétique de l'Église." *Irénikon* 24:289–312 and 440–66.

1952

Beumer, Johannes. "Glaubenssinn der Kirche?" *Trierer theologische Zeitschrift* 61:129–142.

Philips, Gérard. "De leek tegenover het leergezag." *De leek in de kerk.* Leuven: Davidsfonds, 148–68.

1953

Congar, Yves. "les laïcs et la fonction prophétique de l'Église" and "Excursus: Le *sensus fidelium* chez les Pères." *Jalons pour une théologie du laïcat.* Unam Sanctam 23. Paris: Cerf, 367–449 and 450–53.

1954

Dillenschneider, Clément. *Le sens de la foi et le progrès dogmatique du mystère marial.* Rome: Academia Mariana Internationalis.

Philips, Gérard. "Le laïcat devant le magistère." *Le rôle du laïcat dans l'Église.* Tournai: Casterman, 97–113.

1955

Beumer, Johannes. "Glaubenssinn der Kirche als Quelle einer Definition." *Theologie und Glaube* 45:250–60.

1956

Peinador, Máximo. "El 'sensus fidei' y el progreso dogmático en el misterio marial." *Ephemerides Mariologicae* 6:463–73.

Philips, Gérard. "The Laity and the Magisterium." *The Role of the Laity in the Church.* Trans. John R. Gilbert and James W. Moudry. Chicago: Fides, 70–82.

1957

Congar, Yves. "The Laity and the Church's Prophetical Function." *Lay People in the Church: A Study for a Theology of Laity.* Trans. Donald Attwater. London: Geoffrey Chapman, 258–308. 2nd ed., Westminster, MD: The Newman Press, 271–323.

1958

Loncke, J. "*Sensus Ecclesiae* en Marilogie." *Standard van Maria* 34:57–73.

1960

García Extremeño, Claudio. "El *sentido de la fe*, criterio de la tradición." *La Ciencia Tomista* 87:569–605.

Schmaus, Michael. *Katholische Dogmatik*, vol. 1. 6th ed.; Munich: Max Hueber. 154–57 ["Der Träger der Überlieferung"].

Seckler, Max. "Glaubenssinn." In *Lexikon für Theologie und Kirche*, vol. 4. Ed. Josef Höfer and Karl Rahner. 2nd ed.; Freiburg: Herder, cols. 945–48.

1961

Camelot, Pierre-Thomas. "Le sens de l'Église chez les Pères Latins." *Nouvelle revue théologique* 83:367–81.

Coulson, John. "Introduction." John Henry Newman, *On Consulting the Faithful in Matters of Doctrine.* New York: Sheed & Ward, 1–49.

1962

Thils, Gustave. "L'infaillibilité de l'Église 'in credendo' et 'in docendo.'" *Salesianum* 24:298–336.

1963

Bartolomei, Tommaso M. "L'influsso del 'Senso della Fede' nell'esplicitazione del dogma dell' Immaculta Concepzione della B. Vergine degna Madre di Dio." *Marianum* 25:297–346.

———. "Natura, realtà, genesi e valore del 'Sensus fidei' nell'esplicitazione delle virtualità dei dommi." *Asprenas: Rivista di teologia* 10:269–94.

Congar, Yves. *La Tadition et les traditions: Essai théologique.* Paris: Fayard, 81–101 ["*L'Ecclesia*, sujet de la Tradition"] and 101–8 ["Le Saint-Esprit, sujet transcendant de la Tradition. Son actualité dans l'Église-Corps du Christ"].

Ratzinger, Joseph. "Sentire ecclesiam." *Geist und Leben* 36:321–26.

Thils, Gustave. "L'infaillibilité de l'Église dans la Constitution 'Pastor Aeternus' du Ier Concile du Vatican." In *L'infaillibilité de l'Église. Journées oecuméniques de Chevetogne, 25–29 Septembre 1961.* Chevetogne, 147–82.

1964

Bartolomei, Tommaso M. "L'influsso del 'senso della fede' nell'esplicitazione del domma dell' Assunzione corporale di Maria." *Ephemerides Mariologicae* 14:5–38.

1965

Hammans, Herbert. "Der Glaubenssinn." *Die neueren katholischen Erklärungen der Dogmenentwicklung.* Essen: Ludgerus-Verlag Hubert Wingen, 242–62.

Löhrer, Magnus. *Mysterium Salutis. Grundriss heilsgeschichtlicher Dogmatik.* 5 vols. Ed. J. Feiner and M. Löhrer. Einsiedeln: Benziger, 1:545–47 ["Die Funktion der Kirche als ganzer"] and 547–55 ["Das christliche Volk und die Offenbarungsvermittlung"].

1966

Congar, Yves. *Tradition and Traditions: An Historical and a Theological Essay.* Trans. Michael Naseby and Thomas Rainborough. New York: Macmillan, 314–38 ["The 'Ecclesia' as the Subject of Tradition"] and 338–46 ["The Holy

Spirit, the Transcendent Subject of Tradition. His Active Presence in the Church the Body of Christ"].

Geiselmann, Josef Rupert. *The Meaning of Tradition.* Quaestiones Disputatae 15. Trans. W. J. O'Hara. New York: Herder and Herder, 19–23 ["Interior tradition. The *sensus fidelium*"].

1967

Femiano, Samuel D. *Infallibility of the Laity: The Legacy of Newman.* New York: Herder and Herder.

Grillmeier, Aloys. *Commentary on the Documents of Vatican II,* 5 vols., ed. Herbert Vorgrimler. New York: Herder and Herder, 1:164–65 [Commentary on LG 12].

Philips, Gérard. *L'Église et son mystère au IIe Concile du Vatican. Histoire, texte et commentaire de la Constitution* Lumen Gentium. 2 vols. Paris: Desclée, 1:167–74 ["Le sens de la foi dans le peuple fidèle"].

1968

Glaser, John. "Authority, Connatural Knowledge, and the Spontaneous Judgment of the Faithful." *Theological Studies* 29:742–51.

Read, Denis William. *Sensus fidei: Practical Faith-Knowledge in Moral Theology. A Study of Moral Theological Methodology in the Writings of John Henry Cardinal Newman.* Rome: Academia Alfonsiana.

1969

Oehler, Klaus. "Der Consensus Omnium als Kriterium der Wahrheit in der antiken Philosophie und der Patristik." *Antike und Abendland* 10:103–29.

Philips, Gérard. "The Sense of Faith and the Cult of Mary." *The Marian Era* 9:8–10, 55–62.

1970

Morales, J. "Nota historico-doctrinal sobre las relaciones entre magisterio eclesiástico, oficio teológico y sentido popular de la fe." *Scripta Theologica* 2:481–99.

1971

Beinert, Wolfgang. "Bedeutung und Begründung des Glaubenssinnes (Sensus fidei) als eines dogmatischen Erkenntniskriteriums." *Catholica* 25:271–303.

Gill, James. "The Representation of the *universitas fidelium* in the Councils of the Conciliar Period." *Studies in Church History* 7:177–95.

Koster, Mannes D. "Der Glaubenssinn der Hirten und Gläubigen." Reprinted in *Volk Gottes im Werden: Gesammelte Studien.* Ed. H.-D. Langer and O. H.

Pesch. Wahlberger Studien der Albertus-Magnus-Akademie, 7. Mainz: Matthias-Grünewald, 131–50.

1973

Penaskovic, Richard. *Open to the Spirit: The Notion of the Laity in the Writings of J.H. Newman.* Ph.D. dissertation, Ludwig-Maximilians-Universität Munich, 187–98.

Thompson, William M. "*Sensus Fidelium* and Infallibility." *The American Ecclesiastical Review* 167:450–86.

1974

Fernekess, Peter. *Der Glaubenssinn der Gläubigen in der Traditionslehre bei M. J. Scheeben.* Landau i. d. Pfalz.

1975

Hitchcock, James. "Thomas More and the *Sensus fidelium.*" *Theological Studies* 36:145–54.

Seybold, Michael. "Kirchliches Lehramt und allgemeiner Glaubenssinn. Ein Reformatorisches Anliegen aus der Sicht des I. und II. Vatikanischen Konzils." *Theologie und Glaube* 65: 266–77.

Tillard, J. M. R. "À propos du 'sensus fidelium.'" *Proche-Orient chrétien* 25:113–34.

———. "*Sensus Fidelium.*" *One in Christ* 11:2–29.

1976

D'Aragon, Jean-Louis. "Le '*sensus fidelium*' et ses fondements néotestamentaires." In *Foi populaire, foi savante.* Cogitatio Fidei 87. Paris: Cerf, 41–48.

Dumont, Fernand. "Remarques critiques pour une théologie de 'consensus fidelium.'" In *Foi populaire, foi savante.* Cogitatio fidei 87. Paris: Cerf, 49–60.

Fairweather, Eugene R. "Le '*sensus fidelium*': un point de vue anglican." In *Foi populaire, foi savante.* Cogitatio Fidei 87. Paris: Cerf, 61–66.

Lamirande, Emilien. "La théologie du 'sensus fidelium' et la collaboration de l'historien." In *Foi populaire, foi savante.* Cogitatio fidei 87. Paris: Cerf, 67–72.

Tillard, J. M. R. "Le '*sensus fidelium*'. Réflexion théologique." In *Foi populaire, foi savante.* Cogitatio fidei 87. Paris: Cerf, 9–40.

1977

Fic, Leonard. "'*Sensus fidei*' jako kryterium wiary według M. D. Kostera." *Studia Theologica Varsoviensia* 15/1:77–94.

Foley, Edward. "Passing the Torch: Full, Prophetic and Ecclesial Participation." *Worship* 86:386–402, at 394–400.

1978

Eno, Robert B. "Consensus and Doctrine: Three Ancient Views." *Église et Théologie* 9:473–83.

1979

Rahner, Karl. "Einleitende Überlegungen zum Verhältnis von Theologie und Volksreligion." In *Volksreligion—Religion des Volkes*. Ed. Karl Rahner, Christian Modehn, and Michael Göpfert. Stuttgart: Kohlhammer, 9-16. Reprinted as "Zum Verhältnis von Theologie und Volksreligion." *Schriften zur Theologie*. 16 vols. Einsiedeln: Benziger, 1984, 16:185–95. English translation [E.T.] "The Relation between Theology and Popular Religion." *Theological Investigations*. 23 vols. Trans. Joseph Donceel. New York: Crossroad, 1991, 22:140–47.

Sancho Bielsa, Jesús. *Infalibilidad del Pueblo de Dios. 'Sensus fidei' e infalibilidad orgánica de la Iglesia en la Constitución 'Lumen Gentium' del Concilio Vaticano II*. Pamplona: Ediciones de Universidad de Navarra, S.A.

Wagner, Harald. "Glaubenssinn, Glaubenszustimmung und Glaubenskonsens." *Theologie und Glaube* 69:263–71.

1980

Emilianus, Metropolitan. "Consensus in the Formulation of Doctrine." *The Greek Orthodox Theological Review* 25:21–36.

Fernández de Trocóniz y Sasigain, Luis María. "Recurso al 'sensus fidei' en la teología católica de 1950 a 1960." *Scriptorium Victoriense* 27:142–83 (Part 1).

Granfield, Patrick. "The Sensus Fidelium in Episcopal Selection." In *Electing Our Own Bishops*. Concilium 137. Ed. Peter Huizing and Knut Walf. New York: Seabury, 33–38.

1981

Biser, Eugen. "Der Glaubenssinn. Ein begriffskritischer Rettungsversuch." *Stimmen der Zeit* 199:678–84.

Fernández de Trocóniz y Sasigain, Luis María. "Recurso al 'sensus fidei' en la teología católica de 1950 a 1960." *Scriptorium Victoriense* 28:39–75 (Part 2).

Moltmann, Jürgen, and Hans Küng, eds. *Who Has the Say in the Church?* Concilium 148. New York: Seabury.

Sancho Bielsa, Jesús. "Santo Tomás y el *'sensus fidei'* del Concilio Vaticano II." In *Prospettive teologiche moderne. Atti dell' VIII Congresso Tomistico Internazionale*, vol. 4. Vatican City: Libreria Editrice Vaticana, 381–89

Sartori, Luigi. "What Is the Criterion for the Sensus Fidelium?" In *Who Has the Say in the Church?* Concilium 148. Ed. Jürgen Moltmann and Hans Küng. New York: Seabury, 56–60.

Weis, Norbert. *Das prophetische Amt der Laien in der Kirche. Eine rechtstheologische Untersuchung anhand dreier Dokumente des Zweiten Vatikanischen Konzils.* Rome: Università Gregoriana Editrice.

1982

Ardusso, F. "Il 'senso della fede' e il 'consenso dei credenti.'" *Credere oggi* 2, no. 2:15–26.

Brauchart, Peter. *Die Lehre vom 'Glaubenssin' (Sensus fidei) in ihrer Bedeutung für die gegenwärtige Ekklesiologie.* Graz: dbv-Verlag.

Fernández de Trocóniz y Sasigain, Luis María. "La teologia sobre el 'sensus fidei' de 1960 a 1970." *Scriptorium Victoriense* 29:133–79.

O'Leary, Paul. "Authority to Proclaim the Word of God and the Consent of the Church." *Freiburger Zeitschrift für Philosophie und Theologie* 29:239–51.

Swidler, Leonard. "*Demo-Kratia,* The Rule of the People of God, or *Consensus Fidelium.*" In *Authority in the Church and the Schillebeeckx Case.* Eds. Leonard Swidler and Piet F. Fransen. New York: Crossroad, 226–43.

Tillard, J. M. R. "Théologie et vie ecclésiale." In *Initiation à la pratique de la théologie,* 5 vols. Eds. Bernard Lauret and François Refoulé. Paris: Cerf, 1:161–82.

1984

Fernández de Trocóniz y Sasigain, Luis María. "La teologia sobre el 'sensus fidei' de 1960 a 1970." *Scriptorium Victoriense* 31:5–55.

Rahner, Karl. "Offizielle Glaubenslehre der Kirche und faktische Gläubigkeit des Volkes." In *Theologie in Freiheit und Verantwortung.* Ed. Karl Rahner and Heinrich Fries. Munich: Kösel. Reprinted in *Schriften zur Theologie.* 16 vols. Einsiedeln: Benziger, 16:217–30. E.T. "What the Church Officially Teaches and What the People Actually Believe." *Theological Investigations.* 23 vols. Trans. Joseph Donceel. New York: Crossroad, 1991, 22:165–75.

1985

Duquoc, Christian. "An Active Role for the People of God in Defining the Church's Faith." In *The Teaching Authority of Believers.* Eds. J. B. Metz and E. Schillebeeckx, 73–81.

Fiorenza, Elisabeth Schüssler. "Claiming Our Authority and Power." In *The Teaching Authority of Believers.* Eds. J. B. Metz and E. Schillebeeckx, 45–53.

Fries, Heinrich. "Is There a *Magisterium* of the Faithful?" In *The Teaching Authority of Believers.* Eds. J. B. Metz and E. Schillebeeckx, 82–91.

Metz, Johann Baptist, and Edward Schillebeeckx, eds. *The Teaching Authority of Believers* Concilium 180. Edinburgh: T.&T. Clark.

Schillebeeckx, Edward. "The Teaching Authority of All—A Reflection about the Structure of the New Testament." In *The Teaching Authority of Believers*. Eds. J. B. Metz and E. Schillebeeckx, 12–22.

Sobrino, Jon. "The 'Doctrinal Authority' of the People of God in Latin America." In *The Teaching Authority of Believers*. Eds. J. B. Metz and E. Schillebeeckx, 54–62.

Vorgrimler, Herbert. "From *Sensus Fidei* to *Consensus Fidelium*." In *The Teaching Authority of Believers*. Eds. J. B. Metz and E. Schillebeeckx, 3–11.

Waldenfels, Hans. "Authority and Knowledge." In *The Teaching Authority of Believers*. Eds. J. B. Metz and E. Schillebbeckx, 31–42.

———. *Kontextuelle Fundamentaltheologie*. Paderborn: Schöningh, 469–72 ["Zur Autorität des Gottesvolkes"].

Walgrave, Jan. "Newman's 'On Consulting the Faithful in Matters of Doctrine.'" In *The Teaching Authority of Believers*. Eds. J. B. Metz and E. Schillebeeckx, 23–30.

1986

Bertolino, Rinaldo. "Sensus fidei et coutume dans le droit de l'Église." *Freiburger Zeitschrift für Philosophie und Theologie* 33:227–43.

Dulles, Avery. "Sensus Fidelium." *America* 155:240–42, 263.

Frank, Karl Suso. "Bischöfe und Laien in der Glaubensüberlieferung." *Diakonia: Internationale Zeitschrift für die Praxis der Kirche* 17:149–56.

1987

Camilleri, René. *The 'Sensus fidei' of the Whole Church and the Magisterium: From the Time of Vatican I to Vatican Council II*. Rome: Gregorian University Press.

Frank, Karl Suso. "Bishops and Laity in the Faith Tradition." *Theology Digest* 34:37–41.

Granfield, Patrick. *The Limits of the Papacy: Authority and Autonomy in the Church*. New York: Crossroad, 134–47 ["The Sense of the Faithful"].

Miller, Edward Jeremy. *John Henry Newman on the Idea of Church*. Shepherdstown, WV: Patmos, 69–75 ["*Sensus Fidelium*: The Witness to Revelation"] and 116–21 ["Ecclesial Reception: *Securus Judicat Orbis Terrarum*"].

O'Collins, Gerald. "Note a proposito della consultazione dei fedeli." *La Civiltà Cattolica* 138/4:40–45.

Sancho Bielsa, Jesús. "El *sensus fidei* en los laicos." In *La misión del laico en la Iglesia y en el mundo. VIII Simposio Internacional de Teología de la Universidad de Navarra*. Eds. Augusto Sarmiento, Tomás Rincon, José María Yanguas, and Antonio Quiros. Pamplona: Ediciones Universidad de Navarra, 545–51.

Sartori, Luigi. "Il 'sensus fidelium' del popolo di Dio e il concorso dei laici nelle determinazione dottrinali." *Studi Ecumenici* 6:33–57.

Scheffczyk, Leo. "Sensus fidelium—Zeugnis in Kraft der Gemeinschaft." *Internationale katholische Zeitschrift: Communio* 16:420–33.

Tillard, J. M. R. *Église d'églises. L'ecclésiologie de communion.* Cogitatio fidei 143. Paris: Cerf, 143–54.

1988

Alszeghy, Zoltán. "The *Sensus Fidei* and the Development of Dogma." In *Vatican II: Assessment and Perspectives Twenty-Five Years After (1962–1987)*, 3 vols. Ed. René Latourelle. New York: Paulist Press, 1:138–56.

Dobbin, Edmund J. "*Sensus fidelium* as a Source for Theology." *Catholic Theological Society of America Proceedings* 43:112–15.

Fernández de Trocóniz y Sasigain, Luis María. "La teologia sobre el 'sensus fidei' de 1960 a 1970." *Scriptorium Victoriense* 35:33–58.

Fries, Heinrich. "Sensus fidelium. Der Theologe zwischen dem Lehramt der Hierarchie und dem Lehramt der Gläubigen." In *Theologe und Hierarch.* Ed. J. Pfammater and E. Christen. Theologische Berichte 17. Einsiedeln: Benziger, 55–77.

Kerkofs, Jan. "Le Peuple de Dieu est-il infaillible? L'importance du *sensus fidelium* dans l'Église postconciliaire." *Freiburger Zeitschrift für Philosophie und Theologie* 35:3–19.

Mucci, Giandomenico. "L'infallibilità della Chiesa, magistero e autorità dottrinale dei fedeli." *La Civiltà Cattolica* 139/1:431–42.

Scheffczyk, Leo. "*Sensus fidelium*—Witness on the Part of the Community." *Communio* 15:182–98.

Tillard, J. M. R. "Autorité et mémoire dans l'Église." *Irénikon* 61:336–46 and 481–84.

1989

Beinert, Wolfgang. "Das Finden und Verkünden der Wahrheit in der Gemeinschaft der Kirche." *Catholica* 43:1–30.

Dobbin, Edmund J. "Sensus Fidelium Reconsidered." *New Theology Review* 2/3:48–64.

Lindbeck, George A. "Scripture, Consensus, and Community." In *Biblical Interpretation in Crisis: The Ratzinger Conference on Bible and Church.* Ed. Richard John Neuhaus. Grand Rapids, MI: Wm. B. Eerdmans, 74–101.

1990

Costigan, Richard F. "The Consensus of the Church: Differing Classical Views." *Theological Studies* 51:25–48.

McGinniss, Michael J. "*Sensus Fidelium*, USA: Laity and Church Structures for the Future." *Listening* no. 25, 71–85.

1991

Beinert, Wolfgang. S.v. "Glaubenssinn der Gläubigen." In *Lexikon der katholischen Dogmatik*. Ed. W. Beinert. 2nd ed.; Freiburg: Herder, 200–201.

Hartin, Patrick J. "*Sensus fidelium*: A Roman Catholic Reflection on Its Significance for Ecumenical Thought." *Journal of Ecumenical Studies* 28:74–87.

Merrigan, Terrence. *Clear Heads and Holy Hearts: The Religious and Theological Ideal of John Henry Newman*. Louvain: Peeters, 229–36 ["The Mind of the Church"], 236–40 ["The Unity Founding the Mind of the Church"], and 240–42 ["Rationality and the Mind of the Church: Theology and the Sense of the Faithful"].

1992

Biemer, Günter. "Die Gläubigen in Dingen der Lehre befragen? John Henry Newmans Auffassung von der Bedeutung der Laien für die Glaubensüberlieferung." *Münchener theologische Zeitschrift* 43:437–48.

Burkhard, John J. "*Sensus fidei*: Meaning, Role and Future of a Teaching of Vatican II." *Louvain Studies* 17:18–34.

Crowley, Paul G. "Catholicity, Inculturation and Newman's *sensus fidelium*." *The Heythrop Journal* 33:161–74.

———. "The *Sensus Fidelium* and Catholicity: Newman's Legacy in the Age of Inculturation." In *John Henry Newman: Theology and Reform*. Eds. Michael E. Allsopp and Ronald R. Burke. New York: Garland, 109–29.

Heft, James L. "'Sensus Fidelium' and the Marian Dogmas." In *Mater fidei et fidelium: Collected Essays to Honor Théodore Koehler on His 80th Birthday*. Marian Library Studies, vol. 17–23. Dayton, OH: University of Dayton, 767–86. Reprinted in *One in Christ* 28:106–25.

Nichols, Aidan. "The Sense of the Faithful." *The Shape of Catholic Theology*. Collegeville, MN: Liturgical Press, 221–31.

Scharr, Peter. *Consensus fidelium. Zur Unfehlbarkeit der Kirche aus der Perspektive einer Konsenstheorie der Wahrheit*. Würzburg: Echter.

Sesboüé, Bernard. "Le 'sensus fidelium' en morale à la lumière de Vatican II." *Le Supplément* 181:153–66. Reprinted as "Le *sensus fidelium* en morale. Un exemple: le prêt à l'intérêt" in idem, *Le magistère à l'épreuve: Autorité, vérité et liberté dans l'Église*. Paris: Desclée de Brouwer, 2001, 95–108.

Tillard, J. M. R. *Church of Churches: The Ecclesiology of Communion*. Trans. R. C. De Peaux. Collegeville, MN: Liturgical Press, 108–18.

1993

Beinert, Wolfgang. "Der Glaubenssinn der Gläubigen in der systematischen Theologie." In *Mitsprache im Glauben? Vom Glaubenssinn der Gläubigen* Ed. Günter Koch, 51–78.

———. "Die Beziehungen zwischen kirchlichen Lehramt, wissenschaftlichen Theologie und dem Glaubenssinn der Gläubigen." *Anzeiger für die Seelsorge* Heft 1:3–8.

Fernández de Trocóniz y Sasigain, Luis María. "El 'sensus fidei' según Sto. Tomás de Aquino." *Scriptorium Victoriense* 40:195–208.

Fisichella, Rino. "Il teologo e il 'sensus fidei.'" In CDF, *"Donum veritatis." Istruzione e commenti (24 maggio 1990)*. Vatican City: Libreria Editrice Vaticana, 97–103.

Heft, James L. "'Sensus Fidelium' and the Marian Dogmas." *One in Christ* 28:106–25.

Kirchschläger, Walter. "Was das Neue Testament über den Glaubenssinn der Gläubigen sagt." In *Mitsprache im Glauben? Vom Glaubenssinn der Gläubigen*. Ed. Günter Koch, 7–24.

Koch, Günter, ed. *Mitsprache im Glauben? Vom Glaubenssinn der Gläubigen*. Würzburg: Echter.

———. "Glaubenssinn—Wahrheitsfindung im Miteinander. Theologische Grundlagen—pastorale Konsequenzen." In *Mitsprache im Glauben? Vom Glaubenssinn der Gläubigen*. Ed. G. Koch, 99–114.

Martin, Stefania. "Sul concetto teologico-canonistico di sensus fidei." In *Studi sul primo libro del Codex Iuris Canonici*. Ed. Sandro Gherro. Padua: CEDAM, 137–61.

Miller, Edward Jeremy. "Newman's *Sensus Fidelium* and Papal Fundamentalism." In *The Struggle Over the Past: Fundamentalism in the Modern World*. Ed. William M. Shea. Annual Publication of the College Theology Society 35. Lanham, MD: University Press of America, 289–304.

Riedel-Spangenberger, Ilona. "Der Verkündigungsdienst (*munus docendi*) der Kirche und der Glaubenssinn des Volkes Gottes." In *Wege der Evangelisierung. Heinz Feilzer zum 65. Geburtstag*. Ed. Andreas Heinz, Wolfgang Lentzen-Deis, and Ernst Schneck. Trier: Paulinus, 193–206.

Slusser, Michael. "Does Newman's 'On Consulting the Faithful in Matters of Doctrine' Rest Upon a Mistake?" *Horizons* 20:234–40.

Steinruck, Josef. "Was die Gläubigen in der Geschichte der Kirche zu vermelden hatten." In *Mitsprache im Glauben? Vom Glaubenssinn der Gläubigen*. Ed. Günter Koch, 25–50.

Vitali, Dario. *Sensus fidelium: Una funzione ecclesiale di intelligenza della fede*. Brescia: Morcelliana.

Wiederkehr, Dietrich. "Glaubenssinn des Gottesvolkes: Einbahnstrasse oder Gegenverkehr?" In *Mitsprache im Glauben? Vom Glaubenssinn der Gläubigen*. Ed. Günter Koch, 79–98.

1994

Baumer, Iso. "Glaubenssinn—Kirchensinn: Konkrete Annäherungen. Träger. Muster und Bedeutungen in kollektiven religiösen Äusserungen." In *Der Glaubenssinn des Gottesvolkes—Konkurrent oder Partner des Lehramts?* Ed. Dietirch Wiederkehr, 21–65.

Beinert, Wolfgang. "Der Glaubenssinn der Gläubigen in Theologie- und Dogmengeschichte. Ein Überblick." In *Der Glaubenssinn des Gottesvolkes— Konkurrent oder Partner des Lehramts?* Ed. Dietrich.Wiederkehr, 66–131.

Bertolino, Rinaldo. "*Sensus fidei*, Charismen und Recht im Volk Gottes." *Archiv für katholisches Kirchenrecht* 163:28–73.

Böckenförde, Werner. "Statement aus der Sicht eines Kirchenrechtlers." In *Der Glaubenssinn des Gottesvolkes—Konkurrent oder Partner des Lehramts?* Ed. Dietrich Wiederkehr, 207–13.

Kaufmann, Franz-Xaver. "Glaube und Kommunikation: eine soziologische Perspektive." In *Der Glaubenssinn des Gottesvolkes— Konkurrent oder Partner des Lehramts?* Ed. Dietrich Wiederkehr, 132–60.

Pemsel-Maier, Sabine. "Differenzierte Subjektwerdung im Volke Gottes." In *Der Glaubenssinn des Gottesvolkes—Konkurrent oder Partner des Lehramts?* Ed. Dietrich Wiederkehr, 161–81.

Wiederkehr, Dietrich, ed. *Der Glaubenssinn des Gottesvolkes—Konkurrent oder Partner des Lehramtes?* Quaestiones Disputatae 151. Freiburg: Herder.

———. "Vorwort: 'Glaubenssinn des Gottesvolkes': Aufarbeitung von Realitätsdefiziten." In *Der Glaubenssinn des Gottesvolkes—Konkurrent oder Partner des Lehramtes?* Ed. Dietrich Wiederkehr, 9–19.

———. "Sensus vor consensus: auf dem Weg zu einem partizipativen Glauben— Reflexionen einer Wahrheitspolitik." In *Der Glaubenssinn des Gottesvolkes— Konkurrent oder Partner des Lehramtes?* Ed. Dietrich Wiederkehr, 182–206.

1995

Beinert, Wolfgang. Art. "Sensus Fidelium." In *Handbook of Catholic Theology.* Eds. Wolfgang Beinert and Francis Schüssler Fiorenza. New York: Crossroad, 655–57.

———. "Der Glaubenssinn der Gläubigen." In *Glaubenszugänge. Lehrbuch der katholischen Dogmatik,* 3 vols. Ed. Wolfgang Beinert. Paderborn: F. Schöningh, 1:167–82.

Bertolino, Rinaldo. "'*Sensus fidei,*' carismi e diritto nel popolo di Dio." *Ius Ecclesiae* 7:155–98.

Bourgeois, Henri. "Les chrétiens et le sens de la foi." *Études* 382:669–79.

Fic, Leonard. *Il "sensus fidei" nel pensiero di M. D. Koster e nel Vaticano II.* Włocławek: Włocławskie Wydawnictwo Diecezjalne.

Haight, Roger. S.v. *"Sensus fidelium."* In *The HarperCollins Encyclopedia of Catholicism.* Ed. Richard P. McBrien. San Francisco: HarperSanFrancisco, 1182–83.

Hattrup, Dieter. "Amt und Volk in der Kirche. Zum Sinn des Sensus Fidei." *Theologie und Glaube* 85:337–64.

Knoch, Wendelin. "Sensus fidelium—Eine bindende und verbindene Glaubensnorm." In *Theologia et Jus canonicum. Festgabe für Heribert Heinemann zur Vollendung seines 70. Lebensjahres.* Ed. Heinrich J. F. Reinhardt. Essen: Ludgerus, 73–83.

Pié-Ninot, Salvador. S.v. "Sensus Fidei." In *Dictionary of Fundamental Theology.* Ed. René Latourelle and Rino Fisichella. New York: Crossroad, 992–95.

Tillard, J. M. R. *L'Église locale. Écclésiologie de communion et catholicité.* Cogitatio Fidei 191. Paris: Cerf, 314–24 ["'Sensus fidei', 'sensus fidelium', mémoire'"].

Vergauwen, Guido. "Sensus fidei—consensus fidelium im ökumenischen Dialog heute." In *Ökumene, das eine Ziel—die vielen Wege: Festschrift zum dreissigjährigen Bestehen des Institutum Studiorum Oecumenicorum der Universität Freiburg (Schweiz).* Ed. Iso Baumer and Guido Vergauwen. Freiburg: Universitätsverlag, 23–47.

Wiedenhofer, Siegfried. "Sensus fidelium—Demokratisierung der Kirche?" In *Surrexit dominus vere: die Gegenwart des Auferstandenen in seiner Kirche. Festschrift für Johannes Joachim Degenhardt.* Ed. Josef Ernst and Stephan Leimgruber. Paderborn: Bonifatius, 457–71.

1996

Böttigheimer, Christoph. "Mitspracherecht der Gläubigen in Glaubensfragen." *Stimmen der Zeit* 214:547–54.

Brereton, Andrew J. *"Sensus Fidelium*: Why the Church Needs It." *Church* 12/3:15–20.

Finucane, Daniel J. *Sensus Fidelium: The Use of a Concept in the Post-Vatican II Era* [Ph.D. dissertation, St. Louis University, 1993]. San Francisco-London-Bethesda: International Scholars Publications.

Mišerda, Marko. *Subjektivität im Glauben. Eine theologisch-methodologische Untersuchung zur Diskussion über den 'Glaubens-Sinn' in der katholischen Theologie des 19. Jahrhunderts.* Frankfurt: Peter Lang.

O'Donnell, Christopher. Art. "Sense of the Faith—Sense of the Faithful." *Ecclesia: A Theological Encyclopedia of the Church.* Collegeville, MN: Liturgical Press, 422–24.

Pottmeyer, Hermann Josef. "Die Mitsprache der Gläubigen in Glaubenssachen. Eine alte Praxis und ihre Wiederentdeckung." *Internationale katholische Zeitschrift* 25:134–47.

1997

Böttigheimer, Christoph. "Lehramt, Theologie und Glaubenssinn." *Stimmen der Zeit* 215:603–14.

Espín, Orlando O. "Tradition and Popular Religion: An Understanding of the *Sensus Fidelium*." *The Faith of the People: Theological Reflections on Popular Catholicism*. Maryknoll, NY: Orbis Books, 63–90.

Gaillardetz, Richard R. *Teaching with Authority: A Theology of the Magisterium in the Church*. Collegeville, MN: Liturgical Press, 230–35 ["The *Sensus Fidelium*"].

Legrand, Hervé. "Reception, *Sensus Fidelium*, and Synodal Life: An Effort at Articulation." *The Jurist* 57:405–31.

Rush, Ormond. *The Reception of Doctrine: An Appropriation of Hans Robert Jauss' Reception Aesthetics and Literary Hermeneutics*. Tesi Gregoriana, Serie Teologia 19. Rome: Gregorian University Press, 213–16, 300–303, 317–19, and 336–38.

Wehrle, Paul. "Pastoral im Hören auf das Volk Gottes. 'Der Glaubenssinn der Gläubigen.'" In *Hören und Dienen. Pastorales Handeln im Umbruch*. Ed. Paul Wehrle, Josef Müller, and Philipp Müller. Freiburger Texte 27. Freiburg: Erzbischöfliches Ordinariat, 35–57.

1998

Brosse, Richard. "Consensus fidelium: un dialogue? Réflexions herméneutiques sur la théologie fondamentale et l'ecclésiologie." *Revue théologique de Louvain* 29:331–44.

Parmentier, Élisabeth. "Le témoignage chrétien au crible du *sensus fidelium*." *Positions luthériennes* 46:273–90.

Schmucker, Robert W. *Sensus Fidei. Der Glaubenssinn in seiner vorkonziliaren Entwicklungsgeschichte und in den Dokumenten des Zweiten Vatikanischen Konzils*. Theorie und Forschung, Theologie, Bd. 36. Regensburg: S. Roderer Verlag.

Tillard, J. M. R. "How Is Christian Truth Taught in the Roman Catholic Church?" *One in Christ* 34:293–306.

1999

Anglican-Roman Catholic Dialogue. "The Gift of Authority." In *Growth in Agreement III: International Dialogue Texts and Agreed Statements, 1998–2005*. Ed. Jeffrey Gros, Thomas F. Best, and Lorelei F. Fuchs. Grand Rapids, MI: Wm. B. Eerdmans, 2007, 60–81 [§§ 29–31, 36, 38, 43].

Ohly, Christoph. *Sensus fidei fidelium. Zur Einordnung des Glaubenssinnes aller Gläubigen in die Communio-Struktur der Kirche im geschichtlichen Spiegel dogmatisch-kanonistischer Erkenntnisse und der Aussagen des II. Vaticanum*.

Münchener Theologische Studien, III. Kanonistische Abteilung, vol. 57. St. Ottilien: EOS Verlag.

———. "Der Glaubenssinn der Gläubigen. Ekklesiologische Anmerkungen zum Verständnis eines oft missverstandenen Phänomens im Beziehungsverhältnis von Dogmatik und Kanonistik." *Archiv für katholisches Kirchenrecht* 168:51–82.

Vergauwen, Guido. "Sensus Fidei: Consensus Fidelium in Ecumenical Dialogue Today." *Melita Theologica* 50:3–24.

2000

Hünermann, Peter. S.v. "Sensus fidei." In *Lexikon für Theologie und Kirche*, 3rd ed., vol. 9. Ed. Walter Kasper. Freiburg: Herder, cols. 465–67.

Puthenpurackal, Matthias. *Sensus Fidei and Satyagraha: A Theological Dialogue with Mahatma Gandhi*. Hamburg: Kovac.

2001

Rush, Ormond. "*Sensus Fidei*: Faith 'Making Sense' of Revelation." *Theological Studies* 62:231–61.

Vitali, Dario. "*Sensus fidelium* e opinione pubblica nella Chiesa." *Gregorianum* 82:689–717.

2002

Burghardt, Dominik. *Institution Glaubenssinn. Die Bedeutung des* sensus fidei *im kirchlichen Verfassungsrecht und für die Interpretation kanonischer Gesetze*. Paderborn: Bonifatius. Reviewed by Norbert Lüdecke, *Theologische Revue* 99 (2003): cols. 319–23.

Sullivan, Francis A. "The Sense of Faith: The Sensus/Consensus of the Faithful." In *Authority in the Roman Catholic Church: Theory and Practice*. Ed. Bernard Hoose. Burlington, VT: Ashgate, 85–93.

Wohlmuth, Josef. "Sensus fidei (fidelium)." *Pastoraltheologische Informationen* 22:17–35.

2003

Burkhard, John J. "*Sensus fidelium*." *New Catholic Encyclopedia*, vol. 12. 2nd ed. Detroit: Gale Group and Catholic University of America, 916–18.

Kerkofs, Jan. "[Introduction to the Readings on] The *Sensus Fidelium* and Reception of Teaching." In *Readings in Church Authority: Gifts and Challenges for Contemporary Catholicism*. Ed. Gerard Mannion, Richard Gaillardetz, Jan Kerkhofs, and Kenneth Wilson. Burlington, VT: Ashgate, 291–92.

Pelikan, Jaroslav. "Between Ecumenical Councils: The Orthodoxy of the Body of the Faithful." *Greek Orthodox Theological Review* 48:93–103.

Rush, Ormond. "The Offices of Christ, *Lumen Gentium* and the People's Sense of the Faith." *Pacifica* 16:137–52.

Song, Johannes Yong-Min. *"Glaubenssinn" und "Inkulturation": Eine Studie zum "Glaubenssinn der Glaubenden" (sensus fidelium) unter besonderer Berücksichtigung der Volksfrömmigkeit in Korea*. Bonn: Borengässer.

2004

Beinert, Wolfgang. "Was gilt in der Kirche und wer sagt uns das? Im Spannungsfeld von Lehramt, Theologie und Glaubenssinn." In *Theologie im Dialog. Festschrift für Harald Wagner*. Eds. Peter Neuner and Peter Lüning. Münster: Aschendorff, 159–79.

Demel, Sabine. "Dringender Handlungsbedarf. Der Glaubenssinn des Gottesvolkes und seine rechtliche Umsetzung." *Herder Korrespondenz* 58:618–23.

———. "Sensus fidelium. Der Glaubenssinn des ganzen Gottesvolkes: Fromme Floskel oder erfahrbare Wirklichkeit? Vortrag auf der 16. Bundesversammlung der KirchenVolksbewegung Wir Sind Kirche am 23 Okt. 2004, Regensburg." Published by KirchenVolksbewegung Wir sind Kirche (Munich).

Hünermann, Peter. *Herders theologischer Kommentar zum Zweiten Vatikanischen Konzil*, vol. 2. Freiburg: Herder, 383–86, 434–44, and 472–76 ["Kommentierung" LG 12, LG 25, and LG 35].

2005

Burkhard, John J. "*Sensus Fidei*: Recent Theological Reflection (1990–2001). Part I." *The Heythrop Journal* 46:450–75.

Costigan, Richard F. *The Consensus of the Church and Papal Infallibility: A Study in the Background of Vatican I*. Washington, D.C.: Catholic University of America Press.

Lawler, Michael G. "Reception and *Sensus Fidei*." *What Is and What Ought to Be: The Dialectic of Experience, Theology, and Church*. New York: Continuum, 119–42.

Napiwodzki, Piotr. "*Sensus fidei* und seine ekklesiologische Bedeutung." *Eine Ekklesiologie im Werden. Mannes Dominikus Koster und sein Beitrag zum theologischen Verständnis der Kirche*. S.T.D. dissertation, University of Fribourg, Switzerland. Available online at https://doc.rero.ch/record/5056/files /1_NapiwodzkiP.pdf, 115–65.

Vitali, Dario. "*Universitas fidelium in credendo falli nequit* (LG 12). Il *sensus fidelium* al concilio Vaticano II." *Gregorianum* 86:607–28.

Voss, Gerhard. "Sensus fidelium—der 'Glaubenssinn' der Gläubigen." *Una Sancta* 60:110–18.

2006

Albano, Gerardo. *Il sensus fidelium: la partecipazione del popolo di Dio alla funzione profetica di Cristo.* Naples: Pontificia Facoltà Teologica dell'Italia Meriodionale.

Bausenhart, Guido. "Evangelisierung in der communio aller Getauften." In *Herders theologischer Kommentar zum Zweiten Vatikanischen Konzil,* vol. 5: *Theologische Zusammenschau und Perspektiven.* Eds. Peter Hünermann and Bernd Jochen Hilberath. Freiburg: Herder, 277–86 [on *sensus fidelium* and *consensus fidelium*].

Böckenförde, Werner. "Statement aus der Sicht eines Kirchenrechtlers aus der Jahrestagung des Arbeitsgemeinschaft Katholischer Dogmatiker und Fundamentaltheologen zum Thema 'Der Glaubenssinn des Gottesvolkes.'" In *Freiheit und Gerechtigkeit in der Kirche. Gedenkschrift für Werner Böckenförde.* Ed. Norbert Lüdecke and Georg Bier. Würzburg: Echter, 161–66.

Brereton, Andrew J. "The *Sensus Fidelium* and the Sacramentality of the Teaching Church: A Model Based on the Theology of Louis-Marie Chauvet." Ph.D. dissertation, Fordham University.

Burkhard, John J. "*Sensus Fidei*: Recent Theological Reflection (1990–2001). Part II." *The Heythrop Journal* 46:38–54.

Compagnoni, Francesco. "'*Sensus fidelium*' e discernimento morale, in Paul Valadier (Francia), Giuseppe Angelini (Italia), Nathaniël Yaovi Soede (Costa d'Avorio)." *Rivista di teologia morale* 38:533–39.

Miller, Edward Jeremy. "Newman on the Voice of the Laity: Lessons for Today's Church." *Newman Studies Journal* 3/2:16–31.

Smith, Janet E. "The *Sensus Fidelium* and *Humanae Vitae.*" *Angelicum* 83:271–97.

2007

Angelini, Giuseppe. "Il *sensus fidelium* in materia morale." *Teologia* 32:56–70.

———. "The *Sensus Fidelium* and Moral Discernment." In *Catholic Theological Ethics in the World Church: The Plenary Papers from the First Cross-Cultural Conference on Catholic Theological Ethics.* Ed. James F. Keenan. New York: Continuum, 202–9.

Mason, Denis. "On Consulting the Faithful in Matters of Sexual Teaching." *Doctrine and Life* 57/4:50–62.

Soédé, Nathanaël Yaovi. "The *Sensus Fidelium* and Moral Discernment: The Principle of Inculturation and of Love." In *Catholic Theological Ethics in the World Church: The Plenary Papers from the First Cross-cultural Conference on Catholic Theological Ethics.* Ed. James F. Keenan. New York: Continuum, 193–201.

Stenger, H. "Gemeinsames Hirtentum aller Christen: Reform der Kirche im Respekt für den sensus fidelium." *Herder Korrespondenz* 58:357–60.

Valadier, Paul. "Has the Concept of *Sensus Fidelium* Fallen into Desuetude?" In *Catholic Theological Ethics in the World Church: The Plenary Papers from the First Cross-Cultural Conference on Catholic Theological Ethics*. Ed. James F. Keenan. New York: Continuum, 187–92.

Walter, Peter. "Bischöfliche Leitungsvollmacht—Ohnmacht des Gottesvolkes. Zum 'sensus fidelium' als verdrängten locus theologicus." In *"[. . .] in voller Wahrheit Vorsteher des Volkes." Der Dienst des Bischofs im Wandel. Paul Wehrle zum silbernen Bischofsjubiläum*. Ed. Thomas Herkert, Karsten Kreutzer, and Tobias Licht. Freiburg: Verlag der Katholischen Akademie der Erzdiözese Freiburg, 23–40.

2008

Albano, Gerardo. *Il sensus fidelium: la partecipazione del popolo di Dio alla funzione profetica di Cristo*. Naples: Pontificia Facoltà Teologica dell'Italia Meriodionale.

Bier, Georg. "Wir sind Kirche. Der Glaubenssinn des Gottesvolkes in kirchen-rechtlicher Sicht." In *Rezeption des Zweiten Vatikanischen Konzils in Theologie und Kirchenrecht heute. Festschrift für Klaus Lüdicke zur Vollendung seines 65. Lebensjahres*. Ed. Dominicus Meier, Peter Platen, Heinrich J. F. Reinhardt, and Frank Sanders. Beihefte zum Münsterischen Kommentar 55. Essen: Ludgerus Verlag, 73–97.

Burkhard, John J. "The *Sensus Fidelium*." In *The Routledge Companion to the Christian Church*. Ed. Gerard Mannion and Lewis S. Mudge. New York: Routledge, 560–75.

DelMonico, Marc. "'There is Something in the Breathing Together of the Pastors and the Faithful Which is Not in the Pastors Alone': The Normative Significance of the *Sensus Fidei*." *Chicago Studies* 48:85–109.

Mushy, Prosper. "The Primacy of Sensus Fidei in the Discernment of Tradition: Perspectives from John Thiel's '*Senses of Tradition: Continuity and Development in Catholic Faith*.'" *African Christian Studies* 24/1:56–66.

———. "The 'Sense of the Faithful' as a *Locus* for Inculturation in Africa: Bridging Faith and Culture." *African Christian Studies* 24/3:7–27.

Rush, Ormond. "Receptive Ecumenism and the *Sensus Fidelium*: Expanding the Categories for Catholic Ecclesial Discerning." In *Receptive Ecumenism and Ecclesial Learning: Learning to Be Church Together. Joint 2nd International Receptive Ecumenism Conference*. Ed. Paul D. Murray. New York: Oxford University Press.

Silva, Joaquín. "Teología, magisterio y sentido de la fe: Un desafío de diálogo y communión." *Teologia y Vida* 49:551–73.

2009

Baggett, Jerome P. *Sense of the Faithful: How American Catholics Live Their Faith.* New York: Oxford University Press.

Mushy, Prosper. "The 'Sense of the Faithful' as a Criterion for Inculturation: Bridging the Gulf between Faith and Culture." *Vidyajyoti. Journal of Theological Reflection* 73/3:179–201.

Rush, Ormond. *The Eyes of Faith: The Sense of the Faithful and the Church's Reception of Revelation.* Washington, D.C.: Catholic University of America Press.

Vecchi, Fabio. "Dell'annuncio della 'parola' nella crisi della fede e delle culture." In *Parola di Dio e missione della Chiesa: aspetti giuridici.* Ed. Davide Cito and Fernando Puig. Milan: Giuffrè Editore, 385–402.

2010

McCann, Pamela. "The *Sensus fidei* and Canon Law." *Studia Canonica* 44:211–58.

Mushy, Prosper. Sensus fidelium *as a Locus for Theology: Some Perspectives on the Use of the Concept in Ecumenical Dialogue.* Saarbrücken, Germany and San Bernardino, CA: LAP Lambert Academic Publishing.

2011

McCann, Pamela. "Karl Rahner as a Resource for the Theology of the *Sensus Fidelium*: The Canonical Implications of His Vision." Ph.D. dissertation, University of St. Michael's College, 2010. Ann Arbor, MI: UMI Dissertation Services.

Vitali, Dario. "Il *sensus fidelium* tra modelli di interpretazione della fede e processi di partecipazione." *Rivista di Scienze Religiose* 25/1:39–55.

2012

Böttigheimer, Christoph. Art. "Glaubenssinn der Gläubigen." In *Neues Lexikon der katholischen Dogmatik.* Ed. Wolfgang Beinert and Bertram Stubenrauch. Freiburg: Herder, 272–74.

Foley, Edward. "Passing the Torch: Full, Prophetic and Ecclesial Participation." *Worship* 86:386–402, at 394–400.

Geissler, Hermann. "The Witness of the Faithful in Matters of Doctrine according to John Henry Newman," 1–17 at http://www.newmanfriendsinternational .org/newman/wp-content/uploads/2012/06/on-consulting-english1.pdf.

Noceti, Serena. "Laici e *sensus fidei* (LG 12)." In *I laici dopo il Concilio. Quale autonomia?* Ed. Cettina Militello. Bologna: Edizioni Dehoniane, 87–101.

Rush, Ormond. "The Prophetic Office in the Church: Pneumatological Perspectives on the *Sensus Fidelium*-Theology-Magisterium Relationship." In *When the Magisterium Intervenes: The Magisterium and Theologians in Today's Church.* Ed. Richard R. Gaillardetz. Collegeville, MN: Liturgical Press, 89–112.

2013

Ekpo, Anthony. "Canon Law and the Agents of the *Sensus Fidelium*: A Theological and Canonical Exploration." *The Canonist* 4/1:65–86.

———. "From *Sensus Fidei* to *Sensus Legis*: Reconciling Faith and Law in the Church." *The Canonist* 4/2:157–68.

Hahnenberg, Edward P. "How Is the *Sensus fidelium* Identified and Determined by Catholics?" Paper delivered to the U.S. Lutheran-Catholic Dialogue— Round XII, Section Two: April 11–14. Unpublished paper. 21 pages.

Lawler, Michael G., and Todd A. Salzman. "The Normativity of History That Shapes Tradition: Human Experience, *Sensus Fidei*, and Sociology." In *The Shaping of Tradition: Context and Normativity*. Ed. Colby Dickinson with the collaboration of Lieven Boeve and Terrence Merrigan. Leuven: Peeters, 27–42.

Long, David P. "John Henry Newman and the Consultation of the Faithful." *Newman Studies Journal* 10:18–31.

McCann, Pamela. "Karl Rahner and the *Sensus Fidelium*." *Philosophy & Theology* 25:311–35.

Vorgrimler, Herbert. "Die Lehrautorität der Gläubigen: Karl Rahners Überlegungen zum 'sensus fidelium.'" Foreward by Andreas R. Batlogg. In *Rahner Lecture 2013*. Veröffentlichung des Karl Rahner-Archivs München im Verlag der Universitätsbibliothek, Freiburg im Breisgau. 30 pages.

Wijlens, Myriam. "Sensus fidelium—Authority: Protecting and Promoting the Ecclesiology of Vatican II with the Assistance of Institutions?" In *Believing in Community: Ecumenical Reflections on the Church*. Ed. Peter De Mey, Pieter De Witte, and Gerard Mannion. Leuven: Peeters, 207–28.

2014

Autiero, Antonio. "*Sensus fidelium* e Magistero dal Concilio ad oggi." Prolusione, XXV Congresso nazionale ATISM, Agrigento, 2 luglio 2014.

Ekpo, Anthony. *The Breath of the Spirit in the Church: The* Sensus Fidelium *and Canon Law*. Strathfield, NSW: St Pauls.

———. "The Structures of the *Sensus Fidelium* and Canon Law: Part I." *Australian eJournal of Theology* 21/1:29–48.

———. "The Structures of the *Sensus Fidelium* and Canon Law: Part II." *Australian eJournal of Theology* 21/2:94–107.

Gelpi, Albert, and Barbara C. "*Sensus fidelium*." In *From Vatican II to Pope Francis: Charting a Catholic Future*. Ed. Paul Crowley. Maryknoll, NY: Orbis Books, 170–80.

Grümme, Bernhard. "Kinder im sensus fidei. Ein Versuch, ihren ekklesiologischen Ort zu bestimmen." In *Glaube in Gemeinschaft. Autorität und Rezeption in der Kirche*. Ed. Markus Knapp and Thomas Söding, 228–40.

Hahn, Judith. "Lehramt und Glaubenssinn. Kirchenrechtliche Überlegungen zu einem spannungsreichen Verhältnis – aus aktuellen Anlass." In *Glaube in Gemeinschaft. Autorität und Rezeption in der Kirche*. Ed. Markus Knapp and Thomas Söding, 182–212.

International Theological Commission. *Sensus Fidei in the Life of the Church*. London: Catholic Truth Society. Or see www.vatican.va/roman_curia/congregations /cfaith/cti_documents/rc_cti_20140610_sensus-fidei_en.html.

Knapp, Markus, and Thomas Söding, eds. *Glaube in Gemeinschaft. Autorität und Rezeption in der Kirche*. Freiburg: Herder.

McNamara, Tony. "*Sensus Fidelium* and the Synod on the Family." *Doctrine and Life* 64/1:16–22.

Monson, Paul G. "*Sentire cum concilio*. Vatican II and the *Sensus fidelium* in the Thought of Avery Cardinal Dulles, S.J." *Gregorianum* 95:39–58.

Rahner, Johanna. "Lehramt und Glaubenssinn. Anmerkungen zu einem zunehmend schwieriger werdenden dogmatischen Lehrstück." In *Glaube in Gemeinschaft. Autorität und Rezeption in der Kirche*. Ed. Markus Knapp and Thomas Söding, 165–81.

Rush, Ormond. "*Sensus fidelium* und Katholizität: Ortskirche und Universalkirche im Gespräch mit Gott." In *Die wechselseitige Rezeption zwischen Ortskirche und Universalkirche. Das Zweite Vatikanum und die Kirche im Osten Deutschlands*. Ed. Myriam Wijlens. Erfurter Theologische Schriften 46. Würzburg: Echter, 151–60.

Schambeck, Mirjam. "Reli-Lehrer(in) sein zwischen Lehre und Leere? Wie eine korrelative Theologie das Verhältnis von Theologie und Spiritualität klären könnte. Auch ein Frage nach der Beziehung von Lehramt und Glaubenssinn." In *Glaube in Gemeinschaft. Autorität und Rezeption in der Kirche*. Ed. Markus Knapp and Thomas Söding, 241–58.

2015

Autiero, Antonio. "The *Sensus Fidelium* and the Magisterium from the Council to the Present Day: Moral-Theological Reflections." *Asian Horizons* 9/1:57–75.

Beinert, Wolfgang. "Einstimmen oder übereinstimmen? Die Aufgabe des Glaubenssinnes der Gläubigen." In *Zerreissprobe Ehe. Das Ringen der katholischen Kirche um die Familie*. Ed. Ulrich Ruh and Myriam Wijlens. Freiburg: Herder, 27–43.

Burkhard, John J. "The *Sensus Fidelium*: Old Questions, New Challenges." *Catholic Theological Society of America Proceedings* 70:27–43.

Carter, David. "*Sensus Fidei* in the Life of the Church 2." *Ecumenical Trends* 44/2:6–11, 15.

Ekpo, Anthony. "From Amnesia to Anamnesis: The *Sensus Fidei* and the Eucharist." *Australian eJournal of Theology* 22/2:120–27.

———. "The *Sensus Fidelium* and the Threefold Office of Christ: A Reinterpretation of *Lumen Gentium* No. 12." *Theological Studies* 76:330–46.

Rush, Ormond. "The Church Local and Universal and the Communion of the Faithful." In *A Realist's Church: Essays in Honor of Joseph A. Komonchak.* Ed. Christopher D. Denny, Patrick J. Hayes, and Nicholas K. Rademacher. Maryknoll, NY: Orbis Books, 117–30.

Wood, Susan K. "The *Sensus Fidelium*: Discerning the Path of Faith." In *Catholic Theological Society of America Proceedings* 70:72–83.

2016

Aihiokhai, SimonMary A. "A Mosaic of Identities of the *Sensus Fidelium*: The Realities of African Ecclesial Communities in Diaspora." In *Learning from All the Faithful.* Ed Bradford E. Hinze and Peter C. Phan, 226–36.

Arabome, Anne. "How Are Theologians Challenged and Informed by Their Engagement with the Sense of the Faithful in the Local/Global Church?" In *Learning from All the Faithful.* Ed. Bradford E. Hinze and Peter C. Phan, 360–66.

Bingemer, Maria Clara Lucchetti. "The *Sensus Fidei* in the Recent History of the Latin American Church." In *Learning from All the Faithful.* Ed. Bradford E. Hinze and Peter C. Phan, 329–43.

Böhnke, Michael. "Gerichtetheit im Handeln, Wahrheit des Gewissens, Berufung zur Freundschaft und Gewissheit der Erlösung. Dimensionen des *sensus fidei.*" In *Der Spürsinn des Gottesvolkes. Eine Diskussion mit der Internationalen Theologischen Kommission.* Ed. Thomas Söding, 285–302.

Burkhard, John J. "The *Sensus Fidelium*: Old Questions, New Challenges." In *Learning from All the Faithful: A Contemporary Theology of the Sensus Fidei.* Ed. Bradford E. Hinze and Peter C. Phan, 125–42.

Canaris, Michael M. "A Rahnerian Reading of '*Sensus Fidei* in the Life of the Church.'" In *Learning from All the Faithful.* Ed. Bradford E. Hinze and Peter C. Phan, 196–209.

Chia, Edmund Kee-Fook. "Discerning the *Sensus Fidelium* in Asia's Narrative Theologies." In *Learning from All the Faithful.* Ed. Bradford E. Hinze and Peter C. Phan, 295–311.

Chiron, Jean-François. "*Sensus fidei* et vision de l'Église chez le pape François." *Recherches de science religieuse* 104:187–205.

Choi, Hoon. "Storytelling as an Expression of *Sensus Fidelium*." In *Learning from All the Faithful.* Ed. Bradford E. Hinze and Peter C. Phan, 312–28.

Copeland, M. Shawn. "The Institute for Black Catholic Studies: Culture, the *Sensus Fidelium*, and Practical Theological Agency." In *Learning from All the Faithful.* Ed. Bradford E. Hinze and Peter C. Phan, 237–54.

Cortegiano, Robert. "The Use of Sociology in the Study of the *Sensus Fidelium*: An Evaluation of the Contribution of Jerome Baggett." In *Learning from* All *the Faithful*. Ed. Bradford E. Hinze and Peter C. Phan, 103–21.

Cruz, Gemma Tulud. "Theology as Conversation: *Sensus Fidelium* and Doing Theology on/from the Margins." In *Learning from* All *the Faithful*. Ed Bradford E. Hinze and Peter C. Phan, 344–59.

Famerée, Joseph. "*Sensus fidei, sensus fidelium*. Histoire d'une notion théologique discutée." *Recherches de science religieuse* 104:167–85.

Fischer, Irmtraud. "Geist Gottes und *sensus fidei* im Gottesvolk. Alttestamentliche Perspektive." In *Der Spürsinn des Gottesvolkes. Eine Diskussion mit der Internationalen Theologischen Kommission*. Ed. Thomas Söding, 107–20.

Fletcher, Jeannine Hill. "Supremacy in the Sense of the Faith: Theological Anthropology and the 'Various Ranks' (*Lumen Gentium* 13)." In *Learning from* All *the Faithful*. Eds. Bradford E. Hinze and Peter C. Phan, 53–66.

George, William P. "Who Are the *Fideles* and What Is Their *Sensus*? Insights from Bernard Lonergan." In *Learning from* All *the Faithful*. Ed. Bradford E. Hinze and Peter C. Phan, 184–95.

Gerwing, Manfred. "*Sensus fidei* und *consensus fidelium*. Bemerkungen zum Glaubenssinn der Gläubigen in der Theologie des Mittelalters." In *Der Spürsinn des Gottesvolkes. Eine Diskussion mit der Internationalen Theologischen Kommission*. Ed. Thomas Söding, 190–212.

Grieser, Heike. "Hören auf das Gottesvolk? Bemerkungen aus kirchenhistorischer Perspektive zu einer Herausforderung seit frühchristlicher Zeit." In *Der Spürsinn des Gottesvolkes. Eine Diskussion mit der Internationalen Theologischen Kommission*. Ed. Thomas Söding, 159–89.

Hahnenberg, Edward P. "Learning to Discern the *Sensus Fidelium Latinamente*." In *Learning from* All *the Faithful*. Ed. Bradford E. Hinze and Peter C. Phan, 255–71.

Hinze, Bradford E., and Peter C. Phan, eds. *Learning from* All *the Faithful: A Contemporary Theology of the Sensus Fidei*. Eugene, OR: Pickwick Publications.

Imperatori-Lee, Natalia. "Latina Lives, Latina Literature: A Narrative Camino in Search of the *Sensus Fidelium*." In *Learning from* All *the Faithful*. Ed. Bradford E. Hinze and Peter C. Phan, 272–80.

Knapp, Markus. "Der 'Ort' des Glaubenssinns. Melchior Cano und das 2. Vatikanische Konzil." In *Der Spürsinn des Gottesvolkes. Eine Diskussion mit der Internationalen Theologischen Kommission*. Ed. Thomas Söding, 213–32.

Knop, Julia. "*Sensus* und Auftrag der Kirche. Der Glaubenssinn der Gläubigen in der Ekklesiologie des II. Vatikanischen Konzils." In *Der Spürsinn des Gottesvolkes. Eine Diskussion mit der Internationalen Theologischen Kommission*. Ed. Thomas Söding, 235–57.

Kowalski, Beate. "Die Verheissung der Wahrheit. Der johanneische Impuls." In *Der Spürsinn des Gottesvolkes. Eine Diskussion mit der Internationalen Theologischen Kommission*. Ed. Thomas Söding, 137–56.

Mannion, Gerard. "*Sensus Fidelium* and the International Theological Commission—Has Anything Changed between 2012 and 2014?" In *Learning from All the Faithful*. Ed. Bradford E. Hinze and Peter C. Phan, 69–88.

Marr, Ryan. "John Henry Newman on Consulting the Faithful: An Idea in Need of Development." In *Learning from All the Faithful*. Ed. Bradford E. Hinze and Peter C. Phan, 42–52.

Massingale, Brian N. "Beyond 'Who Am I to Judge?' The *Sensus Fidelium*, LGBT Experience, and Truth-Telling in the Church." In *Learning from All the Faithful*. Ed. Bradford E. Hinze and Peter C. Phan, 170–83.

Ormerod, Neil. "*Sensus Fidei* and Sociology: How Do We Find the Normative in the Empirical?" In *Learning from All the Faithful*. Ed. Bradford E. Hinze and Peter C. Phan, 89–102.

Osheim, Amanda C. *A Ministry of Discernment: The Bishop and the Sense of the Faithful*. Collegeville, MN: Liturgical Press.

Phan, Peter C. "*Sensus Fidelium, Dissensus Infidelium, Consensus Omnium*: An Interreligious Approach to Consensus in Doctrinal Theology." In *Learning from All the Faithful*. Ed. Bradford E. Hinze and Peter C. Phan, 213–25.

Rush, Ormond. "The Church as a Hermeneutical Community and the Eschatological Function of the *Sensus Fidelium*." In *Learning from All the Faithful*. Eds. Bradford E. Hinze and Peter C. Phan, 143–54.

Ryan, Thomas. "Sensuous History: The Medieval Feast of Corpus Christi as an Expression of the *Sensus Fidelium*." In *Learning from All the Faithful*. Ed. Bradford E. Hinze and Peter C. Phan, 27–41.

Schockenhoff, Eberhard. "Der Glaubenssinn des Volkes Gottes als ethisches Erkenntniskriterium? Zur Nicht-Rezeption kirchlicher Lehraussagen über die Sexualmoral durch die Gläubigen." *Theologie und Philosophie* 91:321–62. Abridged version in *Der Spürsinn des Gottesvolkes. Eine Diskussion mit der Internationalen Theologischen Kommission*. Ed. Thomas Söding, 305–30.

Söding, Thomas, ed. *Der Spürsinn des Gottesvolkes. Eine Diskussion mit der Internationalen Theologischen Kommission*. Questiones Disputatae 281. Freiburg: Herder.

Tamisiea, David A. "Vatican II, St. Thomas Aquinas, and the *Sensus Fidelium*." In *Wisdom and The Renewal of Catholic Theology: Essays in Honor of Matthew L. Lamb*. Ed. Thomas P. Harmon and Roger W. Nutt. Eugene, OR: Pickwick Publications. 175–204.

Tan, Jonathan Y. " 'Who Do You Say that I Am?' Uncovering the Chinese *Sensus Fidelium* in Images of Jesus in Pre-Communist Chinese Catholic Devotional

Art from the 1930s to 1940s." In *Learning from All the Faithful*. Ed. Bradford E. Hinze and Peter C. Phan, 281–94.

Theobald, Christoph. "*Sensus fidei fidelium*. Enjeux d'avenir d'une notion classique." *Recherches de science religieuse* 104:207–36.

Traina, Cristina L. H. "Whose *Sensus*? Which *Fidelium*? Justice and Gender in a Global Church." In *Learning from All the Faithful*. Ed. Bradford E. Hinze and Peter C. Phan, 155–69.

Werner, Gunda. "Gewissensfreiheit und Lehrautorität—Spannungsfelder des *sensus fidei fidelis*?" In *Der Spürsinn des Gottesvolkes. Eine Diskussion mit der Internationalen Theologischen Kommission*. Ed. Thomas Söding, 258–84.

Wiemeyer, Joachim. "Soziallehre der Kirche—als Ausdruck des Galubenssinns des Gottes-volkes." In *Der Spürsinn des Gottesvolkes. Eine Diskussion mit der Internationalen Theologischen Kommission*. Ed. Thomas Söding, 331–49.

2017

Blanchard, Shaun. "The Minority Report at Trent and the Vatican Councils: Dissenting Episcopal Voices as Positive Sources for Theological Reflection." *New Blackfriars* 98:147–56.

Boss, Sarah Jane. "Deification: The Mariology of the Ordinary Faithful." *New Blackfriars* 98:188–202.

Costigane, Helen. "Sensus Fidelium and Canon Law: Sense and Sensitivity?" *New Blackfriars* 98:157–70.

Curran, Charles E., and Lisa A. Fullam, eds. *The* Sensus Fidelium *and Moral Theology*. Readings in Moral Theology 18. New York: Paulist Press.

Llywelyn, Dorian. "Devotion, Theology and the *Sensus Fidelium*." *New Blackfriars* 98:171–87.

Mannion, Gerard. "Making Sense of the Faith: The Dynamics of *Sensus Fidelium* and the Role of Reception." *Ecclesiology* 13:379–85.

O'Loughlin, Thomas. "Are 'the Bishops . . . the "High Priets" Who Preside at the Eucharist'?: A Note on the Sources of the Text of *Sensus Fidei*." *New Blackfriars* 98:232–38.

Poulsom, Martin G. "Schillebeeckx and the *Sensus Fidelium*." *New Blackfriars* 98:203–17.

Rush, Ormond. "Inverting the Pyramid: The *Sensus Fidelium* in a Synodal Church." *Theological Studies* 78:299–325.

———. "Receptive Ecumenism and Discerning the *Sensus Fidelium*: Expanding the Categories for a Catholic Reception of Revelation." *Theological Studies* 78:559–72.

———. "A Synodal Church: On Being a Hermeneutical Community." In *Beyond Dogmatism and Innocence: Hermeneutics, Critique, and Catholic Theology*.

Ed. Anthony J. Godzieba and Bradford E. Hinze. Collegeville, MN: Liturgical Press, 160–75.

Strange, Roderick. "Newman on Consulting the Faithful: Context, Content, and Consequences." *New Blackfriars* 98:134–46.

Suchart, Verena. "*Sensus Fidelium* and the Old Testament: Learning from the Faith of Israel." *New Blackfriars* 98:218–31.

Wijlens, Myriam. "Reforming the Church by Hitting the Reset Button: Reconfiguring Collegiality within Synodality because of *Sensus Fidelium.*" *The Canonist* 8:235–61.

2018

Curran, Charles E. "*Humanae Vitae* and the *sensus fidelium.*" *National Catholic Reporter* 54/19 (June 29–July 12): 6–7.

Gaillardetz, Richard R. "What Is the Sense of the Faithful?" In *By What Authority? Foundations for Understanding Authority in the Church.* 2nd ed.; Collegeville, MN: Liturgical Press, 179–99.

Mignozzi, Vito. "Esiste un'autorità dei *christifideles laici* nella Chiesa? Linee interpretative (sostenibili) in prospettiva ecclesiologica." *Apulia Theologica: Rivista della Facoltà Theologica Pugliese* 4:151–72.

Moons, Jos. " 'Aroused and Sustained by the Holy Spirit'? A Plea for a Pneumatological Reconsideration of *Sensus Fidei* on the Basis of *Lumen Gentium* 12." *Gregorianum* 99:271–92.

2019

Go, Johnny C. *Religious Education from a Critical Realist Perspective: Sensus Fidei and Critical Thinking.* New York: Routledge.

Meszaros, Andrew. "The Body of Christ the Teacher: The Church's Prophetic Office." *Angelicum* 96:203–36.

Wijlens, Myriam. "De kerk hervormen door een 'herconfiguratie' van de leer. De collegialiteit van bisschoppen situeren binnen de synodaliteit van het hele kerk wegens de *sensus fidei fidelium.*" *Collationes. Tijdschrift voor Theologie en Pastoraal* 49:5–28.

2020

Bauer, Christian. "Leutetheologien, ein *locus theologicus*? Ein kartographischer Vorschlag mit M.-Dominique Chenu und Michel de Certeau." In *Der Glaubenssinn der Gläubigen als Ort theologischer Erkenntnis: Praktische und systematische Theologie im Gespräch.* Ed. Agnes Slunitschek and Thomas Bremer, 35–68.

Böhnke, Michael. " 'Wo aber der Geist des Herrn ist, da ist Freiheit' (2 Kor 3,17). Wie die vielfältigen Glaubenszeugnisse in Theologie und kirchlichen Lehrdiskurs einzubeziehen sind." In *Der Glaubenssinn der Gläubigen als Ort theologischer Erkenntnis: Praktische und systematische Theologie im Gespräch.* Ed. Agnes Slunitschek and Thomas Bremer, 243–54.

Bremer, Thomas. "Der Glaubenssinn der Gläubigen als Ort theologischer Erkenntnis. Ein Problemaufriss." In *Der Glaubenssinn der Gläubigen als Ort theologischer Erkenntnis: Praktische und systematische Theologie im Gespräch.* Ed. Agnes Slunitschek and Thomas Bremer, 15–31.

Eckholt, Margit. "Die Gläubigen als Ort theologischer Erkenntnis. subjektwerdung im Glauben in Gemeinschaft und theologische Erkenntnis." In *Der Glaubenssinn der Gläubigen als Ort theologischer Erkenntnis: Praktische und systematische Theologie im Gespräch.* Ed. Agnes Slunitschek and Thomas Bremer, 96–122.

Kling-Witzenhausen, Monika. "Die Stimmen der Gläubigen hörbar machen. Leutetheologien von Schwellenchrist(inn)en und ihre Implikationen für akademische Theolog(inn)en." In *Der Glaubenssinn der Gläubigen als Ort theologischer Erkenntnis: Praktische und systematische Theologie im Gespräch.* Ed. Agnes Slunitschek and Thomas Bremer, 195–215.

Slunitschek, Agnes. "Der Glaubenssinn des Gottesvolkes: Einmütig, einstimmig?" *Herder Korrespondenz* 74/8:45–48.

———. "Die Gläubigen als Ort theologischer Erkenntnis. Subjektwerdung im Glauben in Gemeinschaft und theologische Erkenntnis." In *Der Glaubenssinn der Gläubigen als Ort theologischer Erkenntnis: Praktische und systematische Theologie im Gespräch.* Ed. Agnes Slunitschek and Thomas Bremer, 96–122.

Slunitschek, Agnes, and Thomas Bremer, eds. *Der Glaubenssinn der Gläubigen als Ort theologischer Erkenntnis: Praktische und systematische Theologie im Gespräch.* Quaestiones Disputatae 304. Freiburg: Herder.

General Bibliography

This bibliography contains only the most general or frequently referenced works. Other books and articles can be located in the footnotes of the text after consulting the authors in the index of authors. Books and articles on the "sense of the faith" are located in the specialized chronological bibliography on the "sense of the faith."

Primary Sources

Abbot, Walter M., ed. *The Documents of Vatican II, with Notes and Comments by Catholic, Protestant, and Orthodox Authorities*. Translation editor Joseph Gallagher. New York: Guild Press/America Press/Association Press, 1966.

Acta et documenta Concilio Oecumenico Vaticano II apparando. Vatican City: Typis Polyglottis Vaticanis, 1969.

Acta Synodalia Sacrosancti Concilii Oecumenici Vaticani II. Vatican City: Typis Polyglottis Vaticanis, 1970–1978.

Alberigo, Giuseppe, and Franca Magistretti, eds. *Constitutionis Dogmaticae Lumen Gentium: Synopsis Historica*. Bologna: Istituto per le Scienze Religiose, 1975.

Aquinas, Thomas. *The Summa Theologica of St. Thomas Aquinas*. American edition. 3 vols. New York: Benziger Brothers, 1947.

Aristotle. *The Basic Works of Aristotle*. Ed. Richard McKeon. New York: Random House, 1941.

Bettenson, Henry, and Chris Maunder, eds. *Documents of the Christian Church*. 3rd ed. New York: Oxford University Press, 1999.

Carlen, Claudia, ed. *The Papal Encyclicals*. 5 vols. Ann Arbor, MI: Pierian Press, 1990.

Catechism of the Catholic Church. 2nd ed. Washington, DC: United States Catholic Conference, 1997.

Code of Canon Law, Latin-English Edition: New English Translation. Washington, DC: Canon Law Society of America, 2017.

Code of Canons of the Eastern Churches, Latin-English Edition. Washington, DC: Canon Law Society of America, 2001.

Congregation for the Doctrine of the Faith. *Instruction on the Ecclesial Vocation of the Theologian.* Washington, DC: United States Catholic Conference, 1990.

Denzinger, Henricus, and Adolfus Schönmetzer, eds. *Enchiridion symbolorum, definitionum et declarationum de rebus fidei et morum.* 33rd ed. Freiburg: Herder, 1965.

Elliott, J. K., ed. *The Apocryphal New Testament: A Collection of Apocryphal Christian Literature in an English Translation Based on M. R. James.* Oxford: Clarendon Press, 2009.

Flannery, Austin, ed. *Vatican Council II: Constitutions, Decrees, Declarations; The Basic Sixteen Documents.* Collegeville, MN: Liturgical Press, 2014.

Francis of Assisi, Saint. *Francis of Assisi: Early Documents.* Vol. 1: *The Saint.* Ed. Regis J. Armstrong, J. A. Wayne Hellmann, and William J. Short. New York: New City Press, 1999.

Francis, Pope. *The Joy of the Gospel.* Boston: Pauline Books & Media, 2013.

Hennecke, Edgar, and Wilhelm Schneemelcher, eds. *New Testament Apocrypha.* 2 vols. Philadelphia: Westminster Press, 1963.

International Theological Commission. *Theology Today: Perspectives, Principles, and Criteria.* Washington, DC: Catholic University of America Press, 2012.

———. *Sensus Fidei in the Life of the Church.* London: Catholic Truth Society, 2014.

———. *Synodality in the Life and Mission of the Church.* Available at www.vatican .va/roman_curia/congregations/cfaith/cti_documents/re_cti_20180302 .sinodalita_en.html#.

John Paul II, Pope. *Theotókos: Woman, Mother, Disciple.* Boston: Pauline Books & Media, 2000.

———. *The Redeemer of Man (Redemptor hominis).* Boston: Pauline Books & Media, 1979.

———. *The Role of the Christian Family in the Modern World (Familiaris consortio).* Boston: Pauline Books & Media, 1981.

———. *The Lay Members of Christ's Faithful People (Christifideles laici).* Boston: Pauline Books & Media, 1988.

———. *The Splendor of Truth (Veritatis splendor).* Boston: Pauline Books & Media, 1993.

———. *On Reserving Priestly Ordination to Men Alone (Ordinatio sacerdotalis).* London: Catholic Truth Society, 1994.

———. *The Gospel of Life (Evangelium vitae).* Boston: Pauline Books & Media, 1995.

———. *On Commitment to Ecumenism (Ut Unum Sint).* Boston: Pauline Books & Media, 1995.

———. *On Protecting the Faith (Ad tuendam fidem).* Boston: Pauline Books & Media, 1998.

Mansi, Johannes-Dominicus. *Sacrorum conciliorum et decretum collectio nova et amplissima collectio.* 53 vols. Florence/Venice/Paris/Leipzig, 1759–1927.

Migne, Jacques-Paul. *Patrologiae Cursus Completus: Series Graeca.* 162 vols. Paris, 1857–1886.

———. *Patrologiae Cursus Completus: Series Latina.* 221 vols. Paris, 1844–1891.

Pius XII, Pope. *Munificentissimus Deus.* In *Acta Apostolicae Sedis* 42 (1950): 753–92.

Scotus, John Duns. *Four Questions on Mary.* Trans. Allan Wolter. Santa Barbara, CA: Old Mission Santa Barbara, 1988.

Tanner, Norman P., ed. *The Decrees of the Ecumenical Councils.* 2 vols. Washington, DC: Georgetown University Press, 1990.

Secondary Sources

Alberigo, Giuseppe, and Joseph A. Komonchak, eds. *History of Vatican II.* 5 vols. Maryknoll, NY: Orbis Books, 1995–2006.

Alberigo, Giuseppe, Jean-Pierre Jossua, and Joseph A. Komonchak, eds. *The Reception of Vatican II.* Washington, DC: Catholic University of America Press, 1987. See Rinaldo Bertolino, Dominik Burghardt, Eugenio Corecco, and Christoph Ohly.

Anderson, H. George, J. Francis Stafford, and Joseph A. Burgess, eds. *The One Mediator, the Saints, and Mary.* Lutherans and Catholics in Dialogue 8. Minneapolis: Augsburg Press, 1992.

Baillie, John. *The Idea of Revelation in Recent Thought.* New York: Columbia University Press, 1956.

Beal, John P., James A. Coriden, and Thomas J. Green, eds. *New Commentary of the Code of Canon Law.* New York: Paulist Press, 2000. See Robert J. Kaslyn.

Beatrice, Pier Franco. *The Transmission of Sin: Augustine and the Pre-Augustinian Sources.* Trans. Adam Kamesar. New York: Oxford University Press, 2013. See Jesse Couenhoven, Gisbert Greshake, Matthew Levering, Brian O. McDermott, James P. O'Sullivan, Karl Rahner, Athanase Sage, Alfred Vanneste, Karl-Heinz Weger, and Siegfried Wiedenhofer.

Beinert, Wolfgang, ed. *Glaube als Zustimmung: Zur Interpretation kirchlicher Rezeptionsvorgänge.* Quaestiones Disputatae 131. Freiburg: Herder, 1991.

Bilateral Working Group of the German National Bishops' Conference and the Church Leadership of the United Evangelical Lutheran Church of Germany. *Communio Sanctorum: The Church as the Communion of Saints.* Trans. Mark W. Jeske, Michael Root, and Daniel R. Smith. Collegeville, MN: Liturgical Press, 2004.

Bolewski, Jacek. *Der reine Anfang: Die Dialektik der Erbsünde in marianischer Perspektive nach Karl Rahner.* Frankfurt: Josef Knecht, 1991.

Boman, Thorleif. *Hebrew Thought Compared with Greek.* Philadelphia: Westminster Press, 1960. See A. Debrunner and H. Kleinknecht.

Boss, Sarah Jane, ed. *Mary: The Complete Resource.* New York: Oxford University Press, 2007.

Boureux, Christophe, and Christoph Theobald, eds. *Original Sin: A Code of Fallibility.* Concilium 2004, no. 1. London: SCM, 2004.

Brown, Peter. *Augustine of Hippo: A Biography.* New ed. Berkeley, CA: University of California Press, 2000.

Burigana, Riccardo. *La Bibbia nel Concilio: La redazione della costituzione "Dei Verbum" del Vaticano II.* Bologna: Il Mulino, 1998.

Butler, Cuthbert. *The Vatican Council 1869–1870, Based on Bishop Ullathorne's Letters.* Ed. Christopher Butler. London: Collins and Harville, 1962.

Carey, Patrick W., and Joseph T. Lienhard, eds. *Bibliographical History of Christian Theologians.* Peabody, MA: Hendrickson Publishers, 2002.

Carnley, Peter. *The Reconstruction of Resurrection Belief.* Eugene, OR: Cascade Books, 2019.

Cenalmor Palanca, Daniel. *La Ley Fundamental de la Iglesia: Historia y análisis de un proyecto legislativo.* Pamplona: Ediciones Universidad de Navarra, 1991. See Thomas J. Green and Winfried Aymans.

Cerbelaud, Dominique. *Marie, un parcours dogmatique.* Cogitatio Fidei 232. Paris: Cerf, 2003.

Chupungco, Anscar J., ed. *Handbook for Liturgical Studies.* 5 vols. Collegeville, MN: Liturgical Press, 1997–2000.

Congar, Yves. *Lay People in the Church: A Study for a Theology of Laity.* Rev. ed. Westminster, MD: Newman Press, 1965. See Gabriel Flynn, Étienne Fouilloux, Elizabeth T. Groppe, Bernard Lauret, Louis Ligier, Charles MacDonald, Aidan Nichols, Jean Puyo, André Vauchez, and Cornelis Th. M. van Vliet.

———. *Tradition and Traditions: An Historical Essay and a Theological Essay.* New York: Macmillan, 1966.

———. *Vraie et fausse réforme dans l'Église.* Rev. ed. Paris: Cerf, 1968.

———. *L'ecclésiologie du haut moyen âge: de saint Grégoire le Grand à la désunion entre Byzance et Rome.* Paris: Cerf, 1968.

———. *L'Église de saint Augustin à l'époque moderne.* Paris: Cerf, 1970.

———. *Ministères et communion ecclésiale.* Paris: Cerf, 1971. See Rémi Chéno, Joseph Famerée, and A. N. Williams.

———. *I Believe in the Holy Spirit.* 3 vols. New York: Seabury Press, 1983.

———. *Diversity and Communion.* Mystic, CT: Twenty-Third Publications, 1985. See Denis Carroll, William Henn, and George Tavard.

———. *My Journal of the Council.* Ed. Éric Mahieu. Collegeville, MN: Liturgical Press, 2012.

———. *Journal of a Theologian (1946–1956)*. Ed. Étienne Fouilloux. Hindmarsh, SA: ATF Theology, 2015.

Coriden, James A., Thomas J. Green, and Donald E. Heintshel, eds. *The Code of Canon Law: A Text and a Commentary*. New York: Paulist Press, 1985. See John A. Alesandro.

Costigan, Richard F. *The Consensus of the Church and Papal Infallibility: A Study in the Background of Vatican I*. Washington, DC: Catholic University of America Press, 2005.

Daley, Brian E. *On the Dormition of Mary: Early Patristic Homilies*. Popular Patristic Series 18. Crestwood, NY: St. Vladimir's Seminary Press, 1998.

Davies, Brian. *The Thought of Thomas Aquinas*. Oxford: Clarendon Press, 1992. See Charles E. Bouchard, Bonnie Kent, Jacques Maritain, Edward D. O'Connor, Thomas F. O'Meara, and Servais Pinckaers.

Denaux, Adelbert, and Nicholas Sagovsky, ed. *Studying Mary: The Virgin Mary in Anglican and Roman Catholic Theology and Devotion. The ARCIC Working Papers*. New York: T&T Clark, 2007. See Sara Butler and Liam G. Walsh.

Dietrich, Donald J., and Michael J. Himes. *The Legacy of the Tübingen School: The Relevance of Nineteenth-Century Theology for the Twenty-First Century*. New York: Crossroad, 1997.

Donnelly, Doris, Adelbert Denaux, and Joseph Famerée, eds. *The Holy Spirit, the Church and Christian Unity: Proceedings of the Consultation Held at the Monastery of Bose, Italy (14–20 October 2002)*. Leuven: Peeters, 2005.

Dulles, Avery. *Revelation Theology: A History*. New York: Herder and Herder, 1970. See Wolfgang Beinert, Avery Dulles, Heinrich Fries, H. Richard Niebuhr, Ormond Rush, and John B. Webster.

———. *The Survival of Dogma*. Garden City, NY: Doubleday & Company, 1971.

———. *The Craft of Theology: From Symbol to System*. Expanded ed. New York: Crossroad, 1995.

———. *John Henry Newman*. 2nd ed. New York: Continuum, 2009.

Fantappiè, Carlo. *Storia del diritto canonico e delle istituzioni della Chiesa*. Bologna: Il Mulino, 2011.

Flynn, Gabriel, and Paul D. Murray, eds. *Ressourcement: A Movement for Renewal in Twentieth-Century Catholic Theology*. New York: Oxford University Press, 2012.

Fransen, Piet. *The New Life of Grace*. Tournai: Desclée Company, 1969. See Piet Fransen and Karl Rahner.

Franzelin, Johann Baptist. *Tractatus de divina traditione et scriptura*. Rome: Typis S. C. de Propaganda Fidei, 1870. See T. Howland Sanks, Leo Scheffczyk, and Peter Walter.

Fries, Heinrich, and Georg Schwaiger, eds. *Katholische Theologen Deutschlands im 19. Jahrhundert*. 3 vols. Munich: Kösel, 1975.

Fuchs, Josef. *Magisterium, Ministerium, Regimen. Vom Ursprung einer ekklesiologischen Trilogie.* Cologne, 1941. See Juan Alfaro, Yves Congar, Joseph H. Crehan, Peter De Mey, Peter Drilling, Ludwig Hödl, John Henry Newman, and Ludwig Schick.

Gadamer, Hans Georg. *Truth and Method.* Rev. English ed. New York: Crossroad, 1989.

Gaillardetz, Richard R., ed. *When the Magisterium Intervenes: The Magisterium and Theologians in Today's Church.* Collegeville, MN: Liturgical Press, 2012.

Gambero, Luigi. *Mary and the Fathers of the Church: The Blessed Virgin in Patristic Thought.* San Francisco: Ignatius Press, 1999.

———. *Mary in the Middle Ages: The Blessed Virgin Mary in the Thought of Medieval Latin Theologians.* San Francisco: Ignatius Press, 2005.

Gasser, Vincent. *The Gift of Infallibility: The Official Relatio on Infallibility of Bishop Gasser at Vatican Council I.* Boston: St. Paul Editions, 1986.

Geiselmann, Josef Rupert. *Lebendiger Glaube aus geheiligter Überlieferung: Der Grundgedanke der Theologie Johann Adam Möhlers und der katholischen Tübinger Schule.* Mainz: Matthias-Grünewald, 1942.

———. *The Meaning of Tradition.* New York: Herder and Herder, 1966. See also the articles by Geiselmann from 1956, 1957, 1961, and 1962.

Greshake, Gisbert. *Leben – stärker als der Tod: Von der Christlichen Hoffnung.* Freiburg: Herder, 2008.

———. *Maria-Ecclesia: Perspektiven einer marianisch grundierten Theologie und Kirchenpraxis.* Regensburg: F. Pustet, 2014.

Greshake, Gisbert, and Gerhard Lohfink. *Naherwartung, Auferstehung, Unsterblichkeit: Untersuchungen zur christlichen Eschatologie.* Quaestiones Disputatae 71. 5th ed. Freiburg: Herder, 1986. See Alexander Lahl, Ulrich Lüke, Thomas Schärtl, and Josef Wohlmuth.

Greshake, Gisbert and Jacob Kremer. *Resurrectio mortuorum: Zum theologischen Verständnis der leiblichen Auferstehung.* Darmstadt: Wissenschaftliche Buchgesellschaft, 1986.

Groupe des Dombes. *Mary in the Plan of God and in the Communion of Saints.* New York: Paulist Press, 2002.

Haight, Roger. *The Experience and Language of Grace.* New York: Paulist Press, 1979.

Hammans, Hubert. *Die neueren katholischen Erklärungen der Dogmenentwicklung.* Essen: Ludgerus-Verlag Hubert Wingen, 1965. See Karl Rahner and Edward Schillebeeckx.

Hermisson, Hans-Jürgen, and Eduard Lohse. *Faith.* Biblical Encounters Series. Nashville, TN: Abingdon, 1981. See Jürgen Becker, Peter Carnley, James D. G. Dunn, Gerhard Schneider, and Giuseppe Segalla.

Himes, Michael J. *Ongoing Incarnation: Johann Adam Möhler and the Beginning of Modern Ecclesiology.* New York: Crossroad, 1997.

Hoping, Helmut, and Michael Schulz, eds. *Unheilvolles Erbe? Zur Theologie der Erbsünde.* Quaestiones Disputatae 231. Freiburg: Herder, 2009.

Horst, Ulrich. *The Dominicans and the Pope: Papal Teaching Authority in the Medieval and Early Modern Thomist Tradition.* Notre Dame, IN: University of Notre Dame Press, 2006.

Hünermann, Peter, and Dietmar Mieth, eds. *Streitgespräch um Theologie und Lehramt: Die Instruktion über die kirchliche Berufung des Theologen in der Diskussion.* Frankfurt: J. Knecht, 1991.

Hünermann, Peter, and Bernd Jochen Hilberath, eds. *Herders theologischer Kommentar zum Zweiten Vatikanischen Konzil.* 5 vols. Freiburg: Herder, 2004–2006.

Jedin, Hubert, and John Dolan, eds. *Handbook of Church History.* 10 vols. New York: Herder and Herder, 1965–1981.

Johnson, Maxwell E. *The Rites of Christian Initiation: Their Evolution and Interpretation.* Expanded ed. Collegeville, MN: Liturgical Press, 2007.

Jugie, Martin. *La mort et l'assomption de la Sainte Vierge: Étude historico-doctrinale.* Studi e testi 114. Vatican City: Biblioteca Apostolica Vaticana, 1944. See Josef Rupert Geiselmann (1951).

Kasper, Walter. *Die Lehre von der Tradition in der Römischen Schule.* Walter Kasper Gesammelte Schriften 1. Freiburg: Herder, 2011.

Kavanagh, Aidan. *On Liturgical Theology.* New York: Pueblo Publishing, 1984. See Maïeul Cappuyns, Kevin W. Irwin, and Edward J. Kilmartin.

Kelly, J. N. D. *The Oxford Dictionary of the Popes.* New York: Oxford University Press, 1986.

Kennedy, Philip. *Deus Humanissimus: The Knowability of God in the Theology of Edward Schillebeeckx.* Fribourg, CH: University Press, 1993.

———. *Schillebeeckx.* Outstanding Christian Thinkers Series. Collegeville, MN: Liturgical Press, 1993.

Ker, Ian. *John Henry Newman: A Biography.* Oxford: Clarendon Press, 1988.

Kilby, Karen. *Karl Rahner: Theology and Philosophy.* New York: Routledge, 2004.

Koster, Dominikus M. *Volk Gottes im Werden.* Mainz: Matthias-Grünewald, 1971. See Karl Adam, Johannes Beumer, Sophronius Classen, Yves Congar, Leonard Fic, Francis X. Lawlor, Piotr Napiwodzki, Michael Schmaus, and Hartmut Westermann.

Lacey, Michael J., and Francis Oakley, eds. *The Crisis of Authority in Catholic Modernity.* New York: Oxford University Press, 2011. See Richard R. Gaillardetz and John E. Thiel.

Lamy, Marielle. *L'Immaculée Conception: Étapes et enjeux d'une controverse au moyen-âge (XIIe-XVe siècles).* Collection des Études Augustiniennes,

Série Moyen Âge et Temps Modernes 35. Paris: Institut d'Études Augustiniennes, 2000. See Daniel P. Horan and Dominic Unger.

Lane, Dermot A. *Keeping Hope Alive: Stirrings in Christian Theology*. New York: Paulist Press, 1996.

La Soujeole, Benoît-Dominique de. *Initiation à la théologie mariale*. Paris: Parole et Silence, 2007.

Laurentin, René. *A Short Treatise on the Virgin Mary*. Washington, NJ: AMI Press, 1991.

Legrand, Hervé, Julio Manzanarez, and Antonio García y García, eds. *Reception and Communion among Churches*. Washington, DC: Canon Law Department of the Catholic University of America, 1997. See Yves Congar and John Zizioulas.

Lennan, Richard, and Nancy Pineda-Madrid, eds. *The Holy Spirit: Setting the World on Fire*. New York: Paulist Press, 2017.

Lenoble, Robert. *Essai sur la notion d'expérience*. Paris: J. Vrin, 1943.

Lohfink, Gerhard. *Is This All There Is? On Resurrection and Eternal Life*. Collegeville, MN: Liturgical Press, 2018.

Lohfink, Gerhard, and Ludwig Weimer. *Maria – nicht ohne Israel: Eine neue Sicht der Lehre von der Unbefleckten Empfängnis*. Freiburg: Herder, 2008. See Juan Alfaro, Roger Aubert, Siegfried Gruber, René Laurentin, and Gerhard Müller.

Lonergan, Bernard. *Insight: A Study of Human Understanding*. New York: Philosophical Library, 1958.

———. *Method in Theology*. New York: Herder and Herder, 1972.

———. *Collection*. Collected Works of Bernard Lonergan 4. Toronto: University of Toronto Press, 1993.

———. *A Second Collection*. Ed. William F. J. Ryan and Bernard J. Tyrell. Philadelphia: Westminster Press, 1974.

Manoir, Hubert du, ed. *Maria: Études sur la sainte Vierge*. 8 vols. Paris: Beauchesne, 1949–1971. See Bernard Capelle, Édouard Cothenet, and Severien Salaville.

Marín-Sola, Francisco. *L'Évolution homogène du dogme catholique*. 2 vols. Fribourg, CH: Imprimerie et Librairie de l'Oeuvre de Saint-Paul, 1924.

Marthaler, Berard. *The Catechism Yesterday and Today: The Evolution of a Genre*. Collegeville, MN: Liturgical Press, 1995.

Martimort, Aimé Georges. *The Church at Prayer*. 4 vols. Collegeville, MN: Liturgical Press, 1985–1988.

Matuscheck, Dominik. *Konkrete Dogmatik: die Mariologie Karl Rahners*. Innsbrucker theologische Studien 87. Innsbruck: Tyrolia, 2012.

Maunder, Chris, ed. *The Origins of the Cult of the Virgin Mary.* London: Burns and Oates, 2008. See Ignazio M. Calabuig, Pierre Jounel, Kilian McDonnell, and Philippe Rouillard.

Mazza, Enrico. *Mystagogy: A Theology of Liturgy in the Patristic Age.* New York: Pueblo Publishing, 1989.

McCool, Gerald. *Catholic Theology in the Nineteenth Century: The Quest for a Unitary Method.* New York: Seabury Press, 1977.

McKenzie, John L. *Myths and Realities: Studies in Biblical Theology.* Milwaukee, WI: Bruce, 1963. See J. Bergman, H. Lutzmann, W. H. Schmidt, Jerome Kodell, and Bruce Vawter.

Menke, Karl-Heinz. *Fleisch geworden aus Maria: Die Geschichte Israels und der Marienglaube der Kirche.* Regensburg: F. Pustet, 1999.

Merkle, Judith A. *Beyond Our Lights and Shadows: Charism and Institution in the Church.* New York: Bloomsbury T&T Clark, 2016.

Mimouni, Simon Claude. *Dormition et Assomption de Marie: histoire des traditions anciennes.* Théologie historique 98. Paris: Beauchesne, 1995.

———. *Les traditions anciennes sur la Dormition et l'Assomption de Marie: Études littéraires, historiques et doctrinales.* Supplements to *Vigiliae Christianae* 104. Leiden: Brill, 2011.

Möhler, Johann-Adam. *Unity in the Church or the Principle of Catholicism: Presented in the Spirit of the Church Fathers of the First Three Centuries.* Washington, DC: Catholic University of America Press, 1996.

———. *Symbolism: Exposition of the Doctrinal Differences between Catholics and Protestants as Evidenced by the Symbolical Writings.* New York: Crossroad, 1997.

Moran, Gabriel. *Theology of Revelation.* New York: Herder and Herder, 1966.

Mouroux, Jean. *The Christian Experience: An Introduction to a Theology.* New York: Sheed and Ward, 1954.

Nabert, Jean. *L'expérience de la liberté.* Paris: Presses Universitaires de France, 1923.

Nedungatt, George, ed. *A Guide to the Eastern Code: A Commentary on the Code of Canons of the Eastern Churches.* Rome: Pontificio Istituto Orientale, 2002.

Newman, John Henry. *The Arians of the Fourth Century.* 2nd ed. London: J. G. & F. Rivington, 1842. See Michel R. Barnes and Daniel H. Williams, Hanns Christof Brennecke, R. P. C. Hanson, Thomas A. Kopecek, Michel Meslin, and Rowan Williams.

———. *An Essay on the Development of Christian Doctrine.* London: Longmans, Green, and Co., 1878. See Owen Chadwick, Nicholas Lash, and Jan H. Walgrave.

———. *On Consulting the Faithful in Matters of Doctrine.* Kansas City, MO: Sheed and Ward, 1961. See John T. Ford, Hermann Geissler, Ian Ker, Lawrence J. King, David P. Long, Terrence Merrigan, Edward Jeremy Miller, Richard J. Penaskovic, C. Michael Shea, and Michael Slusser.

Nitsche, Bernhard, ed. *Atem des sprechenden Gottes: Einführung in die Lehre vom Heiligen Geist.* Regenburg: F. Pustet, 2003. See Raymond E. Brown, Stefano Cucchetti, Richard R. Gaillardetz and Catherine E. Clifford,Walter Kasper, Karl Rahner, Ormond Rush, and Thomas Söding.

Norelli, Enrico. *Marie des apocryphes: enquête sur la mère de Jésus dans le christianisme antique.* Christianismes antiques. Geneva: Labor et Fides, 2009.

O'Collins, Gerald. *Tradition: Understanding Christian Tradition.* New York: Oxford University Press, 2018. See Avery Dulles, Richard R. Gaillardetz and Catherine E. Clifford, and Ormond Rush.

O'Gara, Margaret. *Triumph in Defeat: Infallibility, Vatican I, and the French Minority Bishops.* Washington, DC: Catholic University of America Press, 1988.

O'Malley, John W. *What Happened at Vatican II.* Cambridge, MA: Belknap Press, 2008.

———. *Trent: What Happened at the Council.* Cambridge, MA: Belknap Press, 2013.

———. *Vatican I: The Council and the Making of the Ultramontane Church.* Cambridge, MA: Belknap Press, 2018.

Perrin, Norman. *Jesus and the Language of the Kingdom: Symbol and Metaphor in New Testament Interpretation.* Philadelphia: Fortress Press, 1976. See Avery Dulles and Karl Rahner.

Philips, Gérard. *The Role of the Laity in the Church.* Chicago: Fides Publishers, 1955.

Pius XII, Pope. *Munificentissimus Deus.* See *American Ecclesiastical Review* 124 (1951) 1–17. See Berthold Altaner, Joseph Coppens, and Johannes Ernst.

Pottmeyer, Hermann Josef. *Unfehlbarkeit und Souveränität. Die päpstliche Unfehlbarkeit im System der ultramontanen Ekklesiologie des 19. Jahrhunderts.* Mainz: Matthias-Grünewald, 1975.

Rahner, Karl. *Mary, Mother of the Lord: Theological Meditations.* New York: Herder, 1963.

———. *The Christian Commitment: Essays in Pastoral Theology.* New York: Sheed and Ward, 1963.

———. *On the Theology of Death.* New York: Herder and Herder, 1965. See the index under Rahner for articles from 1949, 1963, 1966, 1969, 1978, 1981, 1983. See also Pierre Benoît, Jacek Bolewski, Donal Flanagan, and Otto Karrer.

———. "Assumptio-Arbeit." Ed. Regina Pacis Meyer. In *Maria, Mutter des Herrn; Mariologische Studien*. Karl Rahner Sämtliche Werke 9. Freiburg: Herder, 2004. 3–393.

———. *Foundations of Christian Faith: An Introduction to the Idea of Christianity*. New York: Seabury Press, 1978.

Ratzinger, Joseph. *Theological Highlights of Vatican II*. New York: Paulist Press, 1966.

———. *Daughter Zion: Meditations on the Church's Marian Belief*. San Francisco: Ignatius Press, 1983. See Franz Courth, Angelus Häussling, and Anton Ziegenaus.

———. *Eschatology: Death and Eternal Life*. Expanded ed. Washington, DC: Catholic University of America Press, 1988. See Ratzinger for individual articles from 1970, 1972, 1973, 1980. See also Terrence P. Ehrman, Karl-Heinz Menke, and Bernard P. Prusak.

———. *In the Beginning . . . : A Catholic Understanding of the Story of Creation and the Fall*. Grand Rapids, MI: Eerdmans, 1995.

Ratzinger, Joseph, and Karl Rahner. *Revelation and Tradition*. Quaestiones Disputatae 17. New York: Herder and Herder, 1966.

Remenyi, Matthias. *Auferstehung denken: Anwege, Grenzen und Modelle personal-eschatologischer Theoriebildung*. Freiburg: Herder, 2016.

Reynolds, Brian K. *Gateway to Heaven: Marian Doctrine and Devotion, Image and Typology in the Patristic and Medieval Periods*. Hyde Park, NY: New City Press, 2012.

Routhier, Gilles. *La réception d'un concile*. Cogitatio Fidei 174. Paris: Cerf, 1993.

Rovira, German, ed. *Im Gewande des Heils: die Unbefleckte Empfängnis Mariens als Urbild der menschlichen Heiligkeit*. Essen: Ludgerus, 1980.

Rush, Ormond. *The Reception of Doctrine: An Appropriation of Hans Robert Jauss' Reception Aesthetics and Literary Hermeneutics*. Rome: Gregorian University Press, 1997.

———. *The Vision of Vatican II: Its Fundamental Principles*. Collegeville, MN: Liturgical Press, 2019.

Sanks, T. Howland. *Authority in the Church: A Study in Changing Paradigms*. Missoula, MT: American Academy of Religion, 1974.

Sauter, Gerhard. *The Question of Meaning: A Theological and Philosophical Orientation*. Grand Rapids, MI: Eerdmans, 1995.

Schatz, Klaus. *Papal Primacy: From Its Origins to the Present*. Collegeville, MN: Liturgical Press, 1996.

Scheeben, Matthias Joseph. *Handbook of Catholic Dogmatics*. Steubenville, OH: Emmaus Academic, 2019–2021. See Norbert Brox, Michael Fiedrowicz, Peter Fernekess, Robert M. Grant, Marko Mišerda, Aidan Nichols, Ulrich Sander, and Eberhard Schockenhoff.

Schillebeeckx, Edward. *Menschliche Erfahrung und Glaube an Jesus Christus: eine Rechenschaft*. Freiburg: Herder, 1979.

———. "The Authority of New Experiences." *Christ: The Experience of Jesus as Lord*. New York: Seabury Press, 1980. 30–64. See Mary Catherine Hilkert, Patrick Jacquemont, Jean-Pierre Jossua, and Bernard Quelquejeu.

Schnackenburg, Rudolf. *God's Rule and Kingdom*. New York: Herder and Herder, 1963.

Seewald, Michael. *Dogma im Wandel: Wie Glaubenslehren sich entwickeln*. Freiburg: Herder, 2018.

Semmelroth, Otto. *Mary, Archetype of the Church*. New York: Sheed and Ward, 1963. See Patrick J. Beardsley, Brian E. Daley, and Elizabeth A. Johnson.

Shoemaker, Stephen J. *Ancient Traditions of the Virgin Mary's Dormition and Assumption*. Oxford Early Christian Studies. New York: Oxford University Press, 2002.

———. *Mary in Early Christian Faith and Devotion*. New Haven, CT: Yale University Press, 2016. See Henri Barré, Ignazio M. Calabuig, Pierre Jounel, Giuseppe Quadrio, Albert Ripberger, and Philippe Rouillard.

Smith, John E. *Experience and God*. New York: Oxford University Press, 1968. See Robert O. Johann.

Söding, Thomas, ed. *Die Rolle der Theologie in der Kirche. Die Debatte über das Dokument der Theologenkommission*. Quaestiones Disputatae 268. Freiburg: Herder, 2015. See Lieven Boeve.

Söll, Georg. *Mariologie*. Handbuch der Dogmengeschichte, III/4. Freiburg: Herder, 1978.

Spendel, Stefanie Aurelia, and Marion Wagner, eds. *Maria zu lieben: Moderne Rede über eine biblische Frau*. Regensburg: F. Pustet, 1999. See Marion Wagner.

Stacpoole, Alberic, ed. *Mary's Place in Christian Dialogue: Occasional Papers of the Ecumenical Society of the Blessed Virgin Mary, 1970–1980*. Middlegreen, Slough: St. Paul Publications, 1982. See Manfred Hauke, Myrrha Lot-Borodine, Virginia M. Kimball, and Kallistos Ware.

Taylor, Charles. *Philosophical Papers*. Vol. 1: *Human Agency and Language*. Vol. 2: *Philosophy and the Human Sciences*. New York: Cambridge University Press, 1985.

———. *Dilemmas and Connections: Selected Essays*. Cambridge, MA: Belknap Press, 2011.

———. *The Language Animal: The Full Shape of the Human Linguistic Capacity*. Cambridge, MA: Belknap Press, 2016. See Martin Heidegger and Hans-Georg Gadamer.

Thiel, John E. *Senses of Tradition: Continuity and Development in Catholic Faith.* New York: Oxford University Press, 2000. See Walter Kasper and articles by John E. Thiel.

Thils, Gustave. *L'infaillibilité du peuple chrétien "in credendo." Notes de théologie posttridentine.* Bibliotheca Ephemeridum Theologicarum Lovaniensium 21. Louvain: E. Warny, 1963. See Marc Caudron, Antoine Chavasse, Yves Congar, Georges Dejaifve, Heinrich Fries, Otfried Müller, P. Nau, Bernard Sesboüé, Gustave Thils, and J.-M.-A. Vacant.

Torrell, Jean-Pierre. *A Priestly People: Baptismal Priesthood and Priestly Ministry.* New York: Paulist Press, 2013. See Bernard Botte, Bernard Capelle, Lucien Cerfaux, Yves Congar, Paul Dabin, Peter Ketter, Engelbert Niebecker, Paul F. Palmer, Laurence Ryan, and Gustave Thils.

Vorgrimler, Herbert, ed. *Commentary on the Documents of Vatican II.* 5 vols. New York: Herder and Herder, 1967–1969.

Weis, Norbert. *Das prophetische Amt der Laien in der Kirche. Eine rechtstheologische Untersuchung anhand dreier Dokumente des Zweiten Vatikanischen Konzils.* Analecta Gregoriana 225. Rome: Gregorian University Press, 1981.

Wenger, Antoine. *Assomption de la T. S. Vierge dans la tradition byzantine du VIe au Xe siècle.* Archives de l'Orient Chrétien 5. Paris: Institut Français des Études Byzantines, 1955. See Michel van Esbroeck.

Wicks, Jared. *Investigating Vatican II: Its Theologians, Ecumenical Turn, and Biblical Commitment.* Washington, DC: Catholic University of America Press, 2018.

Wiederkehr, Dietrich, ed. *Wie geschiet Tradition? Überlieferung im Lebensprozess der Kirche.* Quaestiones Disputatae 133. Freiburg: Herder, 1991.

Witherup, Ronald D. *Scripture: Dei Verbum.* Rediscovering Vatican II. New York: Paulist Press, 2006. See Bernard-Dominique Dupuy, Johannes Feiner, Rino Fisichella, Charles Moeller, Joseph Ratzinger, Hanjo Sauer, and Jared Wicks.

Yarnold, Edward J. *The Awe-Inspiring Rites of Initiation: The Origins of the R.C.I.A.* 2nd ed. Collegeville, MN: Liturgical Press, 1994.

Yates, Stephen. *Between Death and Resurrection: A Critical Response to Recent Catholic Debate Concerning the Intermediate State.* London: Bloomsbury Academic, 2017.

Index of Names

Index of Subjects

faith: as content/doctrine (*fides quae*), 5, 11,
17–21, 25, 31–33, 53–54, 62–63, 68–69,
89–95, 96–97, 100–101, 106, 112–14, 119,
128, 140, 166, 176–77, 184, 190, 229, 242,
248, 351; as act of faith (*fides qua*), 127,
126, 140, 148–49, 179, 245–46, 295, 330,
381; and understanding, 149–52, 156,
252, 258–59, 266, 287, 293, 311, 341–42;
as obedience, 106–7; and dialogue, 311;
and the Holy Spirit, 115, 117–19, 138,
146, 151, 173, 202, 311, 364, 369
"faith and morals," 124, 222, 225, 234, 244,
249, 278, 283, 292, 350, 370, 375, 382
faith and reason, 41, 57, 111, 113, 147, 308
faithful, the (ordinary), 4–8, 11–16, 18–22, 30,
33–34, 36–37, 41, 47, 54–55, 60–62, 63–
64, 69–71, 88–96, 99–101, 106–9, 114–17,
119, 127, 131, 136–37, 141–43, 149–56,
158–59, 162–64, 167, 169, 174, 176,
180–81, 200–203, 219, 225–27, 238–39,
241, 246, 251, 253–59, 266, 279, 281–85,
291–93, 299, 312, 314, 318, 339, 342, 355,
365, 368, 370, 375, 378–80, 381–85
Familiaris consortio, 289, 291, 416
Fathers of the Church, 3, 11, 20, 25, 86, 104,
118–19, 138, 155–56, 173, 202, 310
Febronianism, see Gallicanism
Ferrara-Florence, Council of, 7, 9, 53
fideism, 352
fittingness (*convenientia*), the argument
from, 196, 199, 201

Gallicanism: 8, 123, 127, 130; the Gallican
Articles, 127; Febronianism, 123, 127;
Josephenism, 123
Gaudium et Spes, 1, 237, 285, 287, 298, 321,
335–36, 369
Gelasian sacramentary, 44
general judgment, the, 156, 209
gifts of the Holy Spirit, 7, 136–40, 148, 155,
159, 221, 243, 311
grace, 28–29, 43, 48–50, 55, 69, 72–75,
77–78, 80, 83–84, 111–12, 118, 136,
138, 140–42, 148, 156, 164, 166, 176–77,
214–15, 242, 244–45, 250, 254, 311, 315,
320, 325–26, 338, 351, 353, 366, 384

Grave nimis, 54
Great Western Schism, xii, 2, 53
Gregorian sacramentary, 45
Groupe des Dombes, 82, 84

habit (*habitus*), 136, 138–39, 146, 148, 159,
221, 233, 311
hierarchy (ecclesiastical), 26, 32, 33, 38–40,
68, 88, 92, 103, 108–9, 125, 142, 158,
162, 166–67, 169, 230, 236, 241, 256,
258–59, 267, 309, 313–14, 341–42, 363,
368, 380, 383
hierarchy of truths, 171, 175–76
historical consciousness, 336–39
historical-critical method, 20, 352
historicity, 49, 141, 171, 249, 252, 313, 339,
349, 359
history, 20, 26–27, 70, 73, 79, 134, 147, 162,
169, 173, 199, 212, 215, 241, 313, 321,
337–39, 350–52, 355, 357, 359
holiness, 101, 236, 254, 316, 320; (universal
call to) 230, 235–36
holiness of Mary, 20, 42–47, 71, 81, 173;
perfect holiness of Mary (*panhagia*), 43,
79, 81, 201
Holy Spirit, 7, 14, 18, 23, 26–27, 49, 98, 108,
115–19, 136–40, 142, 146, 148, 151, 155,
157, 159, 162–64, 173–75, 177, 181, 215,
221, 225, 227, 237–38, 243, 245, 249–51,
259, 266, 288, 292–93, 298, 301, 311,
317, 320, 322, 335, 342, 356, 363–71,
375–76, 380; pneumatological deficit,
363, 369–70
hope, 79, 192, 215, 217, 219, 256, 258, 294,
307, 325, 334, 348, 371, 384
Humanae vitae, 356, 403, 412

iconoclast controversy, 156, 188
imagination, 101, 180, 190, 214–15, 337;
and metaphor, 38, 214–15, 219, 231,
245, 345–46, 377, 424; and symbol, 91,
114, 150, 214–15, 219, 237, 321, 324,
329–30, 342, 344–46, 352, 359
immaculate conception of Mary, xii, 20,
63–70, 72–75; and typology, 76–78; and
holy remnant; and holiness, 80–81; and